# Geoactive 2

## STAGE 5 AUSTRALIAN GEOGRAPHY

**Third edition**

Susan **Bliss** | John **Paine**

Contributing author
Paul **McCartan**

jacaranda *plus*

Third edition published 2010 by
John Wiley & Sons Australia, Ltd
42 McDougall Street, Milton, Qld 4064

First edition published 2000
Second edition published 2005

Typeset in 9.5/12.5 pt LinoLetter

© Susan Bliss, John Paine 2000, 2005, 2010

The moral rights of the authors have been asserted.

National Library of Australia
Cataloguing-in-publication entry

| | |
|---|---|
| Author: | Bliss, Sue, 1944– |
| Title: | Geoactive 2: stage 5 Australian geography/ Susan Bliss, John Paine. |
| Edition: | 3rd ed. |
| ISBN: | 978 1 7421 6008 5 (pbk) |
| | 978 1 7421 6143 3 (eBook) |
| Notes: | Includes index. |
| Target audience: | For secondary school age. |
| Subjects: | Physical geography — Australia — Textbooks. Australia — Geography — Textbooks. |
| Other authors/ contributors: | Paine, J. (John) |
| Dewey number: | 919.4 |

**Reproduction and communication for educational purposes**
The Australian *Copyright Act 1968* (the Act) allows a maximum of one chapter or 10% of the pages of this work, whichever is the greater, to be reproduced and/or communicated by any educational institution for its educational purposes provided that the educational institution (or the body that administers it) has given a remuneration notice to Copyright Agency Limited (CAL).

**Reproduction and communication for other purposes**
Except as permitted under the Act (for example, a fair dealing for the purposes of study, research, criticism or review), no part of this book may be reproduced, stored in a retrieval system, communicated or transmitted in any form or by any means without prior written permission. All inquiries should be made to the publisher.

Cover image: © Digital Stock/Corbis Corporation; © Paddy Ryan

Internal design images: © Digital Stock/Corbis Corporation; © Digital Vision

Cartography by MAPgraphics Pty Ltd, Brisbane and the Wiley Art Studio

Illustrated by Philip Blythe, Gary Collett, Shane Collinge, Mike Golding, Craig Jackson, Paul Lennon, Glenn Lumsden, Janice McCormack, Rob Poulton, Bronwyn Searle, Terry St Ledger, Graeme Tavendale and the Wiley Art Studio

Printed in China by
Printplus Limited

20 19 18 17 16 15 14 13 12 11 10 9

This textbook contains images of Indigenous people who are, or may be, deceased. The publisher appreciates that this inclusion may distress some Indigenous communities. These images have been included so that the young multicultural audience for this book can better appreciate specific aspects of Indigenous history and experience.

In this book, the word *Aborigine* rather than *Koori* is used when referring to Indigenous Australians. The issues raised are not unique to the Indigenous people of New South Wales and so the Australia-wide reference has been maintained.

It is recommended that teachers should first preview resources on Aboriginal topics in relation to their suitability for the class level or situation. It is also suggested that Aboriginal parents or community members be invited to help assess the resources to be shown to Aboriginal children. At all times the guidelines laid down by the Department of Education should be followed.

# Contents

*Preface* vi
*About eBookPLUS* vii
*How to use this book* viii
*Coverage of syllabus* x
*Acknowledgements* xii

## TOPIC 1
## INVESTIGATING AUSTRALIA'S PHYSICAL ENVIRONMENTS

### Chapter 1 The Australian continent 2

1.1 Australia's geographical dimensions 4
1.2 Locating Australia 6
1.3 Origins of the continent: Aboriginal perspective 8
1.4 Origins of the continent: geographical perspective 10
1.5 Climate and sea level changes shaped our continent 14

**Working geographically 16**

### Chapter 2 Physical characteristics that make Australia unique 18

2.1 Major landforms and drainage basins 20
2.2 Topographic maps 24
2.3 *GEOskillbuilder* — Using topographic maps 26
2.4 *GEOskillbuilder* — Understanding landforms: Walls of Jerusalem 30
2.5 *GEOskillbuilder* — Constructing a cross-section 32
2.6 Australia's pattern of climate and vegetation 34
2.7 Impact of climate change on Australia 38
2.8 Understanding weather maps 40
2.9 Australia's pattern of natural resources 42
2.10 Australia's unique flora and fauna 46
2.11 Flora and fauna of the Daintree rainforest 48

**Working geographically 50**

### Chapter 3 Natural hazards in Australia 52

3.1 Natural hazards and natural disasters 54
3.2 Natural hazards: droughts 56
3.3 Causes of drought in Australia 58
3.4 The drought of 1991–95 60
3.5 Bushfires as natural hazards 62
3.6 From hazard to disaster 64
3.7 Black Saturday, Victoria 2009 66
3.8 Natural hazards: storms 70
3.9 The Sydney hailstorm, 1999 72
3.10 Natural hazards: tropical cyclones 74
3.11 Floods as natural hazards 78
3.12 *GEOskillbuilder* — Research and presentation: earthquakes in Australia 82
3.13 Natural hazards: earthquakes 84

**Working geographically 87**
**ICT activities 90**

### TOPIC 2
## CHANGING AUSTRALIAN COMMUNITIES

### Chapter 4  Australia's population  92
4.1 Australia's unique character  94
4.2 Changing settlement patterns  96
4.3 Population change in Australia  98
4.4 Changes to Australia's population structure  100
4.5 Changes to ethnic composition  102
4.6 Changes in the Indigenous population  104
4.7 Australians on the move  106
4.8 Australia's changing nature and identity  108
Working geographically  110

### Chapter 5  Australian communities  112
5.1 Forming communities  114
5.2 A sporting community: Terrigal Surf Life Saving Club  116
5.3 Rural communities  118
5.4 Indigenous communities  120
5.5 Culturally diverse communities  122
Working geographically  124

### Chapter 6  Factors causing change in Australian communities  126
6.1 Overview of change in Australian communities  128
6.2 Gold Coast: lifestyle expectations  132
6.3 Cabramatta: a culturally diverse community  136
6.4 The Mirarr community and Jabiluka  140
Working geographically  144
ICT activities  146

### TOPIC 3
## ISSUES IN AUSTRALIAN ENVIRONMENTS

### Chapter 7  Geographical issues  148
7.1 What are geographical issues?  150
7.2 Air quality  156
7.3 Managing air quality  158
7.4 Urban growth and decline  162
7.5 Urban growth and decline in Sydney  166
7.6 Redeveloping the Ultimo–Pyrmont area  170
7.7 Spatial inequality: overview  172
7.8 Nature and impacts of poverty  174
7.9 A 'fair go' for all Aussies: citizenship  176
7.10 Nature of wastes  178
7.11 Waste management  180
7.12 Sewage: going to waste?  182
7.13 Nuclear waste: a permanent problem  184
7.14 Australia's nuclear industry  186
Working geographically  188

### Chapter 8  Land and water management  190
8.1 Land and water interactions  192
8.2 Land degradation  194
8.3 Soil erosion  196
8.4 Salinity  198
8.5 Sustainable land management  200
8.6 Nature and impacts of tourism on land  202
8.7 Ecotourism: the sustainable alternative  204
8.8 Managing the Australian alps  206
Working geographically  208
8.9 Water: nature, impacts and management  210
8.10 Rivers out of balance  212
8.11 The Georges River catchment  214
8.12 Managing Sydney's water  216
8.13 Nature of wetlands and inland rivers  218
Working geographically  220

### Chapter 9  Coastal management  222
9.1 Coastal management: a geographical issue  224
9.2 Coastal landforms  226
9.3 Transportation processes  228
9.4 Processes of coastal erosion  232
9.5 Processes of coastal deposition  234
Working geographically  236
9.6 Managing the impact of global warming on coasts  238
9.7 Coastal pollution: nature, impacts and management  240
9.8 Coastal management case study: Wamberal and Terrigal  242
9.9 Managing Sydney Harbour: a geographical issue  246
9.10 *GEOskillbuilder* — Coastal fieldwork and research action plan  248
Working geographically  250
ICT activities  252

## TOPIC 4

## AUSTRALIA IN ITS REGIONAL AND GLOBAL CONTEXTS

**Chapter 10  Australia in its regional and global contexts   254**

- 10.1 Australia's place in the world: territorial boundaries   256
- 10.2 Protecting territorial boundaries   258
- 10.3 Australia's changing place in a globalised world   260

- 10.4 Strengthening links in the Asia–Pacific region   262
- 10.5 Australia's connection to ASEAN countries: Indonesia   264
- 10.6 Links with a future superpower: China   266

**Working geographically   268**

- 10.7 Our Pacific island neighbours: Nauru and Tuvalu   270
- 10.8 Communication links   274
- 10.9 Australia's cultural links   276
- 10.10 Australia's migration links   278
- 10.11 Australia's tourism links   280
- 10.12 Future tourism links and trends   282
- 10.13 Australia's sporting links   284
- 10.14 Strengthening future sporting links   286

**Working geographically   288**

**Chapter 11  Trade, aid, defence: global regional links   290**

- 11.1 Australia's changing trade links   292
- 11.2 Australia's main trading links: countries, goods and services   294
- 11.3 Australia's trade agreements   296
- 11.4 Fair trade: equity and social justice   298
- 11.5 Helping hand: Australia's foreign aid links   300
- 11.6 Australian government aid links at work   302
- 11.7 Indonesia–Australia aid links   304
- 11.8 Australian government links with Papua New Guinea   306
- 11.9 A non-government organisation: World Vision Australia   308
- 11.10 Australia's defence links   310
- 11.11 Australia's defence agreements   312
- 11.12 From frontline to peace building   314
- 11.13 Global links: the war on terrorism   316
- 11.14 Regional defence links: helping a friend   318

**Working geographically   320**

**Chapter 12  Future challenges: population   322**

- 12.1 Australia's population is growing   324
- 12.2 Age structure trend: fewer babies   326
- 12.3 Implications of an ageing population   328
- 12.4 Government migration policies   330
- 12.5 Humanitarian migration   332
- 12.6 Culturally diverse Australia   334
- 12.7 Where we live: spatial distribution   336
- 12.8 Population movements   338
- 12.9 Population movement and urban planning   340
- 12.10 Urban planning for the future: Sydney   342
- 12.11 Ecological sustainability   344
- 12.12 Towards the ecocity: sustainable Sydney   346

**Working geographically   348**

**Chapter 13  Challenges: human rights and reconciliation   350**

- 13.1 Everyone, everywhere has human rights: agreements   352
- 13.2 Abuse of human rights: global community   354
- 13.3 Human rights for Australians   356
- 13.4 Human rights and refugees: Australia responds   358
- 13.5 Gender: women's rights   360
- 13.6 Freedom of expression   362
- 13.7 Indigenous Australians: many nations, one people   364
- 13.8 Strategies to 'close the gap'   366
- 13.9 Comparisons: international indigenous communities   368
- 13.10 Challenge: walking together for reconciliation   370
- 13.11 Challenges and strategies for a better future   374

**Working geographically   376**

**ICT activities   378**

*Glossary   380*
*Index   386*

# Preface

*Geoactive 2, third edition* has been written for the NSW Stage 5 Australian Geography syllabus. This syllabus incorporates Civics and Citizenship. The needs of students and teachers have been carefully researched, with meetings, surveys and reviews used to revise the text, activities, illustrations and layout of this third edition. The core idea of the text is to engage students in different forms of learning as they acquire the skills to work geographically, and to ensure that the activities form the basis of learning how to learn.

The sample spreads on pages viii–ix and the overview of the exciting new eBookPLUS on page vii explain the main features of this print and digital package of student resources and teacher support.

The following are some of the highlights of this new edition of the student text.

- The textbook features a more student-friendly layout, with text, activities and a range of visual information. Particular attention has been paid to literacy and reading level in all chapters, with shorter paragraphs and greater use of bullet points to enhance understanding and highlight concepts.
- Most of the text is in double-page format but, where the topic is large, a four-page format is used.
- *Geoterms* on pages provide definitions of geography-specific terms in context as they are used. As well, a full list of *Key terms* appears in the chapter opener and in a combined glossary at the end of the book.
- *Geofacts* have been included on many pages to interest and engage students in bite-sized geography facts.
- A comprehensive range of *GEOskillbuilder* features is included in relevant sections according to syllabus requirements. These skillbuilders provide a detailed step-by-step guide to important practical geographical skills. *GEOskills toolbox* features provide additional information on key skills.
- The student *Activities* are divided into three sections: *Understanding* revises basic concepts and terms; *Thinking and applying* requires higher levels of understanding and often calls on students to apply different intelligences; and *Using your skills* applies the skills learned in the section or revises those skills learned in previous sections. Short and extended responses are included to give students practice in communicating geographical information.
- *Working geographically* pages allow students to practise concepts and skills developed within chapters. These pages also introduce broadsheets in School Certificate format and multiple-choice questions.
- There are many new, up-to-date and topical sample studies, graphs, statistics, maps and diagrams.
- An increased emphasis on the Asia–Pacific region has been included in chapters 10, 11 and 12.
- A new and exciting dimension in the teaching and learning of Geography is provided through a range of online resources for each focus area in eBookPLUS (see page vii). These innovative tools for the Geography teacher use the full potential of digital media to integrate ICT and stimulate students in inquiry-based learning.

# About eBookPLUS

## jacaranda plus
### Next generation teaching and learning

This book features eBookPLUS: an electronic version of the entire textbook and supporting multimedia resources. It is available for you online at the JacarandaPLUS website (www.jacplus.com.au).

## Using the JacarandaPLUS website

To access your eBookPLUS resources, simply log on to www.jacplus.com.au using your existing JacarandaPLUS login and enter the registration code. If you are new to JacarandaPLUS, follow the three easy steps below.

### Step 1. Create a user account
The first time you use the JacarandaPLUS system, you will need to create a user account. Go to the JacarandaPLUS home page (www.jacplus.com.au), click on the button to create a new account and follow the instructions on screen. You can then use your nominated email address and password to log in to the JacarandaPLUS system.

### Step 2. Enter your registration code
Once you have logged in, enter your unique registration code for this book, which is printed on the inside front cover of your textbook. The title of your textbook will appear in your bookshelf. Click on the link to open your eBookPLUS.

### Step 3. View or download eBookPLUS resources
Your eBookPLUS and supporting resources are provided in a chapter-by-chapter format. Simply select the desired chapter from the drop-down list. Your eBookPLUS contains the entire textbook's content in easy-to-use HTML. The student resources panel contains supporting multimedia resources for each chapter.

## Using eBookPLUS references
eBookPLUS logos are used throughout the printed books to inform you that a multimedia resource is available for the content you are studying.

Searchlight IDs (e.g. **INT-0001**) give you instant access to multimedia resources. Once you are logged in, simply enter the searchlight ID for that resource and it will open immediately.

## Minimum requirements
JacarandaPLUS requires you to use a supported internet browser and version, otherwise you will not be able to access your resources or view all features and upgrades. Please view the complete list of JacPLUS minimum system requirements at http://jacplus.desk.com/customer/portal/articles/463717.

## Troubleshooting
- Go to the JacarandaPLUS help page at www.jacplus.com.au/jsp/help.jsp.
- Contact John Wiley & Sons Australia, Ltd.
  Email: support@jacplus.com.au
  Phone: 1800 JAC PLUS (1800 522 7587)

> Once you have created your account, you can use the same email address and password in the future to register any JacarandaPLUS titles you own.

# How to use this book

The following examples highlight the structure and main features of this textbook and eBookPLUS.

Chapters begin with *Inquiry questions* based on the syllabus.

A short section introduces each chapter.

Skills covered are listed at the beginning of each chapter.

The *Key terms* used in the chapter are clearly defined.

Presentation within chapters is in two-page or four-page sections for ease of study and teaching.

To aid literacy, dot points are used to break up blocks of text.

*GEOskills toolbox* features explain geographical skills and tools. Some chapters have step-by-step *GEOskillbuilder* features to teach skills.

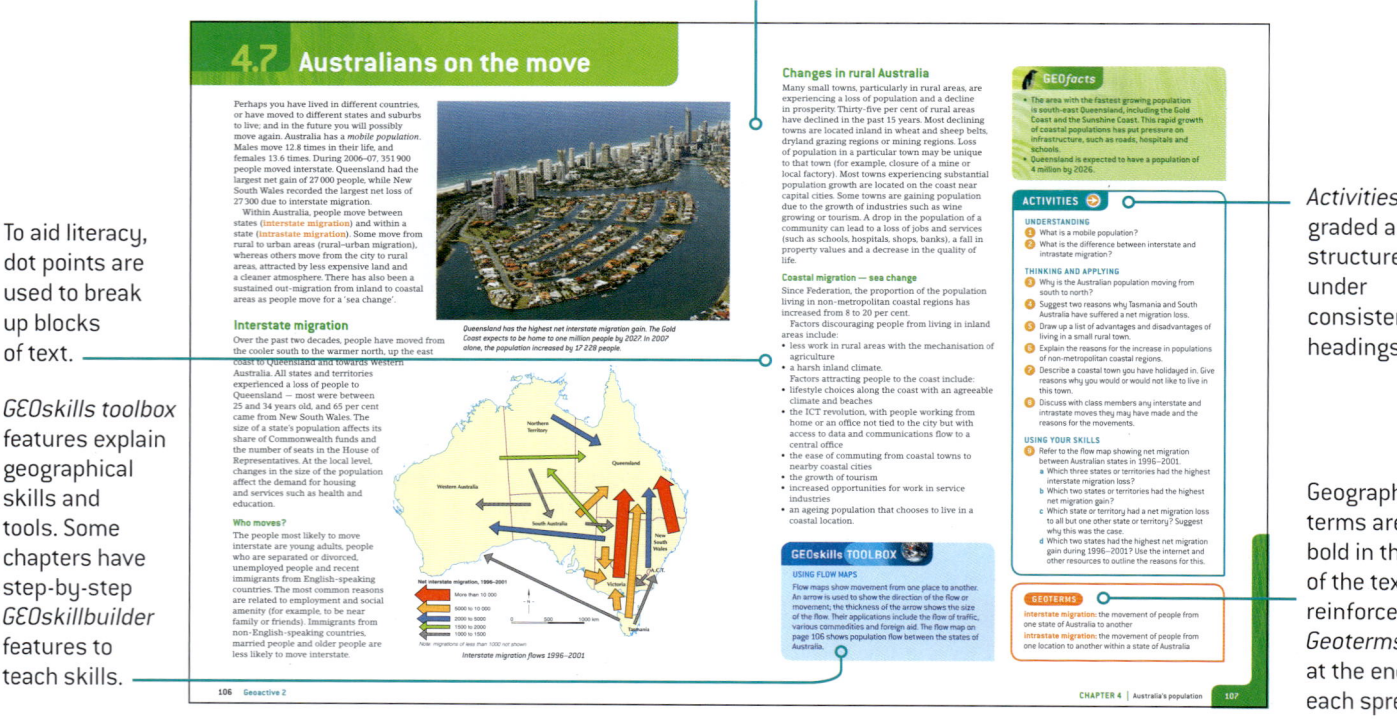

*Activities* are graded and structured under consistent headings.

Geographical terms are in bold in the body of the text and reinforced in a *Geoterms* box at the end of each spread.

*Working geographically* pages focus on students' understanding and analysis of stimulus material to prepare for the School Certificate.

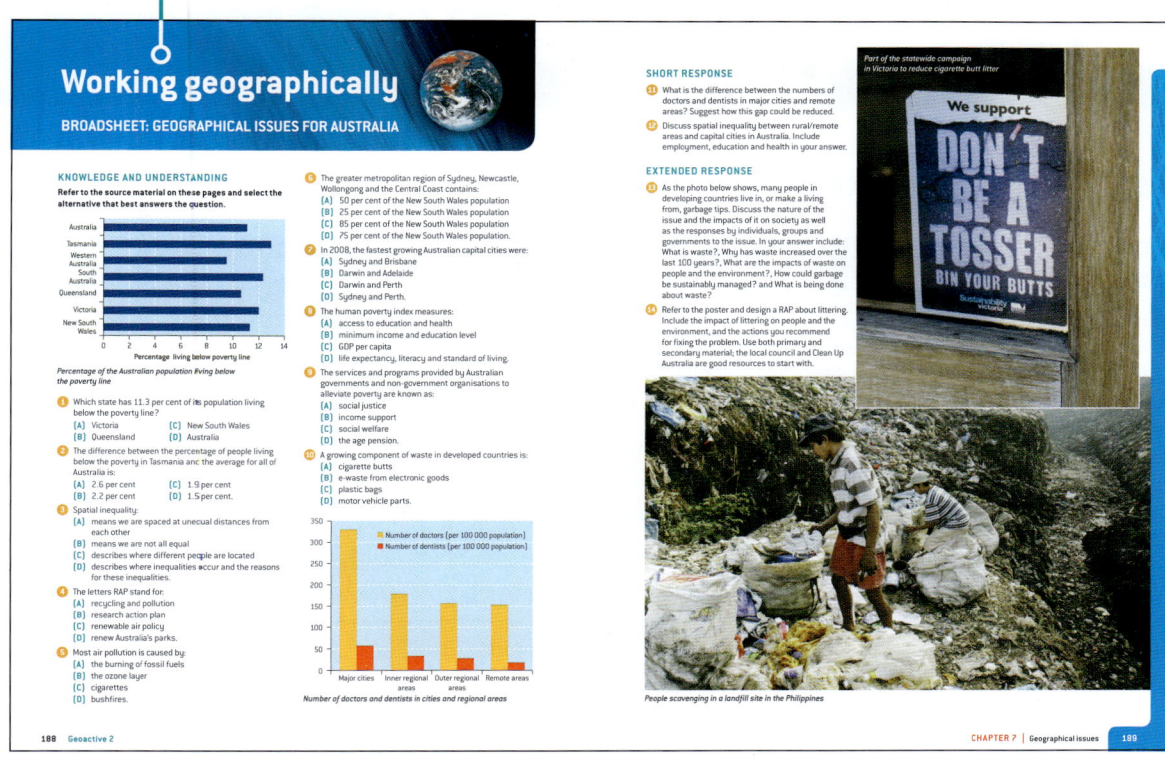

*ProjectsPLUS* is a new research management system, featuring media, templates and video introductions to a unique ICT project. Each project is specifically designed to inspire and engage students while providing quality assessment support for teachers.

Targeted *ICT activities* are available on eBookPLUS.

How to use this book  ix

# Coverage of syllabus

## Stage 5 Mandatory outcomes

| Outcomes | | Focus areas and chapter coverage | | | |
|---|---|---|---|---|---|
| A student: | | 5G1 | 5G2 | 5G3 | 5G4 |
| 5.1 | identifies, gathers and evaluates geographical information | Chapters 1–3 | Chapters 4–6 | Chapters 7–9 | |
| 5.2 | analyses, organises and synthesises geographical information | Chapters 1–3 | Chapters 4–6 | Chapters 7–9 | Chapters 10–13 |
| 5.3 | selects and uses appropriate written, oral and graphic forms to communicate geographical information | Chapters 1–3 | Chapters 4–6 | Chapters 7–9 | Chapters 10–13 |
| 5.4 | selects and applies appropriate geographical tools | Chapters 1–3 | Chapters 4–6 | Chapters 7–9 | Chapters 10–13 |
| 5.5 | demonstrates a sense of place about Australian environments | Chapters 1–3 | | Chapters 7–9 | |
| 5.6 | explains the geographical processes that form and transform Australian environments | Chapters 1–3 | | Chapters 7–9 | |
| 5.7 | analyses the impacts of different perspectives on geographical issues at local, national and global scales | | Chapters 4–6 | Chapters 7–9 | Chapters 10–13 |
| 5.8 | accounts for differences within and between Australian communities | | Chapters 4–6 | | Chapters 10–13 |
| 5.9 | explains Australia's links with other countries and its role in the global community | | Chapters 4–6 | | Chapters 10–13 |
| 5.10 | applies geographical knowledge, understanding and skills with knowledge of civics to demonstrate informed and active citizenship | Chapters 1–3 | Chapters 4–6 | Chapters 7–9 | Chapters 10–13 |

# Geographical tools

| GEOskillbuilder[a] | Chapter, section, page |
|---|---|
| **Using topographic maps** | Chapter 2, 2.3, pages 26–9 |
|     Calculating gradient | Chapter 2, 2.3, page 27 |
|     Finding local relief | Chapter 2, 2.3, page 28 |
|     Finding the aspect of a slope | Chapter 2, 2.3, page 28 |
|     Drawing a transect | Chapter 2, 2.3, page 28 |
| **Understanding landforms** | Chapter 2, 2.4, pages 30–1 |
|     Calculating the area of a feature | Chapter 2, 2.4, pages 30–1 |
| **Constructing a cross-section** | Chapter 2, 2.5, pages 32–3 |
| **Research and presentation** | Chapter 3, 3.12, pages 82–3 |
| **Constructing a population pyramid** | Chapter 4, 4.4, page 101 |
| **Using fieldwork techniques to collect data** | Chapter 6, 6.3, page 139 |
| **Developing a research action plan** | Chapter 7, 7.1, page 155 |
| **Coastal fieldwork and research action plan** | Chapter 9, 9.10, pages 248–9 |

| GEOskills toolbox | Chapter, section, page |
|---|---|
| Locating features on a map using latitude and longitude | Chapter 1, 1.2, page 7 |
| Creating a document containing weblinks | Chapter 1, 1.3, page 9 |
| Using physical maps | Chapter 2, 2.1, page 22 |
| Interpreting climatic graphs | Chapter 2, 2.6, page 37 |
| Interpreting synoptic charts | Chapter 2, 2.8, page 41 |
| Comparing satellite images | Chapter 3, 3.2, page 57 |
| Interpreting a newspaper article | Chapter 3, 3.4, page 61 |
| Interpreting a satellite image | Chapter 3, 3.7, page 69; chapter 6, 6.1, page 129 |
| Working with thematic maps | Chapter 3, 3.9, page 72 |
| Flow charts and diagrams | Chapter 3, 3.11, page 80 |
| Calculating population density | Chapter 4, 4.1, page 94 |
| Locating features using latitude and longitude | Chapter 4, 4.1, page 95 |
| Identifying large-scale and small-scale maps | Chapter 4, 4.2, page 96 |
| Working with compound column or bar graphs | Chapter 4, 4.5, page 103 |
| Using flow maps | Chapter 4, 4.7, page 107 |
| Constructing land use maps | Chapter 5, 5.3, page 119 |
| Interpreting a column graph | Chapter 5, 5.4, page 120 |
| Using choropleth maps | Chapter 5, 5.5, page 122 |
| Comparing a graph with a table | Chapter 6, 6.1, page 131 |
| Using the internet for newspaper articles | Chapter 6, 6.4, page 142 |
| Using a geographical issues scaffold | Chapter 7, 7.1, page 150 |
| Measuring bearings on a map | Chapter 7, 7.6, page 171 |
| Collecting and using digital images | Chapter 8, 8.4, page 199 |
| Reading and interpreting a synoptic chart | Chapter 9, 9.3, page 228 |
| Interpreting a vegetation transect | Chapter 9, 9.5, page 235 |
| Using latitude and longitude | Chapter 11, 11.14, page 319 |
| Statistical data and combined graphs | Chapter 12, 12.1, page 325 |
| Constructing a population pyramid | Chapter 12, 12.3, page 329 |

(a) *GEOskillbuilder* features take students step by step through key geographical skills.

# Acknowledgements

The authors would like to thank Pamela McAlister for her valuable contribution and consistent support. Thanks also to the staff of John Wiley & Sons Australia for their commitment to quality, particularly Jan Cousens for her dedication and creativity.

The authors and publisher would like to thank the following copyright holders, organisations and individuals for their assistance and for permission to reproduce copyright material in this book.

**Images:**
• Andrew D. Short, Senior Coastal Scientist **239** (bottom left) • Andrew Weldon **297** (bottom) • Australian Bureau of Meteorology **228** • Australian Bureau of Statistics/ABS data used with permission from the Australian Bureau of Statistics (www.abs.gov.au): /ABS Year Book Australia 2008 **105** (top left); /Cat. 4713 — Table 2.4 Estimated Resident Population, by Remoteness Areas (27 March 2008) **120** (middle right); /Map redrawn by MAPgraphics Pty Ltd, Brisbane **123** (bottom); **133** (top right); **135** (top left); /Map redrawn by MAPgraphics Pty Ltd, Brisbane **137** (bottom); **268** (bottom); **289** (bottom left); /Cat. 4901.0 — Children's Participation in Cultural and Leisure Activities, Australia April 2006 **289** (top left); /Cat. 3222.0 — Population Projections, Australia, 2006 to 2101 **324** (top right); /Cat. 3222.0 — Population Projections 1999–2101 **326** (top right); /Cat. 3222.0 — Population Projections 2002–2101 **328** (middle left); /Cat. 3412.0 — Migration **330** (middle right); /Cat. 3412.0 — Migration 2006–07 **330** (top left); /Cat. 4102.0 — Housing and Services in Remote Aboriginal and Torres Strait Islander Communities, Australian Social Trends, 2008 **337** (middle right); /2003 Population Projections Australia 2002–2101 **338** • Australian Conservation Foundation and the Australian Medical Association, Dr Rosalie Woodruff, Dr Simon Hales, Dr Colin Butler and Professor Anthony McMichael. Reproduced by permission of the Australian Conservation Foundation. **39** (bottom) • Australian Council of Social Service (ACOSS) **175** (middle left); **188** (bottom right) • Australian Koala Foundation/Artwork: John Garnsworthy & Associates. Reproduced with permission from the Australian Koala Foundation (www.savethekoala.com) **209** • AusAID: /Roger Wheatley **290–1**; **301** (top left) • AAP Image: /Wildlight/Willem van den Bosch **46**; /Brent Bignell **114**; /Liz Thompson **126–7**; /David Hancock **141** (bottom right); /Brian Harvey **146** (bottom); /Tourism NSW **147** (middle right); **161**; /AFP/William West **175** (bottom left); /Laura Freizer **187**; AP/Jamie Alexander **197** (top left); /Wildlight/ Bill Bachman **202** (bottom); /AP/Tertius Pickard **241** (inset, right); /Dave Hunt **241** (right); /AFP **258** (bottom right); /Jiri Rezac **259** (top right); /AFP/William West **260**; /Lloyd Jones **319** (middle left); /Wildlight/ Jason Busch **322–3**; /AP **355** (bottom left); /Wildlight/Penny Tweedie **365** (middle left); /Wildlight **365** (middle) • ANTPhoto.com.au: / Kelvin Aitken **51** (inset); /JP & ES Baker **206** (middle left); /Peter Atkinson **224** (bottom right); /Otto Rogge **232**; /P&M Walton **233**; /Natfoto **234** (bottom right); /JP & ES Baker **235** • Bali Discovery Tours (www.balidiscovery.com) **265** (middle left) • Barry Skipsey **124** • © Brand X Pictures **26** • Brice Peired **256** • © City of Sydney **247** (left); **247** (right) • Bureau of Meteorology, © Commonwealth of Australia, reproduced by permission: /Annual Australian Climate Statement 2005 **39** (middle); /Annual Climate Statement 2005 **39** (top); **40**; **67** (top right); /Greg Holland **75** (bottom); /GMS-5: Satellite image originally processed by Australian Bureau of Meteorology from the geostationary satellite GMS-5 operated by the Japan Meteorological Agency **76** (bottom right); **192**; **251** • The Treasury, © Commonwealth of Australia, reproduced by permission **176** • Department of the Environment, Water, Heritage and the Arts, © Commonwealth of Australia, reproduced by permission/Map redrawn by MAPgraphics Pty Ltd, Brisbane **236** (left) • Australian Customs and Border Protection Service, © Commonwealth of Australia, reproduced by permission **258** (middle left) • Department of Foreign Affairs and Trade, © Commonwealth of Australia, reproduced by permission: /Australia–China Free Trade Agreement, 2008 **267**; /Composition of Trade Australia 2007–2008, p. 4 **293** (bottom left); /Composition of Trade Australia 2007–2008, p. 3 **293** (middle left); /Composition of Trade Australia 2007–2008, p. 24 **295** (bottom left); /Composition of Trade Australia 2007–2008, p. 24 **295** (middle left); /Composition of Trade Australia 2007–2008, p. 24 **295** (top left); /Composition of Trade Australia 2007–2008, p. 22 **295** (top middle); /Country, Economy & Regional Information **321** (left) • Department of Agriculture, Fisheries and Forestry, © Commonwealth of Australia, reproduced by permission **297** (top), **298** • AusAID, © Commonwealth of Australia, reproduced by permission **300**, **304** (top right), **306**, **307** (top) • Australian Institute of Family Studies, © Commonwealth of Australia, reproduced by permission **326** (top left), **328** (right) • Department of Immigration and Citizenship, © Commonwealth of Australia, reproduced by permission **330** (bottom right), **333** (bottom left), **333** (middle left), **335** (middle left), **335** (top left) • © Commonwealth of Australia, Geoscience Australia: **22** (bottom left); /2009 **22** (bottom middle); /2009/Map redrawn by MAPgraphics Pty Ltd, Brisbane **66** (bottom left); /2009 **125**; **145**; /Bureau of Meteorology, Emergency Management Australia **250**; /Map redrawn by MAPgraphics Pty Ltd, Brisbane **349** • © Commonwealth of Australia, reproduced by permission: **301** (middle right); **301** (top right); /Map redrawn by MAPgraphics Pty Ltd, Brisbane **302**; **311** (top); /Map redrawn by MAPgraphics Pty Ltd, Brisbane **337** (top right); **376** (bottom right); **377** (bottom left); **377** (middle left); **377** (top left) • Coo-ee Picture Library: **189** (top right); **105** (bottom left) • Corbis: /Nick Rains **1**, **9** (top right); /J. Carnemolla **58** (top left); **85** (middle right); /Reuters/Daniel Munoz **148–9**; /Ecoscene/Nick Hawkes **212** (middle right); /Paul A. Souders **233**; /Yann Arthus-Bertrand **237** (top left); /Patrick Robert **274**; /Erol Gurian **308** (bottom right); /Clifford White **368** (bottom left); /Atlantide Phototravel/ Mario Cipriani **369** (middle left); /Ulises Rodriguez **369** (top left); /dpa/Erwin Patzelt **369** (top right); /John Van Hasselt **372** (bottom left); /Andrew Brownbill/epa **52–3** • © Corbis Corporation **153** (bottom right); **309** (top left) • The Courier-Mail, 13 March 2009 **241** (bottom left) • © CSIRO Marine and Atmospheric Research, reproduced with permission from http://www.cmar.csiro.au/e-print/open/hennessy_2003a.pdf **207** (bottom left) • CSIRO Publishing: /© CSIRO/Gregory Heath **196** (middle right); /© CSIRO 2005/Photo by Pauline English **198** (bottom left) • © Cynthia Wardle **83** (middle) • © Denis Couch **61** (top right) • Department of Environment, Climate Change and Water **160** (bottom right), **193** • Department of Environment and Conservation, based on 1995 paper 'The use of ecological footprint methodology for regional analysis' by R. Simpson, A. Petroeschevsky, K. Gaschk, S. Rutherford, presented to the Regional Science Conference, Brisbane. **344** (bottom right) • Courtesy of Department of Primary Industries, Victoria/Photo by Ian Sargeant **196** (bottom right) • Base map reproduced with the permission of TASMAP, State of Tasmania **31** • © The State of Queensland (Department of Environment and Resource Management), 2009 **200** (bottom right), **200** (top right) • © Digital Vision: /Stephen Frink **50** (middle right); **308** (middle right) • © Earth Vistas **4** (bottom) • Eastview Cartography, map redrawn by MAPgraphics Pty Ltd, Brisbane **269** • © EcoSTEPS **344** (left) • Reprinted with permission from Elsevier. Reprinted from The Lancet, Vol. 367, 'Lancet Series on Indigenous Health', p. 2022, June 2006. **376** (middle right) • ESRI (www.esri.com) **313** (middle left) • Fairfax Photo Library: /The Sun Herald **11** (middle right); /Robert Pearce **56**, **73**, **123** (top right); /Jason South **63**; **66** (top right); /Craig Abraham **67**; /Peter Morris **79**; /Rick Stevens **92–3**, **370**; **102** (middle right); /Sandy Scheltema **142** (bottom left); /Louise Kennerley **146** (top right); /Andrew Taylor **152** (top right); /Dallas Kilponen **153** (middle left); /Wayne Taylor **153** (top right); /Jenny Evans **179** (middle right); **183**; /Kate Geraghty **197** (bottom right); /Andrew Meares **238** (bottom left), **371**; /Jojin Kang **238** (bottom right); /Justin McManus **350–1**; /Mike Bowers **373** • Franco Vairani/MIT Smart Cities Group **346** (right) • Data supplied and processed by Geoimage www.geoimage.com.au/Landsat **111**, **129** • Georges River Environmental Education Centre: /Sharyn Cullis **215** (bottom left), **215** (middle right); /David Barnett **215** (middle left); /Ron Israel **215** (top left); /Georges River Environmental Education Centre/Debbie Andrew **215** (top right) • Getty Images: /AFP/Antonia Scorza **254–5**; /Ezra Shaw **284**; /Lisa Maree Williams **302** (top

right); /AFP/William West **303** (top left); /Paula Bronstein **303** (top right); /AFP/Jewel Samad **305**; /Uriel Sinai **317**; /AFP/Philippe Hugeun **355** (top left); /AFP/Stringer **356**; /Matt Turner **365** (middle right); /Ian Waldie **367**; /Andrew Sheargold/Stringer **375** • © Google **236** (right) • © Gundjehmi Aboriginal Corporation **141** (top right) • Horwath HTL **281** (bottom), **281** (middle right) • Hunter Development Corporation **164–5** • © Iain Meyer **249** • © www.imageaddict.com.au **327** (top right) • © Image 100 **244** (upper middle left) • Internet World Stats **131** • International Atomic Energy Agency (IAEA) — Power Reactor Information System **184** • © IAG, map redrawn by MAPgraphics Pty Ltd, Brisbane **72** • IPCC **239** (top left) • John Oxley Library/Sydney Hughes Greetings **202** (top right) • © John Wiley & Sons Australia/Vikki Steele **82** (middle right) • Jojin Kang **68** • © Joli **229** (middle left) • Judy Mraz **30** • The Kobal Collection/20th Century Fox/Bazmark Films **283** (top left) • © Land and Property Management Authority 2009 (www.lpma.nsw.gov.au) **88** (bottom), **89**, **119**, **208** • Map courtesy of Land Information Services, Department of Primary Industries, Water & Environment, Hobart **29** • Lend Lease Development Pty Ltd, Map Illustration Holcam Creative 02 9326 2559 **171** • Darren Jew/Living Image **229** (bottom left), **229** (top left) • Lochman Transparencies: /© Marie Lochman **45** (middle left); /© Jiri Lochman **50** (bottom left), **50** (bottom middle), **50** (bottom right); /© Col Roberts **140** • Lonely Planet Images/Peter Solness **307** (right) • © Ludo Kuipers, OzOutback Internet Services **151** • MAPgraphics Pty Ltd, Brisbane **4** (bottom), **4** (top right), **5, 6–7, 10, 17, 20** (bottom), **21** (top right), **32, 34** (left), **35** (right), **36** (top right), **36** (left), **44** (bottom right), **45** (bottom), **51, 55, 61** (top left), **62, 75** (top left), **76** (top left), **83** (left), **83** (right), **85** (bottom left), **87** (bottom left), **87** (bottom right), **87** (middle right), **94** (top right), **95, 96** (left), **96** (right), **106** (bottom right), **110, 115, 132** (top left), **136** (top left), **142** (bottom right), **196** (bottom left), **198** (top right), **206** (top right), **215** (centre), **217** (top left), **219** (top left), **230** (bottom middle), **243** (top right), **256, 264, 288, 347, 353, 354–5** (middle), **363**; /E. Pluribus Anthony/Map redrawn by MAPgraphics Pty Ltd, Brisbane **262** • Photo by Mary E. White in *Listen our Land is Crying* **212** (middle left) • Matthias Loster **43** (top) • Murray–Darling Basin Authority/Map redrawn by MAPgraphics Pty Ltd, Brisbane **199** • Murray–Darling Basin Commission/MAPgraphics Pty Ltd, Brisbane **221** (inset) • Murray–Darling Basin Committee/ MAPgraphics Pty Ltd, Brisbane **220** • © Newcastle Region Library **86** • Newspix: /Chris Hyde **42** (middle right); /Steve Brennan **49** (left); /David Caird **66** (bottom right); /Patrick Hamilton **71**; /Anna Rogers **74**; /Marc McCormack **77**; /Karen Brook **81** (middle); /Liam Driver **94** (middle); /David Caird **98** (left); /Phil Hillyard **105** (top right); /Isabella Lettini **109** (top right); /Brendan Radke **135** (top right); /John Fotiadis **136** (top right), **137** (inset), **138** (bottom left), **138** (top right); /Clive Hyde **142** (top right); /Bob Finlayson **150**; /John Grainger **160** (bottom left); /Renee Nowytarger **167** (top left); /Jim Trifyllis **167** (top right); /Dean Marzolla **168**; /Geoff Ward **170** (top right); /Richard Cisar-Wright **177** (top right); /AFP/Thomas Coex **180**; /Alan Pryke **186**; /Kelly Barnes **219** (top left); **243** (top left); /Kym Smith **266**; /Toby Zerna **277, 280**; /Stephen Cooper **287**; /AFP/William West **312**; /Elsby James **327** (bottom left); **330** (top right); /David Geraghty **332**; /Robert McKell **339**; /Jason Busch **342**; /AFP/ Giulio Napolitano **354** (top right); /Antony Dickson **355** (top right); /Kelly Barnes **357**; /AFP/Timothy A. Clary **360**; /Ray Strange **362**; /AFP/ **366** (bottom right); /Eddie Safarik **366** (top right); /David Sproule **369** (centre); /Jamie Wicks **372** (bottom right) • NASA: /NASA's Goddard Space Flight Center, MODIS Rapid Response Team **69**; **81** (top right); **321** • Graph produced by the Centre for Epidemiology and Research, NSW Department of Health using data produced by the Australian Bureau of Statistics (ABS 2001 and 2006 Census Basic Community Profiles) **334** • NSW Department of Planning: **168** (middle left); /*City of Cities — A Plan for Sydney's Future*, December 2005, p. 19 • NSW Department of Planning, map by MAPgrpahics Pty Ltd, Brisbane **343** • © State of NSW through the NSW Office of Water 2009 **217** (bottom left) • © The Australian National University: 'Reviving Growth in the Pacific Islands: Are we Swimming or Sinking?' Biman Chand Prasad and Paresh Kumar Narayan, *Pacific Economic Bulletin* Volume 23 Number 2 2008 **270** • Panos Pictures: /Jocelyn Carlin **271**; /Jane Hahn **299** (top right); /Mark Henley **313** (middle); /Paul Weinberg **369** (middle right) • Parliament of Australia, Parliamentary Library **177** (top left) • Penny van Oosterzee **12** • Perri Winter/Just Salvos (www.justsalvos.com) **299** (middle left) • Cartoon by Peter Nicholson from *The Australian* (www.nicholsoncartoons.com.au) **289** (top right) • Photo Index **50** (middle left) • © Photodisc **82** (bottom), **152** (bottom right), **244** (bottom left), **244** (bottom right), **244** (lower middle left), **244** (middle right), **244** (top left), **244** (top right), **308** (top right), **309** (top right), **327** (top right) • Photolibrary: /Geoff Higgins **2–3, 203**; /Brian Lovell **20** (top); /Javier Larrea **42** (bottom left); /Photononstop/Jacques Loic **42** (bottom right); /Oxford Scientific Films/Konrad Wothe **49** (right); /Peter Harrison **106** (top right), **133** (left), **163, 216, 230**; /Roel Loopers **109** (middle left); /Phillip Hayson **112–3, 222–3**; /Robin Smith **118** (bottom right), **202** (middle right), **207** (top right); /David Messent **134, 225**; **144**; /Science Photo Library/Peter Menzel **189** (bottom); **234** (middle right); /John Warburton-Lee Photography/Andrew Watson **237** (bottom right) • Population projections for Sunshine Coast DGP, by age and sex, 2005 and 2020, *Population Health Profile of the Sunshine Coast Division of General Practice: Supplement, Population Profile Series: 83A*, PHIDU, March 2007, p. 2 **348** • Qasco **170** (bottom right) • © Refugee Council of Australia **358** • Rhett A. Butler **259** (bottom left) • Richard Woldendorp **224** (top right) • © Sash Whitehead **70** • D.L. Dunkerley/Monash University/School of Geography and Environmental Science. Boucher 1990/Photography by Tony Miller. **196** (top right) • Used under license from Shutterstock.com 2009: /Julian Weber **252–3** (bottom); /© Cheryl Casey **91** (middle left), **253** (middle right); /© Neale Cousland **90** (middle); /© Stephen Finn **379** (middle right); /© Leisa Hennessy **378–9** (bottom); /© Idiz **378** (top); /© Roger Rosentreter **90** (bottom); /© twobluedogs **378–9** (middle) • © The Smith Family, data sourced from ABS 1997–98 Survey of Income and Housing Costs, updated by NATSEM to May 1999. **172** • Snowy Hydro Limited **43** (bottom) • Télécoms Sans Frontières and www.tsfi.org **275** • Tasmanian Photo Library **204** • Terrigal Surf Life Saving Club/Vesna Tindall **116** (bottom left), **116** (middle right), **117** (bottom left), **117** (top) • Tourism Australia, reproduced by permission **268** (top right), **283** (top right) • Globalis. UNEP/GRID-Arendal: /Common Database (UN Population Division estimate) **162**; /Philippe Rekacewicz **185** • © Viewfinder Australia Photo Library **iii** (left), **8, 152** (middle), **246** (bottom right), **246** (top right) • Warringah Council **225** (top left) • Wildlight Photo Agency: /© The Right Image/Wildlight.net **18**; /© Bill Bachman/Wildlight.net **21** (top left); /© Hugh Brown/Wildlight.net **44** (left); /© Penny Tweedie/Wildlight.net **120** (bottom); /© Kevin McGrath/Wildlight.net **130**; /© Bill Bachman/Wildlight.net **190–1**; /© Bill Bachman/Wildlight.net **221** (bottom) • World Trade Organization /Map redrawn by MAPgraphics Pty Ltd, Brisbane **294**

**Text:**

• Asa Wahlquist, *The Australian*, 16 December 2008 **220**; *The Australian*, 8 August 2008 **221** • Asa Wahlquist and Sonya Sandham, *The Sydney Morning Herald*, 27 May 1994 **60** • Association of Surfing Professionals (ASP) **285** • Australian Bureau of Statistics, ABS data used with permission from the Australian Bureau of Statistics (www.abs.gov.au): /Cat.1301.0 — Year Book Australia, 2005 **100** /Cat. 4713 — Population Characteristics: Aboriginal and Torres Strait Islander Australians **104**; /Cat. 1301.0 — Year Book Australia, 2008 **338** • © Australian Strategic Policy Institute **68** • Reproduced with permission from AusAID **302, 303** • © ABC 2009. All rights reserved. **237** • © 2003 Board of Studies NSW for and on behalf of the Crown in right of the State of New South Wales **x** • Attorney-General for Australia, © Commonwealth of Australia **251** • Department of Foreign Affairs and Trade, © Commonwealth of Australia, reproduced by permission: /Australia–China Free Trade Agreement, 2008 **267**; /Country, Economy & Regional Information, **264**; /Country, Economy & Regional Information **271** • Department of Immigration and Citizenship, © Commonwealth of Australia, reproduced by permission **359** • The *Australian Declaration Towards Reconciliation* (2000) was published and presented by the Council for Aboriginal Reconciliation, which ended its 10-year term at the end of the year 2000. For further information visit www.reconciliation.org.au. **371** • Brian Williams and Robyn Ironside, *The Courier-Mail*, 18 November 2008 **71** • Daniel Dasey, *Sun Herald*, 20 August 2006, p. 36 **11** • Ecotourism Australia **205** • *The Guardian*, 30 May 2007 **143** • International Atomic Energy Agency — Power Reactor Information System **184** • Richard Macey and Natasha Wallace, *The Age*, 24 September 2009 **197** • © NSW Department of Planning/*City of Cities — A Plan for Sydney's Future*, December 2005, p. 18 **343** • Daryl Passmore, *The Sunday Mail* (Brisbane), 15 March 2009 **151** • Tourism Australia, reproduced by permission **283**

Every effort has been made to trace the ownership of copyright material. Information that will enable the publisher to rectify any error or omission in subsequent reprints will be welcome. In such cases, please contact the Permission Section of John Wiley & Sons Australia, Ltd.

Geography poses fascinating questions about who we are and how we got to be that way, and then provides clues to the answers.

Kenneth C. Davis, *Don't know much about geography* (2004)

# 1 The Australian continent

### INQUIRY QUESTIONS
+ What are Australia's geographical dimensions?
+ What is Australia's relative size and shape compared with other continents and countries?
+ How do we locate Australia in the world?
+ How can we explain the origins of the Australian continent?

Australia is a unique continent. It is not only the smallest continent but also the driest and the flattest inhabited continent. In this chapter, we locate Australia and its place on the Earth using latitude and longitude. We study its geographical dimensions such as its relative size and shape compared with other countries. We also explore the origins of the continent from both Aboriginal and geographical perspectives.

### GEOskills TOOLBOX
+ Locating features on a map using latitude and longitude (page 7)
+ Creating a document containing weblinks (page 9)

*Australia has many spectacular landforms that are recognised both by Australians and people in other countries. One such landform is Kata Tjuta in the Northern Territory's 'red centre'.*

### KEY TERMS

**continent:** one of the seven great main landmasses on the Earth

**continental drift:** the theory that describes how continents broke away and drifted from an original landmass

**continental shelf:** the part of a continent found under a shallow sea

**Dreaming:** stories that describe the Dreamtime, a time in which the Aboriginal peoples believe the Earth came to have its present form and in which life and nature began

**erosion:** the wearing away of soil and rock by natural elements such as wind and water

**gross national income (GNI) per capita:** total value of goods and services produced in a country in one year per person plus net income from abroad

**ice age:** a time in which the Earth was colder, resulting in the expansion of glaciers and ice sheets and a fall in sea level

**Indigenous people:** the descendants of the original inhabitants of an area

**latitude:** location represented by imaginary lines drawn around the Earth from east to west, which show the distance north or south of the Equator, measured in degrees, minutes and seconds

**longitude:** location represented by imaginary lines drawn around the Earth from north to south, which show the distance east or west of the Prime Meridian, measured in degrees, minutes and seconds

**mantle:** the layer of rock between the Earth's crust and the core

**sacred sites:** places where important events in the Dreaming took place

**sediment:** material deposited by a stream or other body of water

**tectonic plates:** the various slow-moving plates that make up the Earth's crust. Volcanoes and earthquakes often occur at the edge of plates.

**topography:** physical features (height and shape) of an area of land

**weathering:** the breakdown of bare rock by water and temperature changes

# 1.1 Australia's geographical dimensions

## Size and shape

Australia is one of the seven continents of the world. The landmass of the Australian **continent** extends over an area of about 7682 million square kilometres. This is almost as great as the area of the United States of America (excluding Alaska), a little more than one-third of the size of Russia and about thirty-two times greater than the United Kingdom.

If you travelled in a straight line from Australia's east coast to the west coast at its widest point, you would cover a distance of almost 4000 kilometres. You would also pass through three time zones — on the west coast the sun rises two hours later than it does on the east. A journey from south to north through the 'red centre' would cover over 2500 kilometres and pass through several climate zones, from the cooler and temperate south to the hot, humid tropics in the north.

### GEO*facts*

- Australia is the smallest of the seven continents of the world.
- Australia is the sixth-largest country.
- The population of Australia grew to over 22 million people in 2007.

*The relative size of Australia*

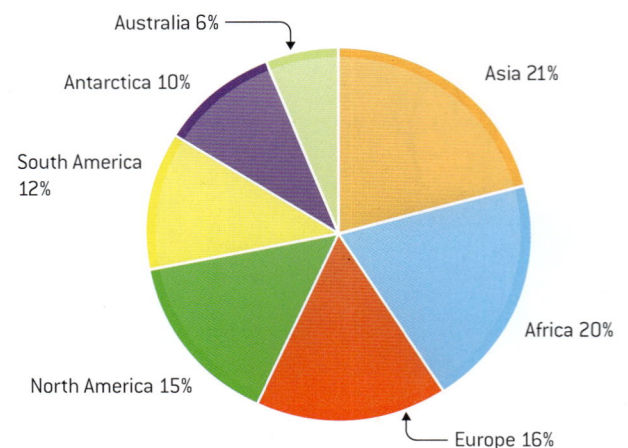

*The relative size of the continents*

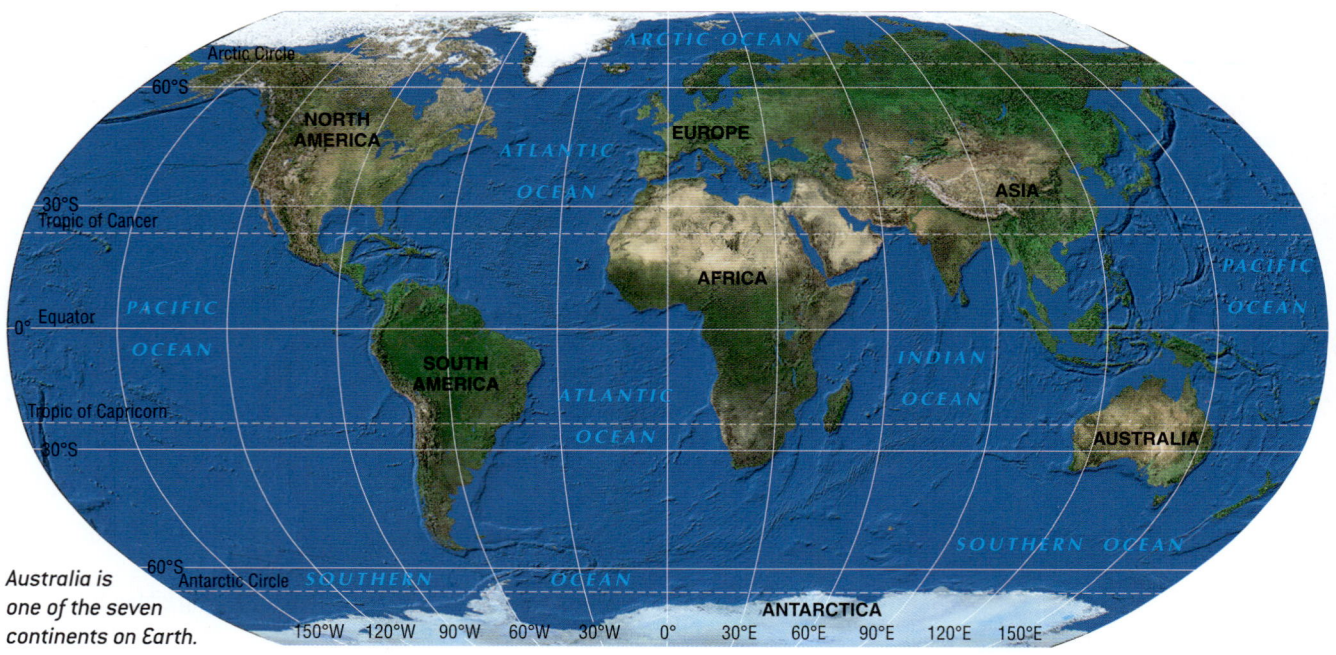

Australia is one of the seven continents on Earth.

# Commonwealth states and territories

The Commonwealth of Australia is made up of six states and two territories. Each state and territory has its own internal government and capital city.

The federal capital of Australia is Canberra. Australia also has seven external territories: Norfolk Island; Christmas Island; the Cocos (Keeling) Islands; the Coral Sea Islands Territory; the Territory of Ashmore and Cartier Islands; the Australian Antarctic Territory; and Heard Island and McDonald Islands.

# Exclusive economic zone

Australia's territorial maritime (sea) boundaries extend about 200 nautical miles (or 370 kilometres) out from the coastline of Australia. Most of the area within the maritime boundary is the exclusive economic zone (EEZ). Australia has exclusive rights to explore, exploit, conserve and manage all natural marine resources within the zone. In 2008, the United Nations granted Australia another 2.5 million square kilometres of the **continental shelf**. This included the seabed within 200 nautical miles of Australia and all its external territories. It enlarged the area of potential gas, oil and mineral deposits available to Australia.

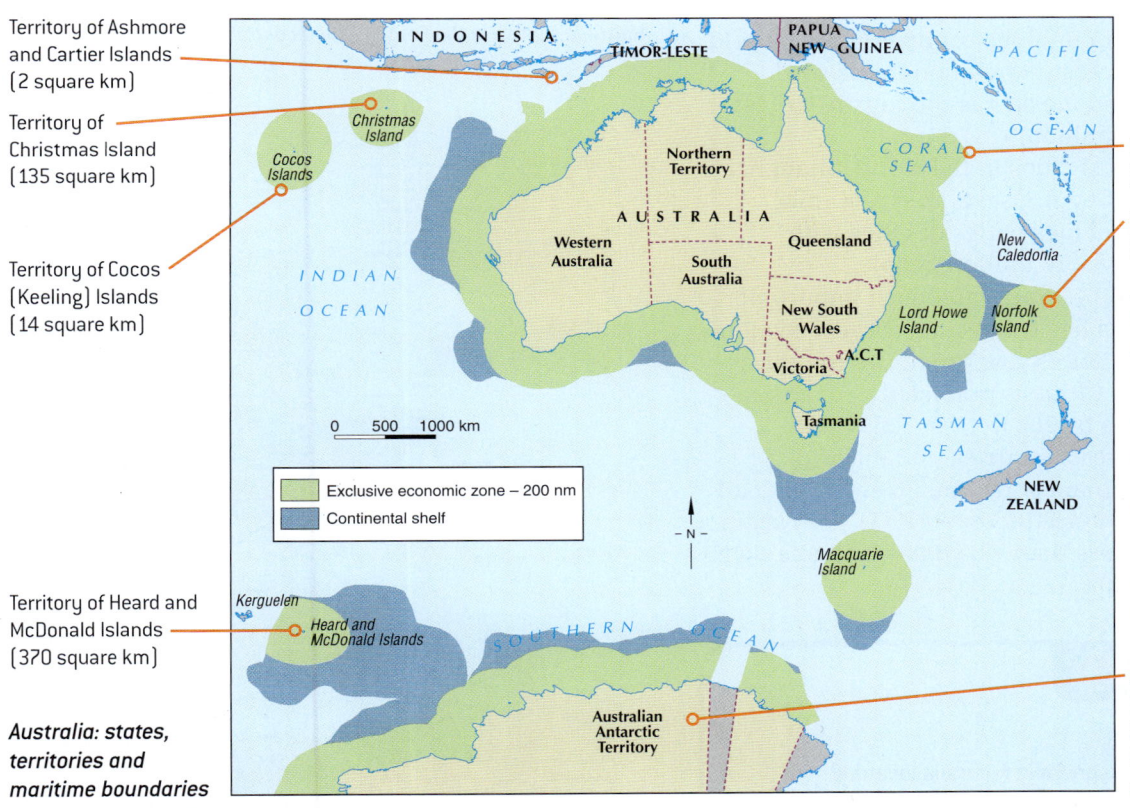

Territory of Ashmore and Cartier Islands (2 square km)
Territory of Christmas Island (135 square km)
Territory of Cocos (Keeling) Islands (14 square km)
Territory of Heard and McDonald Islands (370 square km)

*Australia: states, territories and maritime boundaries*

Coral Sea Islands Territory (approx. 81 square km)
Norfolk Island (35 square km)

**Areas of the states and territories**
ACT: 2 358 square km
Northern Territory: 1 420 970 square km
NSW: 809 444 square km
Queensland: 1 852 642 square km
South Australia: 1 043 514 square km
Tasmania: 90 758 square km
Victoria: 227 600 square km
Western Australia: 2 645 615 square km
Australian Antarctic Territory (6 100 000 square km, including sea; 5 896 500 square km, excluding sea)

## ACTIVITIES

### UNDERSTANDING

1. List the continents of the world in order from largest to smallest.
2. How would you describe Australia's size relative to Russia's?
3. What is the Exclusive Economic Zone?

### USING YOUR SKILLS

4. Refer to the world map on the previous page. Which continents are crossed by the:
   a Equator
   b Tropic of Cancer
   c Tropic of Capricorn?

5. Refer to the map of Australia above.
   a List the states and mainland territories in order of size from largest to smallest.
   b Identify and list Australia's seven external territories.
   c Estimate which external territory is closest to and which is furthest from Australia's mainland.

### GEOTERMS

**continent:** one of the seven great main landmasses on the Earth
**continental shelf:** the part of a continent found under a shallow sea

CHAPTER 1 | The Australian continent

# 1.2 Locating Australia

Australia is located in the Southern Hemisphere, a location it shares with the continents of Africa, South America and Antarctica, as well as many islands in the South Atlantic, Indian and South Pacific oceans. We also refer to Australia as being located in the Eastern Hemisphere, which it shares with East Asia and South Asia, New Zealand, the Pacific Islands and part of Antarctica. The dividing line between the Eastern and Western Hemispheres is known as the Prime Meridian.

To the north of Australia lie:
- some of the most populous countries in the world. China has the largest population in the world (1330 million); Indonesia has the fourth-largest population (238 million).
- some of the largest cities in the world. Shanghai, Beijing, Tianjin, Seoul, Osaka, Tokyo, Manila and Jakarta are all megacities or cities with populations of over 10 million people.
- some of the world's largest and most important economies. China has the second-largest economy after the United States, and Japan has the third-largest economy. China is predicted to overtake the United States by 2025.
- some of the poorest countries in the world. Timor-Leste, Vietnam and Papua New Guinea all have a **gross national income (GNI) per capita** (per person) of less than US$1000. Australia's GNI is over US$36 000.

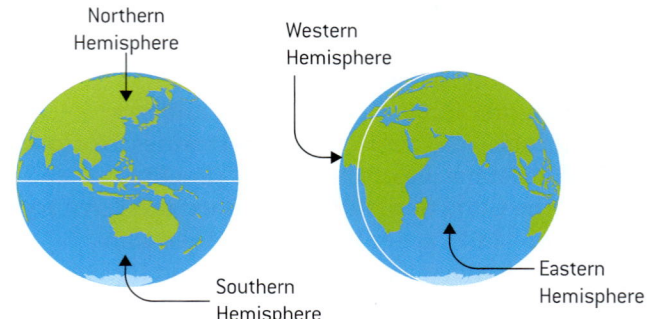

*Australia's place in the Southern and Eastern Hemispheres*

*World political map*

## ACTIVITIES

### UNDERSTANDING
1. In which hemisphere is Australia located?
2. Name two megacities that are located to Australia's north.

### USING YOUR SKILLS
3. Refer to the world political map opposite. Estimate the distance in a straight line from:
   a. the easternmost part of Australia to the closest part of the United States
   b. the northernmost part of Australia to the closest part of Indonesia
   c. the westernmost part of Australia to the closest part of the United Kingdom.
4. Give the location using latitude and longitude of:
   a. Australia
   b. New Zealand
   c. Papua New Guinea
   d. China.

6  Geoactive 2

## GEOskills TOOLBOX

### LOCATING FEATURES ON A MAP USING LATITUDE AND LONGITUDE

To locate places, geographers use a grid made up of lines of **latitude** and **longitude**. These lines are shown in the diagram. The map below shows these lines combined as a grid. Latitude and longitude are measured in degrees. Each degree can be further divided into 60 minutes. Latitude and longitude allow us to locate any place on Earth. For example, Japan is located between latitudes 30°N and 40°N and between longitudes 135°E and 150°E. Latitude is always given before longitude.

### Latitude

Imaginary lines running across the world are called parallels of latitude. They measure how far north or south of the Equator (0° latitude) a place is located. Places south of the Equator are shown with an 'S'. Places north of the Equator are shown with an 'N'.

### Longitude

Imaginary lines running from the South Pole to the North Pole are called meridians of longitude. One of these lines has been chosen as the Prime Meridian (0° longitude). It runs through Greenwich in England. All the other lines of longitude are given a number between 0° and 180°. They measure how far east or west of the Prime Meridian a place is located. Places east of this line are marked with an 'E'. Places west of this line are marked with a 'W'.

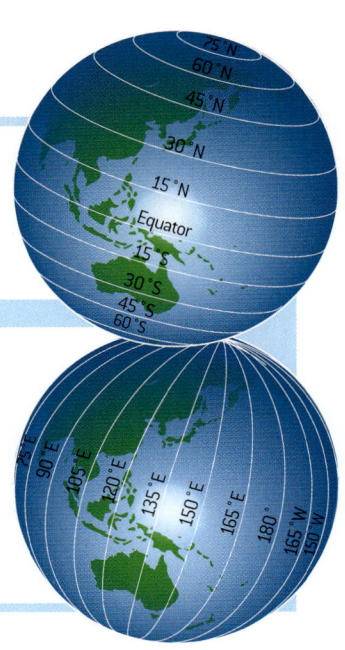

**CHAPTER 1** | The Australian continent

# 1.3 Origins of the continent: Aboriginal perspective

## The Dreaming and the land

The oral history of Australia's Aboriginal and Torres Strait Islander peoples — its **Indigenous people** — tells of a Dreamtime when all things began. Stories of this time have been passed down by word of mouth over thousands of years. Dreamtime stories explained how the world came to be, providing a basis for people's spirituality. They also provided rules to live by and sometimes warned of danger. Not everyone had the same **Dreaming**, as the people spoke many different languages and had differing customs. But the strong link between the people and their land was common to all. The land provided everything they needed to survive, and connected them and all living things with their powerful ancestral beings.

 **GEO*facts*** From archaeological sites, we know that Indigenous people have lived in Australia for at least 40 000 years. This is a very long time compared with the time that Europeans have lived in Australia. Think of a clock — if Indigenous people have lived here for one hour, Europeans have been here for only 15 seconds.

## Creation of a continent

The ancestral beings of Indigenous people were believed to have emerged during the Dreamtime. Some came up from the ground; others came from the sky and across the seas. Many could change their form back and forth, from human to plant or animal. As they journeyed over what was then a flat land, they sang into being both the landscape features and all life forms.

When their creation work was finished, the ancestral beings disappeared. Some went back into the sky. Many merged into the landforms they had created, such as mountains, gorges, rivers, trees and waterholes. There, according to traditional belief, they live today, continuing to influence life on Earth.

## Map Dreaming

An important record of the Dreaming is preserved today in the traditional paintings of Aboriginal artists and in their decorated artefacts. Many Aboriginal paintings are like maps, depicting the landscape and events of the Dreaming from an aerial perspective. The painting opposite shows landforms and other features around Kiwirrkura, in the Gibson Desert near the border of the Northern Territory and Western Australia. Paintings of this type are plan views, providing a map of **sacred sites** and hunting grounds. Aboriginal people have long used symbols in their artworks, but only those people directly involved in creating a painting can give its full meaning. Some symbols have many meanings; a series of circles within circles, for example, could mean a camp fire, cave, waterhole, tree or hill.

### A Dreamtime story of The Three Sisters

According to an Aboriginal Dreamtime story, this huge rock formation in the Blue Mountains was once three beautiful sisters. The sisters, Meehni, Wimlah and Gennedoo, lived in the Jamison valley as members of the Katoomba tribe. The sisters fell in love with three brothers from the Nepean tribe, but tribal law would not allow their marriage. The three brothers did not accept this law and decided to use force to capture the three sisters. A major tribal war broke out. To protect the lives of the three sisters, a witchdoctor from their Katoomba tribe decided to turn them into rocks. The witchdoctor intended to reverse the spell but was killed during the battles. As a result, the sisters were preserved forever in the magnificent rock formation known as The Three Sisters.

*The Three Sisters formation in the Blue Mountains*

*Donkeyman Lee Tjupurrula*
*Kukatja (c. 1921)–1994*
**Tingari Dreaming at Walawala** *1989*
*synthetic polymer on canvas, 119.7 × 179.3 cm*
*National Gallery of Victoria, Melbourne*
*Purchased from Admission Funds, 1989*
*© Donkeyman Lee Tjupurrula, licensed by VISCOPY, Australia, 2009*

|  Man |  Two men sitting |  Footprints | 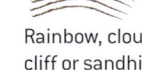 Rainbow, cloud, cliff or sandhill |
|---|---|---|---|
|  Water, rainbow, snake, lightning, string, cliff or honey store |  Waterholes connected by running water | | 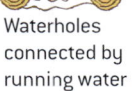 Campsite, stone, waterhole, rock hole, breast, fire, hole or fruit |

**Symbols commonly used in Aboriginal art**

*Rock art depicting a Wandjina figure, a cloud or rain spirit. Wandjina style art is found in the Kimberley region of Western Australia.*

### GEOskills TOOLBOX

**CREATING A DOCUMENT CONTAINING WEBLINKS**

Weblinks are also called hyperlinks. In documents and web pages, they are often shown as coloured or underlined text. Clicking on a weblink takes the user to a different location, such as a page on the internet.

You can easily create weblinks in your own documents or web pages. In software such as Microsoft Word, you can type the address into your document and Word will automatically format the address as a weblink. To find out more, use your computer's Help file.

## ACTIVITIES

### UNDERSTANDING

1. Describe the importance of Dreaming stories for Aboriginal people.
2. Why are there so many different Dreaming stories and creation ancestors? What link do they all have in common?
3. Name at least two different ways in which stories of the Dreaming could be passed on from one group of people to another.

### USING YOUR SKILLS

4. Refer to the painting *Tingari Dreaming at Walawala* above.
   a. How can some Aboriginal artworks also be used as maps?
   b. How many waterholes like this  can you count in the painting?
   c. Sketch the three central circles joined by lines in the centre of the painting. What do you think these represent?
   d. List the similarities and differences between the painting and other maps.
5. Draw a map of your local area in the style of an Aboriginal painting. Use some conventional Aboriginal symbols as well as some of your own.
6. Create a document or web page containing weblinks that help other people understand more about Dreaming creation stories. Use the internet to research Dreaming stories and to find websites to use as your weblinks. Your final document should include:
   - a Dreaming story that describes the creation of a landform
   - the location where the story is set (you might like to include a map)
   - photographs or paintings of the landform
   - at least one weblink that provides more information about Dreaming stories
   - at least one weblink to a site that presents an Aboriginal perspective of the origins of the Australian continent.

# 1.4 Origins of the continent: geographical perspective

## Continental drift

The broad shape of Australia and its distinctive landforms have been influenced over long periods by earth movements that cause the breaking and bending of the Earth's crust. Geographers call these movements tectonic processes.

The Earth's crust is made up of many individual moving pieces called **tectonic plates**. There are nine large plates and about a dozen smaller ones. The larger plates contain the continents and oceans. These plates 'float' on the dense layer of rock below.

Geographers have long been aware that, if the continents were rearranged and repositioned, they would fit together like a jigsaw. Scientists believe that, about 225 million years ago, the continent of Australia was joined to all the other continents. This supercontinent (called Pangaea) then split into:
- Gondwana (now South America, Africa, Antarctica and Australia)
- Laurasia (now North America, Asia and Europe).

As the plates have slowly moved, the continents have broken up and moved apart. Movements of molten rock known as convection currents caused the plates to move slowly around the surface of the Earth. This is called the theory of **continental drift**.

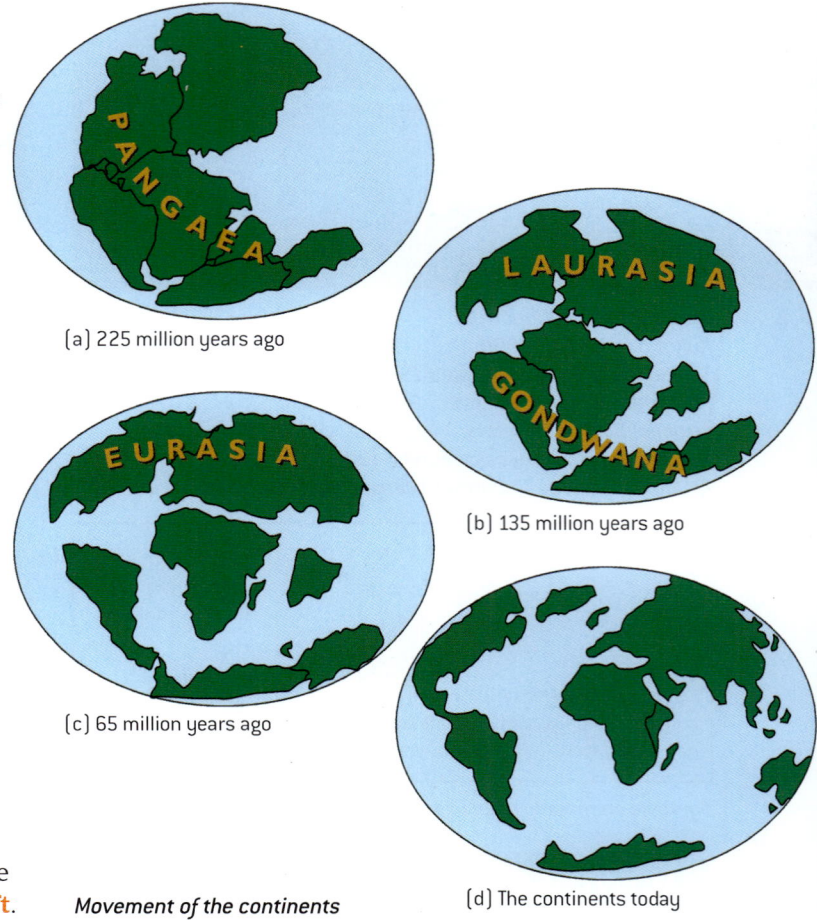

(a) 225 million years ago

(b) 135 million years ago

(c) 65 million years ago

(d) The continents today

Movement of the continents

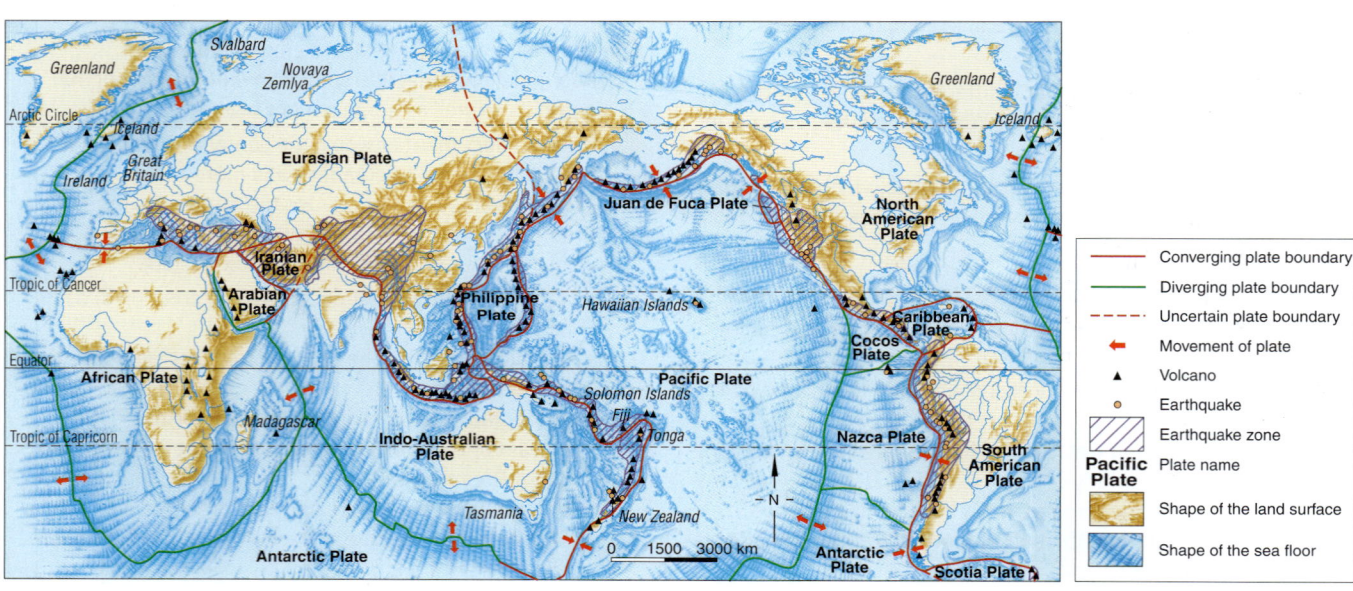

The Earth's continental plates

## The big bangs that made Australia

These days not much changes in the arid desert south of Alice Springs.

But new research has shown it was once one of the most dynamic places on the face of the planet, filled with erupting volcanos and newly forming mountain ranges.

A study by a University of Adelaide academic shows the region was the scene of a massive collision between the continents more than 1.6 billion years ago, during Australia's early formation.

Kate Selway's research clearly shows the impact zone when northern Australia slammed into central Australia with a grind of continental plates.

'These big collision zones, when they are active, are full of magmas and faults which can be very instrumental in [locating] mineral deposits,' she said.

The findings are helping to reshape our understanding of early Australia and could have implications for mining companies looking for minerals ...

Selway said the findings sat well with the emerging view on how the Australian continent formed.

'In the 1980s, people thought Australia had pretty well much always existed as it is today,' she said.

'From the 1980s on, most people have questioned that a fair bit and thought we came together from different continents.'

Selway believes that originally western Australia, southern Australia, central Australia and northern Australia were distinct land masses, separated by bodies of water.

'If you looked south from Alice Springs you would have seen an ocean,' she said.

About 1.64 billion years ago northern Australia collided with the central Australian continent.

Selway's study surprisingly appeared to show that the northern Australian continental plate slipped under the central Australian plate.

'Most of the models suggested the central Australian side would go under the northern Australia side,' she said.

Further studies were needed to find what roles the continents that became western and southern Australia played in the collision. Eastern Australia joined the mass at a later stage.

The period of Selway's study predates the creation of the southern supercontinent Gondwanaland.

Source: *Sun Herald*, 20 August 2006.

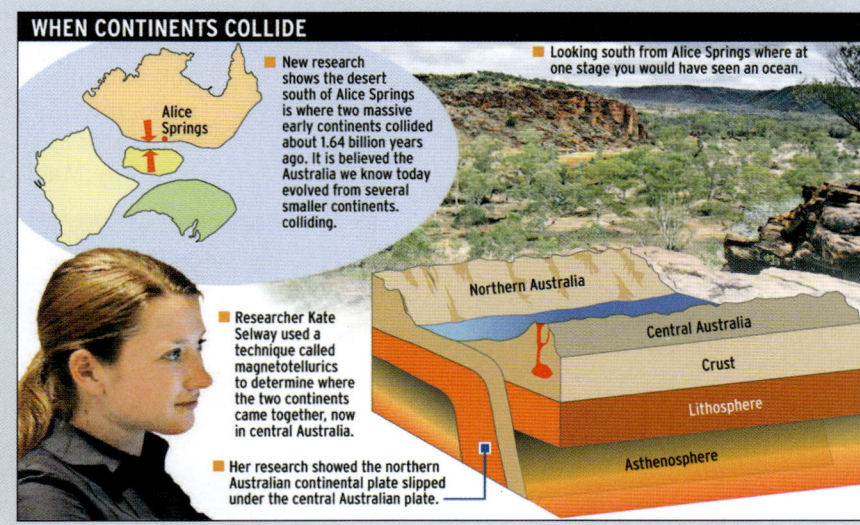

## ACTIVITIES

### UNDERSTANDING

1. What are tectonic plates?
2. Identify the supercontinent that contained all present continents.
3. Make up a mnemonic that will help you remember how to spell *Pangaea*, for example: 'Pretty and nice girls always eat apples'.
4. Read the newspaper article 'The big bangs that made Australia' and answer the following questions.
   a Describe what the desert region south of Alice Springs was like around 1.6 billion years ago.
   b Explain the reason for the region being very different then from what it is today.
   c Explain the connection between continental drift and Kate Selway's findings.

### THINKING AND APPLYING

5. Why might an understanding of the early formation of the Australian continent be important for mining companies searching for mineral deposits?

### USING YOUR SKILLS

6. Refer to the diagrams on the previous page showing the movement of the continents.
   a Which three continents were still connected about 65 million years ago?
   b Describe the sequence of events that resulted in the break-up of Pangaea.
7. Refer to the map of the Earth's continental plates on the previous page.
   a On which plate is Australia located?
   b In which direction is this plate moving?

## Mountain building

The movement of the Earth's plates explains both the present location of continents and the processes of mountain building and volcanic activity.

When two plates collide, mountain ranges are formed. They are formed by either folding or faulting. Fold mountains are formed when one plate slides down under another. Some rocks are forced down while others are forced upwards and bent into wave-like forms. Fault mountains are formed when layers of rock are fractured and one section moves down and another section moves up. Many of Australia's mountain ranges are the result of folding and faulting — for example, the Flinders Ranges (South Australia) and the Stirling Ranges (Western Australia).

*The formation of fold mountains*

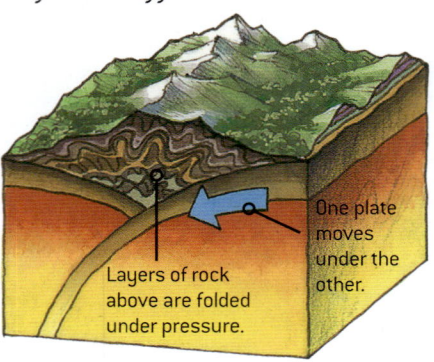

*The formation of fault mountains*

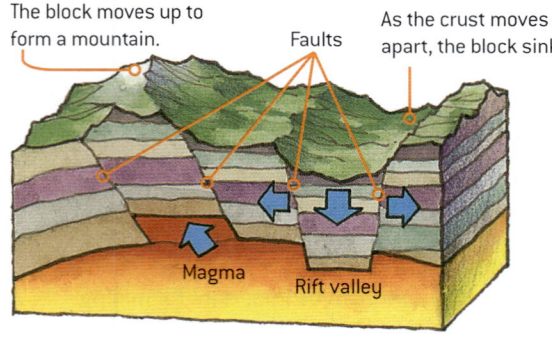

## Formation of the MacDonnell Ranges

Until about 600 million years ago, the area of the Northern Territory where the MacDonnell Ranges now lie was covered by shallow seas. Then, movements of the continental plates caused folding that formed the ranges.

The present MacDonnell Ranges have been significantly eroded by running water. **Erosion** is the wearing away of soil and rock by natural elements such as wind and water. Erosion acts quickly on softer rocks. Harder rocks erode more slowly and they are left as mountains and hills.

The photo below shows the present MacDonnell Ranges, while the two diagrams at the foot of the page show stages in the formation of the MacDonnell Ranges. Diagram A shows folding from volcanic activity occurring between 400 and 100 million years ago, buckling the sedimentary rocks into anticlines. In diagram B, the tops of these anticlines have eroded over millions of years to form the MacDonnell Ranges we know.

*The MacDonnell Ranges*

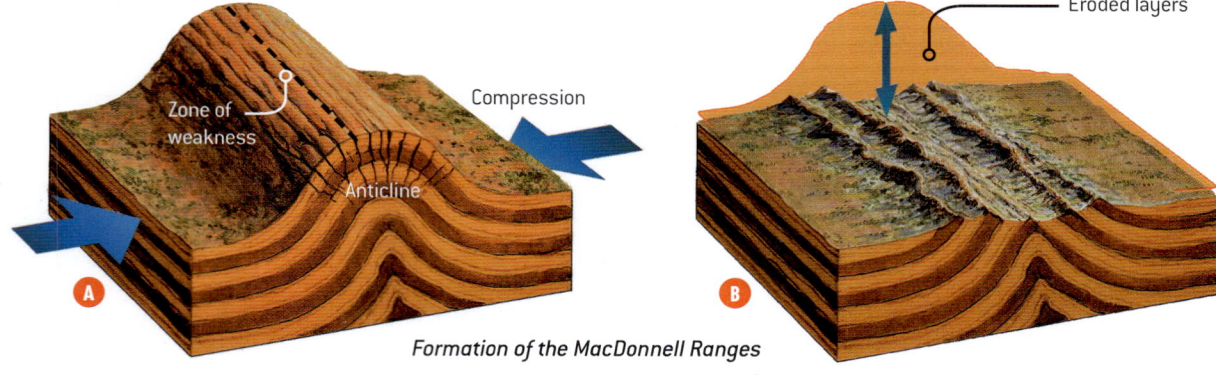

*Formation of the MacDonnell Ranges*

## Volcanic mountains

Mountains can be formed by folding and faulting processes, and also by volcanic activity, which normally takes place around the margins of moving plates. In the past, there was extensive volcanic activity in Australia even though the continent is not situated on the edge of a moving plate. There were volcanoes the size of the modern Mount Vesuvius, and huge lava plains covered considerable areas. Some vulcanologists suggest that these volcanoes occurred as the continent drifted north and moved over a hot spot in the **mantle**.

Hot spot volcanoes form in the middle of tectonic plates directly above a source of magma (molten lava) located deep beneath the Earth. A hot spot stays still, but the tectonic plate above it keeps moving.

1. A crater lake forms when a caldera fills with water. Mount Eccles in Victoria and Blue Lake in Mount Gambier in South Australia are examples.
2. A caldera is formed when a volcano erupts violently, resulting in the cone collapsing into the magma chamber below. Tower Hill in Victoria is a caldera.
3. Cinder cones are formed when layers of ash and cinders build up a cone with a large crater.
4. Magma can make rocks arch up and fill the space to produce an upside-down bowl of rock called a laccolith.
5. A batholith is a huge body of granite rock, beneath the Earth's surface, that used to be a magma chamber supplying lava to the surface.
6. Cracks that are formed when the land is pulling apart can be filled with magma. When this cools and becomes rock, a dyke is formed.
7. A sill is formed from cooled magma (igneous rock) that forces rock layers apart and hardens in a horizontal layer.
8. A lava dome is formed when lava flows so slowly that it piles up around the vent rather than flowing away.
9. Pluton is rock that was once lava forced between other rocks and cooled under the ground. The You Yangs near Geelong in Victoria are the exposed portion of a pluton.
10. A volcanic plug is a feature that remains after a volcano has eroded.

About 33 million years ago — as Australia was drifting northwards after splitting from Antarctica — the continent passed over a large hot spot. Over the next 27 million years, about 30 volcanoes erupted while they were above these hot spots. The oldest eruption was 35 million years ago at Cape Hillsborough in Queensland; the last was the Macedon volcano in Victoria around 6 million years ago. Over millions of years, this hot spot process form a chain of volcanoes, including those in eastern and south-eastern Australia. At present, the hot spot responsible for all this activity is probably beneath Bass Strait.

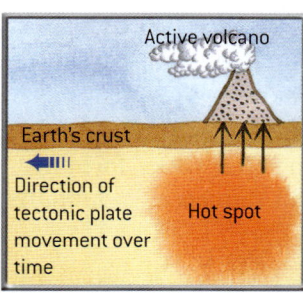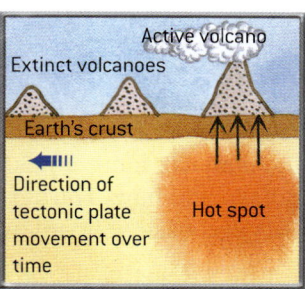

*How hot spot volcanoes form on a drifting landmass*

### ACTIVITIES

**UNDERSTANDING**

1. What processes form (a) fold mountains and (b) fault mountains?
2. Where does volcanic activity normally take place?
3. Describe the formation of the MacDonnell Ranges.

**THINKING AND APPLYING**

4. Explain why Australia had volcanic activity even though it was not located on a plate edge.

**USING YOUR SKILLS**

5. Refer to the diagram of volcanic landforms on the left. Briefly describe the formation of the following landforms:
   a caldera
   b crater lake
   c cinder cone
   d sill
   e batholith
   f dyke.

### GEOTERMS

**continental drift:** the theory that describes how continents broke away and drifted from an original landmass

**erosion:** the wearing away of soil and rock by natural elements such as wind and water

**mantle:** the layer of rock between the Earth's crust and the core

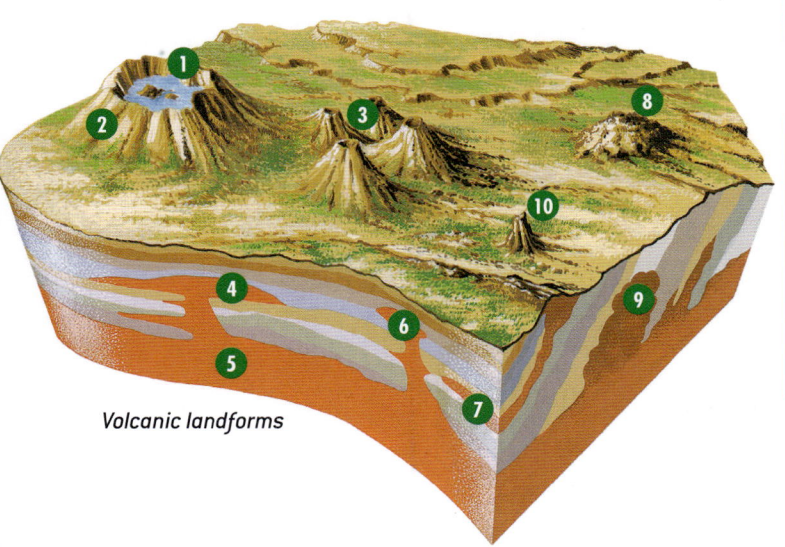

*Volcanic landforms*

CHAPTER 1 | The Australian continent

# 1.5 Climate and sea level changes shaped our continent

## An ancient land

Australia is an ancient landmass. The Earth is about 4600 million years old and the Australian continent is about 4300 million years old. Over millions of years, Australia has undergone many changes — mountain ranges and inland seas have come and gone. As mountain ranges eroded, **sediments** many kilometres thick were laid down over vast areas. These sedimentary rocks were then subjected to folding, faulting and uplifting. Over time, the forces of **weathering** and erosion wore these down again. Erosion acts more quickly on softer rocks, forming valleys and bays. Harder rocks remain as mountains, hills and coastal headlands.

## Lowest and flattest

Because it is located in the centre of a tectonic plate, rather than at the edge, Australia has no active volcanoes on its mainland and has very little tectonic lift from below. It therefore experiences relatively little volcanic and earthquake activity. This means its raised landforms, such as mountains, have been exposed to weathering forces longer than those of some other continents. Hence they are more rounded or worn down. In fact, Australia is the lowest and flattest of all the continents.

The present **topography** results from the erosion caused by a huge icecap about 290 million years ago. After the ice melted, parts of the continent subsided and were covered by sediment to form sedimentary basins such as the Great Artesian Basin.

### GEOfacts

- Australia is the continent with the lowest average elevation. The average altitude of the Australian landmass is only 300 metres. North America has an average elevation of 790 metres.
- Only 0.5 per cent of the Australian continent is above 1000 metres.
- Australia's highest point is Mt Kosciuszko, with an elevation of 2228 metres above sea level. Mt Everest, the world's highest mountain, is 8848 metres above sea level.
- Australia's lowest point is Lake Eyre, which is 15 metres below sea level.

## Climate change

During the last **ice age**, temperatures were much lower, and vast amounts of water became trapped in ice sheets and glaciers. The sea level was 100 metres lower than it is today. New Guinea and Tasmania were attached to mainland Australia. The climate was much colder in the south and much wetter in the centre. Temperatures in the inland were temperate to subtropical. There were great rivers and lakes, and lush vegetation teeming with bird and animal life.

With the end of the ice age, about 15 000 years ago, higher temperatures led to the retreat of ice sheets and glaciers, and sea levels gradually rose to their present levels. Australia took on its present shape and became isolated, with Tasmania and New Guinea cut off from the mainland. Some of the lower valleys were drowned, making fine harbours such as Sydney Harbour. As the sea level rose, other valleys filled with alluvium, forming the typical lowland valleys around the Australian coast. Higher temperatures meant changes in climate, and the physical environment of the inland was transformed into the harsh desert and semidesert that we know today.

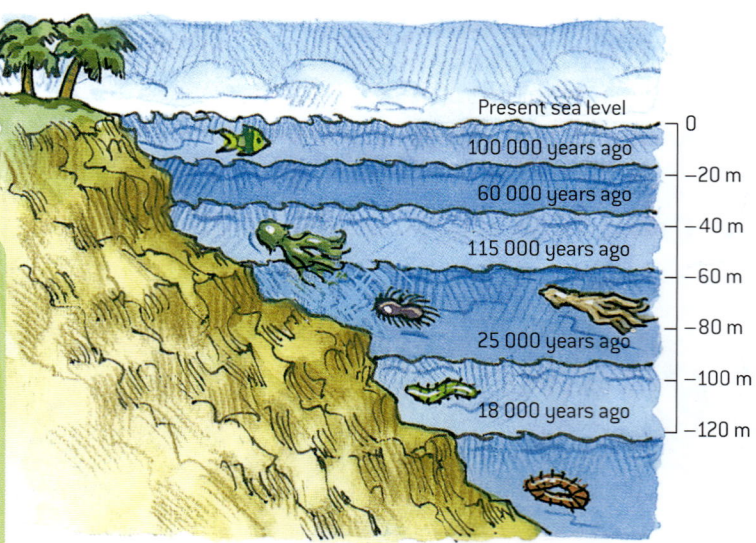

Sea levels have changed several times over thousands of years. About 18 000 years ago, the sea level was at least 120 metres lower than it is today. Yet, if we look back as far as 100 000 years ago, seas were only 20 metres lower than today.

## Land bridges

Many scientists believe that Aboriginal people are descended from people who migrated to Australia from southern Asia. This was possibly the earliest large-scale migration in human history. It is believed to have begun about 50 000 years ago, during the last ice age. The first people to reach Australia could have simply walked most of the way across the land bridge between New Guinea and Australia. During that ice age, the islands of Indonesia were closer together, making it possible for the migrants to 'island-hop' their way to Australia. The longest water crossing involving canoes was possibly only from Timor to Australia. Making such a journey in a canoe would still have been dangerous, however, due to the risk of sudden storms and rough seas.

*Land surface during the last ice age and possible migration routes taken by Aboriginal people*

Image © WorldSat International Inc., 2001 — www.worldsat.ca — All rights reserved.
Overlay by MAPgraphics Pty Ltd, Brisbane.

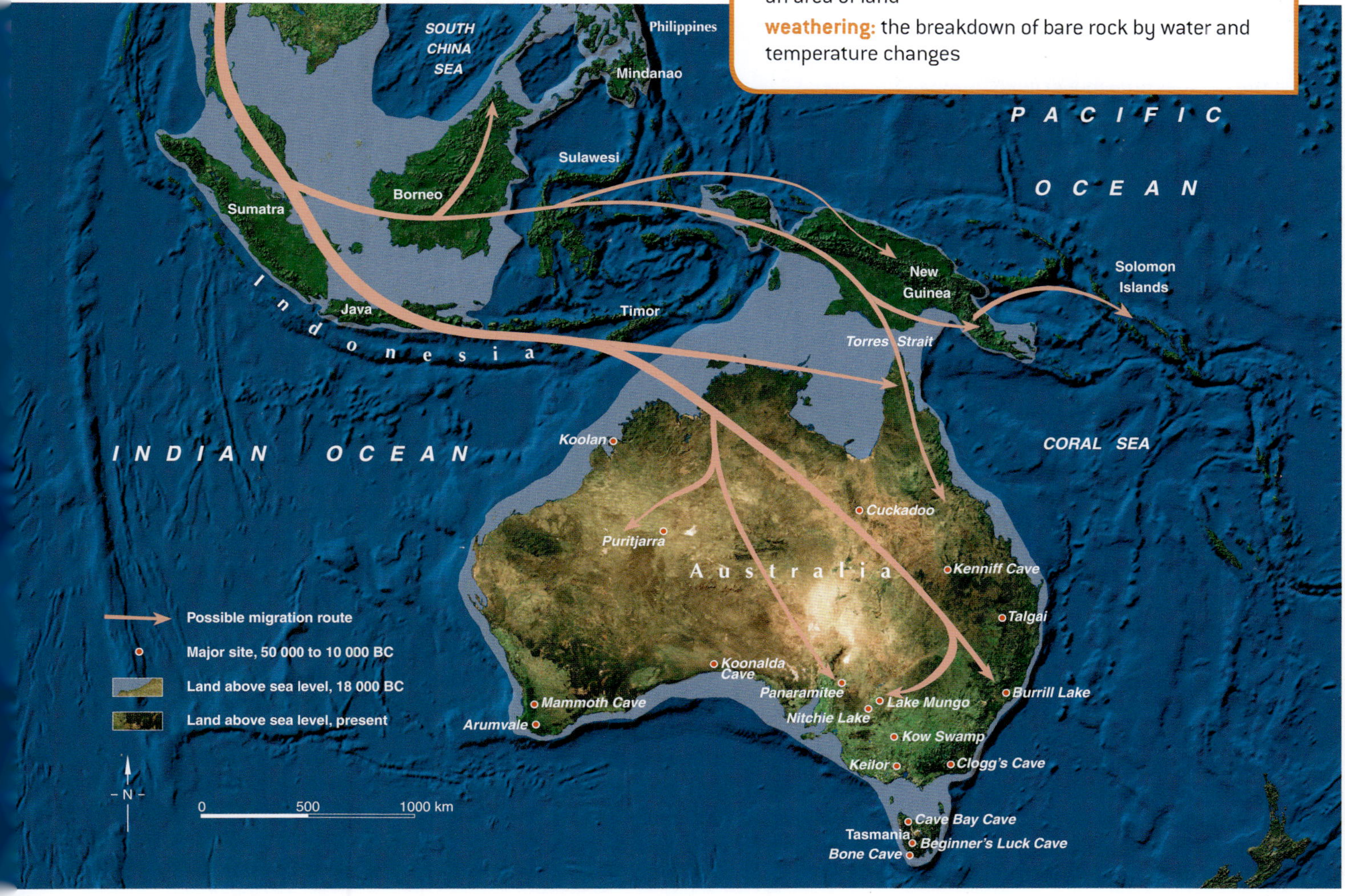

### ACTIVITIES

**UNDERSTANDING**
1. How old is the Australian continent?
2. Define the term 'ice age'.
3. When do scientists think the ancestors of Aboriginal people began to migrate to Australia?

**THINKING AND APPLYING**
4. How can the changes in sea levels over time be explained?

**USING YOUR SKILLS**
5. Refer to the map on this page.
   a. Estimate how far Aboriginal people might have sailed between Timor and Australia during the last ice age.
   b. Estimate the distance they would have to travel today.

### GEOTERMS

**topography:** physical features (height and shape) of an area of land

**weathering:** the breakdown of bare rock by water and temperature changes

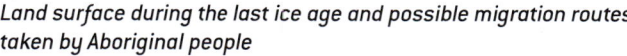

CHAPTER 1 | The Australian continent

# Working geographically

## BROADSHEET: AUSTRALIA — OVERVIEW

### KNOWLEDGE AND UNDERSTANDING

Refer to the diagram on this page, and select the alternative that best answers the question.

1. Around 550 million years ago, the Uluru alluvial fan was formed from:
   - (A) ancient igneous rock
   - (B) arkose (sedimentary rock)
   - (C) sediment from the Petermann Ranges
   - (D) folding and faulting.

#### Formation of Uluru and Kata Tjuta

Uluru is an inselberg, or isolated rocky outcrop that resists erosion. The rock is mostly arkose, a type of sandstone. It covers an area of 3.3 square kilometres and is nearly 10 kilometres around its base. Uluru rises 348 metres above the flat plains, but this is only the tip — it probably extends several kilometres below the surface. Kata Tjuta, located 35 kilometres from Uluru, is a mountain range of large rounded boulders. It is made up of conglomerate. The conglomerate probably extends 6 kilometres beneath Mount Olga, the highest peak. Many gorges are located in this landform.

2. Between 65 and 70 million years ago:
   - (A) part of the area was still covered by water
   - (B) there was no water over the area
   - (C) continual deposition of sediment formed Mount Currie
   - (D) sand dunes began to form.

3. Over the time period shown in the diagrams:
   - (A) the whole area has risen
   - (B) the whole area has been eroded
   - (C) the whole area has become wetter
   - (D) the whole area has become drier.

4. Uluru has been formed by a combination of the following processes:
   - (A) folding and faulting
   - (B) erosion and deposition
   - (C) erosion, folding and faulting
   - (D) erosion, deposition, folding and faulting.

Answer the following two questions by writing two or three paragraphs.

5. Outline a geographical explanation of how Kata Tjuta and Uluru were formed.

6. Describe a possible Aboriginal explanation of the formation of these two landforms.

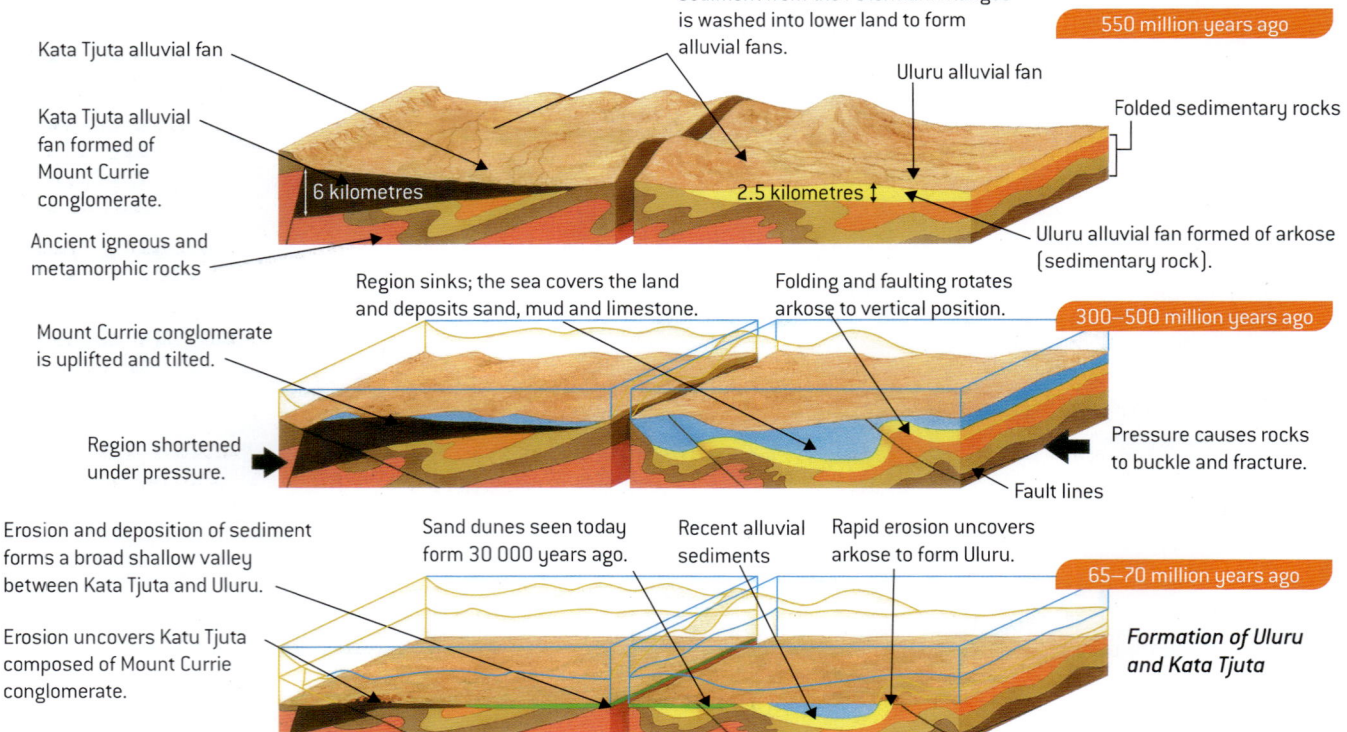

Formation of Uluru and Kata Tjuta

**Refer to the map, and select the alternative that best answers the question.**

7. A plane flying from 42.50°S 147.15°E to 35.17°S 149.08°E would cross:
   (A) Bass Strait
   (B) Lake Eyre
   (C) the Indian Ocean
   (D) the Atlantic Ocean.

8. The latitude and longitude of Sydney are:
   (A) 33.55°S 151.13°E
   (B) 30.22°S 153.26°E
   (C) 34.43°S 153.26°E
   (D) 35.24°S 154.17°S.

9. The latitude and longitude of Broken Hill are:
   (A) 32.57°S 140.25°E
   (B) 31.58°S 141.27°E
   (C) 31.56°S 142.28°E
   (D) 34.45°S 140.24°E.

10. The latitude and longitude of Townsville are:
    (A) 19.16°S 146.49°E
    (B) 22.34°S 145.35°E
    (C) 17.45°S 141.34°E
    (D) 21.34°S 149.32°E.

11. The city closest to the Tropic of Capricorn is:
    (A) Alice Springs
    (B) Gladstone
    (C) Rockhampton
    (D) Dubbo.

12. The city closest to longitude 140°E is:
    (A) Broken Hill
    (B) Mount Isa
    (C) Griffith
    (D) Whyalla.

13. What direction is Broken Hill from Sydney?
    (A) North-east
    (B) North-west
    (C) South-east
    (D) South-west

14. Approximately how far is Cairns from Dubbo?
    (A) 900 km
    (B) 1200 km
    (C) 1800 km
    (D) 2000 km

*Central and eastern Australia*

CHAPTER 1 | The Australian continent

# 2 Physical characteristics that make Australia unique

### INQUIRY QUESTIONS
+ How can we explore Australia's physical features using maps?
+ How are the elements of Australia's physical environment interrelated?
+ How have Australia's flora and fauna developed?

Australia is the only continent that is both an island and one nation, and it is particularly noted for physical characteristics that make it unique. In this chapter, we focus on Australia's physical environment, including major landforms and drainage basins, climate patterns, vegetation and natural resources, and flora and fauna.

### GEOskills TOOLBOX

**GEOskillbuilder** Using topographic maps (pages 26–9)
Calculating gradient (page 27)
Finding local relief (page 28)
Finding the aspect of a slope (page 28)
Drawing a transect (page 28)

**GEOskillbuilder** Understanding landforms (pages 30–1)
Calculating the area of a feature (page 30)

**GEOskillbuilder** Constructing a cross-section (pages 32–3)
+ Using physical maps (page 22)
+ Interpreting climatic graphs (page 37)
+ Interpreting synoptic charts (page 41)

*Red kangaroos move through the reed beds of the Macquarie Marshes, New South Wales.*

## KEY TERMS

**climate:** the long-term variation in the atmosphere, relating mainly to temperature and precipitation

**drainage basin:** the area of land that feeds a river with water, or the whole area of land drained by a river and its tributaries

**drought:** a prolonged period of below-average precipitation

**ecosystem:** a system formed by the interactions between living organisms (plants, animals and humans) and physical elements of the environment

**endemic:** native to a particular area and found nowhere else

**isobar:** line drawn on a map joining places of equal barometric pressure

**marsupial:** mammal that keeps and feeds its young in a pouch for a few months after birth

**monotreme:** mammal that lays eggs; the only species are the platypus and echidna

**monsoon:** the seasonal change in wind direction that is experienced in much of the tropics

**regolith:** the layer of broken rock and soil on top of the solid rock of the Earth's crust; also known as mantle rock

**species:** a group of plants or animals of the same kind that are able to breed with each other

**synoptic chart:** weather map that uses isobars and other symbols to show the movement of weather systems and patterns of temperature and rainfall

**topographic map:** a map that shows the relief of an area by use of contour lines

# 2.1 Major landforms and drainage basins

The tectonic forces of folding, faulting and volcanic activity have created many of Australia's major landforms. Other forces that work on the surface of Australia and give our landforms their present appearance are weathering, mass movement, erosion and deposition.

- Weathering is the breakdown of bare rock by water and temperature changes at the Earth's surface. This process converts solid rock into a layer of **regolith**, or broken rock and soil, which is more easily moved by other processes.
- The gravitational movement of rock and soil downslope is called mass movement. This contributes to the appearance of local landforms. For example, the steep sides of parts of the Blue Mountains are formed by a combination of weathering and mass movement.
- The main force that has created the present appearance of our topography is erosion. Erosion is the wearing away of soil and rock by natural elements, such as water, ice and wind. Water erosion by rivers and streams has been responsible for the carving of many valleys in Australia's higher areas. Small parts of the Australian alps and Tasmania have been eroded by glaciers during the last ice age. Drier parts of Australia have experienced some wind erosion.
- When streams, glaciers and winds slow down, they deposit or 'drop' the load of rock, soil and particles they have been carrying. This is called deposition. Many broad coastal and low-lying inland valleys have been created by stream deposition. These areas are called flood plains. Wind deposition has created many sand dunes along beaches and in desert areas.

## Major landform regions

The topography or landforms of Australia can be divided into four major regions: the Coastal Plains, the Eastern Highlands, the Central Lowlands and the Western Plateau.

- The Coastal Plains around Australia's edge are narrow and discontinuous. The plains often take the form of river valleys, such as those of the Hunter Valley near Newcastle.
- The Eastern Highlands region (which includes the Great Dividing Range) is mainly a series of tablelands and plateaus. Most of the area is very rugged because rivers have cut deep valleys. It is the source of most of Australia's largest rivers including the Fitzroy, Darling and Murray. The highest part is in the south-east where a small alpine area is snow-covered for more than half the year.

*Erosion and weathering have shaped the 450-km long Bungle Bungle Range in Western Australia. Its beehive shapes rise up to 300 metres above the surrounding plain.*

- The Central Lowlands is a vast area of very flat, low-lying land that contains three large **drainage basins**: the Carpentaria lowlands in the north, the Lake Eyre basin in the centre, and the Murray–Darling Basin in the south (see sample study).
- The Western Plateau is a huge area of tablelands, most of which is about 500 metres above sea level. It includes areas of gibber (or stony) deserts and sandy deserts. There are several rugged upland areas, including the Kimberley and MacDonnell ranges.

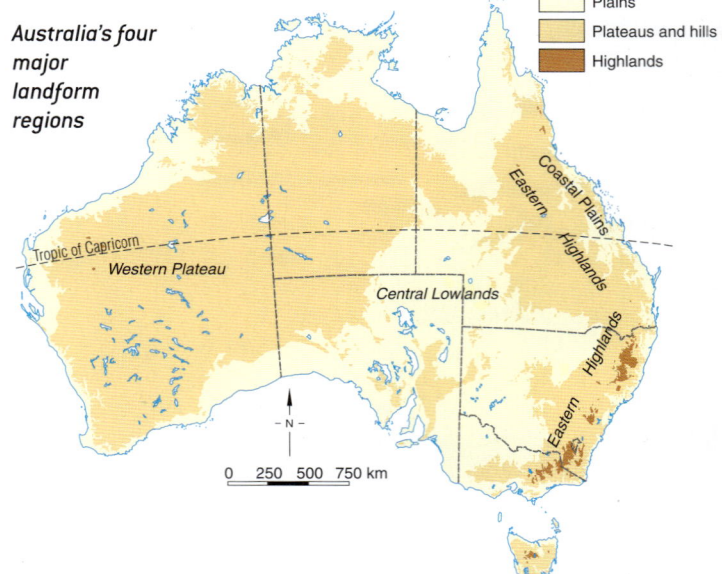

*Australia's four major landform regions*

Aerial view of the mouth of the Murray River, where it enters the Coorong and Lake Alexandrina in South Australia

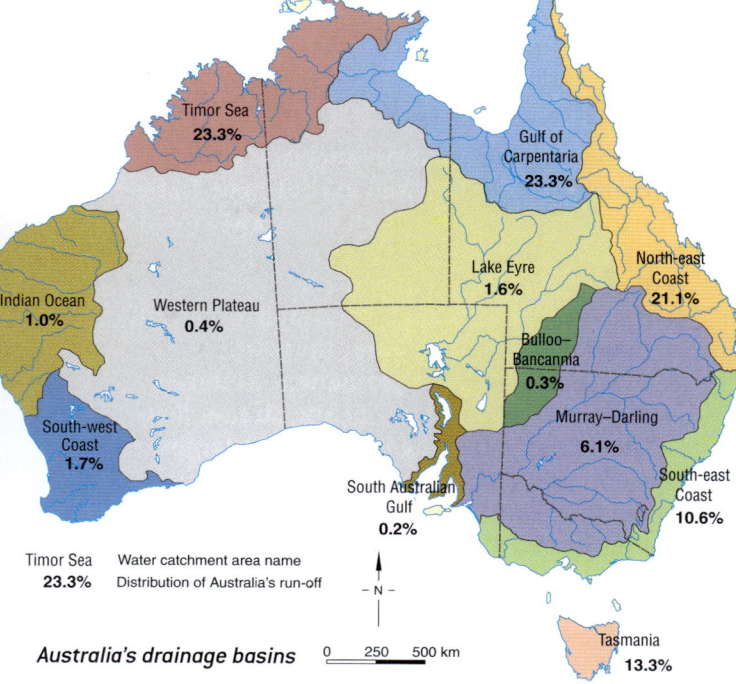

Australia's drainage basins

Timor Sea 23.3%
Gulf of Carpentaria 23.3%
Indian Ocean 1.0%
Western Plateau 0.4%
Lake Eyre 1.6%
North-east Coast 21.1%
Bulloo–Bancannia 0.3%
South-west Coast 1.7%
Murray–Darling 6.1%
South Australian Gulf 0.2%
South-east Coast 10.6%
Tasmania 13.3%

## SAMPLE STUDY

### The Murray–Darling Basin

The Murray–Darling Basin covers about one million square kilometres and is drained by more than twenty major rivers. It has a wide variety of environments ranging from alpine areas in the east to plains in the west. The basin produces 43 per cent of Australia's food and over 40 per cent of Australia's total agricultural income.

The Murray–Darling drainage basin is the largest and most important in Australia, covering one-seventh of the continent. However, the amount of water flowing through it in one year is about the same as the daily flow of the Amazon River.

The basin is facing severe problems:

- Only about 20 per cent of the water flowing through the basin ever reaches the sea. The rest is diverted for agriculture, industry and domestic use.
- The Murray supplies about 40 per cent of Adelaide's drinking water. The quality of the water continues to decline, mainly because of salinity levels.
- Approximately 50–80 per cent of the wetlands in the basin has been severely damaged or destroyed, and more than one-third of the native fish species are threatened with extinction.
- In 2008, inflows to the river system were at their lowest since records began 117 years earlier.
- An estimate of weather trends shows that the flow to the Murray River mouth may be reduced by a further 25 per cent by 2030. However, with the added problem of climate change, it is predicted that precipitation in the Murray–Darling catchment will decrease, so the reduction in flow to the mouth could be as high as 70 per cent.

## ACTIVITIES

### UNDERSTANDING

1. List Australia's four main landform regions.
2. Identify Australia's largest drainage basin.

### THINKING AND APPLYING

3. Explain which process or processes you consider to be most influential in the formation of Australia's landforms.
4. The Murray–Darling Basin has a wide variety of environments. Explain how this would affect the potential for agriculture.

### USING YOUR SKILLS

5. Refer to the map of Australia's drainage basins above. Rank the drainage basins from highest to lowest run-off.
6. Use Google Earth to view any part of the Murray–Darling Basin. Describe the landscape that you see.
7. Refer to the map of Australia's major landform regions on the previous page.
   a. Briefly describe the location of Australia's four major landform regions.
   b. Identify the largest and the smallest in area.

## GEOTERMS

**drainage basin:** the area of land that feeds a river with water, or the whole area of land drained by a river and its tributaries

**regolith:** the layer of broken rock and soil on top of the solid rock of the Earth's crust; also known as mantle rock

## Rivers and lakes

Permanent rivers and streams flow in only a small proportion of the Australian continent. In fact, Australia is the driest of all the world's inhabited continents. It has:
- the lowest amount of run-off
- the lowest percentage of rainfall as run-off
- the least amount of water in rivers
- the smallest area of permanent wetlands
- the most variable rainfall and stream flow.

The Murray–Darling is Australia's largest river system. Other significant rivers are:
- the Burdekin River in Queensland
- the Hunter River in New South Wales
- the Murchison, Gascoyne, Ashburton, Fortescue, De Grey, Fitzroy, Drysdale and Ord rivers in the north-west region
- the Victoria and Daly rivers in the Northern Territory
- the Leichhardt, Norman, Gilbert and Mitchell rivers in the Gulf of Carpentaria
- the Tamar, Derwent and Gordon rivers of Tasmania, although these are relatively short.

Australia has many lakes but they hold little water compared with those found on other continents. The largest are Lake Eyre and Lake Torrens in South Australia. During dry seasons, these become beds of salt and mud. Yet an inland sea did once exist in this area. It covered about 100 000 square kilometres around present-day Lake Eyre and Lake Frome. South Australia is Australia's driest state and has very few permanent rivers or streams.

Satellite image of Lake Eyre, March 1985. Once a freshwater lake, the region is now normally an evaporated saltpan. The crust of salt is shown as white in the image.

Satellite image of Lake Eyre, February 1984. Three or four times each century, the lake fills with water, transforming it into a haven for wildlife. Deep water is shown as black in the image.

### GEOskills TOOLBOX

**USING PHYSICAL MAPS**

The natural features of a region are shown on physical maps. Mountain ranges, plateaus, rivers, seas and other physical features are highlighted. Information about towns and cities is kept to a minimum. The map below was constructed using a satellite image with labels overlaid by the cartographer.

Australia — physical map

## ACTIVITIES

### USING YOUR SKILLS

1. Refer to the physical map of Australia on these pages and list the following:
   a. the three highest mountain peaks in the Great Dividing Range
   b. two deserts in the Central Lowlands
   c. four mountain ranges on the Western Plateau
   d. three rivers in the Murray–Darling drainage basin
   e. three rivers in the Indian Ocean drainage basin (see map on page 21).

2. Using information from the map, explain why Lake Torrens and Lake Eyre usually contain so little water.

3. Use information from the text and from the map to explain why the Murray–Darling river system has a small discharge relative to the size of its catchment and length.

4. On an outline map of Australia complete the following.
   a. Draw the Great Dividing Range and the Murray–Darling Basin on your map.
   b. Add Mount Kosciuszko to your map.
   c. Shade the areas of desert.
   d. Mark the locations of four seas near Australia.
   e. Show the approximate location of the area shown in the photographs on the opposite page. Add a label for this place.
   f. Provide a title, scale and key for your map.
   g. Use the scale to estimate the width of Australia at its widest point and the distance from the most northerly point of Australia to the most southerly point.

**CHAPTER 2** | Physical characteristics that make Australia unique

# 2.2 Topographic maps

## What is a topographic map?

A **topographic map** shows the actual shape of the landscape and the various heights of the landscape. Topographic maps are used to:
- find location, direction and distance
- describe the distribution of physical and human features
- show interrelationships between features such as landforms and settlement patterns.

*A topographic map represents a three-dimensional landscape on a flat surface. Contour lines are like horizontal slices of a landscape.*

## How topographic maps show height and shape

Topographic maps use *contour lines* to join places of equal height or elevation above sea level.

The height difference between the contour lines is called the *contour interval*. The map on the opposite page has various contour lines with an interval of 50 metres. The numbers on the contour lines show how high the land is above sea level. Mt Florence, for example, is more than 400 metres above sea level.

The map also shows that some contour lines are close together while other contour lines are far apart. Close contours mean that the slope of the land is steep; contours well apart mean that the slope of the land is gentle. The closer the contours, the steeper the slope. The further apart the contours, the flatter the slope. Therefore, on the map on this page, the land around X is steeper than the land around Y. The relative steepness of the slope is called the *gradient*. See page 27 to learn how to calculate a gradient.

## How topographic maps show the physical and human features of the landscape

Topographic maps use a key or legend of conventional signs and symbols to show:
- physical features, such as rivers, lakes, swamps, hills and beaches
- human features, such as roads, towns, railways and dams.

### Colours

Different colours are also used on topographic maps to indicate certain features. For example:
- brown is used for natural features, including contour lines
- blue is used for all water and river features
- green is used for vegetation and ground cover
- black and red are used for human features such as roads, railways and buildings.

## How topographic maps help us locate places on a map

Topographic maps use a system of grid lines overprinted on the map to allow us to give either area or grid references for places. These grid lines are given as two-digit numbers that appear on the margins of the map. The lines that run up and down the map (north–south) are called *eastings* because the numbers increase the further east they are. The lines that run across the map horizontally (east–west) are called *northings* because the numbers increase the further north they are. When stating location, the eastings are given first and then the northings.

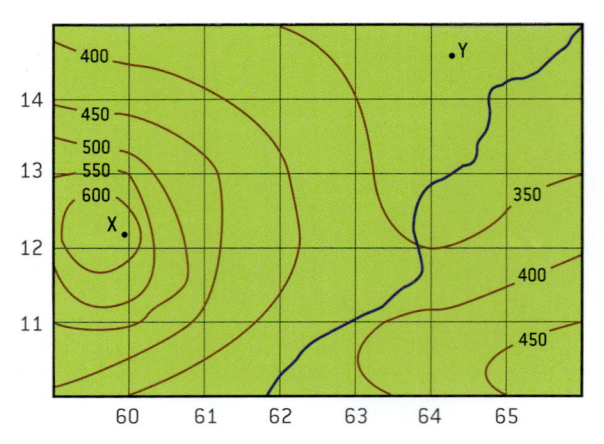

*Area references and contour lines on a topographic map*

An *area reference* is a four-figure reference that tells us the grid square in which to find a feature. On the map below, the railway station is located at 8640. The letters AR are usually placed in front of an area reference, so the area reference for the railway station is AR8640.

A *grid reference* is a six-figure number that shows an exact point in the grid square. The third and sixth figures represent one-tenth of the distance between the two grid numbers. However, these are not written on the map, so they must be estimated. The letters GR are used in a grid reference. The grid reference for point Y on the map on page 24 is GR643146. There are no spaces between the digits in references.

> **GEOTERMS**
>
> **topographic map:** a map that shows the relief of an area by use of contour lines

## ACTIVITIES

### USING YOUR SKILLS

The map below is a topographic map showing contours, grid references and a legend. Examine the map carefully and answer these questions.

1. What is the area reference for each of the following points marked on the map? The first one is done for you.
   a A is AR8348
   b D
   c G
   d B
   e E
   f F
   g C
   h H
2. What are the grid references for the points in question 1? A is GR835486.
3. In which direction would you have to travel to reach point D from:
   a B
   b C
   c E?
4. Use the legend to describe what is at each of these points.
   a A
   b B
   c C
   d D
   e E
   f F
5. What is the height of the land at each of points B, C, F and G on the contour map?
6. How high is Mt Florence? Which side of Mt Florence is the steepest?
7. If you walked from the railway station to Mt Florence:
   a would you be travelling uphill or downhill
   b which part would be the flattest section of your journey
   c how many metres would you have to walk to reach Mt Florence?
8. Which human features can be found at the following area references?
   a AR8640
   b AR8940
   c AR8441
9. Measure the distance between GR802440 and GR890453.

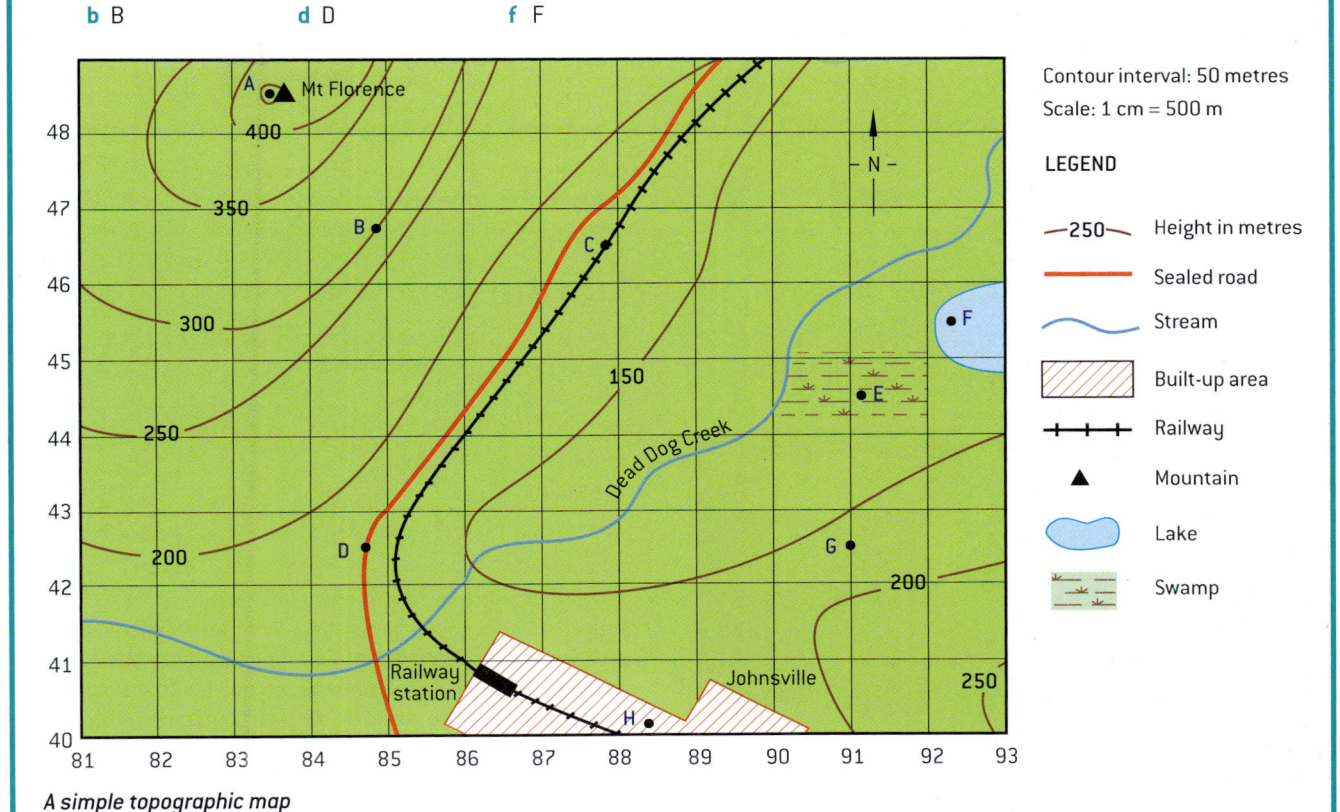

*A simple topographic map*

**CHAPTER 2** | Physical characteristics that make Australia unique

# 2.3 GEOskillbuilder

# Using topographic maps

## Direction on topographic maps

Direction is a geographical tool for locating places. You will notice that north is always at the top of a topographic map. All the easting lines on a topographic map run north–south. This is referred to as *grid north*. *True north* is the actual direction of Earth's geographical north pole, while *magnetic north* is the direction in which the magnetic needle of a compass points. Magnetic north varies due to the spinning of the Earth.

## Bearings

Geographers use compass points, such as NE and SW, to give directions and work out the location of features. When using topographic maps, a *bearing* (or angle) is given for greater accuracy.

*North is 0°, north-east is 45° and east is 90°.*

- A bearing is the angle, measured in a clockwise direction, that a line between one place and another makes with a fixed north line, which is at 0°.

*Geographers use compass points to work out the location of features*

- Bearings range from 0° degrees (north) to 360° (which is also north).
- Bearings are always measured clockwise. Therefore, the bearing of any location to the east of the north–south line is between 0° and 180°; the bearing of any location to the west of the north–south line is between 180° and 360°.

To accurately measure a bearing, a protractor is used, as shown below.

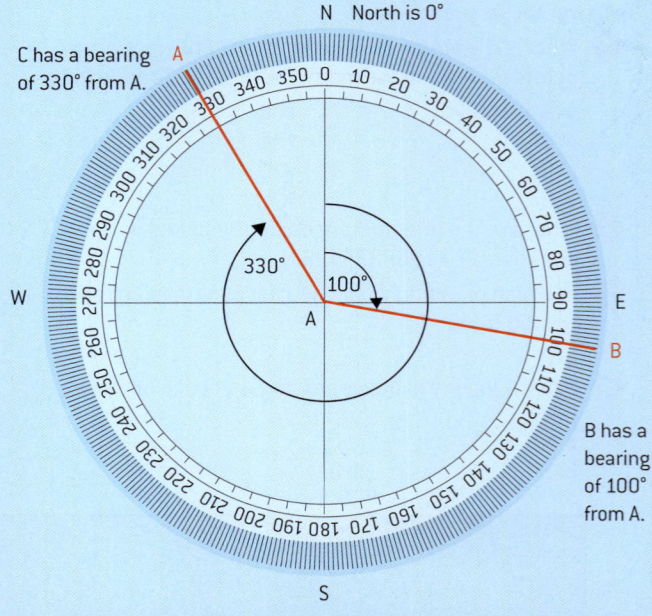

*The bearing of location A from location B is the number of degrees measured in a clockwise direction between north and B (100°). The bearing of location C from location A is 330°.*

## Contours

Contours are used on topographic maps to show both the height and shape of the land. Contours are shown as numbered lines that join places of equal height above sea level. Their spacing and pattern can show the shape and type of landform and also the:

- slope of the land
- the *gradient* of the slope
- the *aspect* of the slope

On any topographic or contour map, evenly spaced contours mean an even slope, close contours mean a steeper slope, and widely spaced contours mean a gentle slope or flat area. The difference in height between one contour line and the next is always the same on any particular map. This is known as the *vertical interval* or *contour interval*. *Spot heights* are also given to show the actual height of particular locations on a topographic map. Usually only the highest points, such as mountains or hills, have a spot height shown.

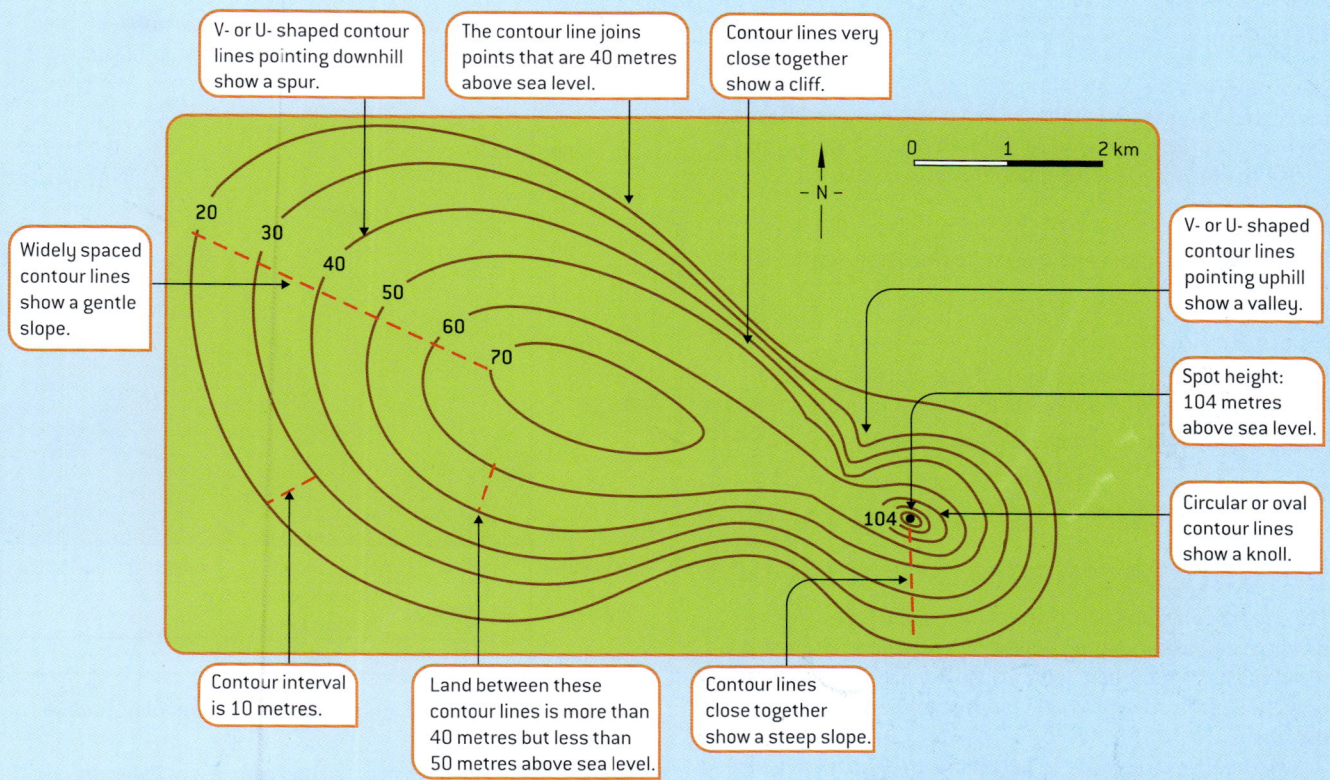

*How contour lines show the shape of the land*

Labels on diagram:
- V- or U- shaped contour lines pointing downhill show a spur.
- The contour line joins points that are 40 metres above sea level.
- Contour lines very close together show a cliff.
- Widely spaced contour lines show a gentle slope.
- V- or U- shaped contour lines pointing uphill show a valley.
- Spot height: 104 metres above sea level.
- Circular or oval contour lines show a knoll.
- Contour interval is 10 metres.
- Land between these contour lines is more than 40 metres but less than 50 metres above sea level.
- Contour lines close together show a steep slope.

# Calculating gradient

*Gradient* measures the steepness of a slope between two points or locations. It is usually expressed as a ratio. For example, a 1 in 2 gradient means that a slope rises 1 metre for every 2 metres travelled. Such a gradient would indicate a very steep slope. A slope of 1 in 40 is a gentle slope. To work out the gradient of a slope using a topographic map, follow these steps.

### STEP 1
Calculate the difference in height between two places on the slope. This can be found by subtracting the lower point from the higher point.

### STEP 2
Calculate the horizontal distance between two places on the slope. This can be found by measuring the distance between the two points on the map and using the map's scale to work out the actual difference.

### STEP 3
Calculate the gradient using the following formula.
Divide the difference in height by the horizontal distance:

$$\text{gradient} = \frac{\text{difference in height}}{\text{horizontal difference}}$$

The gradient is expressed as a fraction with a numerator of 1. For example:

$$\text{Gradient A to B} = \frac{40}{400} = \frac{1}{10} \text{ (or 1 in 10)}$$

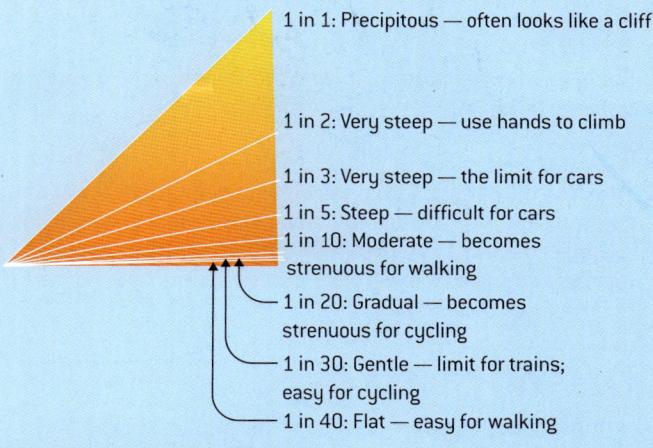

*Descriptions of land gradients:*
- 1 in 1: Precipitous — often looks like a cliff
- 1 in 2: Very steep — use hands to climb
- 1 in 3: Very steep — the limit for cars
- 1 in 5: Steep — difficult for cars
- 1 in 10: Moderate — becomes strenuous for walking
- 1 in 20: Gradual — becomes strenuous for cycling
- 1 in 30: Gentle — limit for trains; easy for cycling
- 1 in 40: Flat — easy for walking

## ACTIVITIES

### USING YOUR SKILLS
Refer to the topographic map extract of Walls of Jerusalem National Park on page 31.

1. Calculate the gradients of the slopes between:
   a. GR438693 and Mount Jerusalem
   b. GR433697 and Mount Jerusalem
   c. Pool of Siloam GR418705 and Zion Hill GR423704
   d. Pool of Siloam GR418705 and Mount Ophal GR413708.
2. Describe the gradients for each of the above, (a) to (d).
3. Classify slopes (a) to (d) in ascending order of steepness.

## Finding local relief

*Local relief* is a measure of the difference in height between the highest and lowest points within a relatively small area, such as a valley. It is useful for describing local landforms.

Use the following steps to find the local relief.

### STEP 1
Determine the highest and lowest points using contours and spot heights.

### STEP 2
Calculate the difference between these two points. If the highest point is 130 metres and the lowest point 10 metres:

local relief = highest point − lowest point
= 130 − 10
= 120 metres

## Finding the aspect of a slope

The *aspect* of a slope is the direction a slope faces. For example a house might be built with a southerly aspect to avoid the heat of the sun for much of the day. A field for crops might have a northerly aspect in order to receive more sun on the plants.

Use the following steps to determine the aspect of a slope.

### STEP 1
Study the contour patterns to find the slope's highest and lowest points.

### STEP 2
Work out the direction from the highest point to the lowest (downhill). This is the direction the slope is said to face. If, for example, the slope runs downhill to the south-east from its highest point to its lowest, then it faces south-east and is said to have a south-easterly aspect.

## Drawing a transect

A *transect* is a diagram that shows the relationship between different features on a topographic map. It is based on a cross-section diagram (see pages 32–3 for how to draw a cross-section) but adds other descriptive information about the area covered by the cross-section. When a transect diagram is complete, a geographer can identify how certain features, such as landforms, have influenced other features, such as land use.

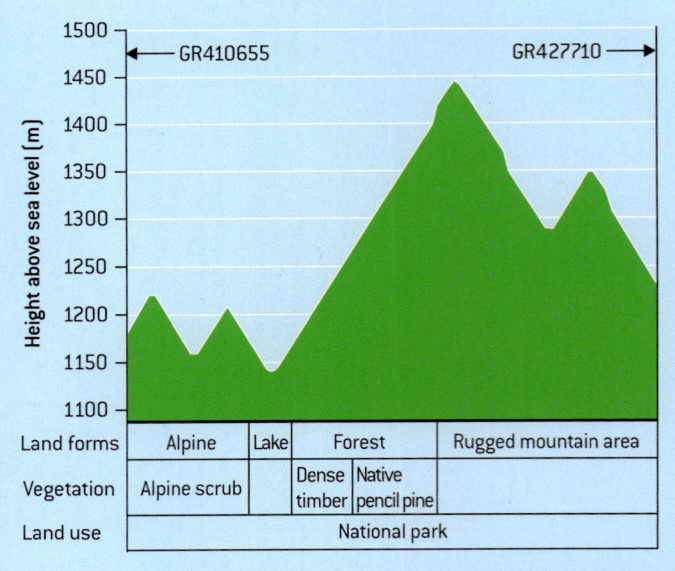

*Cross-section of Walls of Jerusalem National Park (see page 31)*

Use the following steps to construct a transect diagram.

### STEP 1
Select the two points at each end of the transect.

### STEP 2
Draw up a table similar to the one above.

### STEP 3
Draw a cross-section of the land in the middle of the table.

### STEP 4
Place a piece of paper between the two points along the cross-section and identify the landforms and their location along the cross-section. Write the information in the table below the cross-section.

### STEP 5
Complete the other features of the transect diagram, including vegetation and land use.

## ACTIVITIES

### USING YOUR SKILLS

Refer to the topographic map extract of Walls of Jerusalem National Park, Tasmania on page 31.

1. Calculate the bearings from The Temple GR423694 to:
   a. Zion Hill GR423705
   b. Dixons Kingdom Hut GR426688
   c. Mount Moriah GR412679
   d. King Davids Peak GR407702.

2. Calculate the local relief from:
   a. Damascus Gate GR418693 to Solomons Throne GR416693
   b. Lake Salome GR413705 to King Davids Peak GR407702.

3. What is the aspect of each of the following slopes?
   a. King Davids Peak GR407702 to Lake Salome GR413705
   b. King Davids Peak GR407702 to Damascus Gate GR418693
   c. Dixons Kingdom Hut GR426688 to Mount Moriah GR412679

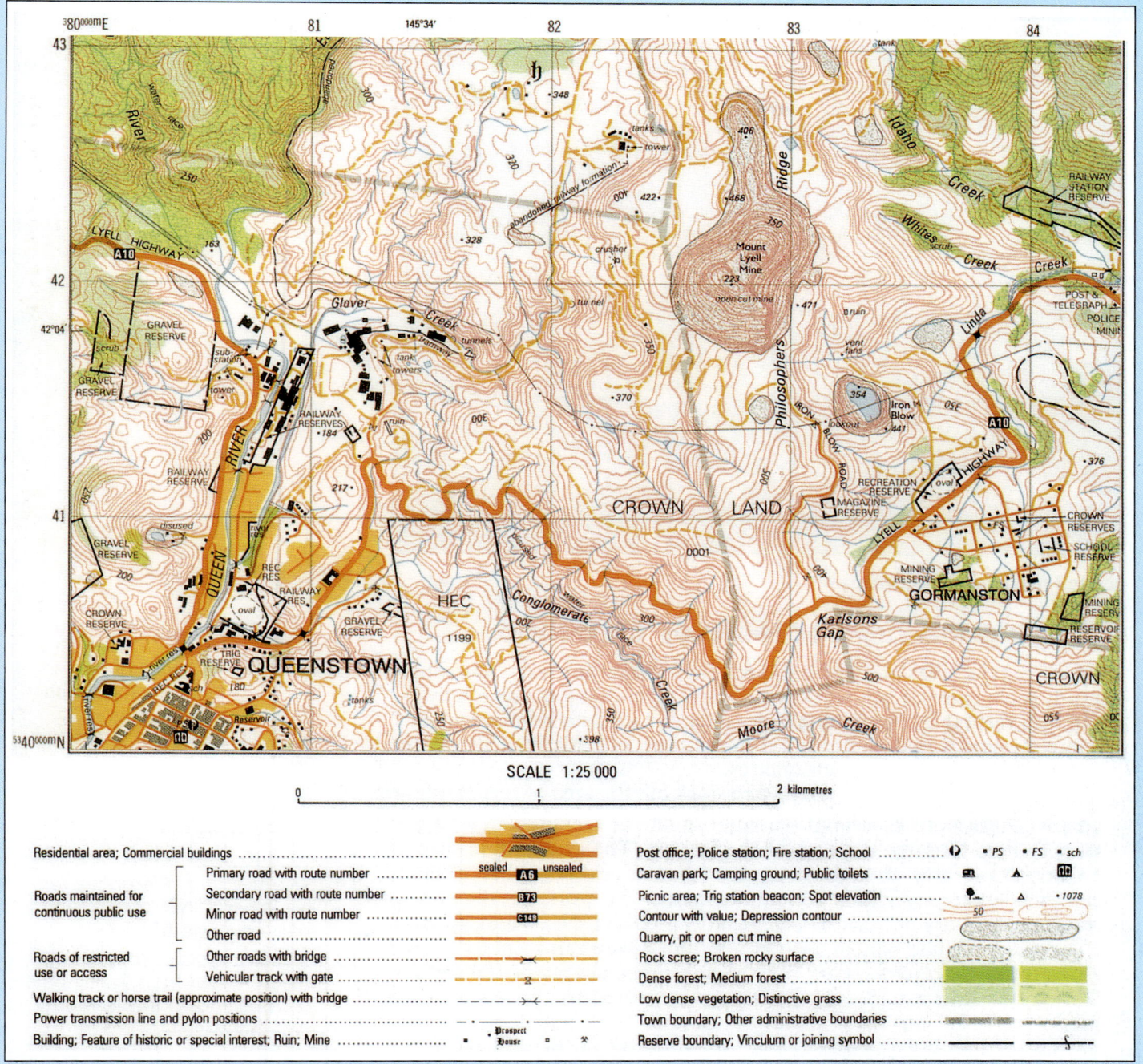

*Topographic map extract of Queenstown, Tasmania*

4. **a** Draw a transect from GR407687 to GR437689.
   **b** Label the landforms and vegetation along the transect.

Refer to the topographic map extract of Queenstown above to answer the following questions.

5. What is the contour interval of the map?
6. Calculate the bearings from Mt Lyell Mine GR828421 to:
   **a** Magazine Reserve GR832411
   **b** Queenstown oval GR807406.
7. Calculate the gradients of the slopes between Karlsons Gap GR831406 and the knoll at GR828409.
8. Calculate the area of Mt Lyell Mine.
9. Draw a cross-section (see pages 32–3) from Queenstown Trig Reserve GR807404 to Reservoir Reserve GR841405.
10. What is the distance from Queenstown to Iron Blow?
11. What direction is Gormanston from Queenstown?

CHAPTER 2 | Physical characteristics that make Australia unique

# 2.4 GEOskillbuilder

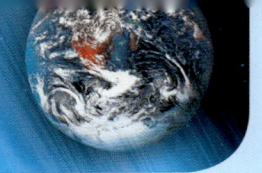

## Understanding landforms: Walls of Jerusalem

The spectacular Walls of Jerusalem National Park is located in the Central Plateau area of Tasmania. Topographic maps are an essential item for bushwalkers who visit this area.

*Looking from Mount Jerusalem towards the West Wall, with Lake Salome, Zion Hill, part of The Temple and Herods Gate*

## Calculating the area of a feature

The area of a feature can be calculated using the line scale or the grid pattern on a map. It is easier to calculate area if the feature is a square or rectangular shape such as a settlement.

Use the following steps to calculate the area of a square or rectangular feature.

**STEP 1**
Use the line scale to estimate the length and width of the feature in kilometres.

**STEP 2**
Multiply these two figures to give the area in square kilometres. For example, a feature 2 kilometres long and 2 kilometres wide would cover an area of 4 square kilometres.

Use the following steps to calculate the area of an irregular shape such as a lake.

**STEP 1**
Use the grid squares across the map to count the number of complete grid squares covered by the feature.

**STEP 2**
To estimate the area of the incomplete squares covered by the feature, count them as half squares; that is, halve the number of incomplete squares. Add this to the number of complete squares to arrive at a total. For example, 10 complete grid squares and 4 incomplete squares would total 12 complete grid squares.

**STEP 3**
Multiply the number of complete grid squares by the area of each grid (use the scale to find the area of each grid). For example, 12 complete squares with an area of 0.5 kilometres each would cover an area of 6 square kilometres.

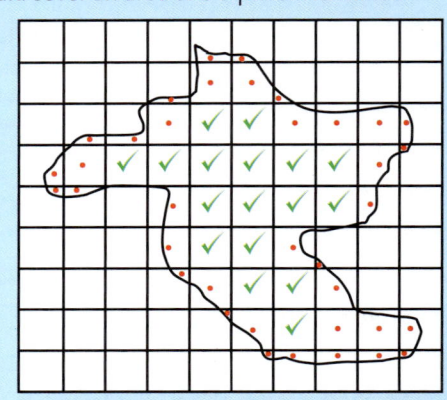

*In this example, there are 17 complete grid squares and 37 incomplete grid squares. Halving the number of incomplete grid squares and adding this number (18.5) to 17 gives a total of 35.5 complete squares.*

### ACTIVITIES

**USING YOUR SKILLS**

1. Use the map on the next page to calculate the areas of (a) The Temple and (b) Lake Ball.

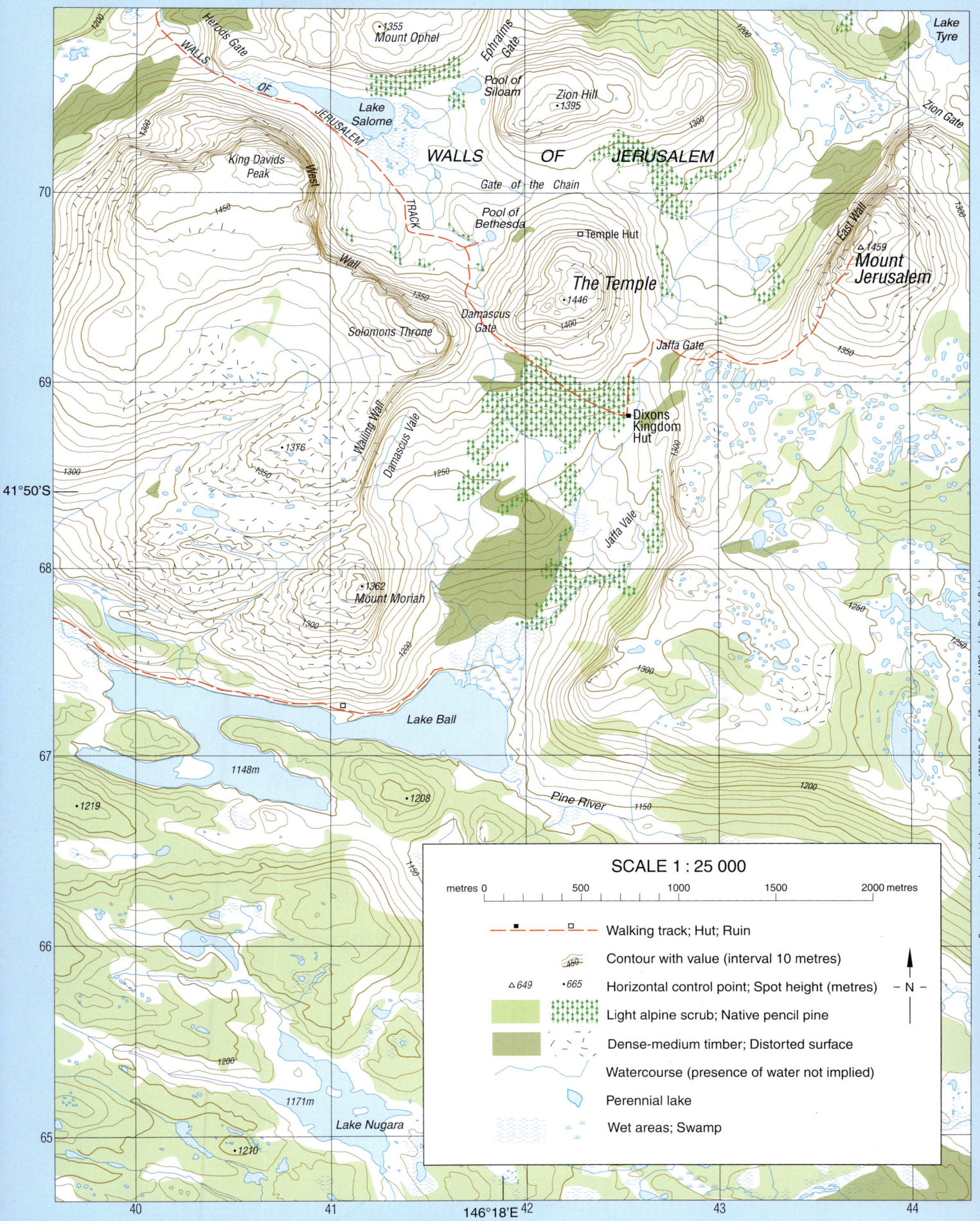

Topographic map extract of Walls of Jerusalem National Park, Tasmania

CHAPTER 2 | Physical characteristics that make Australia unique

# 2.5 GEOskillbuilder

## Constructing a cross-section

To help show the shape of the land and look more closely at the slope, a cross-section can be drawn. A *cross-section* shows the shape of a feature from the side, as if it had been sliced with a knife.

Cross-sections are useful for:
- helping identify the shape of the land
- showing the changing shape of the land
- planning constructions, such as houses, on sloping blocks
- planning a walk in a mountainous area
- showing areas of land that cannot be seen.

The map of Thredbo below provides a good opportunity to look at how we can make our own cross-sections to show the slope of the land.

We will use the contour lines on the Thredbo map to construct a cross-section along the path of Merritt's chairlift. The contour interval tells us the vertical distance between the unlabelled lines. The contour interval for the Thredbo map is 20 metres.

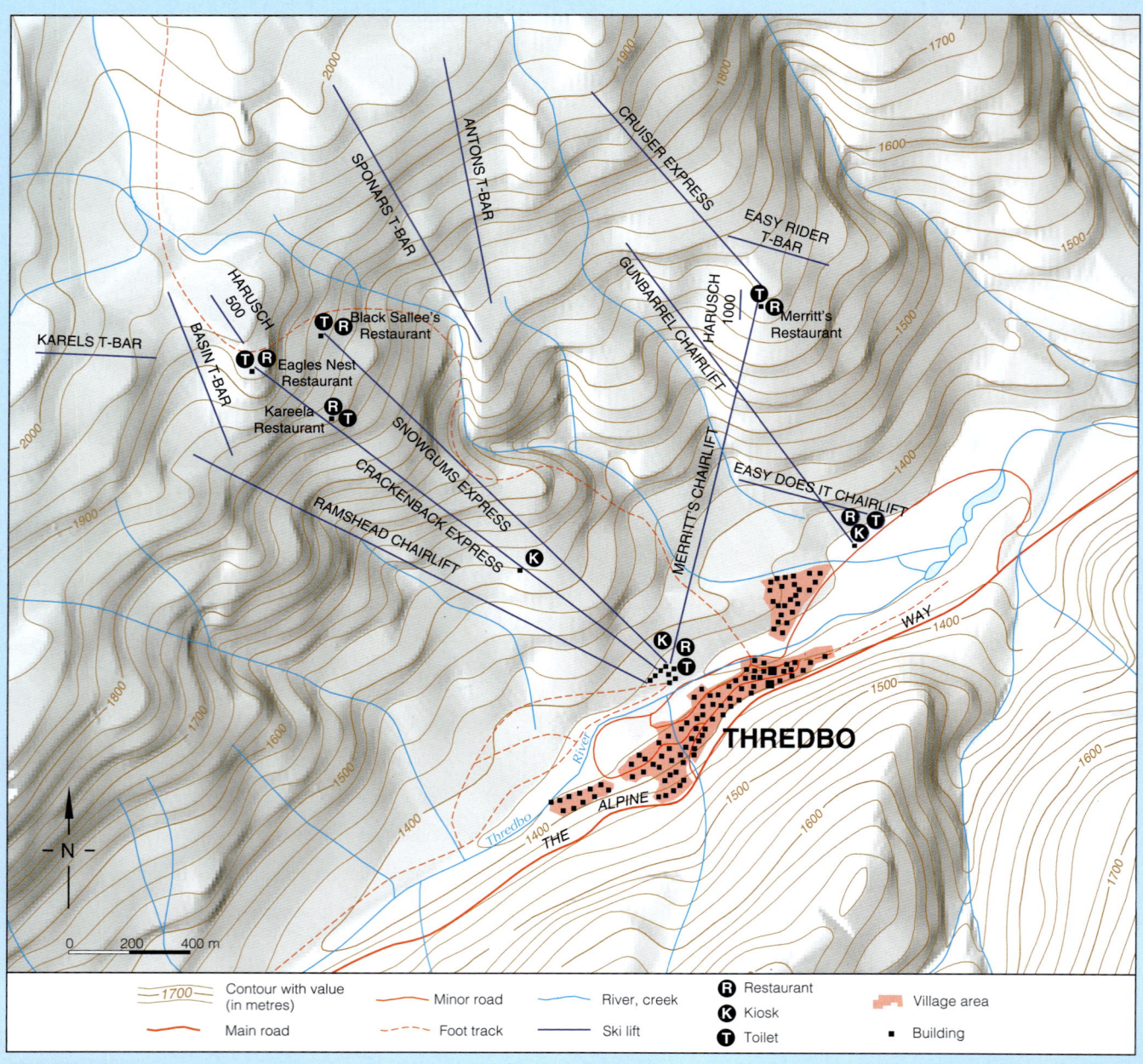

*Map of Thredbo*

### STEP 1
Place the straight edge of a piece of clean paper along the path of Merritt's chairlift. Mark each contour line at the point it touches the edge of your paper as shown below. Against each stroke indicate the height of the contour line it stands for.

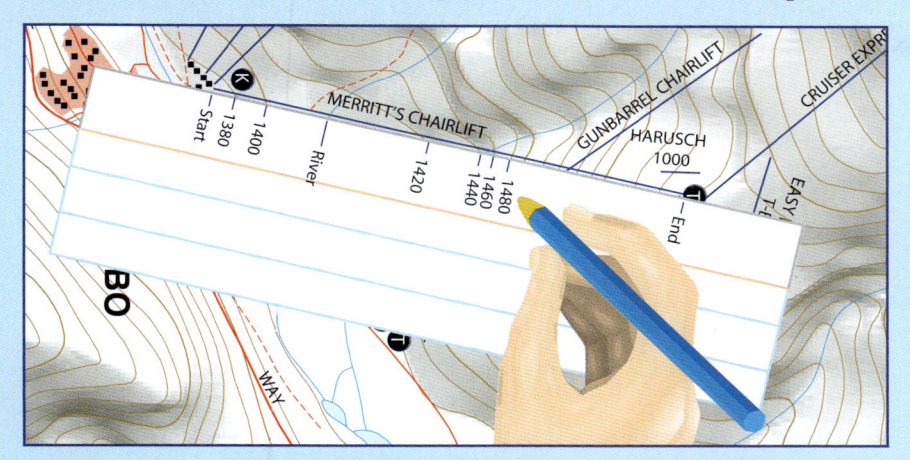

### STEP 2
On a sheet of graph paper draw a suitable vertical scale for your cross-section. Here, we have used 1 centimetre to represent 100 metres. This gives a realistic impression of what the slope might look like.

### STEP 3
Place the marked edge of the paper at the base of the vertical scale and mark the appropriate height directly above each stroke with a dot. Join the dots with a smooth line to show the slope of the land.

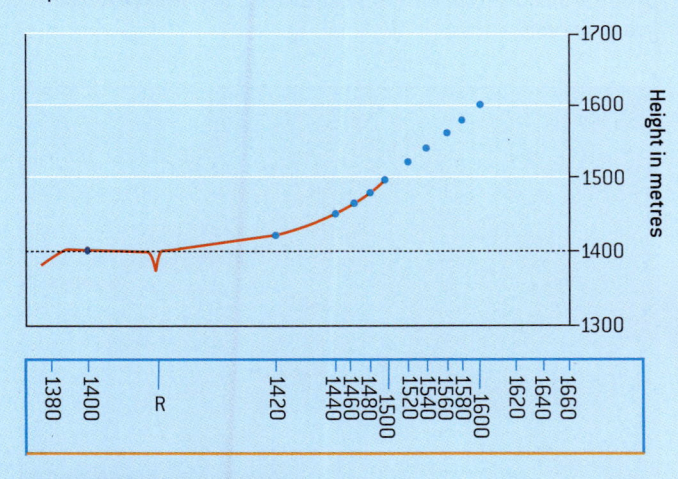

### STEP 4
Add a title for the vertical axis.

### STEP 5
Work out the vertical exaggeration for the cross-section. Vertical exaggeration is used to make sure your cross-section doesn't look as flat as a pancake. It is the number of times your vertical scale is exaggerating the horizontal scale. In this case the horizontal scale for the map is 1 centimetre = 200 metres and the vertical scale is 1 centimetre = 100 metres. The vertical exaggeration of 2 is found by dividing the horizontal scale by the vertical scale.

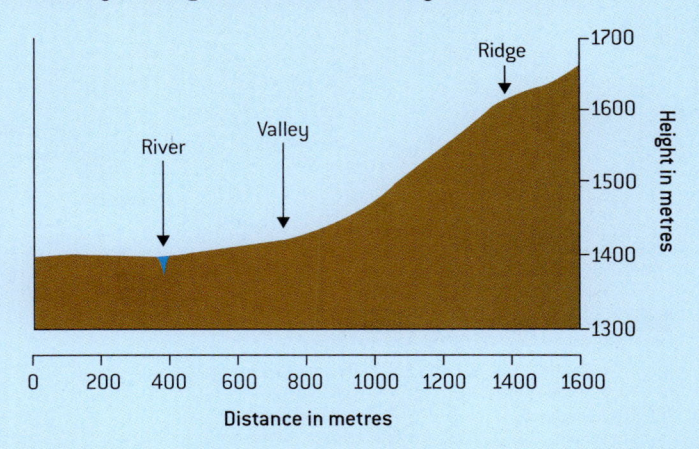

## ACTIVITIES

### USING YOUR SKILLS

1. Refer to the topographic map of Thredbo on the previous page.
   a. What is the length of Merritt's chairlift?
   b. Are there any longer chairlifts in Thredbo?
   c. What is the approximate height of Merritt's Restaurant?
   d. What is the aspect from Merritt's Restaurant as you look down to Thredbo?

2. Refer to the cross-section above. Calculate the local relief of the cross-section.

3. Refer to the instructions above for constructing a cross-section.
   a. Construct a cross-section along Snowgums Express ski lift.
   b. Compare this cross-section with that for Merritt's chairlift.
   c. Calculate the vertical scale of your cross-section from part (a).

CHAPTER 2 | Physical characteristics that make Australia unique

# 2.6 Australia's pattern of climate and vegetation

## Climate and rainfall

The size and location of Australia ensures that it has a wide range of **climates**. These can be seen on the map of climatic zones below. Australia is widely known as the 'dry continent'. Around 80 per cent of Australia has a rainfall of less than 600 mm per year and 50 per cent has less than 300 mm. The rainfall is not only low but also highly variable, and **droughts** are a common occurrence.

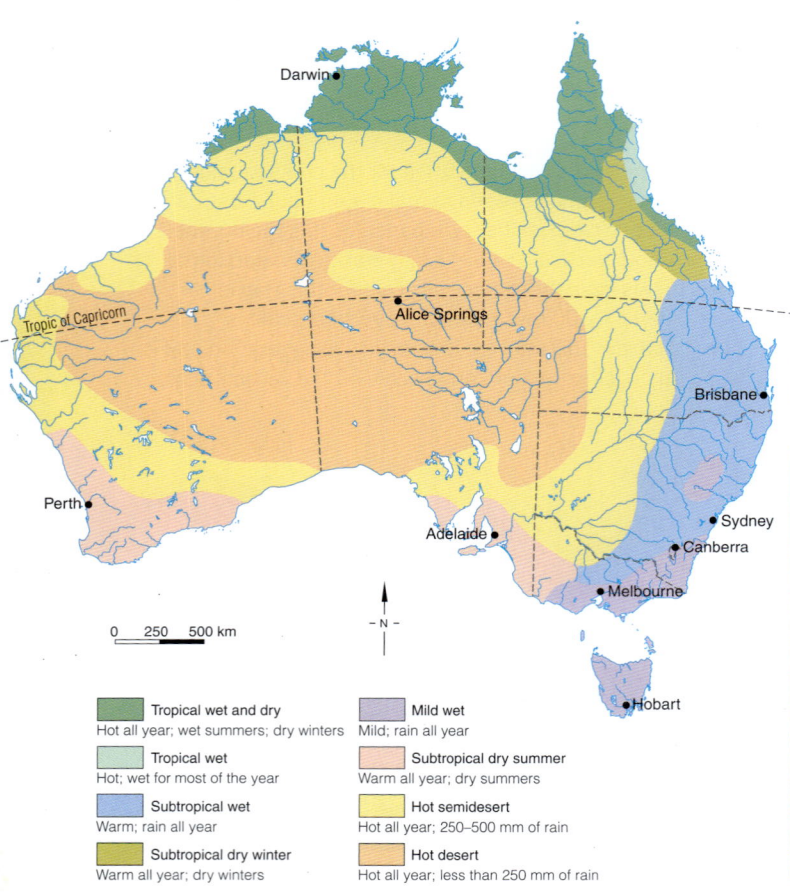

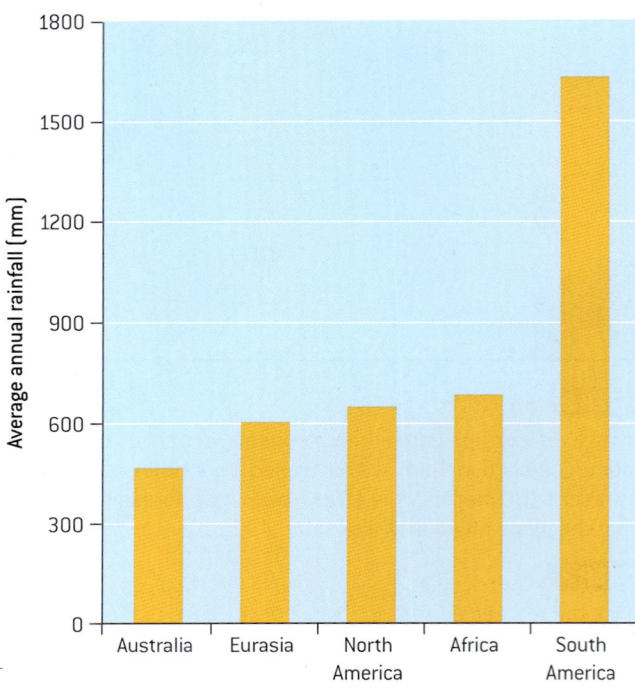

*Of all the inhabited continents, Australia has the lowest average yearly rainfall.*

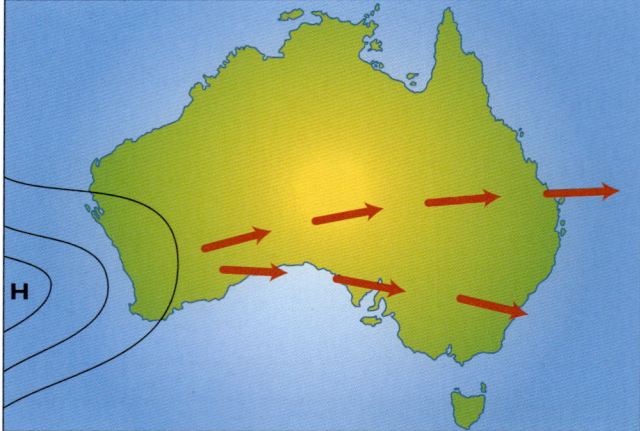

**Australian climatic zones**

- Tropical wet and dry — Hot all year; wet summers; dry winters
- Tropical wet — Hot; wet for most of the year
- Subtropical wet — Warm; rain all year
- Subtropical dry winter — Warm all year; dry winters
- Mild wet — Mild; rain all year
- Subtropical dry summer — Warm all year; dry summers
- Hot semidesert — Hot all year; 250–500 mm of rain
- Hot desert — Hot all year; less than 250 mm of rain

*The movement of high pressure systems across the continent is the main reason Australia is so dry.*

## Pressure systems

The main reason Australia is so dry is that much of the continent lies in an area dominated by high pressure for most of the year. High pressure systems drift from west to east across the continent bringing dry, stable, sinking air. This results in atmospheric conditions that are not favourable for rainfall (see the weather map above right).

As the rainfall maps opposite show, the wettest parts of Australia are the northern and eastern coastal areas and the west coast of Tasmania. The northern part of Australia generally has a summer rainfall maximum. In summer, a trough of low pressure can extend south from the Equator, bringing moist, unstable air in north-westerly winds over the area (see the weather map that follows).

This can lead to widespread rain, particularly near the coast. This is often referred to as the north-west **monsoon**.

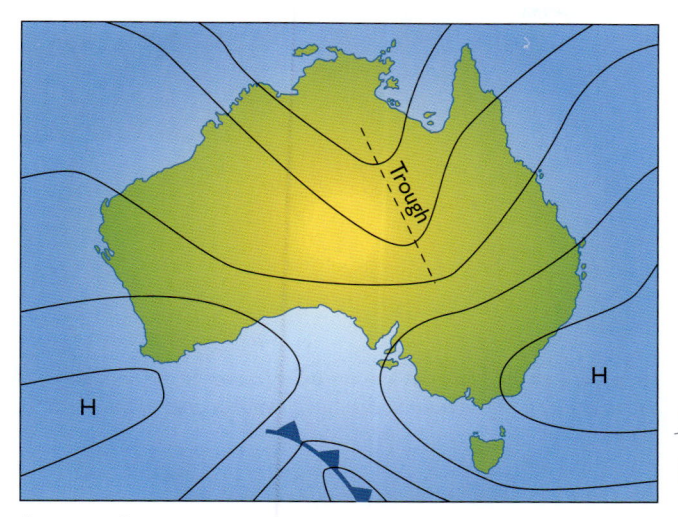

*A summer low pressure trough brings rain to northern Australia.*

Also during the summer and autumn, tropical cyclones can develop off the coast of northern Australia and bring heavy rain, especially to coastal areas. During winter much of the area is dominated by high pressure systems that have moved further north. Dry and stable air from the interior of Australia dominates the area and there is little rainfall.

The southern part of Australia generally has more rain in winter. During winter, cold fronts in association with low pressure systems move further north over this area and bring cool moist air and rain as the cold fronts pass through. The heaviest rain falls on the coastal margins, including the west coast of Tasmania.

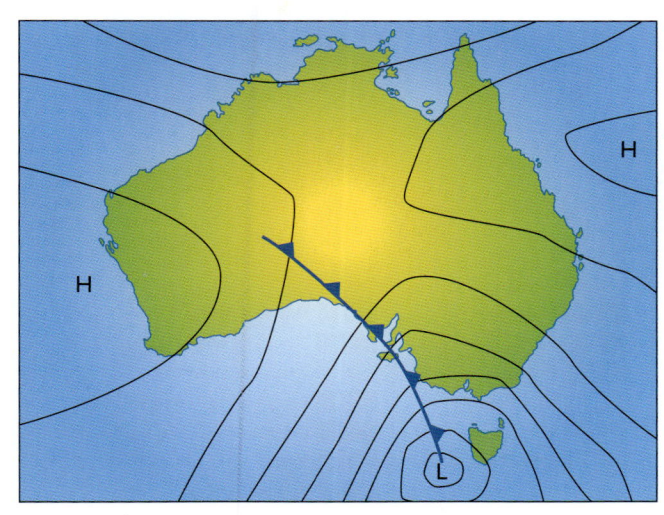

The east coast receives rainfall throughout the year. Much of this rain is brought by moist easterly winds. The heavier falls of rain are generally confined to the coast and highlands as the western side of the highlands lies in a rainshadow area from the moist easterlies.

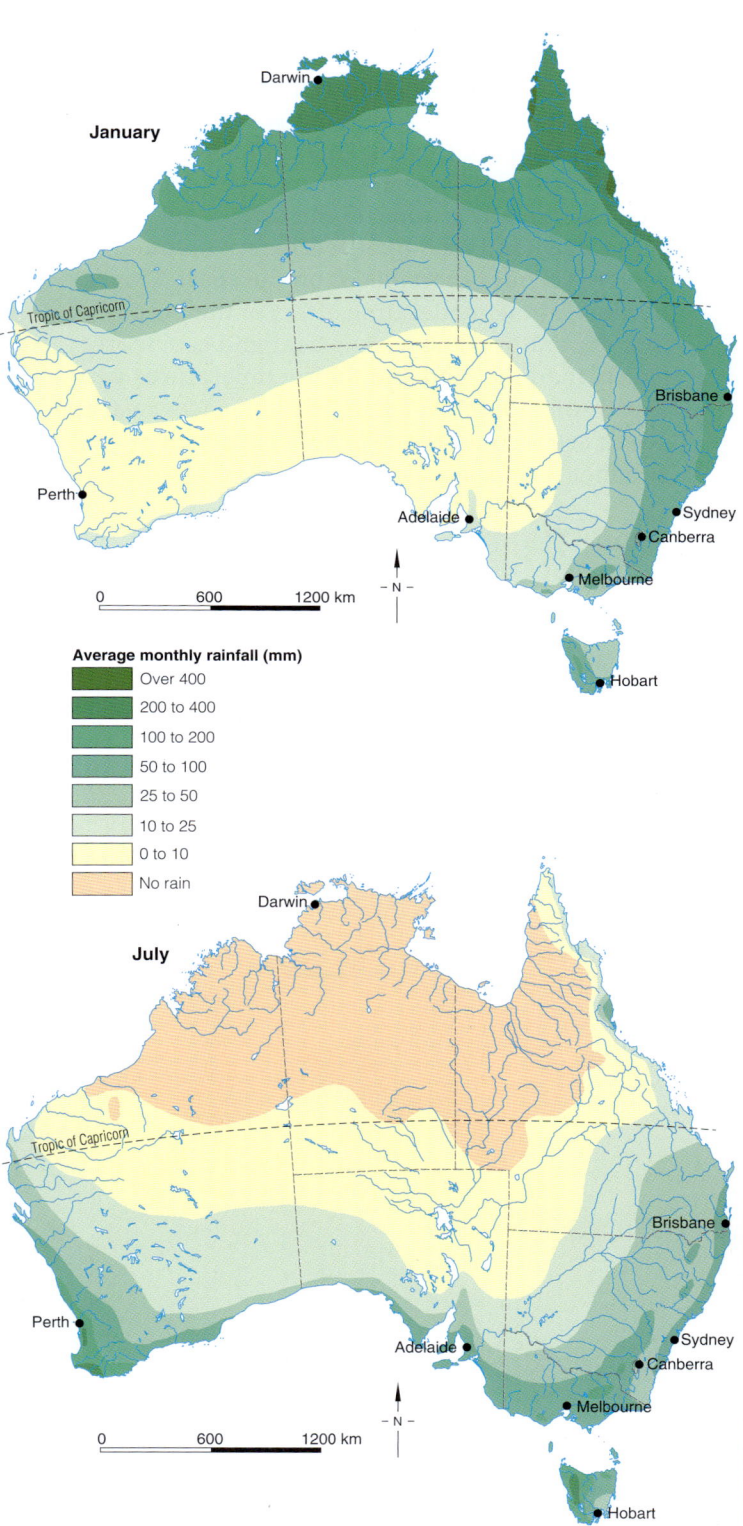

**Average monthly rainfall (mm)**
- Over 400
- 200 to 400
- 100 to 200
- 50 to 100
- 25 to 50
- 10 to 25
- 0 to 10
- No rain

*The passage of a cold front over southern Australia in winter brings cool, moist air.*

*Average rainfall in Australia for January and July*

CHAPTER 2 | Physical characteristics that make Australia unique    35

## Temperature

The maps below show the seasonal distribution of temperature in Australia for January and July. Variations in temperature occur for several reasons. One reason is that at higher latitudes on the Earth's curved surface, solar radiation (heat from the sun) is spread more widely than at places at lower latitudes (see the diagram at right). The sun's rays that reach the Earth near the Equator (that is, at low latitudes) have a smaller area to heat than rays reaching the Earth at higher latitudes. This explains why Darwin experiences higher temperatures than Melbourne (see the climatic graphs on the next page).

Places inland tend to be warmer in summer and cooler in winter than places on the coast. This is because of the moderating effect of the oceans on temperature. The oceans heat and cool more slowly than the land and their temperatures vary less throughout the year. In winter, places near the ocean are warmer than places inland, whereas in summer they are cooler.

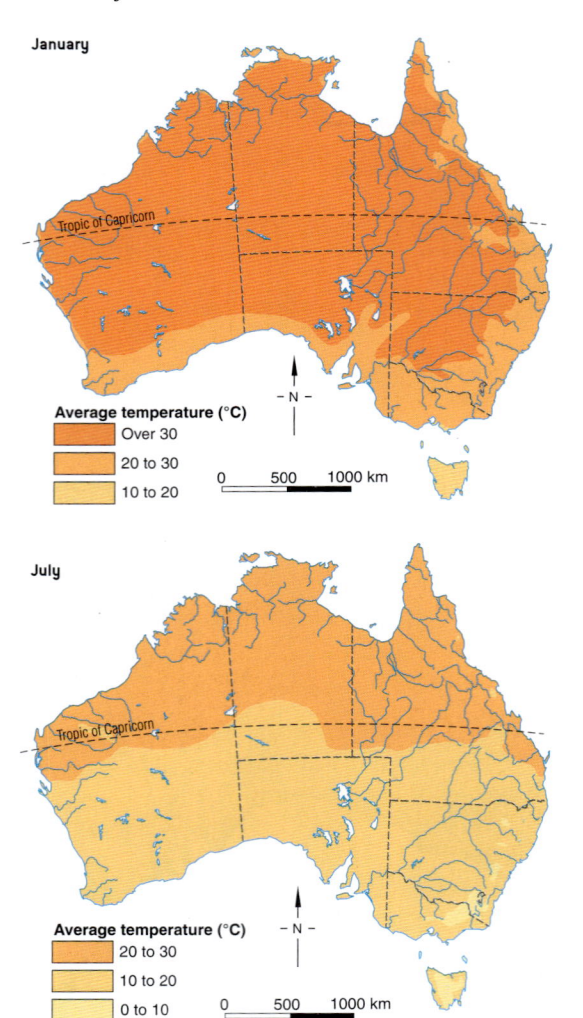

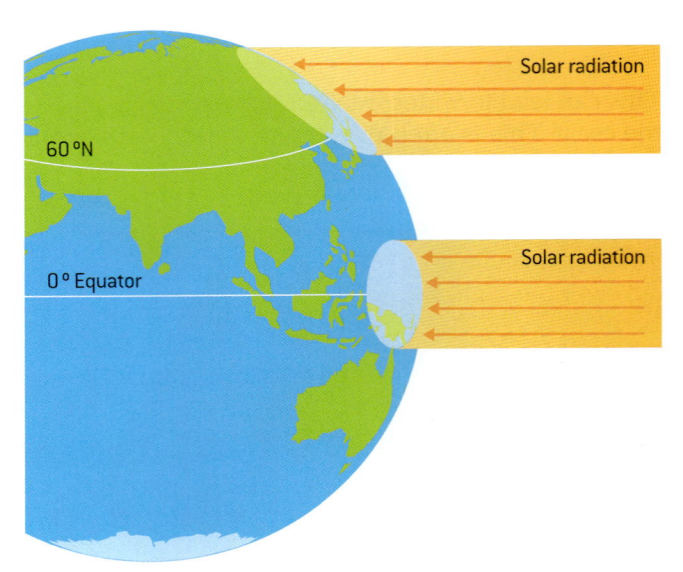

*Temperatures are higher at low latitudes (closer to the Equator) because incoming solar radiation has a smaller area of the Earth to heat.*

## Australia's pattern of vegetation

The size and latitudinal extent of Australia has resulted in a wide variety of vegetation. Because of the dry climate, about 40 per cent of Australia is covered by grassland and shrubs. In higher rainfall areas, trees dominate. In the medium to high rainfall areas, much of the natural vegetation has been cleared for agricultural and urban development.

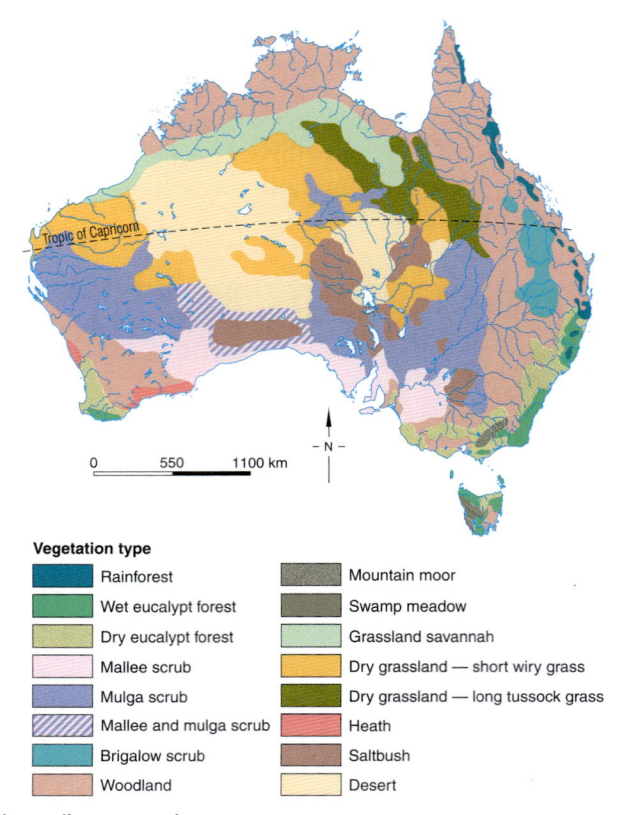

**January**

**Average temperature (°C)**
- Over 30
- 20 to 30
- 10 to 20

**July**

**Average temperature (°C)**
- 20 to 30
- 10 to 20
- 0 to 10

*Average temperatures in Australia for January and July*

**Vegetation type**
- Rainforest
- Wet eucalypt forest
- Dry eucalypt forest
- Mallee scrub
- Mulga scrub
- Mallee and mulga scrub
- Brigalow scrub
- Woodland
- Mountain moor
- Swamp meadow
- Grassland savannah
- Dry grassland — short wiry grass
- Dry grassland — long tussock grass
- Heath
- Saltbush
- Desert

*Australian vegetation*

36　Geoactive 2

## GEOskills TOOLBOX

### INTERPRETING CLIMATIC GRAPHS

A climatic graph is a combination of a bar graph and a line graph. Climatic graphs show the climate of a place over a 12-month period. The line graph section always shows average monthly temperature, and the bar graph represents average monthly rainfall. Be careful to read from the correct scale when studying climatic graphs. The right-hand scale represents average rainfall in millimetres. The left-hand scale represents temperature in degrees Celsius.

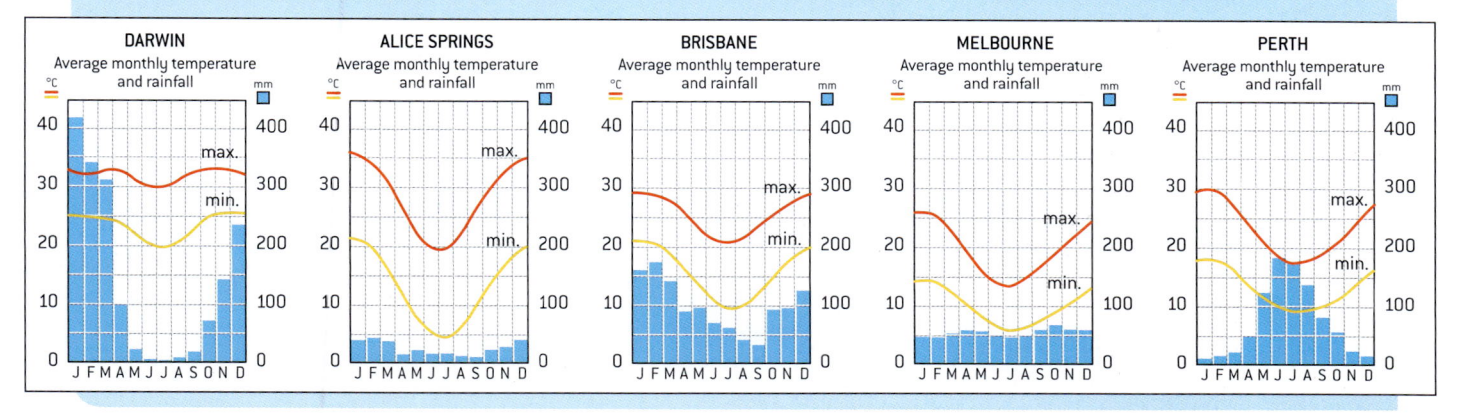

## ACTIVITIES

### UNDERSTANDING

1. Explain why Australia has a wide range of climates.
2. State whether each of the following statements is true or false.
   a. The wettest parts of Australia are in the inland areas.
   b. High pressure systems move from west to east across the Australian continent.
   c. About 40 per cent of Australia is covered in trees.

### USING YOUR SKILLS

3. Refer to the map on page 34 in the right-hand column.
   a. Describe the movement of high pressure systems across Australia.
   b. How do high pressure systems contribute to Australia's dryness?
4. Refer to the maps on page 35 showing Australia's average rainfall for January and July.
   a. Moving in a line from Adelaide to Darwin, describe the changes in rainfall that occur in January.
   b. Moving in a line from Brisbane to Perth, describe the changes in rainfall that occur in January.
   c. Moving in a line from Hobart to Darwin, describe the changes in rainfall that occur in July.
   d. Using the maps on page 35 showing a summer low pressure trough and the passage of a winter cold front, explain the main reasons for the distribution of rainfall over Australia in January and July.
5. Refer to the maps on page 36 showing average temperatures in Australia in January and July.

   With the aid of an atlas:
   a. rank the following towns and cities from the warmest to the coolest for temperatures in January: Perth, Mount Isa, Mount Gambier, Hobart
   b. rank the following towns and cities from coldest to warmest for temperatures in July: Alice Springs, Hobart, Darwin, Melbourne, Mackay
   c. explain why Alice Springs has higher average daily temperatures in July than Mackay, even though Mackay has a slightly lower latitude.
6. Refer to the map of Australian vegetation on the previous page. Moving in a line from Adelaide to Darwin, describe the changes in vegetation type. Account for these changes.
7. Refer to the climatic graph for Alice Springs.
   a. What type of climate is this?
   b. Describe the climate in terms of temperature and rainfall.
8. Refer to the climatic graphs for Perth, Darwin, Melbourne and Brisbane.
   a. What type of climate does each of these cities have?
   b. Describe the climate of each of these cities including temperature, seasonal distribution of temperature, rainfall and seasonal distribution of rainfall.

### GEOTERMS

**climate:** the long-term variation in the atmosphere, relating mainly to temperature and precipitation

**drought:** a prolonged period of below-average precipitation

**monsoon:** the seasonal change in wind direction that is experienced in much of the tropics

# 2.7 Impact of climate change on Australia

In 2006, the Bureau of Meteorology announced that 2005 was the warmest year on record in Australia. The annual mean temperature was 1.09°C above average. This is the equivalent of many southern Australian towns shifting northward by about 100 kilometres. An increase of 4°C would mean that temperatures in Melbourne could be similar to those now experienced in Moree, in northern New South Wales.

There were regional differences in the amount of warming and the impact on rainfall. The general trend in 2005 showed increases in average temperatures in all states, and decreases in rainfall, except in Tasmania.

| Global Temp. rise | Tourism | Water and primary industries | Infrastructure and insurance |
|---|---|---|---|
| <1°C | • Regular bleaching of 60% of the Great Barrier Reef<br>• Snow-covered alpine areas shrink by 10 to 40%<br>• Area of montane tropical rainforest in northern Australia decreases by 50%<br>• Vertebrates in the World Heritage Wet Tropics lose half their habitat | • Melbourne's water supply falls 3 to 11%<br>• Droughts in NSW 70% more frequent and more widespread<br>• Native pasture growth falls by 8% (based on 11% decrease in precipitation)<br>• Cows in NSW Hunter Valley produce 250 to 310 litres less milk a year<br>• 14% of Victoria's marine invertebrates lose their habitat | • 10 to 20% increase in extreme rainfall in NSW<br>• 25% more days above 35°C in NT<br>• 18% more days above 35°C in SA<br>• Peak electricity demand in Adelaide and Brisbane increases by 2 to 5%<br>• Peak electricity demand in Melbourne and Sydney decreases by up to 1%<br>• Demand for natural gas heating in Melbourne decreases |
| 1–2°C | • Bleaching of 60 to 80% of the Great Barrier Reef each year<br>• Vertebrates in the World Heritage Wet Tropics lose 90% of core habitat<br>• Loss of 80% of Kakadu freshwater wetlands due to 30 cm sea level rise | • Flows in the Murray–Darling fall 12 to 25%<br>• Melbourne's water supply falls 7 to 35%<br>• 91% chance of wheat exports falling below current level<br>• $12.4 million per year to manage southward spread of Queensland fruit fly<br>• $5.7 million per year benefit due to reduction in apple moth | • Twice as many people exposed to flooding<br>• Malaria zones spread southward<br>• Population at risk of dengue fever increases from 0.17 million to 0.75–1.6 million<br>• Rise in refugees from Pacific Islands<br>• Peak electricity demand in Adelaide and Brisbane increases by 4 to 10%<br>• Peak electricity demand in Melbourne and Sydney decreases by 1% |
| 2–3°C | • Bleaching of 97% of the Great Barrier Reef each year<br>• Victoria's montane tropical vertebrate species lose 30 to 70% of core habitat | • Flows in the Macquarie River basin (NSW) fall 5 to 35%<br>• Pasture growth slows by 31%<br>• Livestock-carrying capacity falls by 40% | • 10% increase in forest fire danger<br>• 15% increase in 100-year storm tides along eastern Victorian coast<br>• 20 to 30% increase in tropical cyclone rainfall and 5 to 10% increase in wind speed<br>• 17% increase in road maintenance costs across most of Australia |
| 3–4°C | • Distribution of Great Barrier Reef species shrinks by 95%<br>• Area of snow-covered alpine shrinks by 20 to 85%<br>• Area of '60-day' snow cover shrinks by 40 to 95% | • Flows in the Murray–Darling fall 30 to 70%<br>• Australian primary production falls 6%<br>• Eucalypts lose 55% of their core habitat<br>• Timber yields in SA rise by 25 to 50%, but fall by similar margin in north Queensland and the Top End | • Oceania experiences a net loss of GDP<br>• Dengue fever transmission zone reaches Brisbane and possibly Sydney<br>• Temperature-related deaths of people over 65 rise by 200%<br>• Peak electricity demand increases in Adelaide, Brisbane and Melbourne by 5 to 20% |
| >4°C | • Most Australian vertebrates lose 90 to 100% of their core habitat | • 32% chance of decreased wheat production<br>• 45% chance of wheat crop value being below current level | • 25% increase in extreme rainfall in Victoria<br>• 30% increase in 100-year storm tides along eastern Victorian coast<br>• 150% increase in annual days above 35°C in SA<br>• Peak electricity demand increases in Adelaide, Brisbane and Melbourne by 9 to 25% |

*Potential effects in Australia of various temperature increases*

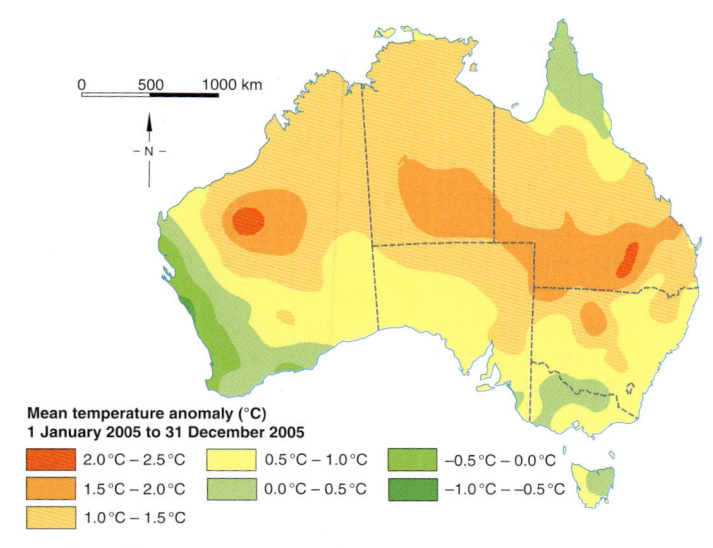

There will be a variety of climate change impacts in Australia, depending on a range of possible global temperature changes. Climate change will affect natural environments, our water supply, health, agriculture and industry.

**Mean temperature anomaly (°C)**
**1 January 2005 to 31 December 2005**

- 2.0 °C – 2.5 °C
- 1.5 °C – 2.0 °C
- 1.0 °C – 1.5 °C
- 0.5 °C – 1.0 °C
- 0.0 °C – 0.5 °C
- −0.5 °C – 0.0 °C
- −1.0 °C – −0.5 °C

*Annual mean temperatures for Australia in 2005 compared to normal trends*

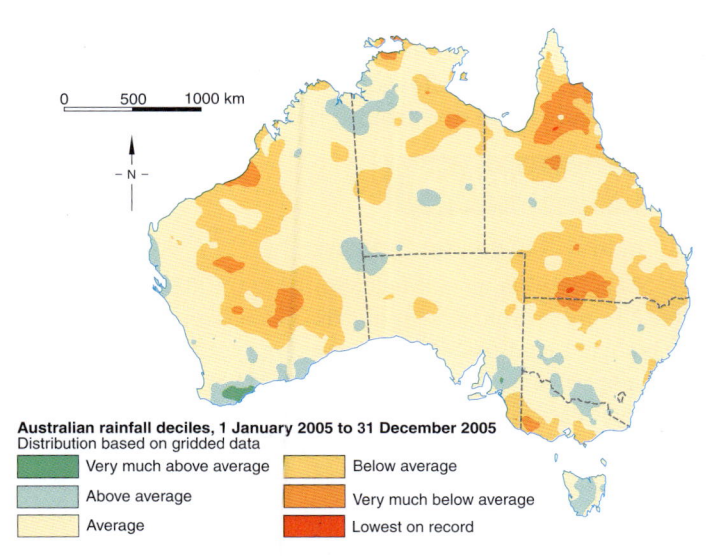

**Australian rainfall deciles, 1 January 2005 to 31 December 2005**
Distribution based on gridded data

- Very much above average
- Above average
- Average
- Below average
- Very much below average
- Lowest on record

*2005 rainfall compared with historical rainfall records*

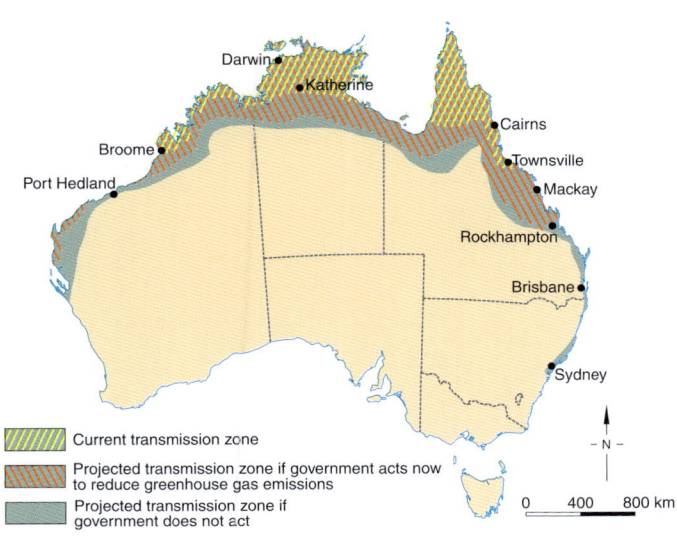

- Current transmission zone
- Projected transmission zone if government acts now to reduce greenhouse gas emissions
- Projected transmission zone if government does not act

*Potential dengue fever transmission zones*

## GEOfacts

- In January 2009, Melbourne and Adelaide experienced heatwaves with temperatures of 44–45°C for over four consecutive days. The national capital city record for the highest temperature is held by Perth, which had a temperature of 46.2°C in 1991.
- The extreme temperatures in Victoria contributed to the Black Saturday bushfires: Australia's worst natural disaster.
- In January 2009, after weeks of rain, around 200 people in the Cairns region were infected with dengue fever. The disease is expected to move as far south as Sydney in the future. This is because the increased temperatures and rainfall associated with global warming create new habitats in which dengue-carrying mosquitoes can breed.

## ACTIVITIES

### UNDERSTANDING

1. Refer to the table on the previous page.
   a. Outline four possible impacts on Australia's tourism industry as a result of climate change.
   b. List three possible benefits of climate change to Australia.

### USING YOUR SKILLS

2. Refer to the temperature and rainfall maps on this page.
   a. Describe the general pattern of temperature and rainfall experienced in Australia in 2005.
   b. What type of temperature and rainfall was experienced where you live? How was this different from the normal and historical figures?
   c. Use an atlas to name two locations experiencing conditions that were:
      - warmer and drier
      - warmer and wetter
      - cooler and wetter.

3. Refer to the map of the potential dengue fever transmission zones. Describe the potential spread of the disease according to two possible futures.

**CHAPTER 2** | Physical characteristics that make Australia unique

# 2.8 Understanding weather maps

Weather maps, or **synoptic charts**, can appear rather complicated. But when you know what the lines and symbols mean you will find these maps easy to use.

## Pressure systems

One of the most important features of the atmosphere, and one that is very frequently measured, is *air pressure*, or the weight of the air. All air has weight. While we can't feel it because we are constantly surrounded by it, sensitive instruments called barometers can measure the air pressure. Atmospheric air pressure measurements are given in hectopascals (hPa). Several times a day, air pressure is read at various weather stations around the world. Many observers around Australia measure air pressure and other aspects of the weather and send them to the national and regional centres of the Bureau of Meteorology. These observations are combined with others made from satellites, aircraft, ships at sea and in other countries to prepare weather maps.

The main lines that we see on weather maps are called **isobars**. Isobars are lines joining places of equal or constant barometric pressure. These lines never cross or touch.

## Highs and lows

The average weight of air at sea level is 1013 hPa. If air pressure measures more than 1013 hPa, it is usually an area of sinking air and is generally an area of high pressure. High pressure systems are often called *anticyclones*. You can see from the table opposite how a high pressure system is shown on a weather map and the anticlockwise direction in which the air travels in a high pressure system. The moving air, known as wind, always moves *out* of a high and *into* a low pressure system.

If air pressure measures below 1013 hPa, it is usually an area of rising air, and is generally an area of low pressure. Low pressure systems are often called *cyclones*. You can see in our table how a low pressure system is shown and the clockwise direction in which the air travels in a low pressure system.

Pressure systems generally move from west to east as they move across Australia (see map on page 34) and around the world. As they move they change in shape and often change their latitudinal position.

## Air masses and fronts

Sometimes people confuse pressure systems with air masses. An *air mass* is a large section of the atmosphere containing air with a similar temperature and moisture content. A line drawn on a weather map to show where two different air masses meet is called a *front*. There are two main types of fronts: cold fronts and warm fronts.

## Winds and temperature

When we look at the direction of winds on a weather map we can work out if temperatures are warmer, cooler or about normal for the time of year. In Australia, a northerly wind (coming from the north) means higher than normal temperatures and a southerly wind means lower than normal temperatures. Easterlies and westerlies mean temperatures that are around normal.

### SAMPLE STUDY

**Coldest July day for 21 years**

The weather map below for 18 July 2007 shows a cold front moving into the Tasman Sea that brought a cold 'snap' to south-eastern Australia. Cold, moist air from the ocean to the south of Australia moved across Tasmania, Victoria and New South Wales, bringing extensive snowfalls to the higher parts of the tablelands and ranges. One weather station at Thredbo recorded a temperature below that at Australia's base in Antarctica. In the coldest rural areas, roads were closed by snow and ice.

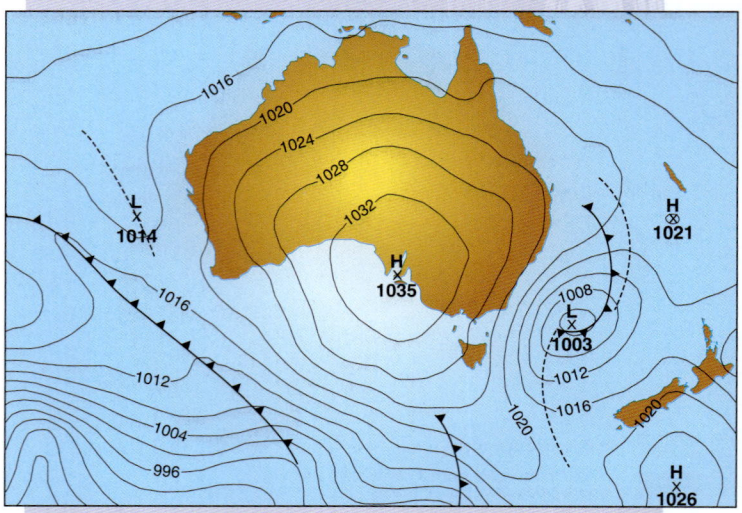

Weather map, 18 July 2007

## GEOskills TOOLBOX
### INTERPRETING SYNOPTIC CHARTS

| Symbol | Name | Description | Associated weather |
|---|---|---|---|
| (isobar lines 1020, 1018, 1016) | Isobars | Lines joining places of equal pressure | The closer the isobars are, the stronger the winds are. |
| (H with concentric circles 1014, 1016, 1018) | High pressure system | Area of sinking air | Generally fine weather. Winds rotate around these systems in an anticlockwise direction. |
| (L with concentric circles 1012, 1010, 1008) | Low pressure system | Area of rising air | Generally cloudy weather and a good chance of rain. Winds rotate around these systems in a clockwise direction. |
| T.C. Pamela (concentric circles 1002, 1000, 998) | Tropical cyclone | Area of rapidly rising air | Torrential rain, very strong and destructive winds in a clockwise direction. Cyclones are given a name (e.g. Tropical Cyclone Pamela). |
| (blue line with triangles) | Cold front | Separates warm and cold air, with the cold air behind the front | Fall in temperature; may bring rain and storms. Front moves in the direction of the arrowheads. |
| (red line with semicircles) | Warm front | Separates warm and cold air, with the warm air behind the front | Increase in temperature; may bring light showers; uncommon in Australia |

## ACTIVITIES

### UNDERSTANDING

1. What is another name for a weather map?
2. List three differences between low and high pressure systems.
3. What does a weather map indicate when:
   a isobars are close together
   b isobars are well apart?
4. What do we call the lines that are drawn on weather maps to separate different air masses?

### USING YOUR SKILLS

5. Refer to the weather map below.

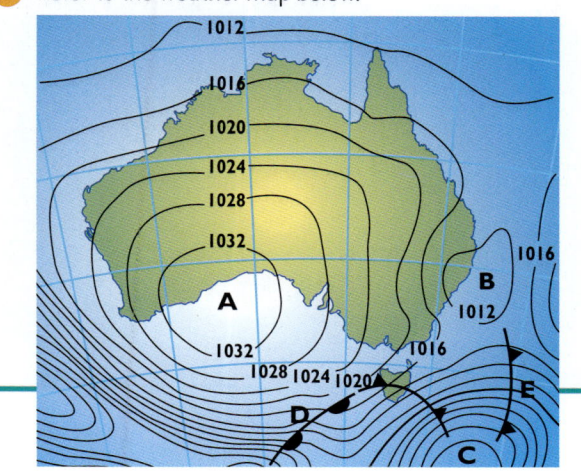

   a Estimate the wind direction in Adelaide. Is it windy or calm?
   b Identify the pressure systems at A, B and C.
   c Identify the types of fronts at D and E.
   d Describe the temperatures at Brisbane, Sydney, Melbourne, Adelaide and Perth, using the terms *warmer*, *cooler* and *normal for the time of year*.
   e Name any of the cities in part (d) in which you think it could be raining and give reasons for your answer.
   f Which capital city will soon experience a cool change?

6. Refer to the sample study on the previous page.
   a What is the central pressure of the high pressure system over South Australia?
   b What is the weather system that passed over south-eastern Australia in July 2007?
   c Using your own words, describe the weather being experienced over south-eastern Australia. Make sure you mention wind strength and direction, cloud cover, precipitation including snowfall and the temperature for this time of the year.
   d Why did the weather situation bring widespread snowfalls?

### GEOTERMS

**isobar:** line drawn on a map, joining places of equal or constant barometric pressure

# 2.9 Australia's pattern of natural resources

Natural resources are the wealth supplied by nature that is available for human use. Natural resources include water, soil, forests, fish, energy and mineral deposits, wildlife and natural scenery. Australia has a greater value of natural resources per head of population than any other country in the world. The main reason for this is that we have a small population in a very large country. The United States and China, for example, are far better endowed with natural resources than Australia, but they have much larger populations.

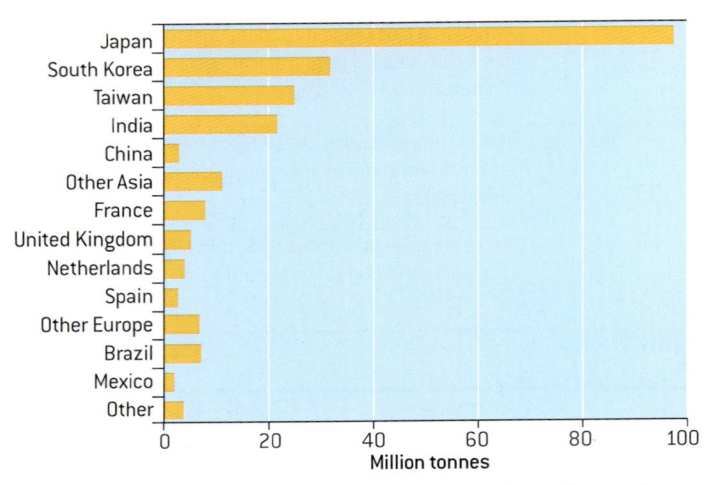

Australia is the world's largest coal exporter. Australia supplies more than 35 countries around the world.

Data derived from Australian Coal Association.

## Renewable energy

Global warming and increased emission of greenhouse gases have prompted more research and development in renewable energy resources. Some renewable types of energy that could be sustainable in Australia include the following.

- Geothermal energy: Australia has huge underground energy resources known as 'hot rocks'. Water is heated by pumping it underground through these hot rocks. The resulting steam then drives a turbine to generate electricity.

- Wind power: a typical wind turbine can meet the energy needs of up to 1000 homes.

- Tidal power: waves can drive turbines to produce electricity. Tidal power is especially suitable for desalination plants.

- Biomass energy: this is produced from the combustion of organic matter. Biomass can be used to produce electricity as well as liquid fuels such as ethanol and biodiesel.

- Solar power: solar energy technologies harness the sun's heat and light to provide heating, lighting and electricity. Two types of solar technologies are currently under development in Australia:
  - Photovoltaic cells convert solar energy directly into electricity.
  - Solar thermal systems use the sun's heat to generate electricity by first heating a fluid such as water, which drives a turbine to generate electricity.
  
  Australia has abundant solar radiation and, therefore, great potential for the development of solar energy.
- Hydro-electric power: most of Australia's hydro-electric power is generated in Tasmania and by the Snowy Mountains Hydro-electric Scheme. Around 10 per cent of Australia's electricity comes from hydro-electric power but there is limited opportunity to increase this because of the lack of water resources.

*Jounama is one of the artificial dams created for the Snowy Mountains Hydro-electric Scheme.*

The use of sustainable energy is in its infancy but is growing rapidly in China, the United States and Europe. Fossil fuels are cheaper and more convenient than renewable energy sources. The reason that fossil fuels are so cheap is that we do not pay the real cost of their use; we do not pay for the huge cost of dumping waste products into the atmosphere. In the future, a carbon tax or restrictions on the use of fossil fuels will increase their costs relative to renewable energy.

Most countries realise there is a real threat of serious global warming. Despite the cost of renewable energy, it should be the main source of power for households and industry in the future.

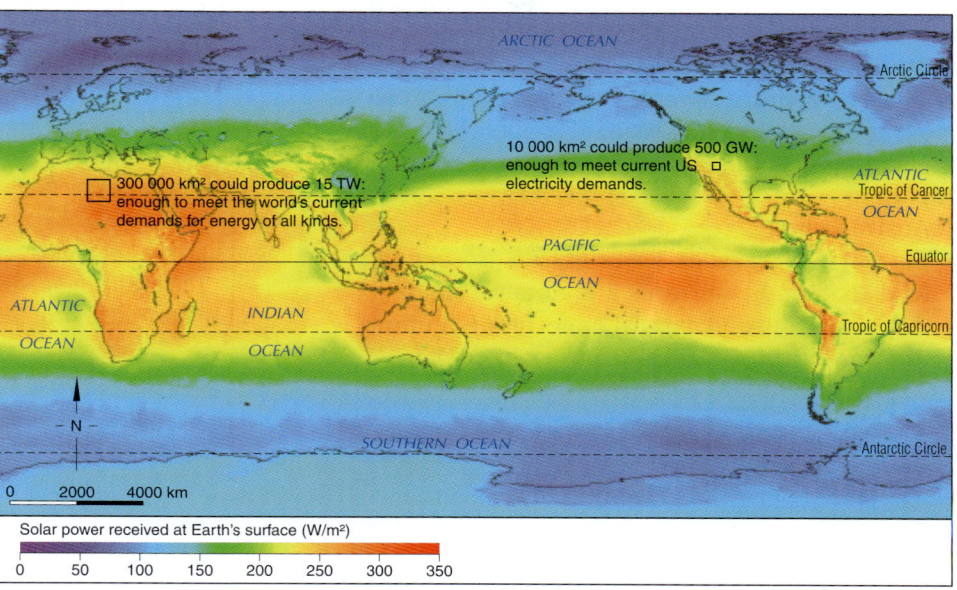

*A large enough area of photovoltaic cells could supply all the electricity for the most energy-hungry countries on Earth or even meet the whole world's energy needs. (© Matthias Loster 2006)*

## ACTIVITIES

### UNDERSTANDING

1. Why is Australia considered to be rich in natural resources?
2. In which energy resources is Australia (a) rich and (b) poor?

### THINKING AND APPLYING

3. Define the term *renewable energy*. List the main forms of renewable energy. Why is renewable energy not widely used?
4. What are two types of solar technology?
5. Form groups of three to four.
   a. Research the advantages and disadvantages of using nuclear energy as a source of power for the future.
   b. Present your findings to the class on a poster or display.

### USING YOUR SKILLS

6. Refer to the graph of Australia's coal exports by destination on the previous page.
   a. List the five top destinations for Australia's coal exports.
   b. In which geographic region are these nations located?
   c. How many million tonnes of coal does Australia supply to Brazil?

## Minerals

Australia is also rich in mineral resources. The Pilbara region in Western Australia has some of the largest reserves of iron ore in the world. Large reserves of bauxite and aluminium exist at Weipa in Queensland and the Gove Peninsula in the Northern Territory. Australia also produces many other minerals, including silver, copper, nickel and tin. The main goldfields are located in Western Australia.

Australia is:
- the world's largest exporter of iron ore, bauxite, lead, diamonds, zinc ores and mineral sands
- the world's second-largest exporter of alumina
- the world's third-largest exporter of gold.

*Mount Tom Price is a huge iron ore mine in the Pilbara region in Western Australia. To learn more, use the Mining weblink in your eBookPLUS.*

## Soils

Australia has generally poor soils, especially when compared with those found on other continents, such as North America and Europe. Most Australian soils are low in nutrients, and in some parts of the continent, particularly the more arid areas, high salt content is also a problem. Most parts of Australia are suitable for only sheep and cattle grazing, rather than intensive agriculture, due to the combination of low rainfall and poor soils.

There are patches of good soil scattered throughout the continent. These include soils formed on rock of volcanic origin, such as those on the Darling Downs in Queensland and around Orange in New South Wales. Alluvial soils are also found in river valleys, such as those along the Clarence River in New South Wales and around the Margaret River in Western Australia.

## SAMPLE STUDY

### The Pilbara

Most of Australia's iron ore reserves are found in the Pilbara region in Western Australia. The Pilbara accounts for 98 per cent of the country's production and 96 per cent of its iron ore exports. Iron ore is the raw material from which iron is made. Although iron in its cast form has many uses, its main use is in steelmaking. Steel is the main structural metal in engineering, building, ship building, automobiles and machinery.

The major companies operating in the Pilbara are BHP Billiton and Rio Tinto. There are many mines in the Pilbara including those at Mount Tom Price, Marandoo, Channar, Newman and Robe River.

The iron ore is relatively easy to mine. It is also high quality so there is strong demand from many countries including Japan, China and South Korea.

**World's major iron ore producers, 2006 (million tonnes)**

| Country | Production |
|---|---|
| Australia | 570 |
| China | 520 |
| Brazil | 300 |
| India | 150 |
| Russia | 105 |
| Ukraine | 73 |
| United States | 54 |
| South Africa | 40 |
| Canada | 33 |
| Sweden | 24 |

*Source: US Geological Survey.*

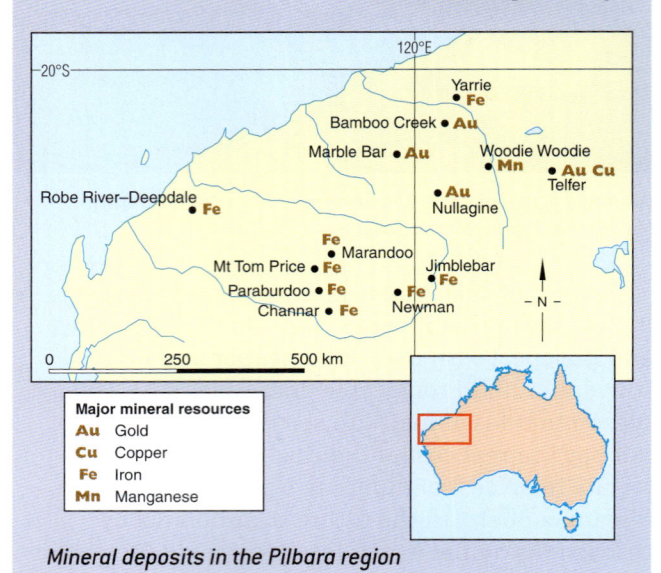

*Mineral deposits in the Pilbara region*

## Natural scenery

Australia, with its unique flora and fauna, has many places of great natural beauty. The spectacular scenery attracts tourists from all over the world. Australia has several sites on the World Heritage List. This means that they are recognised as being of global importance because they are places of great natural or cultural significance. For example, Kakadu National Park is recognised as a World Heritage area because of its natural significance (including exceptional natural beauty and biological diversity) and cultural significance (including Aboriginal rock art and ceremonial sites). Other places of unique natural scenery are Fraser Island and the Blue Mountains.

## Forests

Apart from Antarctica — which has no trees — Australia is the world's least forested continent. The prevailing vegetation in Australia is woodland and shrubland. Before European settlement only about nine per cent of Australia was forested. Today, about five per cent of the country is forested. Even though Australia exports timber and timber products, large amounts of timber, particularly softwoods, have to be imported.

*A World Heritage rainforest, Lamington National Park, south-east Queensland*

### ACTIVITIES

#### UNDERSTANDING

1. Outline the main mineral resources of Australia.
2. Refer to the sample study on page 44.
   a. What is the location of Australia's main iron ore production?
   b. What is the main use of iron ore?
   c. List the five main producers of iron ore.
   d. Why is there strong demand overseas for Australian iron ore?
3. Refer to the photo of Mount Tom Price on page 44. Use Google Earth to view Mount Tom Price. Describe what you see in the two images.
4. Explain why many Australian soils are suitable only for grazing.
5. Explain why Australia's scenery attracts many overseas visitors.

#### USING YOUR SKILLS

6. List three locations in the Pilbara where there are deposits of iron ore.
7. Which state of Australia has the most World Heritage sites?

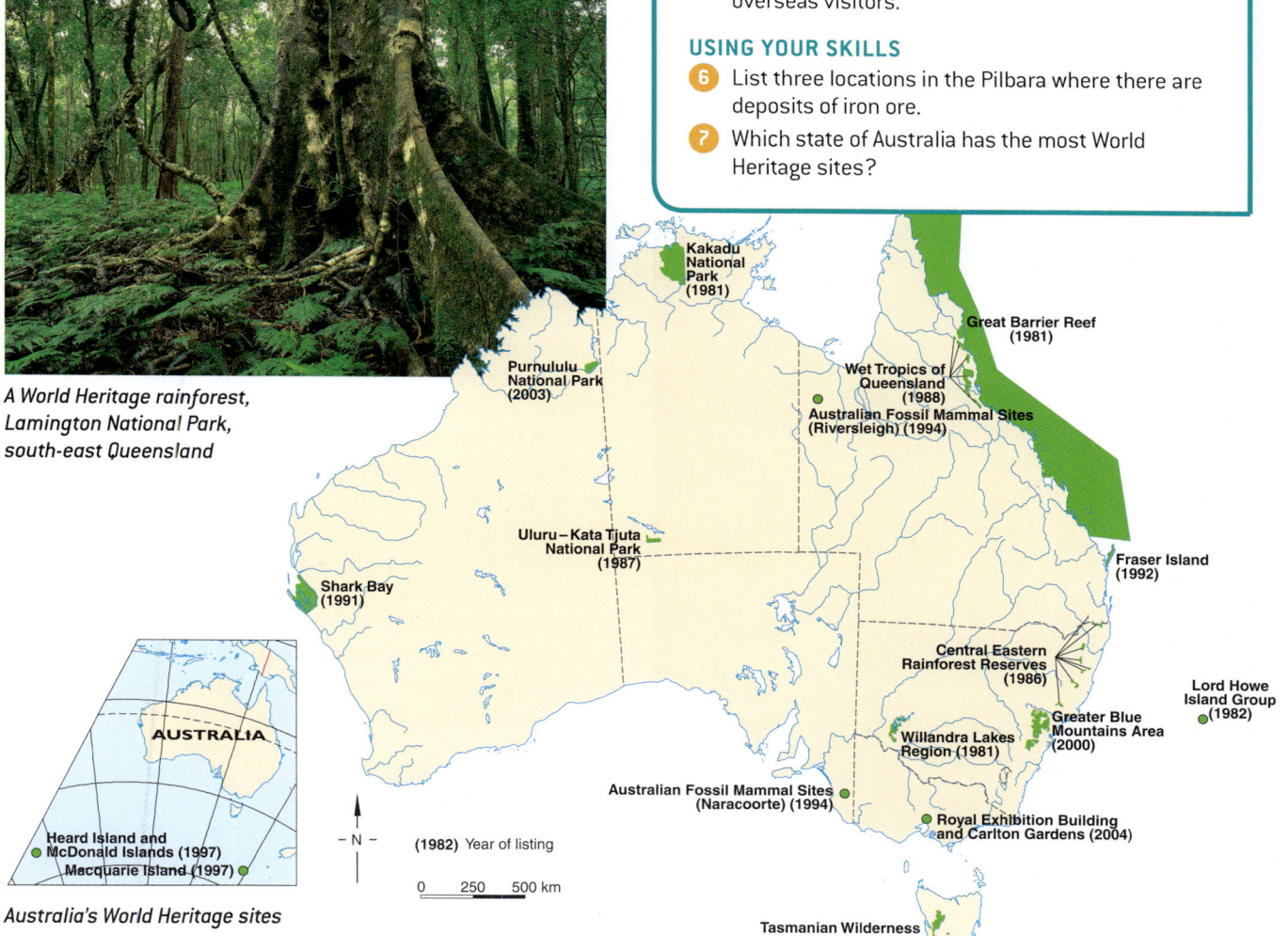

*Australia's World Heritage sites*

- Kakadu National Park (1981)
- Great Barrier Reef (1981)
- Purnululu National Park (2003)
- Wet Tropics of Queensland (1988)
- Australian Fossil Mammal Sites (Riversleigh) (1994)
- Uluru–Kata Tjuta National Park (1987)
- Fraser Island (1992)
- Shark Bay (1991)
- Central Eastern Rainforest Reserves (1986)
- Lord Howe Island Group (1982)
- Willandra Lakes Region (1981)
- Greater Blue Mountains Area (2000)
- Australian Fossil Mammal Sites (Naracoorte) (1994)
- Royal Exhibition Building and Carlton Gardens (2004)
- Heard Island and McDonald Islands (1997)
- Macquarie Island (1997)
- Tasmanian Wilderness (1982)

(1982) Year of listing

CHAPTER 2 | Physical characteristics that make Australia unique

# 2.10 Australia's unique flora and fauna

The long geographic isolation of Australia from other continents has resulted in an exceptional variety of plant and animal life. From arid central Australia to the tropical forests of north Queensland, no other country has such a variety. More than 80 per cent of Australia's flora and fauna is found nowhere else in the world. The estimated number of native and introduced **species** living in Australia — about one million — is more than twice the number of species in North America and Europe combined.

## Unique flora

Due to the generally low amounts of rainfall and its unreliability, most of the flora in Australia is characterised by drought-resistant qualities. The Australian land flora comprises over 12 000 species and many of these are **endemic** to Australia — that is, they occur naturally in Australia and nowhere else in the world. For example, most of Australia's 500 different species of *Eucalyptus* (gum trees) are endemic. Some plant species are not only unique to Australia but also unique to small areas of Australia. For example, about 75 per cent of the flowering trees and shrubs in the south-west corner of Australia have been found to be unique to this area.

The distribution of vegetation in Australia is strongly influenced by climate. Only about five per cent of Australia is forested. Most of this forest vegetation occurs along the wetter eastern coast and highlands area. The forests are dominated by eucalypt trees, which are tough and durable and able to withstand the frequent fires that occur. As rainfall decreases inland, trees decrease in number and become smaller and further apart. Eucalypts are still the main types of tree found there. Further inland, as the climate becomes increasingly dry, grasslands and shrubs begin to dominate.

## Unique fauna

Most of the world's **marsupials** are found in Australia. They include the bandicoot, koala, kangaroo, wallaby, wombat and the Tasmanian devil. Marsupials have pouches in which they suckle and carry their young. Marsupial babies are born in a tiny immature state and complete much of their development in the pouch.

Despite the number of unique marsupials in Australia, most of our native animals are not marsupials. Most are placental, which means that the young remain in the womb for much longer than marsupials and there is no pouch. Australian placental animals include bats and rodents and such marine mammals as seals, dugongs and dolphins.

Most mammals reproduce by giving birth to live young. **Monotremes** are unique in being the only mammals that lay eggs. There are only three species of monotreme in the world: the platypus and two species of echidna. One echidna species occurs in New Guinea but the platypus and the other species of echidna are uniquely Australian.

Loss of species in Australia has been largely caused by habitat destruction and degradation and this problem is still occurring. Because most Australian species are found nowhere else, we have a special responsibility to conserve them.

*Grass trees (Xanthorrhea spp.) are among the many plant species that are endemic to Australia.*

**GEOfacts** There are the same number of species of reptiles in an average Australian backyard as there are in the whole of England.

# ACTIVITIES

## UNDERSTANDING

1. Define the terms *endemic*, *marsupial* and *monotreme*.
2. What is the major reason for Australia's wide variety of unusual plant and animal life?
3. What is the main characteristic of flora in Australia?
4. Account for the distribution of vegetation in Australia.
5. Select two animals and explain how they have adapted to survive in the desert.

## THINKING AND APPLYING

6. Use your knowledge of the evolution of the Australian continent to explain why echidnas are found in New Guinea as well as Australia.
7. Create a colourful poster, web page or report that explains the adaptation of flora and fauna to the Australian environment.
   - Select two species: one animal or plant from inland areas and one animal or plant from coastal areas.
   - Use your library or the internet to research the two species.
   - Include labelled sketches to draw attention to the appearance and main characteristics of the two species.
   - Include distribution maps and interesting statistics.
   - Write a paragraph describing the habitat and some of the characteristics that indicate how the two species have adapted to their environments.

Find out more about Australia's plants and animals by using the **Flora and fauna** weblink in your eBookPLUS.

## GEOTERMS

**species:** a group of plants or animals of the same kind that are able to breed with each other

---

Budgerigars feed on seeds produced by native plants. They are nomads, and in large flocks of a few thousand or more they follow the flowering cycles.

The camel has a double row of eyelashes on each eye to keep out glare and grit. It stores energy as fat in its hump and can swallow around 100 litres of water at a time.

Mulga have specially shaped leaves and branches that funnel rainfall to the base of the tree.

Termites live in tall mounds of clay. They are protected inside the mound from the hot, dry desert winds.

Spinifex leaves roll into tight cylinders during the hot desert day to reduce the surface area exposed to the sun. Spinifex roots spread deep and wide to pick up both ground and surface water.

Rock wallabies rest in shady caves and crevices during the hottest part of the day. When no grasses are available, they can eat leaves, bark and roots.

Death adders are commonly found at night, soaking up the heat from roads.

Bilbies always stay close to one of several burrows they dig. These protect them from desert heat and predators.

The spinifex hopping mouse does not sweat, its droppings are dry and its urine is very concentrated. A female feeds her young on concentrated milk and drinks their urine.

Honey ants store food and water in their abdomen, which swells up like a plastic bubble. When food is scarce, they vomit up the nectar to feed the colony.

The marsupial mole is blind because it has no need for eyesight when living underground. It moves underground by 'swimming' through the sand.

*Life is rather tough in a desert environment. Desert plants and animals face extremes of temperature, food shortages and a lack of readily available water. To survive, they have had to adapt to these harsh conditions.*

South Australia's desert spadefoot toad hibernates in burrows for most of the year, coming out to breed and lay eggs only when it rains.

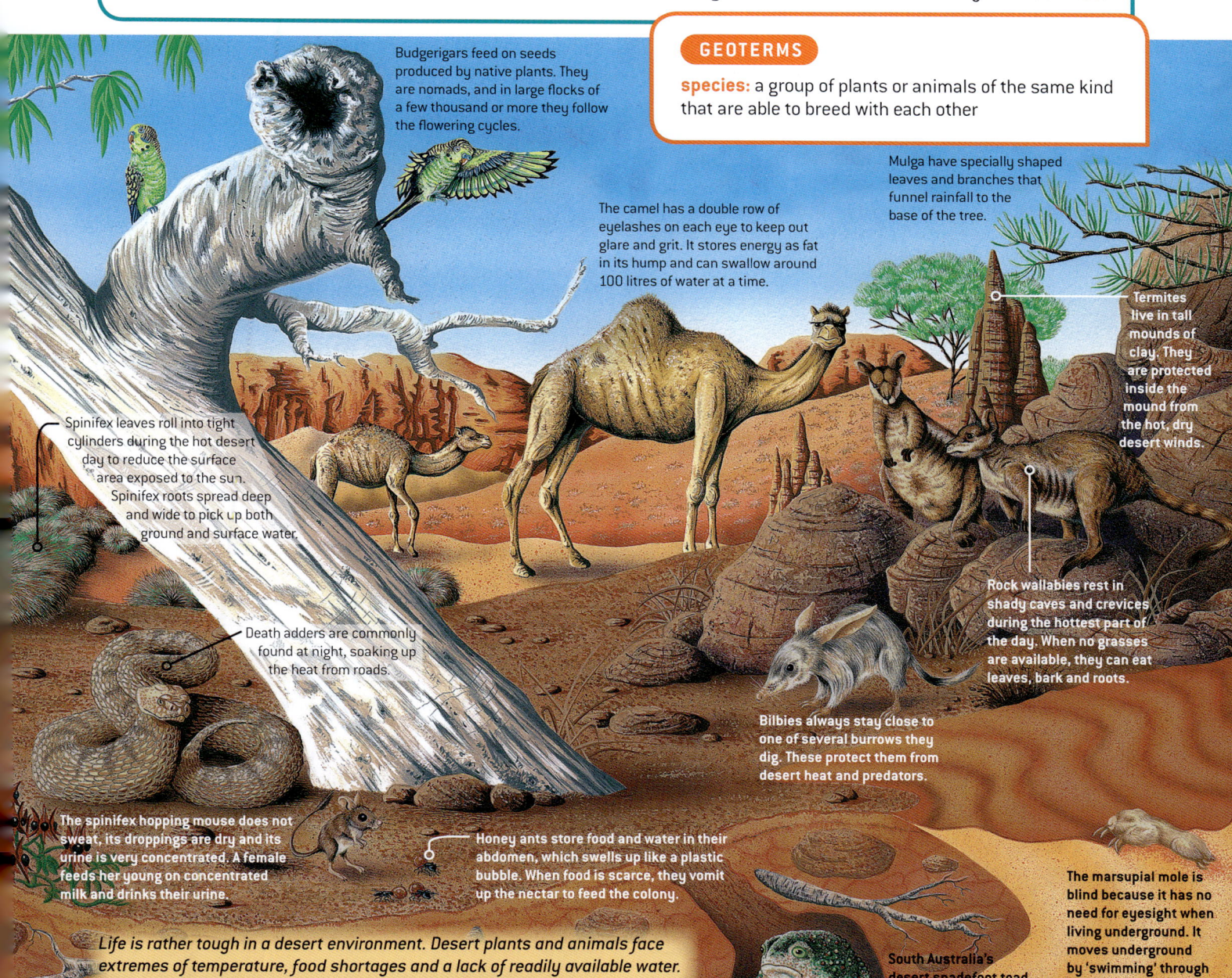

# 2.11 Flora and fauna of the Daintree rainforest

The Daintree rainforest is located about two hours' drive north of Cairns in Queensland. The northern section near Cape Tribulation borders the Great Barrier Reef. The Daintree River flows through much of the rainforest. The Daintree is part of the Wet Tropics World Heritage site, listed in 1988 because it satisfied the following four criteria:
- it shows major changes in the Earth's evolution
- it shows ongoing evolution
- it has outstanding aesthetic value
- it is the home of endangered species including the cassowary.

Much of the Daintree is inaccessible wilderness in the higher areas, but very accessible in the hills and river flats of the lower eastern parts. It has one of the wettest and warmest climates in Australia. Over 400 species of trees have been identified in the Daintree and a substantial number are found only within its borders. There are many other ferns, orchids, palms, mosses and lichens.

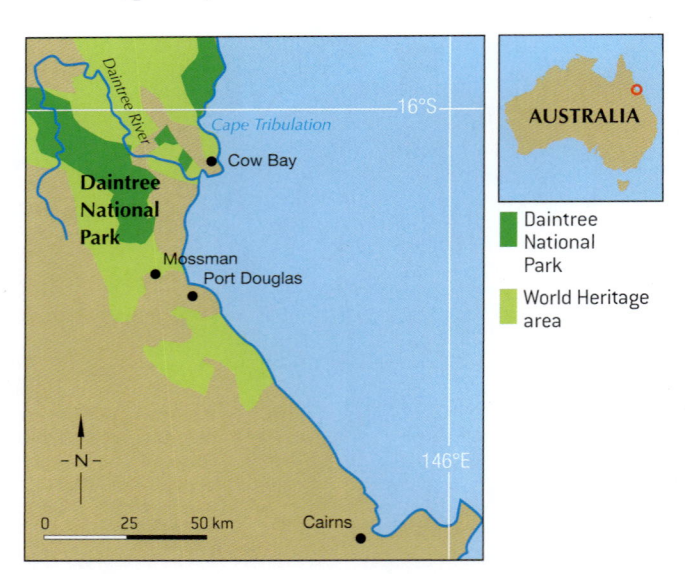

*The Daintree National Park is located within the Wet Tropics World Heritage area.*

## The disappearing rainforest

Over the last 200 years, human activity has reduced the Daintree rainforest to one-fifth of its original area. This has resulted in plant and animal species becoming endangered and extinct. The rainforest has been cleared for timber, mining, farming, roads and tourism.

Clearing the rainforest has resulted in:
- changes to food webs and **ecosystems**
- the lower storey receiving more sunlight, allowing eucalypts to enter the rainforest
- less leaf litter and therefore fewer nutrients
- fertilisers from farms running off into the sea, killing coral
- the invasion of exotic plants and feral animals
- more fires.

## Animals in the rainforest

Some rare animals live in the forest, including two species of tree kangaroos and the Daintree ring-tailed possum. The rainforest houses the world's largest moth and the smallest bat. The cassowary is endangered, with only about 50 birds remaining in the Daintree. There are 1.5 million identified species of animals in the Daintree. It is estimated that there are six million unidentified species of animals.

Humans have introduced animals into the environment, such as cats and pigs, which kill native animals or destroy the native habitat. The fruit bat has been affected by the introduced paralysis tick. Introduced animals also spread diseases.

## Crocodiles and mangroves

In the lowland rainforest areas of the Daintree, sometimes referred to as jungle, along the rivers and creeks there is a large variety of animals and plants. Two of the best known are crocodiles and mangroves.

### Crocodiles

Only one type of crocodile inhabits coastal north-eastern Queensland: the dangerous estuarine crocodile. It is the world's largest crocodile. These crocodiles inhabit the tidal rivers and creeks but can occur kilometres upstream in fresh water. They take a variety of prey such as crabs, fish, birds, wallabies and domestic dogs, and humans on rare occasions. Larger crocodiles are scavengers and can walk several hundred metres from water and drag back a dead animal. They are also cannibals and eat many smaller crocodiles.

### Mangroves

Mangrove forests are dense communities of plants, consisting of different species of trees, creepers, vines, lichen, algae and sea grasses. They live in saline waterlogged soils where conditions fluctuate between high and low tide. They form an almost impenetrable maze of root systems along the shores of the waterways. Mangrove ecosystems have important functions in the rainforest.

- They are vital spawning grounds for fish, crabs and prawns.
- They support a large variety of specialist life forms such as birds, mammals and insects.
- Flying foxes or fruit bats commonly feed on blossoms and establish camps.
- They protect the coastline from strong winds and erosion.
- They trap sediments that would otherwise be washed into the sea, thus protecting many fragile marine habitats.
- The mangroves of the Daintree are an essential part of the habitat of estuarine crocodiles, which feed on the rich food sources within the water.

## SAMPLE STUDY

### The southern cassowary

A survey in 1993 by CSIRO, Australia's largest scientific research organisation, found that the number of cassowaries in the Daintree rainforest had declined to only 54. The decline was due to collisions with motor vehicles as they crossed roads, attacks by dogs and through accidental trapping intended for feral pigs. A conservation program has seen numbers of this shy flightless bird rise to over 1000, although the bird's status is still endangered because of habitat loss through land clearing.

Cassowaries are vital to the survival of the rainforest because only they can disperse the seed of large rainforest fruits through their dung. They can grow up to 2 metres tall and weigh as much as 80 kilograms. With a ground speed of up to 50 km/h and a dagger-like claw on each foot, they can be very dangerous. In 1926, a 16-year-old boy was killed near Mossman by a bird that he and his dogs had been attacking. The life span of a cassowary in the wild is uncertain but it is thought they may reach 40 years of age.

## ACTIVITIES

### UNDERSTANDING

1. Describe the climate of the Daintree.
2. List the adverse results of clearing the rainforest.
3. List the main reasons why the cassowary is endangered.
4. Why is the cassowary vital to the plant species in the Daintree rainforest?
5. Why was the Wet Tropics area placed on the World Heritage List?
6. Why do estuarine crocodiles thrive in the lowland forest of the Daintree?
7. Explain why mangrove forests are so important in lowland areas.

### THINKING AND APPLYING

8. Imagine you are lobbying the government to develop stronger conservation policies for the Daintree. Outline the main arguments you would use.

### GEOTERMS

**ecosystem:** a system formed by the interactions between living organisms (plants, animals and humans) and physical elements of the environment

# Working geographically

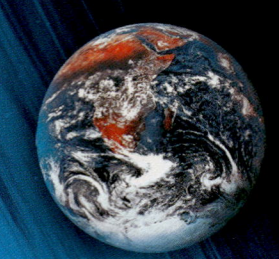

## BROADSHEET: SHARK BAY

### KNOWLEDGE AND UNDERSTANDING

**Refer to the map and photos and select the alternative that best answers the question.**

1. What is the distance from Denham to Monkey Mia?
   - (A) 20 kilometres
   - (B) 26 kilometres
   - (C) 32 kilometres
   - (D) 37 kilometres
2. What is the distance from Denham to Hamelin by road?
   - (A) 105 kilometres
   - (B) 111 kilometres
   - (C) 131 kilometres
   - (D) 141 kilometres
3. Wooramel Seagrass Bank stretches 129 kilometres from Gladstone Bay almost to:
   - (A) Long Point
   - (B) Bush Bay
   - (C) Carnarvon
   - (D) Dubaut Point.
4. In what direction would a boat travel from Carnarvon to Dorre Island?
   - (A) West
   - (B) East
   - (C) North-west
   - (D) South-west
5. What have tourists to the south-eastern shore of Shark Bay come to see?
   - (A) Dugongs
   - (B) Stromatolites
   - (C) Dolphins
   - (D) Burrowing bettong
6. What have tourists to the eastern shore of the Peron Peninsula come to see?
   - (A) Dugongs
   - (B) Stromatolites
   - (C) Dolphins
   - (D) Burrowing bettong
7. What important habitat is found on Bernier and Dorre islands?
   - (A) Cliffs
   - (B) Mountains
   - (C) Sandhills
   - (D) Trees

### SHORT RESPONSE

8. Outline why Bernier and Dorre islands are home to a number of endangered species.
9. Suggest three reasons why Shark Bay was given World Heritage status in 1991.

*Stromatolites growing in Hamelin Pool are among the oldest forms of life on Earth.*

*The largest population of dugong in the world is found in Shark Bay where they graze on the seagrass.*

*Once common over southern Western Australia, the banded hare-wallaby is now restricted to scrub on Bernier and Dorre islands in Shark Bay. Its decline was mainly due to the spread of farming.*

*The burrowing bettong was once found over most of mainland Australia. The introduction of foxes, rabbits and the use of poison grain have contributed to its decline. It is now found only on Bernier, Dorre, Barrow and Boodie islands.*

*Once abundant in arid Australia, the western barred bandicoot is now found only in the sandhills on Bernier and Dorre islands. It is thought the introduction of feral goats and pigs, rabbits, foxes and cats was responsible for its decline.*

At Monkey Mia, where hand-feeding of dolphins is a popular attraction, tourist numbers increased from 10 000 in 1984 to over 86 000 in 2005–06. Numbers peaked at 108 000 in 2003–04.

Shark Bay, on the west coast of Western Australia

**CHAPTER 2** | Physical characteristics that make Australia unique

# 3 Natural hazards in Australia

### INQUIRY QUESTIONS

+ What natural hazards is Australia at risk from?
+ What geographical processes are involved in natural hazards?
+ How can we prepare for, and minimise, the impacts of natural hazards?

Australia faces a range of serious hazards and disasters. Crops and animals can be destroyed by drought; beaches savagely eroded and buildings damaged by storms and cyclones; settlements drowned by floods; lives and forests lost through bushfires; and, less commonly, buildings destroyed by earthquakes. In this chapter, we look at the causes of natural hazards and describe their economic, environmental and social impacts. We also investigate the response of individuals, community-based groups and the different levels of government to natural hazards.

### GEOskills TOOLBOX

**GEOskillbuilder** Research and presentation (pages 82–3)
+ Comparing satellite images (page 57)
+ Interpreting a newspaper article (page 61)
+ Interpreting a satellite image (page 69)
+ Working with thematic maps (page 72)
+ Flow charts and diagrams (page 80)

*Firefighters try to control a fire in the Bunyip State Forest near Tonimbuk, Victoria, 7 February 2009.*

## KEY TERMS

**alluvium:** the loose material brought down by a river and deposited on its bed, flood plain or delta

**blocking high pressure system:** a persistent high pressure system that occurs on a large scale, remaining stationary for a period of time, compressing and warming the air below

**bushfire:** a fire burning out of control in the open; also called a wildfire

**cold front:** a surface where a cool air mass meets a warmer mass, into which it is advancing

**drought:** a prolonged period of below average precipitation

**earthquake:** shaking of the ground that is generated by disturbances in the Earth's crust

**El Niño event:** the reversal (every few years) of the more usual direction of winds and surface currents across the Pacific Ocean. This change causes drought in eastern Australia and heavy rain in South America.

**epicentre:** the point on the Earth's surface directly above the focus of an earthquake

**fire front:** the edge of a fire that spreads fastest

**firebrand:** aerially burning fuel that blows ahead of a fire front

**firestorm:** an intense fire that may generate strong convection currents and violent winds causing long-range spotting and flame spirals

**flood:** an unusual accumulation of water that overflows from rivers, lakes and the ocean onto land that is not normally covered by water

**flood mitigation:** measures aimed at preparing for floods and trying to reduce their effects, such as constructing artificial levees, strengthening bridges, raising road levels and enlarging drains

**flood plain:** part of a river valley covered by water during floods

**heatwave:** a prolonged period of very hot weather

**La Niña event:** a period of well above average rainfall in eastern Australia that often brings floods

**natural disaster:** an extreme event that is the result of natural processes and causes serious material damage or loss of life

**natural hazard:** an extreme event that is the result of natural processes and has the potential to cause serious material damage and loss of life

**Richter scale:** used to measure the energy of earthquakes

**sclerophyll:** plants found in low rainfall areas; their leathery leaves help reduce water loss

**southern oscillation:** a major air pressure shift between the Asian and east Pacific regions. Its most common extremes are El Niño events.

**storm surge:** a rise in sea level above the normal tide caused by very low atmospheric pressure and the stress of strong winds on the sea surface when a tropical cyclone approaches or crosses a coastline

**thunderstorm:** a storm associated with lightning and thunder, occurring with cumulonimbus clouds

**tropical cyclone:** a severe weather event that occurs where warm, moist, rising air begins to spiral upwards. Tropical cyclones are often accompanied by very strong winds, heavy rain and rough seas.

# 3.1 Natural hazards and natural disasters

There is a difference between **natural hazards** and **natural disasters**. A hazard is an event or object that is a potential source of harm to a community. A disaster occurs as the result of a hazardous event that dramatically affects a community. There are four broad types of natural hazards:
1. *Atmospheric* — for example, cyclones, hailstorms, blizzards and bushfires
2. *Hydrological* — for example, flooding, wave action and glaciers
3. *Geological* — for example, earthquakes and volcanoes
4. *Biological* — for example, disease epidemics and plagues.

It should be noted that some natural hazards are influenced by the actions and locations of people. For example, the severity of bushfires depends not only on the amount of fuel available or the strength and humidity of the wind. Humans influence bushfires through carelessness in the use of fire, inadequate preparation of their property in the event of a bushfire and poor disaster planning. Some bushfires are deliberately lit.

## Assessing the risk

Risk analysis is concerned with the chance of a hazardous event occurring and whether or not it could result in a disaster. The map opposite shows those areas of Australia that are vulnerable to the threat of natural disaster. It shows that different types of hazards and disasters are prevalent in different parts of Australia. For example, cyclones located to the north of Australia are associated with the warm tropical ocean; bushfires to the south of Australia are associated with dry vegetation. People who move to such an area have usually decided that the benefits of living and working there outweigh the risk.

## Coping with disasters

Few Australian communities are free of the risk of natural disasters, but some are more vulnerable than others. Vulnerability varies according to:
- the location of the community and the hazardous event
- the magnitude of the hazardous event
- the potential amount of damage.

When disasters occur in unpopulated areas, people are rarely killed or injured, and the damage to property is small. However, when hazardous events take place in populated areas, a disaster can occur.

## Managing hazards

Effective management of hazards requires that individuals, communities and governments:
- prepare for hazards — for example, by clearing vegetation around homes in bushfire-prone areas
- prevent hazards — for example, by avoiding establishing settlements on flood plains
- recognise and respond to hazards quickly so they do not turn into disasters.

Emergency management procedures involve gathering information, pre-disaster planning, responding, recovery and reconstruction. A disaster involves the coordination of voluntary organisations (such as the State Emergency Service), charities (such as the Salvation Army), financial assistance and donations, and government support (such as the army).

### Australia not ready for a major natural disaster: think tank
BY LEIGH SALES

A report to be released today finds Australia has more to fear from natural disasters than a terrorist attack.

The Australian Strategic Policy Institute (ASPI) report says Australia is not well placed to deal with a natural disaster and governments need to pay more attention to emergency response management.

The report says that since September 11, 2001, governments have spent around $10 billion on counter-terrorism initiatives, but only $500 million on emergency response capabilities.

*Source:* ABC News, 7 May 2008.

### GEOfacts

**Australia's worst natural disasters**
- *Bushfire:* Black Saturday, Victoria 2009 — 173 deaths, 3500 buildings destroyed, $1.5 billion cost
- *Cyclone:* Cyclone Tracy, Darwin 1974 — 65 deaths, 10 800 buildings destroyed, $4180 million cost
- *Hailstorm:* Sydney 1999 — 1 death, 24 800 buildings damaged, $2000 million cost
- *Earthquake:* Newcastle 1989 — 13 deaths, 50 000 buildings damaged, more than $4000 million cost

## Australia's natural hazards and disasters

**Floods**
- ≈ Potential flash flooding
- ≈ Potential flash flooding (greater frequency)
- ▲ Major flood

**Cyclones** — Approximate number of coastal crossings since 1959
- 6 to 10
- 11 to 16
- → Major cyclone

**Severe storms**
- ↗ At least one recorded severe thunderstorm (non-tornadic)
- ↗ At least one recorded tornado
- ↗ At least one severe thunderstorm per year (on average)
- ↗ At least one severe thunderstorm per year (on average) and at least one recorded tornado

**Bushfires**
- Areas subject to forest, grass and scrub fires of moderate risk to people
- Areas subject to disaster fires
- Major bushfire

**Earthquakes**
- Risk area
- Major earthquake

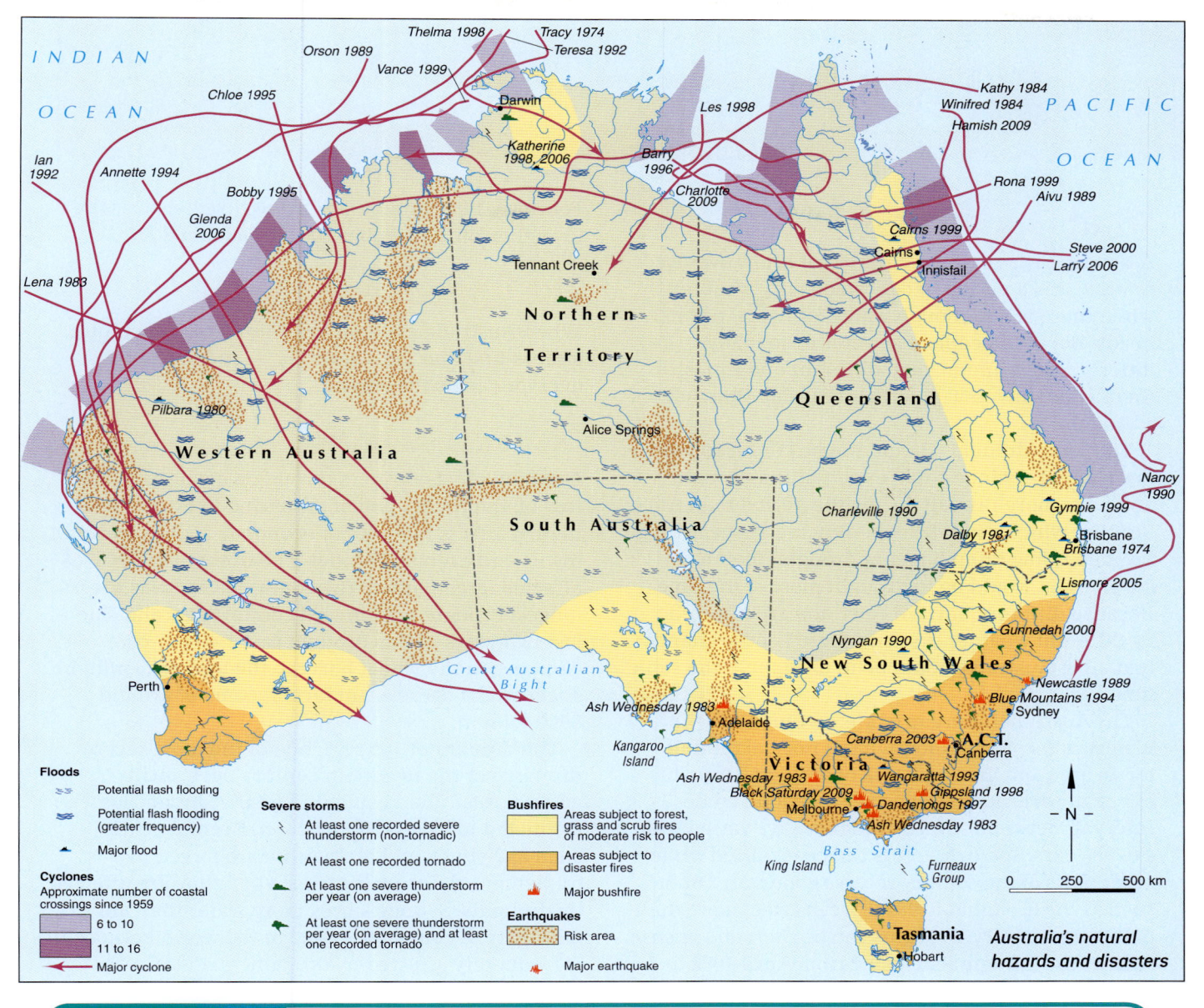

## ACTIVITIES

### UNDERSTANDING

1. What is the difference between a natural hazard and a natural disaster?

### THINKING AND APPLYING

2. Explain how a bushfire can be both a natural and human hazard.
3. Why does the risk of experiencing a natural disaster depend on the geographical location of a community?
4. Read the article 'Australia not ready for a major natural disaster'.
   a. Give reasons why more is spent on possible terrorist attacks than emergency response management.
   b. With a partner, prepare an argument justifying more spending on emergency response management.

### USING YOUR SKILLS

5. Refer to the map of natural disasters and hazards on this page.
   a. What types of natural disasters occur most often in Australia?
   b. Describe the location of Australia's cyclone hazard zone.
   c. Give one example of a community that has suffered a bushfire disaster.
   d. What type of hazard are communities around Newcastle subject to?
   e. What would be the likely impact of a large earthquake occurring in the earthquake hazard zone of central Australia?

6. With the assistance of the internet, answer the following key geographical questions in relation to the flood disaster in Katherine in 1998.
   a. How did the disaster occur?
   b. What was the impact of the disaster on the community?
   c. Why do people risk living there?

CHAPTER 3 | Natural hazards in Australia

# 3.2 Natural hazards: droughts

## What is a drought?

A *drought* is a prolonged period of *below average rainfall*. It is a period of continuous dry weather when there is not enough water for users' normal needs. Because people use water in so many different ways and in such different quantities, there is no universal amount of rainfall that defines a drought.

The term 'drought' should not be confused with low rainfall. Sydney could experience a drought and have more rainfall during the period than Alice Springs, which could be experiencing above average rainfall. If low rainfall meant drought, then most of Australia would be in drought most of the time. Because different parts of Australia are affected by different weather systems, there is little chance that all of Australia would be in drought at the same time.

The Australian Bureau of Meteorology has historical records to show what is normal rainfall for an area and the area's risk of drought. Droughts affect all parts of Australia over a period of time. Intervals between severe droughts have varied from 4 to 38 years. Some droughts can be localised while other parts of the country receive good rain. Others, such as the drought of 1982–83, can affect more than half of the country. Droughts can be *short and intense*, such as the drought that lasted from April 1982 to February 1983; or they can be *long lived*, such as the drought from November 2001 to October 2007.

## The impact of drought

When Australia experiences a drought, agriculture suffers first and most severely — and eventually everyone feels the impact.

### Economic impacts

Drought affects farmers through a decline in, or a loss of, the production of crops and livestock. This in turn affects the level of economic activity in rural towns and even large cities. The drought of 1963–68 affected large parts of the continent and was the longest drought ever in arid central Australia. The last two years of this drought saw a 40 per cent decrease in the wheat harvest, the loss of 20 million sheep and a decrease in farm income of around $500 million.

The drought of 1991–95, one of the most severe droughts of the twentieth century over north-eastern Australia, resulted in total economic losses estimated in excess of $5 billion. Even big cities such as Sydney and Melbourne are forced to implement water restrictions when they are affected by droughts. Sydney stores more water than any other city of comparable size in the world because it is frequently affected by drought.

*Aerial photograph of Warragamba Dam, June 2004. The dam is the main source of Sydney's water supply. The water level in the dam became alarmingly low as drought conditions persisted in Australia from 2001 to 2007.*

## Social impacts

The greatest social impact is the loss of income. This loss affects not only the farmers, but also communities. In rural towns, for example, jobs may be lost and businesses may fail. People may be forced to leave drought-affected areas in search of other work. Many never return. Prolonged drought and the heartbreak associated with it can result in the breakup of families and severe depression in individuals.

### GEOskills TOOLBOX

**COMPARING SATELLITE IMAGES**

Satellite images often use false colours to highlight particular features. These satellite images, from two different years, show how drought is spreading in Australia. Red areas indicate healthy vegetation.

**SEPTEMBER 2000**

**SEPTEMBER 2002**

*Source:* © CNES/SPOT. Image reproduced with permission from SPOT Imaging Services/ Analysis by Agrecon.

## Environmental impacts

Droughts have a large impact on topsoil in Australia. During drought conditions, millions of tonnes of topsoil are blown away. This loss takes many years to replace naturally, if it is ever replaced. This loss of topsoil can result in large areas that are far less productive. Many crop cultivation methods in Australia are not suitable in a country that is often affected by drought. Prolonged droughts are usually associated with the outbreak of serious bushfires as in Victoria in February 2009. These bushfires can have severe environmental impacts, even though much natural vegetation can benefit from fires.

### ACTIVITIES

**UNDERSTANDING**

1. Define the term *drought*.
2. What is the difference between drought and low rainfall?
3. How often might droughts be expected to occur in Australia?
4. State how droughts in Australia can be divided by their duration into two main types.
5. Describe the economic impacts of two droughts that have occurred in Australia.
6. Why does Sydney store more water than any other city in the world of similar size?
7. Explain how droughts can result in decreased soil fertility.

**THINKING AND APPLYING**

8. Explain why there is little chance that all of Australia would be affected by drought at the same time.

**USING YOUR SKILLS**

9. Refer to the two maps on this page to answer the following questions.
   a. Approximately what proportion of Australia had healthy vegetation in September 2000?
   b. Describe the location of the main areas with healthy vegetation in September 2002.
   c. Approximately what proportion of Australia's healthy vegetation was affected by drought in September 2002?

### GEOTERMS

**drought:** a prolonged period of below average precipitation

# 3.3 Causes of drought in Australia

## A dry continent

Australia is the driest continent. The main reason Australia is so dry is that much of the continent lies in an area dominated by high atmospheric pressure for most of the year (see page 34). Australia also experiences considerable variation in its rainfall. If we looked at a typical ten-year period, we would see about four years of above average rainfall, three years of average rainfall and three years of below average rainfall.

*When there is no longer natural feed available for cattle, farmers have to buy it — often at great expense.*

## Southern oscillation

Fluctuations in rainfall have several causes that are not fully understood. Probably the main cause of major rainfall fluctuations in Australia is the **southern oscillation**, which is a major air pressure shift between the Asian and east Pacific regions. The strength and direction of the southern oscillation is measured by a simple index called the Southern Oscillation Index (SOI). The SOI is calculated from monthly or seasonal fluctuations in air pressure between Tahiti and Darwin.

In an average rainfall year with 'typical' pressure patterns, the SOI is between −10 and +10. If the SOI is strongly negative, less than −10, this means that the air pressure at sea level in Darwin is higher than in Tahiti, and an **El Niño event** occurs. During an El Niño event, less than average rainfall falls over much of Australia. If the SOI becomes strongly positive, above +10, this means that the air pressure in Darwin is much lower than normal and a **La Niña event** occurs.

*Typical pattern of eastern and northern Australian rainfall and the SOI during an El Niño and a La Niña event*

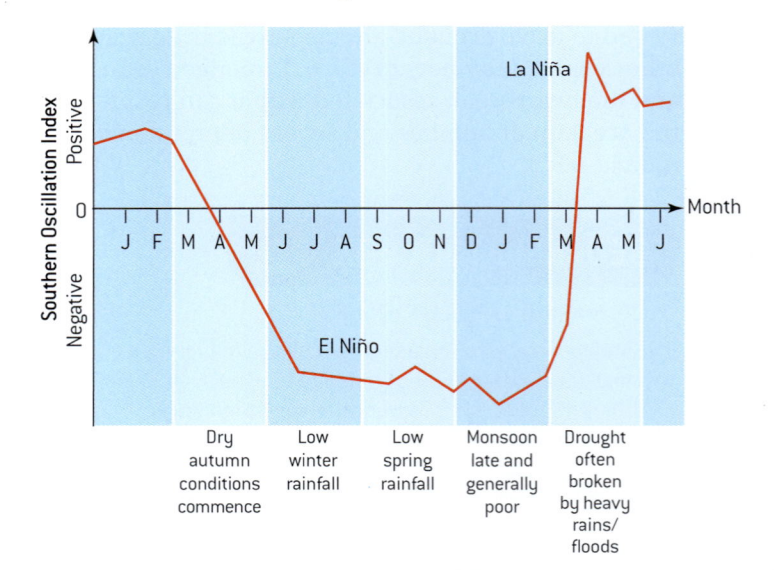

*The SOI, El Niño and La Niña (eastern and northern Australia)*

## El Niño

Probably the main cause of drought in eastern Australia is El Niño — a warm ocean current in the Pacific. At irregular intervals, it spreads further south and the water in the central and eastern Pacific becomes much warmer, bringing heavy rainfall and floods to arid parts of South America.

At the same time, normally warm water in the oceans to the east and north of Australia are replaced by much cooler water as the warm water

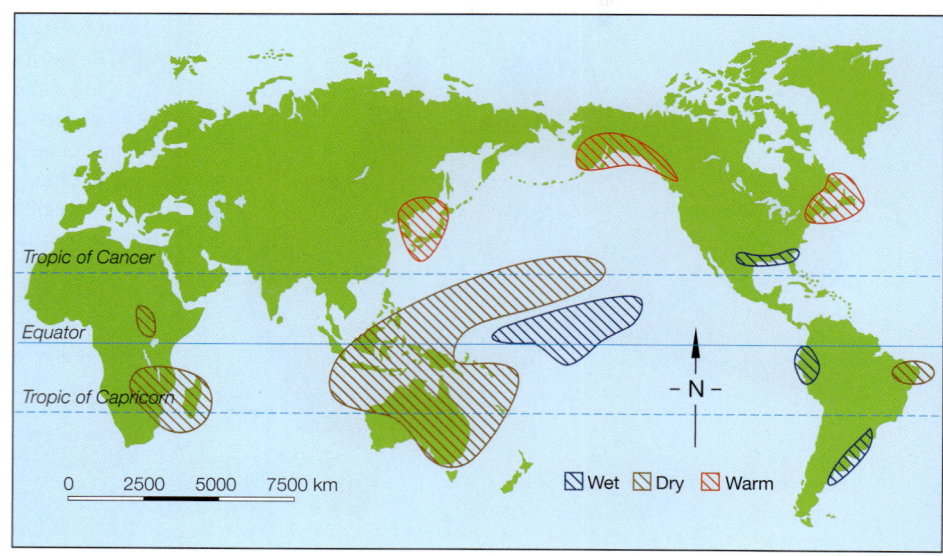

*Areas affected by El Niño*

spreads east. As well, the easterly trade winds that normally blow across the Pacific Ocean bringing warm, moist air to Australia reverse their direction. There is an accompanying reversal of air pressure across the Pacific, resulting in strong high pressure systems building up over most of Australia. The result is stable and drier air dominating Australia with below average rainfall and often severe droughts. El Niño brings significant climatic change, not only to Australia but also to other parts of the world.

In recent years, scientists have made great advances in understanding and forecasting El Niño and southern oscillation events. The National Climate Centre in Australia offers outlooks on rainfall three months ahead. These outlooks are proving to be of great value to farmers and especially valuable for ecologically sustainable development in rural areas.

> Australian scientists have discovered a new villain that they believe is responsible for record droughts in south-eastern Australia in recent years. This is the Indian Ocean dipole (or IOD), a cycle of warming and cooling of water in the Indian Ocean. In its positive phase, it reduces moisture-bearing winds, which are needed to bring rain across Australia. The IOD has been in its positive phase since 1992 — the longest period since records began in the late nineteenth century.

## ACTIVITIES

### UNDERSTANDING

1. Why is Australia so dry?
2. What is SOI and how is it calculated?
3. What do the following SOIs indicate?
   a Between +10 and −10
   b >+10
   c <−10
4. Refer to the diagram on this page comparing conditions during a normal year and an El Niño year, and study the text. Use these words to complete the following sentences: stable, moist, cooler, east, droughts, Tahiti, drier, warm, north, Darwin.

   During an El Niño event, the normally _____ sea in the oceans to the _____ and _____ of Australia are replaced by much _____ water. The air pressure in _____ begins to fall relative to the air pressure in _____. The normal _____ easterly trade winds change their direction. The result is _____ and _____ air and severe _____.

### THINKING AND APPLYING

5. Refer to the graph on the previous page.
   a Describe the seasonal conditions that prevail during an El Niño event.
   b What happens to the SOI when a drought breaks?
   c What would be happening to the air pressure in Darwin as the SOI rises?

### USING YOUR SKILLS

6. Refer to the map on the previous page showing the areas affected by El Niño. Describe the areas that become (a) wetter, (b) drier and (c) warmer during an El Niño event.

### GEOTERMS

**El Niño event:** the reversal (every few years) of the more usual direction of winds and surface currents across the Pacific Ocean. This change causes drought in eastern Australia and heavy rain in South America.

**La Niña event:** a period of well above average rainfall in eastern Australia that often brings floods

**southern oscillation:** a major air pressure shift between the Asian and east Pacific regions. Its most common extremes are El Niño events.

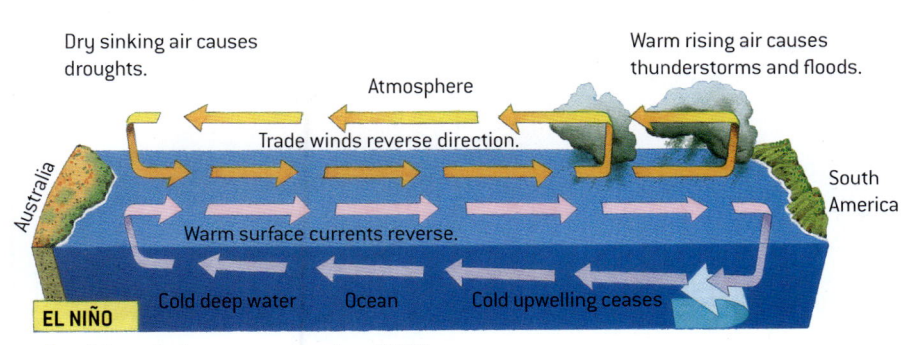

*Conditions during a normal and an El Niño year*

CHAPTER 3 | Natural hazards in Australia

# 3.4 The drought of 1991–95

Australia's drought of March 1991 to December 1995 was a long-lived, El Niño related drought. It was one of the longest of the twentieth century and one of the most destructive to the physical environment. Large areas of topsoil were lost and there was some damage to vegetation and wildlife.

As droughts occur frequently in Australia, most native plants and animals are usually well equipped to deal with them. However, introduced crops and animals can be severely affected, leading to crop failures, minimal planting of new crops and the death of introduced stock, such as sheep and cattle. Consequently, droughts have the most impact on areas given over to cropping or intensive grazing. The drought of 1991–95 had a devastating impact on such areas.

As the map opposite shows, the drought had its greatest impact on north-eastern Australia, particularly Queensland. Most of eastern Australia experienced below average rainfall for much of the period of the drought.

The cause of the drought was clearly El Niño related, as the graph of the SOI for the period shows. For nearly all of the period, the SOI was below zero and for many months it was in the range < –10.

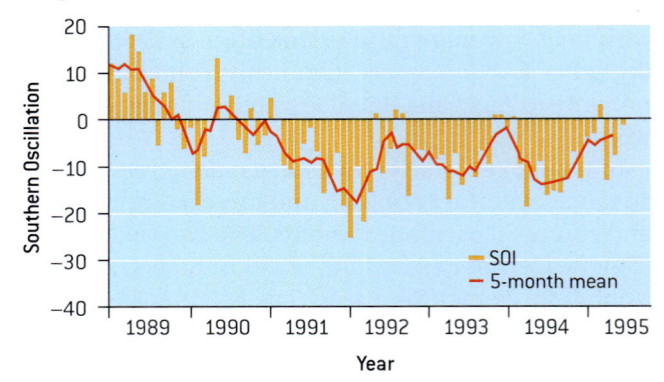

*Southern Oscillation Index, 1989–95*

One of the most dramatic consequences of severe drought is the dust storm. When the soil lacks moisture and dries out, plants and tree roots that normally hold the soil together wither and die. The dry soil particles on the surface are easily lifted into the air by strong winds, and topsoil can be carried across huge distances.

## Dust disaster to cost hundreds of millions

BY ASA WAHLQUIST AND SONYA SANDHAM

The massive wind storm that has blown millions of tonnes of dust across south-eastern Australia this week was a natural disaster that could cost grain growers hundreds of millions of dollars in lost production, a senior CSIRO scientist has warned.

'The estimated lost production value runs to perhaps 10 per cent of the value of the crops,' Dr Michael Raupach, an environmental scientist, said. Grain crops grown in south-eastern Australia were worth about $2 billion last year.

A thick cloud of dust hung over Sydney yesterday morning as gale-force winds carried more than one million tonnes of topsoil over the city. At dawn the cloud was 500 kilometres long, 300 kilometres wide and 1.3 kilometres deep but by 11 am it had dissipated to a depth of 2.5 kilometres.

A senior research officer with the Department of Conservation and Land Management, Mr John Leys, said between 1 million and 1.5 million tonnes of topsoil blew over the city, enough to fill 42 000 semi-trailers.

Farmers have already had to delay crop planting because of dry conditions and now fear a drought. 'It's a combination of strong winds, both north-westerly and westerlies, with dry conditions which make the surface layer of the soil friable and easy to lift off ...' Dr Raupach said. 'The other factor that has aggravated the situation is that some farmers have been burning off stubble, because of the mouse plagues in north-western Victoria. The combination has left us pretty vulnerable.'

Dr Rapauch said the dust lifted into the storm comprised the finer particles. 'They preferentially contain the nutrients, especially nitrogen and phosphorus, and have a lot to do with the water-holding capacity of the soil. That means that when we lose a tonne of dust from the soil we are in fact losing nutrient from between two and three tonnes of soil; we are winnowing the soil of its nutrients.'

One tonne of dust carries nutrients worth $1.50. 'So if we have lost 20 million tonnes we have lost $30 million of nutrients ...'

*Source: The Sydney Morning Herald, 27 May 1994.*

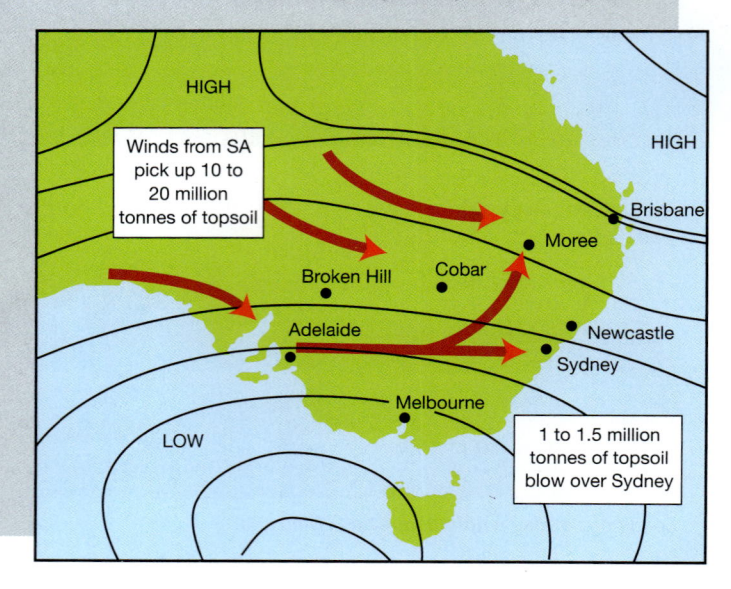

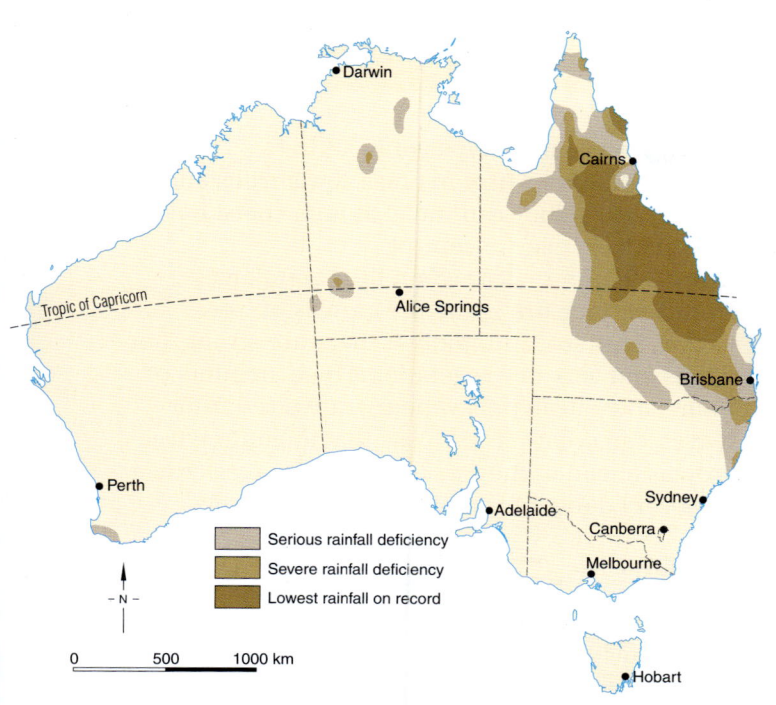

*Areas of Australia most affected by the drought of 1991–95*

Map legend:
- Serious rainfall deficiency
- Severe rainfall deficiency
- Lowest rainfall on record

*Dust storm approaching the town of Griffith, New South Wales. The dust was picked up by 90-kilometre winds from drought-affected farms. Dust storms carry away millions of tonnes of precious topsoil.*

## GEOskills TOOLBOX

### INTERPRETING A NEWSPAPER ARTICLE

Newspapers often provide valuable information on contemporary geographical issues. Daily newspapers are usually up to date and accurate, and we can obtain additional information from them in the form of photographs, graphs, diagrams and maps. The article on the previous page about the dust storms of 1994 presents an important geographical issue and is a strong reminder of the destructive power of droughts on the physical environment.

## Response to the drought

Farmers reduced their stock numbers and decreased the amount of land under crops. Some left drought-affected areas permanently. Farmers attempted to reduce the impact of drought by improving their farming methods, including the use of conservation techniques and fodder production systems. Community-based groups such as farming organisations lobbied for financial assistance from governments and provided assistance for individual farmers. The Commonwealth Government provided $590 million in drought relief from 1992 to 1995. The government has now developed the National Drought Policy, which provides a range of subsidies and direct financial assistance. It also encourages farmers to be more self-reliant, through risk management and farm plans.

## ACTIVITIES

### UNDERSTANDING

1. What was the cause of the drought of 1991–95?
2. Outline the main effects of the 1991–95 drought.
3. Refer to the graph of the Southern Oscillation Index, 1989–95.
   a. What indications were there that a drought would occur in 1991?
   b. According to the SOI, which were the two worst drought years?
   c. Describe the movement in the 5-month mean of the SOI over the period shown in the graph.

### THINKING AND APPLYING

4. In small teams, investigate how Australians respond to droughts. Decide which one of the following groups your team will focus on:
   - individuals
   - community-based organisations
   - governments.
   Summarise your findings in a poster, PowerPoint display or report, and present it to the class. After the presentations, explain how the responses of two of these groups demonstrate active citizenship.

### USING YOUR SKILLS

5. Refer to the map above left. Describe the areas affected by drought. Use the map scale to estimate the size of the area that experienced the lowest rainfall on record.
6. Read the newspaper article opposite.
   a. Use a diagram and the text of the article to describe the passage of the dust storm across south-eastern Australia.
   b. What were the impacts of the wind storm on agriculture?

CHAPTER 3 | Natural hazards in Australia

# 3.5 Bushfires as natural hazards

## Bushfires

A **bushfire** is a fire burning out of control in the open. Bushfires can burn using grass, scrub or forest (or a combination of these) for fuel. Unless quickly controlled, bushfires can become large, spreading to affect forests, wildlife, crops, houses and other buildings, and human life.

Fires are not a recent occurrence in Australia. Since the last ice age, bushfires have influenced the development of the Australian land. Fires are an essential element in some Australian ecosystems, which need the intense heat of bushfires to release the seeds from plants and replenish growth. Australian Aborigines used fires to assist them in their hunting activities. It is believed that the fire activities of Aborigines contributed to the development of an open woodland ecosystem in parts of south-eastern Australia.

Early European settlers also used fire to assist in the clearing of land for crops and as a means of removing stubble following cropping. Laws have now been passed restricting the lighting of fires for these purposes. This has led to a more dense vegetation in many rural areas and more leaf and bark litter on the ground. The litter provides a significant amount of fuel for fires if they do start.

There are two main types of bushfires:
- *Surface bushfires* burn in grass, low shrubs and ground litter. They can travel at high speed but are relatively easy to control.
- *Crown bushfires* occur when heat and flames from a surface fire ignite the crowns of trees. Crown fires spread rapidly if there are strong, hot winds and very dry vegetation. Huge amounts of flammable eucalyptus vapour, transpired from leaves, can create **firebrands** that engulf the tree crowns ahead of the **fire front**. This makes crown fires very dangerous and difficult to control.

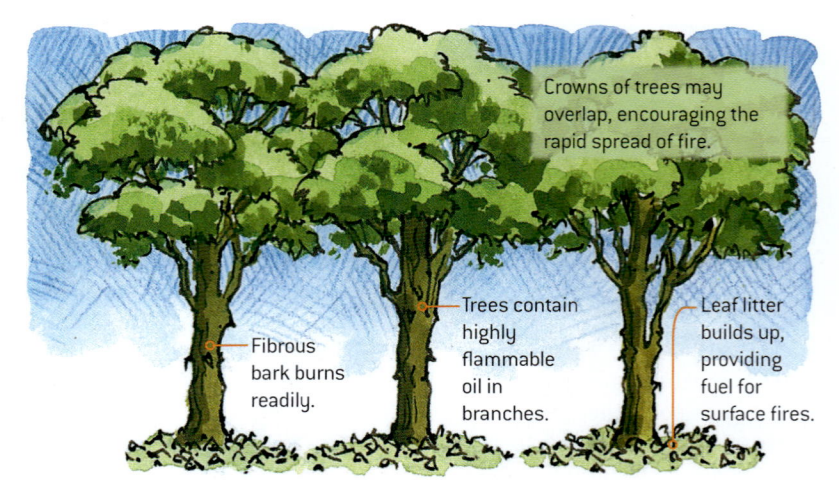

*Eucalypts and bushfires*

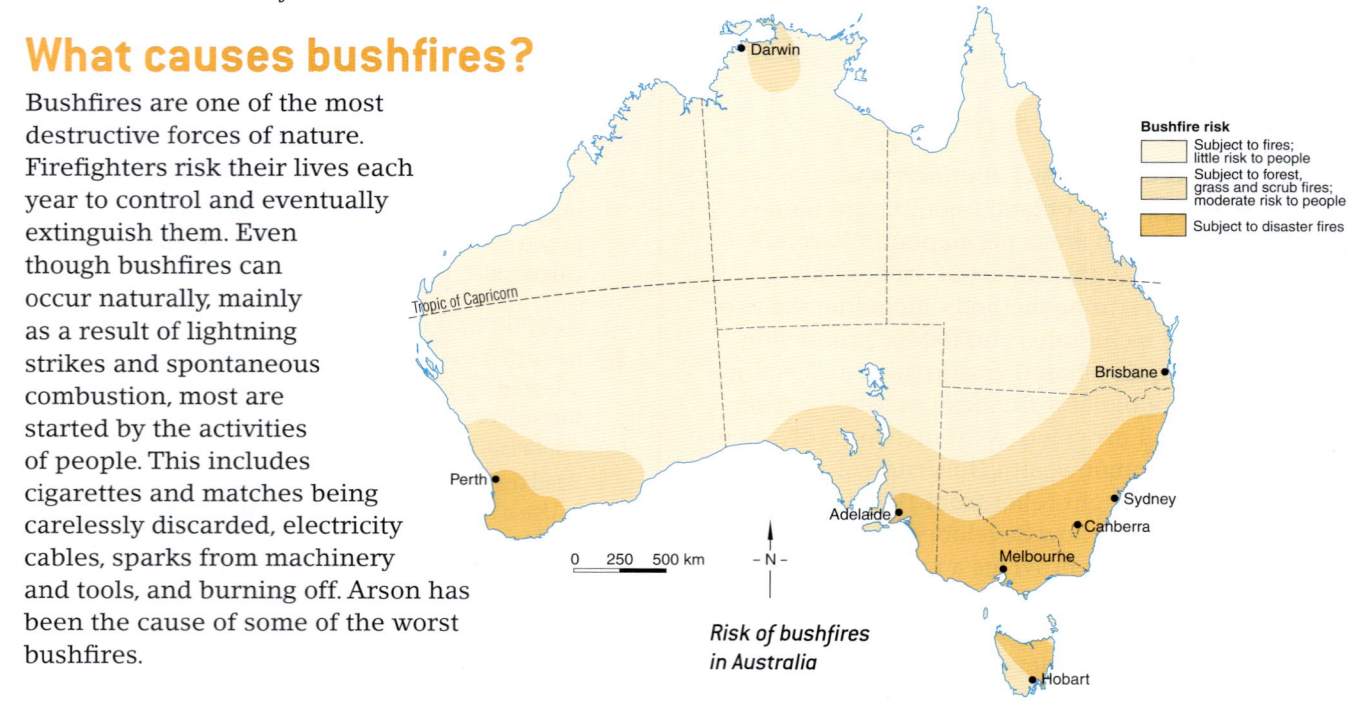

- Crowns of trees may overlap, encouraging the rapid spread of fire.
- Fibrous bark burns readily.
- Trees contain highly flammable oil in branches.
- Leaf litter builds up, providing fuel for surface fires.

## What causes bushfires?

Bushfires are one of the most destructive forces of nature. Firefighters risk their lives each year to control and eventually extinguish them. Even though bushfires can occur naturally, mainly as a result of lightning strikes and spontaneous combustion, most are started by the activities of people. This includes cigarettes and matches being carelessly discarded, electricity cables, sparks from machinery and tools, and burning off. Arson has been the cause of some of the worst bushfires.

*Risk of bushfires in Australia*

Bushfire risk:
- Subject to fires; little risk to people
- Subject to forest, grass and scrub fires; moderate risk to people
- Subject to disaster fires

## Where do bushfires occur?

As the map opposite shows, bushfires usually occur in the less arid parts of Australia. Arid areas tend not to have enough fuel to sustain fires for any length of time. South-eastern Australia is particularly subject to bushfires. There are several reasons for this, including the following:

1. Large areas are covered with **sclerophyll** vegetation. The dominant trees are eucalypts, which have highly flammable oil in their branches. Eucalypts burn readily and can become so hot during fires that their sap boils and the whole tree or shrub can explode in flames. This is not a problem for the plant species as most eucalypt varieties burn hot and fast as a means of releasing seeds onto the fire-cleared ground. Some burnt trees simply send up new shoots from their stumps or roots and grow to full-size trees again.
2. The area is also subject to prolonged periods of below average rainfall and droughts. Many of the most severe bushfires have occurred during droughts and El Niño events. Bushfires and drought often occur together.
3. South-eastern Australia is also subject to **heatwaves** and strong northerly winds during the summer months. Two or three days of heatwave weather can often provide conditions suitable for bushfires to occur. This was the case in Australia's worst bushfires in Victoria in February 2009 (see pages 66–9).
4. Climate change scientists have forecast that south-eastern Australia is likely to become hotter and drier in the future. They estimate that the number of 'very high' and 'extreme' fire danger days could increase by 4–25% by 2020 and 15–70% by 2050. The potential exists therefore for more bushfire disasters.

## Response to bushfires

Bushfires can bring massive destruction, loss of life and personal hardship to families and communities. Individuals, community-based groups and governments have responded to this hazard in many ways.

There are over 70 000 individuals who are volunteer members of bushfire brigades. They do most of the fighting of bushfires. During times of severe bushfires they can be on duty for days at a time, sometimes facing extreme danger. They make a highly significant contribution to community safety.

The government has set up many agencies that work to protect the community when bushfires occur. These include fire brigades, police and ambulance services, welfare agencies and the State Emergency Service. Governments can provide emergency financial assistance in severe bushfires. The Bureau of Meteorology provides short- and long-term weather forecasts to warn of bushfire dangers.

*Bushfire brigade volunteers risk their lives to save people, animals and property from bushfires.*

### ACTIVITIES

#### UNDERSTANDING
1. Define the term *bushfire*.
2. How have bushfires been essential to some Australian ecosystems?
3. How did the activities of Aboriginal people affect ecosystems?

#### THINKING AND APPLYING
4. How can climate change in south-eastern Australia affect the risk of bushfires?

#### USING YOUR SKILLS
5. Refer to the map opposite showing the risk of bushfires in Australia. Describe the distribution of the risk areas. Why is south-eastern Australia particularly subject to bushfires?

### GEOTERMS

**bushfire:** a fire burning out of control in the open; also called a wildfire
**firebrand:** aerially burning fuel that blows ahead of a fire front
**fire front:** the edge of a fire that spreads fastest

# 3.6 From hazard to disaster

Bushfires are one of the most common natural disasters faced by Australians. Along with floods and droughts, they are part of the way our physical environment functions.

The effects of bushfires are widespread; they cost lives, destroy property and devastate forests and farmland.

Dry conditions caused by drought, searing temperatures and strong, hot northerly winds cure the bush, making it so dry that a spark can ignite a major bushfire. Grasses die off and the soil is easily blown away.

High temperatures, low relative humidity and strong winds combine to create high fire danger days.

Crown bushfires spread through the treetops or 'crowns' of forests. Before long, a wide blanket of forest is fully ablaze.

Many animals perish, as fire fronts often move too quickly for them to escape.

## ACTIVITIES

### UNDERSTANDING
1. What is a crown bushfire?
2. List the firefighting techniques shown here.
3. Why do many animals die in bushfires?
4. Why do bushfires often occur in times of drought?
5. Explain how eucalypt trees help bushfires spread.

### THINKING AND APPLYING
6. Imagine a small fire front with a long flank. The fire is being pushed by winds from the north. Suddenly the wind changes and starts blowing from the west. Will the people on the west or on the east of the original fire now be in danger?
7. Write a news report of the scene shown on these pages. Outline the effects on people and wildlife. Include interviews and describe the fire using key terms explained in this chapter.
8. How could you make your home and community safer in a bushfire? Think about terrain, climate, vegetation, access to water, firefighting resources and so on. Design a poster outlining one of your ideas. It should be eye-catching and contain a short clever message. Use the **Fire prevention** weblink in your eBookPLUS and information on these pages to help you.

What was the flank or side of a bushfire can become the new fire front if there is a wind change.

Australia's eucalypt forests not only tolerate fire but also need it in order to survive! The seeds of some eucalypts need the heat of a bushfire to be able to open and grow. The low moisture content of eucalypts means they ignite and burn easily. Their fibrous bark is highly combustible.

Special helicopters can scoop up to 9500 litres of water in 45 seconds and dump the whole lot in just 3 seconds.

Dry forests provide plenty of fuel. Surface bushfires quickly ignite dry, flammable grass, twigs and branches on the ground.

A firebrand is burning fuel that is pushed ahead of the fire front by the wind. Firebrands have been known to travel kilometres from their original source. A spot fire is a new bushfire started by firebrands.

By using the wrong building materials, planting eucalypts close to the house and stacking firewood against the house, people can actively contribute to the spread of a bushfire.

Properties are more likely to survive if gutters are clear of leaves, lawns and shrubs are trimmed, and there is access to water and hoses. People who defend their house must cover up with cotton or woollen clothing.

CHAPTER 3 | Natural hazards in Australia  65

# 3.7 Black Saturday, Victoria 2009

Saturday 7 February 2009 saw the onset of Australia's worst natural disaster; raging bushfires in Victoria killed 173 people. The fires that burned for days afterwards also destroyed 2029 homes in many towns including Marysville, Kinglake and Whittlesea and displaced 7000 Victorians. An estimated 1 million native animals were lost.

## Causes of the bushfires

1. *Heatwaves*. In the weeks preceding the bushfires, there had been a series of exceptional heatwaves in south-eastern Australia and particularly Victoria. The heatwave that accompanied the bushfires on Black Saturday smashed records. Much of Victoria, including Melbourne and 20 other centres registered unprecedented maximum temperatures. Melbourne reached 46.4° Celsius, the highest in 154 years of record keeping. The cause of the heatwaves were **blocking high pressure systems** over the Tasman Sea, which channelled hot, dry tropical air over south-eastern Australia.

2. *Low rainfall*. The soaring temperatures were preceded by months of very low rainfall and periods of drought in much of Victoria. The result was tinder-dry fuel that was very easily ignited but very difficult to extinguish.

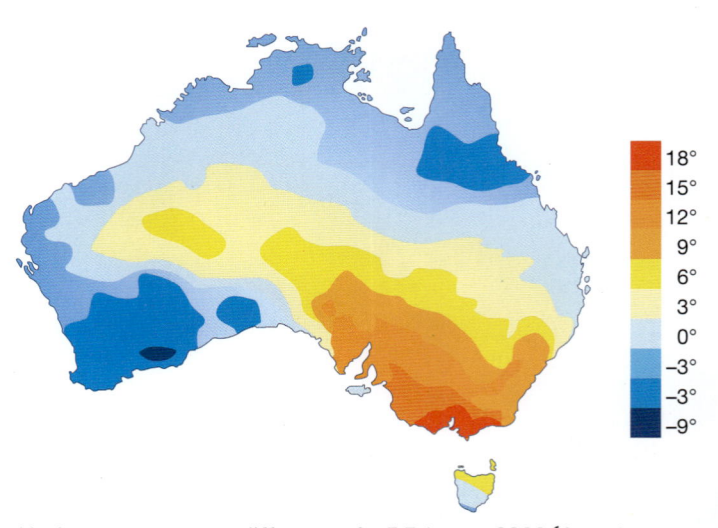

*Maximum temperature differences for 7 February 2009 (from the 1971–2000 average)*

Source: Bureau of Meteorology.

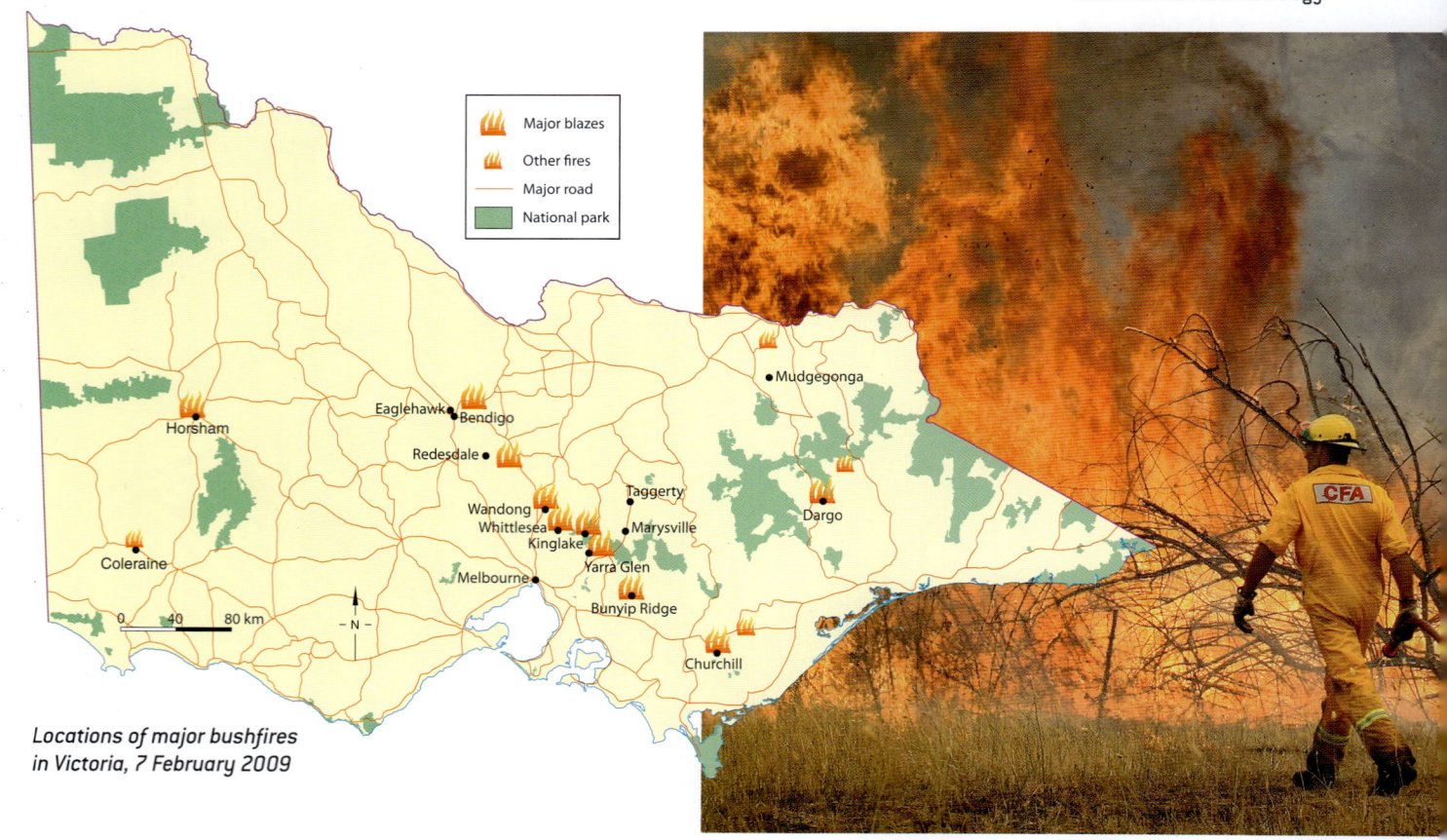

*Locations of major bushfires in Victoria, 7 February 2009*

*A CFA firefighter defends a property at Mudgegonga, Victoria, 2009.*

3. *Winds*. There were strong, dry north-westerly winds on early Saturday ahead of a cold front. As the cold front moved through late on 7 February, it changed the direction of the wind and the fire fronts, threatening many towns. Very strong winds of up to 120 kilometres per hour resulted in fires that spread very rapidly as burning embers were carried up to 15 kilometres ahead to start secondary fires. Gradually, over the following days the weather cooled and firefighters were able to slowly bring many fires under control.
4. *Low humidity*. Record low levels of relative humidity were set with Melbourne recording only 5 per cent humidity in the late afternoon of 7 February.
5. *Topography*. The hilly nature of the topography of Victoria's Central Highlands played a part. The fires spread more quickly up slopes.
6. *Human factors*. As Melbourne's population has grown, more people have chosen a 'tree-change' lifestyle, moving to hilly bushland areas within driving distance of Melbourne. This exposed many more people to the fires. One or more of the fires may have been the result of arson — the intentional, unlawful burning of property.

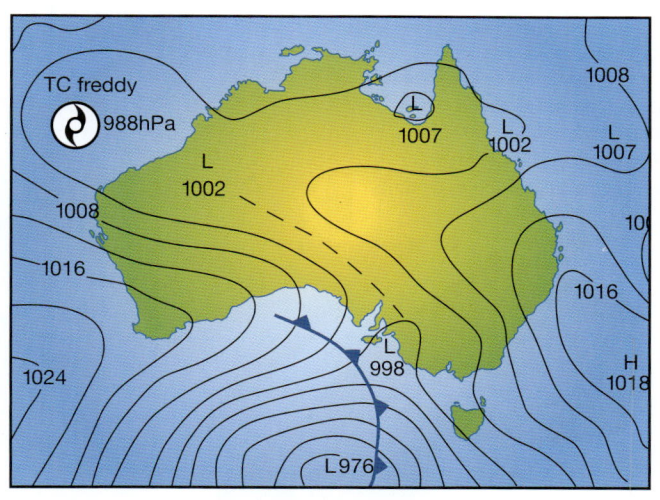

*Synoptic chart for noon on 7 February 2009*

*Aerial view of Marysville, Victoria, on 11 February 2009, four days after the Black Saturday bushfires*

**Fuel**
Months of drought and weeks of extreme heat produced very dry fuel. High temperatures dried the fuel even more, making it easier for the fire to spread.

**Cold change**
As the cold front passed in the early evening, the wind direction changed suddenly by about 90° so that the fire flank became a wide fire front. This caused a sudden increase in the speed and intensity of the fire.

**Air**
Turbulence from the mid 40° heat drew super dry air from 4 to 5 kilometres above the ground. This increased the dryness of the air and gustiness of winds.

**N–NW winds**
North and north-westerly winds bring very dry, hot air from the inland. Winds were very strong and gusty ahead of the cool change.

*Narrow fire front*

*Wind and fire fronts in Victoria on 7 February 2009*

## Response to the fire

The immediate response to the fires was from the Country Fire Authority (CFA) who coordinated the efforts of volunteers to fight the fires. Many locals fought fires on their own properties. Volunteers, men and women from across Australia and New Zealand, joined the battle.

The Victorian and Australian governments provided many services in the aftermath of the fires including food, accommodation, counselling and emergency cash assistance. Australian Prime Minister Kevin Rudd said, 'Together we'll rebuild each of these communities — brick by brick, school by school, community hall by community hall.'

Charity organisations, including the Red Cross and the Salvation Army, offered immediate and short-term assistance. Many corporations, foreign governments and thousands of individuals made cash donations. The Red Cross received over $245 million to assist the rehabilitation of the bushfire victims.

In the aftermath of the fires, a royal commission looked at planning regulations, building standards and whether fire breaks or bunkers should be built. It also reviewed the existing advice to property owners of 'stay and defend' when a bushfire threatens. The Premier of Victoria said after the fires, 'If you are going, you've got to go early … If you stay, you must have in place the best possible fire plan.'

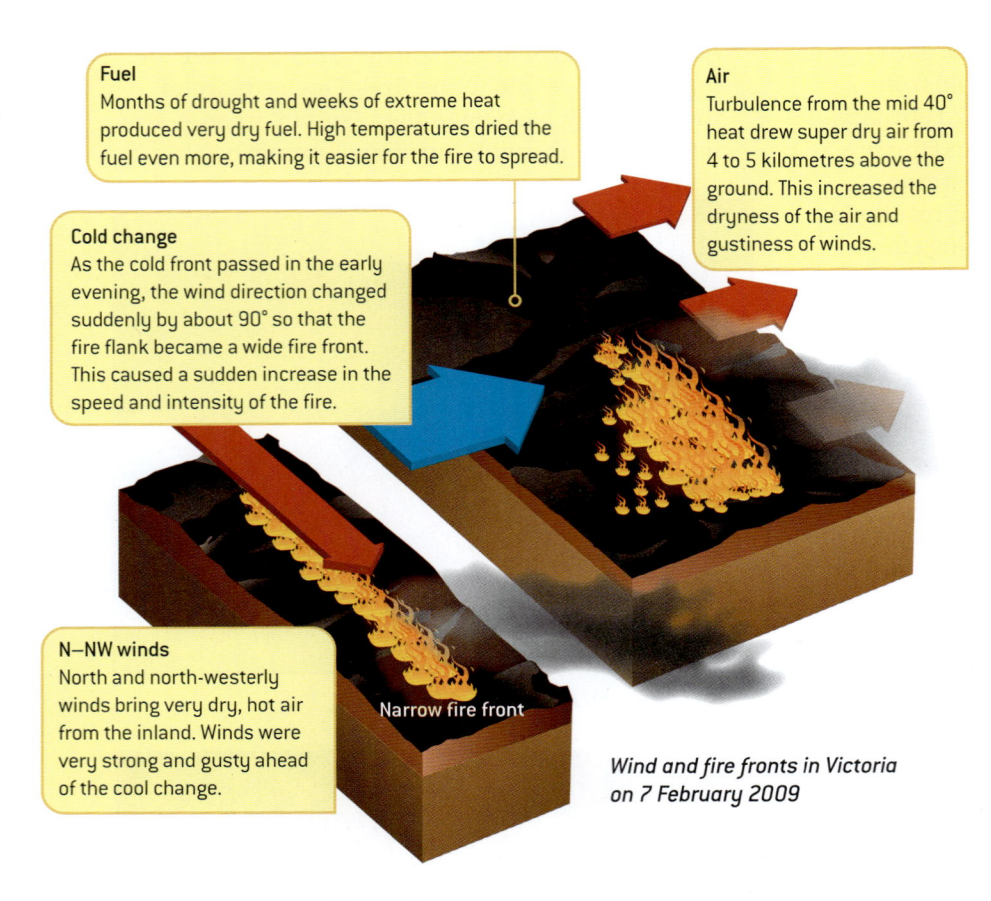

## Changing fire fronts

Most of the damage was caused by two massive **firestorms** with broad fire fronts fuelled by winds and the tinder-dry vegetation. The fire front's movement and size are strongly influenced by the wind direction and speed. Early on Black Saturday, the winds blew in a northerly and north-westerly direction, and most of the existing fires had a narrow front.

As the cold front passed, the wind direction changed 90 degrees, which broadened the front and quickly increased the intensity and speed of the fire. Towns that had not been threatened by the fires were now faced with a wall of flames.

As the front broadened, the heat increased producing fire tornadoes: areas of intense heat, updraughts, downdraughts and great turbulence.

## Counting the cost

The following table shows that Victoria's 2009 losses exceed those caused by previous bushfire disasters in Australia and overseas.

**Losses from bushfire disasters in selected locations**

| Location | Date | Deaths | Homes lost | Hectares burned | Cost at the time |
| --- | --- | --- | --- | --- | --- |
| Tasmania | February 1967 | 62 | 1300 | 260 000 | $45 million |
| Victoria | February 1983 | 75 | 2400 | 500 000 | $400 million |
| Portugal | August 2003 | 15 | 500 | 140 000 | US$1 billion |
| California | October 2007 | 23 | 1500 | 200 000 | US$1 billion |
| Greece | August 2007 | 64 | 1500 | 11 000 | US$1.2 billion |
| Victoria | February 2009 | 173 | 2029 | 450 000 | $1.5 billion |

*Source:* Australian Strategic Policy Institute.

## GEOskills TOOLBOX

### INTERPRETING A SATELLITE IMAGE

Satellite images allow large areas of the Earth to be shown in one image. In the satellite image on the right, false colour is used to show areas of active fire. These appear in red near the centre of the image and to the north-east near Dederang. Smoke can be seen drifting north from Marysville and Kinglake.

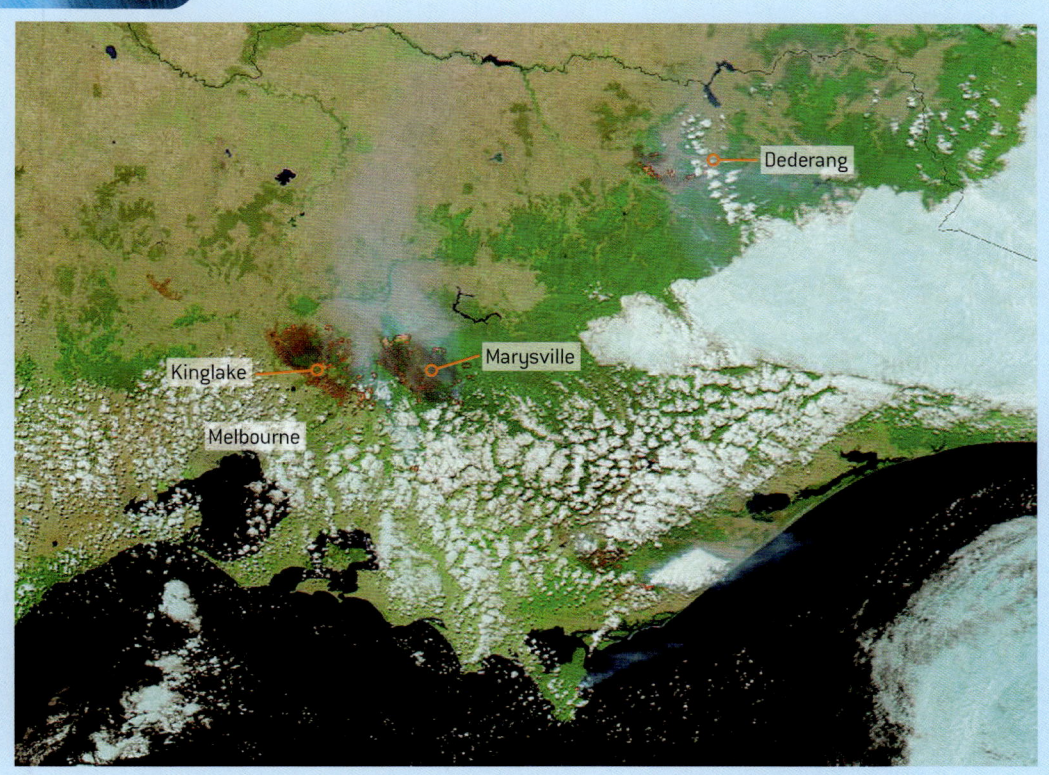

*Satellite image of central Victoria, 9 February 2009*

## ACTIVITIES

### UNDERSTANDING

1. By what criteria was Black Saturday Australia's worst natural disaster?
2. Describe the destruction caused by the bushfires.
3. Explain how weather conditions before and during the fires contributed to the critical fire situation in Victoria.
4. How did individuals, government and non-government agencies respond to the fires?

### THINKING AND APPLYING

5. Could residents in the areas of Victoria affected by the fires have prepared for such intense and fast-moving fires? Suggest strategies that may have helped.
6. The prevailing advice for people facing a bushfire threat is to 'stay and defend' their properties. What do you think of this advice in light of the death toll in the Black Saturday Victorian fires?
7. Should people living in fire-prone areas be allowed to clear away native vegetation from around their homes?

### USING YOUR SKILLS

8. Refer to the map of Victoria flashpoints on page 66. Describe the location of the fires. Is there any pattern to their location?
9. Refer to the map of 'temperature anomalies' on page 66. Describe the distribution of temperature anomalies in south-eastern Australia, and suggest how this contributed to the disaster.
10. Refer to the satellite map above showing the fires.
    a. Where are the fires located in relation to Melbourne?
    b. Which direction is the wind coming from?
    c. Estimate the proportion of the land area that shows burning.
11. Use the table on page 68 to answer the following questions.
    a. Compare the scale of the Victorian bushfires of 7 February 2009 with two other bushfires.
    b. Outline the problem with the data for comparing bushfires. How could this problem be overcome?

### GEOTERMS

**blocking high pressure system:** a persistent high pressure system that occurs on a large scale, remaining stationary for a period of time, compressing and warming the air below

**firestorm:** an intense fire that may generate strong convection currents and violent winds causing long-range spotting and flame spirals

# 3.8 Natural hazards: storms

A storm is any violent disturbance of the atmosphere and the effects associated with it. The main types of storms are thunderstorms, tropical cyclones, cold fronts and tornadoes (twisters). In this section, we look at thunderstorms and their effect on people's activities.

## What is a thunderstorm?

A **thunderstorm** is a storm associated with lightning and thunder and occurring with cumulonimbus clouds. Cumulonimbus clouds can develop singly or extend over an area of 100 kilometres or more. Thunderstorms result when cumulonimbus clouds build up enough static electricity to produce lightning. Lightning instantly heats the air through which it travels to about 20 000° Celsius — more than three times as hot as the surface of the sun. This causes the air to expand so quickly that it causes an explosion (thunder). The time between a lightning flash and the crash of thunder tells you how far away the lightning is (5 seconds = 1.6 kilometres).

### GEO*facts*

- Some 1000 years or so ago, the Vikings thought thunder was the rumbling of Thor's chariot. (He was their god of thunder and lightning.) Lightning marked the path of his mighty hammer, Mjöllnir, when he threw it across the sky at his enemies.
- An average of about 100 severe thunderstorms are reported in Australia each year.

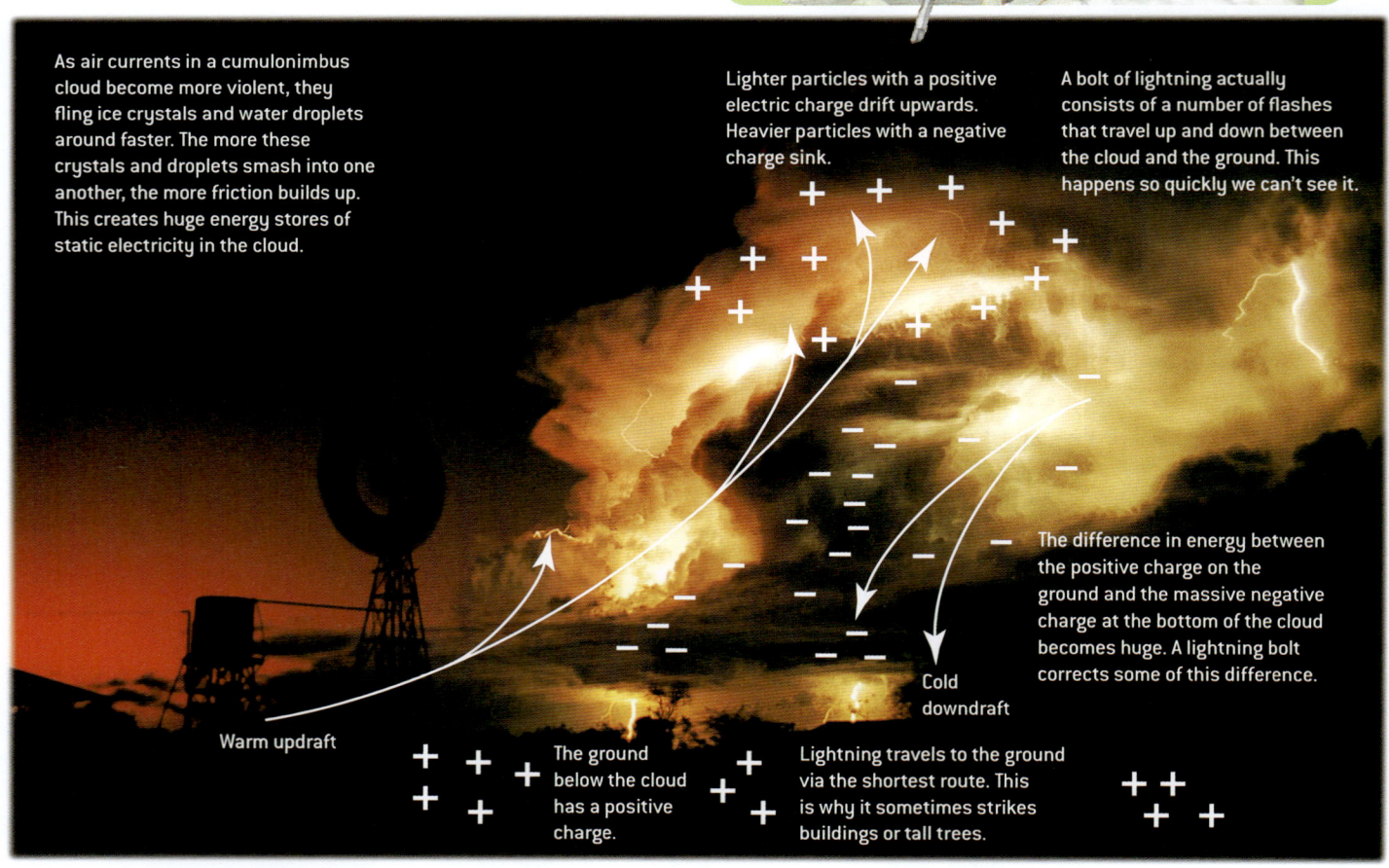

---

As air currents in a cumulonimbus cloud become more violent, they fling ice crystals and water droplets around faster. The more these crystals and droplets smash into one another, the more friction builds up. This creates huge energy stores of static electricity in the cloud.

Lighter particles with a positive electric charge drift upwards. Heavier particles with a negative charge sink.

A bolt of lightning actually consists of a number of flashes that travel up and down between the cloud and the ground. This happens so quickly we can't see it.

The difference in energy between the positive charge on the ground and the massive negative charge at the bottom of the cloud becomes huge. A lightning bolt corrects some of this difference.

Warm updraft

Cold downdraft

The ground below the cloud has a positive charge.

Lightning travels to the ground via the shortest route. This is why it sometimes strikes buildings or tall trees.

*How a thunderstorm works*

## Ingredients of disaster

BY BRIAN WILLIAMS AND ROBYN IRONSIDE

WEATHER bureau meteorologists have rated the storm that hit Brisbane on Sunday as the worst since 2004.

But they will reappraise its severity when the final insurance bill is calculated.

Severe weather meteorologist Tony Wedd said the storm was large and unusual because it hit Brisbane suburbs such as The Gap, Ferny Grove and Keperra, areas that did not often get big storms.

'It would have been a real eye-opener for people living out there,' he said. 'It's not like Esk or Gatton, which are used to being hit by storms like this.

'It was really a line of storms that covered the northern suburbs. Cells waxed and waned, which is why you've got different pockets of damage, as cells reached peak intensity.'

Forecaster Geoff Doueal said between 10 and 20 storms formed across the southeast after temperatures soared into the 30s and humidity rose to the high 90s.

'Storms were popping up all over the place and then dying until they finally formed a line of squalls,' he said.

Queensland Parks and Wildlife regional manager Jason Jacobi said extensive damage had been done to reserves in Brisbane's western and northern suburbs and on the Gold Coast hinterland, including Brisbane Forest Park, Samford State Forest, Bunyaville Forest Reserve and D'Aguilar Range including Mt Mee State Forest, and Lamington and Springbrook national parks.

Energex, Brisbane City Council and State Emergency Service crews worked through Sunday night and all day yesterday to clear a path through the debris. The SES took more than 15,000 calls and sent crews to more than 100 households to help with sand-bagging and repairing damaged roofs and windows.

Brisbane Lord Mayor Campbell Newman said 300 staff and 100 vehicles had been deployed along with crews from Logan and Redland city councils and the Queensland Parks and Wildlife Service . . .

Source: *The Courier-Mail*, 18 November 2008.

*The extensive damage in places like The Gap is now thought to have been caused by a 'microburst', which is a concentrated severe downdraft that can cause damaging winds at ground level.*

## Severe thunderstorms

Severe thunderstorms can be a serious natural hazard because they can bring one or more of the following features:
- *hailstones*, which are two centimetres or more in diameter
- *wind gusts* of 90 kilometres or more per hour
- *tornadoes*, which are rapidly rotating columns of air that descend in a funnel shape from thunderstorm clouds
- *very heavy rain*, which can result in flash flooding. A thunderstorm often moves slowly, dropping a lot of precipitation in one area. The rain or hail may be too heavy and prolonged for the ground to absorb the moisture. The water runs off, quickly flooding local areas.

### GEOTERMS

**thunderstorm:** a storm associated with lightning and thunder, occurring with cumulonimbus clouds

### ACTIVITIES

**UNDERSTANDING**

1. Define the following terms:
   a storm
   b thunderstorm
   c severe thunderstorm
2. How can severe thunderstorms develop?
3. Refer to the diagram on the opposite page of how a thunderstorm works, and use information in the text to explain:
   a what causes static electricity in a cloud
   b what causes thunder and lightning
   c why a lightning bolt travels between the clouds and the ground.
4. Read the article above about severe storms in Brisbane in November 2008.
   a Why was the storm unusual?
   b What factors contributed to the storms?
   c What were the main impacts of the storms? Use the text of the article and the photograph in your response.

# 3.9 The Sydney hailstorm, 1999

At about 7.30 pm on 14 April 1999, a freak hailstorm hit Sydney. It affected more houses and people than any previous natural disaster in Australia's history. With a ferocity that shocked the unsuspecting residents and in the space of only 45 minutes, more than 500 000 tonnes of hailstones — some the size of cricket balls — destroyed homes and property. One person was killed. More than 24 000 buildings were damaged. About 60 000 cars were damaged, with one-third so badly damaged they were written off by the insurance companies. The total cost of the hailstorm was $2000 million.

## Anatomy of a hailstorm

In thunderstorms, when warm air rises above freezing level, water droplets can freeze and fall as hail. However, the hailstorm that hit Sydney in April 1999 was caused by a much more powerful thunderstorm — known as a super-cell. The very strong updraft of air in a super-cell storm keeps hailstones suspended inside the cloud for a much longer time than in regular storms. The smaller hailstones join together and grow before becoming too heavy and falling.

1. As the ice crystals rise and fall with the updrafts, they collide with water droplets that freeze around them, forming hailstones.
2. Hail begins to form when strong updrafts lift moist air into the freezing zone in cumulonimbus clouds. Here, the moisture in the air turns to ice crystals.
3. The more the hailstones rise and fall, the larger they become.
4. A supercell storm has extremely strong updrafts. These keep hailstones suspended longer than regular storms, allowing hailstones to grow bigger. To form cricket-ball sized hailstones, there must be updrafts of around 160 km/h.
5. Hailstones fall to Earth (at speeds of around 160 km/h) when they become too heavy or are caught in a downdraft.

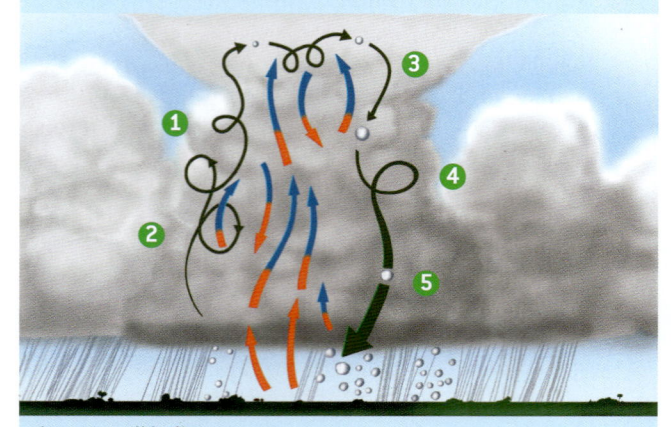

*A super-cell hailstorm*

A super-cell thunderstorm is a particularly rare storm, marked by its severity. Super-cells are characterised by the fact that they last much longer than normal thunderstorms. The 14 April 1999 storm in Sydney lasted approximately five and a half hours. In contrast, a normal thunderstorm might last one hour. Super-cells bring the most extreme weather, such as large hailstones, high winds, flash flooding and sometimes tornadoes.

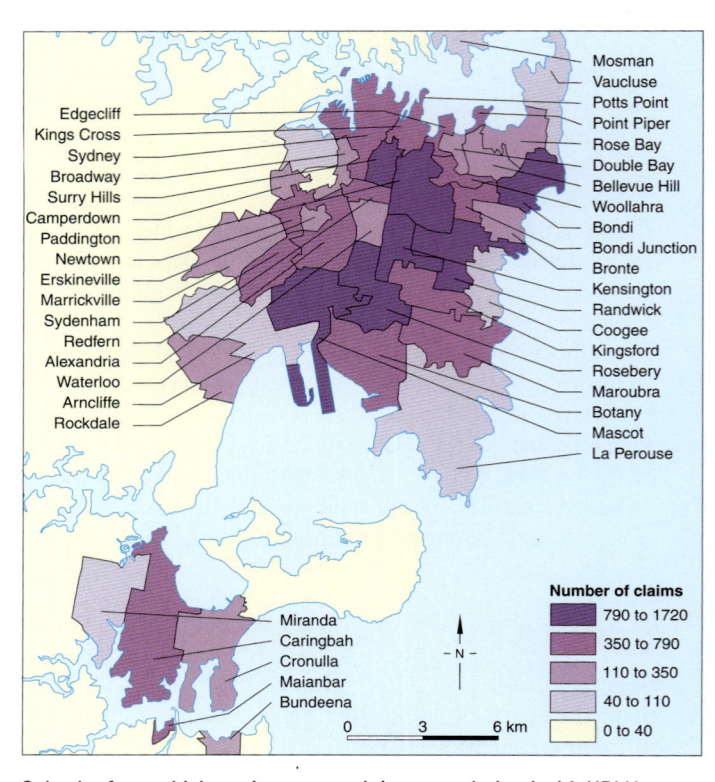

**Number of claims**
- 790 to 1720
- 350 to 790
- 110 to 350
- 40 to 110
- 0 to 40

*Suburbs from which car insurance claims were lodged with NRMA Insurance by 20 April 1999*

### GEOskills TOOLBOX

**WORKING WITH THEMATIC MAPS**

Choropleth maps are a special type of thematic map that shows patterns. The choropleth map of car insurance claims resulting from the Sydney hailstorm gives a good picture of the path and severity of the storm. The map has been coloured to show the number of claims in each suburb. The darker shades show the highest number of claims and the lighter colours show the least number of claims. The colours have been carefully selected so that the observer can instantly see a pattern.

*The dramatic aerial view of Kensington suggests the extent of the impact on the lives of residents. The patchwork of coloured tarpaulins over Sydney suburbs exceeded 90 000. More than 20 000 homes as well as schools and businesses suffered damage in an area concentrated on the eastern suburbs but stretching from Bundeena (south of the city centre) to the north shore.*

## Stormtroopers cover Sydney

Army troops have been called in belatedly to help protect the homes of Sydney's distressed residents from further damage after the disastrous hailstorm. They will join the State Emergency Service and relief workers from the Rural Fire Service and New South Wales Fire Brigade, almost doubling the number of workers to 5000 over the weekend.

The premier conceded that his government may not have acted quickly enough to help storm victims deal with Sydney's biggest-ever storm disaster. The finger has also been pointed at forecasters at the Bureau of Meteorology. By the time the direction and intensity of the storm cell was identified, it was already battering Sydney's eastern suburbs. A new radar warning system designed to issue alerts to forecasters was installed at Kurnell one month ago, but meteorologists at the Weather Bureau had not been fully trained to use it.

Many homes will need to be revisited in a month to have tarpaulins replaced as hundreds of tarpaulins ordered from China have been found to be below standard. Shortages of terracotta tiles and skilled labour mean that many families face at least a six-month delay for permanent roof repairs and possibly a wait of several weeks for glass and carpet replacement . . .

## ACTIVITIES

### UNDERSTANDING

1. By what criteria was the Sydney hailstorm rated as Australia's worst natural disaster up to that time? List the types of damage it caused.
2. Read the text and refer to the diagram of a super-cell storm. Write a paragraph explaining why the hailstones were larger than normal.
3. Read the report 'Stormtroopers cover Sydney'.
   a Explain what is meant by the title of the article.
   b What change did the storm bring to the affected communities of Sydney?
   c Which community groups were involved in the disaster relief?
   d What problems were faced in repairing the damage?

### THINKING AND APPLYING

4. Imagine you were premier of New South Wales. What action would you take to change the way disasters are handled?
5. What lessons do you think organisations such as insurance companies and community groups would have learned from the Sydney hailstorm?

### USING YOUR SKILLS

6. Refer to the aerial photograph of Kensington above.
   a How many roofs are not covered by tarpaulins?
   b What other features in the photograph are likely to be damaged by hail?
7. Refer to the map opposite then complete a paragraph describing the number of insurance claims made in Sydney's suburbs. Ensure you include in your description the names of some suburbs and their location.

CHAPTER 3 | Natural hazards in Australia

# 3.10 Natural hazards: tropical cyclones

A **tropical cyclone** is a particular type of low pressure system. It is called a hurricane in the United States and a typhoon in Asia. Tropical cyclones are areas of warm, moist air rising rapidly. The upward flow of air is deflected by the Coriolis effect (winds deflected by the Earth's rotation), creating a rotation around a central core, known as the 'eye'. Tropical cyclones are often accompanied by very strong winds (gusts of over 300 kilometres per hour have been recorded), torrential rain (1800 millimetres in 24 hours have been recorded) and very rough seas.

A **storm surge** resulting in a sudden rise in sea level can occur when a tropical cyclone approaches or crosses a coastline. Among the destructive and death-dealing features of tropical cyclones, storm surges and floods are ranked as more significant than winds.

Tropical cyclones need the energy provided by warm water vapour (sea waters of at least 27° Celsius). Usually they die out if they move inland away from the water vapour, or out of the tropics, away from the warmth. This is why tropical coastal areas, such as the Caribbean Sea (Central America), the north-west Pacific and north-east Australia, between 5° and 15° north and south of the Equator, are commonly affected by tropical cyclones.

The amount of energy released in a tropical cyclone in one day is about the equivalent of the energy released by 400 twenty-megatonne hydrogen bombs. If tropical cyclones occur near large population centres, they can cause extensive damage to property and the loss of life.

A tropical cyclone may exist for only a few days or as long as a few weeks. It can behave unpredictably, moving forward, hardly moving, changing direction and even doubling back on itself.

The map opposite shows the paths of major Australian cyclones since 1970. Tropical cyclones occur in northern Australia between December and April, with the greatest activity usually occurring between January and March. The number of cyclones varies considerably from year to year, the frequency usually determined by the temperature

| Australia's deadly cyclones | |
|---|---|
| Most deadly | Cyclone Mahina killed more than 300 in December 1899 at Bathurst Bay, north Queensland. |
| Most costly | Cyclone Tracy destroyed $800 million worth of property (1974 figures) on 24 December 1974 in Darwin. |
| Strongest winds | Cyclone Larry gusted up to 300 km/h in March 2006 in Innisfail, north Queensland. |
| Heaviest rainfall | Cyclone Naomi unleashed 202 mm of rain in 24 hours in December 1993 in Western Australia. |

*The formation of a tropical cyclone*

*Strong winds and high seas are among the effects of tropical cyclones.*

of the oceans in the tropical waters around northern Australia. The Australian Bureau of Meteorology tracks an average of ten cyclones per year in the Australian region. Of these, six may be expected to cross the Australian coast. We will examine two major tropical cyclones that have hit different parts of Australia and their effects on people.

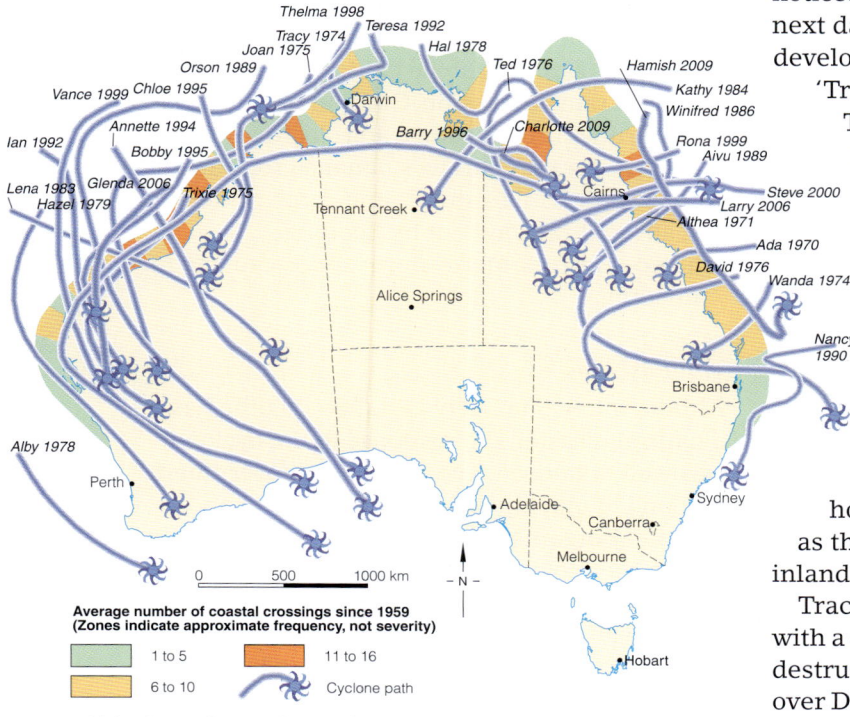

*Major Australian cyclones since 1970*

# Tropical Cyclone Tracy, Northern Territory, December 1974

On 20 December 1974, a low pressure system several hundred kilometres north of Darwin was noticed by the Bureau of Meteorology. By late the next day, satellite pictures indicated that it had developed into a tropical cyclone. It was named 'Tracy', and a warning was issued by the Tropical Cyclone Centre in Darwin. Tracy intensified over the next two days as it moved south-west and then curved south-east towards Darwin. The cyclone was tracked continuously by the Bureau of Meteorology at Darwin Airport.

Soon after midnight on Christmas Day, the cyclone approached the city with wind gusts in excess of 100 kilometres per hour, and the destruction of the city began. Tracy passed directly over Darwin. It had wind gusts ranging from 217 to 240 kilometres per hour. Winds were abating in Darwin by 6.30 am as the cyclone weakened and moved further inland and degenerated into a rain depression.

Tracy was a small cyclone in area but very intense, with a central pressure of 950 hectopascals. Its destructive effect was total, because it passed directly over Darwin and hit just as the residents of the city were preparing to enjoy themselves at Christmas.

*Some of the destruction caused by Tropical Cyclone Tracy*

CHAPTER 3 | Natural hazards in Australia

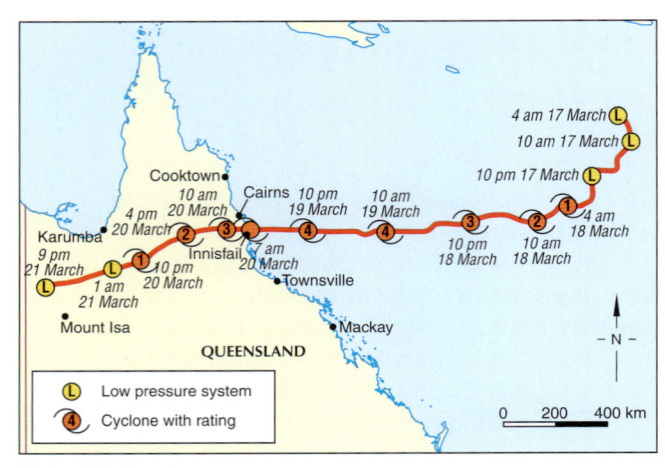

*Path of Cyclone Larry*

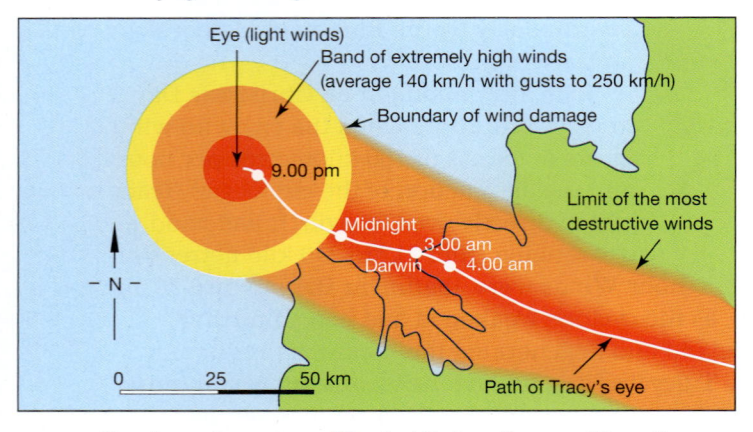

*The size and structure of Tropical Cyclone Tracy and its path over Darwin on 25 December 1974*

## Impacts and responses

Tracy was Australia's most destructive cyclone. It caused the deaths of 65 people — of these, 16 were reported missing at sea. As well, there were 145 serious injuries and over 500 minor injuries. Between 50 and 60 per cent of buildings were damaged beyond repair. Damage from the cyclone was over $4180 million in today's estimates. Following the cyclone, more than 35 000 people had to be evacuated — few of them still had homes, there were no essential services and the threat of disease was a major problem.

Many people reacted heroically, working at great risk to rescue trapped people. Government response included the provision of emergency services and the building of a new Darwin — one that should be better able to withstand any future tropical cyclones. After Tropical Cyclone Tracy, new building codes were introduced. Roofs for new houses had to be tied to the foundations, and cladding was required to protect homes from flying debris.

# Tropical Cyclone Larry, Queensland, March 2006

Cyclone Larry began as a low pressure system over the Coral Sea. On the morning of 20 March 2006, the cyclone crossed the north Queensland coast near Innisfail. It brought with it winds of up to 300 kilometres per hour and a path of destruction, but no deaths. The category 5 cyclone reduced much of the Innisfail area to rubble before it deteriorated into a tropical rain depression. Other impacts included:

- powerlines brought down and electricity supply lost
- 80 per cent of Australia's banana crops and 20 per cent of Australia's sugar cane crops ruined
- roads and railways cut by flooding
- a two- to three-metre storm surge, causing further flooding.

## Responses

Although Cyclone Larry certainly qualified as a natural disaster, the response to the cyclone was well organised. The Australian government responded quickly with army personnel and volunteer organisations placed on standby even before the cyclone struck. Food, water, medical supplies, fuel, tarpaulins, generators and aircraft were organised for the rescue, evacuation and later rebuilding efforts. Australians also rallied with donations totalling almost $20 million within two months of the disaster.

*Satellite image of Cyclone Larry crossing the Queensland coast at 7.30 am, 20 March 2006*

Innisfail High School, 20 March 2006

## ACTIVITIES

### UNDERSTANDING

1. Define the term *tropical cyclone*.
2. Outline why tropical cyclones usually die out if they move inland.
3. Make a simple drawing showing the movement of winds around a tropical cyclone.
4. List the effects or impacts of a tropical cyclone when it crosses the coast.

### THINKING AND APPLYING

5. Tracy was only a small cyclone in area. Why do you think it caused so much damage?
6. Research the US government's response to Hurricane Katrina. Why do you think they failed to respond as promptly and with as much planning and organisation as the Queensland and federal governments did in the case of Larry?

### USING YOUR SKILLS

7. Refer to the map on page 75 showing major Australian cyclones since 1970 and briefly describe the path of the following three cyclones: (a) Annette, (b) Rona, (c) Hamish.
8. Refer to the map on the opposite page showing Tropical Cyclone Tracy's size, structure and path over Darwin.
   a. What was the general direction of Tracy's path over Darwin?
   b. How wide was the belt of extremely high winds?
   c. About how far did Tracy travel from midnight to 4.00 am?
9. Refer to the satellite image of Cyclone Larry on page 76. Describe its location and appearance. Use an atlas to list six coastal settlements other than Innisfail that you would expect to be directly affected.
10. Compare the photo of Innisfail High School with the photo of destruction after Cyclone Tracy. What similarities can you see?

### GEOTERMS

**tropical cyclone:** a severe weather event that occurs where warm, moist rising air begins to spiral upwards. Tropical cyclones are often accompanied by very strong winds, heavy rain and rough seas.

CHAPTER 3 | Natural hazards in Australia

# 3.11 Floods as natural hazards

Even though Australia is the driest of all the world's inhabited continents and has the lowest percentage of rainfall as run-off, there are periods of very heavy rainfall and **floods**. A flood is an unusual accumulation of water that overflows from rivers, lakes or the ocean onto land that is not normally covered by water.

## Types of floods

There are three main types of flood:

1. *Slow-onset floods*. These occur along the flood plains of inland rivers, such as the Darling and Namoi, and may last for weeks and even months. They are caused by heavy rain and run-off upstream, and the water can take days and even weeks to affect farms and towns downstream. The Great Floods of 1990 are an example of a slow-onset flood (see the Geofacts panel opposite).
2. *Rapid-onset floods*. These occur in mountain headwater areas of larger inland rivers or rivers flowing to the coast. The rivers are steeper and the water flows more rapidly. Rapid-onset floods are often more damaging because there is less time to prepare.
3. *Flash floods*. These occur due to heavy rainfall of short duration, such as in a severe thunderstorm. This type of flooding causes the greatest risk of property damage and loss of life as it can happen so quickly. It can be a serious problem in urban areas where drainage systems are inadequate.

**GEOfacts** The Great Floods of 1990 in eastern Australia during April and May covered more than one million square kilometres of Queensland and New South Wales. In both states there was extensive damage to transport links and severe loss of stock. Many towns were invaded by floodwaters, and communities were isolated for long periods.

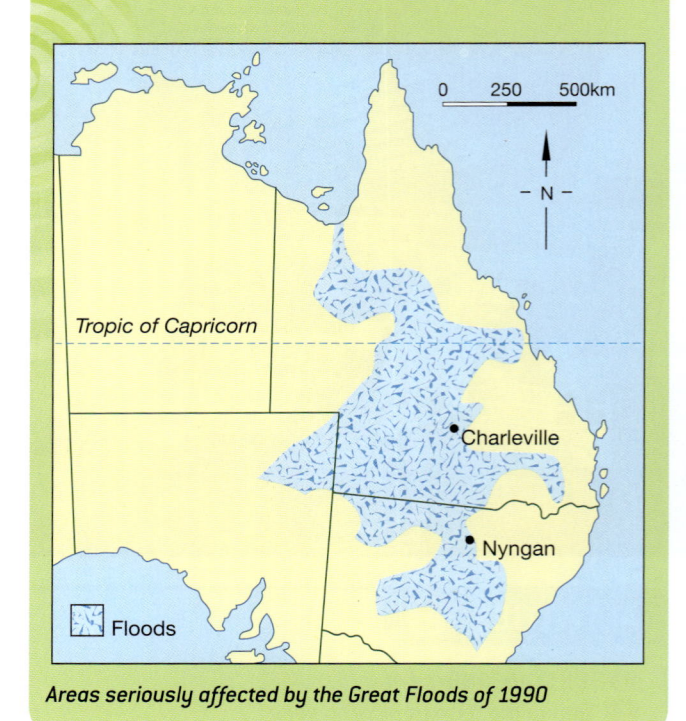

*Areas seriously affected by the Great Floods of 1990*

◀ Rivers begin in mountains. The force of water rushing down the steep slopes erodes vertically and carries the material away. Mountain river valleys are steep-sided and 'V'-shaped.

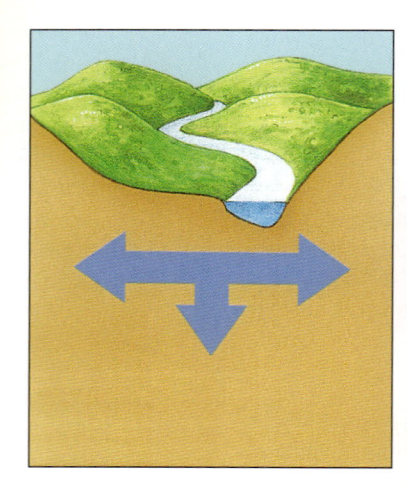

◀ A river is in the valley section when it reaches lower land downstream from the mountains. The valleys are deeper but wider as the river erodes both the floor and sides of the valley.

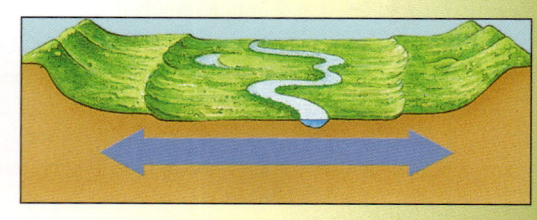

▲ On the flood plain, the stream erodes horizontally causing a river valley that is broad and flat. The river can no longer hold all the sediment it carries and deposits material to form flood plains and deltas.

*The life of a river*

## Floods and flood plains

Floods are a natural occurrence, but they are a natural hazard to humans who have built farms, towns and transport routes in areas, such as **flood plains**, which are subject to flooding. A flood plain is an area of relatively flat land that borders a river and is covered by water during a flood. Flood plains are formed when the speed of the water in the river slows down on flatter areas. The river begins to meander and gradually deposits **alluvium**. During this process, a flood plain and other landforms such as deltas are built up by the river. These fertile, flat areas have become favoured for farming and settlement around the world. In Australia many of our richest farming areas are on flood plains. There are many towns in Australia that have been built on flood plains close to rivers. Parts of many towns are still located on flood plains and are subject to flooding.

Floods are not confined to flood plains. If there is sufficient volume of water, they can occur in the lower parts of valleys and even on hill slopes during periods of torrential rain.

## La Niña and floods

A La Niña event in Australia is often associated with floods. La Niña translates from Spanish as 'the girl child'. A La Niña event is indicated by a rise in the Southern Oscillation Index to well into the positive (see the diagram of El Niño and the SOI, page 60). La Niña is virtually the opposite of El Niño. Very cold waters dominate the eastern Pacific, and the oceans off Australia are warmer than normal. Large areas of low pressure extend over much of Australia; warm, moist air moves in and above average rainfall occurs. There can also be torrential rain and widespread floods.

Recent La Niña events in Australia occurred in 1998 and 2007–08 when many parts of coastal Queensland and New South Wales were flooded. The flooding of the Richmond River occurred during the 2007–08 La Niña.

*The flat, fertile lands of the river flood plain are favoured areas for farming and settlement. The newer parts of towns are often built above the flood plain.*

Northern New South Wales was declared a natural disaster area in January 2008 when severe thunderstorms caused extensive flooding in Coraki in the Richmond River valley. The valley floods rapidly when very heavy rain falls in the watershed of the Richmond River.

## Weather systems and floods

The flooding of streams is caused by a number of factors, the most important being a high intensity of rainfall into a catchment or drainage basin. High-intensity rains may occur as a result of:
- *storms* — thunderstorms, tropical cyclones or rain depressions (the remains of tropical cyclones after they have moved inland)
- *low pressure systems* that cross Australia in the cooler months, including those associated with cold fronts and east coast depressions.

**Cold fronts** can bring heavy rainfall to southern Australia, particularly during winter and spring. East coast depressions can bring heavy rain to the coast of New South Wales in autumn and winter.

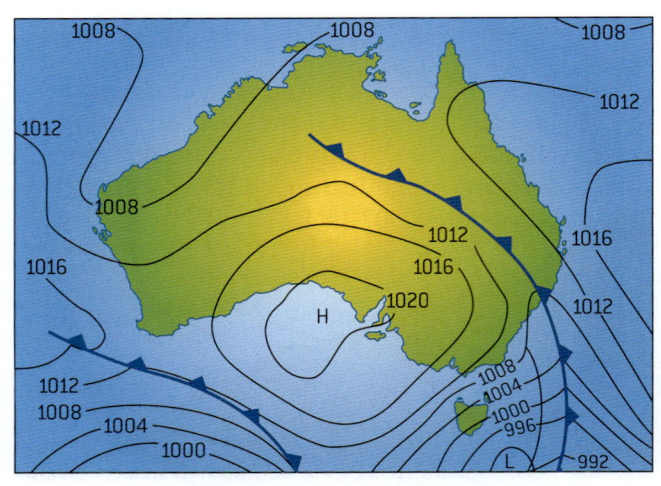

*Cold fronts move from west to east across southern Australia, bringing cooler weather and rain.*

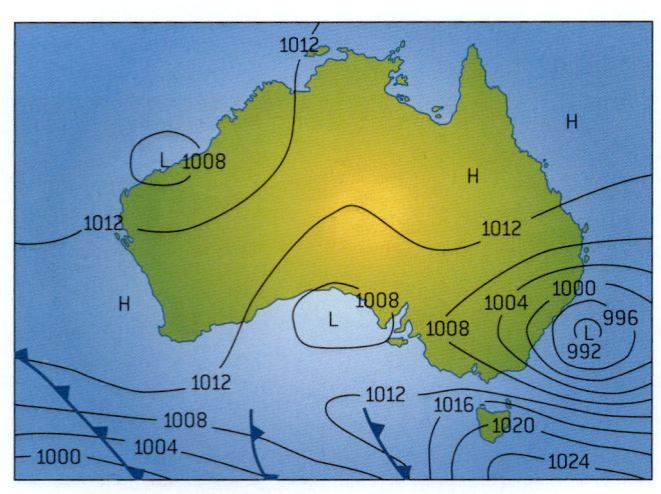

*East coast depressions form off the coast of New South Wales and can bring heavy rain and flooding.*

The possibility of flood is also increased when vegetation in catchment areas has been cleared or modified. Native vegetation can slow down the run-off and reduce the chance of flooding.

## GEOskills TOOLBOX

### FLOW CHARTS AND DIAGRAMS

Flow charts are a useful diagrammatic tool showing the steps in a process and how they fit together.

A well-constructed flow chart builds step by step to define and analyse a process or cause and effects. Boxes, circles and arrows can be used in a horizontal or vertical arrangement.

The chart should be kept simple so that the main ideas or steps are easily seen.

Flow charts can also be pictorial, such as the flow chart showing the life of a river on page 78.

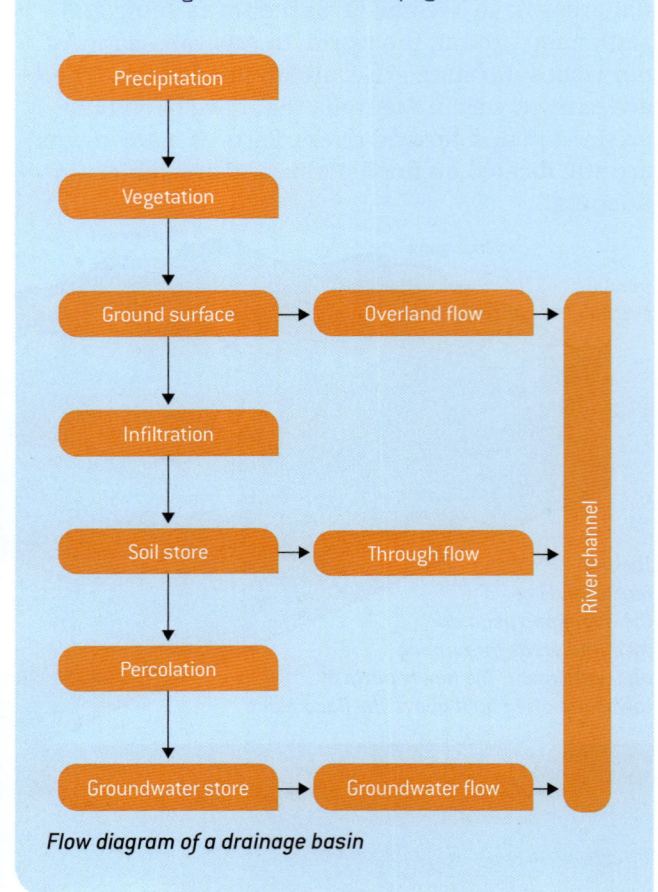

*Flow diagram of a drainage basin*

## Floods and communities

People could be discouraged from farming and living on flood plains but this is not always practical — especially as flood plains provide some of the best areas and soils for farming. Communities can, however, prepare for floods and try to reduce their effects. This is called **flood mitigation**. Flood mitigation programs include artificial levees (as built in Nyngan, see page 88) to protect low-lying urban areas from flooding, strengthening bridges, raising road levels and constructing large drains to move floodwaters more rapidly.

### Floods in northern and outback Queensland 2009

The biggest wet in living memory swamped over 60 per cent of Queensland from the Gulf of Carpentaria into South Australia when rain fell over a two-month period from early January 2009. The rain was the result of a severe monsoon season. Climate change scientists say we can expect such events to happen more often in the future. Communities like Bedourie (pictured) and Birdsville were cut off, thousands of cattle were drowned or starved, and crops were ruined. Damage to roads exceeded $65 million. The floods also brought an end to a long crippling drought and will ensure good seasons for the cattle industry. As a result of the floods in the Georgina and Diamantina rivers and Eyre Creek, water flowed into Lake Eyre, almost filling it. It last filled in 1989.

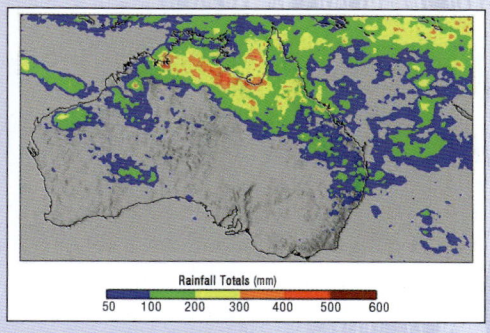

*Multi-satellite analysis showing rainfall across Australia from 24 December 2008 to 7 January 2009*

*The settlement of Bedourie in Queensland's Channel Country sits in flooded isolation in February 2009.*

## ACTIVITIES

### UNDERSTANDING

1. Define the term *flood*.
2. What are the three main types of floods?
3. Outline the main causes of high-intensity rainfall in Australia.
4. Describe the actions that can be taken by communities to reduce the impact of floods.

### THINKING AND APPLYING

5. What is La Niña? Why are floods often associated with a La Niña event? To find out more, use the **Flood** weblink in your eBookPLUS.
6. Explain why floods occur on flood plains and in deltas.

### USING YOUR SKILLS

7. Refer to the flow diagram of the life of a river on page 78.
    a. How are river valleys formed?
    b. How are flood plains and deltas formed?
8. Construct a simple flow diagram to show the process of a La Niña event.
9. Read the sample study on the floods in Queensland in 2009 and answer the following questions.
    a. Refer to the photograph of the flooded community. What type of photograph is this? Describe the scene.
    b. Refer to the satellite image. Which parts of Australia were affected by the monsoonal rain?

### GEOTERMS

**cold front:** a surface where a cooler air mass meets a warmer mass, into which it is advancing

**flood:** an unusual accumulation of water that overflows from rivers, lakes and the ocean onto land that is not normally covered by water

CHAPTER 3 | Natural hazards in Australia

# 3.12 GEOskillbuilder

## Research and presentation: earthquakes in Australia

One of the most important skills in geography is to research a given topic and then present your research in an interesting and informative way.

The topic below is one that geography teachers love to set as an assignment because it means you have to look at both sides of the issue.

### Research and present a topic

The clue for this assignment is the word *discuss*. In other words, you first have to find some information that supports the view that a major Australian city will suffer a major earthquake; then you must find some information that says the opposite. At the end of it all, you have to give your opinion, based on the information you have found.

For a topic like this one, other useful places to find information are:

1. a good atlas, to show plate boundaries and Australia's location
2. some good reference books to find out what causes earthquakes and whether Australian cities have experienced them in the past
3. journal or magazine articles such as those in *Australian Geographic* or *National Geographic*. Your librarian can help you to use an index system for magazines and journals.

> Discuss the likelihood of a large earthquake striking a major Australian city in the next 100 years.

### STEP 1

#### RESEARCH

Use a variety of sources to find your information. The internet is a good place to find a lot of information quickly, but you need to make sure it's reliable. This is because anyone can publish material on the internet without having to prove what they are saying. Much of this information can be wrong.

Two useful techniques when using the internet for research are:

1. Use at least four different sites to check your information (this is called **cross-checking**).
2. Try to find educational (edu.) or government (gov.) sites. For example, a reliable site for researching this topic is www.ga.gov.au.

82 Geoactive 2

### STEP 2

**ORGANISE YOUR INFORMATION**

This is a most important step. Sometimes students leave it out because they run out of time. However, their final assignment can suffer as a result. It is important because this is where you sort out your information. A good way to do this is to use a table like the one on the right. Add notes around your table, as in the example given, to remind yourself of what you have to do.

Use visual material of previous earthquakes.

Check atlas to find distance to nearest boundary edge.

Check facts with my teacher.

| Evidence FOR a major earthquake | Evidence AGAINST a major earthquake |
|---|---|
| • We have had earthquakes before, e.g. Newcastle, 1989. 13 dead. | • Most earthquakes occur on plate boundaries. |
| • Australia has many fault lines. | • Australia is a long way from a plate boundary. |
| • Any earthquake would be devastating because Australia is poorly prepared for one. | • Australia is such a big country that even if we did have an earthquake it probably wouldn't strike a major city. |
| • Not all of the world's earthquakes occur on plate boundaries. | • We have many small earthquakes and these relieve pressure in the crust. |
| • Maybe the pressure is building up. | |

Use a labelled map (with key) to demonstrate this for known major earthquakes over last century. Check internet and library references for earthquake details.

Find other supporting references to back this up.

### STEP 3

**PRESENTATION**

There are many ways to present information in an interesting way, such as a PowerPoint presentation, a series of 'television' interviews, a newspaper spread or an oral presentation. However, a particularly useful style of presentation that geographers use is an **annotated visual display** (AVD). A typical example is shown here.

You can write directly onto the card or stick paper onto it.

Break your information down into several sections rather than having lots of writing.

Spread your maps and photos out to make the presentation interesting.

Don't forget your list of references. If there are lots of references, you can put them on the back.

Remember for every map:
**B**order,
**O**rientation,
**L**egend,
**T**itle,
**S**cale and
**S**ource.

Use a large, coloured piece of card from the newsagent for your backing.

---

### ACTIVITIES

1. What do you have to do if an assignment question asks you to 'discuss' an issue?
2. Explain why you have to be careful about material you find on the internet. What are two useful things you should do if using the internet for factual research?
3. Explain in your own words the meaning of the term 'annotated visual display'.
4. Use the techniques outlined on these two pages to research and present information on one of these topics:
   a Discuss the likelihood of a severe cyclone occurring along the east coast of Australia that could damage towns and cities.
   b Bushfires are impossible to prevent in Australia's unique physical environment. Explain.

# 3.13 Natural hazards: earthquakes

**Earthquakes** are shakings of the ground that are generated by disturbances in the Earth's crust.

## What causes earthquakes?

Scientists now believe that the Earth is made up of a series of layers.

The mantle, which makes up the bulk of the Earth's interior, is semi-molten. This means that it is a very slow-moving liquid. It circulates slowly between the very hot inner core (3700° Celsius) and the very cold outer crust (as cold as 0°). The crust on which we live is very thin and brittle. Over the last few billion years it has broken up into a series of huge plates (called tectonic plates). These fit together like a giant jigsaw puzzle. Because the plates float on the mantle, they move. This movement is what scientists believe causes an earthquake.

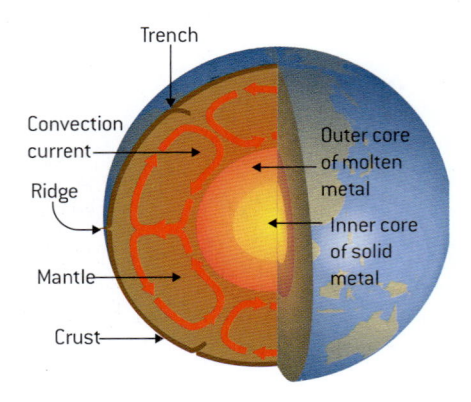

*The structure of the Earth is a bit like an apple: it has a core at the centre and a thin crust (skin) on the outside.*

About 95 per cent of all earthquakes occur where two plates push together or rub past each other. New Zealand, Japan and California sit on the edges of two or more plates, while Australia sits much more safely in the middle of a plate.

Earthquakes are unpredictable and strike without warning. They range in strength from slight tremors to severe shocks and can last from just a few seconds to as long as several days. All earthquakes have a focus, which is the area underground where the Earth's crust has snapped, sending shock waves to the surface. The point on the Earth's surface above the focus is called the **epicentre**. This is where the greatest amount of damage occurs. From the epicentre, shock waves radiate out like ripples in a pond (see the following diagram). The shocks are less intense the further they are from the epicentre.

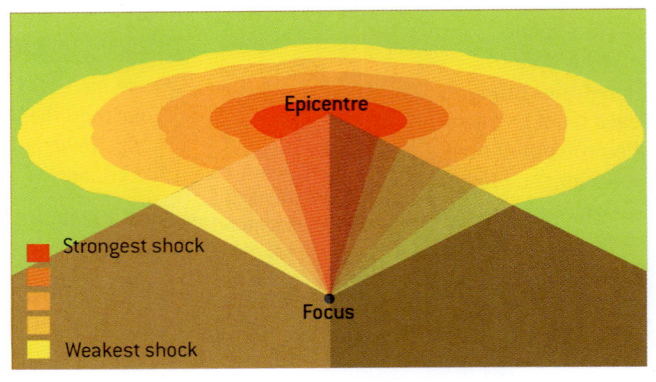

*The focus and epicentre of an earthquake*

## Measuring earthquakes

Earthquakes are measured according to their magnitude and intensity. Magnitude (or energy released by an earthquake) is measured by the **Richter scale**. This scale is open-ended as there is no upper limit to the amount of energy an earthquake might release. The most severe earthquakes so far have not exceeded 9.5 on this scale. An increase of 1.0 on the scale indicates 30 times greater magnitude. For example, the energy released at a magnitude of 6.0 is 30 times greater than the energy released at 5.0.

The intensity of an earthquake is measured on the Modified Mercalli scale. It rates the amount of damage caused and uses Roman numerals at each level (see the diagram on the opposite page). The intensity varies according to such factors as the nature of buildings and the time of day. Intensity can vary for any given earthquake whereas magnitude does not.

> **GEOfacts** Since the start of the twentieth century, there have been only 18 earthquakes in Australia measuring 6.0 or more on the Richter scale. This rate of occurrence of fewer than one every five years contrasts with a world average of about 140 major earthquakes per year.

## Impact of earthquakes

An earthquake can cause massive damage. Buildings can be demolished; electricity and telephone lines cut; and gas, sewer and water mains can be damaged. Landslides, subsidence and tsunamis can also be triggered. Most injuries and deaths result from falling objects and debris in and around buildings.

| Modified Mercalli scale | II | III | IV | V | V–VI | VI | VII–VIII | IX–XII |
|---|---|---|---|---|---|---|---|---|
| Reaction of people and buildings | Not felt by people generally. Just recordable by seismograph. | A few people indoors notice a slight vibration. | Sleeping persons wake. Hanging items like lamps swing. | Things indoors fall over. | Old buildings suffer considerable damage — houses generally some damage. | Houses suffer damage. A few collapse. | Most houses damaged heavily or collapse. | Houses everywhere collapse. Complete destruction. |

*The Modified Mercalli scale*

## Australia's risk areas

Earthquakes happen a lot in some places, and hardly at all in other places. We are fortunate in Australia because, unlike many other countries in the world, earthquake activity here is low. In fact, until the Newcastle earthquake in 1989, most people thought that earthquakes were not a serious natural hazard in Australia.

Our most severe earthquakes have usually occurred in unpopulated areas, but several have caused damage in urban areas and others have come very close. For example, an earthquake occurred near Sydney on 17 March 1999. The epicentre was near the town of Wilton, in the Southern Highlands between Sydney and Goulburn. The earthquake measured 4.7 on the Richter scale, not quite strong enough to cause structural damage. However, power was cut for over an hour, dams and pipelines were inspected for cracks, and coalmines were evacuated.

*The San Francisco earthquake of 1906 killed over 3000 people and made more than half the population homeless, as 28 000 buildings were destroyed — mainly by fire.*

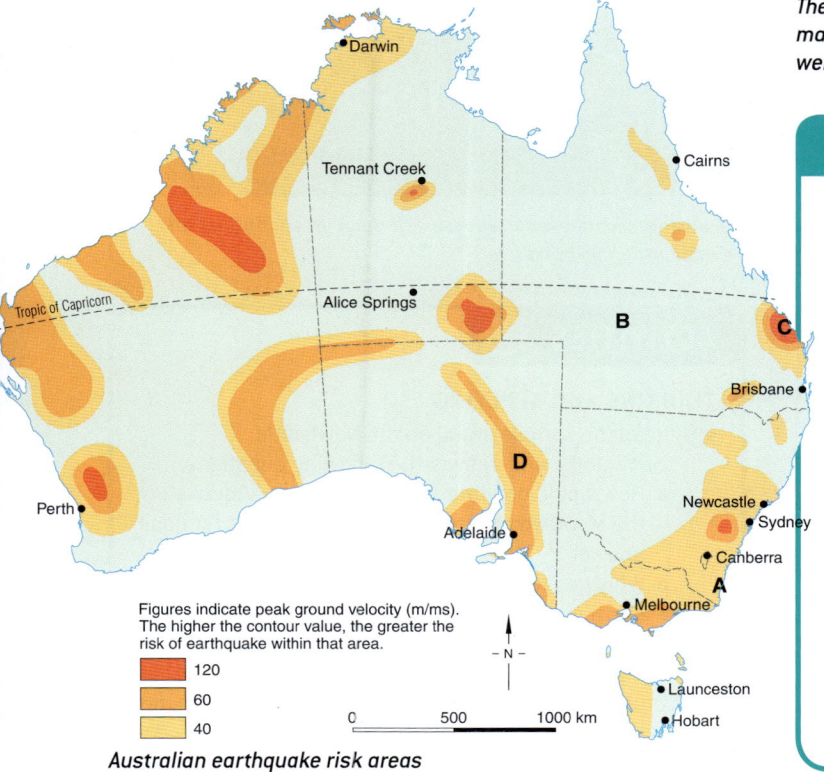

### ACTIVITIES

#### UNDERSTANDING

1. Define the term *earthquake*.
2. Explain the difference between the Richter scale and the Modified Mercalli scale.
3. How much greater is the magnitude of an earthquake of 8.0 on the Richter scale than one of 7.0?
4. Describe the damage caused by earthquakes with the following measurements on the Modified Mercalli scale: **a** II **b** V **c** VI **d** IX–X.

#### USING YOUR SKILLS

5. Refer to the map of Australian earthquake risk areas on the left and the locations marked A, B, C and D.
   **a** List these locations in order of highest to lowest earthquake risk.
   **b** Locate where you live on the map. How great is the risk where you live?

*Australian earthquake risk areas*

Figures indicate peak ground velocity (m/ms). The higher the contour value, the greater the risk of earthquake within that area.
- 120
- 60
- 40

CHAPTER 3 | Natural hazards in Australia | 85

## SAMPLE STUDY

### Newcastle earthquake, 28 December 1989

A killer earthquake occurred in Australia without warning at 10.27 am on 28 December 1989, smashing into the city of Newcastle. Although it was only a moderate earthquake, with a magnitude of 5.6 on the Richter scale, the shock waves were felt up to 500 kilometres away, across more than one-quarter of New South Wales. In Sydney, 160 kilometres to the south, there were reports of house wall cracks and computer screens trembling in city skyscrapers.

### Impacts of the earthquake

It was the first earthquake since European settlement in Australia to cause fatalities. There were 13 deaths. Nine people were crushed when a large section of the Newcastle Workers Club collapsed, three were killed when shopfronts collapsed in Beaumont Street, and one person died from shock. More than 160 people were injured. The loss of life could have been much greater if the earthquake had struck during school term and not the Christmas holidays. More than 40 schools suffered structural damage, some so badly that they had to be demolished. More than 50 000 buildings were moderately to seriously damaged. The total cost of damage was more than $4 billion, and the event caused the largest insured loss due to disasters in Australian history at that time.

There was unusually extensive damage for such a relatively small magnitude earthquake. This unusual damage was due to an underlying thin layer of silt and sand, covering a former course of the Hunter River and a swamp. This appeared to magnify the shaking or ground motion.

### Response to the earthquake

Due to the extent of the damage in such a low seismic risk area, seismic activity is now closely monitored. Since 1994, regulations have required that all buildings must be constructed to withstand earthquakes.

*The epicentre and seismic aftershocks*

*The earthquake caused irreparable damage to shopfronts and other commercial buildings.*

## ACTIVITIES

### THINKING AND APPLYING

1. Read the sample study on the Newcastle earthquake and answer the following questions.
   a. How would you rate the Newcastle earthquake on the Modified Mercalli scale? Give reasons for your answer.
   b. Why was there so much damage when the earthquake measured only 5.6 on the Richter scale?
   c. Using information in the sample study and the photograph, describe the impact of the Newcastle earthquake.

### GEOTERMS

**earthquakes:** shakings of the ground that are generated by disturbances in the Earth's crust

**epicentre:** the point on the Earth's surface directly above the focus of an earthquake

# Working geographically

## BROADSHEET: NYNGAN FLOOD

**KNOWLEDGE AND UNDERSTANDING**

Select the alternative that best answers the question.

Refer to the rainfall graph.

1. In which month does Nyngan normally experience its highest rainfall?
   - (A) January
   - (B) February
   - (C) April
   - (D) October

2. How much rain was recorded at Nyngan in April 1990?
   - (A) 30 millilitres
   - (B) 60 millilitres
   - (C) 375 millilitres
   - (D) 600 millilitres

Refer to the map showing rainfall depths.

3. The highest rainfall during April 1990 was recorded to the:
   - (A) east of Nyngan
   - (B) west of Nyngan
   - (C) south-west of Nyngan
   - (D) south-east of Nyngan.

4. In April 1990 how much rainfall did the town of Tottenham receive?
   - (A) 350 millimetres
   - (B) Between 300 and 350 millimetres
   - (C) 300 millimetres
   - (D) Between 250 and 300 millimetres

Refer to the map of flood warning stations and the table.

5. Where was the flood volume greatest?
   - (A) Nyngan
   - (B) Neurie Plains
   - (C) Dandaloo
   - (D) Peak Hill

6. A discharge of 1610 m$^3$/s was recorded:
   - (A) at Nyngan
   - (B) 90 kilometres from Nyngan
   - (C) 155 kilometres from Nyngan
   - (D) 370 kilometres from Nyngan.

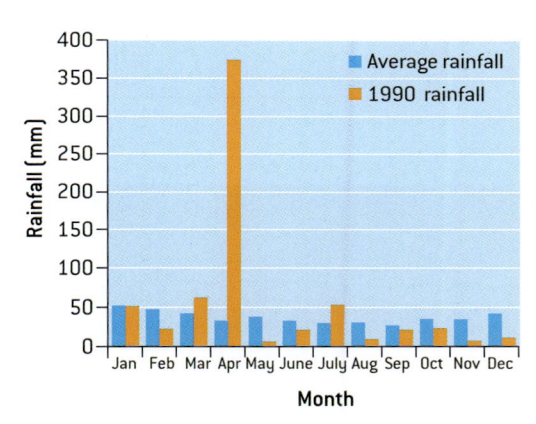

*Graph of Nyngan rainfall*

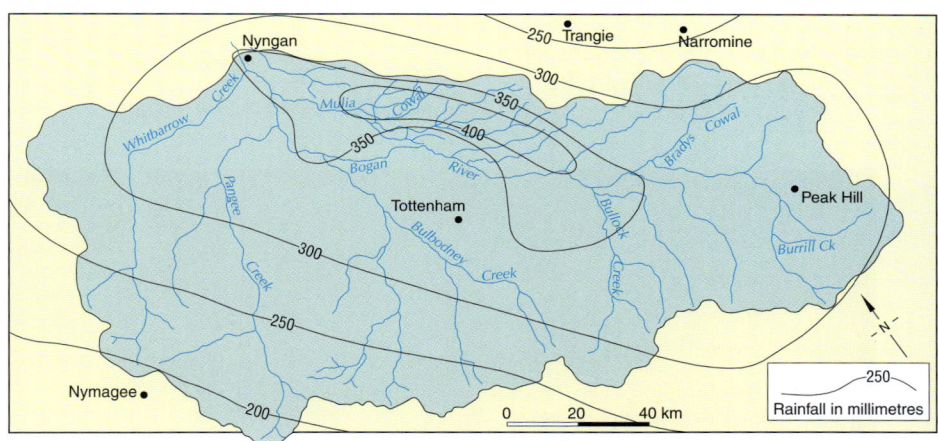

*Nyngan catchment rainfall depths, April 1990*

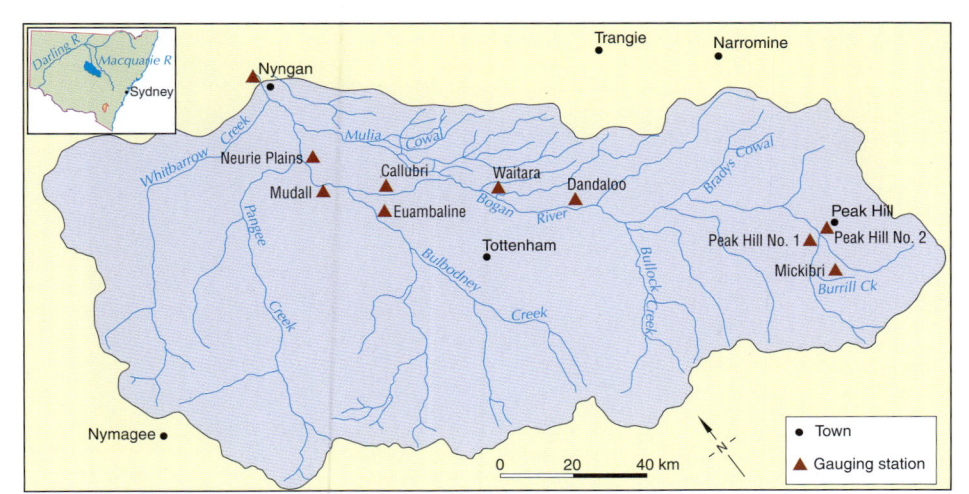

*Location of flood warning stations in the Nyngan catchment. Inset map shows catchment location.*

*Nyngan location map*

**Peak discharges (cubic metres per second), April 1990**

| Peak Hill | 344 |
|---|---|
| Dandaloo | 1610 |
| Neurie Plains | 678 |
| Nyngan | 2080 |

CHAPTER 3 | Natural hazards in Australia

**Refer to the aerial photograph and map of levee breaches.**

7. A levee is a bank that protects an area from flooding. Most floodwater flowed over or through levees to the:
   (A) north of Nyngan
   (B) south of Nyngan
   (C) east of Nyngan
   (D) west of Nyngan.

8. Which feature runs along the top of one levee?
   (A) The railway line
   (B) Dandaloo Street
   (C) The airport
   (D) The racecourse

## SHORT RESPONSE

**Refer to the map of Nyngan and other resources.**

9. Describe the area subject to flooding shown on the map.
10. Suggest two reasons why Nyngan received the worst flooding in the region.
11. Find two examples of transport routes cut by the April 1990 floods in Nyngan.

*Map of levee breaches in Nyngan*

*Aerial photograph of Nyngan in flood, 24 April 1990*

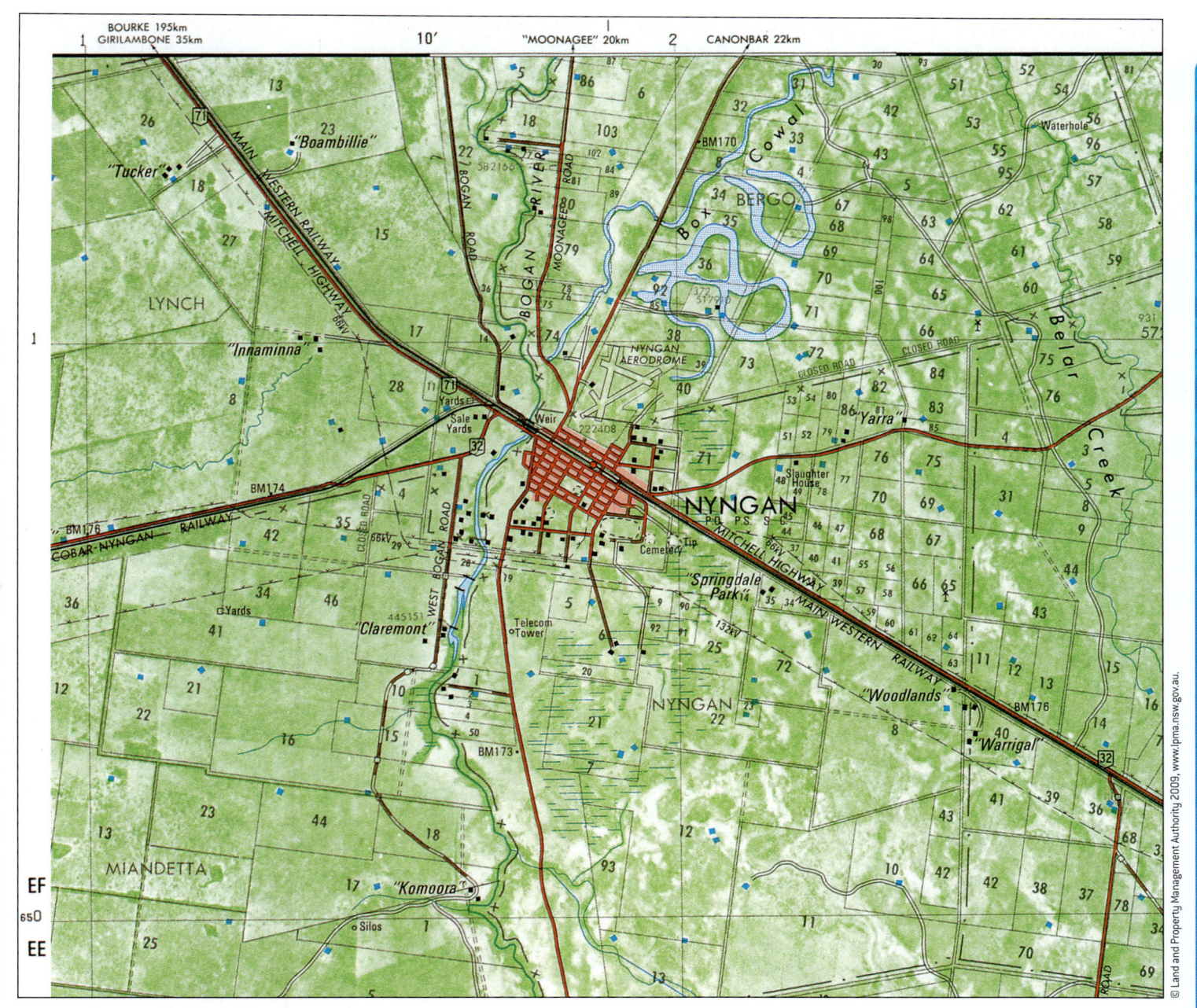

Topographic map of Nyngan

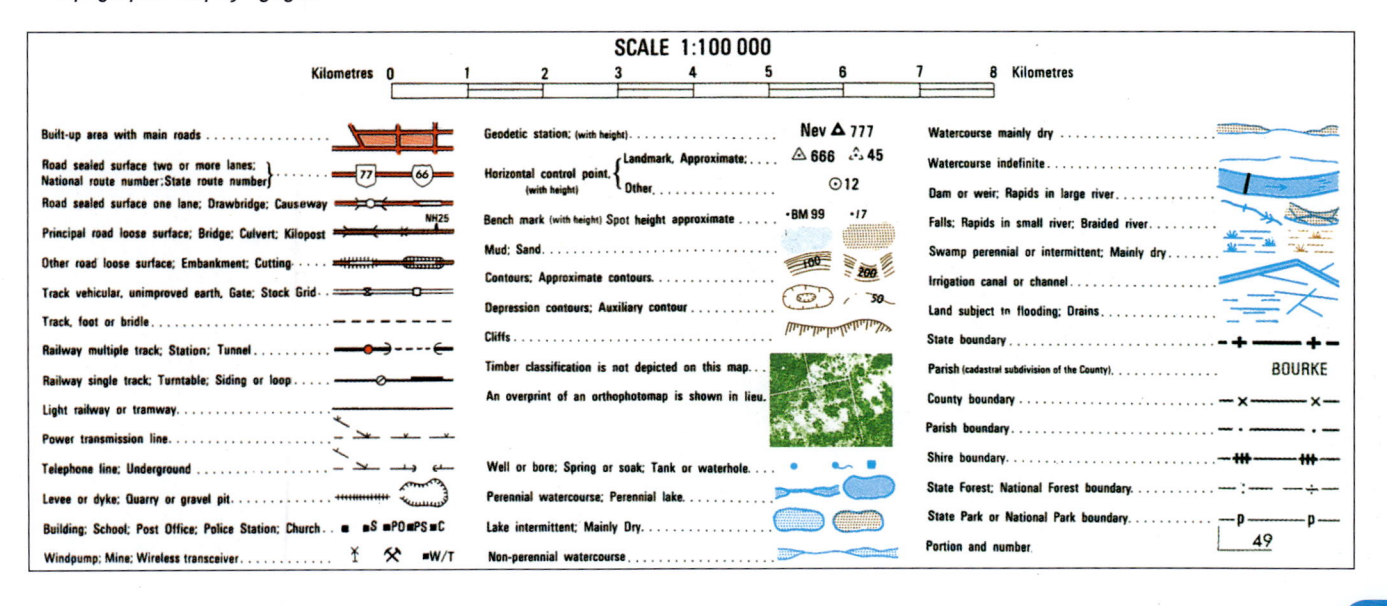

**CHAPTER 3** | Natural hazards in Australia

# ICT activities

## projectsplus

## Preparing for an emergency
SEARCHLIGHT ID: PRO-0031

### SCENARIO
You are a member of the advertising and marketing team for EMA (Emergency Management Australia). In light of the recent increased risks of natural hazards in Australia, the federal government has mandated that emergency services brochures must be produced for all major newspapers to provide more detailed information on how the general public should manage risks and respond to specific natural hazards.

The brief provided by the Attorney-General's Department outlines that the Australian public has become too comfortable with the risks associated with natural hazards. Research has also found that there are varying messages provided by different states and territories on how to respond to a specific hazard. The brochure must therefore provide a clear message that can be used in each state and territory. It must also be general enough to cater for a wide and varied audience.

### YOUR TASK
Create an emergency services brochure that provides information on how to prepare for and manage the risk of a specific natural hazard in Australia. Your brochure should include images, artwork, statistics and ideas. Your aim is to educate the general public in an interesting way.

Your choice of natural hazards in Australia includes:
- a tropical cyclone in northern Australia (e.g. Cairns)
- a bushfire on the rural–urban fringe of a major city (e.g. Sydney or Brisbane)
- an earthquake in an urban area (e.g. Newcastle)
- a severe thunderstorm in an urban area (e.g. Melbourne)
- drought in an urban area (e.g. Sydney, Brisbane, Melbourne or Adelaide)
- drought in a farming community (e.g. Mildura, the Darling Downs or western New South Wales).

### PROCESS
- Open the ProjectsPLUS application for this chapter, located in your eBookPLUS. Watch the introductory video lesson and then click the 'Start Project' button to set up your project group. You can complete this project individually or invite other members of your class to form a group. Save your settings and the project will be launched.

Your ProjectsPLUS application is available in this chapter's Student Resources tab inside your eBookPLUS. Visit www.jacplus.com.au to locate your digital resources.

**SUGGESTED SOFTWARE**
- ProjectsPLUS
- Photoshop
- Microsoft Publisher or InDesign

- Navigate to your Media Centre and use the weblinks provided to view a series of old community service announcements. These should give you an idea of the type of information that you need to include in your brochure.
- Navigate to your Research Forum where your choice of natural hazards has been pre-loaded as topics. Choose a topic for your brochure and delete the others. Begin your research by considering what information the general public will need to know — for example, what the hazard is, why it occurs, what risks are associated with it, and how and when they will need to respond to the hazard. Remember that you are developing an informative resource for a very specific section of the community; farmers, people from urban areas and those on the rural–urban fringe all have different needs and are all affected differently by these hazards. Enter your findings as articles in the Research Forum. You can view and comment on other group members' articles and rate the information they have entered.
- When your research is complete, write the text for your brochure. You might like to include features such as 'Did you know?' or 'Staggering statistics' boxes, but remember that the aim of the brochure is to provide your audience with the important, potentially life-saving, information that could help them in a disaster.
- Navigate to your Media Centre. A selection of images has been provided for you to download and use in your brochure. You may also choose to take some of your own photographs or source other images. Don't forget to record the source of any image you use as you always need to credit other people's work.
- Plan the design of your brochure and think about the visual appeal. Consider the font to be used and your headings.
- Create your brochure using Microsoft Publisher or InDesign. If you don't have either of these programs, you could create your brochure in Microsoft Word.
- Print out your research report from ProjectsPLUS and hand it in to your teacher with your brochure.

**MEDIA CENTRE**

Your Media Centre contains:
- images to use in your brochure
- weblinks to research sites and other community service advertisements
- an assessment rubric.

## Interactivity

### LABEL: 'AUSTRALIAN LANDFORMS'

This interactive Label game will test your ability to identify and correctly name common Australian landforms. You will race against the clock to drag the labels to their correct position on the image. Be careful because any wrong moves will lose you time, but get them right and you'll receive a bonus chunk.

SEARCHLIGHT ID: INT-0776

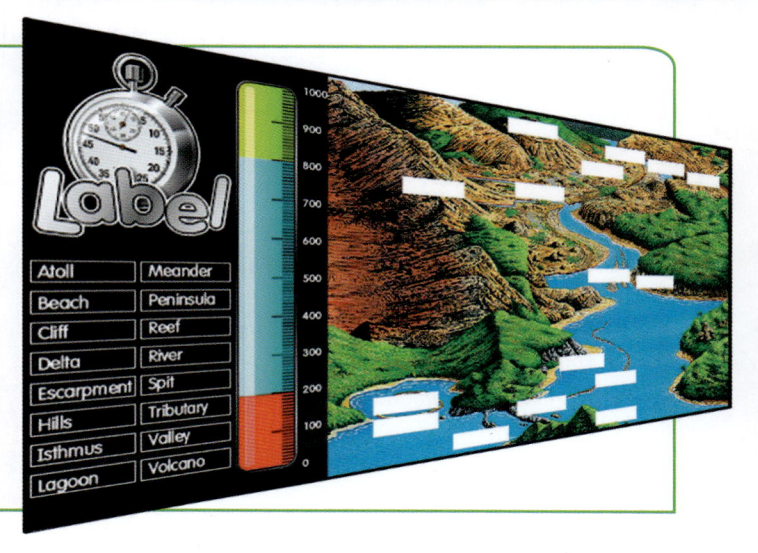

**CHAPTER 3** | Natural hazards in Australia

# 4 Australia's population

**INQUIRY QUESTIONS**

+ How is the population of Australia changing?
+ Where do people live?
+ How have Australia's demographic characteristics influenced the nature and identity of Australian society?

Although Australia has a population that is small in number, it is even smaller in comparison to its area. However, Australia's population is increasing due to an increase in both the birth rate and immigration rate. While the population is spread over many different physical and human environments, there is a growing tendency for it to be concentrated in coastal and urban areas. As a result, some rural towns are facing decreasing populations and a loss of resources such as schools and hospitals. Planning for future population growth and distribution will help Australia achieve sustainable resource use in the future.

## GEOskills TOOLBOX

**GEOskillbuilder** Constructing a population pyramid (page 101)

+ Calculating population density (page 94)
+ Locating features using latitude and longitude (page 95)
+ Identifying large-scale and small-scale maps (page 96)
+ Working with compound column or bar graphs (page 103)
+ Using flow maps (page 107)

*Australians gather in their tens of thousands to enjoy events such as this cricket match at the Sydney Cricket Ground.*

### KEY TERMS

**Anglo-Celtic:** describes a person whose origin is the British Isles
**census:** the counting of a population, along with details on age, sex, jobs and other relevant information
**crude birth rate:** the number of live births per 1000 population
**crude death rate:** the number of deaths per 1000 population
**demography:** the study of populations, including patterns and trends in population data
**emigration:** the movement of people out of a country
**ethnically diverse:** describes a population composed of people from different ethnic backgrounds or origins
**fertility rate:** the average number of babies born to women during their reproductive years
**immigration:** the movement of people into a country
**Indigenous people:** the descendants of the original inhabitants of an area
**infant mortality rate:** the number of deaths per 1000 babies under one year of age
**interstate migration:** the movement of people from one state of Australia to another
**intrastate migration:** the movement of people from one location to another within a state of Australia
**migration:** the permanent or semi-permanent movement of people from one location to another
**natural increase:** the excess of births over deaths, usually expressed as a percentage
**net overseas migration:** the number of people migrating to a country minus the number of people emigrating to live in other countries; it is expressed as a percentage of the total population
**population density:** the number of people living in a given area, usually a square kilometre
**population pyramid:** set of bar graphs that show the age and sex distribution of a population
**referendum:** a process through which change can be made to the Constitution, in which electors vote on a particular change
**refugee:** a person who, owing to religious persecution or political troubles, seeks shelter or protection in a foreign country
**replacement rate:** a total fertility rate of 2.1. When a population reaches this level, it will remain stable (assuming no immigration or emigration takes place).
**rural settlement:** site where most of the people are engaged in primary industry, such as farming, fishing or mining
**settlement:** a group of people living in one place or location
**standard of living:** the amount of goods and services, mainly food, clothing, housing, education and health, that is available for use in the community per head of population
**sustainable development:** development that meets the needs of the present population without endangering the ability of future generations to meet their own needs
**urban settlement:** site where most of the population is engaged in tertiary industries, such as commerce, administration and transport

# 4.1 Australia's unique character

Australia is the only continent that consists of just one country. It is also the world's driest inhabited continent with a larger proportion of desert than any other continent. Australia has one of the lowest **population densities** in the world. Only a few areas along or near the coasts receive enough rainfall to support a large population. Today, most Australians live in a narrow coastal strip extending from Brisbane to Adelaide. Eighty-six per cent of Australians live in towns that have populations of more than 1000.

Australia is a developed country with busy cities and highly productive farms and mines. It is the world's leading exporter of wool and bauxite (the ore from which aluminium is made). The income from these and other exports has made it possible for most Australians to enjoy a high **standard of living**.

Until 1788 Indigenous people alone occupied Australia. They had lived and prospered in Australia for at least 50 000 years before the first white settlers arrived. Britain settled Australia as a prison colony in 1788 and, as the numbers of British migrants increased, the proportion of Indigenous people in the population decreased. Since 1945, **immigration** — from southern European nations such as Greece and Italy and more recently from Asian nations — has turned Australia into one of the most **ethnically diverse** countries in the world.

Australia's population density

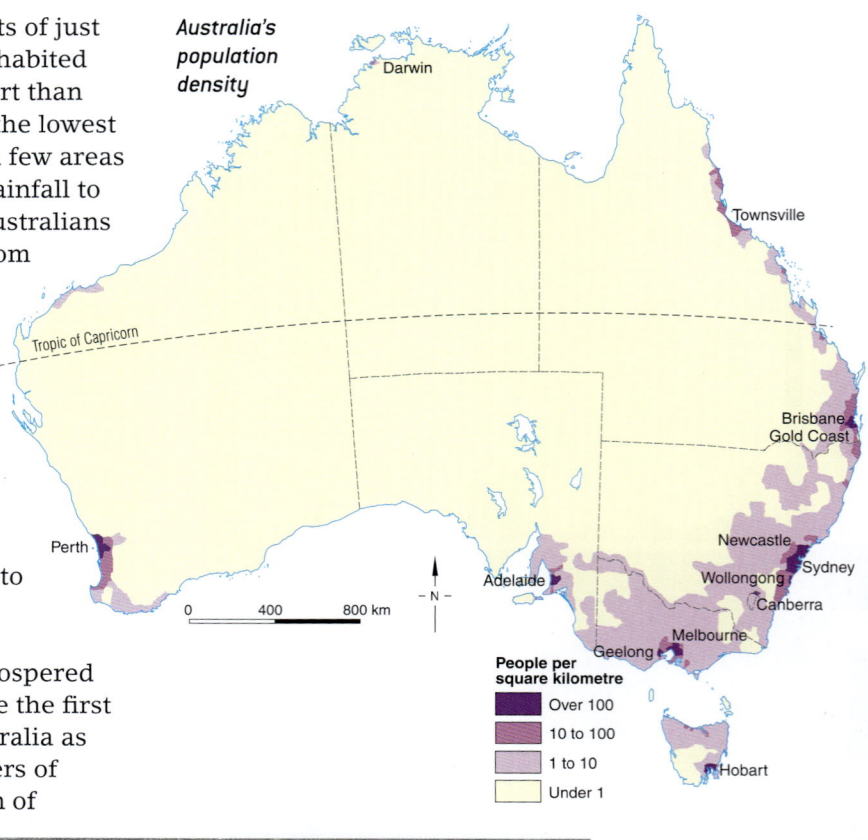

People per square kilometre
- Over 100
- 10 to 100
- 1 to 10
- Under 1

Many Australians live in coastal cities such as Newcastle.

## Where is Australia's population growing?

Much of Australia's population growth occurs in and around towns and cities that have a population of 1000 or more people. The fastest growing areas are generally those on the fringes of capital cities. New suburbs grow into areas that were previously used for farming. As people move into new housing estates, shops are built to cater for their needs. As the population continues to grow, other amenities such as schools, medical services and sporting facilities are built.

### GEOskills TOOLBOX

**CALCULATING POPULATION DENSITY**

Population density is the number of people living in a given area of land — usually one square kilometre. The following formula can be used to work out population density:

$$\text{population density} = \frac{\text{population}}{\text{area}}$$

This means Australia, with a population of 21 million and an area of 8 million square kilometres, has a population density of approximately 2.6.

*Australian settlement*

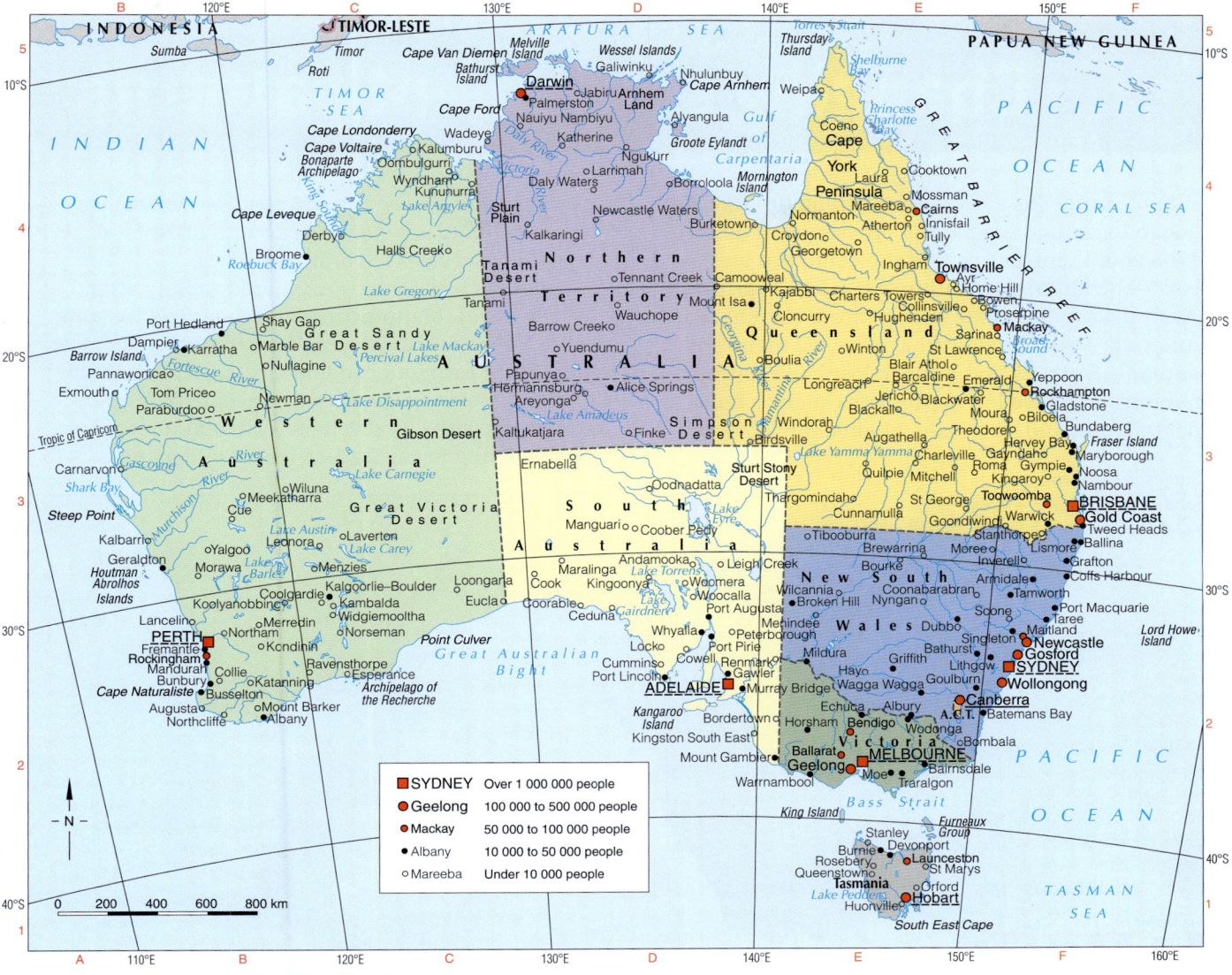

## GEOskills TOOLBOX

### LOCATING FEATURES USING LATITUDE AND LONGITUDE

Latitude and longitude help you pinpoint places with great accuracy. Lines running east–west across a map are called parallels of latitude. They are measured in degrees north and south of the Equator (0° latitude). Lines running north–south on a map are called meridians of longitude. They are measured in degrees east and west of Greenwich, near London (0° longitude).

Latitude is always given before longitude. To give accurate locations, each degree is divided into 60 minutes ('). For example, Sydney is located at 33° and 55' south of the Equator, and 151° and 13' east of the Prime Meridian. An atlas would show this as 33.55s 151.13e.

### GEOTERMS

**ethnically diverse:** describes a population composed of people from different ethnic backgrounds or origins
**immigration:** the movement of people into a country
**population density:** the number of people living in a given area, usually a square kilometre

## ACTIVITIES

### USING YOUR SKILLS

1. Refer to the population density map of Australia on page 94.
   a Where is the most densely populated area?
   b Which areas have a population density higher than 100 people per square kilometre?
   c What do you think the population density of the area shown in the photograph would be?

2. Which part of capital cities are generally growing at the fastest rate?

3. Find the following Australian communities using the Australian settlement map above.
   a 20.02S 140.02E        c 29.28S 149.51E
   b 34.56S 138.36E        d 17.58S 122.14E

4. Give the approximate latitude and longitude for the following Australian communities.
   a Broome (C4)           c Moura (F3)
   b Broken Hill (E2)      d Newman (B3)

CHAPTER 4 | Australia's population

# 4.2 Changing settlement patterns

When Europeans arrived in Australia in 1788, they began to change the natural environment. Before 1788 about nine per cent of the continent was covered with forests. Within 200 years, nearly half of Australia's forest areas disappeared. The changes to Australia's environments have caused many species of plants, animals and birds to lose their natural habitats and have led to problems such as land degradation and decreased biodiversity.

*Stages in European land settlement in Australia*

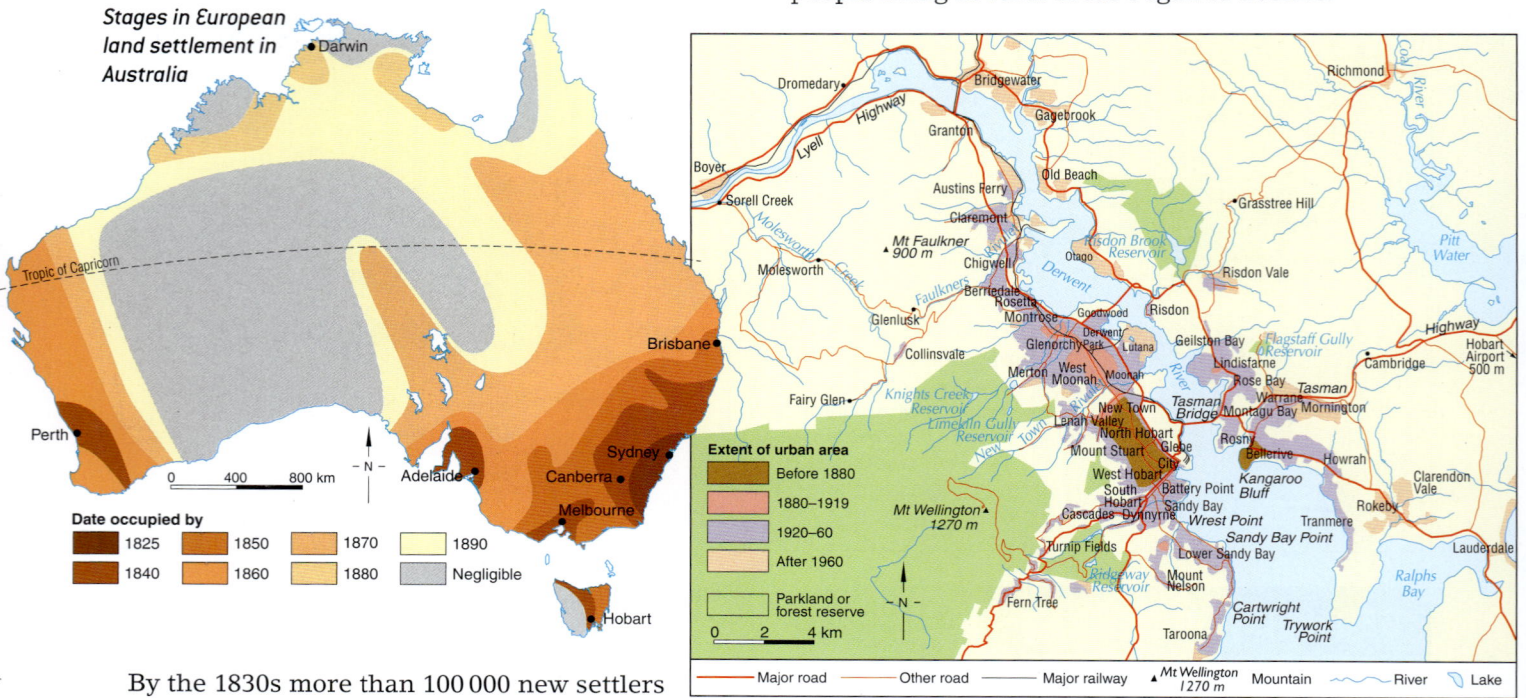

By the 1830s more than 100 000 new settlers had come to Australia, and the development of new technologies encouraged the wheat and wool industries to expand. Between 1851 and 1860, about 600 000 migrants came to Australia, attracted by the discovery of gold and the economic development that followed. The expansion of railways enabled farmers to move further inland. Irrigation schemes, which were set up in the 1880s, allowed areas of more intensive agriculture and settlement to develop. Many new towns grew and prospered, providing services to rural industries.

Cities such as Sydney expanded rapidly after World War II. Manufacturing and services became more important, displacing agriculture as the most significant form of economic activity. This had the effect of lowering the average income of farmers compared with city dwellers. The total number of people living in rural areas began to decline.

*The first settlement in Hobart was established in 1804.*

## What is a settlement?

A **settlement** is a group of people living in one place or location. There may be a collection of buildings and transport links within and between settlements. There are two main types of settlements: rural and urban. In **rural settlements** most of the population is engaged in primary economic activities, such as farming, fishing and mining. In **urban settlements** most of the population is engaged in secondary and tertiary economic activities, such as transportation, commerce and administration.

The position of a settlement includes both its site and situation. Site is the area occupied by a settlement. For example, settlements may be located close to a reliable water supply, near a port or on a plain. Situation is the position of a settlement in relation to access to the surrounding areas and its location in relation to other settlements.

## GEOskills TOOLBOX

### IDENTIFYING LARGE-SCALE AND SMALL-SCALE MAPS

Large-scale maps show detailed information about a small area, such as a suburb, small city or town. Small-scale maps show broad patterns and large areas such as major cities, countries or continents. A map at a scale of 1 : 500 000 (1 centimetre represents five kilometres, or 500 000 centimetres) or smaller is usually considered a small-scale map.

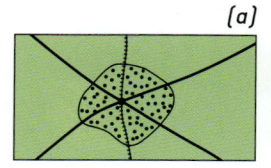

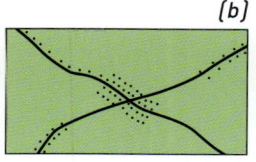

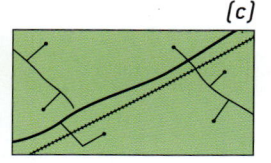

Examples of settlement patterns: (a) nucleated or cluster, (b) linear, (c) dispersed

Originally settlements grew unplanned, but now they are mostly planned. They may take one of three forms, as shown in the diagram on the left. Nucleated (or cluster) settlements have a centre point that historically was the centre of the settlement. In a linear settlement, the buildings are located along a main transport route. When individual farms are scattered, the settlement pattern is said to be 'dispersed'. Planned settlements, on the other hand, usually form more regular, organised patterns.

**Key reasons for the location of settlements in Australia**

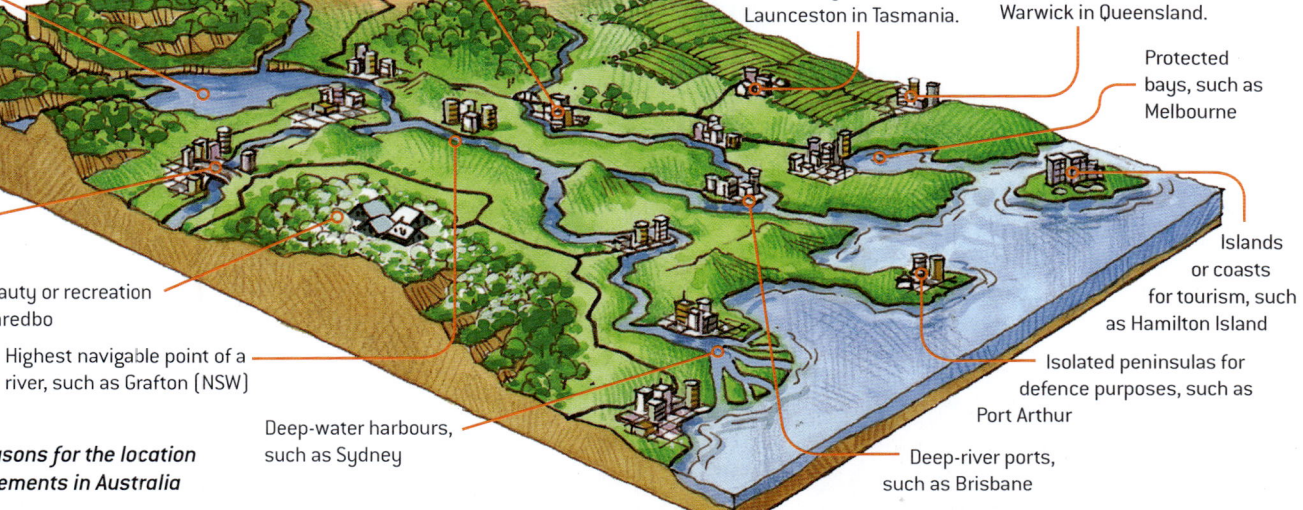

- The sites of mineral resources become industrial centres, such as Mount Isa in Queensland.
- Intersection of transport routes, such as Albury–Wodonga
- In hilly or mountainous areas towns are built in valleys, such as Launceston in Tasmania.
- Fertile soils attract farms and towns, such as Warwick in Queensland.
- A lake or reservoir, such as Lake Argyle in Western Australia
- Protected bays, such as Melbourne
- River crossings, such as Perth
- Areas of natural beauty or recreation centres, such as Thredbo
- Highest navigable point of a river, such as Grafton (NSW)
- Deep-water harbours, such as Sydney
- Islands or coasts for tourism, such as Hamilton Island
- Isolated peninsulas for defence purposes, such as Port Arthur
- Deep-river ports, such as Brisbane

## ACTIVITIES

### UNDERSTANDING
1. Define the terms *settlement*, *rural settlement* and *urban settlement*.
2. What was the key economic activity in Australia before World War II?

### THINKING AND APPLYING
3. Give two reasons to explain why settlement after 1788 had a great impact on the natural environment.
4. Suggest reasons why people were attracted to migrate to Australia.

### USING YOUR SKILLS
5. Refer to the map of Hobart on the previous page.
   a. On which bank of the Derwent River did Hobart's first settlement begin?
   b. In which direction did the population spread between 1880 and 1919?
   c. Why has Hobart's population not spread to the west of the city?
6. Refer to the map on the previous page showing the stages in European land settlement of Australia.
   a. When was the area surrounding Sydney settled?
   b. Which of the cities shown on the map was settled most recently?
   c. In which direction did land settlement expand in Western Australia?
7. Refer to the diagram above showing the reasons for the location of settlements.
   a. Give two examples of locations based on natural resources.
   b. Give two examples of locations based on transport.
8. Refer to the maps of Australia and Hobart on the previous page. Which scale is larger?
9. Convert the scales for the two maps from line scales into representative fractions. (To do this you must convert kilometres into centimetres.)
10. Is the Hobart map a small- or large-scale map?
11. Would a map showing bus routes in a local suburb be a large- or small-scale map?
12. Which type of map shows the larger area: small-scale or large-scale?

### GEOTERMS

**settlement:** a group of people living in one place or location

# 4.3 Population change in Australia

Every five years the Australian Bureau of Statistics (ABS) conducts a census on the population of Australia to determine its size, rate of increase, age and sex distribution, life expectancy and migration, and where people live. Such information helps governments to decide where to build new schools, hospitals and roads, and where there is a need for retirement homes and kindergartens.

## Population growth

In 2008, Australia had a population of more than 21 million. The population of Australia increased rapidly during the twentieth century, being about five times greater at the end of the twentieth century than it was in 1900. There have been two main reasons for this increase:
- *Natural increase*. This occurs when the number of people born (birth rate) is higher than the number of people dying (death rate).
- *Migration*. The proportion of Australia's population born overseas increased from less than 10 per cent in 1947 to 23 per cent in 1996.

Figures released by the Australian Bureau of Statistics show that the number of births in 2006 was 265 922, the second highest figure on record. It was the highest in 36 years, with more babies born than in any one year since 1971.

## Natural increase

From 1861, natural increase has been the major component of Australia's total population growth. Natural increase is the excess of births over deaths, and is usually expressed as a percentage. Fertility and births are measured and compared by using the crude birth rate, which is the number of live births per 1000 population. Mortality or death is commonly measured by the crude death rate, which is the number of deaths per 1000 population. To show how the rates are used, imagine a population of 2000 that has had 32 births and 17 deaths in a year. The crude birth rate (CBR) for the year is 16 and the crude death rate (CDR) is 8.5. The rate of natural increase is (CBR16 – CDR8.5) = 7.5 per 1000 = 0.75 per cent. The difference between CBR and CDR is divided by 10 because the rate of natural increase is expressed as a percentage, whereas the CBR and CDR are numbers per 1000 population.

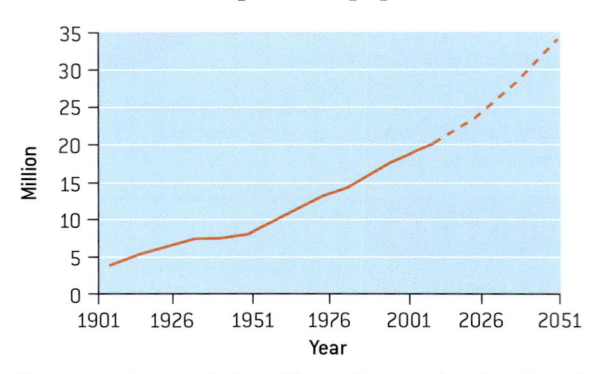

Changes to the population of Australia, actual and projected, 1901– 2051

*Source:* Australian Bureau of Statistics.

## Migration

Australia's net overseas migration is the number of people migrating to live in Australia minus the number of people emigrating from Australia to live in other countries. Net overseas migration is expressed as a percentage of the total population. For example, in 2002–03 Australia's net overseas

### Australia's changing population rate

| Year | Live births '000 | Deaths '000 | Natural increase '000 | Net overseas migration '000 | Population '000 | Growth rate % |
|---|---|---|---|---|---|---|
| 2001 | 247.5 | 128.9 | 118.6 | 135.7 | 19 413.2 | 1.36 |
| 2003 | 247.4 | 132.2 | 115.2 | 116.5 | 19 902.7 | 1.26 |
| 2006 | 264.3 | 133.1 | 131.2 | 134.8 | 20 701.5 | 1.43 |

*Source:* Data derived from Australian Bureau of Statistics.

migration was 139 000 and its total population was 19 881 500. Divide the net overseas migration by the total population (139 000/19 881 500) and multiply by 100 to achieve a percentage rate for net overseas migration in 2002–03 (0.7 per cent).

Migration to Australia began more than 50 000 years ago when the sea level was 60 metres lower than it is today. Aborigines are thought to have walked most of the way to Australia to become the first migrants to the continent. The second phase of migration began with the arrival in Australia of the British in 1788. Immigration to Australia by Europeans provided more people for the population than natural increase before 1861.

### GEOfacts

In Australia in 2008, there was an overall population increase of one person every 1 minute and 37 seconds. This resulted from:
- one birth every minute and 55 seconds
- one death every 3 minutes and 58 seconds
- a net gain of one international migrant every 2 minutes and 51 seconds.

*Source:* Data derived from Australian Bureau of Statistics.

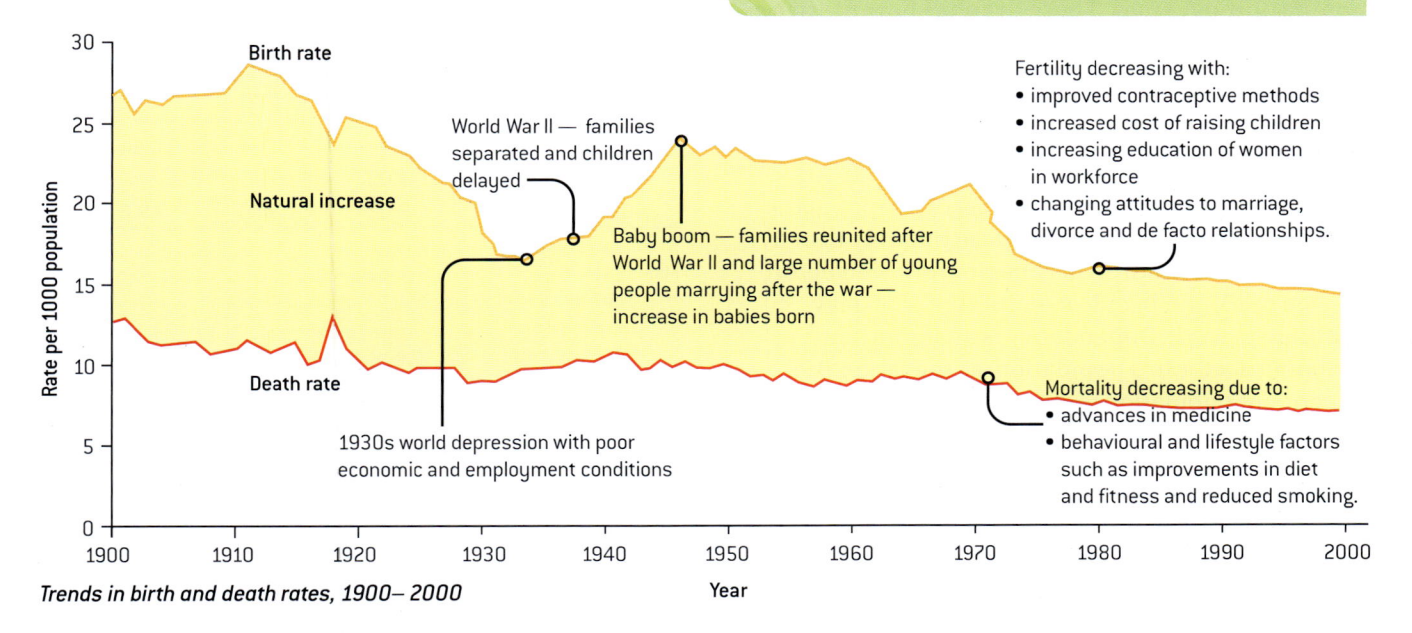

*Trends in birth and death rates, 1900– 2000*

Labels on graph:
- Birth rate
- Natural increase
- Death rate
- World War II — families separated and children delayed
- Baby boom — families reunited after World War II and large number of young people marrying after the war — increase in babies born
- 1930s world depression with poor economic and employment conditions
- Fertility decreasing with:
  - improved contraceptive methods
  - increased cost of raising children
  - increasing education of women in workforce
  - changing attitudes to marriage, divorce and de facto relationships.
- Mortality decreasing due to:
  - advances in medicine
  - behavioural and lifestyle factors such as improvements in diet and fitness and reduced smoking.

## ACTIVITIES

### UNDERSTANDING

1. What have been the two main reasons for the increased population of Australia?
2. What determines the natural increase in population?

### THINKING AND APPLYING

3. Why is sustainable population growth important?

### USING YOUR SKILLS

4. Refer to the graph of the change to the population of Australia 1901–2051.
   a. What is the difference between the populations in 1901 and 2001?
   b. When did Australia's population begin to increase rapidly?
   c. What is likely to happen to Australia's population growth between 2001 and 2051?

5. Refer to the table on the previous page showing Australia's population change.
   a. What was Australia's total population in 2006?
   b. How many live births were there in 2006?
   c. Calculate Australia's crude birth rate for 2006.
   d. Calculate Australia's crude death rate for 2006.
   e. Calculate Australia's natural increase for 2006.
   f. Calculate Australia's net overseas migration in 2006.
   g. Describe the trends in natural increase and migration from 2001 to 2006. Account for the changes.

6. Refer to the graph showing trends in birth and death rates between 1900 and 2000.
   a. What has been the overall trend in death rates in the twentieth century?
   b. Suggest reasons for this trend.
   c. Describe the trend in birth rate in Australia during the twentieth century.
   d. Suggest reasons why the birth rate has declined since 1970.

### GEOTERMS

**census:** the counting of a population, along with details on age, sex, jobs and other relevant information

CHAPTER 4 | Australia's population

# 4.4 Changes to Australia's population structure

Accurate calculation of the current and future age and sex structure of a population is important when predicting the uses of resources such as schools and hospitals, the labour force and recreational facilities. The age and sex distribution of a population is usually presented as a set of graphs known as a **population pyramid**. These graphs show the age and sex of the population, tell us about the past, and make predictions for the future.

In Australia, people in the 0–15 and over 65 age groups are known as the dependent population, because they are generally not part of the labour force and are supported by the rest of the population. In other countries, especially those that rely heavily on agriculture, children may begin work well before the age of 15, and people over the age of 65 may continue to work. Dependency is an important economic factor in a population, as the larger the dependent population grows, the greater the pressure is on the working population to support them.

## An ageing population

During the twentieth century, the population of Australia gradually aged. In 1900, 4 per cent of the population was over 65 years; in 2001 it was 14 per cent. The reasons for the change in Australia's population structure are:

1. Australia has one of the lowest crude death rates (7 per 1000) in the world.
2. Australia has one of the lowest crude birth rates (12 per 1000) in the world.
3. Australia has one of the highest life expectancies (78 for men and 83 for women).
4. Children of the postwar baby boom are reaching retirement age in the year 2010.
5. Twenty-five per cent of Australian women are electing not to have children. Other women are having fewer children and giving birth at an older age. For example, in 1979, 25 per cent of births were to women over 30 years compared with 50 per cent today.

The consequences of an ageing Australian population are numerous. Taxpayers will need to provide more funds for pensions, because there will be more people collecting a pension, and they will be collecting it for a longer time. Governments are also faced with increasing expenditure in the areas of health and welfare for the elderly.

**Projected population of Australia, 2051**

| Age group (years) | Males (%) | Females (%) | Age group (years) | Males (%) | Females (%) |
|---|---|---|---|---|---|
| 85+ | 1.63 | 2.92 | 35–39 | 3.07 | 3.00 |
| 80–84 | 1.71 | 2.15 | 30–34 | 3.07 | 2.98 |
| 75–79 | 2.24 | 2.52 | 25–29 | 3.04 | 2.92 |
| 70–74 | 2.53 | 2.65 | 20–24 | 2.98 | 2.83 |
| 65–69 | 2.89 | 2.92 | 15–19 | 2.81 | 2.66 |
| 60–64 | 3.07 | 3.05 | 10–14 | 2.72 | 2.57 |
| 55–59 | 3.16 | 3.12 | 5–9 | 2.67 | 2.53 |
| 50–54 | 3.13 | 3.07 | 0–4 | 2.64 | 2.50 |
| 45–49 | 3.11 | 3.05 | | | |
| 40–44 | 3.08 | 3.02 | **Total** | **49.6** | **50.5** |

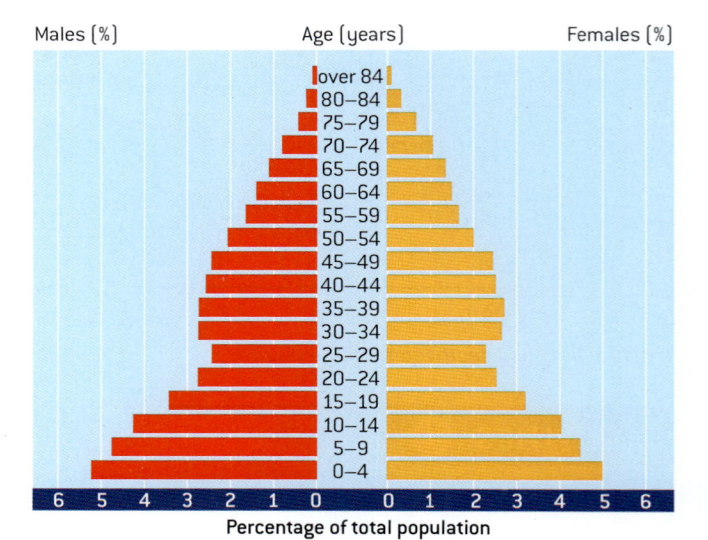

*Australia's population structure, 1961*

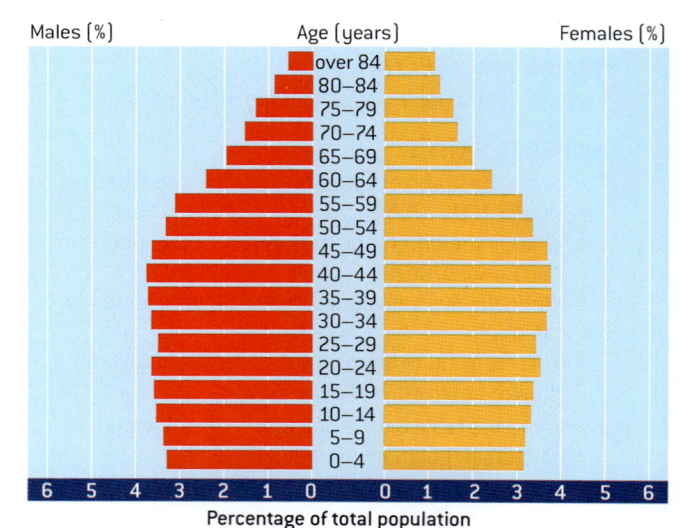

*Australia's population structure, 2006*

# Changing fertility rates

Fertility in Australia reached a low point of 2.1 babies per woman during the 1930s Great Depression. At the height of the 'baby boom' in 1961, the **fertility rate** reached 3.5 babies per woman. In the 1970s, changing laws and social attitudes allowed women greater reproductive choice and freedom to pursue an education and a job. As a result, fertility declined below the **replacement rate** of 2.1 babies per woman to the present rate of 1.8.

These trends have resulted in 'family-friendly' policies — such as paid parental leave, subsidised childcare and the government's baby bonus — which aim to enable parents, especially mothers, to combine work and family. From 2011, all Australian mothers (or fathers) in the workforce will be entitled to 18 weeks paid parental leave.

## GEO skillbuilder

### CONSTRUCTING A POPULATION PYRAMID

Population pyramids are simply two bar graphs that are drawn on a vertical axis. They show the age and sex distribution of the population and the size of the dependent population as a proportion of the total population. Young populations are indicated by a wide base. Old populations are indicated by a vase shape, with a small base, larger middle and small top.

Refer to the table of population data for Australia, 2051 on the previous page. Your task is to present this information as a a population pyramid, like the examples of Australia in 1961 and 2006. Follow these steps.

**STEP 1**

On a piece of graph paper draw in the base for your pyramid. Males are represented on the left and females on the right. Label the horizontal axes as Males (%) and Females (%).

**STEP 2**

Draw the two vertical axes and label the age groups.

**STEP 3**

Divide each horizontal axis into equal sections starting from 0. Mark each from 0 to 4 (because the highest percentage in the table is less than 4 but greater than 3).

**STEP 4**

Use the percentage columns in the table to draw horizontal bars for males and females in each age group.

**STEP 5**

After completing the pyramid, shade the male and female sides. Add a title.

## ACTIVITIES

### UNDERSTANDING

1. What does a population pyramid show?
2. Define the following terms:
   a *fertility rate*
   b *replacement rate*.
3. Who are Australia's dependent population?
4. Why has Australia's fertility rate dropped?

### THINKING AND APPLYING

5. In pairs or small groups, discuss the challenges an ageing population presents for governments and other planners.
6. Should governments pay pensions to elderly pensioners or should they have to provide for themselves?

### USING YOUR SKILLS

7. Refer to the 1961 population pyramid.
   a In which years were people in the 0–14 age group born?
   b Why is this group so large?
   c Explain why the 25–29 age group is smaller than the groups either side of it.
   d Why is there a greater percentage of elderly women than elderly men?
8. Refer to the 2006 population pyramid.
   a Locate your age and sex group on the population pyramid. What percentage of the total population in 2006 was made up by your age and sex group?
   b Which age group represents the largest percentage of Australia's population in 2006?
   c How has Australia's population profile changed since 1961? Suggest two reasons for this change.
9. Refer to the pyramid you drew in the GEOskillbuilder and answer the following questions.
   a Which age group is likely to be the largest in 2051?
   b What facilities is this group likely to need?
   c To which age group will you belong in 2051?
   d Estimate the dependent population in 2051.

## GEOTERMS

**fertility rate:** the average number of babies born to women during their reproductive years

**replacement rate:** a total fertility rate of 2.1 is considered to be the replacement rate. When a population reaches this level, it will remain stable (assuming no immigration or emigration takes place).

**CHAPTER 4** | Australia's population

# 4.5 Changes to ethnic composition

Migration is the permanent or semi-permanent movement of people from one location to another. Immigration is the movement of people into a country and **emigration** is the movement of people out of a country. A migrant is different from a **refugee**: migrants elect to move to another country and are free to return. In contrast, refugees are forced to leave their country and cannot return, because of persecution based on their race, religion, nationality, political opinion or membership of a particular social group. In 1948, the Universal Declaration of Human Rights stated that anyone in fear of persecution should be able to seek a safe refuge in another country. This is a basic human right.

Australia has a non-discriminatory immigration policy — this means that anyone from any country can apply to migrate, regardless of ethnic origin, gender, race or religion. Each year, the government decides how many migrants are allowed into Australia and whether they can enter via the family, skilled or humanitarian categories. These decisions are made in consultation with states, territories and local governments, as well as with businesses, trade unions and environmental organisations. This process determines the migration levels that will contribute to **sustainable development**.

## Change over time

Since 1788, immigration has contributed to Australia's increasing population. Over time, however, the number, the country of origin and the reasons people migrate to Australia have changed. In 1947, the proportion of the population born overseas was 10 per cent, and 81 per cent came from English-speaking countries. By 2006, 24 per cent of the population was born overseas, 33 per cent migrated from north-west Europe (mainly the United Kingdom and Ireland), 19 per cent from southern and eastern Europe, and 13 per cent from South-East Asia.

The changes to the immigration pattern started after World War II, when many Australians feared

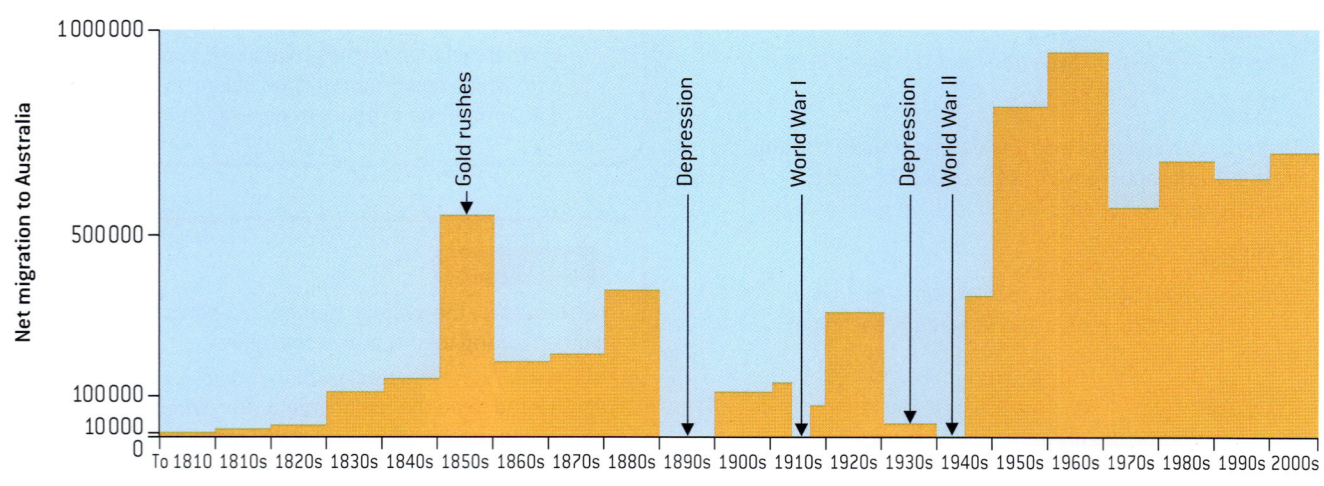

*European immigrants arriving by ship after World War II*

*The pattern of Australian immigration*

an invasion from countries located to the immediate north. The slogan 'populate or perish' was touted, and migrants and refugees from Europe were encouraged. Many British citizens were seduced by advertisements of sun, surf and opportunities, and they emigrated to Australia as 'ten pound tourists'. After the White Australia policy was abandoned in the 1970s, a larger proportion of migrants and refugees arrived from Asia, especially during the Vietnam War. Today the Asian region has become an increasingly important source of migrants, who bring with them a diversity of cultures.

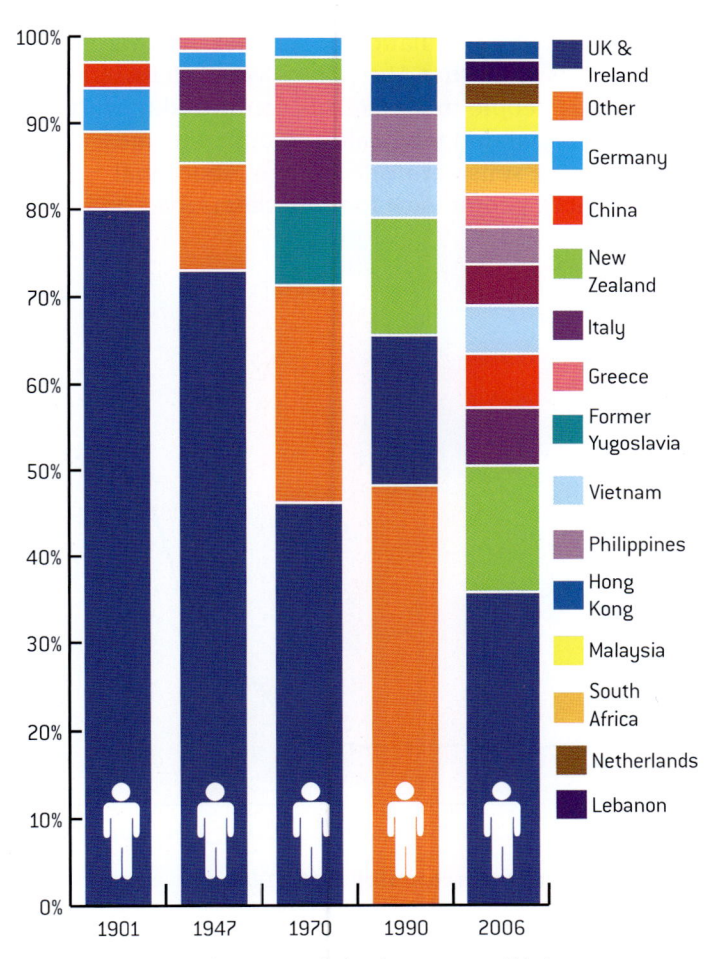

*Australia's immigrant population by country of birth*

### GEOskills TOOLBOX

**WORKING WITH COMPOUND COLUMN OR BAR GRAPHS**

Compound bar graphs are commonly used to compare a number of groups of related information. Each bar or column is divided into segments, with the largest segment at the bottom and the smallest at the top. The full bar or column represents the total amount.

### ACTIVITIES

**UNDERSTANDING**

1. What are the differences between:
   a. a migrant and a refugee
   b. immigration and emigration?
2. Describe the changes in the number and country of origin of migrants entering Australia since 1901.
3. What are the factors that would cause people to migrate to Australia?

**THINKING AND APPLYING**

4. People have different perspectives on whether Australia should increase or decrease the number of immigrants. Suggest what argument might be put forward by:
   a. a refugee from Afghanistan
   b. a Vietnamese restaurant owner
   c. a Department of Immigration employee
   d. an unemployed person
   e. an environmentalist.
5. Imagine you are a non-English-speaking migrant. Describe your life at school and in the Australian community.
6. How have migrants contributed to our ethnically diverse society? Take a tour around your local area and describe the impacts of migration. Illustrate your fieldwork with photographs.

**USING YOUR SKILLS**

7. Refer to the graph on page 102.
   a. What was the net migration to Australia during the gold rush period of the 1850s?
   b. List two factors that have greatly reduced the number of migrants coming to Australia.
8. Refer to the compound bar graphs of Australia's immigrant population.
   a. What was the percentage change in the people born in the United Kingdom and New Zealand between 1901 and 2006? Account for the change.
   b. From which countries did most migrants arrive following the end of World War II in 1945?
   c. List the countries that had the greatest number of migrants to Australia following the end of the White Australia policy in the 1970s.
   d. Name four countries that appear in 2006 but not in 1990. Suggest reasons for this change.

### GEOTERMS

**emigration:** the movement of people out of a country

**refugee:** a person who, owing to religious persecution or political troubles, seeks shelter or protection in a foreign country

**sustainable development:** development that meets the needs of the present population without endangering the ability of future generations to meet their own needs

# 4.6 Changes in the Indigenous population

The **Indigenous people** of Australia are Aborigines and Torres Strait Islanders. Their cultures are some of the oldest in the world. However, they are also one of the most deprived groups in Australia, with many living in poverty. Compared with many other Australians, Indigenous people are disadvantaged with respect to education, income, health, employment and housing.

**An unequal country**

| | Indigenous Australians | Non-Indigenous Australians |
|---|---|---|
| Death rate, males | 19 per 1000 | 7 per 1000 |
| Death rate, females | 12 per 1000 | 5 per 1000 |
| Life expectancy, males | 59 years | 77 years |
| Life expectancy, females | 65 years | 82 years |
| Maternal mortality | 34.8 per 100 000 | 10.1 per 100 000 |
| Incidence of tuberculosis | 15.3 per 100 000 | 1.2 per 100 000 |
| Expenditure by Australian government and the private sector on health services | $3065 per person | $2518 per person |

**Indigenous population distribution in Australia, 2006**

| State/territory | Indigenous population | Proportion of Australian Indigenous population (%) | Proportion of total state/territory population (%) |
|---|---|---|---|
| New South Wales | 148 178 | 28.7 | 2.2 |
| Queensland | 146 429 | 28.3 | 3.6 |
| Western Australia | 77 928 | 15.1 | 3.8 |
| Northern Territory | 66 582 | 12.9 | 31.6 |
| Victoria | 30 839 | 6.0 | 0.6 |
| South Australia | 26 044 | 5.0 | 1.7 |
| Tasmania | 16 900 | 3.3 | 3.4 |
| Australian Capital Territory | 4 043 | 0.8 | 1.2 |
| Other territories | 231 | 0.1 | 9.7 |
| **Australia** | **517 174** | **100.0** | **2.5** |

*Source:* Australian Bureau of Statistics.

## Proud to stand and be counted

After European settlement, the size of Australia's Indigenous population declined dramatically due to introduced diseases and displacement. When the Australian Constitution came into effect in 1901, Aboriginal people were not counted as part of the Australian population. It was not until the 1967 **referendum** that Australians voted to include Indigenous people in the census count. Today, with changing social and political developments and an increasing sense of pride in their Aboriginal origins, more people now identify themselves as Indigenous.

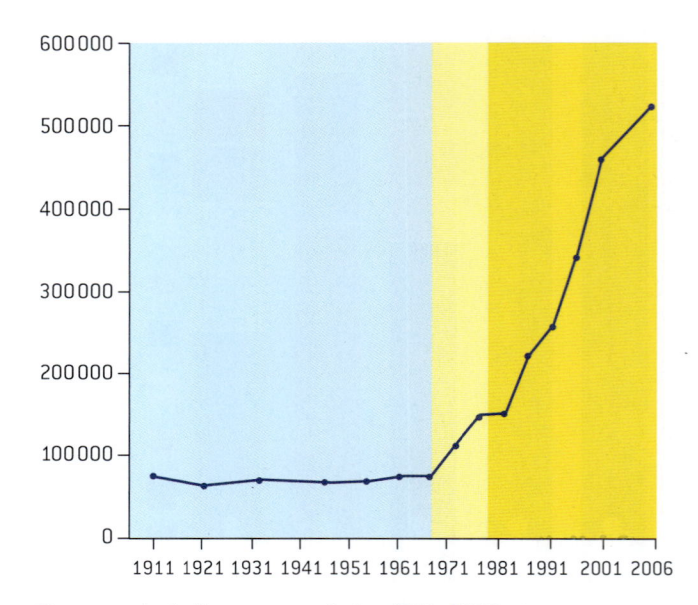

*Change to the Indigenous population 1911–2006*

## More babies but lower life expectancy

The Indigenous age–sex population structure is different from the total Australian structure. Indigenous people have higher fertility and higher death rates, and their population is younger than the total Australian population. Although fertility rates for Indigenous women fell to 2.1 babies per woman by 2006, this is still higher than the fertility rate of 1.7 babies per woman in the total Australian female population.

The high death rate is reflected in a life expectancy of 59 years for males and 65 years for females. Only 3 per cent of the Indigenous population are over 65 years, compared with 13 per cent of the total population. This is a result of poorer health from higher rates of smoking, obesity, diabetes, asthma and kidney diseases compared with the rest of the population. On a positive note, more babies are reaching their fifth birthday with a decrease in the **infant mortality rate**, helped by government health services, non-government organisations (NGOs) and Indigenous community health programs.

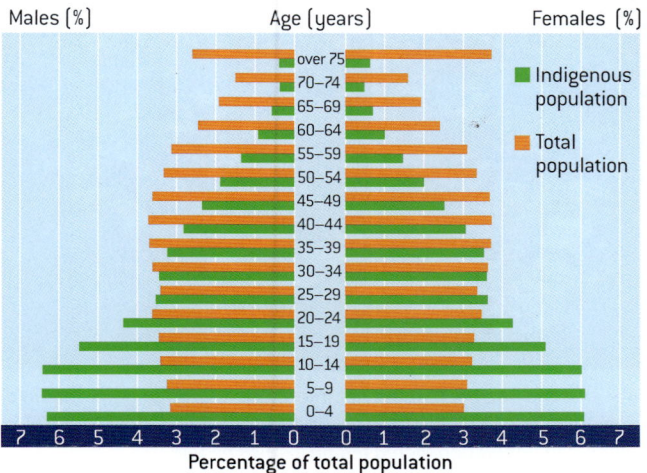

*Many Indigenous Australians are prominent in sport, business and government. Adam Goodes is an outstanding player in the Sydney Swans AFL team.*

*Indigenous and total population, 2006*
Source: Australian Bureau of Statistics.

## Distribution of Indigenous people

Most of Australia's Indigenous people live in major urban and other urban areas. Compared with non-Indigenous people, however, a higher proportion of Indigenous people live in rural and remote areas. Today, more Aboriginal people are moving to rural areas, while the general population is moving to urban areas. About 27 per cent of the Indigenous population live in remote parts of Australia compared with only 2 per cent of non-Indigenous Australians. The remoteness of these communities has meant limited access to health services, adequate housing, education services and employment opportunities.

*The Hermannsburg Aboriginal community in central Australia has a population of only 559. It began as a Lutheran mission in 1877.*

### ACTIVITIES

#### UNDERSTANDING
1. Who are Australia's Indigenous people?
2. How are Indigenous people disadvantaged?
3. Where do most Indigenous people live today?
4. Why did Australia's Indigenous population decline after European settlement?

#### THINKING AND APPLYING
5. What was the trend for the Indigenous population during the twentieth century? Suggest reasons for the trend.
6. What were the difficulties in determining the Indigenous population from 1788 until after the referendum in 1967 to include Indigenous people in the census count?
7. Refer to the table 'An unequal country'. Use the internet and other resources to describe what can be done to improve Indigenous peoples' quality of life.
8. In groups, select a well-known Indigenous person. Use the internet and other resources to describe the selected person. Outline why he or she is well known and the obstacles he or she had to overcome to become successful.

#### USING YOUR SKILLS
9. Refer to the population pyramid. Compare the percentage of Indigenous people with the total Australian population for the following age groups:
   a 0–4 years
   b 45–49 years and over.
   Suggest reasons for the differences.

### GEOTERMS

**Indigenous people:** the descendants of the original inhabitants of an area

CHAPTER 4 | Australia's population

# 4.7 Australians on the move

Perhaps you have lived in different countries, or have moved to different states and suburbs to live; and in the future you will possibly move again. Australia has a *mobile population*. Males move 12.8 times in their life, and females 13.6 times. During 2006–07, 351 900 people moved interstate. Queensland had the largest net gain of 27 000 people, while New South Wales recorded the largest net loss of 27 300 due to interstate migration.

Within Australia, people move between states (**interstate migration**) and within a state (**intrastate migration**). Some move from rural to urban areas (rural–urban migration), whereas others move from the city to rural areas, attracted by less expensive land and a cleaner atmosphere. There has also been a sustained out-migration from inland to coastal areas as people move for a 'sea change'.

*Queensland has the highest net interstate migration gain. The Gold Coast expects to be home to one million people by 2027. In 2007 alone, the population increased by 17 228 people.*

## Interstate migration

Over the past two decades, people have moved from the cooler south to the warmer north, up the east coast to Queensland and towards Western Australia. All states and territories experienced a loss of people to Queensland — most were between 25 and 34 years old, and 65 per cent came from New South Wales. The size of a state's population affects its share of Commonwealth funds and the number of seats in the House of Representatives. At the local level, changes in the size of the population affect the demand for housing and services such as health and education.

## Who moves?

The people most likely to move interstate are young adults, people who are separated or divorced, unemployed people and recent immigrants from English-speaking countries. The most common reasons are related to employment and social amenity (for example, to be near family or friends). Immigrants from non-English-speaking countries, married people and older people are less likely to move interstate.

**Net interstate migration, 1996–2001**
- More than 10 000
- 5000 to 10 000
- 2000 to 5000
- 1500 to 2000
- 1000 to 1500

*Note: migrations of less than 1000 not shown*

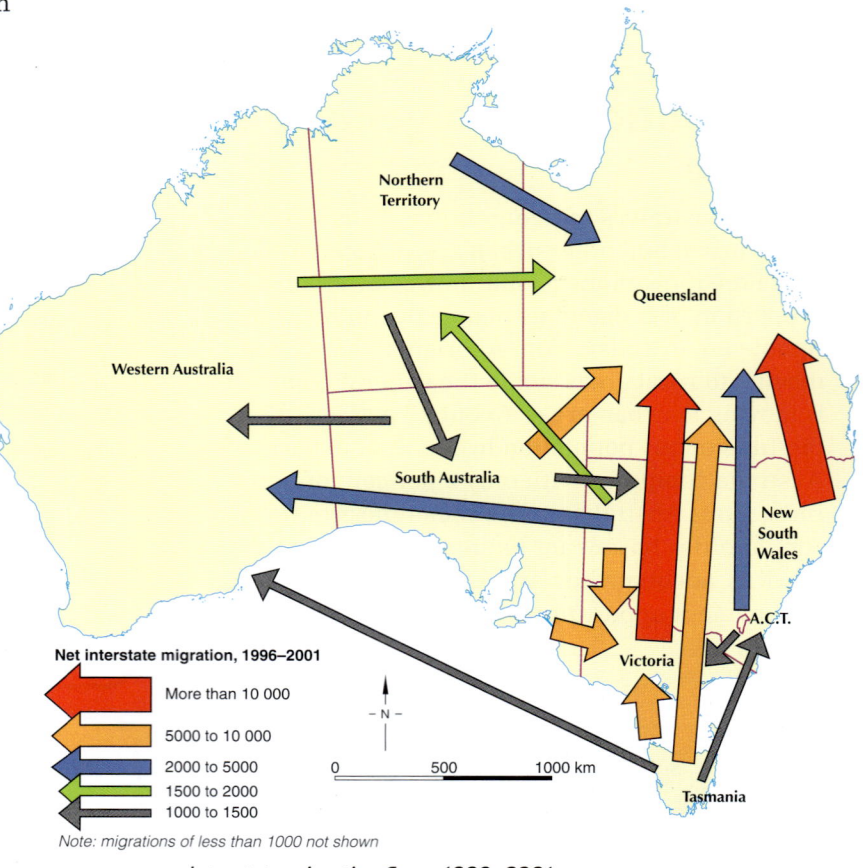

*Interstate migration flows 1996–2001*

## Changes in rural Australia

Many small towns, particularly in rural areas, are experiencing a loss of population and a decline in prosperity. Thirty-five per cent of rural areas have declined in the past 15 years. Most declining towns are located inland in wheat and sheep belts, dryland grazing regions or mining regions. Loss of population in a particular town may be unique to that town (for example, closure of a mine or local factory). Most towns experiencing substantial population growth are located on the coast near capital cities. Some towns are gaining population due to the growth of industries such as wine growing or tourism. A drop in the population of a community can lead to a loss of jobs and services (such as schools, hospitals, shops, banks), a fall in property values and a decrease in the quality of life.

### Coastal migration — sea change

Since Federation, the proportion of the population living in non-metropolitan coastal regions has increased from 8 to 20 per cent.

Factors discouraging people from living in inland areas include:
- less work in rural areas with the mechanisation of agriculture
- a harsh inland climate.

Factors attracting people to the coast include:
- lifestyle choices along the coast with an agreeable climate and beaches
- the ICT revolution, with people working from home or an office not tied to the city but with access to data and communications flow to a central office
- the ease of commuting from coastal towns to nearby coastal cities
- the growth of tourism
- increased opportunities for work in service industries
- an ageing population that chooses to live in a coastal location.

### GEOskills TOOLBOX

**USING FLOW MAPS**

Flow maps show movement from one place to another. An arrow is used to show the direction of the flow or movement; the thickness of the arrow shows the size of the flow. Their applications include the flow of traffic, various commodities and foreign aid. The flow map on page 106 shows population flow between the states of Australia.

### GEOfacts

- The area with the fastest growing population is south-east Queensland, including the Gold Coast and the Sunshine Coast. This rapid growth of coastal populations has put pressure on infrastructure, such as roads, hospitals and schools.
- Queensland is expected to have a population of 4 million by 2026.

### ACTIVITIES

**UNDERSTANDING**
1. What is a mobile population?
2. What is the difference between interstate and intrastate migration?

**THINKING AND APPLYING**
3. Why is the Australian population moving from south to north?
4. Suggest two reasons why Tasmania and South Australia have suffered a net migration loss.
5. Draw up a list of advantages and disadvantages of living in a small rural town.
6. Explain the reasons for the increase in populations of non-metropolitan coastal regions.
7. Describe a coastal town you have holidayed in. Give reasons why you would or would not like to live in this town.
8. Discuss with class members any interstate and intrastate moves they may have made and the reasons for the movements.

**USING YOUR SKILLS**
9. Refer to the flow map showing net migration between Australian states in 1996–2001.
   a. Which three states or territories had the highest interstate migration loss?
   b. Which two states or territories had the highest net migration gain?
   c. What are the limitations of flow maps such as the one on page 106? Suggest other ways that the data could be displayed to give more precise figures for interstate migration.
   d. Which two states had the highest net migration gain during 1996–2001? Use the internet and other resources to outline the reasons for this.

### GEOTERMS

**interstate migration:** the movement of people from one state of Australia to another

**intrastate migration:** the movement of people from one location to another within a state of Australia

# 4.8 Australia's changing nature and identity

The nature of Australia's population has changed dramatically over the last 200 years. It went from an almost totally Aboriginal population in 1800 to a predominantly **Anglo-Celtic** population by 1900. Currently, it is about 74 per cent Anglo-Celtic, 19 per cent other European and 4.5 per cent Asian.

## Population growth

In 2008, Australia's population was over 21 million. Natural increase has contributed around two-thirds of the population growth over the past 100 years. Immigration has contributed about one-third to Australia's population growth, but the contribution was reduced during the Great Depression and two World Wars. During the twenty-first century, there has been a resurgence in immigration. In 2008, immigration was the biggest contributor to the increase in Australia's population.

The benefits of immigration include:
- greater skills base in the population
- increased cultural diversity
- reduced ageing of the population.

## Population structure

The Australian population has gradually aged during the last 50 years.
- In 1956, the largest age group was 0–4 years old.
- In 2006, the largest age group was 40–44 years old.

This ageing is a characteristic of all developed countries and is the result of a decreased fertility rate and the postponement of the birth of the first child. Australia's population has aged more slowly than that of France and Japan because of the influx of young migrants.

Government policies in recent years have been directed towards encouraging families to have more children. Peter Costello, Federal Treasurer until 2007, exhorted Australians to have 'one for Mum, one for Dad, and one for the country'.

**Change in life expectancy in Australia**

| Year | Male | Female |
|---|---|---|
| 1858 | 52.5 | 55.0 |
| 1901 | 55.2 | 58.8 |
| 1960 | 67.9 | 74.2 |
| 2005 | 77.0 | 83.0 |
| 2051 (estimated) | 84.2 | 87.7 |

*Source: Australian Bureau of Statistics.*

## Ethnic composition

In Australia today, nearly one in four people were born overseas; in fact, 43 per cent of all Australians were born overseas or have at least one parent who was born overseas. In recent years, people from around 185 different countries have made their home in Australia.

Australia is one of the most ethnically diverse nations on Earth, and it has been able to absorb this diversity with a minimum of strife. A few of the advantages of this characteristic include:
- a wide number of languages being spoken fluently, which helps commerce
- overseas links, especially with China and India, for government and commerce
- a wide variety of ethnic foods.

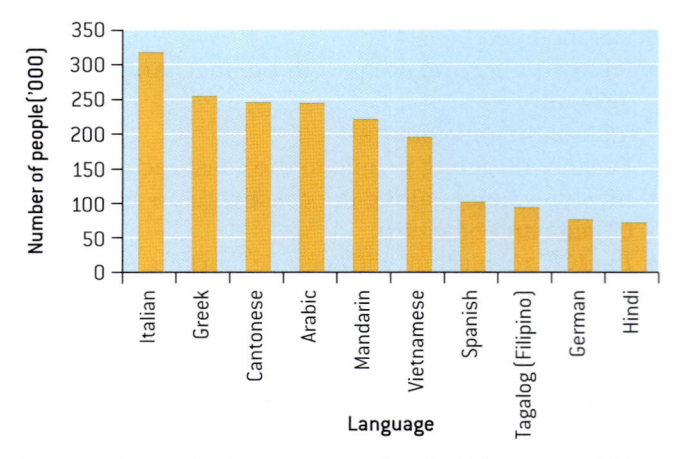

*Persons who speak a language other than English at home 2006*

## Changes in the Indigenous population

The Indigenous population has grown from fewer than 100 000 in 1911 to over 517 200 in the 2006 census. Indigenous Australians are found in all cities and rural areas, but they are still disadvantaged economically and in health compared with most other Australians. A recent study shows that Indigenous Australians are 13 times more likely than non-Indigenous Australians to go to jail. On the positive side, an increasing number of Indigenous people are continuing tertiary studies and graduating with a broad range of qualifications before taking up new career paths.

# Changing settlement patterns

Over the last century, there has been a reduction in the percentage of the population residing in rural areas, with increased settlement in coastal areas. The main changes in Australia's **demography** in the last century include:
- a different ethnic composition
- a declining birth rate
- an ageing population
- a larger Indigenous population
- a population that is overwhelmingly concentrated on the coast.

*Australia's ethnic composition has changed.*

*Perth is the capital city with the most rapidly increasing population.*

## ACTIVITIES

### UNDERSTANDING
1. What is an Anglo-Celtic?
2. Define the term *demography*.
3. Outline the main sources of Australia's population growth.
4. How does immigration benefit the recipient country?
5. Outline changes to Australia's population structure since 1900.
6. Why has Australia's population aged?
7. What are the disadvantages for Australia of an ageing population?
8. Australia has emerged as an ethnically diverse society. Outline the benefits and possible disadvantages of ethnic diversity.

### THINKING AND APPLYING
9. Imagine you are walking down a main street of a capital city in Australia. Describe what you would see that is typical of three of Australia's demographic characteristics.

### USING YOUR SKILLS
10. Refer to the table 'Change in life expectancy in Australia'. Describe the change in life expectancy from 1858 to 2051. What do you notice about the life expectancy of males and females?

### GEOTERMS

**demography:** the study of populations, including patterns and trends in population data

# Working geographically

## BROADSHEET: PERTH

### KNOWLEDGE AND UNDERSTANDING

**Refer to the population pyramid for Perth and select the alternative that best answers the question.**

1. The main change in the age–sex distribution of Perth's population between 1991 and 2006 was the:
   - (A) decreased proportion of the population aged over 70 years
   - (B) decreased proportion of the population aged between 45 and 54 years
   - (C) increased proportion of the population aged between 45 and 54 years
   - (D) increased proportion of the female population aged between 0 and 9 years.

2. The population of Perth is an example of:
   - (A) an ageing population
   - (B) a young population
   - (C) a dependent population
   - (D) an Indigenous population.

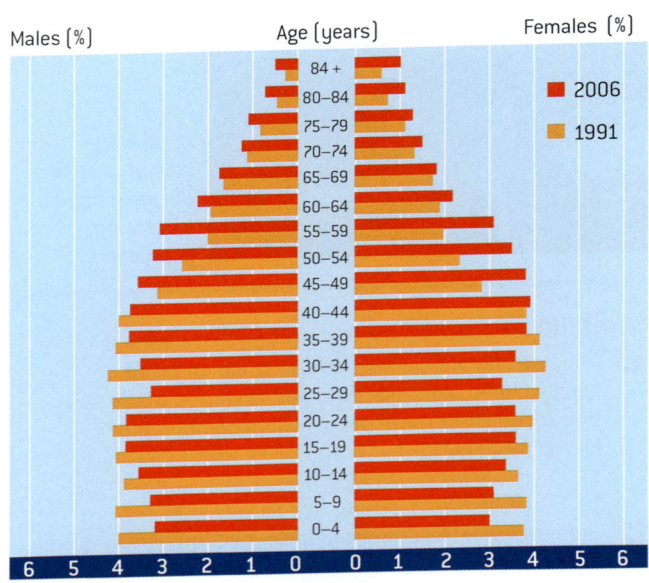

*Population pyramid, Perth*

**Refer to the urban area map for Perth (above right) and select the alternative that best answers the question.**

3. An area developed before 1880 was:
   - (A) Rockingham
   - (B) Quinns Rocks
   - (C) Dalkeith
   - (D) Perth's inner city.

4. In which two main directions did the population of Perth expand between 1880 and 1919?
   - (A) North and south
   - (B) East and west
   - (C) North-east and south-west
   - (D) North-west and south-east

5. How far do the suburbs of Perth spread between the city and Neerabup (to the north-west)?
   - (A) 20 kilometres
   - (B) 30 kilometres
   - (C) 35 kilometres
   - (D) 40 kilometres

*Urban area map for Perth*

**Refer to the map above and the satellite image of Perth and select the alternative that best answers the question.**

6. The area directly south of the Perth Airport is:
   - (A) a very densely settled urban area
   - (B) a sparsely settled urban area
   - (C) farmland
   - (D) wetlands.

110 Geoactive 2

**7** Perth's urban growth to the east is moving into:
 (A) coastal regions
 (B) farmland
 (C) forest
 (D) forest and farmland.

**8** In the satellite image, rural settlements can be clearly seen to the:
 (A) north, north-east and south
 (B) south, north and north-west
 (C) south-east, north and north-east
 (D) south, east and north-east.

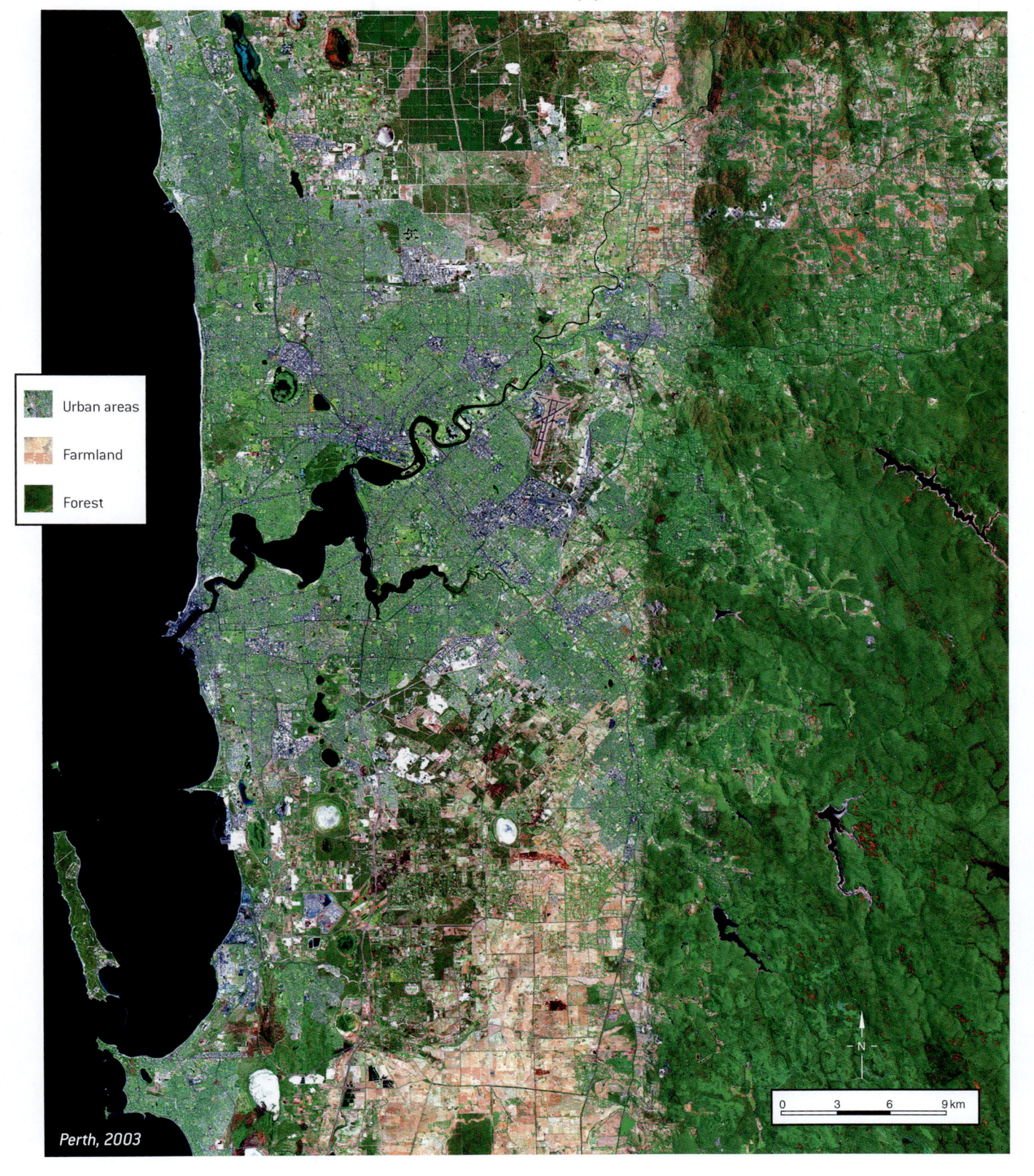

*Perth, 2003*

Legend:
- Urban areas
- Farmland
- Forest

**CHAPTER 4** | Australia's population

# 5 Australian communities

## INQUIRY QUESTIONS
- What are communities?
- How is a community formed?
- What are the significant differences with and between Australian communities?
- What are Indigenous communities?

People belong to many different communities. A wide diversity of cultural groups exist within Australian communities. However, communities are not based only on culture. In this chapter, we look at a range of factors that contribute to the Australian sense of community. Communities are formed by people with something in common. The communities we belong to contribute to our sense of identity and allow us to live our lives among other people with whom we share something in common. As we investigate communities, we will become increasingly aware of the many different communities to which we belong.

## GEOskills TOOLBOX
- Constructing land use maps (page 119)
- Interpreting a column graph (page 120)
- Using choropleth maps (page 122)

*Aerial view of Tuggerah Lake, New South Wales*

### KEY TERMS

**commodity:** an article such as a raw foodstuff (for example, wheat), or material (such as wool, coal or gold) which is traded internationally

**community:** a group formed by people with something in common and based on shared space and social organisation

**culturally diverse:** describes a society that includes many different cultural groups

**demographic characteristics:** characteristics of a population described by statistics such as births, deaths, marriages and so on

**heritage:** assets, traditions or culture that belong to a person, community or nation

**immigrant:** person who has come to live in a new country

**kinship:** being in a family relationship. A kinship system is the system of relationships traditionally accepted by a particular culture, and the rights and obligations that they involve.

**life expectancy:** the average number of years a person can be expected to live; affected by nutrition, occupation, hereditary and other factors

**outstation:** area where a small community of Aboriginal people lives away from larger settlements

**rural:** describes areas where people live in population clusters of fewer than 1000 people and where primary industry is the main activity

**standard of living:** (or living standard), the amount of goods and services available for use in the community per head of population; mainly concerned with food, clothing, housing, education and health

**surf lifesaving club:** a club dedicated to the prevention of aquatic injury and drowning through lifesaving and education practices

**transnational corporation (TNC):** a company or organisation that possesses and controls the means of production, such as factories, mines, farms and financial organisations, in more than one country

**urban:** describes areas where people live in population clusters of more than 1000 people and where either secondary or tertiary industry is the main activity

# 5.1 Forming communities

## Differences between Australian communities

A **community** is a group formed by people with something in common and based on shared space and social organisation. People with similar interests often get together to form communities. Members of a community who share something in common often share an identity too. For example, the communities you belong to now or in the future might be identified by the school you go to; where you live; the religious beliefs that you have; the country in which you were born; or the sporting team you belong to or support. You can belong to several communities at the same time — but each group you belong to is made up of people who feel a sense of 'community' with each other.

Some of the factors that can contribute to a sense of identity and community include:
- culture
- **heritage**
- place
- occupation
- gender
- religion
- hobbies
- sports.

*Meeting places encourage a sense of community.*

The culture and experiences we share in common as members of a community have a major influence on how we see the culture and experiences of other people.

Communities can often be described by their **demographic characteristics**. The Australian Bureau of Statistics gathers and publishes data about the demographic characteristics of the Australian population, including age, sex, income, employment status, occupation, number of children, religion, marital status, home ownership and level of education.

## Communities are changing

We all belong to the larger Australian community. Since 1788, **immigrants** from many different countries have settled in Australia, creating diverse communities. In recent years, many **urban** areas on the coast and on the fringes of Australia's major cities have grown rapidly. These communities are experiencing change due to population growth (discussed in detail in chapters 4 and 12). Meanwhile, many inland towns are experiencing rural decline.

Communities in **rural** areas tend to be close-knit communities where most people know each other. In contrast, some urban communities are loose-knit communities and members may have little contact even with their neighbours. This growing isolation became obvious in the aftermath of the hailstorm that devastated parts of Sydney in April 1999. Workers from the State Emergency Service came across people who were alone in their wrecked homes with no-one even aware that they were in trouble. Many people also intentionally isolate themselves behind high walls protected by alarm and intercom systems. In recent years, security concerns have led to more private housing estates and gated communities with private security guards.

## Communities based on occupation

The communities that people form at work can have a major impact on their lives. A person who works for a **transnational corporation (TNC)** might know hundreds of people in different occupations and from different cultures. A person employed in a specialised field or in an isolated location might have only a few co-workers. As the following sample study suggests, shared space and social organisation in the workplace can encourage a sense of community.

## SAMPLE STUDY

### Working at Mawson Station, Antarctica

Australia's Mawson Station, established in 1954, is the longest continually operating research station on Antarctica. The Mawson community is made up of scientists and support staff. During the summer months from October to March, the scientists conduct field research, studying the ice sheet and Antarctica's geology. Physicists and astronomers are also researching cosmic rays and auroras. The community lives and works in buildings made from prefabricated panels bolted to steel frames. The inner walls are polystyrene and the outer walls are made of enamel. Each scientist has a private bed-sit room, and the station has excellent library and recreational facilities.

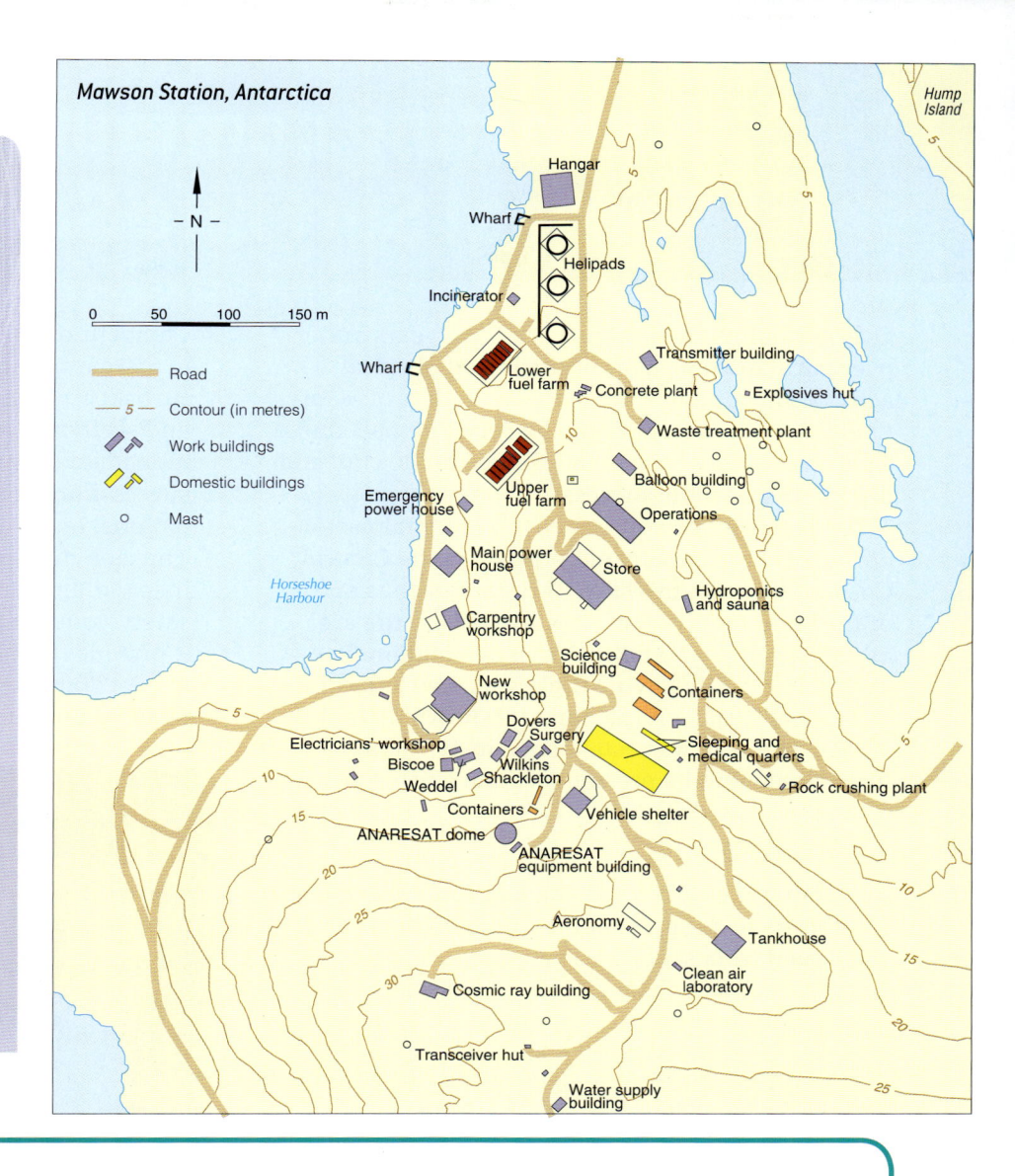

*Mawson Station, Antarctica* — map showing roads, contours (in metres), work buildings, domestic buildings and masts. Features include: Hump Island, Hangar, Wharf, Helipads, Incinerator, Transmitter building, Lower fuel farm, Concrete plant, Explosives hut, Waste treatment plant, Upper fuel farm, Balloon building, Emergency power house, Operations, Main power house, Store, Hydroponics and sauna, Horseshoe Harbour, Carpentry workshop, Science building, New workshop, Containers, Electricians' workshop, Dovers, Surgery, Sleeping and medical quarters, Biscoe, Wilkins, Shackleton, Weddel, Rock crushing plant, Containers, Vehicle shelter, ANARESAT dome, ANARESAT equipment building, Aeronomy, Tankhouse, Cosmic ray building, Clean air laboratory, Transceiver hut, Water supply building.

## ACTIVITIES

### UNDERSTANDING

1. What is a community?
2. List eight factors that can contribute to a sense of community.
3. Give three examples of a community to which you belong.
4. Outline the ways in which Australian communities are changing.

### THINKING AND APPLYING

5. How do culture and heritage contribute to a sense of community?
6. Investigate an occupation that involves geography (for example, meteorologist, National Parks ranger, marine biologist, travel agent).
   a. Find out the qualifications required for the role.
   b. Describe some of the activities that might be carried out on a typical day.
   c. Describe how shared space and/or shared social organisation could contribute to a sense of community among the workers in this occupation.

### USING YOUR SKILLS

7. Refer to the map above of Mawson Station, Antarctica.
   a. What evidence can you find to support the idea that Mawson Station is a research community?
   b. Suggest five different occupations represented at Mawson Station.
   c. Find the highest point of Mawson Station. What do physicists study in the building located at this site?
   d. What is the approximate area of the large sleeping quarters building?
   e. Is the land an area of steep or gentle slope?

### GEOTERMS

**community:** group formed by people with something in common and based on shared space and social organisation

**rural:** describes areas where people live in population clusters of fewer than 1000 people and where primary industry is the main activity

**urban:** describes areas where people live in population clusters of more than 1000 people and where either secondary or tertiary industry is the main activity

# 5.2 A sporting community: Terrigal Surf Life Saving Club

Over six million Australians aged five years and over participate in sport or organised physical activity. Many people are active members of teams or clubs, such as swimming, soccer or netball clubs. This means they have an allegiance to the club and are interested in its success.

Terrigal Surf Life Saving Club is a vital part of the local community of Terrigal, on the Central Coast of New South Wales. Terrigal Beach is one of the main family beach destinations in the area as well as a very popular tourist destination. The Terrigal Surf Life Saving Club is located adjacent to Terrigal Beach on the north-eastern side of the village. The club was established in 1925 and has been situated in its present location since 2001.

## The club

The club has grown from a small group of dedicated supporters to the present membership of around 1000, aged from six to 90. The members of the Terrigal Surf Life Saving Club provide safety and security for the beach-going public. There are 15 active patrols (over 250 members) on a roster to help protect the beach on weekends and public holidays. Active lifesaver patrols provide a service to over 150 000 visitors to Terrigal Beach every year, and help to maintain equipment and facilities. Lifesavers undergo testing, education and skill development each year.

The club also provides other benefits for the local community:
- Education — there are a range of surf lifesaving skills taught, leading up to the Bronze Medallion Award. Other skills that are taught include how to use an inflatable rescue boat (IRB), and courses in first aid and advanced resuscitation.

*Terrigal Surf Club*

- Competition — people of many ages (from eight to 65 years) compete in swimming, board and surf ski, ironman, IRB racing, lifesaving, first aid and surfboat events. There are various team and individual events. Members have participated successfully in competitions from a local to a national level.
- The club provides opportunities for a healthy lifestyle, a social outlet, self-discipline, security, safety, youth and adult activities. Most importantly it provides members with skills they can use to contribute to the local community, and it is a meeting point for many residents of Terrigal.

*Patrol training for surf rescue*

## The club as a community

The club is a diverse community bringing together people who have a love of surfing and a sense of duty to the wider community. The youngest members are Nippers, aged from six years old, who engage in a wide range of skill development and gradually increase their participation in competitions. Some of the older members also engage in competitions, and many are attracted by the sense of community at the club. Among the older members is a loose group called the 'Terrigal Tremblers', who swim every morning in summer and winter. The club reflects the community of Terrigal, embracing everyone with an interest in community service and a love of surfing.

*Surf skis are popular for recreation and competition.*

The club has a code of conduct for the guidance of members:
- Respect the rights, dignity and worth of others.
- Be fair, considerate and honest in all dealings with others.
- Be professional in, and accept responsibility for, your actions.
- Make a commitment to providing quality service.
- Be aware of and adhere to Surf Life Saving Australia (SLSA) standards, rules, regulations and policies.
- Operate within the rules of surf life saving that govern SLSA.

**Nippers on Terrigal Beach**

The club's code of conduct affects all members of the community, providing members with a safe and healthy environment for leisure and community service.

## ACTIVITIES

### UNDERSTANDING

1. What is a surf life saving club?
2. Why do you think so many Australians participate in a sport or organised physical activity?
3. Who makes up the membership of the Terrigal Surf Life Saving Club? Why is it a community?
4. Describe the benefits the club provides to the local community.
5. Define the term 'allegiance'. Why do club members have an allegiance to their club?
6. What are the main activities of club members?
7. Why do club members require training in many skills to be a member of active patrols?
8. In groups, discuss the club's code of conduct. How does this code promote a sense of community?
9. Describe a sporting group or club to which you belong. Why did you join? Does this club provide a service to the wider community?

**CHAPTER 5** | Australian communities

# 5.3 Rural communities

Rural communities depend on the success of the area's main activity, whether it is agriculture, fishing, logging, mining or tourism. For example, if farmers do well, the rest of the community will benefit because the farmers have more money to spend in the local area's shops and businesses. However, during the last 25 years, many rural communities have experienced decreasing incomes and increasing unemployment. Several factors have contributed to this process including globalisation, falling **commodity** prices, prolonged droughts and job losses due to technological advances. As more people have moved to urban centres in search of jobs, these communities have suffered rural decline.

Some communities have been able to maintain their **standard of living** by changing the way the land is used. In locations where soil and climatic conditions are favourable, farmers have tried new crops such as grapes or sunflowers. In some areas, profitability has been increased by consolidating smaller farms into larger and more efficient farms. In other areas, productivity has been raised by using new technologies such as satellites to monitor the health of crops or the spread of salinity. In areas that have the potential to attract tourists, some unproductive farms have taken on a new life as profitable bed-and-breakfast accommodation.

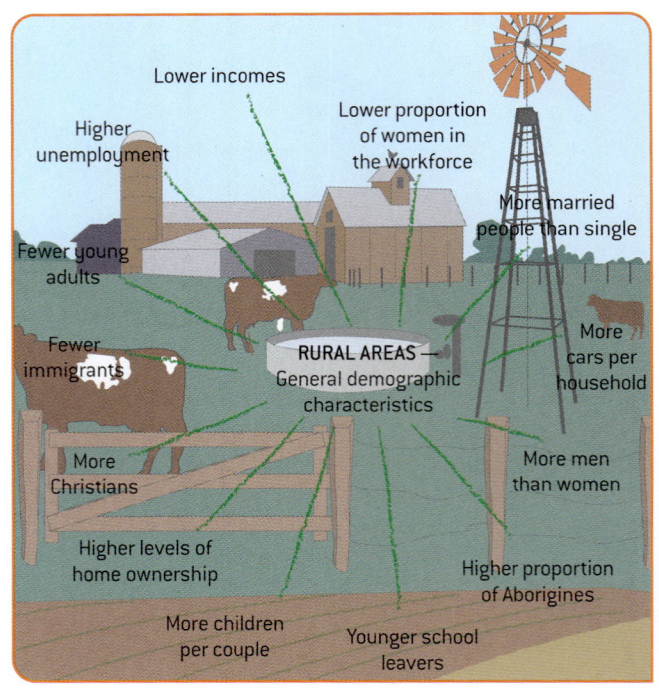

*A general picture of the demographics of rural communities as opposed to urban communities*

Rural areas — General demographic characteristics:
- Lower incomes
- Higher unemployment
- Lower proportion of women in the workforce
- More married people than single
- Fewer young adults
- Fewer immigrants
- More cars per household
- More Christians
- Higher levels of home ownership
- More children per couple
- Younger school leavers
- Higher proportion of Aborigines
- More men than women

## SAMPLE STUDY

### German heritage in the Barossa Valley

German settlers came to the Barossa Valley in the 1840s when religious persecution 'pushed' them from their homeland. They established close-knit communities and built cottages with steep pitched roofs and stone walls like the homes in a German village. In 1839, a German geologist observed that the Barossa Valley had similar characteristics to the Rhine Valley in Germany. He predicted the Barossa would produce excellent wines similar to those produced in the Rhine. The first grapes were planted in 1847. The rich soils, warm dry summers and wet winters were ideal for grapes. Today, tourism and winemaking generate income for the community. People come to experience German architecture and food, visit the wineries and take part in festival events such as grape-treading competitions.

*Vineyards in the Barossa Valley*

## SAMPLE STUDY

### Tamworth — a 'country capital'

The city of Tamworth is located on fertile agricultural plains on the banks of the Peel River in northern New South Wales. Some characteristics of this rural community are: 89.7 per cent are Australian born, only 2 per cent of the community speak a language other than English in the home and only 0.7 per cent are non-Christians. This is reflected in the largely Anglo-Australian culture within the community of about 57 200 people, and it may have led to the community's interest in country music. What began as a few performers entertaining local fans has now grown into a 10-day festival. It attracts 50 000 tourists and 1000 performers every January. Tamworth is now identified as the Country Music Capital of Australia. The Country Music Festival makes a significant contribution to Tamworth's sense of community and to the local economy.

*Aerial photograph of Tamworth*
Source: Department of Lands, Panorama Avenue, Bathurst 2795 www.lands.nsw.gov.au.

## GEOskills TOOLBOX

### CONSTRUCTING LAND USE MAPS

As the name suggests, land use maps show how land is being used. Land use maps give a quick impression of the patterns of natural and human environments.

## ACTIVITIES

### UNDERSTANDING

1. Describe how a rural community is different from an urban community.
2. What factors have contributed to a recent rural decline?
3. Describe the influence of German heritage and culture on communities in the Barossa Valley.
4. How has culture affected the rural community of Tamworth?
5. What action has Tamworth taken to improve its economic and community identity?
6. Suggest reasons for the location of Tamworth using the information provided in the aerial photograph.

### USING YOUR SKILLS

7. Draw a scale outline map of Tamworth using the aerial photograph provided.
   a. Mark in the key rivers and roads as a guide and provide a direction arrow and title.
   b. Colour in the area covered by the settlement of Tamworth and provide a legend to show this type of land use.
   c. Show other types of land use on your map — such as agriculture, forest and recreation — and add them to your legend.

**CHAPTER 5** | Australian communities

# 5.4 Indigenous communities

Diversity has always been a feature of Indigenous communities. The size of the Australian continent meant that many different survival skills, languages and social organisations were developed throughout the country. Songs, stories, art styles and ceremonies varied widely. However, despite this diversity, Indigenous communities shared the same belief that their spiritual ancestors created the natural features on Earth and the Aboriginal people.

Before colonisation, ceremonial meetings took place in all parts of Australia when seasonal conditions were suitable and abundant food was available. Indigenous people walked hundreds of kilometres, and thousands would gather for some weeks on such occasions. These gatherings were a chance to exchange goods, ideas and news. People's relationships with each other and with the land were strengthened by dancing, singing and performing ceremonies. **Kinship** plays an important part in Aboriginal social organisation and encourages a sense of community.

## Demographic characteristics

Today Indigenous people make up 2.5 per cent of the Australian population. The majority of Aboriginal people prefer to live in country areas and only 25 per cent live in cities of more than 100 000 people. About 70 per cent of the Indigenous population is less than 30 years old. This is partly due to the fact that Aboriginal **life expectancy** is 15–20 years less than for other Australians. (See chapter 12 for more on this.) Incomes are up to 50 per cent lower. The Aboriginal community of Redfern in Sydney, for example, experiences higher unemployment, lower incomes, poorer housing and lower life expectancy than other Australians.

### GEOskills TOOLBOX

**INTERPRETING A COLUMN GRAPH**

A column graph is a graph that has vertical columns. Column graphs are often used in geography to compare things. This graph is comparing resident population by remoteness area.

A column graph has both a vertical and horizontal axis. In this graph:
- the vertical axis shows the percentage of the population
- the horizontal axis shows the remoteness of areas.

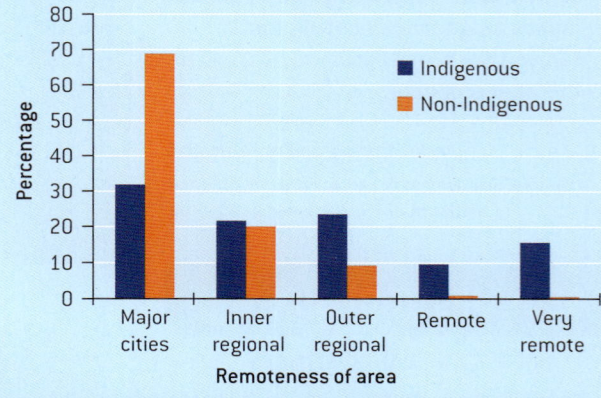

*Estimated resident population by remoteness of areas as a percentage of the total population group, 30 June 2006*

Source: ABS, Population Characteristics: Aboriginal and Torres Strait Islander Australians, Catalogue No. 4713, Table 2.4 Estimated Resident Population, by Remoteness Areas (27 March 2008), p. 18.

*Children from the Ramingining community in Arnhem Land enjoy a cool dip in the local creek.*

### SAMPLE STUDY

**Ramingining: a traditional community**

Ramingining is an Aboriginal community in Arnhem Land, located about 400 kilometres east of Darwin and 22 kilometres inland from the Arafura Sea. The climate is monsoonal with a temperature range of 16 to 38 degrees. The dry season extends from May to September. Between October and April the weather is very hot and humid.

The Ramingining community was founded in the early 1970s. About one-third of the population of 750 live on **outstations** in their traditional country. Services available in the community include a school and a clinic. Children at the Ramingining school are keen computer users, and other favourite interests include basketball and line dancing. Technological changes, such as satellite communication and solar power, have penetrated even to the outstations.

The people live within a law and kinship system practised for thousands of years. They pass on traditions through song, dance, art and ritual. Elders teach young people about the seasons and where, when and how to find food and materials at different times of the year.

The area's isolation and its unsuitability for cattle have helped the people sustain their traditional way of life. Even so, Aboriginal communities have had a long struggle to retain their rights to self-determination. When Arnhem Land became an Aboriginal reserve in 1913, the Commonwealth Government took control of the people's lives. Permission was required to enter or leave the area. Part-Aboriginal children were taken away from their parents and placed in institutions. This practice persisted even until the 1970s and victims of it have become known as the Stolen Generations.

When the *Aboriginal Land Rights Act (Northern Territory)* was passed in 1976, the people gained freehold title to their land. They began to leave the large mission stations and set up communities such as Ramingining, where they live in smaller clans and follow a more traditional lifestyle. The people have taken more control of their future by learning how to manage Australia's legal and government systems. For example, the Northern Land Council negotiates mining royalties and represents the interests of traditional owners in land claims.

### SAMPLE STUDY

**Hermannsburg: a changing rural community**

Hermannsburg is an Aboriginal community located in central Australia about 124 kilometres south-west of Alice Springs. It was established as a Lutheran mission in 1877. In the late 1800s Hermannsburg had a cattle station, tannery and school, and was also a camel train terminal. The famous painter Albert Namatjira was born at the mission in 1902.

In 1982, the Lutheran Church handed over the lease to the Aranda tribe. Thousands of tourists now visit this small community every year. They come to see the old mission buildings and beautiful artworks created by the area's Indigenous people. Besides traditional Aboriginal culture, the community's interests include country music, rodeos and football. To find out more about the community or see some of the artworks, use the **Hermannsburg** weblink in your eBookPLUS.

### ACTIVITIES

**UNDERSTANDING**

1. What is meant by 'Indigenous community'?
2. Define the term *kinship*.
3. Where is the Hermannsburg Aboriginal community? Describe how the Hermannsburg Aboriginal community has changed over time.
4. What happened in 1976 that was important to the Ramingining community? Explain why it was important to the community.

**THINKING AND APPLYING**

5. What evidence is there of diversity within the Aboriginal culture before European settlement?
6. Describe the factors which contributed to a sense of unity among Aboriginal people before colonisation.
7. Explain why the Redfern Aboriginal community is an example of social injustice.

**USING YOUR SKILLS**

8. Refer to the column graph in the GEOskills Toolbox.
   a. What percentage of the non-Indigenous population lives in major cities?
   b. What percentage of the Indigenous population lives in major cities?
   c. What are the main advantages of living in major cities for the population?
   d. What percentage of the non-Indigenous population lives in remote or very remote areas?
   e. What percentage of the Indigenous population lives in remote or very remote areas?
   f. How would you explain the large percentage of the Indigenous population living in remote or very remote areas?
   g. List the advantages and disadvantages of Indigenous people living in remote or very remote areas.

# 5.5 Culturally diverse communities

## Cultural diversity

Australia's migration policies have created a culturally diverse nation with an abundance of different languages and religions, types of literature, and music and architectural styles. Many things that we take for granted are a result of our **culturally diverse** heritage. For example, we enjoy a variety of international foods, among them Italian, Chinese, Japanese, Thai and Indian. The New South Wales Government's Community Relations Commission states on its website: 'Each community treasures its unique cultural heritage. By building relationships we share our riches to strengthen our own community, and the unity of our society at large. Through mutual respect and recognition we use and celebrate our diversity as a resource and an asset.'

## Cultural links

Immigrants from the same country of origin tend to concentrate in a particular area. They join communities that provide familiarity and support and allow them to retain elements of their own original culture and heritage.

People like to live in a neighbourhood where they can do things that they enjoy or are important to them. The factors that attract people to a certain area might include:
- entertainment
- restaurants
- places of worship
- traditional festivals
- employment and networking opportunities
- access to transport
- the presence of family or friends.

People's cultural tastes and requirements in food and clothing are more likely to be available in neighbourhoods where there are enough people who want the same types of goods. This pattern is observed all over Australia. Germans settled in the Barossa Valley, Vietnamese came to Cabramatta in Sydney and Springvale in Melbourne, and people from the Middle East settled around the Sydney suburb of Auburn. Over time, these communities disperse into the wider community, leaving their influence behind — for example, Chinatown near Darling Harbour and the Italian restaurants in Norton Street, Leichhardt.

## Migrant distribution in Sydney

Sydney is a powerful magnet for new migrants because of family and community ties and job opportunities. At the 2006 Census, 37 per cent of the total population of Sydney were born overseas: 15.7 per cent in North-East Asia, 15.6 per cent in South-East Asia, 15.3 per cent in Southern and Eastern Europe, 13 per cent in the United Kingdom and 6 per cent in New Zealand.

### GEOskills TOOLBOX

**USING CHOROPLETH MAPS**

Choropleth maps show the spatial pattern of statistics. These maps use shades of one colour or similar colours to show a pattern. Darker colours represent the most or the biggest, and lighter colours show the least or the smallest. The choropleth map opposite shows the pattern of people not fluent in English in the Sydney metropolitan area. Information about communities in five different suburbs is also given.

### ACTIVITIES

**UNDERSTANDING**

1. What has created cultural diversity in Sydney?
2. Explain why different migrant groups are attracted to various locations.

**THINKING AND APPLYING**

3. Use the data and map in the **CRC** weblink in your eBookPLUS to create a culturally diverse profile for a local government area in New South Wales.

**USING YOUR SKILLS**

4. Refer to the map and answer the following questions.
   a. In which areas are the highest percentage of people not fluent in English: (i) the northern suburbs (ii) the north-western suburbs (iii) the western suburbs?
   b. Suggest two reasons to explain the pattern.
   c. Forty-two per cent of the population of Cabramatta are not fluent in English. Why do you think this is the case?
   d. Which of the highlighted suburbs had the lowest percentage of the population not fluent in English? Why might this be so?

### BLACKTOWN
Twenty-five per cent of all Filipinos living in Sydney reside in Blacktown. They were originally attracted to the reasonable property prices and good transport links, but now the strong cultural links provided by the Filipino community provide a further magnet to migrants from the Philippines.

### CABRAMATTA
Asian culture is evident in the architecture of Freedom Plaza in the town centre, the variety of Asian restaurants and shops, and the availability of alternative medical practitioners such as acupuncturists and herbalists. Today Cabramatta has a high rate of population growth, low incomes, high unemployment, inadequate and expensive transport and lack of employment opportunities for young people.

*Several Australian mosques are examples of very fine architecture, such as this one in the suburb of Auburn.*

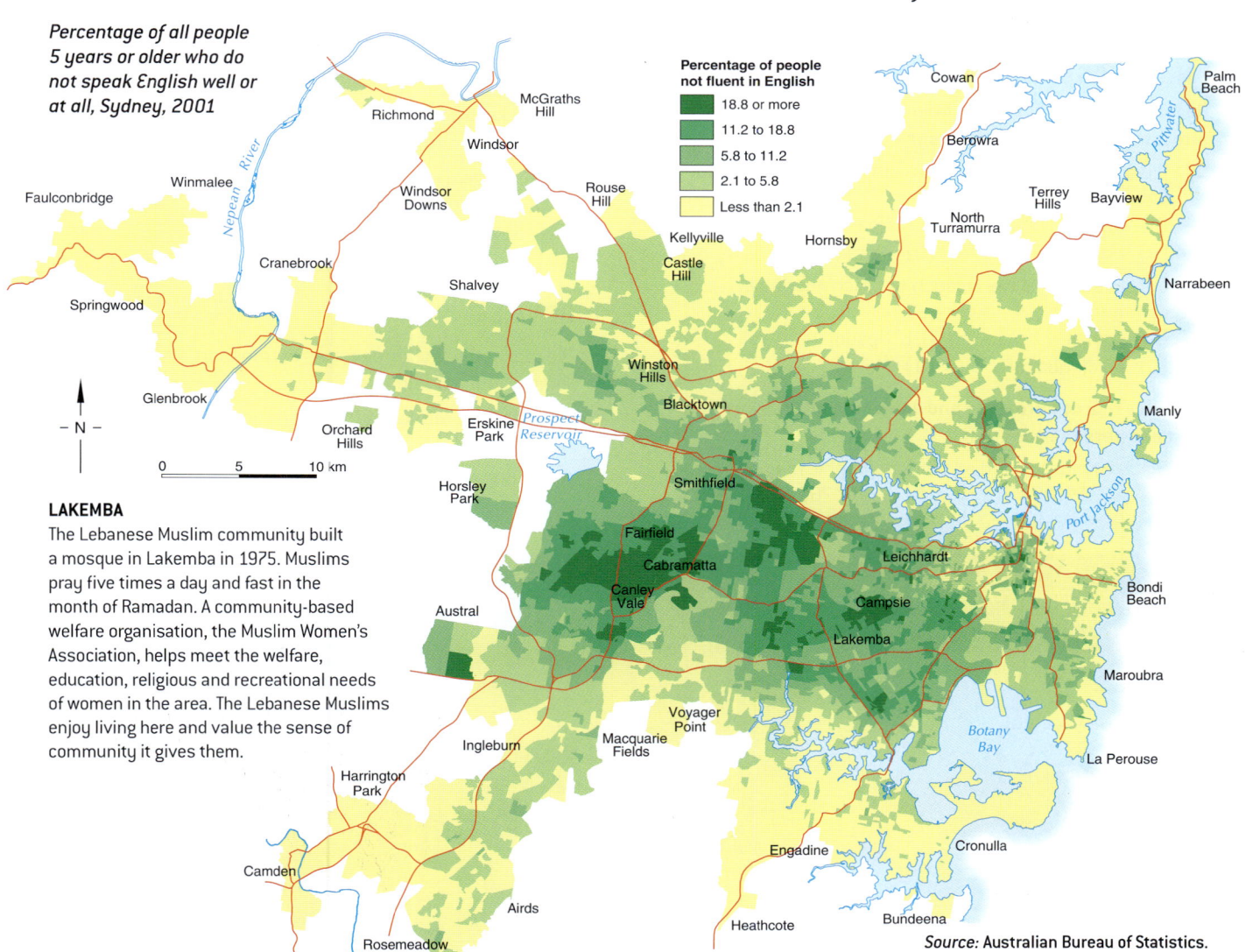

*Percentage of all people 5 years or older who do not speak English well or at all, Sydney, 2001*

**Percentage of people not fluent in English**
- 18.8 or more
- 11.2 to 18.8
- 5.8 to 11.2
- 2.1 to 5.8
- Less than 2.1

### LAKEMBA
The Lebanese Muslim community built a mosque in Lakemba in 1975. Muslims pray five times a day and fast in the month of Ramadan. A community-based welfare organisation, the Muslim Women's Association, helps meet the welfare, education, religious and recreational needs of women in the area. The Lebanese Muslims enjoy living here and value the sense of community it gives them.

*Source:* Australian Bureau of Statistics.

### LEICHHARDT
About 40 per cent of Leichhardt's population was born overseas. Italian-Australians are the largest group and the area has many Italian-style coffee shops and restaurants. During the last ten years, fewer immigrants have come from Italy and more have come from Asia, particularly Vietnam and Hong Kong.

### CAMPSIE
Successive waves of immigrants have come to Campsie since World War II. Many people came from Greece and Italy, and Lebanese immigrants came during the 1960s. Asian immigrants came in the 1970s and 1980s. Within the last ten years, the Korean population in Campsie has increased from a few hundred to over 8000. The Korean church is the core of the community's social and cultural life.

# Working geographically

## BROADSHEET: COBOURG PENINSULA

The Cobourg Peninsula is 200 kilometres north-east of Darwin and is home to four Aboriginal clans. The peninsula and adjacent waters and islands are within the Gurig National Park and the Cobourg Marine Park. The parks are jointly managed by the Aboriginal custodians and the Northern Territory Parks and Wildlife Commission. Fishing is a key source of food and recreation for the small communities on the peninsula.

## KNOWLEDGE AND UNDERSTANDING

Refer to the Aboriginal clan map below and select the alternative that best answers the question.

1. Which Aboriginal clan occupies the eastern part of the Cobourg Peninsula?
   - (A) Agalda
   - (B) Madjunbalmi
   - (C) Ngandjarr
   - (D) Muran

2. Gul Gul station is the location of which Aboriginal community?
   - (A) Agalda
   - (B) Madjunbalmi
   - (C) Ngandjarr
   - (D) Muran

Use all resources provided and select the alternative that best answers the question.

3. Black Point is located on the topographic map at:
   - (A) GR765188
   - (B) GR188766
   - (C) GR184765
   - (D) GR765184.

4. Which Aboriginal outstation is located near Black Point?
   - (A) Gumeragi
   - (B) Gul Gul
   - (C) Marraya
   - (D) Araru

5. What type of vegetation surrounds the Black Point community?
   - (A) Rainforest
   - (B) Dense forest
   - (C) Medium forest
   - (D) Plantations

6. What is the distance between the Gumeragi and Gul Gul outstations?
   - (A) 6 kilometres
   - (B) 13 kilometres
   - (C) 22 kilometres
   - (D) 130 kilometres

7. What danger (see the topographic map) do fishermen in boats face near Gul Gul on Danger Point?
   - (A) Shallow water
   - (B) Crocodiles
   - (C) Sharks
   - (D) Rocks

## SHORT RESPONSE

8. Locate and name three forms of transport available to the Black Point community.

9. Give the grid reference for Victoria Settlement, abandoned in 1849.

10. What feature can be found at grid reference 186747?

*Oblique aerial photograph with Black Point Ranger Station and Gurig Store visible in the foreground near the jetty*

**Aboriginal clan areas**
- Agalda
- Shared Madjunbalmi and Agalda
- Madjunbalmi
- Ngandjarr
- Muran
- ● Aboriginal outstation

*Aboriginal clans of the Cobourg Peninsula*

*Extract from topographic map of the Cobourg Peninsula*  © Commonwealth of Australia, Geoscience Australia. All rights reserved.

**CHAPTER 5** | Australian communities

# 6 Factors causing change in Australian communities

### INQUIRY QUESTIONS
+ What factors have contributed to the community's sense of identity?
+ What factors are causing change in Australian communities?
+ How is change affecting communities?
+ How are different levels of government involved in the process of change?
+ How do community groups respond to change?

Australia's communities are changing. When Europeans occupied Australia over 200 years ago, they began to change the physical and human environments that had existed here for thousands of years. During the nineteenth century, settlements spread rapidly across the country. The main economic activities in rural areas were farming, grazing and mining. Communities developed in towns and cities to serve the needs of the population. Australia's population has grown and changed rapidly in the last 50 years. In this chapter, we look at how change has affected communities, including Indigenous communities, and how they are responding to change.

### GEOskills TOOLBOX

**GEOskillbuilder** Using fieldwork techniques to collect data (page 139)

+ Interpreting a satellite image (page 129)
+ Comparing a graph with a table (page 131)
+ Using the internet for newspaper articles (page 142)

*The owners of a Turkish restaurant in Surry Hills, Sydney*

### KEY TERMS

**Anglo-Celtic:** describes a person with a British origin

**cultural integration:** communities and governments working together to celebrate diversity, improve community services, meet diverse community needs and address community problems

**demographic change:** a change in the characteristics of a population, such as rates of growth, birth, death and migration

**globalisation:** greater movement of people, goods, money and ideas around the world.

**internet café:** a place where a person can buy time on a computer with internet access. Often it serves as a regular café serving food and drinks.

**Mabo:** a court case in 1992 in which the High Court of Australia ruled that *terra nullius* (the concept that the land was owned by no-one before European settlement) did not apply

**migration:** the permanent or semipermanent movement of people from one location to another

**multiculturalism:** a policy of including many different cultural groups in a society

**native title:** the name given by Australian law to Indigenous peoples' traditional rights to their lands and waters

**wetlands:** areas that are covered permanently, occasionally or periodically by fresh or salt water up to a depth of six metres

**White Australia policy:** a law that existed from 1901 to 1973 that restricted the entry of non-white migrants

**World Heritage site:** a place recognised as being of such great value that it should be preserved for all people for all time

# 6.1 Overview of change in Australian communities

All communities undergo change, some more rapidly than others. Many factors cause changes in Australian communities. Some of the more important are discussed on these pages.

## Changing nature and patterns of work

In Australia people are employed in four main industry sectors — primary industry, secondary industry, tertiary industry and quaternary (or information) industry. These sectors are described in the following diagram.

**Primary industry** 
Produces raw materials, such as wool, iron ore, meat, wheat, oil, timber, fish and uranium.

**Secondary industry** 
Makes goods by hand or machinery from raw materials from primary industries — for example, milk is turned into cheese and butter.

**Tertiary industry** 
Does not produce goods but provides a skill or service, including banking, transport, building and retailing. Salespeople, doctors, electricians and bus drivers are examples of jobs in the services sector.

**Quaternary industry** 
Also called the information industry, as its workers produce information in various forms — for example, people working in media and telecommunications.

*The four main industry sectors that employ people in Australia*

The proportion of the workforce employed in each of these sectors has changed significantly from the middle of the twentieth century. During the 1950s, service jobs in the tertiary and quaternary sector industries began to expand, and this change has continued, with:
- a steady decline in work in the primary and secondary sectors particularly in developed countries
- paticularly rapid expansion in the tertiary and quaternary sectors.

There have also been changes in work patterns:
- There is greater flexibility in the number and timing of working hours, including part-time work, job sharing, temporary work, contract work and videoconferencing.
- More individuals are self-employed in work such as franchises, freelancing, consulting and home-based industries.

These changes have had a major impact on communities including an increase in the size of urban communities, with a decrease in rural communities, an increase in the participation of women in the workforce and the establishment of work-related communities.

## Cultural integration

**Cultural integration** can result when communities and governments work together to celebrate diversity, improve community services, meet diverse community needs and address community problems. There are many examples of cultural integration in Australia. For example, the Chinese community has retained its broad identity in many places in Australia, including Epping in Sydney, while still being part of the diverse Australian community. Also, later in this chapter, we will examine cultural integration of the Vietnamese community in Cabramatta (see pages 136–39).

## Demographic change

**Demographic change**, including changes in the rates of growth, birth, death and **migration**, is one of the major factors affecting Australian communities today.

One aspect of demographic change is the growth of Australia's capital cities. Along with Perth, Brisbane and Melbourne, Sydney has experienced large population increases, affecting established communities and creating new communities. Sydney's suburbs have spread in a westerly direction from the central business district (CBD). The greatest increases in population since 2000 have been recorded in western suburbs such as Blacktown, Liverpool and Baulkham Hills. Sydney's urban sprawl has created new communities and changed existing communities.

## GEOskills TOOLBOX

### INTERPRETING A SATELLITE IMAGE

Satellite images show a much larger area of the Earth's surface than photographs taken from an aircraft. The satellite records bands of light reflected from the Earth. These are coloured to clearly show features. Some of the common colours used on satellite images include:
- black or dark-blue — representing deep water because it absorbs light energy
- purple, light-blue or grey — representing urban areas
- bright green or pink — crops or other vegetation usually in a high rainfall or irrigated area
- darker green — forests
- white — beaches, deserts or bare areas with high amounts of reflection.

Look carefully at the satellite image of Sydney. Copy and complete the description below using the following words:

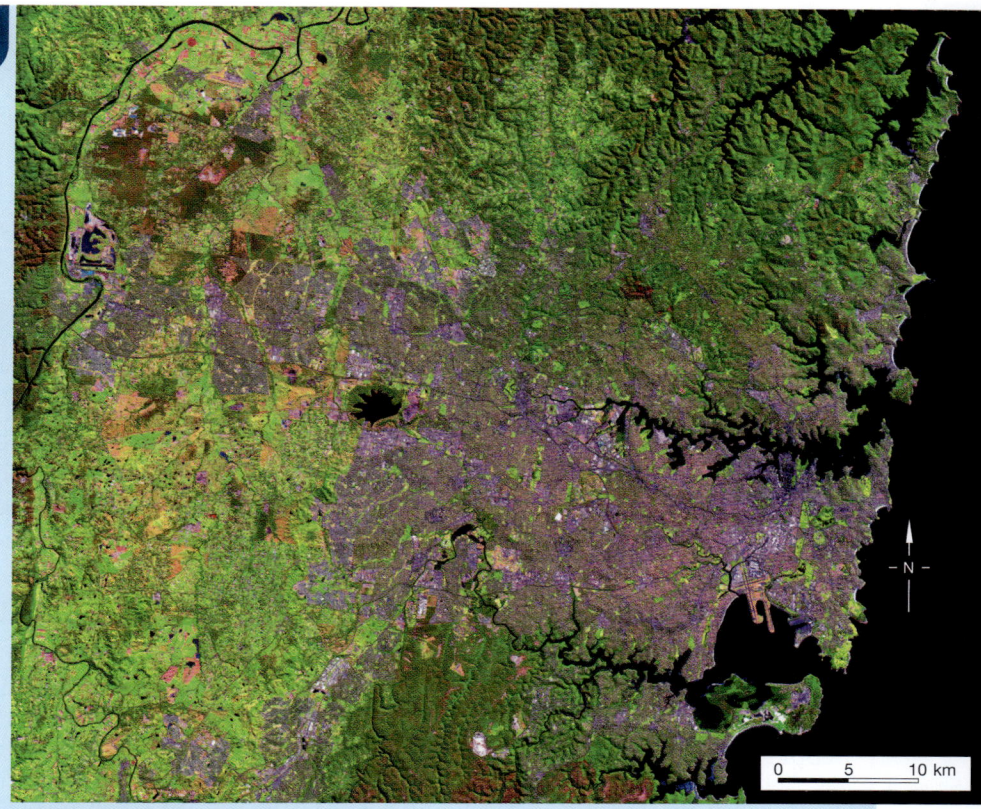

*suburbs, airport, purple, forests, sixty, Blue Mountains, black, darker*

The sprawling Sydney suburbs show up as _____ on the 2002 satellite image. They stretch for _____ kilometres from the coastline to the _____, following the Parramatta River and the Great Western Highway. More densely populated areas show as _____ patches within the urban area. _____ on the rural–urban fringe are represented by bright green on the image. Mountains and _____ in the north of the image have restricted the spread of population in this direction. Botany Bay shows as a large area of _____ in the south-east of the image. An _____ can be clearly seen jutting out into the bay.

*Satellite image of Sydney, 2002*

## Globalisation of economic activity

**Globalisation** is a trend that sees people, goods, money and ideas moving around the world faster and much more cheaply than before. Communication and transport between countries improved significantly during the twentieth century as a result of new technologies. Air travel now brings people together within a few hours, and satellite telecommunications link businesses internationally by phone, fax and the internet. Governments and business worldwide have been encouraged to think 'globally', and stronger links have been forged between countries.

Communities have been affected by this globalisation. One disadvantage has been a reduction in job opportunities in some industries as local industries go overseas. An advantage is that some communities feel less isolated and become part of the 'global village'.

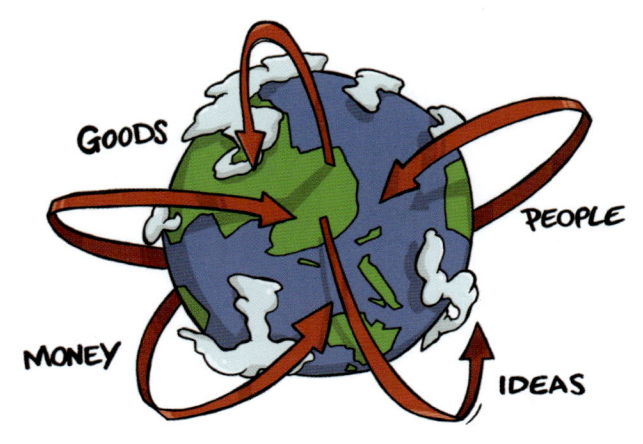

*The global economy in action*

## Lifestyle expectations

Lifestyle expectations are the living standards expected by an individual or community. These expectations are affected by factors such as:
- geographic location. Many Australians prefer the temperate climate, scenic beauty and clean air close to the sea. Locations with the fastest rate of population increase include the Sunshine Coast and the Gold Coast (see pages 132–35).
- socioeconomic status. A person's position within a social structure depends on a number of variables including income, occupation, education, wealth and place of residence. Often people move to a community that reflects their socioeconomic status, such as a wealthy suburb of Sydney or a house with a view.
- culture and religion. People within a community often reflect that community's culture and religion. Many people of Chinese origin in Sydney live in Castle Hill, and their restaurants and other buildings reflect their culture. Deeply religious people often move into communities with other people of the same religion.

## Recognition of native title

'Native title' is the name given by Australian law to Indigenous peoples' traditional rights to their lands and waters. Those rights can range from a relationship similar to full ownership of the land through to the right to go onto the land for ceremonies or to hunt, fish or gather foods and bush medicines. To have their native title rights recognised, the Indigenous group has to prove they still have a connection with their country according to their traditional laws. The recognition of native title affects Indigenous and non-Indigenous communities (see the case study on pages 140–43).

> **GEOfacts** Native title rights can range from a relationship similar to full ownership of the land through to the right to go onto the land for ceremonies or to hunt, fish or gather foods and bush medicines.

## Resource depletion

Over time, non-sustainable resources become depleted. For example, when a gold mine is depleted, there is no longer employment at the mine and most of the population moves on. There are many cases in Australia where a thriving community disappears when the resource that it is based on for prosperity becomes depleted. During the latter part of the nineteenth century, Gulgong in New South Wales was a large town. The resource (gold) had became depleted; now it is a small town, with a community largely dependent on tourism.

*Shopfronts in Gulgong*

## New technologies

Technology is the application of science to industry. New technologies bring change to communities because these developments result in a more efficient and productive way of doing things.

> **SAMPLE STUDY**
>
> ### Neighbourhoods become global communities
>
> Neighbourhood meeting places have traditionally encouraged a sense of community. The local park, hotel, church and coffee shop have provided places where people can get together and exchange news, ideas and gossip. Today, people across the globe can be linked by the internet. Individuals can establish a social network. This is a social structure made of nodes where individuals or organisations are linked by values, ideas, friendship, kinship, dislike, conflict or trade. A social network service focuses on building online communities of people who share interests and activities, or who are interested in exploring the interests and activities of others. Most social network services are web based and provide various ways of interacting, such as email and instant messaging services.
>
> Individuals and groups can swap ideas and news by email or talk to strangers in other parts of the country and other parts of the world. People with special interests can communicate with other people or communities.
>
> Many people are linked to global communities via MySpace and Facebook. People without internet facilities at home often use an internet café. Many travellers use internet cafés to send information to families and members of their community.

## GEOskills TOOLBOX

### COMPARING A GRAPH WITH A TABLE

Bar graphs are very useful for comparing data. If graphs are supplemented with a table, though, comparisons can become more meaningful because of additional information. For example, the bar graph below shows China as the leader in actual numbers of people using the internet. However, the table shows that only 19 per cent of China's population use the internet.

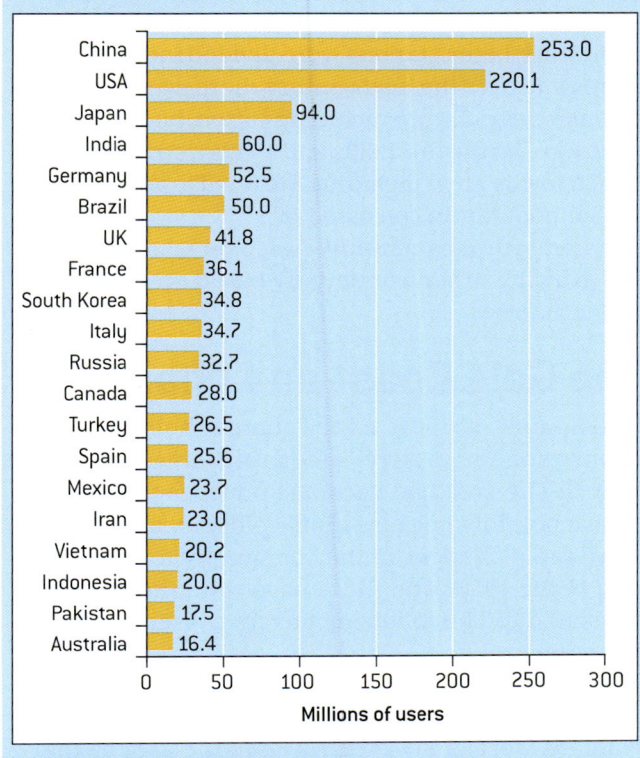

*Countries with the most internet users* (Millions of users):
- China: 253.0
- USA: 220.1
- Japan: 94.0
- India: 60.0
- Germany: 52.5
- Brazil: 50.0
- UK: 41.8
- France: 36.1
- South Korea: 34.8
- Italy: 34.7
- Russia: 32.7
- Canada: 28.0
- Turkey: 26.5
- Spain: 25.6
- Mexico: 23.7
- Iran: 23.0
- Vietnam: 20.2
- Indonesia: 20.0
- Pakistan: 17.5
- Australia: 16.4

**Internet use, 2008**

| Country | % of population that uses the internet | Population (millions) |
|---|---|---|
| Canada | 84.3 | 33 |
| Australia | 79.4 | 21 |
| Japan | 73.8 | 127 |
| United States | 72.5 | 304 |
| South Korea | 70.7 | 49 |
| United Kingdom | 68.6 | 61 |
| Germany | 63.8 | 82 |
| Spain | 63.3 | 40 |
| Italy | 59.7 | 58 |
| France | 58.1 | 62 |
| Turkey | 36.9 | 72 |
| Iran | 34.9 | 66 |
| Brazil | 26.1 | 192 |
| Vietnam | 23.4 | 86 |
| Russia | 23.2 | 141 |
| Mexico | 21.6 | 110 |
| China | 19.0 | 1330 |
| Indonesia | 10.5 | 238 |
| Pakistan | 10.4 | 168 |
| India | 5.2 | 1148 |

*Source:* Data derived from www.internetworldstats.com.

## ACTIVITIES

### UNDERSTANDING

1. List the important factors causing change in Australian communities.
2. Outline how changing the nature and patterns of work causes change in Australian communities.
3. Describe how demographic change causes change in Australian communities.
4. How does globalisation cause change in communities?
5. Read the case study 'Neighbourhood communities become global communities'. Explain how such communities can become global communities.

### THINKING AND APPLYING

6. Interview an older person and ask them how their community has changed over their lifetime. Do they think the community now is better or worse? Record the change on a poster and add a collage of photographs.
7. Refer to the diagram on page 129. Explain the process of globalisation.

### USING YOUR SKILLS

8. List the three countries with the highest number of internet users.
9. For the three countries with the highest number of internet users, state the percentage of the population that uses the internet.
10. Compare Australia's internet use with India's. Account for the difference.

### GEOTERMS

**demographic change:** a change in the characteristics of a population, such as rates of growth, birth, death and migration

**globalisation:** greater movement of people, goods, money and ideas around the world.

**migration:** the permanent or semipermanent movement of people from one location to another

**native title:** the name given by Australian law to Indigenous peoples' traditional rights to their lands and waters

**CHAPTER 6** | Factors causing change in Australian communities

# 6.2 Gold Coast: lifestyle expectations

*The location of the Gold Coast*

The Gold Coast covers 1400 square kilometres of the coastal area in southern Queensland. It is a city and local government area of south-east Queensland.

Before European settlement, the Gold Coast and its hinterland was an area of timbered mountains and hills, river valleys, flood plains, and freshwater and saltwater wetlands. It was the home of the Aboriginal Yugambeh people. They lived in harmony with the natural environment, hunting and collecting. Much of that environment has now changed but the descendants of the Yugambeh people still live on the Gold Coast.

The nineteenth century was a time of great migration from Europe to the countries of the New World including Australia. Settlers, mainly of **Anglo-Celtic** origin, reached the area, then known as the South Coast, and established large cattle stations and cleared much of the land of rainforest. Later, stations were divided into smaller farms and over the next century there was more intensive agriculture including cotton, bananas and avocado. During the 1930s and 1940s a string of small beach towns grew, including Surfers Paradise.

The population consisted of:
- a small rural community based on small farming
- a growing urban community based on tourism and retirees.

## The Gold Coast and change

The South Coast was a very popular holiday destination for ex-servicemen returning from World War II. The area had become known as the Gold Coast, possibly because of its golden beaches. There were rapid changes in the community towards the end of the 1950s and these have continued until the present day. The following factors caused change in the community:
- After World War II, people were generally more prosperous and had higher lifestyle expectations.
- Roads were greatly improved in the area as the family car became more affordable. People from inland and further south travelled to the camping grounds, caravan parks, motels and, later, hotels and apartments.

*Coolangatta in 1952*

- Improvements in communications enabled many people to consult travel agents, who catered for the needs of the holiday maker.
- Along with promotion of the area's natural beauty and subtropical climate came development of holiday apartments, shopping arcades and canal development on waterways. As tourism grew, there were more opportunities for business and investment. By the 1960s, the Gold Coast's infrastructure had grown considerably so high-rise development began. The Gold Coast had become the major tourist destination in Australia, and tourism had become the main industry.
- During the 1980s, the Gold Coast became an established international tourist destination with the development of theme parks such as Dreamworld, Seaworld and Movie World. Japanese investment in high-rise buildings transformed the skyline of the city.
- Many migrants from interstate, and an increasing number from overseas, were attracted by the opportunities of employment and the lifestyle of the Gold Coast.

## Effects of change on the community

The Gold Coast has experienced great change from the small communities before 1950.
- Migration from within Australia and overseas has increased the population to over 500 000 in 2009, making it the sixth largest city in Australia.
- The population has changed from almost all Anglo-Celtic to being more culturally diverse.
- Wetlands have been drained to enable construction of canals and natural waterways have been altered to develop marinas.
- The urban landscape has changed to one of major high-rise development in beachside locations. The Gold Coast has the highest residential building in the world.
- Quality infrastructure, including a hospital and education facilities, has been developed and transport is greatly improved.
- The Gold Coast has become a major tourist destination, attracting more than 10 million overnight and day-trip visitors. It hosts nearly 30 000 visitors each day; 92 per cent come from other areas of Australia and the remainder from overseas, including Japan, New Zealand and China.
- A wide range of work opportunities has been developed.

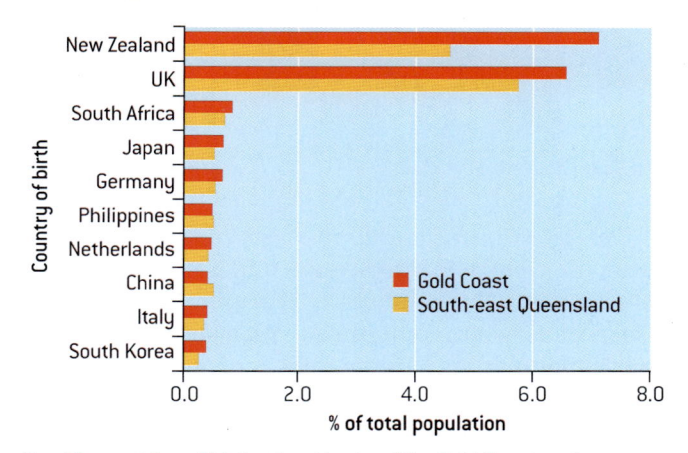

*Top 10 countries of birth of residents of the Gold Coast and south-east Queensland, 2006*

*Source:* Australian Bureau of Statistics.

*Coolangatta in about 2004*

*The Gold Coast skyline*

| Net migration to the Gold Coast, 2001 to 2006 | |
|---|---|
| Other parts of Queensland | 1 283 |
| New South Wales | 20 962 |
| Victoria | 4 811 |
| South Australia | 1 551 |
| Australian Capital Territory | 1 121 |
| Tasmania | 851 |

*Source:* Australian Bureau of Statistics.

The Gold Coast community today reflects the dramatic change in the physical and human environment. The community is primarily a prosperous urban community with a large transient tourist population. Large numbers of people continue to move to the Gold Coast to meet their lifestyle expectations. The Gold Coast retains its position as one of Australia's most visited tourist venues and is the fastest growing region in Australia.

# Government response to change

The three levels of government have supported the development of a tourist industry on the Gold Coast, along with the large increase in population.

## Federal government

Coolangatta Airport was upgraded in the 1980s to allow for international passengers and larger planes. The federal government has also promoted the tourist industry overseas, developed immigration programs and encouraged foreign investment.

## State government

The Queensland state government has developed infrastructure including education, water and sewerage, roads, law and order, and public transport.

## Local government

The Gold Coast City Council (the former Gold Coast Town Council) was officially formed in 1958, and the Gold Coast was proclaimed as a city in 1959. The council has been active in the development of the Gold Coast since then. It is responsible for local infrastructure such as roads, parks, beaches and recreational areas. It has also developed libraries and community centres.

# Response of community groups to change

Many community groups on the Gold Coast have been active during its population increase, change in the physical and human environments and the development of waterways, high-rise buildings and tourist facilities.

- Many community groups, including those involved in 'green' movements and preservation, have opposed change; they have agitated for slower development and preservation of much more of the physical environment.
- Other community groups have advocated more rapid development. Much of the business community and other individuals want a large urban development and the opportunities it brings for employment, education and lifestyle improvement.

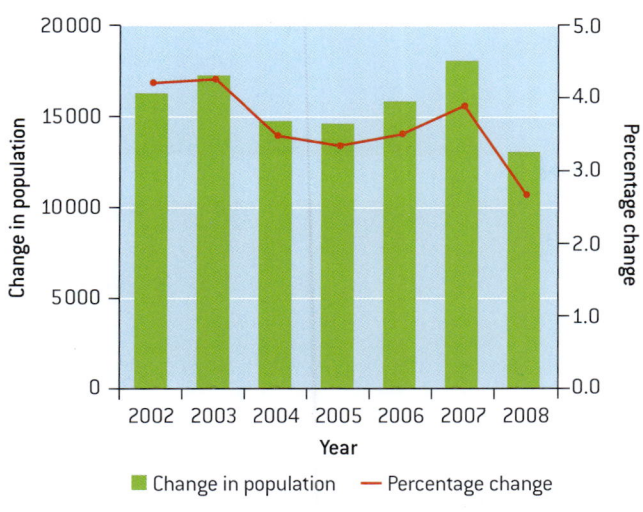

*Changes in estimated resident population, Gold Coast*
Source: Australian Bureau of Statistics.

*Each year, in November and December, around 25 000 Year 12 school leavers from all around Australia arrive on the Gold Coast for Schoolies. Many volunteers from the local community offer support, patrolling beaches and streets to ensure the safety of those celebrating the end of their secondary schooling.*

## ACTIVITIES

### UNDERSTANDING

1. Identify the shared space of the Gold Coast community.
2. How did the Yugambeh people live in harmony with the natural environment?
3. Outline how the European settlers changed the natural environment.
4. Describe the factors causing change in the Gold Coast community after 1950.
5. a Outline the impacts of change on the Gold Coast community.
   b Select one of these impacts and describe how the impact changed the Gold Coast community.
6. Outline how the three levels of government have responded to change in the Gold Coast community.

### THINKING AND APPLYING

7. What do you understand by the term *lifestyle expectations*? Outline the lifestyle expectations of the community in the area in which you live.
8. Discuss the advantages and disadvantages of high-rise buildings in residential areas.
9. Identify two Gold Coast sporting teams in national competitions. Outline how these teams contribute to the feeling of identity of the Gold Coast community.

### USING YOUR SKILLS

10. Refer to the two photographs of Coolangatta Beach on pages 132 and 133.
    a Describe the scene in the 1950s photograph and in the 2004 photograph.
    b What are the main differences between the two photographs? Account for these differences.
11. Refer to the table showing 'Net migration to the Gold Coast, 2001 to 2006'. From which state was the largest migration to the Gold Coast? Suggest reasons for this.
12. Refer to the bar graph showing 'Top 10 countries of birth of residents of the Gold Coast and south-east Queensland, 2006'.
    a Name the three countries of birth that contributed most to the population of the Gold Coast in 2006.
    b Suggest reasons why a greater percentage of people on the Gold Coast than in south-east Queensland were born overseas.
13. Refer to the photograph of the Gold Coast skyline. Make a line drawing of this scene, dividing it into foreground, middle ground and background. Label the drawing.
14. Refer to the graph on this page.
    a What measurement is shown on the left axis of the graph?
    b What measurement is shown on the right axis of the graph?
    c What measurement is shown on the horizontal axis of the graph?
    d Which year had the smallest change in population?
    e Which year had the lowest percentage change in population?
    f What trend can you see in the change in population?
    g What trend can you see in the percentage change in population?
    h How useful is the graph for showing trends?

### GEOTERMS

**wetlands:** areas that are covered permanently, occasionally or periodically by fresh or salt water up to a depth of six metres

# 6.3 Cabramatta: a culturally diverse community

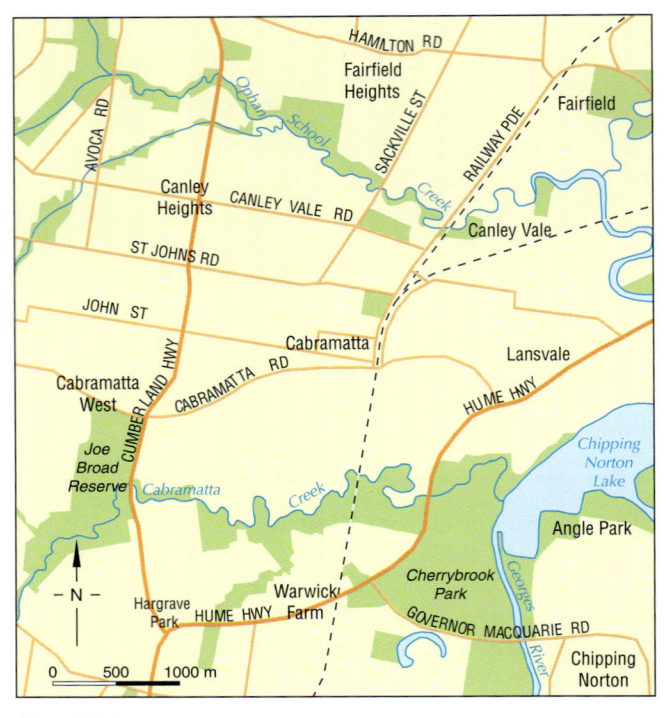

*Map of Cabramatta*

*The central business district of Cabramatta*

Cabramatta is a suburb located in south-western Sydney, about 30 kilometres from Sydney's central business district.

Aboriginal people from the Gandangera tribe have lived in this area for more than 30 000 years. Early development by Europeans was mainly grazing. This gradually gave way to market gardens and sawmills. When a railway line was constructed during the 1850s, clusters of wooden houses grew around the line. It was essentially a rural community until the 1950s when migrant hostels and housing commission developments transformed it into a Sydney suburb.

## Cabramatta and change

The **White Australia policy** was not fully dismantled until 1973; this restricted non-white or non-European migration into Australia, and there were almost no Vietnamese people in Australia. During the late 1970s, Australia began accepting refugees from Vietnam, and Australia began its transformation into a multicultural society. Cabramatta and its surrounding districts had several migrant hostels, and the first Vietnamese immigrants lived there. Gradually they began to settle into Cabramatta and nearby suburbs. Vietnamese people made the suburb their home and they eventually replaced many former migrant groups. By the 1990s, Cabramatta seemed to have developed its own identity with Vietnamese business thriving in shops, restaurants and commercial enterprises. Today in John Street, there are over 800 ethnic businesses offering a wide range of goods and services. Many media commentators unfavourably called the transformed suburb 'Vietnamatta'.

The factors causing changes in the community were:
- the decision by the federal government to allow large numbers of refugees from Vietnam to settle in Australia
- the Vietnamese government allowing refugees to leave the nation and take up residence in Australia
- the movement by previous migrants of European origin to leave migrant hostels and houses in Cabramatta and move to new housing

developments in nearby suburbs such as Smithfield and Bonnyrigg
- the industry and determination by the new migrants to settle in Cabramatta and make it much like their former homeland.

> **GEOfacts** Khoa Do is a young Vietnamese actor, writer and director whose family came to Sydney from Vietnam in 1980. He has worked with Vietnamese youth in Cabramatta, and in 2005 he was awarded Young Australian of the Year. His brother is the comedian Anh Do.

**Vietnamese people in Australia**

| Year | Born in Vietnam ('000s) | Speak Vietnamese ('000s) |
|---|---|---|
| 1976 | 2.4 | – |
| 1981 | 41.1 | – |
| 1986 | 83.0 | – |
| 1991 | 121.8 | 110.8 |
| 1996 | 150.9 | 146.2 |
| 2001 | 154.8 | 174.2 |
| 2006 | 141.8 | 194.9 |

*Source:* Australian Bureau of Statistics.

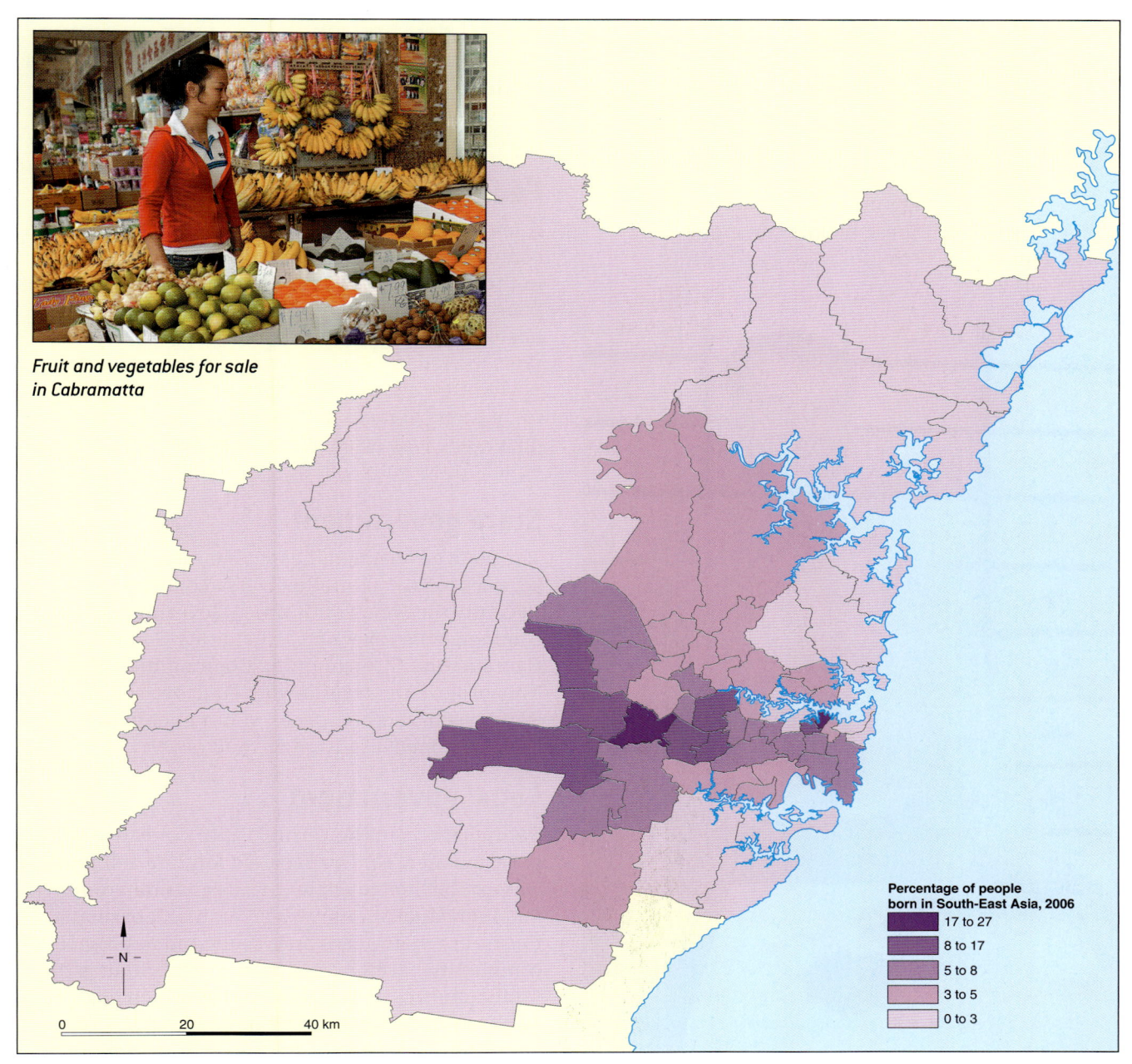

*Fruit and vegetables for sale in Cabramatta*

Percentage of people born in South-East Asia, 2006
- 17 to 27
- 8 to 17
- 5 to 8
- 3 to 5
- 0 to 3

*Map of distribution of people born in South-East Asia, 2006, Sydney*

**CHAPTER 6** | Factors causing change in Australian communities

## Impacts of change on the community

Cabramatta has experienced great change from a community of predominantly European descent in the 1970s and early 1980s.

- In 2006, 27.5 per cent of people resident in Cabramatta were born in Australia, while 31.2 per cent were born in Vietnam, 9.0 per cent in Cambodia, 5.5 per cent in China, 1.6 per cent in Laos and 1.3 per cent in Thailand. In addition, many people born in Australia were of South-East Asian descent.
- Cultural diversity is seen in the Vietnamese restaurants, the Tien Hua and Kwan Yin Buddhist temples, a wide variety of fresh produce and clothing shops, and people working as acupuncturists and selling alternative medicines. The central business district is almost entirely Asian in character.
- In this globalised community, clothes, furniture and newspapers are imported from Asian countries so that these people can enjoy the comforts of both their past and present lifestyles.

*Pai Lau Gate*

*Chinese traditional medicine*

## Government response to change

The three levels of government have been involved in the response to the development of a large increase in immigration from South-East Asia and the development of a culturally diverse community.

### Federal government

A major influence on the change in the Cabramatta community was the federal government's decision in the late 1970s to admit large numbers of refugees from Vietnam and house these people in migrant hostels in the Cabramatta area. Around the same time, the federal government adopted a policy of multiculturalism, which recognised the rights of migrants to maintain their cultural identity, encourage and assist migrants to do so, and promote equal opportunity and access to services.

### State government

The state government has maintained essential services to the culturally diverse community. Recently the New South Wales Government commenced work with Fairfield City Council on Cabramatta's Strengthening Communities project. This project aims to direct its efforts to social issues such as crime, drugs, youth unemployment, socioeconomic disadvantage and poverty.

### Local government

Cabramatta is in the Fairfield City Council local government area. The Fairfield Migrant Interagency was established to allow various cultural groups and individuals in the city, including Cabramatta, to express their needs and issues and to promote community harmony. A similar organisation is the Multicultural Advisory Committee, which enables community representatives and individuals from various migrant groups to provide formal input to the council.

# Community groups and response to change

Various community groups have been established to respond to the great change in the community over 30 years. Two examples are:
- Cabramatta's Moon Festival, which is a traditional annual festival of South-East Asia, is held in September each year.
- the Cabramatta Community Centre, which is a community-based organisation providing a wide range of services including women's support, links to learning, multicultural services, aged care support and housing support.

## GEO skillbuilder

### USING FIELDWORK TECHNIQUES TO COLLECT DATA

Fieldwork involves going out into the field to gather data to bring back into the classroom for further analysis. Successful fieldwork involves good planning, accurate data collection and careful statistical analysis.

A fieldwork study of a local community may be used as a research action plan to improve an aspect of community life. Fieldwork of this nature should involve:
- locating a fieldwork site — for example, a shopping area where the main street is declining
- focus questions to investigate — for example: Is there competition from newer shopping centres with more facilities?
- fieldwork data collection — for example, photographs, car counts, people counts, surveys
- arrangement of raw data into tables and graphs
- presentation of findings in a written report with an action plan for improvement, and a map showing the location of the fieldwork site or area under review.

#### STEP 1
Explore, observe and describe potential sites in your local community that could be improved or used to host a community event.

#### STEP 2
In groups, prepare a SWOT analysis of one of these sites. Place the responses from your group and the wider community under the headings: 'Strengths', 'Weaknesses', Opportunities' and 'Threats'. You could use a large piece of paper for the analysis.

#### STEP 3
Collect and analyse information from your fieldwork.

#### STEP 4
Present your findings as a report, poster or PowerPoint show.

#### STEP 5
As a class, select one project that you believe has the greatest benefit to the local community. Undertake further class fieldwork and research, and present your findings to the local council.

## ACTIVITIES

### UNDERSTANDING
1. Identify the shared space of the Cabramatta community.
2. Define the term *multicultural*.
3. Who were the original inhabitants of Cabramatta?
4. a Identify the factors that led to Cabramatta developing a culturally diverse community.
   b Describe three of the factors.
5. Describe the culturally diverse Cabramatta that had developed by the 1990s.
6. Outline the results of the 2006 census showing the cultural diversity of Cabramatta.
7. What are the streetscape indicators of a culturally diverse community in Cabramatta?
8. Outline the responses to change in the Cabramatta community by the federal government, state government and local government.
9. Describe how two community groups have responded to change in Cabramatta.

### THINKING AND APPLYING
10. Imagine you are going to a Vietnamese restaurant in Cabramatta. In pairs, use the internet or library to research the meal you would choose. Outline the ingredients, method of cooking and likely presentation. Display the meal on a poster.

### USING YOUR SKILLS
11. Refer to the table showing data on Vietnamese people in Australia.
    a Between which years was there the largest increase in people born in Vietnam?
    b Between which years was there the largest decline in people born in Vietnam? Suggest reasons for this.
    c There has been a constant increase in people who speak Vietnamese at home, whereas the number of people born in Vietnam declined after 2001. Suggest reasons for this.

### GEOTERMS

**multiculturalism:** a policy of including many different cultural groups in a society

**White Australia policy:** a law that existed from 1901 to 1973 that restricted the entry of non-white migrants

# 6.4 The Mirarr community and Jabiluka

Jabiluka is a proposed uranium mine in the Northern Territory within Kakadu National Park. It is surrounded by the wetlands, escarpments and sacred sites of one of the world's most famous and most popular **World Heritage sites**. The Jabiluka site is about 20 kilometres north of the Ranger uranium mine. The ore body was discovered in 1971 by Pancontinental Mining Limited. Energy Resources of Australia (ERA) purchased the mineral lease in 1991.

## Change and the Mirarr community

The traditional Aboriginal owners of this land are the Mirarr (or Mirrar) people. The land is communally owned and the community shares the same history, place of birth, kinship system and cultural traditions. Traditionally the Mirarr lived as hunters and gatherers. The land provided food such as wallabies and fruit, the rivers supplied fish and turtles, and the swamps provided abundant lily bulbs and waterfowl. The people had a good standard of living and leisure time to devote to social, cultural and spiritual pursuits.

European settlement in the Northern Territory had an impact on Indigenous communities in many of the same ways as elsewhere in Australia. The people were affected by introduced diseases and the imposition of new rules and ideas by governments and missionaries. Some people left their traditional lands to work in the cattle industry, some became fringe dwellers living in poor conditions on the edges of white settlements, and some part-Indigenous children were taken from their parents and placed in institutions. However, the isolation of the Kakadu region and its unsuitability for farming meant that the people here were more able to maintain their traditional lifestyles and traditions than was the case in densely settled areas such as coastal New South Wales.

The Mirarr's claim to their traditional lands was granted in 1982. It was not called native title, but it recognised the rights subsequently granted under native title. As owners of the land, the Mirarr have the right to lease the land to governments, individuals and corporations. Just before granting the Mirarr's claims, Indigenous leaders had agreed in 1981 to allow a mining company (Pancontinental Mining) to construct an underground uranium mine at Jabiluka. There was considerable doubt over the fairness of the agreement; some maintain that Indigenous leaders were worn down by the negotiation process and compromised in order to reach agreement. The senior traditional owner of the Mirrar land, Yvonne Margarula, claims her father was coerced into signing this agreement.

In the early 1980s, the Ranger uranium mine was established and the township of Jabiru was built.

*The Magela flood plain, Kakadu. The western boundary of the Jabiluka lease adjoins the Magela flood plain.*

## Cultural values threatened

The vast majority of World Heritage sites are listed for natural values. Kakadu was listed for both natural and cultural values. Much of the park is relatively unaffected by human activity, and its native ecosystems remain largely intact. The park contains a rich variety of Indigenous domestic and ceremonial sites and over 7000 rock art sites. A key factor in receiving World Heritage status under the cultural criteria was the ongoing presence in the Kakadu area of Indigenous people for more than 40 000 years.

Many of the Mirarr people regretted signing the agreement to mine uranium. They argued that uranium mining at Jabiluka threatened this living cultural tradition, and therefore the cultural values of Kakadu. In June 1998 the Mirarr people presented their arguments to the UNESCO World Heritage Committee. A UNESCO mission came to Australia and met with government, industry, conservation and Indigenous groups. Extracts from its report are featured below.

> ### JABILUKA WORLD HERITAGE COMMITTEE REPORT NOVEMBER 1998
>
> *Recommendation 2*
> The mission noted the serious concerns and preoccupations expressed by some of Australia's most eminent scientists as to the unacceptably high degree of scientific uncertainties relating to the Jabiluka mine design, tailings disposal and possible impacts on catchment ecosystems.
>
> *Recommendation 4*
> The mission recommends that every effort is made to ensure thorough participation, negotiation and communication with traditional owners, custodians and managers to ensure the compilation of an accurate cultural inventory that will ensure the conservation of cultural sites located within the Jabiluka Mineral Lease.
>
> *Recommendation 7*
> The mission is of the view that it is incumbent on the Australian Government to recognise the special relationship of the Mirarr to their land and their rights to participate in decisions affecting them. Therefore the mission is of the opinion that the Australian Government, along with the other signatories, should reconsider the status of the 1982 agreement and the 1991 transfer of ownership to ensure maintenance of the fundamental rights of the traditional owners.

The World Heritage Committee voted 20–1 for work on Jabiluka to be halted immediately. The growing level of international awareness and concern was demonstrated in April 1999 when Mirarr leaders Yvonne Margarula and Jacqui Katona won the Goldman Environmental Prize in the category of island nations. The Mirarr also received the Friends of the Earth Environmental Award. The Goldman award recognises grassroots environmental campaigners worldwide, and is worth US$150,000.

*Yvonne Margarula (right) and Jacqui Katona (centre) meet Hillary Clinton (wife of the US President Bill Clinton) at the White House after they were awarded the Goldman Environmental Prize in April 1999.*

## Environmental impacts

Enormous quantities of rock have to be mined to retrieve a small amount of uranium oxide. Tailings (the solid wastes left over after mining) retain radioactivity and are easily dispersed in the environment by wind and rain. They can remain dangerous for thousands of years.

Mining and milling uranium also produces contaminated water. Waste water is confined in retention ponds to protect the environment. It is then evaporated or put through wetland filters or treatment plants. In the Kakadu area, the summer monsoon rains can stretch retention ponds to the limit. Leaks and spills have the potential to pollute areas downstream.

*Aerial photograph of the Jabiluka mine site in 2000*

## Responses of individuals, groups and governments

Different people have different perspectives about Jabiluka. Apart from the Mirarr people, other stakeholders include the environmental movement, the World Heritage authorities, the Northern Land Council, the mining company, financiers and investors, the tourism industry and the government. Each group has freedom of speech to express its views in the democratic process in such ways as lobbying, voting, demonstrating and writing letters. Public interest, opinion polls, media coverage and international attitudes can all influence the policies of political parties.

The Mirarr were able to gain widespread international attention and support with little more than a fax machine, email and community-based support. In 1998, the Mirarr invited people to join a non-violent blockade at the entrance to Jabiluka, which attracted more than 5000 supporters as well as media attention. Rallies were held in Germany, Japan and the United Kingdom as well as all over Australia. Support also came from environmental groups including Friends of the Earth and the Wilderness Society who were also opposed to uranium mining at Jabiluka.

In 1999, Aboriginal groups refused to allow uranium ore to be trucked from Jabiluka to Ranger for processing. In 2005, the Jabiluka Long-Term Care and Maintenance Agreement was worked out between ERA, the Northern Land Council and the Mirarr.

*Protest against the Jabiluka mine, 1998*

*Protest banner on the Kakadu escarpment*

### GEOskills TOOLBOX

**USING THE INTERNET FOR NEWSPAPER ARTICLES**

You can use your favourite search engine to read articles from daily Australian and foreign newspapers. Many newspapers also provide articles from past years. Newspapers often give valuable information on contemporary geographical issues. The following article was published by *The Guardian*, a London-based newspaper. Its website can be accessed via the internet.

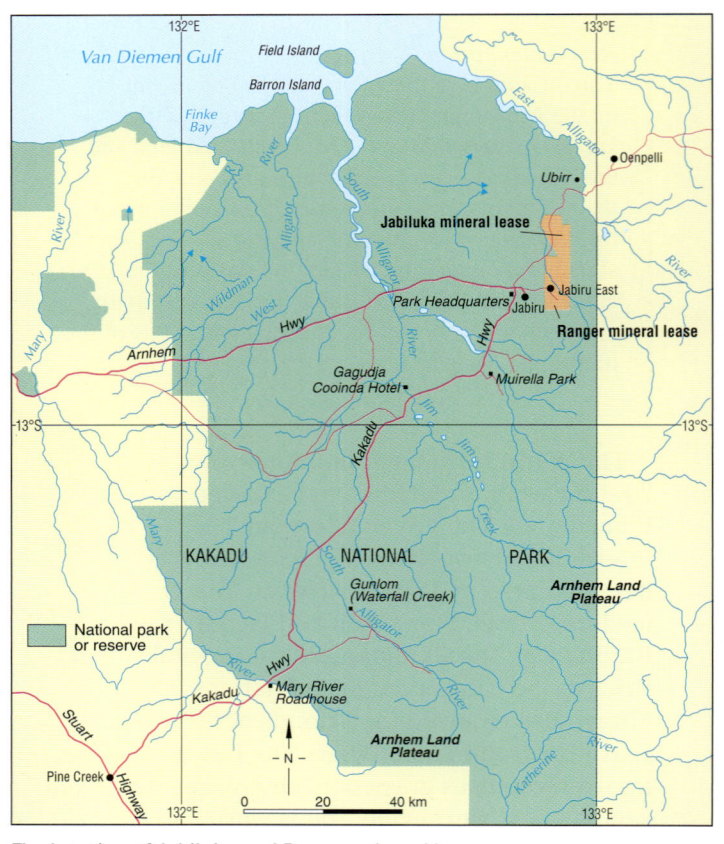

*The location of Jabiluka and Ranger mineral leases*

## Editorial

Two events this week have highlighted the resolve of some Indigenous communities and leaders to defend their long-fought-for rights.

The first is the decision of the Mirarr people of Jabiluka, who have once again stood up to transnational mining corporation Rio Tinto. The mining giant attempted to pressure the community into once again allowing uranium mining on Mirarr traditional lands.

A uranium mine had long been slated at Jabiluka since an unfair contract was pressured on the Mirarr in 1981 by the Federal and Northern Territory Governments. Construction began on the mine in 1998 but after Indigenous and nation-wide protests it was forced to cease and the site was rehabilitated in 2003.

After last week's renewed decision to keep the mine closed, Aboriginal leader Ms Yvonne Margarula said that mining had 'completely upturned our lives, bringing greater access to alcohol and many arguments between Aboriginal people, mostly about money. We stopped the mining here ... Now they have put the ore back in the ground ... it will never again come out. The country is at peace and I am very happy.'

The second event is the much publicized decision of the Tangentyere Council representing Indigenous camp dwellers on the outskirts of Alice Springs.

Using blatant blackmail tactics Howard's Minister for Indigenous Affairs, Mal Brough, attempted to force the Aboriginal people into accepting his proposal for the camps to sub-lease their land for 99 years to the NT Government, along with control over their community housing.

In return for the lease the Government had offered $60 million to provide basic services — services available to other towns and cities without coercion and relinquishing rights. The Government also made clear that another intention of this contract would be to foist private home ownership on the Tangentyere people.

This decision again took immense resolve: the community stood up in the face of a bribe of that magnitude and said 'no' to a despicable and dishonest government intent on permanently wiping away the concept of Native Title.

People and organizations from all over the world wonder how so many Indigenous people in Australia continue to live in appalling Third World conditions in such a rich and prosperous society.

How is it that successive Australian Governments have produced policies that appear dedicated to addressing this issue yet have failed dismally to make any progress? Because to achieve progress in this area would threaten the corporate stranglehold of this country's vast land and resources.

Every victory achieved by Indigenous people is countered by a deliberate reactionary scare campaign. At the time of the **Mabo** land rights decision the Coalition parties rallied a public backlash: 'They can now claim land rights over your backyard!' was the cry.

There is a need for genuine reconciliation, genuine recognition of land rights and fulfillment of all human rights obligations between the Australian Government and the Indigenous people who recognise these as basic steps towards achieving full equality.

This need has long been recognised by progressive community organizations and individuals. Until this is carried out by government policy, little will change.

*Source: The Guardian,* 30 May 2007.

## ACTIVITIES

### UNDERSTANDING

1. Where is the Jabiluka mineral lease located?
2. What mineral is found there and why is it so valuable?
3. Who are the traditional owners of the land?
4. Outline the factors that contribute to the community's sense of identity.
5. Describe the support the Mirarr people gained to help stop the Jabiluka mine.

### THINKING AND APPLYING

6. Suggest three possible ecological impacts of a new mine at Jabiluka.
7. Working with a partner or team, make a list of the different groups who have an interest in Jabiluka. Draw a mind map showing the different perspectives of people about the issue of uranium mining at the site.
8. Investigate the Jabiluka mine issue further. Use the **ERA** and **Mirarr** weblinks in your eBookPLUS.

### USING YOUR SKILLS

9. Refer to the map on page 142 and the photograph of Jabiluka uranium mine on page 141.
    a. What does the green shading on the map represent?
    b. Describe the location of the Jabiluka and Ranger mining leases.
    c. How far is the Jabiluka site from the Ranger mine?
    d. ERA planned to construct a road from Jabiluka to Ranger. Why did the Jabiluka and Ranger sites need to be linked?
10. Refer to the newspaper article and answer the following questions.
    a. List the two events that highlighted the resolve of some Indigenous communities to defend their rights.
    b. Outline why Aboriginal leader Ms Yvonne Margarula wanted to stop mining.
    c. What is the Mabo land rights decision? How important is it to Indigenous people?
    d. Describe the perspective of this article. Do you think this article is biased?

### GEOTERMS

**Mabo:** a court case in 1992 in which the High Court of Australia ruled that *terra nullius* (the concept that the land was owned by no-one before European settlement) did not apply

**World Heritage site:** a place recognised as being of such great value that it should be preserved for all people for all time

# Working geographically

## BROADSHEET: CHANGING COMMUNITIES IN THE CLARE VALLEY

*The Clare Valley is 135 kilometres north of Adelaide.*

### KNOWLEDGE AND UNDERSTANDING

**Refer to the topographic map and select the alternative that best answers the question.**

1. Where is the town of Clare located?
   - (A) AR7853
   - (B) AR7458
   - (C) AR8944
   - (D) AR8843

2. Where is the town of Mintaro located?
   - (A) AR8843
   - (B) AR8944
   - (C) AR8842
   - (D) AR9044

3. Which settlement is located at AR8239?
   - (A) Penwortham
   - (B) Watervale
   - (C) Sevenhill
   - (D) Gully View

4. What is produced at Mintaro?
   - (A) wine
   - (B) clothing
   - (C) slate
   - (D) tin

5. What is the main agricultural activity in the Clare Valley?
   - (A) vineyards
   - (B) pine plantations
   - (C) wheat
   - (D) sugarcane

6. What business can be found at GR811509?
   - (A) Stanley Winery
   - (B) Robertson's Winery
   - (C) a quarry
   - (D) Wendouree Winery

7. What direction is Donnybrook from Clare?
   - (A) SW
   - (B) SE
   - (C) NW
   - (D) NE

### SHORT RESPONSE

8. Where are most of the vineyards located? Outline the reasons for this.
9. Describe the pattern of settlement in the Clare Valley.
10. Give two examples from the map that support the fact that tourism is the major growth industry in the region.

### Legend

Built-up area; Divided highway; Metropolitan route marker
Recreation reserve with oval; Drive-in theatre; Underpass
Sealed road two or more lanes; National route marker
Sealed road one lane; Embankment
Unsealed road two or more lanes
Unsealed road one lane; Cutting
Vehicle track; Road bridge; Gate; Stock grid
Foot track; Foot bridge
Multiple track railway; Station
Single track railway; Light railway
Railway tunnel, bridge, underpass
High voltage transmission line
Fence; Prominent telephone line
Mine; Windmill; Church; Building
Horizontal control point; Spot elevation
Contour with value; Supplementary contour
Depression contour; Sand; Distorted surface
Levee, bank or sand ridge; Joint or rock fissure
High cliff; Escarpment
Vegetation; Dense, medium, scattered
Vegetation distinctive; Distinctive grass
Orchard or vineyard; Line of trees or windbreak
Mangrove swamp; Area subject to inundation
Swamp; Swamp definite boundary
Perennial lake; Watercourse
Intermittent lake; Watercourse
Mainly dry lake; Watercourse
Tank or small dam; Perennial waterhole
Saline coastal flat; Intertidal flat
Navigation light; Intertidal ledge or reef
Pier; Exposed wreck; Prominent submerged wreck
Prominent submerged reef, rock
Indefinite watercourse, shoreline; Rock bare or awash

GRID CONVERGENCE 20 MILS (1.0°)
GRID MAGNETIC ANGLE 110 MILS (6.0°)

TRUE NORTH, GRID NORTH AND MAGNETIC NORTH ARE SHOWN DIAGRAMMATICALLY FOR THE CENTRE OF THIS MAP. MAGNETIC NORTH IS CORRECT FOR 1975 AND MOVES EASTERLY BY 2 MILS (0.1°) IN ABOUT SIX YEARS.
TO CONVERT A MAGNETIC BEARING TO A GRID BEARING ADD GRID MAGNETIC ANGLE.

SCALE 1:100 000
CONTOUR INTERVAL 20 METRES
ELEVATIONS IN METRES

Topographic map of the Clare Valley

# ICT activities

**eBookplus**

**projectsplus**

## The community of Dubbo
SEARCHLIGHT ID: PRO-0016

### SCENARIO
The Dubbo Citizens Association is concerned about the city's future direction and has hired your company to compile a report on the issues facing the community. The state and federal governments have also asked to see copies of the report; they believe Dubbo is representative of the challenges facing many rural communities. You've been in the field compiling information, filming and talking to people in the community and now it's time to write up your report.

### YOUR TASK
Create a report of about 750 words that includes at least three visual supports (graphs, tables, maps) to help make the report findings clear. The report should identify at least two key issues affecting the community and identify how government can respond to the challenges (include recommendations for local, state or federal levels of government). The report should also identify the characteristics of the Dubbo community, and specifically locate Dubbo within Australia.

### PROCESS
- Open the ProjectsPLUS application for this chapter, located in your eBookPLUS. Watch the introductory video lesson and then click the 'Start Project' button to set up your project group. You can complete this project individually or invite other members of your class to form a group. Save your settings and the project will be launched.
- Navigate to your Research Forum. A number of issues within the community of Dubbo have been loaded for you to provide a framework for your research. Explore these issues and gather statistics about Dubbo to help provide a snapshot of the make-up of the community. The weblinks in your Media Centre will help you get started. Share your findings with your group by posting articles under each topic in the Research Forum. You can also rate and comment on the posts made by other members of your group.

Your ProjectsPLUS application is available in this chapter's Student Resources tab inside your eBookPLUS. Visit www.jacplus.com.au to locate your digital resources.

- When your research is completed, navigate to your Media Centre and read the document on report writing. A partial sample report for the fictional community of Dengan Sahat is also available for you to preview.
- Plan your report. You might decide that your report should focus on only two key issues because there is a great deal of information to be included. Check with your teacher to see whether the limits you have considered for your report are suitable.
- Once your plan is finalised and you have brainstormed the relevant material to include, use Microsoft Excel to create graphs and tables to include in your report. As the model report makes clear, graphs are a very useful way of quickly summarising and depicting information. A guide to creating graphs with Microsoft Excel is included in your Media Centre.
- You might also like to include some relevant images from Dubbo in your report. You will find images in your Media Centre that you can download. Be sure to only pick images that reinforce the points you are making in your report.
- When your first draft is completed, you might like to have a peer edit your report.
- Finalise your report based on feedback.
- Print out your research report from ProjectsPLUS and hand it in to your teacher with your completed report.

### SUGGESTED SOFTWARE
- ProjectsPLUS
- Microsoft Word
- Microsoft Excel (for creating graphs)

### MEDIA CENTRE
**Your Media Centre contains:**
- images from the community of Dubbo
- weblinks to research sites
- a document containing hints on writing reports
- a partial sample report for the fictional community of Dengan Sahat
- a guide to creating graphs using Microsoft Excel
- an assessment rubric.

## Interactivity

### AUSTRALIAN POPULATION PYRAMID

See how the population pyramid for Australia would look in any year up to 2055 by manipulating the average crude birth rate over the next 50 years. The crude birth rate is the number of births per 1000 people in any year. Simply input an average crude birth rate for each period and then enter a year and view how Australia's population would look. A worksheet is included to help you explore these concepts.

SEARCHLIGHT ID: INT-1420

### Australian population pyramid

Input an average Crude Birth Rate (CBR) for each or any period on the right. Input the year you would like to see and press the display button to see how your figures affect Australia's population pyramid.

The CBR is the number of births per 1000 people in any year. In 2006, Australia's CBR was 12.8, while the world CBR was estimated to be 20.3.

This interactivity assumes an equal number of males and females will be born each year.

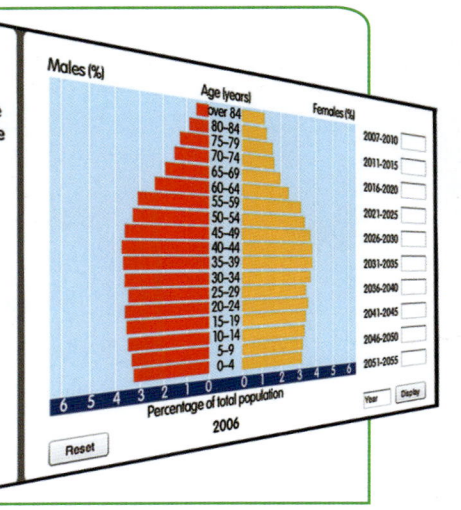

CHAPTER 6 | Factors causing change in Australian communities

# 7 Geographical issues

### INQUIRY QUESTIONS
+ What are the geographical issues affecting Australian environments?
+ What are the responses of individuals, groups and governments to the issue?
+ How can informed, responsible, active citizens promote sustainability, social justice and equity?

Geographical issues are everywhere, in the daily news and everyday conversation. An example of a geographical issue is: Should a resort be allowed in pristine coastal areas near Ningaloo Reef? These and similar issues affect physical or human environments. Geographers investigate such issues using their specialist knowledge, but individuals, groups and governments all play a role in their management. Every Australian citizen has an important responsibility to be part of solutions to geographical issues by being informed and working towards a sustainable and equitable future for all Australians.

## GEOskills TOOLBOX

**GEOskillbuilder** Developing a research action plan (page 155)
+ Using a geographical issues scaffold (page 150)
+ Measuring bearings on a map (page 171)

*People protest at the lack of government action on climate change, Sydney 2009.*

### KEY TERMS

**absolute poverty:** the condition of having so little food, money or resources that the people, no matter where they live in the world, can barely survive

**active citizenship:** involves individuals and groups influencing decision making at local, state, federal and global scales, and actively and responsibly participating in community activities and public affairs

**air pollution:** the build-up of impurities in the air that are likely to be harmful to plants and animals, including humans, once they reach certain concentrations

**bearing:** an angle, given in degrees and minutes, measured clockwise from north on a compass

**boom town:** a community that experiences sudden and rapid population and economic growth

**dormitory town:** a place from which many people travel in order to work in a bigger town or city

**nuclear reactor:** a device where a chain reaction is maintained and controlled for the production of nuclear energy or radioactive isotopes

**relative poverty:** where there is not lack of sufficient resources to meet basic needs, but a lack of resources required to be able to participate in the lifestyle enjoyed by other people in the country

**rural–urban fringe:** an area where growing suburbs meet farmland

**spatial inequality:** the unequal distribution of income, wealth or resources in a geographic area

**urban decay:** occurs when a land use in a part of the city declines where it had previously flourished, leaving behind derelict buildings and vacant sites

**urbanisation:** the process by which the proportion of a country's population in urban areas increases

# 7.1 What are geographical issues?

Geography has something to offer on most current events that appear in the daily news. The issues raised are many and varied. Examples include:
- Why do Indigenous people live, on average, 17 years less than non-Indigenous people?
- Why is the Murray River called an environmental disaster?
- Why should we reduce the use of plastic bags?
- How can urban areas be redeveloped in a sustainable way?

Geographical issues are areas of concern that arise due to changes in environments. They may also arise due to natural and human interaction with environments. These issues can be investigated from spatial and ecological dimensions. A spatial dimension explains where things are and why they are there, and an ecological dimension describes the relationship between people and the environment and the effects they have on each other. Six major issues affecting Australian environments include:
- air quality
- urban growth and decline
- **spatial inequality**
- waste management
- land and water management (see chapter 8)
- coastal management (see chapter 9).

Every Australian is responsible for the management of these issues. As active citizens, we should move from being part of the problem to being part of the solution by promoting sustainability, social justice and equity.

*Newspaper headlines show concern for geographical issues.*

## GEOskills TOOLBOX

### USING A GEOGRAPHICAL ISSUES SCAFFOLD

A geographical issues scaffold provides a useful way of analysing and summarising information sources. It helps geographers focus on the main points and compare different perspectives about an issue. The scaffold below can be used for any geographical issue and for different types of information sources such as newspapers, magazines and the internet.

| |
|---|
| Title, date and author of source |
| Geographical issue |
| Spatial dimension (Where? Why?) |
| Ecological dimension (How do humans interact?) |
| Impacts |
| Key interest groups and contrasting perspectives |
| Responses (Individuals, groups and governments) |
| How successful are their strategies? |
| What are the implications of these processes for sustainability, social justice and equity? |

*Air quality in some Australian cities is affected by pollution.*

# Resort eco watch

BY DARYL PASSMORE

Federal Environment Minister Peter Garrett is being urged to block a $1.5 billion tourism and residential development in north Queensland, to protect endangered turtles.

The area at Ella Bay, 9 km north of Innisfail, is surrounded on three sides by World Heritage-listed wet tropics rainforest and on the other by a 2.5 km beach frontage to the Great Barrier Reef Marine Park.

The proposed development, by Satori Resorts on a 450 ha disused cattle property, has been dubbed 'the new Port Douglas'.

It would include four five-star resorts totalling 860 units and villas, 540 homes, shops, offices, restaurants, a golf course, educational precinct and sports centre.

The largest master-planned community of its type in Australia, the Ella Bay proposal was recognised by the State Government as a project of state significance in 2005 and a decision on the plan from the Co-ordinator-General was expected in May this year.

But its future is now in doubt after Mr Garrett decided to re-evaluate the project under federal environmental legislation following the discovery of marine turtle nesting sites.

Danielle Annese, from Humane Society International, said all six species of marine turtles found in Australia were listed as threatened. 'They are already under intense pressure from development,' she said.

The turtle nests were first spotted in November by Russell Constable, from nearby Bramston Beach, who then conducted a more extensive survey along that stretch of coast.

He is not a member of any environmental group but said he was keen to see the area protected.

But a report commissioned by Satori Resorts last week says only one nest was found within the proposed area and eight more 300 m north.

John Thoroughgood of independent consultants FRC Environmental said the nesting habitat was 'marginal'.

The development, over 10 years, would create 1500 jobs at the peak of construction and 760 once the resort was operating, making it the biggest employer in the Cassowary Coast region.

Satori director Rod Lamb was confident it would go ahead.

A spokesman for Mr Garrett said a decision would be made as soon as possible.

*Source: Sunday Mail, 15 March 2009.*

*'NEW PORT DOUGLAS': A $1.5 billion resort has been proposed for Ella Bay near Innisfail.*

## ACTIVITIES

### UNDERSTANDING

1. What is a geographical issue? Give an example.
2. What is the aim of solving geographical issues?
3. Read the newspaper article on the proposed new resort at Ella Bay and answer the following questions.
   a. Which of the following geographical issues is touched on in the article?
      air quality, coastal management, land and water management, spatial inequality, waste management, urban growth and decline
   b. What is the spatial dimension of the issue?
   c. What is the ecological dimension of the issue?
   d. How have individuals, groups and governments responded to the issue?

### THINKING AND APPLYING

4. Present a scrapbook of newspaper articles over three weeks on the six geographical issues outlined on these pages. Include a source and date for each. Make a collage using the headlines from the articles you collect and display them around the classroom.

### USING YOUR SKILLS

5. Refer to the scaffold in the Geoskills toolbox. Use online newspapers to find articles on three issues from the list on page 150 affecting Australian environments. Copy the scaffold into your workbook and complete it for each of your articles.

### GEOTERMS

**spatial inequality:** the unequal distribution of income, wealth or resources in a geographic area

CHAPTER 7 | Geographical issues  151

# Overview of geographical issues

**Air quality** (see pages 156–61)

| | |
|---|---|
| Spatial dimension | • Air quality differs between places, at different times and under different weather conditions.<br>• Increasing population and demand for more goods puts greater pressure on air quality. |
| Ecological dimension | • Human interactions include transport, industrial activity, smoking, dust storms from overgrazing on marginal land, bushfires and burning fossil fuels. |
| Processes | • The sun is the source of energy for the circulation of the atmosphere and changing weather patterns.<br>• Topography plays an important role in temperature inversions. |
| Impacts | • Smog, enhanced greenhouse effect, asthma, lung cancer, lead poisoning and death of vegetation |
| Responses of individuals and groups | • National Environment Protection Measure, polluter-pays principle, EPA monitoring, unleaded petrol, catalytic converters, increased use of public transport, energy alternatives such as solar power |
| Research action plan questions | • How can renewable energy improve air quality?<br>• How can active citizens work for a cleaner atmosphere?<br>• What laws restrict pollutants entering the air? |

**Coastal management** (see chapter 9)

| | |
|---|---|
| Spatial dimension | • Length of coastline of 30 270 kilometres surrounds continent with cliffs, bays, beaches, lagoons, coral reefs, wetlands and islands.<br>• Ninety per cent of Australians live within 50 kilometres of the coast. |
| Ecological dimension | • Drift of population to the coast and misuse of coastal resources since European settlement<br>• Urban, industrial, agricultural, recreational and tourist activities put additional pressure on coasts. |
| Processes | • Erosion (rock platforms, blowholes)<br>• Transportation (waves, longshore drift)<br>• Deposition (tombolos, spits)<br>• Weathering (corrosion and corrasion)<br>• Atmospheric processes (cyclones, storm surges)<br>• Ocean processes (tides, currents, water temperature, salinity)<br>• Tectonic forces (tsunamis)<br>• Enhanced greenhouse effect (sea level rising) |
| Impacts | • Building on foredunes, clearing of wetlands, sewage disposal, threatening of marine species, oil spills by passing ships, mining for oil and sand |
| Responses of individuals and groups | • Environment Protection Authority (EPA)<br>• Sydney Water (sewage disposal)<br>• Department of Environment and Heritage<br>• Indigenous coastal management, Coastcare<br>• World Heritage site |
| Research action plan questions | • How should urban development, stormwater, sewage, oil spills and litter be sustainably managed?<br>• How can active citizens protect coastal ecosystems?<br>• Why are coastal wetlands cleared?<br>• How should the Great Barrier Reef be managed? |

**Land and water management** (see chapter 8)

| | |
|---|---|
| Spatial dimension | • Australia is the driest inhabited continent on Earth.<br>• There is great variation in topographic features, geology, soils and water availability leading to a wide range of different land uses. |
| Ecological dimension | • Increasing population and poor catchment management since European settlement have led to clearing of vegetation for farms, homes and industries and loss of wildlife habitats.<br>• Increasing demands on water for agriculture, industry and domestic purposes<br>• Protection of areas for conservation<br>• Increasing use of environments for tourism |
| Processes | • Tectonic forces • Erosion<br>• Weathering • Transportation<br>• Deposition |
| Impacts | • Clearing trees leads to increased soil erosion, salinity and sedimentation in rivers, and is linked to enhanced greenhouse warming.<br>• Land degradation leads to decreasing biodiversity, dust storms and desertification.<br>• Polluting and overusing water leads to less ground water, water shortages, water diseases and blue-green algae. |
| Responses of individuals and groups | • Whole farm planning, Farming for the Future • Australian Koala Foundation, ecotourism, Earthwatch<br>• Integrated catchment management • Landcare<br>• Salt Action • Department of Conservation and Land Management<br>• National Soil Conservation Program • Murray–Darling Commission |
| Research action plan questions | • What are the causes of and solutions to salinity, soil erosion and desertification?<br>• What is the impact of population on land and water in urban and rural areas?<br>• What is catchment management and how can it improve land degradation and declining water quality? |

## Urban growth and decline (see pages 162–71)

| | |
|---|---|
| Spatial dimension | • Urban areas grow and decline due to push factors such as unemployment and low socioeconomic status, and pull factors such as employment, lifestyle and educational opportunities.<br>• Growing: Brisbane, Darwin, Sydney and cities along the eastern coast<br>• Declining: Hobart, exploited mining cities and old industrial parts of cities |
| Ecological dimension | • As growth occurs, more stress is placed on the natural environment through increased use of resources and energy and the production of wastes.<br>• In declining areas, environments may be left to decline as the socioeconomic conditions worsen. |
| Processes | • In growth areas, the following processes may occur: urbanisation, development of satellite cities, urban consolidation, gentrification, suburbanisation, reurbanisation and urban renewal.<br>• Declining regions may produce counter-urbanisation or urban decay. |
| Impacts | • Positive impacts include increasing employment opportunities, entertainment, specialist doctors, universities and cultural activities.<br>• Negative impacts include inadequate infrastructure and community services, traffic congestion, deteriorating air quality, high price of homes, urban blight and accumulation of waste. |
| Responses of individuals and groups | • Department of Infrastructure, Planning and Natural Resources (NSW)<br>• Urban Improvement Program NSW, Building Better Cities, Sydney Harbour Foreshore Authority<br>• Community Builders<br>• Local councils |
| Research action plan questions | • What are the effects of urban growth and suburbanisation?<br>• How do groups and governments improve the quality of life of people living in areas of urban decay?<br>• What are the challenges for cities in the twenty-first century? |

## Spatial inequality (see pages 172–77)

| | |
|---|---|
| Spatial dimension | • Clear socioeconomic patterns can be seen in suburbs displaying different levels of income, jobs, education etc.<br>• There is a growing divide between richer urban areas and poorer rural areas as populations drift to city areas. |
| Ecological dimension | • People move out of a community when mines or factories close, or when soils become unproductive. |
| Processes | • People move out of a community in search of work or an improved standard of living.<br>• An unequal society leads to social unrest, a growing dependence on social welfare, a taxation system to redistribute the wealth, programs to improve poor people's quality of life and the growth of non-government organisations (NGOs) such as The Smith Family. |
| Impacts | • Conflict and crime can occur due to social injustice, racism and a socioeconomic divide.<br>• Enclaves of poverty occur spatially and socially (females, Indigenous groups, ethnic groups). |
| Responses of individuals and groups | • Social welfare<br>• Government departments and bodies such as the Australian Institute of Health and Welfare, Community Builders and the NSW Premier's Department<br>• NGOs, such as the Australian Council of Social Service<br>• Care Australia<br>• UnitingCare, Anglicare |
| Research action plan questions | • How can the gap between rich and poor be reduced?<br>• Why do Indigenous people experience a poorer quality of life?<br>• How can active citizens reduce spatial inequality in their community? |

## Waste management (see pages 180–87)

| | |
|---|---|
| Spatial dimension | • Waste is disposed into air, water, land and coasts.<br>• Most waste is produced in cities. |
| Ecological dimension | • Increasing population and unsustainable use of resources leave a large ecological footprint, especially in cities.<br>• In developed countries such as Australia, waste can be directly linked to over-consumption of natural resources. |
| Processes | • Carbon dioxide leads to enhanced greenhouse effect.<br>• Rising polluted air is forced to condense and precipitate as acid rain.<br>• Fertilisers in rivers react with sunlight to cause blue-green algae. |
| Impacts | • Pollutants leach into soil, ground water, rivers and seas to impact on food chains.<br>• Air pollution, enhanced greenhouse effect, acid rain<br>• Polluted rivers and oceans lead to a loss of biodiversity.<br>• Bioaccumulation of toxins in food webs<br>• Algal blooms |
| Responses of individuals and groups | • 'Reduce, reuse, recycle' campaign<br>• Placing home wastes into recycle bins, polluter-pays principle<br>• Local councils dispose of garbage<br>• Management of landfills, Kimbriki Eco Garden<br>• Sewage and stormwater management<br>• Radioactive waste management |
| Research action plan questions | • How can we dispose of waste without polluting the air, water, land and coasts?<br>• What does 'reduce, reuse and recycle' mean?<br>• Who manages waste in your local community? |

CHAPTER 7 | Geographical issues    153

# Active citizenship

**Active citizenship** means being informed about geographical issues — such as salinised soils, mercury in the water and logging of forests — and their effects on environments and people. It involves influencing decision making and organising effective and lawful action. There are a number of ways an active, informed and responsible citizen can participate in the political process. Here are some strategies:

- Understand the parliamentary system.
- Be informed about geographical issues and which government department you need to contact for each geographical issue.
- Write letters to members of parliament, circulate and sign petitions, and organise peaceful demonstrations.
- Contact the ombudsman's office.
- Use the media to highlight issues.
- Boycott a product or service.
- Stand for election, or contribute money or time to a political party or interest group.
- Understand the importance of good *governance* (that is, accountability, transparency, the rule of law, participation of all people, consensus and equity).

# Active civil society

Individuals often join a group in order to influence government decisions on a particular issue such as the absence of health services in a country town. Such groups vary according to their social, economic, environmental and political ideals. Non-government organisations (NGOs) (private, not-for-profit organisations) include the National Council of Churches, Greenpeace, Landcare and Clean Up Australia. NGOs can put pressure on governments to change their policies or decisions.

The National Council of Churches in Australia is an example of an NGO that works to alleviate poverty and promote social justice. It helps refugees to settle in Australia and lobbies governments to ensure that they respect human rights. Landcare is an example of an NGO that works to protect the environment. Landcare groups promote sustainability and have a common concern about geographical issues such as land, water and coastal management.

**Powers of government**

Federal — State — Local

Federal: Taxation (income tax, company tax, customs and excise duties); Immigration (policy on and assistance to migrants); Transport (aviation, shipping); Communication; Trade (exports and imports, duties and tariffs); Health (Medicare, drug control); Social security (age and other pensions, unemployment benefits); Education (universities and colleges, aid to schools); Development (national projects); Antarctica; Foreign affairs (wars, treaties, ambassadors); Aboriginal welfare; Defence (armed forces)

State: Education (primary and secondary schools, teacher training); Transport (state roads, railways); Health (hospitals, nursing services); Local government; Housing; Services (such as electricity); Environment protection; Law and order (police force, crime control, accident prevention); Development (land sales, building projects); Aboriginal welfare

Local: Minor roads; Parks and sporting ovals; Rubbish collection; Swimming pools; Street lighting; Baby health centres

# Individuals make a difference

Many Australians demonstrate active citizenship by recycling their waste, contributing money to the Christmas Bowl Appeal, digging out exotic weeds in parks or buying environmentally friendly products. Individuals do make a difference for a sustainable and equitable society. For example, Ian Kiernan started the Clean Up Australia campaign after he sailed in a yacht race in 1986–87 and noticed rubbish floating in the ocean. On his return, he asked his friends to help him clean up Sydney Harbour. Today, this NGO involves the whole of Australia and has grown into an international event with 45 million people in 120 countries participating in 'Clean Up the World'.

The federal government launched a sustainable schools initiative in 2003 to support schools and their communities in becoming sustainable.

Today, school students have helped to build homes for poor people in Cambodia, raised money for refugee children in Uganda and started recycling paper and planting native vegetation in their school grounds.

## GEOfacts

- In the Murray catchment, Landcare replanted 6000 trees, and at Long Reef they removed bitou bush and revegetated the area with 10 000 flowering coastal shrubs to increase wildlife diversity.
- In Bourke, at the suggestion of the CSIRO, 14 rural properties planted 14 000 saltbush seedlings.

## GEO skillbuilder

### DEVELOPING A RESEARCH ACTION PLAN

A research action plan (RAP) is about understanding an issue, gathering the facts, developing and presenting a plan, and acting as an informed, responsible citizen. A RAP is a systematic inquiry into one of the following Australian geographical issues:
- air quality
- land and water management
- waste management
- coastal management
- spatial inequality
- urban growth and decline.

A RAP involves collecting information on geographical processes and studying their impacts on environments and communities. This information should be collected from a variety of primary and secondary sources to obtain different perspectives and to avoid bias. Primary data is original material collected by the researcher, such as measurements, surveys, photographs and maps. Secondary data is material collected by someone other than the researcher, such as maps, sketches, photographs, newspaper articles and internet material.

When this information has been collated and analysed, the next step is to propose actions by individuals, groups and the three levels of government. Proposed actions should tackle the issues and promote sustainability, social justice and equity.

The final step is to communicate this plan to a variety of audiences (such as classmates) as a written or oral report, PowerPoint display, multimedia presentation, poster, debate, roleplay, model, web page, video/audio tape or simulation. It is important to include geographical tools such as maps, graphs, statistics and photographs.

### FOLLOW THESE RAP STEPS

**Step 1.** Identify the aim or purpose of the investigation.
**Step 2.** Generate a number of focus questions to be answered by the investigation.
**Step 3.** Decide which primary and secondary data are needed to answer the focus questions.
**Step 4.** Identify the techniques that will be used to collect data.
**Step 5.** Collect primary and secondary data.
**Step 6.** Process and analyse the data collected.
**Step 7.** Propose and (where appropriate) take individual or group action in response to the research findings.
**Step 8.** Select presentation methods to communicate your research findings.

### APPLYING FIELDWORK TO THE RAP

It is important to investigate a geographical issue by applying fieldwork techniques. This is an opportunity to put theory into practice by, say, visiting the local river to measure water quality, or observing land and water management on a farm. You could observe and map changes in a new urban area or study the impact of urban renewal in an old industrial area. Other fieldwork suggestions include visiting a sewerage works or garbage dump, measuring air quality in your school or attending a council meeting on waste disposal. To be part of the management process, you could participate in Landcare, Streamwatch or Clean Up Australia or be actively involved in a charity to alleviate poverty.

## ACTIVITIES

### UNDERSTANDING

1. What is a RAP?
2. How can a citizen become active?
3. List the eight steps in a RAP.
4. Describe five fieldwork techniques you could apply to a RAP.

### THINKING AND APPLYING

5. Which level of government would you approach when investigating each of the following issues?
   a. Poor health facilities for rural Indigenous people
   b. Construction of a shopping centre on a coastal foredune
   c. Water diseases in the local swimming pool
   d. Insufficient doctors in small rural towns of New South Wales
6. Waste management is an important issue that relates closely to the other five geographical issues. Provide one impact of three geographical issues that relates to waste management.

### USING YOUR SKILLS

7. Refer to the tables and photographs on pages 152–53.
   a. Sketch, label and describe three photographs.
   b. What are the responses of governments and NGOs to managing three of the issues?
   c. Increasing population contributes to deteriorating air quality, water scarcity, land degradation, waste and urban growth. Explain each of these processes.
   d. Look carefully at the ecological dimensions for each of the issues. Find a connection between four issues — for example, increased transport from urban growth leads to reduced air quality.
8. Select a geographical issue. Use the eight steps in the GEOskillbuilder to prepare your own RAP.

### GEOTERMS

**active citizenship:** involves individuals and groups influencing decision making at local, state, federal and global scales, and actively and responsibly participating in community activities and public affairs

# 7.2 Air quality

## Nature of air quality

**Air pollution** is the accumulation of impurities in the air. Air quality becomes a problem when the extra pollutants in the air are poisonous or concentrated enough to affect life on Earth. Pollutants can have an unpleasant odour, irritate the senses, reduce visibility and damage property. They can even cause death.

Air quality has a spatial dimension. For example, we can test air quality at various sites and locate areas experiencing air pollution. We can map the various air flows that affect an area. Air quality also has an ecological dimension. The way in which people interact with the environment has a major impact on air quality.

Air quality has deteriorated significantly in cities and industrial areas since the Industrial Revolution. At the present time, most air pollution results from burning fossil fuel for transport, power generation and industrial production. In Australia, air quality is primarily a problem affecting large cities and industrial centres. Particular weather conditions can make the situation much worse. For example, on calm days the level of air pollution can be much higher than on windy days.

Compared with many other countries, particularly in the Northern Hemisphere, Australia's air quality is quite good. Australia has the advantage of being an isolated continent and it receives little polluted air directly from other countries. Even so, our cities experience episodes of high pollution each year. Air pollution levels for ozone, in particular, can sometimes approach the levels of cities such as New York or Tokyo.

## Changing nature of air quality

Our sunny climate promotes the formation of photochemical smog. This forms in the atmosphere when sunlight reacts with volatile organic compounds (VOCs) and nitrogen oxides (NOx). Sources of VOCs and NOx include emissions from motor vehicles, power stations and industrial and domestic sources. Ozone is one of the key components of photochemical smog.

Motor vehicles are the most significant source of air pollution in Australian cities. Our dependence on the motor car is linked to our sprawling suburbs. Sydney takes up a larger area than Tokyo even though Sydney has a population of only 4.3 million people compared with Tokyo's 12.5 million. Only 26 per cent of Sydney commuters use public transport.

### GEOfacts

- Of Australian cities, Darwin has the lowest public transport use of 3 per cent.
- Only 1 in 10 commuters in Australian capital cities catches a bus or walks.

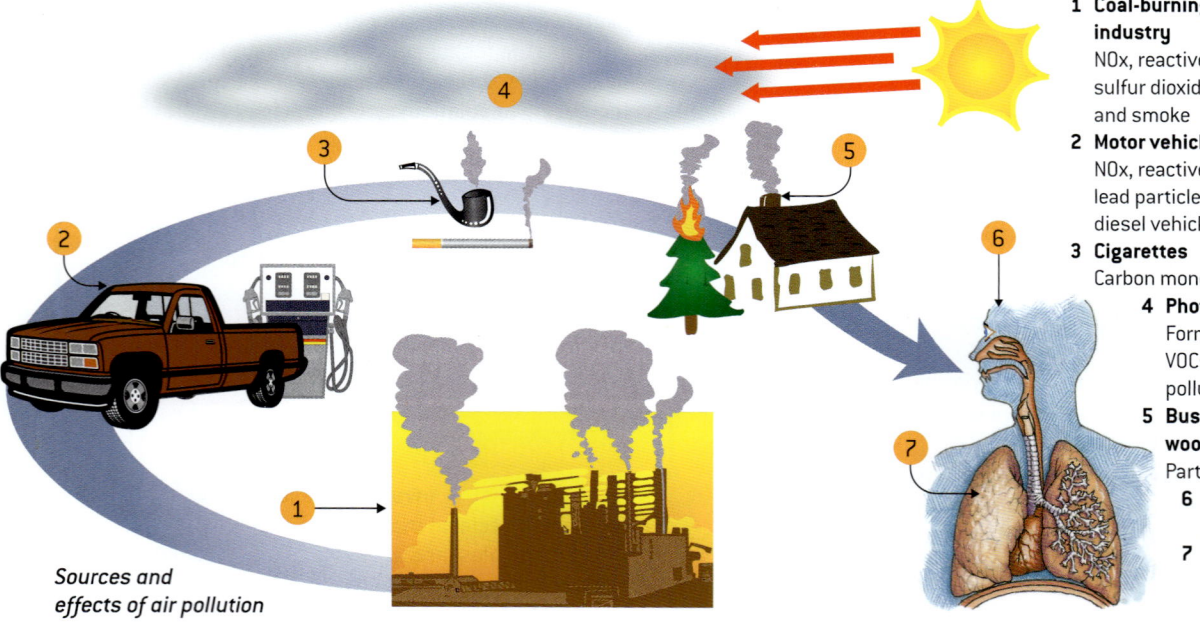

Sources and effects of air pollution

1. **Coal-burning power stations and industry**
   NOx, reactive VOCs, carbon monoxide, sulfur dioxide, particles including soot and smoke
2. **Motor vehicles**
   NOx, reactive VOCs, carbon monoxide, lead particles (produced mainly by diesel vehicles)
3. **Cigarettes**
   Carbon monoxide, smoke
4. **Photochemical smog**
   Formed when sunlight reacts with VOCs and NOx; contains several pollutants including ozone
5. **Bushfires, controlled burning, wood and coal fires, incinerators**
   Particles including smoke and soot
6. **Eye irritation, breathing problems**
7. **Blood carries less oxygen**
   Tiredness, headaches

Coal is used to generate about 93 per cent of electricity used in New South Wales. The process produces ash particles, NOx and reactive VOCs. Solar and wind power are examples of renewable energy resources that do not have a negative impact on air quality. In New South Wales in 2008, over 236 000 residential and commercial customers used Green Power electricity generated from renewable sources. This is an easy and effective way to support the development of renewable energy sources.

Other concerns about air quality include pollutants produced by mining and mineral processing and emissions from factories. Odours are an important issue with the public. Between 30 and 60 per cent of all air quality complaints received by state environmental agencies relate to bad smells.

### Indoor air quality

Most Australians spend more than 90 per cent of their time indoors. Far from being a safe haven from outdoor air pollution, the indoor air quality of our homes, offices, entertainment venues and cars is often worse than outdoors. Factors affecting indoor air quality include cigarette smoke, dust mites, moulds, pesticides and synthetic materials in building products, furnishings, paints and cleaners. Air flow, or the lack of it, is another major contributor to poor indoor air quality. One of the worst sources of indoor air pollution is unflued gas heaters. A flue is like a chimney that ensures that gases are discharged outside the building. Many schools in New South Wales had unflued gas heaters but these are gradually being replaced.

In recent years a cluster of symptoms — sore throat, irritated eyes, runny or blocked nose, skin irritation, headaches — has been termed 'sick building syndrome' by the World Health Organization. The causes are not clearly understood but seem to be associated with air-conditioned office buildings. Outbreaks of a type of pneumonia called legionnaire's disease have occurred occasionally in air-conditioned buildings in Australia.

## Perspectives: global comparison

Sydney's air pollution levels are lower than cities in most other countries. For example, during the 2008 Olympic Games in Beijing, air quality was 1730 micrograms per cubic metre. This was achieved after China had spent $17 billion to improve its air quality by closing industries and reducing the number of cars on the road. This figure is more than 34 times the national Australian level.

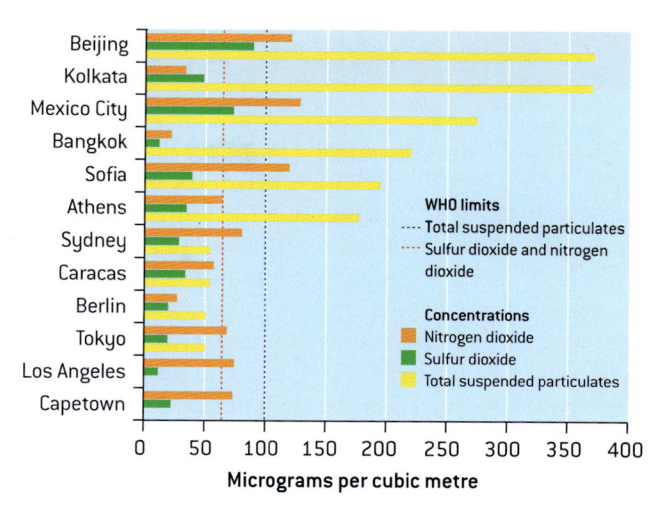

*Concentration of key pollutants in major cities*

### ACTIVITIES

#### UNDERSTANDING

1. Define the term *air pollution*.
2. What are the ecological and spatial dimensions of air quality?
3. Describe how photochemical smog is formed.
4. Explain why indoor pollution is a bigger environmental problem than outdoor pollution.
5. Explain why motor vehicles are the greatest source of air pollution in Sydney. Suggest three ways in which Sydney might reduce motor vehicle pollution.

#### THINKING AND APPLYING

6. Where would you get secondary data for a RAP on air quality?
7. Describe the fieldwork techniques that could be applied to the study of air quality as a RAP.

#### USING YOUR SKILLS

8. Use the diagram on page 156 to write a paragraph on the sources, processes and impacts of air pollution on people and the environment.
9. Refer to the bar graph above of concentration of key pollutants in major cities.
   a. Which countries exceed the WHO limits and in which categories?
   b. Why do you think such limits are set?
   c. Compare key pollutants in Sydney with those in Beijing, and account for the differences.

### GEOTERMS

**air pollution:** the build-up of impurities in the air that are likely to be harmful to plants and animals, including humans, once they reach certain concentrations

# 7.3 Managing air quality

Since the 1980s, some aspects of air quality have improved. Atmospheric lead levels have declined since 1986 with the introduction of catalytic converters (which convert engine exhaust into less harmful substances) on all new motor vehicles and the use of unleaded petrol. Filter systems on industrial smokestacks and the prohibition of backyard burning have also improved air quality. However, these benefits are now being eroded by increasing vehicle use.

Until mid 1998, Australia had no national air quality standards. The National Environment Protection Measure (NEPM) for outdoor air quality now sets maximum concentrations. The standards are based on the need to protect human health. Very little research has yet been done on the effects of air quality on ecosystems, biodiversity or the built environment.

**Typical concentrations of greenhouse gases and pollutants**

| Nature of pollutant | Clean air | Urban air |
|---|---|---|
| Carbon dioxide (ppm) | 360 | 350–600 |
| Methane (ppb) | 1700 | 1700–2500 |
| Nitrous oxide (ppb) | 315 | 315–350 |
| CFC-11 (ppt) | 260 | 300–500 |
| Ozone (ppb) | 15–35 | 0–100 |
| Nitrogen oxides (ppb) | 0.005–0.02 | 1–800 |
| Carbon monoxide (ppm) | 0.03–0.10 | 0.05–50 |
| Aerosol (PM10*) (micrograms per cubic metre) | Less than 10 | 25 |

Notes:
* PM10 aerosol contains atmospheric particles with diameter less than 10 microns. (A micron is a millionth of a metre, or a thousandth of a millimetre. A human hair is about 60 microns wide.)
* ppm is parts per million by volume (360 ppm, for example, represents a concentration of 0.36 per cent by volume)
* ppb is parts per billion by volume
* ppt is parts per trillion by volume

## What can we do to improve air quality?

Strategies that can be used to reduce pollution include the following.
- Improve public transport so it is convenient, safe, reliable and cheap.
- Use some petrol taxes to subsidise improvements to public transport.
- Restrict new housing developments if access to public transport is poor.
- Provide more transit and bus lanes.
- Encourage transport of freight by train.
- Implement stricter emission controls for motor vehicles and industry.
- Provide incentives for research into renewable energy technologies.
- Provide financial incentives for householders to install solar hot-water heaters.
- Use the 'polluter pays' principle, whereby people pay for the pollution and waste they produce.

**Pollutants controlled by the National Environment Protection Measure (NEPM) for outdoor air quality**

| Nature of pollutant | Sources | Impacts on health |
|---|---|---|
| Carbon monoxide | Car exhausts, burning of fossil fuels | Carbon monoxide is absorbed by the blood more readily than oxygen, thus reducing the amount of oxygen being carried through the body. It can produce tiredness and headaches. People with heart problems are particularly at risk. |
| Sulfur dioxide | Coal and oil-burning power stations, mineral ore processing and chemical manufacture | Attacks the throat and lungs. People with breathing problems can suffer severe illness. |
| Nitrogen dioxide | Burning of fossil fuels | Affects the throat and lungs |
| Ozone | Formed from nitrogen oxides and hydrocarbons in sunny conditions. These chemicals are released by motor vehicles and industry. | Ozone attacks the tissue of the throat and lungs and irritates the eyes. |
| Lead | Exhaust gases from motor vehicles that use leaded petrol, smelters | Particles containing lead in the air can enter the lungs. The lead can then be absorbed into the bloodstream. Over a period, lead can affect the nervous system and the body's ability to produce blood. |
| Particles | Motor vehicles, burning of plant materials, bushfires | May cause breathing difficulties and worsen respiratory diseases. Some particles contain cancer-producing materials. |

## SAMPLE STUDY

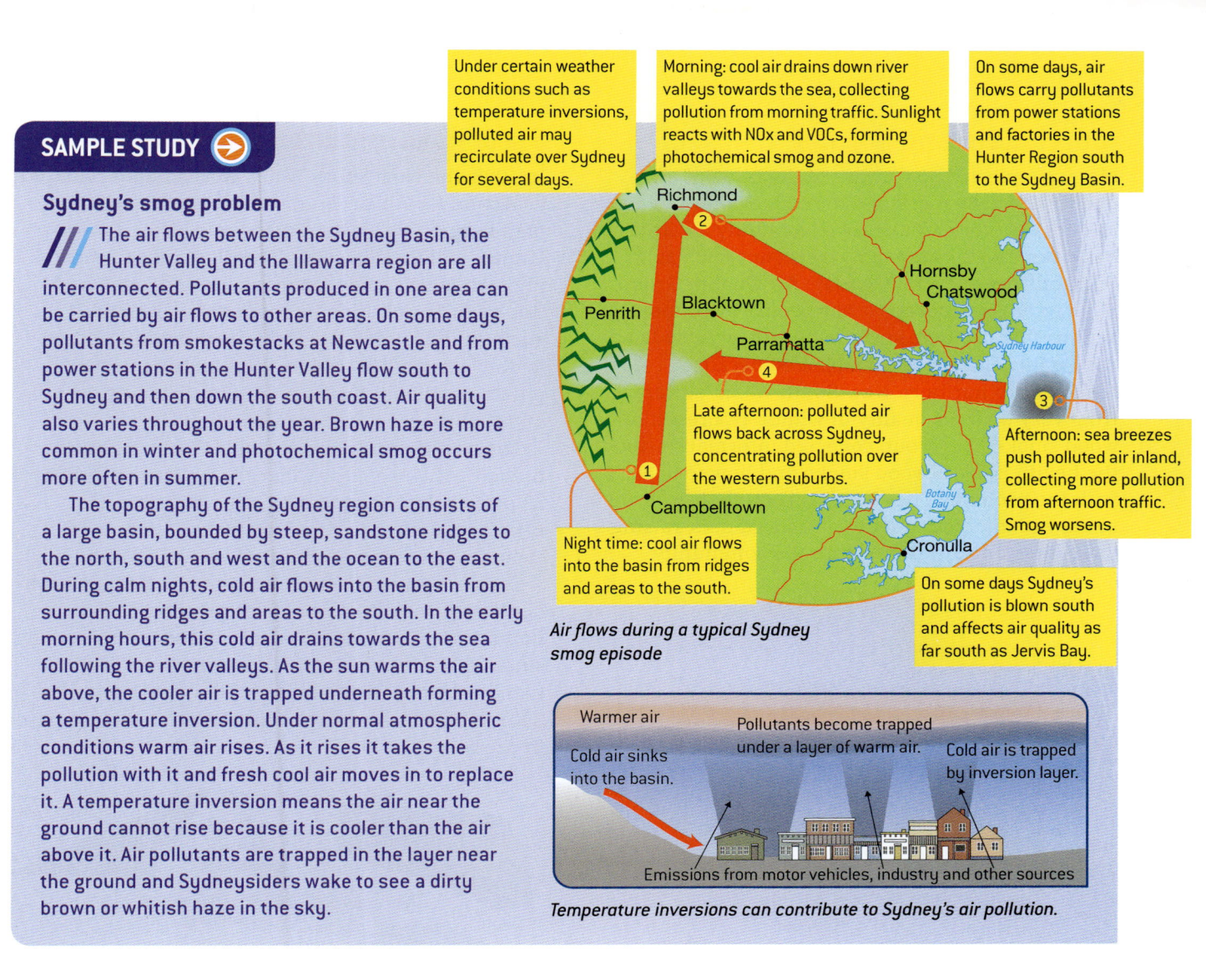

### Sydney's smog problem

The air flows between the Sydney Basin, the Hunter Valley and the Illawarra region are all interconnected. Pollutants produced in one area can be carried by air flows to other areas. On some days, pollutants from smokestacks at Newcastle and from power stations in the Hunter Valley flow south to Sydney and then down the south coast. Air quality also varies throughout the year. Brown haze is more common in winter and photochemical smog occurs more often in summer.

The topography of the Sydney region consists of a large basin, bounded by steep, sandstone ridges to the north, south and west and the ocean to the east. During calm nights, cold air flows into the basin from surrounding ridges and areas to the south. In the early morning hours, this cold air drains towards the sea following the river valleys. As the sun warms the air above, the cooler air is trapped underneath forming a temperature inversion. Under normal atmospheric conditions warm air rises. As it rises it takes the pollution with it and fresh cool air moves in to replace it. A temperature inversion means the air near the ground cannot rise because it is cooler than the air above it. Air pollutants are trapped in the layer near the ground and Sydneysiders wake to see a dirty brown or whitish haze in the sky.

Under certain weather conditions such as temperature inversions, polluted air may recirculate over Sydney for several days.

Morning: cool air drains down river valleys towards the sea, collecting pollution from morning traffic. Sunlight reacts with NOx and VOCs, forming photochemical smog and ozone.

On some days, air flows carry pollutants from power stations and factories in the Hunter Region south to the Sydney Basin.

Late afternoon: polluted air flows back across Sydney, concentrating pollution over the western suburbs.

Afternoon: sea breezes push polluted air inland, collecting more pollution from afternoon traffic. Smog worsens.

Night time: cool air flows into the basin from ridges and areas to the south.

On some days Sydney's pollution is blown south and affects air quality as far south as Jervis Bay.

*Air flows during a typical Sydney smog episode*

*Temperature inversions can contribute to Sydney's air pollution.*

## Measuring air quality

Today, levels of major air pollutants are measured around Australia. The Australian Air Quality Forecasting System (AAQFS) predicts daily levels of photochemical smog, atmospheric particles and 22 other pollutants. The NSW Department of Environment and Climate Change uses an air quality index (AQI) that reports air quality and its effects on health every day. The AQI includes ozone, nitrogen dioxide, visibility, carbon monoxide, sulfur dioxide and particles. It is measured at 24 sites around NSW and is updated hourly.

## Taking action

Air pollution is likely to remain a serious problem due to population growth and our continuing reliance on fossil fuels for transport and electricity. However, the news is not all bad. By the early twenty-first century, emissions in Australia were increasing more slowly than the rate of population or economic growth. This slowdown can be attributed to the actions of individuals, groups and governments.

### Air quality index (AQI)

| Air quality index (AQI) | What action should people take? |
| --- | --- |
| Very good: 0–33 | Enjoy activities |
| Good: 34–66 | Enjoy activities |
| Fair: 67–99 | People sensitive to air pollution: plan strenuous outdoor activities when air quality is better. |
| Poor: 100–149 | Sensitive groups: cut back or reschedule strenuous outdoor activities. |
| Very poor: 150–200 | Sensitive groups: avoid strenuous outdoor activities. Everyone: cut back or reschedule strenuous outdoor activities. |
| Hazardous: 200+ | Sensitive groups: avoid all outdoor physical activities. Everyone: cut back on outdoor physical activities. |

## Individuals and groups

Many people are now aware of the issue of air quality and take measures to reduce pollution and use energy more efficiently. Community awareness has risen due to campaigns by groups such as Smogbusters and the Armidale Air Quality Group. Such groups encourage other people by proposing actions that promote sustainability. The Armidale Air Quality Group was established because Armidale, in northern New South Wales, suffers from very poor air quality in winter as a result of wood smoke. The group collected information about the health risks of wood smoke and how to deal with the problem. They listed this on their website along with daily air quality measurements, raising awareness and support within the community.

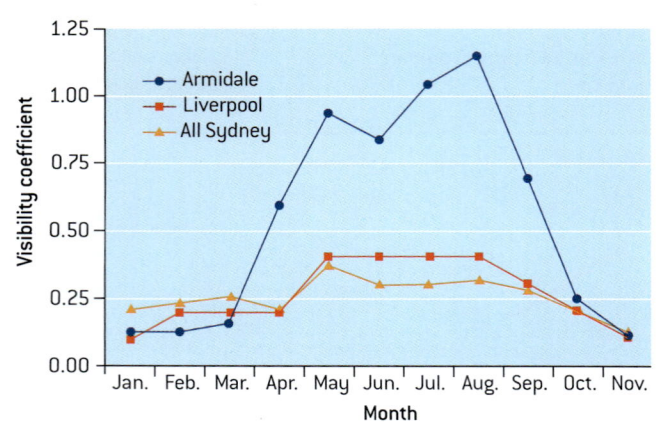

*Wood heaters in Armidale produce more air pollution than in Sydney during winter. It is also high in suburbs such as Liverpool where some people use wood heaters.*

## Local government

Many local councils enforce laws that prohibit backyard burning or incineration of toxic wastes by industry. Some councils are constructing safe bike paths to encourage commuters to use bikes instead of cars. The Commonwealth Government offers funding and assistance to councils to take part in programs to reduce pollution and greenhouse gas emissions. The Cities for Climate Protection program, for example, helps councils to come up with a local action plan. Hundreds of councils have participated, making it one of the most successful programs of its type worldwide.

In New South Wales, local councils have developed air quality management plans that have helped to improved air quality.

*Smog shrouds the city of Sydney.*

## State government

In 1998, the New South Wales Government released its Action for Air program, which is a 25-year plan to improve air quality in Sydney, the Lower Hunter and the Illawarra. The plan aims to control photochemical smog (ozone at ground level) and fine particle pollution by reducing emissions. It encourages community input by providing access to daily air quality reports through the internet. A public air quality forum monitors air quality trends and reports back to the government.

The government aims to improve air quality by reducing the use of private cars: it plans to develop 23 priority bus corridors by 2012; and, through BikePlan, it aims to construct 200 kilometres of cycleways across New South Wales by 2010.

Carbon monoxide concentrations in Sydney have decreased with newer vehicles meeting emission limits and leaded petrol being phased out nationally since 2002. Unfortunately the ozone level is still high in Sydney on a number of days each year. In 2001 and 2002, bushfires contributed to the increase in ozone.

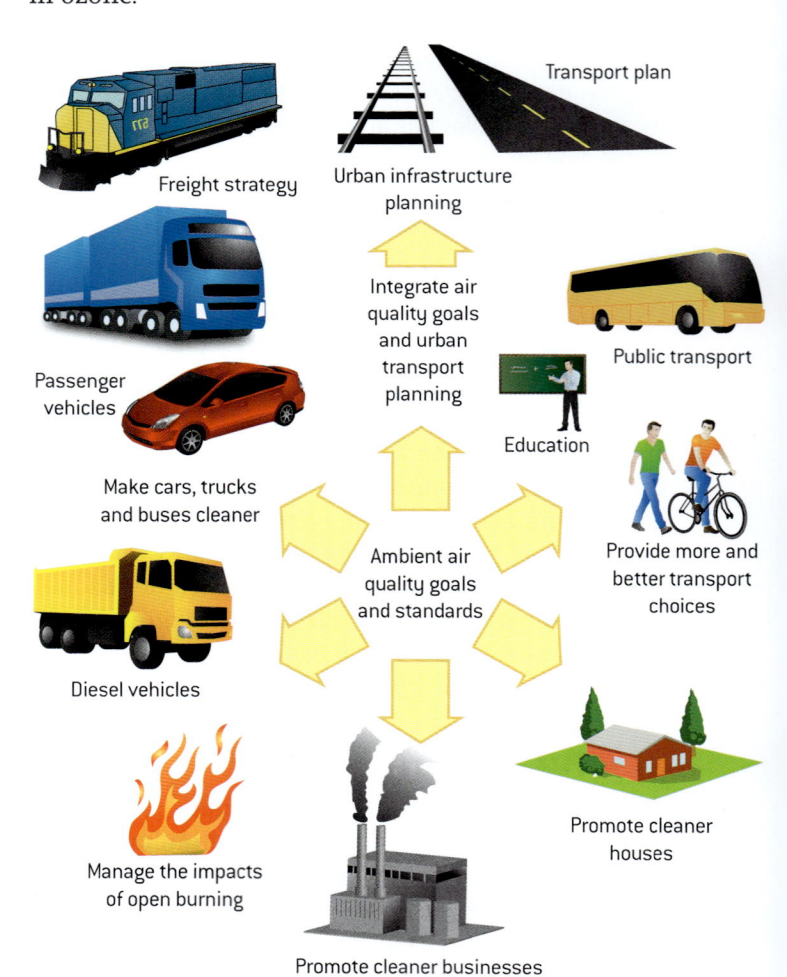

*Framework of the Action for Air program*

## Federal government

Government actions have included the National Environment Protection Measure for outdoor air quality and legislation requiring the use of unleaded petrol and catalytic converters in motor vehicles. Other strategies include the Cities for Climate Protection™ program and the Cool Communities program to reduce greenhouse gas emissions from household energy use, waste and transport. The government supported the development of the Air Quality Forecasting System. This joint project between the CSIRO, the Bureau of Meteorology and Environment Australia supplies 3D forecasts of air quality in major cities and predicts daily levels of photochemical smog. This information is used to:

- enable environment protection agencies and industries to test their management strategies
- advise schools and health institutions to take extra precautions on days experiencing dangerous levels of air pollution.

The CSIRO also works with industry. It has joined forces with General Motors to produce a hybrid car that combines a conventional internal combustion engine with an electric motor to reduce exhaust emissions and maximise fuel economy. The hybrid car is expected to emit less than 70 per cent of the greenhouse gases produced by today's average car. Other cars expected to improve air quality and reduce greenhouse gases include the Honda FCX Clarity and General Motors' Chevy Volt.

The federal government recognises that air quality issues (such as ozone and greenhouse gases) are interconnected and is committed to act both globally and locally. The National Greenhouse Strategy promotes renewable energy sources to reduce greenhouse gases and improve air quality.

*Toyota's Prius — a hybrid electric car*

## ACTIVITIES

### UNDERSTANDING

1. What pollutants are controlled by the National Environment Protection Measure?
2. Outline the impacts of poor air quality on humans.
3. Explain the function of the AQI and how it can help citizens during their daily activities.
4. Discuss the responses of different levels of government to air quality.

### THINKING AND APPLYING

5. Explain how variations in air quality may occur:
   a in a valley surrounded by mountains
   b near industry
   c in a remote rural area.
6. Imagine you are given the task of reducing Sydney's pollution using the NSW Action for Air program. Outline the actions you would take to improve Sydney's air quality.
7. Develop a RAP using fieldwork techniques to discover how the air quality in your local area compares with other places. Answer these key questions before you start the RAP:
   a What is air quality?
   b How does the interaction of the physical and human elements cause air quality to deteriorate?
   c What are the geographical processes relevant to changes in air quality?
   d What are the impacts of poor air quality on people and environments?
   e What are the responses of individuals, groups and governments to poor air quality?
   f What should you do as an active citizen to promote better air quality?
   g What actions are required to promote a sustainable environment?

### USING YOUR SKILLS

8. Refer to the diagram on page 159 showing the movement of polluted air over Sydney.
   a Why does polluted air flow inland in the early afternoon?
   b How does the cool morning air become polluted?
   c How do air flows affect the western suburbs?
   d Name a suburb in Sydney that is likely to have cleaner air than other suburbs. Where should respiratory health services be located?
9. Refer to the diagram on page 159 showing how temperature inversion contributes to air pollution in Sydney.
   a How do pollutants become trapped in the basin?
   b What physical feature forms a barrier to the movement of air?
   c Discuss its impact on health and air flows.
10. Refer to the line graph on page 160 showing air quality in Armidale, Liverpool and Sydney. What is the difference between air quality in Armidale and Sydney in January and August? Account for the difference. Explain how the gap could be reduced.

# 7.4 Urban growth and decline

Australia, with a population of over 21 million people, is one of the world's most urbanised nations. This is in stark contrast to our image as a country of hard-living outback heroes. More than half of the population lives in Sydney, Melbourne, Brisbane, Perth and Adelaide. The greater metropolitan region incorporating Sydney, Newcastle, Wollongong and the Central Coast is home to 4.9 million people or 85 per cent of the New South Wales population. People are drawn to this area because it offers a diverse range of jobs, housing, specialist services and recreational and cultural facilities.

## The nature of urban areas

In Australia an urban centre has a population of over 1000 people and an urban locality has at least 200 people. If a town's population falls below 200, it ceases to exist as an urban locality. Any small town located just beyond the edge of a big city is absorbed into the big city's urban population if the distance between the two places is less than 3 kilometres.

Increasing urbanisation occurred in Australia during the twentieth century. In 1901, Australia's largest centres were Sydney and Melbourne, both with populations of 500 000 people. The proportion of Australians living in large urban areas (100 000 people or more) increased from 34 per cent to 63 per cent over the century. In 2008, the growth rate of the combined capital cities (1.6 per cent) was higher than the growth rate of the rest of Australia (1.4 per cent). The fastest growing capital cities were Darwin (2.6 per cent) and Perth (2.3 per cent). In each state, the highest population growth is in the outer and inner suburbs of capital cities, mining centres (such as Cobar) and some regional centres (such as Albury, Bathurst and Maitland), especially around the coast (such as Byron Bay and Coffs Harbour).

## Urban growth

The number of urban centres and localities in Australia grew from 1725 in 2001 to 1767 in 2008. This represents six new urban centres or localities every year. These new centres have developed through various processes:

- *Suburbanisation* is population growth in the outer suburbs of cities such as Blacktown and Campbelltown in Sydney. As the city sprawls towards the rural–urban fringe, the government provides infrastructure such as water, roads, schools and hospitals.
- Coastal growth is the largest urban growth outside capital cities, especially around south-east Queensland and northern New South Wales (Hervey Bay to Byron Bay), Sydney (Newcastle to Wollongong), Port Phillip Bay in Victoria (Queenscliff to Portsea), and Perth in Western Australia (Wanneroo to Mandurah).
- *Urban consolidation* aims to reduce the environmental impacts and government expenses caused by urban sprawl. By increasing housing density, homes built on 'quarter acre' blocks are subdivided to accommodate units in suburbs such as Chatswood.
- *Urban renewal* is the development of existing urban areas with new buildings and improved infrastructure, such as that at Darling Harbour and the renovation of older homes in Balmain.
- *Exurbanisation* occurs when people move to existing towns within 100 kilometres of a major city and commute to the city regularly (such as the Central Coast, Wollongong and the Blue Mountains near Sydney).

## Impacts of urban growth

By 2050 the number of people living in urban areas in Australia is expected to increase, but the rate of increase is expected to decline. To accommodate the anticipated population, sustainable development policies need to reduce the large urban ecological footprint (EF). There are already high-rise apartments built on sand dunes at Collaroy, and housing developers have cleared wetlands at Sylvania Waters. Urban growth is causing traffic congestion, deteriorating air quality, land and coastal degradation and overuse of scarce water resources.

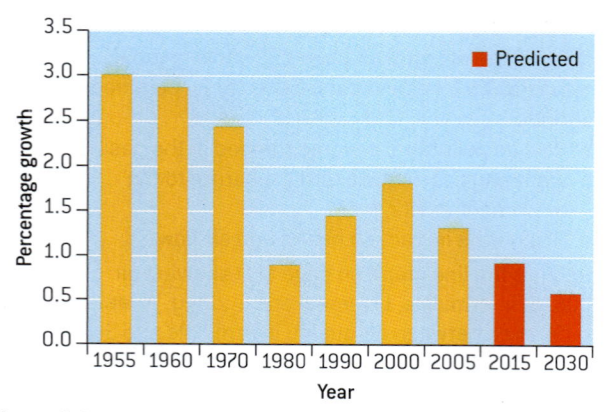

*Australia's past and future urban growth rate*

**Nature of urban growth**

| Reason for urban growth | Nature and examples of urban development |
|---|---|
| Sea change | Movement from suburbs to coastal areas, which has led to increased real estate prices (Newport), high-rise development (Dee Why), tourism development (Terrigal) and development of retirement villas (Terrigal) |
| Hill change | Movement to pleasant environments within a short commuting distance of a city (Blue Mountains, Adelaide Hills) |
| Boom areas | Real estate boom in mining centres (Albany in Western Australia, Mt Isa in Queensland), industrial projects (Wollongong) and historical settlements (The Rocks) |
| Lifestyle features | Location near water, such as harbour (Kirribilli), river, lake and canal; overlooking a national park (Lane Cove) or golf course (Avalon) or near exclusive cafés, shops and schools (Mosman) |
| Blue sky | Prime location on the edge of a city (Dural); beside a river (Woronora); adjoining a beach (Palm Beach); near exclusive schools, cafés and expensive shops (Toorak, Double Bay) |
| Stayers | Areas with character, café culture, quality shopping, schools, transport and close to the inner city for entertainment and work (Balmain) |
| Ripple effect | Increase in property prices in prime suburbs (Surry Hills) leading to movement to less expensive suburbs (Leichhardt) up to the rural–urban fringe (Penrith) |
| Ugly ducklings | Renovation and transformation of inner industrial areas from an ugly duckling to a real estate swan (Richmond in Melbourne, Surry Hills in Sydney) |
| Transport and infrastructure | Increase in urban sprawl by development of roads, bridges, railways, schools and hospitals as well as motorways and expressways that provide fast links to the central business district of a city |

*Oblique aerial photograph of Nelson Bay, Port Stephens, New South Wales. Like many Australian coastal towns, Nelson Bay has experienced a building boom in recent years.*

## Urban decline

Australia loses about five towns a year when the population falls below the 200 threshold. However, of the 66 towns lost in Australia from 2001 to 2006, 41 were absorbed into a larger city. The remaining 25 include Iron Knob in South Australia, Leith in Tasmania, Yuleba in Queensland, Angourie in New South Wales and Peppimenarti in the Northern Territory. The reasons for the decline were mostly to do with changes to the economic base of the community. Some were railway towns (Yelarbon), goldmining towns (Croydon), opalmining towns (Mintabie) and coalmining towns (Cullen Bullen). Others were swept aside by large-scale farming where there is less demand for a local village (Merino). Shifts in Indigenous communities have also reduced some populations (Belyuen).

## Inner-city suburbs

From the 1970s to the 1990s, increased international competition resulted in the closure of many car, clothing and chemical industries in inner-city suburbs. Some industries downsized, some moved to the rural–urban fringe, while others moved offshore to countries with cheaper labour. This restructuring caused urban decline in the La Trobe Valley in Victoria (reliant on coal-based electricity industries) and in Elizabeth and Whyalla in South Australia (reliant on manufacturing). As a result, the population in inner-city suburbs declined by 23 per cent between 1991 and 1996.

There is no single cause of **urban decay**. The Royal Institute of Chartered Surveyors (RICS) report 'Spot the grot, stop the rot' proposes a list of indicators that provide a warning to governments to introduce early prevention techniques, such as the redevelopment of old areas. These indicators include:
- unemployment rates twice the national average
- below average wages
- low property prices
- vacant shops
- more than 200 crimes per 1000 people per year
- a sharp increase in rented housing.

### SAMPLE STUDY

#### Newcastle

Newcastle, the second largest populated area in New South Wales, experienced industrial decline after the 1970s. Unemployment rose to 15 per cent, homes were abandoned and infrastructure decayed. In 1992, the state and federal governments' Building Better Cities program established the Honeysuckle Development Corporation to redevelop 50 hectares of railway and port land adjacent to the CBD. The aim was to increase the population by revitalising the area, creating employment and providing environmental, economic and social benefits.

*Honeysuckle project, Newcastle*

## Drought area decline — mining area boom

Changes to industry (mining) and the environment (climate change) can determine whether an urban population grows or declines. For example, from 2001 to 2008, a prolonged drought affected towns reliant on agriculture so that the population of western NSW decreased by 20 per cent in centres such as Bourke, Moree and Narrabri.

Particularly vulnerable are urban centres dependent on mining. Mines close when resources are depleted, prices fall or global markets are lost. For example in New South Wales, the wealthy towns of Hill End and Newnes, once reliant on goldmining and oil shale respectively, are now ghost towns. Between 2001 and 2008 the population growth of two per cent in 12 **boom towns** may be slowed as a result of the global financial crisis from 2008 onwards.

*Labels on photograph:*
- Housing apartments
- Crown Plaza Hotel
- Proposed multi-purpose site for housing, retail and office space
- Site of medical centre

### GEOfacts
- Angourie had a population of 170 at the 2006 census and the median age was 47.
- Cullen Bullen had a population of 198 at the 2006 census, 107 of whom were male and 91 female.

### ACTIVITIES

#### UNDERSTANDING
1. Explain the following terms: urban centre, urban locality, sea change, boom area, suburbanisation, urban consolidation, urban renewal, exurbanisation, urban decline and urban decay.
2. Describe the changing urban face of Australia from 1901 to 2015.
3. Explain the causes of urban decline.

#### THINKING AND APPLYING
4. Complete a RAP using fieldwork techniques on an area of urban growth in your locality.
5. Refer to the first paragraph on the previous page and locate all the towns on a map of Australia. Find their latitude and longitude. Research two places and discuss the reasons for their population decline.

#### USING YOUR SKILLS
6. Refer to the graph of Australia's past and future urban growth on page 162. In which year was the largest increase in the urban growth rate? Explain the future trends.
7. Refer to the photograph of Nelson Bay on page 163. Draw and label a sketch of Nelson Bay. Why do you think it has experienced a building boom?
8. Refer to the photograph of Newcastle in the sample study. Draw and label a line diagram of the area. What are the government responses to urban decline? List the changes to the site and suggest why residents and businesses might be attracted to the area.

### GEOTERMS

**boom town:** a community that experiences sudden and rapid population and economic growth

**rural–urban fringe:** area where developing suburbs meet farmland or native vegetation

**urban decay:** decline in land use, where it had previously flourished, leaving behind derelict buildings and vacant sites

**urbanisation:** process by which a country's urban population increases

CHAPTER 7 | Geographical issues

# 7.5 Urban growth and decline in Sydney

The spatial nature of Sydney has changed over time. In the 1830s, Sydney was a 'walking' city with densely populated urban areas such as Redfern, Woolloomooloo and Paddington close to the central business district (CBD). After 1880, Sydney evolved into a transit city due to the building of railways, which encouraged the growth of suburbs such as Parramatta. In 1932, the Harbour Bridge was opened, providing a transport link and faster access to North Shore suburbs such as Pymble. The evolution to an automobile city began after World War II and saw the growth of suburbs north (Cherrybrook), south (Menai) and west (St Marys). Faster road and rail links and the availability of cheaper housing eventually led to the development of **dormitory towns** for commuters in the Wollongong, Central Coast and Blue Mountains areas.

## Urban growth

Whether an urban area grows or declines depends not only on the environment, resources, infrastructure and government policies but also on changes to the population such as natural increase (births minus deaths); rural–urban and urban–rural migration (counterurbanisation) and international migration (immigration minus emigration).

Sydney's population is predicted to reach 4.9 million by 2026, an increase of one million in 30 years. The sustainable development of this city requires coordination of individuals, groups and all levels of governments to manage the changing urban processes of:
- urban decay and growth
- urban consolidation
- rural–urban migration
- suburbanisation
- exurbanisation.

These patterns have changed over the last decade with the city's inner- and middle-ring suburbs accommodating a larger share of housing growth. For example, over the past five years, 75 per cent of new dwellings were built in established areas compared with 25 per cent in new release areas.

**Exurbanisation:** e.g. Blue Mountains, associated with fast rail and M4 motorway

**Exurbanisation:** e.g. Gosford, Wyong. This urban growth takes place about 100 km from a major city, associated with a fast rail service and F3 freeway.

**Rural–urban and Urban–rural** (counter-urbanisation)

**Suburbanisation:** e.g. Blacktown, Baulkham Hills, Liverpool, Campbelltown. Movement outwards from the city centre

**Exurbanisation:** e.g. Wollongong, associated with fast rail and F6 freeway

**Natural increase** = births minus deaths

**Migration** = immigration minus emigration

**Urban decline and renewal:** e.g. Paddington, Balmain, Redfern. Marrickville had 500 factories in 1960 but by the 1970s most of the factories had closed, causing unemployment and a decrease in population.

**Sydney CBD:** urban decline in old industrial and port areas and urban renewal in Darling Harbour

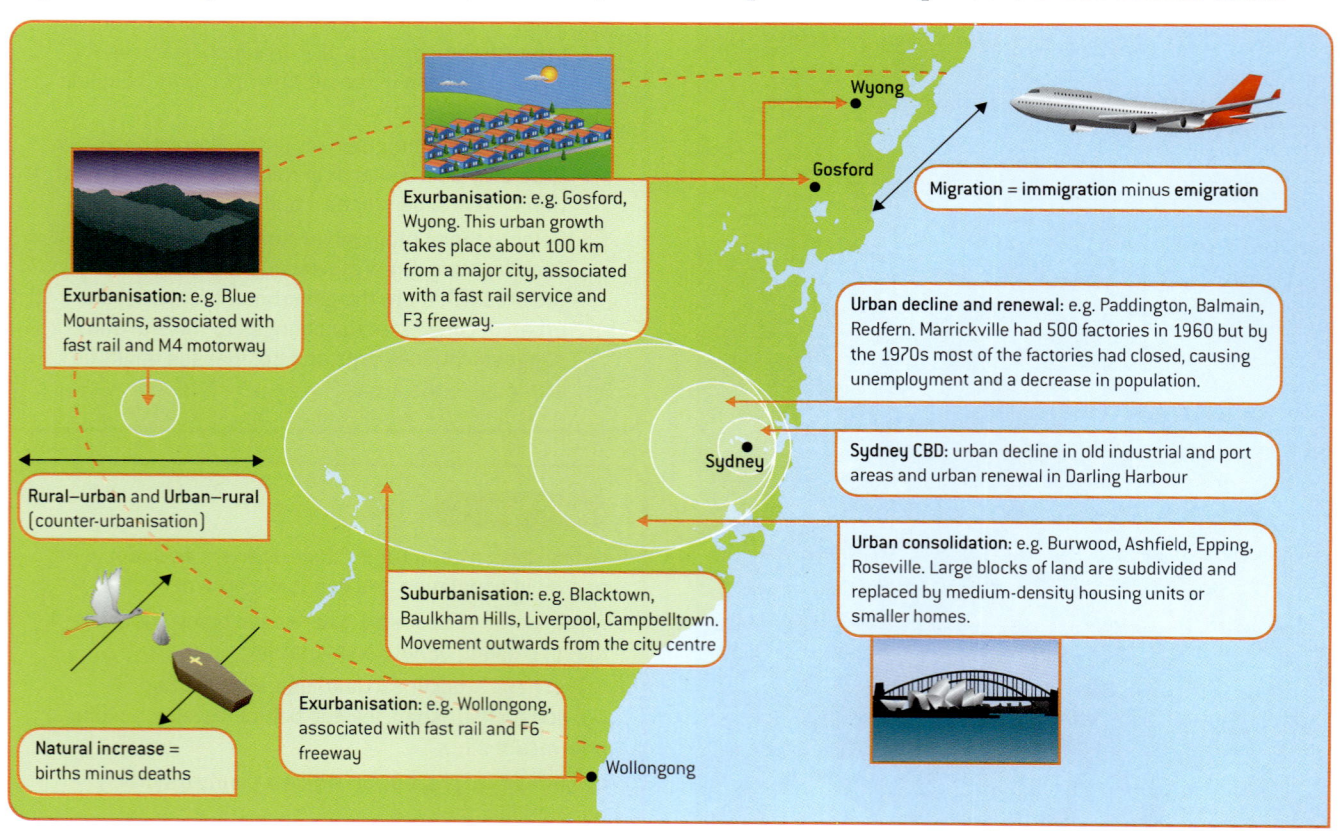

**Urban consolidation:** e.g. Burwood, Ashfield, Epping, Roseville. Large blocks of land are subdivided and replaced by medium-density housing units or smaller homes.

*Map of urban growth and decline in Sydney*

## SAMPLE STUDY

### Redfern: fixing the Block, a $27 million development plan

*Aboriginal leader Lyall Munro outside houses that are typical of the Block in Redfern*

In 1973, a grant to the 8000-square-metres Block in Redfern was given to the Aboriginal Housing Company (AHC). With 102 houses, the Block became the birthplace of urban land rights. Today, only 19 inhabited homes remain; most have been burned and are dilapidated. A plan released in 2006 aims to create 18 000 jobs and a new town centre around Redfern railway station. The New South Wales Government will manage Aboriginal lands on the Block for at least 20 years as part of a redevelopment plan aimed at fixing social problems and lifting the area's property prices.

*A model of the Aboriginal housing project for the Block*

# Urban decline then growth

Improvements in transport and the decentralisation of industry to the outer suburbs meant that people no longer needed to live near the CBD for jobs, shops and services. This led to a shift in the population from the inner to the outer suburbs. Land values near the CBD dropped and neglected areas showed signs of decay. This process was referred to as the *doughnut effect*. For example, in 1960 Marrickville had over 500 factories but by 1970 most of the large factories had closed. As unemployment increased, the population moved out and homes and buildings were neglected. As a result, the population of the inner suburbs declined from 98 000 in 1970 to 78 000 in 1990. Recent urban renewal projects have increased the population to 80 000 in 2009.

Today, suburbs such as the Block in Redfern and the Pyrmont–Ultimo urban villages or 'chic' quarters that were experiencing urban decay are being renewed or *reurbanised*. Young, high-income professionals, sometimes called yuppies, are moving into these inner areas to be close to work and entertainment. Old terraces and industrial blocks have been renovated, leading to the process called *gentrification*. Over time, house prices have increased, forcing people who are less well-off to move to the outer suburbs.

# Urban consolidation

Urban sprawl in Sydney led to environmental degradation (a decrease in quality of land, air and water) and an increased demand for the government to build expensive new infrastructure. To reduce these negative aspects, governments introduced urban consolidation plans. The aim is to increase population density by constructing high-rise apartments and medium-density housing. Despite these planning policies, the majority of Sydneysiders continue to live in low-density outer suburbs.

# Suburbanisation in Sydney

Urban sprawl or suburbanisation occurs when a city spreads outwards to occupy more land. Improved motorways, the widespread use of the motor car, and the release of cheap land and housing packages have contributed to Sydney's urban sprawl. Living in these suburbs has both advantages and disadvantages socially, economically and environmentally. New developments have seen the spread of quickly constructed and needlessly large houses often called McMansions — 'Big Mac burgers of architecture'. Homes positioned side by side on tiny blocks without trees are said to resemble Legoland. By 2008 many of these dwellings had been affected by high interest rates and oil prices.

*Houses known as McMansions in Casula, Sydney*

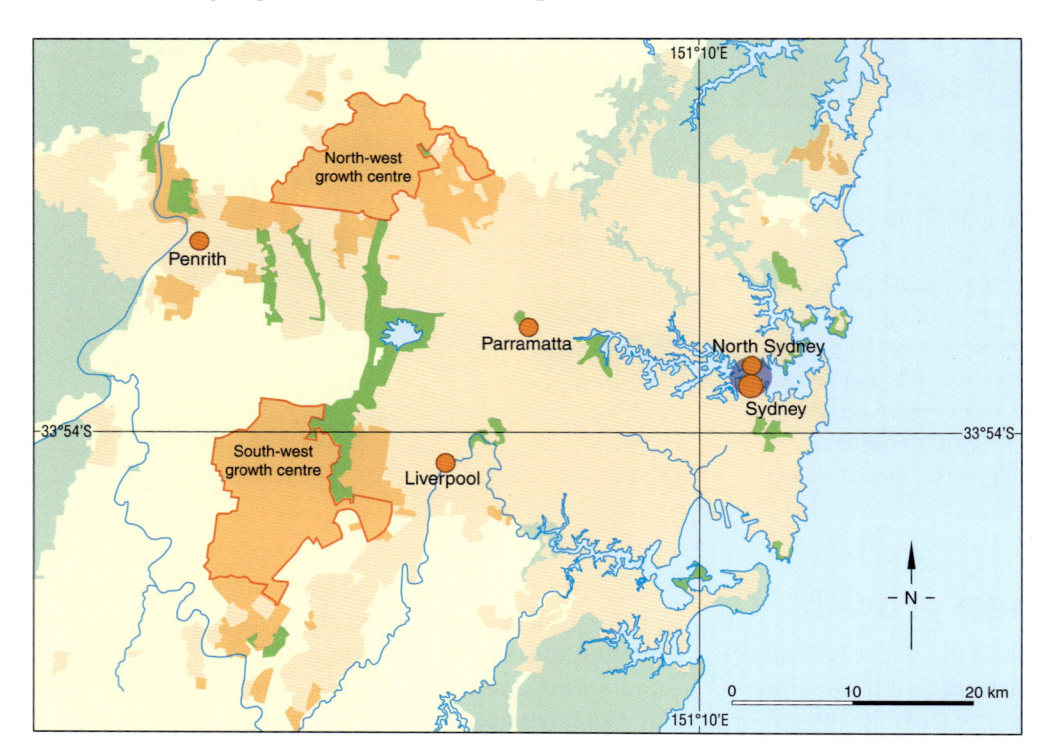

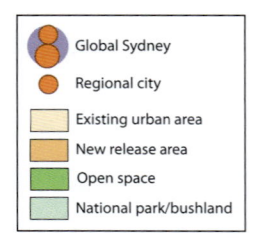

*Map of urban development in new release areas to 2031*

## Suburbanisation

| Disadvantages | Advantages | Government |
|---|---|---|
| • requires:<br>  – more roads<br>  – larger water and sewerage networks<br>  – larger electricity and gas grids<br>  – telephone networks<br>  – health care, education and emergency services<br>  – parking spaces for cars left at railway stations<br>• most cars carry only 1 person, which is not fuel efficient and produces greenhouse gases<br>• women at home isolated as men spend long periods of time travelling to and from work in the CBD<br>• socioeconomic problems, with higher unemployment and lower incomes | • more open spaces<br>• larger homes for lower costs<br>• quieter<br>• more room for children to play | • provides infrastructure<br>• local council provides baby health centres and pre-schools<br>• development of the urban village to overcome disadvantages (mixed land uses, different age groups, bike paths, attractive places for people to meet, commercial and recreational facilities)<br>• encourages businesses to move to areas where land is cheaper, providing jobs for the growing population<br>• more money spent on fast, efficient, cheap public transport |

## North-west region

In Sydney, both the south-west and north-west regions are the major population growth areas. People regard the advantages of living in these areas as:
- the availability of cheaper houses
- being able to have larger backyards.

However the disadvantage is the long distance to the city, often made worse by a lack of public transport.

To accommodate the increasing population in the south-west region (Camden, Campbelltown, Liverpool and Wollondilly), the New South Wales Government plans to build 5700 homes each year until 2031. The north-west region (Baulkham Hills, Blacktown, the Blue Mountains, the Hawkesbury and Penrith) is home to over 760 000 people and is forecast to have the largest share of Sydney's new housing growth (23 per cent) and jobs (24 per cent) over the next 22 years. The 2031 north-west regional plan aims to implement the 2005 'City of cities: a plan for Sydney's future' by providing extra homes, jobs, public transport, services and infrastructure for the increasing population.

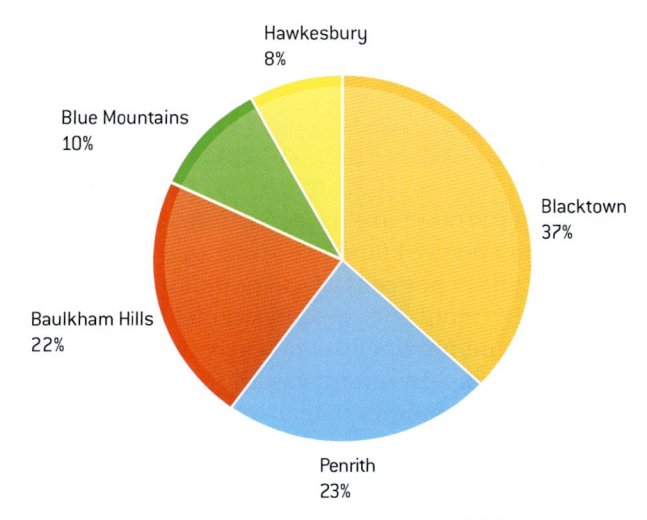

*Graph of % of population in north-west Sydney 2009*

- Hawkesbury 8%
- Blue Mountains 10%
- Blacktown 37%
- Penrith 23%
- Baulkham Hills 22%

As 65 per cent of the residents are in the working age group, the Norwest Business Park provides jobs for an increasingly educated population. Local, state and federal governments work with businesses, groups and individuals to implement the sustainable and equitable plan.

## ACTIVITIES

### UNDERSTANDING

1. Define and give examples of the following terms: dormitory towns, doughnut effect, reurbanisation, gentrification.
2. List three factors that contribute to an increase in the urban population.
3. What is suburbanisation and where does it occur?
4. What are two advantages and two disadvantages of suburbanisation?

### THINKING AND APPLYING

5. Draw a picture to explain the doughnut effect. Provide labels to show both the causes and effects on people, industry, commerce and infrastructure.
6. Discuss the urban processes that have occurred in your local area over the last 20 years.
7. List four primary and four secondary sources of information required to complete a RAP on urban growth or decline in your local area.
8. Explain what is meant by the 'Big Mac burger of architecture'. Why do you think people want to live in one of these residences?

### USING YOUR SKILLS

9. Refer to the map of urban growth and decline in Sydney on page 166.
   a Which areas are experiencing urban growth in Sydney?
   b Explain why you might live in Wollongong or Balmain and work in Sydney.
10. Refer to the photographs of the Block in Redfern.
    a Why is the photograph a good example of spatial inequality?
    b Why is the Block a significant urban site?
    c Explain the responses of the government to urban decline.
    d Write a scenario of this site in 20 years.
11. Refer to the map on the previous page of the north-west and south-west growth centres of Sydney up to 2031.
    a Calculate the area of the newly released land.
    b Calculate the area of the open space.
12. Refer to the pie graph above of the population in north-west Sydney. Rank the suburbs from the highest to lowest population and give each a figure based on a total population in north-west Sydney of 760 000.

### GEOTERMS

**dormitory town:** place from which many people travel in order to work in a bigger town or city

# 7.6 Redeveloping the Ultimo–Pyrmont area

Ultimo and Pyrmont are inner Sydney suburbs on a peninsula about 2 kilometres west of Sydney's CBD. In 2009, 60 per cent of the population living in Ultimo–Pyrmont was aged between 20 and 45 years. In the nineteenth and early twentieth centuries, Ultimo–Pyrmont was an important part of the city's wool storage, sugar refining, flour milling and shipping industries, with a population of nearly 20 000 in 1900. After World War II, the area began slowly decaying. Many industries relocated or closed down when shipping activities declined. By 1954, the population fell to 5000, and by 1978 it was 1800. With the 1980s, property boom, derelict industrial sites began to be redeveloped for residences. By 2001, there were 11 943 residents and a working population of 24 284. The City West Urban Renewal Program aims to transform the area into a sustainable inner-city village, putting people before cars and preserving the heritage. The City of Sydney 2031 Metropolitan Strategy aims to make the area an information technology, communications and media precinct.

Towards the Pyrmont end of the peninsula, the redevelopment plan proposes that 80 000 square metres of space be allocated to commercial, retail and residential projects, as shown on the satellite image.

In 2003, it was proposed that the Elizabeth Macarthur Bay Water Police site be redeveloped. It would contain a 13-storey residential tower plus commercial space. In response, the Friends of Pyrmont Point action group organised a rally to campaign for the return of the Water Police site to public parkland. By 2004, more than 10 000 people had signed the parliamentary petition. In 2005, the City of Sydney purchased the Water Police site for use as a public park.

*Heritage buildings in Ultimo–Pyrmont*

1. Elizabeth Macarthur Bay redevelopment
2. Darling Island
3. 19 Harris Street
4. Fish Market
5. Edwin Davey Flour Mills
6. Goodman Fielder site
7. Festival Records site
8. Winten development

*Eight proposed development sites on the peninsula*

## GEOskills TOOLBOX

### MEASURING BEARINGS ON A MAP

Bearings are used to give greater accuracy when reading a map or using a compass. A **bearing** (or angle) is given in degrees measured clockwise from north.

Compass direction (e.g. NNW)

Bearing (e.g. 270°)

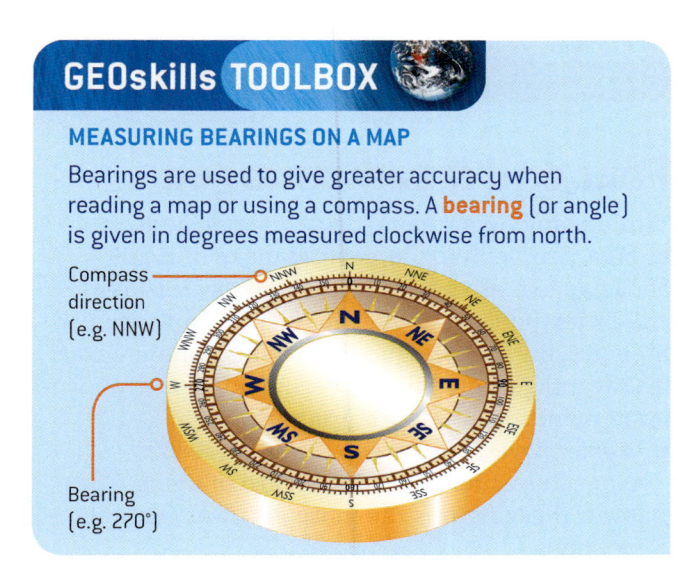

# Redevelopment

The Ultimo–Pyrmont area is the largest urban renewal project in Australia. An area of 140 hectares of former docklands, industry and homes is being redeveloped. To cater for 20 000 residents by 2021, a mixed-use, high-density, medium-rise residential area is planned. To accommodate population growth, the area will require 7500 new dwellings, in addition to 1400 existing dwellings, and affordable housing (or public housing). The Jackson's Landing development situated on the old CSR site has been replaced by one of Australia's most prestigious waterfront redevelopments. It has luxury apartments, shops, cafes and sporting facilities.

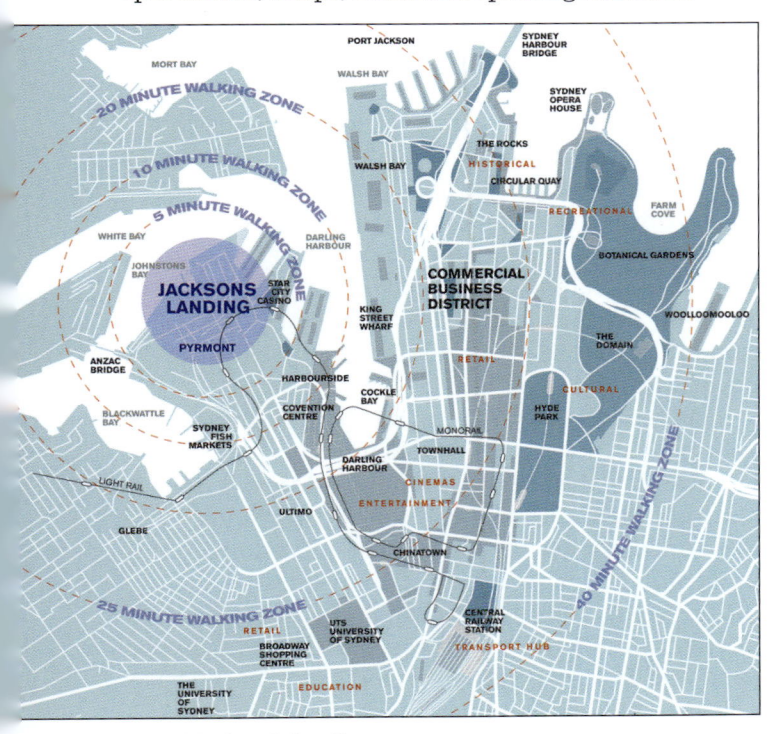

*Map of Jackson's Landing*

## Sustainable urban environment

The Ultimo–Pyrmont renewal project (1994–2004) cleared eight hectares of industrial area for green space. 'Pocket parks' are now accessible by residents and workers within three minutes of their home or workplace. An efficient public transport system includes more buses, a ferry wharf and a light-rail transport system. By providing a pedestrian/cycleway network, limiting parking areas and installing parking meters, it aims to encourage people to use public transport. This has led to a reduced carbon footprint, as 30 per cent of households do not own cars and 42.6 per cent walk to work.

## ACTIVITIES

### UNDERSTANDING

1. Why did the Ultimo–Pyrmont area suffer from urban decline?
2. Discuss why harbour sites close to the CBD are popular for redevelopment.
3. Explain how active citizenship resulted in changes to the redevelopment plan.

### THINKING AND APPLYING

4. Undertake a RAP on urban renewal by researching a site that is changing: for example, from old shops to a one-stop shopping centre, or from industry to residential. Use primary data (interviews, sketch maps, photographs, surveys) and secondary data (maps, graphs, newspaper articles), and visit the local council and developer. After gathering, collating and analysing the information, answer the key geographical issues in a report format.

### USING YOUR SKILLS

5. Study the map showing Jacksons Landing. Imagine you were standing on the letter D of LANDING.
   a. If you walked for 30 minutes at a bearing of 90 degrees, what place would you reach?
   b. What bearing would you follow to reach Darling Harbour? What type of measuring equipment would help you work out your bearing?
   c. If you walked south-east, how long would it take you to reach Chinatown?
6. Using the photograph on page 170, draw a sketch map and label the main roads, bridges and the eight sites to be redeveloped. Discuss the advantages and disadvantages of these sites.

### GEOTERMS

**bearing:** an angle, given in degrees and minutes, measured clockwise from north on a compass

# 7.7 Spatial inequality: overview

Inequality and social injustice can occur when resources and rewards are not distributed evenly within a society. Spatial inequality describes inequalities that occur, for example, between countries, between different areas within a country, between rural and urban settlements, within and between cities, as well as between ethnic groups. In 2009, the non-Indigenous population in Australia earned a higher income and lived on average 17 years longer than Indigenous people. Campaigns to 'Make Indigenous Poverty History' aim to reduce this gap.

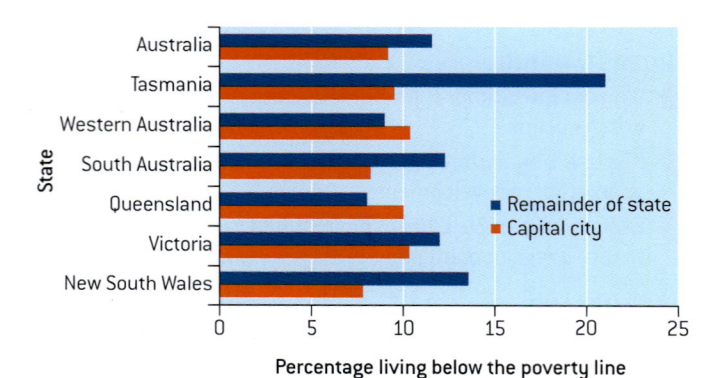

*Graph of poverty gap*

Inequality is found in all societies and is reflected by indicators that include people's income (GDP per person), assets, health, infant mortality rate (IMR) and access to clean water and education. Income is a major determinant of inequality because it influences access to resources. For example, people on low incomes experience lower life expectancy as they cannot afford the same level of health care as people with higher incomes.

**Inequality between Indigenous and non-Indigenous people**

| Indicator | Indigenous people compared with non-Indigenous people |
|---|---|
| Life expectancy | 17 years lower |
| Income | One-third less |
| Circulatory system diseases | 2–10 times higher |
| Renal failure | 2–3 times higher |
| Diabetes | 3–4 times higher |
| Cot death | 2–3 times higher |
| Blindness | 4 times higher |
| Respiratory diseases | 3–4 times higher |

## Poor and disadvantaged

While many Australians juggle the payment of bills, people living in poverty make difficult choices, such as skipping a meal to pay for their child's textbook. To reduce inequality and social injustice, the following indicators determine who is disadvantaged, enabling governments and groups to implement social welfare programs:

- *Human poverty index* (HPI) measures life expectancy, literacy and standard of living. The lower these figures the more disadvantaged the person is.
- *Poverty line* (PL) is the minimum income required to avoid poverty. In 2008, inclusive of housing costs, the poverty line was $714.27 per week for a family comprising two adults, one of whom is working, and two dependent children.
- *Socioeconomic indexes for area* (SEIFA) focus on disadvantaged groups such as those with low income and low educational attainment and the unemployed.
- *The Australian Council of Social Services* (ACOSS) includes additional indicators such as access to dental care, and the ability to raise $500 in an emergency, take a holiday once a year and send a child on school excursions.

## Gap between rich and poor

Australia is a rich, developed country with a high GDP (over $35 000 per person) and high life expectancy (81 years). However, such statistics are only averages and do not show the gap between rich and poor people. In 2008, the wealthiest 20 per cent of the population had 56 per cent of all income, while the bottom 20 per cent had 1 per cent of all income. In 2008, Australia had 12 billionaires while 2 210 000 people (11.1 per cent), including 412 000 children, lived below the poverty line.

Even though every suburb has both rich and poor people, poverty tends to dominate some areas. For example, the areas with the highest poverty rates are Lightning Ridge in New South Wales (26 per cent below the poverty line), Carlton South in Victoria (25 per cent), Gin Gin in Queensland (22 per cent), Ferryden Park in South Australia (30 per cent), Perth city in Western Australia (19 per cent) and St Marys in Tasmania (21 per cent). These poverty rates are more than double the Australian average of 10.2 per cent.

**Spatial inequality across Australia**

| Most disadvantaged | | | | Most advantaged | | | |
|---|---|---|---|---|---|---|---|
| Rank in Australia | Local government area | State | Population | Rank in Australia | Local government area | State | Population |
| 1 | Jilkminggan | NT | 273 | 1 | Barton | ACT | 940 |
| 2 | Belyuen | NT | 173 | 2 | Forrest | ACT | 1 191 |
| 3 | Yarrabah | Qld | 2 372 | 3 | Ku-ring-gai | NSW | 101 084 |
| 4 | Palm Island | Qld | 1 982 | 4 | O'Malley | ACT | 685 |
| 5 | Walangeri Ngumpinku | NT | 463 | 5 | Pullenvale | Qld | 3 153 |
| 6 | East Arnhem—Bal | NT | 6 522 | 6 | Fig Tree Pocket | Qld | 3 259 |
| 7 | Kowanyama | Qld | 1 020 | 7 | Mosman | NSW | 26 236 |
| 8 | Napranum | Qld | 840 | 8 | Chapman | ACT | 2 693 |
| 9 | Daguragu | NT | 543 | 9 | Peppermint Grove | WA | 1 582 |
| 10 | Marngarr | NT | 275 | 10 | Woollahra | NSW | 50 162 |

**Spatial inequality across New South Wales**

| Most disadvantaged | | | Most advantaged | | |
|---|---|---|---|---|---|
| Rank in New South Wales | Local government area | Population | Rank in New South Wales | Local government area | Population |
| 1 | Brewarrina | 1 945 | 1 | Ku-ring-gai | 101 084 |
| 2 | Central Darling | 1 938 | 2 | Mosman | 26 236 |
| 3 | Walgett | 6 944 | 3 | Woollahra | 50 162 |
| 4 | Richmond Valley | 21 312 | 4 | North Sydney | 58 257 |
| 5 | Coonamble | 4 210 | 5 | Lane Cove | 30 427 |
| 6 | Kempsey | 27 386 | 6 | Manly | 37 111 |
| 7 | Nambucca | 17 896 | 7 | Willoughby | 63 604 |
| 8 | Wellington | 8 122 | 8 | Hunter's Hill | 13 242 |
| 9 | Broken Hill | 19 363 | 9 | Baulkham Hills | 159 391 |
| 10 | Tenterfield | 6 533 | 10 | Pittwater | 54 156 |

## ACTIVITIES

### UNDERSTANDING

1. Explain the following terms: spatial inequality, human poverty index, poverty line, socioeconomic indexes for area.
2. List six indicators you would use to measure inequality.
3. Discuss the gap between rich and poor people and communities across Australia.

### THINKING AND APPLYING

4. Explain the meaning of the phrase 'going hungry in rich Australia'.
5. Describe spatial inequality across Australia using examples and statistics.
6. Research the Make Indigenous Poverty History campaign. What are its aims, strategies and achievements so far?
7. Refer to the table on the previous page to give three examples showing inequality between Indigenous and non-Indigenous people. Suggest how this gap could be reduced.

### USING YOUR SKILLS

8. Refer to the bar graph on the previous page showing the poverty gap in Australia.
   a. List the states with the highest poverty in urban areas.
   b. Which state has the highest poverty level?
   c. Which state has the largest difference in poverty between the capital city and the remainder of the state?
9. Refer to the table showing spatial inequality across Australia to answer the following questions.
   a. How many people live in the top ten disadvantaged local government areas?
   b. What two states have the largest number of people living in the top ten most advantaged areas?
10. 'Everyone in New South Wales is equal.' Discuss this statement using statistics from the table above showing spatial inequality across New South Wales.

# 7.8 Nature and impacts of poverty

In Australia, the meaning of poverty is different from the **absolute poverty** that exists in many developing countries. People in rich countries such as Australia may suffer from **relative poverty** — a lack of resources required to participate in the lifestyle enjoyed by other Australians.

Absolute poverty is rare in Australia because social services help to ensure that people have adequate food, clothing and shelter. Nevertheless, many people are still poor relative to others in society. Problems often associated with poverty are unemployment, drug taking, poor health, poor education, crime and lack of opportunities for young people. The challenge for governments is to ensure that people on a low income have access to public transport, affordable housing, employment, education, training, specialist services and opportunities for social participation.

## Who are the poor?

The twenty-first century has seen conflicting trends in Australia's economic and social life. Average real incomes and property markets have risen in the 'lucky country'; yet, for many people, well-paid jobs have disappeared and family incomes have fallen, generating a greater dependence on social services. The people who are missing out on Australia's growing prosperity include Indigenous Australians, the long-term unemployed, children, single-parent families, young people from low-income backgrounds, newly arrived migrants from non-English-speaking backgrounds, unskilled youth, the homeless, caregivers, people with disabilities and those living in remote rural areas.

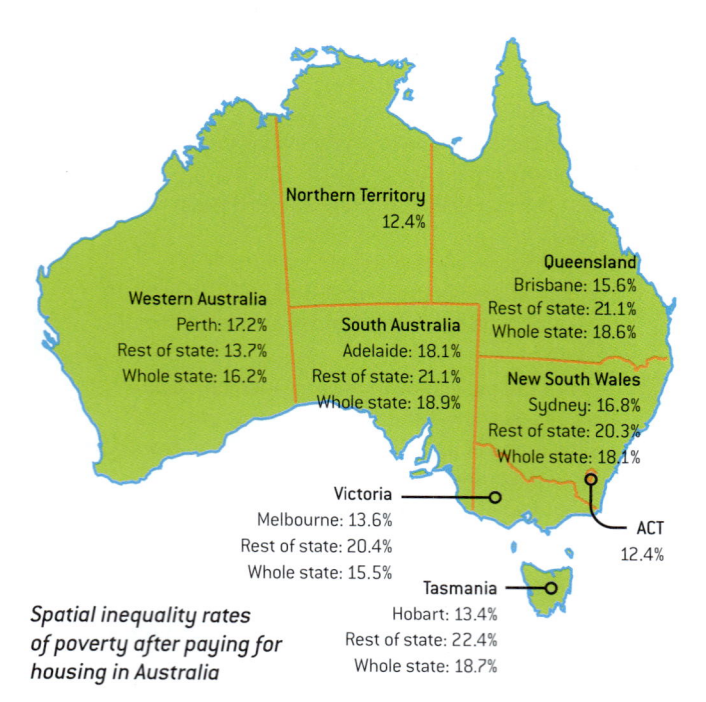

## What are the social impacts?

Changes in the distribution of jobs and earnings over the past two decades have contributed to a social division between the 'haves' and the 'have nots' in Australia. The high cost of housing, food and petrol means that half of Australian households that live on less than $40 000 a year can barely pay the rent, let alone save for a home in capital cities like Sydney and Melbourne. Because of the high cost of housing, 36 per cent of low-income households in Sydney are experiencing housing stress. Many have been forced to approach charities for accommodation, food and clothes. The global financial crisis in 2008–2009 intensified these problems with higher unemployment levels.

However, a job is no longer a guarantee against poverty. The income gap can be attributed to different skills and type of work. Educated workers in the service industries (information technology, law, media, banking) tend to earn more and work in or near the CBD. On the other hand, less-educated, unskilled workers tend to earn less and live in the outer urban suburbs where housing is affordable. In these suburbs, jobs are scarce, public transport inadequate, and car travel expensive.

## Impacts on children and youth

Childhood poverty has both immediate and lasting negative impacts and exists in both developing and developed countries. About 860 000 Australian children live in households where neither parent works and they depend on the government for support. In response, Save the Children Australia funds the Mobile Play Bus program at Redfern and La Perouse. In Western Australia, the Wanneroo Child Health Centre provides Indigenous teenage mothers with education and parenting skills.

Unemployed youth, especially the less educated, are at a high risk of falling below the poverty line. Within Sydney, spatial inequality occurs with teenage full-time unemployment in the inner Sydney suburbs at 30 per cent compared with four per cent in the outer St George/Sutherland area. In response, many organisations and

**Northern Territory** 12.4%

**Queensland**
Brisbane: 15.6%
Rest of state: 21.1%
Whole state: 18.6%

**Western Australia**
Perth: 17.2%
Rest of state: 13.7%
Whole state: 16.2%

**South Australia**
Adelaide: 18.1%
Rest of state: 21.1%
Whole state: 18.9%

**New South Wales**
Sydney: 16.8%
Rest of state: 20.3%
Whole state: 18.1%

**Victoria**
Melbourne: 13.6%
Rest of state: 20.4%
Whole state: 15.5%

**ACT** 12.4%

**Tasmania**
Hobart: 13.4%
Rest of state: 22.4%
Whole state: 18.7%

*Spatial inequality rates of poverty after paying for housing in Australia*

individuals support 'Youth Off The Streets', which aims to reduce the 22 000 young homeless people across Australia, and the Homeless World Cup, which aims to rebuild self-esteem.

Unfortunately, the gap between the rich and poor has led to stereotyping and conflict between groups of young people. The media has contributed to negative images of poor outer suburbs and ignored the diversity of people and cultures that is found in all places.

**Poverty rates of children in Australia**

| Year | % of children who live in single-mother families | % of children who live in poverty | | |
|---|---|---|---|---|
| | | Children in single-mother families | Children in two-parent families | All children |
| 1981 | 51.9 | 9.3 | 9.8 | 13.8 |
| 1985 | 62.2 | 8.4 | 9.5 | 14.0 |
| 1989 | 55.2 | 11.7 | 9.2 | 15.0 |
| 1994 | 46.3 | 10.6 | 11.9 | 15.8 |
| 2004 | 49.2 | 13.1 | 12.0 | 16.0 |
| 2009 | 48.3 | 14.2 | 12.6 | 16.2 |

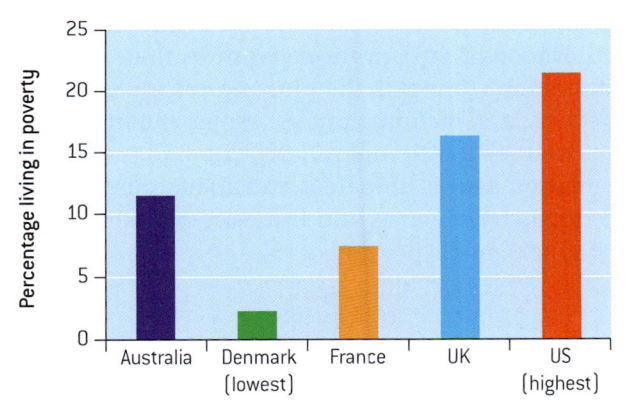

*Child poverty rate in selected countries*

*The Homeless World Cup, played in Melbourne in 2008*

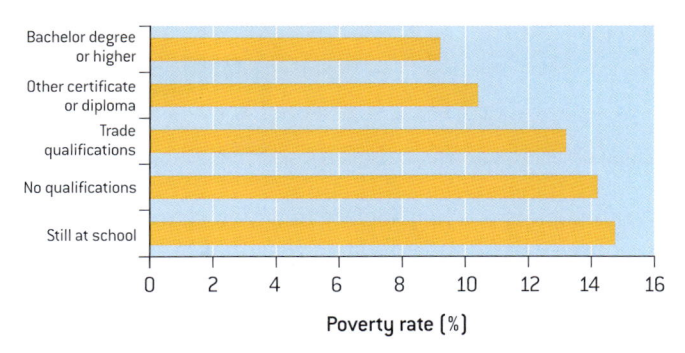

*Poverty rates by educational qualifications in Australia*

## ACTIVITIES

### UNDERSTANDING

1. Distinguish between absolute and relative poverty.
2. Which groups in Australia are disadvantaged?
3. Discuss the economic and social impacts of poverty.
4. Describe how groups can improve the lives of poor and disadvantaged people.

### THINKING AND APPLYING

5. Design a poster for Anti-Poverty Week.

### USING YOUR SKILLS

6. Refer to the map on page 174 to outline the spatial inequality between states and territories. Suggest reasons to explain the highest and lowest figures. Draw a column graph of the after-housing poverty rates in the capital cities.
7. Refer to the table of poverty rates for children in Australia to describe the trend from 1981 to 2009? Which group of parents suffers most poverty? Explain your answer.
8. Refer to the bar graph on the left of Australian child poverty rates compared with other developed countries to estimate the percentage of child poverty in Australia. Write two sentences comparing the percentage with other developed countries.
9. Refer to the bar graph above of poverty rates by educational qualifications to describe the relationship between education and poverty.

### GEOTERMS

**absolute poverty:** lack of sufficient resources to meet basic needs for survival such as food and housing

**relative poverty:** having sufficient resources to meet basic needs, but a lack of resources required to participate in the lifestyle enjoyed by other people in the country

# 7.9 A 'fair go' for all Aussies: citizenship

A fair society is a just society in which scarce resources are distributed in a reasonable and fair manner. It enables harmony and social cohesion within a society. A recent survey found that 91 per cent of Australians thought that a 'fair go' was an important Australian value. Over time, the responsible actions of individuals, groups and governments have given more disadvantaged Australians a 'fair go'.

## Social welfare

Social welfare includes the services and programs provided by governments and non-government organisations (NGOs) to satisfy basic needs and maintain an acceptable quality of life. To achieve an equal, socially just society, the Australian government provides a minimum wage and spends 41 per cent of its yearly budget on social security and welfare such as unemployment benefits. Because of Australia's ageing population, since 1999, an increasing amount of the budget is spent on age pensions. In the 2009 federal budget, pensions were increased in recognition of the struggle faced by elderly people on fixed incomes. The federal government's Department of Family and Community Services (FaCS) provides childcare services and legal aid for homeless people, as well as:
- helping people in rural areas to access basic services
- improving the living conditions of Aboriginal people and Torres Strait Islanders
- encouraging Australians to undertake volunteering activities.

The New South Wales Department of Community Services (DOCS) Community Services Grants Program (CSGP) assists disadvantaged people to maintain their independence. The NSW Commission for Children and Young People 'A head start for Australia: an early years framework' aims to give all children a head start in life to reduce long-term poverty. The Indigenous Small Business Fund (ISBF) helps reduce unemployment, and the Towns and Villages Futures Program fosters job creation in small regional communities.

## Groups: ACOSS and NCOSS

Both the Australian Council of Social Service (ACOSS) and the Council of Social Service of New South Wales (NCOSS) shape government social welfare policies. At the national level, ACOSS is the voice of low-income and disadvantaged people. At the state level, NCOSS supports 900 000 disadvantaged people such as refugees, the aged and the disabled. Escalating house prices in cities and a cut in public housing in rural areas has resulted in people being unable to find affordable accommodation. NCOSS's No Interest Loan Schemes (NILS) offers an interest-free housing loan to low-income households.

## Equity and social justice

Australians rely on non-government social welfare organisations to reduce the impacts of poverty. The National Coalition Against Poverty (NCAP) promotes community action for the eradication of poverty. It believes that an adequate standard of living is a basic human right that includes the right to adequate food, clothing, housing, health care and education. Organisations such as the Brotherhood of St Laurence advocates that long-term unemployment is the most significant cause of poverty, and it campaigns for employment opportunities for all Australians. The Exodus Foundation assists homeless and abandoned youth and runs a free Loaves and Fishes restaurant serving 300 meals per day.

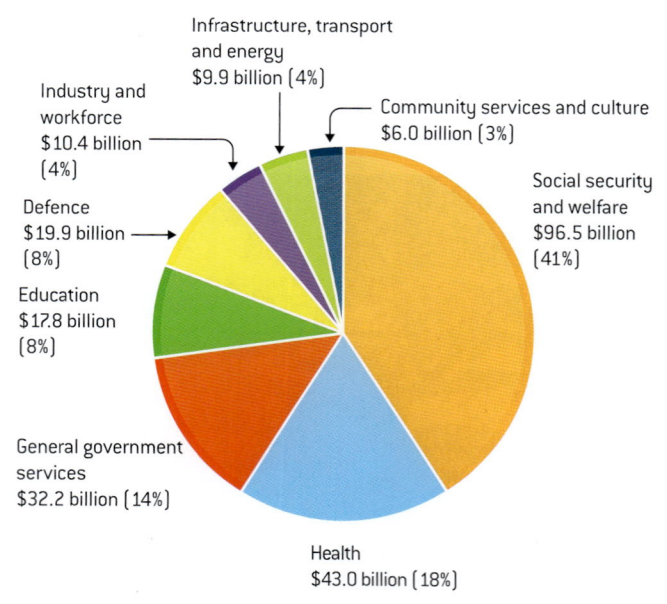

Infrastructure, transport and energy $9.9 billion (4%)
Industry and workforce $10.4 billion (4%)
Community services and culture $6.0 billion (3%)
Defence $19.9 billion (8%)
Education $17.8 billion (8%)
General government services $32.2 billion (14%)
Health $43.0 billion (18%)
Social security and welfare $96.5 billion (41%)

*Federal government budget spending 2007–2008*

## Volunteers make a difference

A volunteer gives unpaid help by way of time, service or skills through an organisation or group. Volunteers work to 'Make Poverty History' both locally and globally. Over the last ten years, volunteers have reduced the impacts of poverty, including the Salvation Army's drought relief campaign. The St Vincent de Paul Society has 40 000 members who help 800 000 people yearly; they run aged-care, migrant and refugee services, homeless person's services and clothing centres.

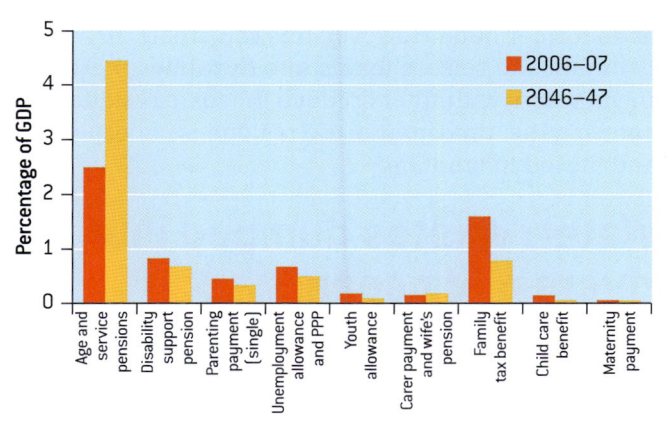

*Bar graph of projected federal government payments to individuals*

*Salvation Army drought appeal*

### Civics and citizenship works to reduce spatial inequality

| Governments | Groups and individuals |
| --- | --- |
| • Family and Community Services (FaCS) <br> • NSW Department of Community Services (NDOCS) <br> • Youth Allowance <br> • Aged pension <br> • Unemployment benefits <br> • Child Care Benefit <br> • Maternity Benefit <br> • Parenting Payment <br> • Commonwealth Family Assistance Office <br> • Austudy <br> • Centrelink <br> • NSW Commission for Children and Young People <br> • communitybuilders.nsw <br> • NSW Department of Aboriginal Affairs | • Australian Council of Social Service (ACOSS) <br> • Council of Social Service of New South Wales (NCOSS) <br> • The Smith Family <br> • St Vincent de Paul Society, Anglicare, Salvation Army, Exodus Foundation <br> • Service clubs such as Rotary, Apex, Lions <br> • Brotherhood of St Laurence <br> • Anti-Poverty Week <br> • Save the Children Australia <br> • National Coalition Against Poverty <br> • Association of Children's Welfare Agencies <br> • Wesley Mission/Wesley Dalmar Accommodation Services <br> • Australian Red Cross <br> • Forum of Non Government Agencies (FONGA) e.g. Federation of Housing Associations (FHA), Western Sydney Community Forum (WSCF), Local Government and Shires Association (LGSA), South West Multicultural and Community Centre |

## ACTIVITIES

### UNDERSTANDING

1. How do the following organisations and programs reduce inequality: DOCS, ACOSS, ISBF, NCOSS, NCAP and NILS?
2. How do the federal and state governments respond to inequality?
3. Describe how individuals and groups address inequality and social injustice.
4. Discuss how volunteers can reduce the gap between the 'haves' and the 'have nots'.

### THINKING AND APPLYING

5. Refer to the table on this page and research two groups or organisations and one government department that work towards equality and social justice. In your answer, include the key geographical questions: what, why and how?
6. Prepare a futures wheel of reducing poverty using the following scenarios.
   a The government reduces taxes on low incomes.
   b The government builds cheaper homes.
   c The government spends more money on education and job training.
   d The government encourages job sharing.
7. Devise a school activity to raise money for disadvantaged children. Prepare a poster promoting the event. Select the organisation that will receive your donations. Give reasons for the selection.

### USING YOUR SKILLS

8. Study the pie graph on page 176.
   a What is the largest expenditure in the federal government budget?
   b Discuss how social welfare is also included in education, health, community services and the workforce.
9. Refer to the bar graph on this page.
   a What are the three largest social welfare payments in 2007 and 2047?
   b Which group will have the largest increase in payments from 2007 to 2047? Account for this increase.

CHAPTER 7 | Geographical issues

# 7.10 Nature of wastes

Wastes are substances that have no further use and, if disposed of in land, water or air, are potentially harmful to humans or the environment. Wastes include:
- solid matter, such as litter, household garbage, industrial and commercial wastes
- liquids, such as sewage and stormwater
- air pollutants, such as greenhouse gases and carbon monoxide.

The physical environment recycles its waste. Over time, the human impact on the physical environment has created waste that cannot be recycled naturally and takes a long time to break down; for example, cigarette butts take one to five years to break down. Dealing with the problem sometimes means dumping waste in the ground, air or water.

## Land: limited landfill sites

If you visit a tip, you will see mountains of rubbish dumped in holes in the ground. This is where most of the waste from the developed world goes. In Australia, 1 tonne per person of solid waste finds its way into Australian landfills each year, which has caused environmental problems. Pollutants, such as chemicals and mercury, leak from rubbish sites, contaminating the soil, the ground water and nearby rivers. Today, landfill sites are covered with soil to prevent smell and dust. The waste decomposes and forms a liquid called *leachate*, which is often nutrient rich. The leachate is pumped to the surface to fertilise plants on top of revegetated landfill sites. As waste decays, methane, a greenhouse gas, escapes into the atmosphere.

Many developed countries have run out of landfill sites and export their toxic rubbish to poorer countries that need the money.

## Air: burning wastes

One of the methods used to get rid of waste is to burn it. Food, wood, paper and plastics are burned, which changes the material into smoke, steam and ash. Burning waste reduces it to about 25 per cent of its former bulk. However, this can create air pollution and release toxins into the atmosphere. Incinerators with filters reduce the toxic residue entering the atmosphere; the residue is collected and buried in landfills.

## Water: wastes dumped into rivers and oceans

Disposing of industrial waste and sewage in rivers and oceans seems an easy option, especially where land is scarce. It is often a case of 'out of sight, out of mind'. Sewage from Sydney is dumped into rivers that eventually enter the ocean. Some radioactive waste is placed in containers and lowered onto the seabed from ships. The United States dumped 60 000 containers of nuclear waste off the Californian coast between 1946 and 1960. In 1977, investigators found that 25 per cent of these containers had leaked. The Russians dumped low-grade nuclear waste in the Sea of Japan. The 1975 international Convention on the Prevention of Marine Pollution by Dumping of Wastes aims to protect marine species from this waste.

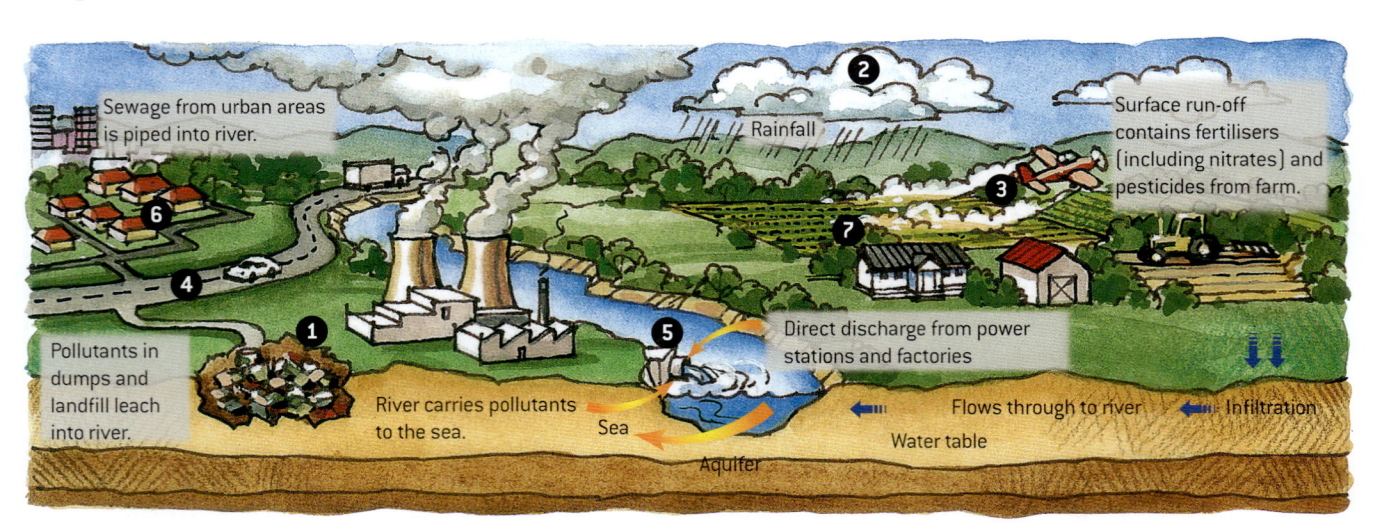

Human wastes and the environment. Wastes often end up in land, air and water.

## SAMPLE STUDY

### E-waste

The drive to have the newest and latest products such as plasma TV sets and mobile phones eventually involves their disposal. This is called e-waste, which is one of the fastest growing waste types. Across Australia there are 10 million computers that will be replaced in a couple of years. E-waste includes toxic waste such as lead, mercury and arsenic that leaches from landfills into ground water and rivers. To avoid this problem, some e-waste is exported to developing countries where the goods are dismantled and their parts recycled, which helps conserve natural resources. The extended producer responsibility (EPR) is a strategy that requires manufacturers to accept responsibility for e-waste and design less wasteful, less toxic and more recyclable products.

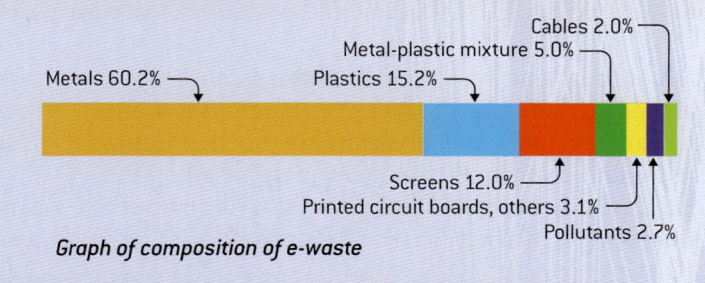

*Graph of composition of e-waste*

Metals 60.2%
Plastics 15.2%
Metal-plastic mixture 5.0%
Cables 2.0%
Screens 12.0%
Printed circuit boards, others 3.1%
Pollutants 2.7%

*Most of our rubbish is disposed of in landfills.*

*The site manager of an e-waste recycling plant in Minto, Sydney*

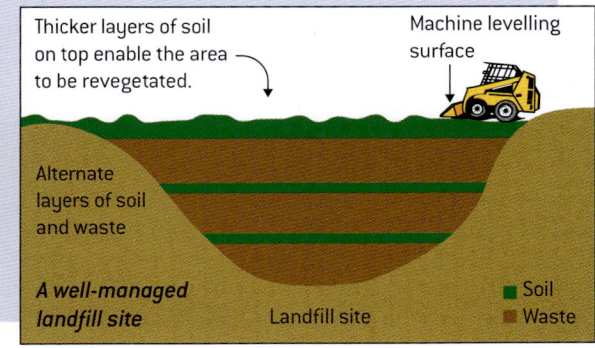

*A well-managed landfill site*

Thicker layers of soil on top enable the area to be revegetated.
Machine levelling surface
Alternate layers of soil and waste
Landfill site
■ Soil
■ Waste

## ACTIVITIES

### UNDERSTANDING

1. Define the term *waste* and provide examples of different types of waste.
2. Explain how the interaction between humans and the physical environment affects land, air and bodies of water.

### THINKING AND APPLYING

3. Discuss the negative effects of backyard burning, dumping nuclear waste into the ocean and the use of cars.
4. Research the disposal of waste in your local area. Present your findings as an oral report.
5. List the technical devices in your home that you expect to dispose of in the future. Suggest how e-waste could be recycled. Why do you think e-waste is sent to developing countries?

### USING YOUR SKILLS

6. Refer to the diagram on page 178 showing human wastes and the environment to answer the following questions.

    a Use the words below to complete the paragraph that follows.

    *fertilisers, pesticides, sewage, water table*

    When waste is dumped as landfill, pollutants can seep into the _____. In many parts of the world, rivers and oceans are still used as convenient dumping places for household _____. Run-off after rainfall flows into rivers and streams and can contain _____ and _____ that are used on farms.

    b Using your own words, write a sentence about what is happening in the diagram at each of the seven points.

CHAPTER 7 | Geographical issues

# 7.11 Waste management

Much of the waste created by humans is not managed sustainably. To conserve the environment, individuals, groups and governments need to follow a sustainable waste management plan based on the internationally accepted hierarchy of 'avoid, reduce, reuse, recycle, recover, treat and dispose'.

## Groups and governments

Few people would argue that trash is a good thing. Broken computers, old mobile phones and toxic chemicals from the illegal burning of tyres pose a challenge. Organisers of events such as the Olympic Games and those held at the Sydney Convention Centre have developed action plans to sustainably manage the huge quantities of waste produced. As Australia is the second highest producer of waste per person in the world, groups and governments aim to manage waste by:

- making the polluter pay: the more you pollute, the larger the payment
- educating citizens and businesses to recycle, reuse and reduce waste
- passing laws to reduce industrial waste
- encouraging polluters to clean up their operations (e.g. mine rehabilitation)
- reducing the use of plastic bags
- reducing unnecessary packaging
- providing recycling centres (e.g. oil, tyres, bricks)
- encouraging the purchase of reuseable green bags
- reducing the burning of waste contributing to greenhouse gases.

## Individuals make a difference

Everyone can contribute to a sustainable environment by reducing the contents in the garbage bin and not throwing rubbish in public areas. Australian John Dobozy won the ABC television 'New Inventors' award with his tyre-recycling technology. The process known as Molectra recycles 100 per cent of the tyre. The tyre is broken down into oil, carbon, rubber granules, steel and plastic fibres, which are made into new products.

## Plastic bags and cigarette butts

Every year, Australians use 4.5 billion plastic bags. As part of the 'Say NO to plastic bags' campaign, Clean Up Australia is working with businesses and governments to eradicate plastic bags. Plastic bags often end up in waterways strangling marine life, or mistaken by animals for food. The 'Say NO to plastic bags' campaign has contributed to a 45 per cent reduction in the number of plastic bags given out by supermarkets in the past few years.

In Australia, 7.2 billion cigarette butts are discarded each year. A 'National Day of Action' aims to educate the community about the impact of discarded cigarette butts on the environment.

### Cigarette butts: what you need to know

- About 7.2 billion cigarette butts are discarded every year. That's 144 000 kilometres of butt litter.
- They harm our environment by:
  - starting 7 per cent of all bushfires
  - taking years to break down
  - leaching chemicals such as cadmium and lead into the water within one hour of contact
  - causing digestive problems in fish, birds, whales and other marine life.
- They can harm young children, who pick them up and swallow them, causing respiration difficulties, cardiac arrhythmia and convulsions.
- They hurt our hip pocket because:
  - councils spend huge amounts of money cleaning them up off the streets, footpaths and beaches
  - they block drainage systems, which costs councils millions of dollars to fix
  - individuals who don't 'bin their butts' can be hit with a penalty for littering.

Civics and citizenship: groups and governments

| Groups and organisations | Governments |
| --- | --- |
| Planet Ark<br>Clean Up Australia<br>Sustainable Schools project<br>Australian Council of Recyclers<br>Waste Management Association of Australia<br>Packaging Council of Australia<br>Recycling at Tamworth Music Festival | **Local governments:** recycle household wastes, provide waste management centres<br>**NSW Government:** Department of Environment and Climate Change; Waste Reduction and Purchasing Policy (WRAPP); online reporting of waste diposal and tracking of waste from producer to receiving agent<br>**Federal government:** Department of the Environment, Water, Heritage and Arts programs; National Day of Action on Cigarette Butt Litter; oil recycling and collection facilities |

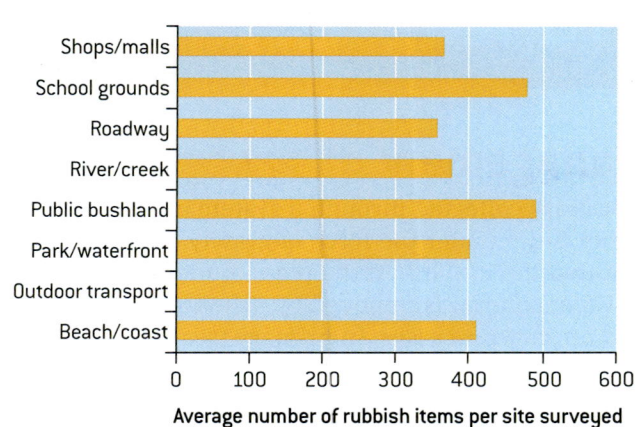

Bar graph of most polluted sites in Australia

## GEOfacts

- Some plastic bags take up to 1000 years to break down, and the energy used to make a plastic bag could drive a car 10 metres.
- Empty chip and confectionery bags account for 49 per cent of all plastic bags, and supermarket bags make up 17 per cent.

Individual action on waste management:
- Choose to buy goods that have less packaging.
- Use public transport.
- Use articles that can be reused or recycled — for example, glass rather than plastic bottles.
- Establish a worm farm.
- Recycle waste water.
- Volunteer to help on Clean Up Australia Day.
- Use phosphate-free detergent (marked NP).
- Join an environmental group.
- Wash the car on the lawn to stop detergents and chemicals going down the drain.
- Dispose of nothing except water in gutters and stormwater drains.
- Put rubbish in the bin instead of in the gutter or toilet.

## ACTIVITIES

### UNDERSTANDING

1. How does Australia rate as a producer of waste?
2. Select either true or false for the statements below.
   a Australia is the highest producer of waste per person in the world. **T/F**
   b Plastic bags are a threat to marine life. **T/F**

### THINKING AND APPLYING

3. Refer to the newspaper article on the previous page. What things does it say are harmed by cigarette butts?
4. Outline the responses of individuals, groups and governments to the sustainable management of waste.
5. Use the **Sustainable Schools Project** weblink in your eBookPLUS to prepare a report of the sustainable management of your school.
6. *Fieldwork and RAP*. Research the waste produced in your local area and how it is managed. Describe the types of waste. Explain its impacts on the physical and human environment. Evaluate the success of individuals, groups and governments in managing the waste. Propose actions to promote sustainability and equity. Apply fieldwork and use your school library or search the internet. Use the **CSIRO** and **New South Wales Government** weblinks in your eBookPLUS and type 'waste' in their search engines.

### USING YOUR SKILLS

7. Refer to the pie graph below.

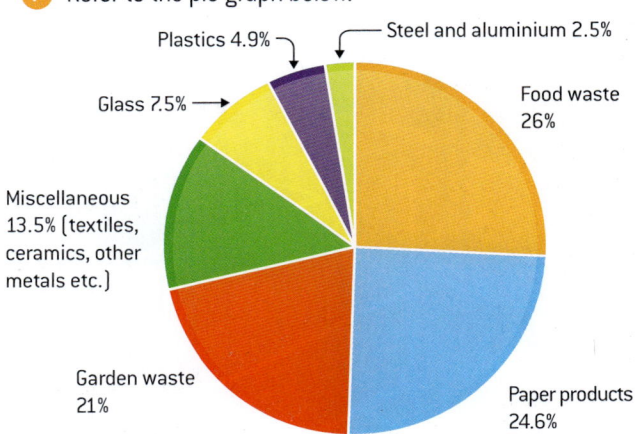

   - Plastics 4.9%
   - Steel and aluminium 2.5%
   - Glass 7.5%
   - Food waste 26%
   - Miscellaneous 13.5% (textiles, ceramics, other metals etc.)
   - Garden waste 21%
   - Paper products 24.6%

   *Analysis of the contents of the average household 'wheelie bin'*

   a What is the main source of waste?
   b What percentage is paper?
   c What type of paper products would you find in the average bin?
   d Explain what your household does with waste such as plastics, glass, steel, aluminium, food, paper and plants.

8. Refer to the bar graph of the most polluted sites in Australia. Rank from one to eight the places where most rubbish is found around Australia.
   a Why do people throw rubbish in public places?
   b What is the impact of this on the environment?
   c Design a poster to stop people littering in public places.

CHAPTER 7 | Geographical issues

# 7.12 Sewage: going to waste?

## What is sewage?

Sewage or waste water is the 'used' water from a community. It contains 99.94 per cent water and 0.06 per cent dissolved or suspended material. While many of us think of sewage as human wastes, the term also includes waste from showers and washing machines. Sewage also comes from businesses, including photocopier toner, and from industry where water is used, such as breweries and dairy factories. In Sydney and New York, each person contributes 250 litres of sewage daily to the sewerage system.

About 42 per cent of the world's population do not have access to a toilet. Instead they defecate in a river, which is used by people downstream as drinking water. Untreated sewage can cause cholera, typhoid and hepatitis, killing millions of people in developing countries. While worldwide sanitation coverage has increased from 49 per cent in 1990 to 62 per cent in 2009, the Millennium Development Goal (MDG) target is 75 per cent by 2015.

## Management of sewage

Sewage is collected through a system of pipes and either flows under the force of gravity or is pumped to a treatment plant. At the plant, undesirable sewage material is removed by primary, secondary and tertiary processes. In primary treatment, sewage is passed through screens to remove solid matter such as paper, condoms, tampons, grease and plastics. The liquid is transferred to a tank where scum is skimmed off the top. Solids settle on the bottom and are removed as sludge. At the end of this process, 60 per cent of solid material and 30 per cent of oxygen-demanding wastes have been removed.

The secondary treatment process uses bacteria to break down inorganic wastes. Most of the oxygen-demanding organic wastes are removed by aeration or by running the sewage through stones. The water left at the end is discharged into rivers and oceans, but it still contains nitrates and phosphates, one of the causes of blue-green algae.

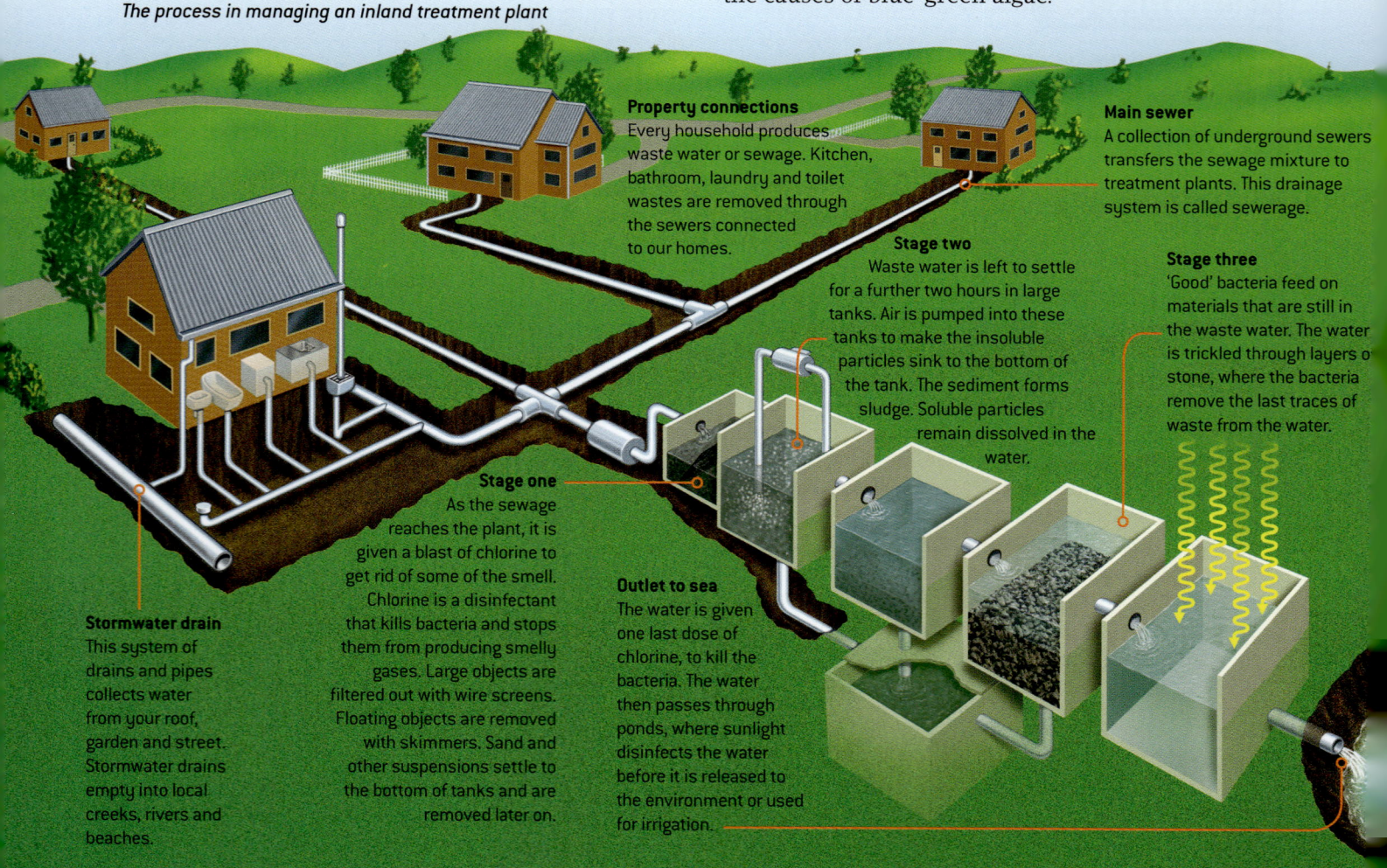

*The process in managing an inland treatment plant*

**Property connections**
Every household produces waste water or sewage. Kitchen, bathroom, laundry and toilet wastes are removed through the sewers connected to our homes.

**Main sewer**
A collection of underground sewers transfers the sewage mixture to treatment plants. This drainage system is called sewerage.

**Stage two**
Waste water is left to settle for a further two hours in large tanks. Air is pumped into these tanks to make the insoluble particles sink to the bottom of the tank. The sediment forms sludge. Soluble particles remain dissolved in the water.

**Stage three**
'Good' bacteria feed on materials that are still in the waste water. The water is trickled through layers of stone, where the bacteria remove the last traces of waste from the water.

**Stage one**
As the sewage reaches the plant, it is given a blast of chlorine to get rid of some of the smell. Chlorine is a disinfectant that kills bacteria and stops them from producing smelly gases. Large objects are filtered out with wire screens. Floating objects are removed with skimmers. Sand and other suspensions settle to the bottom of tanks and are removed later on.

**Outlet to sea**
The water is given one last dose of chlorine, to kill the bacteria. The water then passes through ponds, where sunlight disinfects the water before it is released to the environment or used for irrigation.

**Stormwater drain**
This system of drains and pipes collects water from your roof, garden and street. Stormwater drains empty into local creeks, rivers and beaches.

Tertiary treatment involves precipitation, absorption, electrodialysis and disinfection. The process removes nitrogen, phosphorus, disease-carrying micro-organisms and toxic chemicals from water before it is discharged into the environment or recycled.

## Managing sewage in Sydney

Sydney Water operates the sewerage system that transports and treats sewage through 23 500 kilometres of pipes, 659 pumping stations, 10 coastal treatment plants and 20 inland treatment plants. After treatment, which ranges from primary to tertiary processes, the sewage is reused or discharged into rivers (such as the Hawkesbury River) or the Pacific Ocean. Groups protest and lobby governments to ensure that sewage discharged into water bodies is not hazardous to health or the environment. These discharges are monitored by the Department of Environment and Climate Change (DECC) and Sydney Catchment Authority.

With a focus on sustainable waste-water management, Sydney Water implements projects under WaterPlan 21. Its treatment plants convert sewage sludge into nutrient-rich biosolids, which are used as fertilisers in agriculture, forestry and land rehabilitation. The Waterways Authority maintains sewage pump-out facilities in Sydney Harbour to allow vessels to discharge sewage from holding tanks without polluting the waterways.

Even though Sydney has a good sewerage system, pollution occurs when sewer lines are cracked and sewage overflows after rain. This discharges faecal coliforms (*E. coli*) into water bodies resulting in infections such as *Giardia* and *Cryptosporidium*. Sydney Water monitors *E. coli* in water bodies and, when counts are high, warns citizens not to drink the water or swim in the ocean.

As water is a scarce resource, a 2008 survey found seven in ten people supported recycling sewage. Should we be concerned about the 'yuk factor', that water in the glass might have started off in someone's toilet bowl?

## Managing waste water in Sydney

Used water and sewage enters the waste water or sewerage system that is operated by Sydney Water and monitored by the New South Wales Environment Protection Authority (EPA). The system is made up of sewerage pipes that drain to 10 coastal treatment plants (for example, Bondi, Port Kembla, North Head) and 17 inland treatment plants (for example, Richmond, Blackheath, St Marys). The waste water is then treated (primary, secondary and tertiary) and discharged into waterways or recycled (for example, at Rouse Hill Development Area).

With a focus on sustainable waste-water management, Sydney Water is implementing projects under its WaterPlan 21. Its treatment plants now convert sewage sludge into nutrient-rich biosolids that are used as fertilisers in agriculture, forestry and land rehabilitation. Also in an effort to improve the environment, the Waterways Authority maintains sewage pump-out facilities in Sydney Harbour to allow vessels to discharge sewage from holding tanks without polluting the waterways.

*Sign warning that it is not safe to swim, due to sewage in the water*

### ACTIVITIES

#### UNDERSTANDING

1. Explain the impacts of sewage on people's health and the environment (e.g. blue-green algae).
2. Outline the sewerage management processes used by Sydney Water.

#### THINKING AND APPLYING

3. Conduct a debate on the topic 'Sewage should be recycled as drinking water'.
4. Discuss the unsustainable management of a sewerage system. In your answer, list the causes of sewage spills and suggest how the system could be managed so as to improve health and create a sustainable environment.

#### USING YOUR SKILLS

5. Refer to the diagram on the previous page of processes in managing an inland sewage treatment plant.
   a. Make a list of the sources of waste from a family home that enter the sewerage system.
   b. How does this differ from the waste that enters the stormwater system?
   c. Imagine that the scene in the diagram is a village in a developing country. Sketch the sources of sewage and where it ends up.

# 7.13 Nuclear waste: a permanent problem

## Nature of nuclear waste

We are all exposed to natural forms of radiation from the sun, outer space and substances in the Earth's crust. Today, radioactive material is mined as uranium and processed to produce 'yellow cake' before it is used for medical research, weapons of mass destruction and energy. At present, 220 nuclear reactors power ships and submarines and 443 nuclear power plants supply 16 per cent of the world's electricity. Global warming has resulted in a renewed interest in nuclear energy with 34 nuclear power plants under construction and another 26 anticipated in the next 15 years. As countries move from coal, gas and oil to uranium to produce energy, improved technology for the safe disposal of nuclear waste becomes an urgent issue.

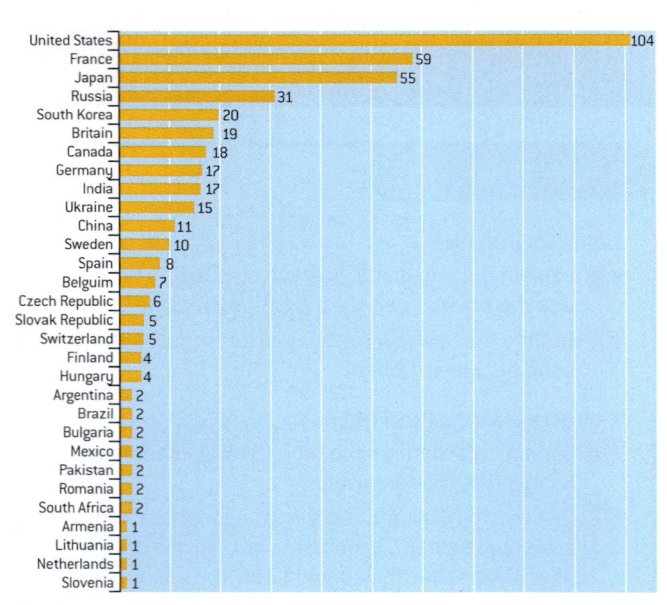

**Nuclear reactors worldwide**

|  |  |
| --- | --- |
| United States | 104 |
| France | 59 |
| Japan | 55 |
| Russia | 31 |
| South Korea | 20 |
| Britain | 19 |
| Canada | 18 |
| Germany | 17 |
| India | 17 |
| Ukraine | 15 |
| China | 11 |
| Sweden | 10 |
| Spain | 8 |
| Belgium | 7 |
| Czech Republic | 6 |
| Slovak Republic | 5 |
| Switzerland | 5 |
| Finland | 4 |
| Hungary | 4 |
| Argentina | 2 |
| Brazil | 2 |
| Bulgaria | 2 |
| Mexico | 2 |
| Pakistan | 2 |
| Romania | 2 |
| South Africa | 2 |
| Armenia | 1 |
| Lithuania | 1 |
| Netherlands | 1 |
| Slovenia | 1 |

## Impacts of nuclear waste

Radioactive material makes its way into air, water, soil, food, animals and human tissue. When it is mined and milled, uranium releases radioactive radon gas into the atmosphere, from where it returns to Earth as rain contaminating soil and water. The solid radioactive wastes from mining, called tailings, can infiltrate the soil and enter the ground water or can be dispersed into the environment by wind. In 1986, a nuclear reactor at Chernobyl in Ukraine exploded. It spread radioactive material over Europe. In 1945, a US uranium-235 bomb exploded in Hiroshima killing 140 000 Japanese. Between 1952 and 1957, the British government carried out 12 atmospheric nuclear explosions in Australia. These tests at Monte Bello Islands (Western Australia), and Emu Field and Maralinga (South Australia), adversely affected the health of Indigenous people.

**Nuclear reactors under construction, 2008**

| Country | Reactors under construction |
| --- | --- |
| Argentina | 1 |
| Bulgaria | 2 |
| China | 6 |
| Finland | 1 |
| France | 1 |
| India | 6 |
| Iran | 1 |
| Japan | 1 |
| South Korea | 3 |
| Pakistan | 1 |
| Russia | 6 |
| Ukraine | 2 |
| United States | 1 |
| Taiwan | 2 |
| **Total** | **34** |

## Management of waste

Radioactive waste is an unavoidable by-product of mining, refining and using uranium. The management of this waste depends on the amount, type, and period of time the waste remains hazardous. For example:

- *Low-level waste* generated from hospitals and industry is buried in shallow landfill sites.
- *Intermediate-level waste* in resins and chemical sludge is buried in concrete or bitumen.
- *High-level waste* in spent fuel rods is transported in thick containers to prevent leaking.

With 150 000 tonnes of used nuclear fuel in the world (increasing daily) individuals, groups and governments are concerned about the lack of a satisfactory disposal system. Methods of managing waste include vitrification, where liquid radioactive waste is mixed with glass and poured into steel

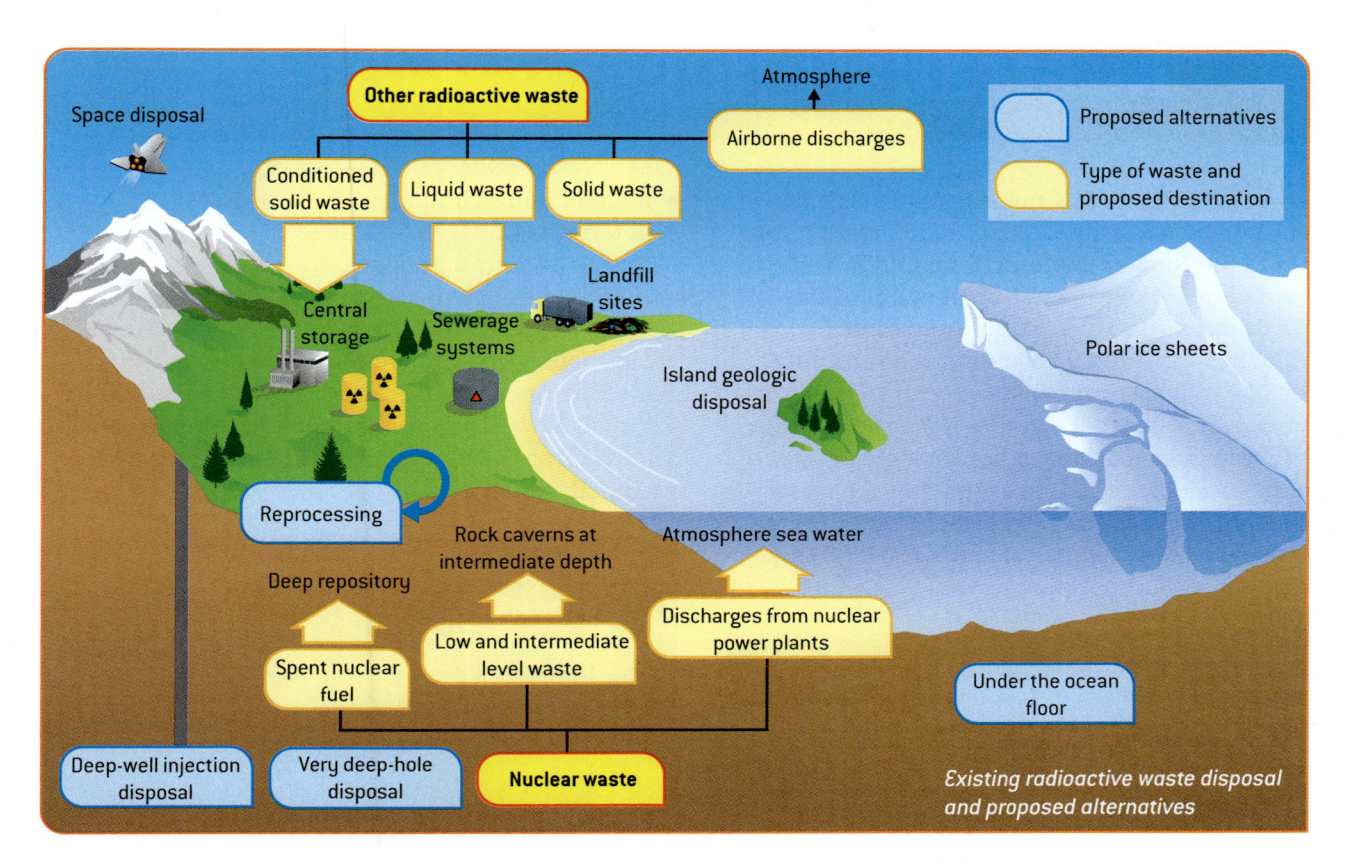

*Existing radioactive waste disposal and proposed alternatives*

drums, and then dug deep into the ground or under the sea floor. Other options include sending waste into space. Individuals and groups, such as Greenpeace, lobby governments to stop construction of nuclear reactors as the first step to solving the nuclear waste problem.

## Responses

Since 1945 there have been 40 nuclear accidents, each releasing radiation waste into the environment. There are now 30 000 nuclear weapons belonging to nine countries. More than 1500 are ready to launch at a moment's notice. Groups such as Greenpeace and the International Physicians for the Prevention of Nuclear War (IPPNW) lobby governments to prevent nuclear war and abolish nuclear weapons.

The International Atomic Energy Agency (IAEA) works for the safe, secure and peaceful use of nuclear technology. The 1970 Treaty on the Non-Proliferation of Nuclear Weapons (NPT) aims to limit the spread of nuclear weapons and promotes the peaceful use of nuclear energy. The treaty is signed by 189 countries, of which five (United States, United Kingdom, France, Russia, and China) have nuclear weapons. In 1996, the United Nations adopted the Comprehensive Nuclear-Test-Ban Treaty (CTBT) to ban all nuclear test explosions. Despite the treaty, North Korea tested nuclear weapons in 2006 and 2009.

## ACTIVITIES

### UNDERSTANDING
1. Describe the nature of nuclear waste.
2. Explain the impacts of nuclear waste on the physical environment (air, water, land, coast, ecosystem).
3. Discuss the responses of non-government organisations and governments to the use of uranium.

### THINKING AND APPLYING
4. Uranium has both positive and negative impacts on people and the environment. Discuss.

### USING YOUR SKILLS
5. Refer to the graph on the previous page of reactors worldwide.
    a. Which continent faces the largest nuclear waste problem? Explain your answer.
    b. List three developing countries that have nuclear reactors.
    c. From the data in the table on the opposite page showing the number of nuclear reactors under construction, draw a column graph.
    d. Account for the recent increase in the number of reactors.
6. Refer to the diagram above of existing radioactive waste disposal and proposed alternatives for storage. Describe the technological solutions to the disposal of nuclear wastes shown in this diagram.

# 7.14 Australia's nuclear industry

The sources of Australia's nuclear waste include hospitals, industries, the Lucas Heights reactor and tailings at the Ranger, Olympic Dam and Beverley uranium mines. Australia has 23 per cent of the world's uranium reserves. From three mines, Australia has exported 52 000 tonnes of uranium (worth $2.6 billion) in the last five years. Uranium is exported on the condition that it is used only for peaceful purposes such as generating electricity and nuclear medicine. Some argue that the waste produced from Australia's exported uranium should be returned to Australia for safe disposal.

**Known uranium reserves**

| Countries | % of world's uranium | Countries | % of world's uranium |
|---|---|---|---|
| Australia | 23 | Niger | 5 |
| Kazakhstan | 15 | Ukraine | 4 |
| Russia | 10 | Jordan | 2 |
| South Africa | 8 | Uzbekistan | 2 |
| Canada | 8 | India | 1 |
| USA | 6 | China | 1 |
| Brazil | 5 | Mongolia | 1 |
| Namibia | 5 | Other | 4 |

*Source:* Data derived from www.world-nuclear.org/info/inf48.html.

## Lucas Heights reactor

The Australian government's only **nuclear reactor** is located at Lucas Heights, 40 kilometres south-west of Sydney's CBD. It is managed by the Australian Nuclear Science and Technology Organisation (ANSTO). The ageing reactor called HIFAR began operation in 1958. It was shut down in 2007 and replaced by the Open Pool Australian Light-water (OPAL) research reactor. Just months after the reactor opened, it had problems with loose fuel plates. It reopened in May 2008.

Some citizens argue against the use of a non-renewable resource and the production of toxic nuclear waste. However, ANSTO makes half a million doses of nuclear medicine every year and its technology can also:

- use radioisotopes to detect when bottles of beer and food containers are filled to the correct level
- reduce pesticides by controlling fruit fly larvae
- irradiate rubber tyres to increase toughness
- power smoke detectors by very small amounts of low-powered radioisotopes
- trace pollution and identify its sources
- determine the ages of artefacts such as Ned Kelly's armour and bones.

ANSTO has developed an emergency plan in case of accidents; this involves the New South Wales police, fire and ambulance services, the State Emergency Service and the Sutherland Shire Council. As well, the Australian Radiation Protection and Nuclear Safety Agency (ARPANSA) monitors radioactive activities.

*Lucas Heights new research reactor*

## Managing nuclear waste

Ensuring that nuclear waste producers are responsible for their waste will encourage waste minimisation. Waste from the Lucas Heights reactor makes up 90 per cent of radioactive waste in Australia and it has to be stored safely. While ANSTO believes that Lucas Heights can store existing and future waste on site, other sites have been sought for Australia's nuclear waste. The traditional owners, Kupa Piti Kungka Tjuta, of a site in South Australia successfully stopped a high-level waste dump being built on their land in 2005. Activists have continued to protest over a suggested waste dump for the Northern Territory; it has been proposed that this dump would receive waste from Lucas Heights over the next 40 years.

## Responses to nuclear waste

Environmentalists argue that uranium mining makes up 1 per cent of Australia's GDP, but waste storage also needs to be considered as a cost to taxpayers for thousands of years. The United Nations World Summit on Sustainable Development stressed to governments the importance of improving the handling, transport and disposal of nuclear waste to protect human health and the environment. This is supported by Australia's *Environment Protection (Nuclear Codes) Act 1978*. Active Australian citizens successfully protested against the mining of uranium at Jabiluka, highlighting the problems of waste moving into the surrounding wetlands. Other citizens who do not want radioactive waste stored close to where they live lobby for wastes to be transported overseas. Such a solution could create an environmental disaster for countries along the transport route.

| Positive arguments for an Australian nuclear reactor | Negative arguments for an Australian nuclear reactor |
|---|---|
| • It creates 85 per cent of Australia's medical isotopes for hospitals and medical clinics.<br>• It is necessary for medical research, biotechnology and environmental science.<br>• The reactor is used commercially to create irradiated silicon for Japan and Europe.<br>• ANSTO claims the reactor is safe and productive.<br>• There are cheaper alternatives to nuclear medicine but they are not as effective.<br>• The 1.6-kilometre buffer zone around the reactor exceeds distance requirements for research reactors overseas.<br>• Radioisotopes are used for checking bridges and aircraft engines, sterilising insect pests, monitoring soil moisture and tracking ground water. | • Lucas Heights is the nuclear waste dump of Australia, storing 3500 cubic metres of radioactive waste and 1600 highly radioactive fuel rods.<br>• There is no known safe disposal method for the high-level waste.<br>• A nuclear accident would cause irreversible harm to the community and the environment.<br>• Water could leak out of the waste dump and contaminate the environment.<br>• Nuclear waste is transported across Australia, through populated areas that don't have adequate emergency facilities.<br>• The reactor may be a terrorist target.<br>• Natural disasters such as bushfires or earthquakes may cause a nuclear accident. |
| *The construction of a new research reactor at Lucas Heights will build on Australia's life-saving nuclear medicine capabilities.*<br>Former Federal Science Minister, Peter McGauran | *The reactor poses the single greatest radiological threat to the largest number of Australians.*<br>Greenpeace nuclear campaigner, James Courtney |

*Protesters at the Lucas Heights facility*

## ACTIVITIES

### UNDERSTANDING

1. Outline the functions of the old and new nuclear reactors at Lucas Heights.
2. Describe the nature and impact of nuclear waste in Australia.
3. Discuss the problems surrounding the management of nuclear waste in Australia.

### THINKING AND APPLYING

4. The Lucas Heights reactor is visible on Google Earth. Why might this be a concern?
5. What perspectives would the following people have on the construction of the new Lucas Heights nuclear reactor?
   a A person dying from cancer requiring radiotherapy for survival
   b An environmentalist
   c A mother with four children living in a nearby suburb
   d A nuclear scientist working at Lucas Heights
   e A firefighter
6. *Fieldwork and RAP:* ANSTO offers guided tours of its Lucas Heights site, Australia's only nuclear science and technology complex. To gather information for a RAP before a fieldwork visit to Lucas Heights, you need to consider the following issues:
   a What are the effects of nuclear waste leaching into the soil and ground water?
   b What are the effects of a nuclear accident on air quality?
   c How would an accident at the reactor affect the community's health?
   d What could happen to people and the environment if there is a terrorist attack on Lucas Heights?
   e Should Lucas Heights have the new reactor?
   f Where will its waste go?
   g Describe why waste should not be dumped in remote areas that may be Aboriginal traditional lands.
   h What are the advantages of nuclear medicine?
   i Why is transport of high-level nuclear waste potentially hazardous?
7. In 2009, the federal government announced a new uranium mine in South Australia. Research the current policies of the major political parties on uranium mining in Australia.

### USING YOUR SKILLS

8. Refer to the table on the previous page of known uranium reserves. Use the information to draw a bar graph.
9. Refer to the photograph of protesters on the left. How would you describe the response of groups to the Lucas Heights reactor. What is the issue surrounding renewable energy?

# Working geographically

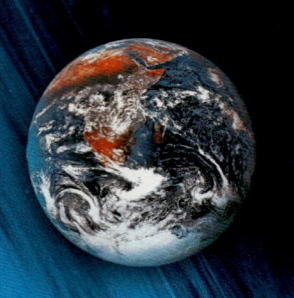

## BROADSHEET: GEOGRAPHICAL ISSUES FOR AUSTRALIA

### KNOWLEDGE AND UNDERSTANDING

Refer to the source material on these pages and select the alternative that best answers the question.

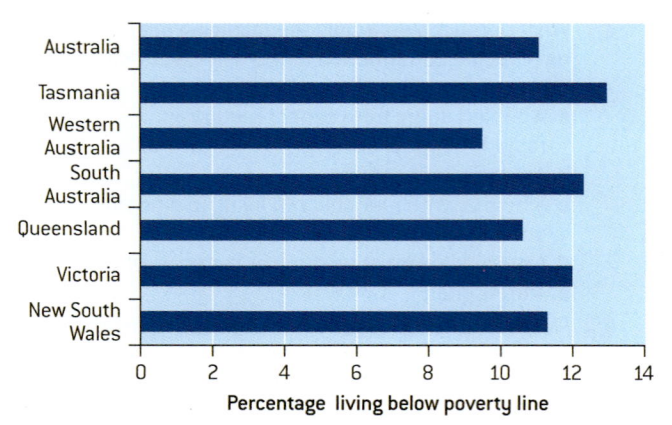

*Percentage of the Australian population living below the poverty line*

1. Which state has 11.3 per cent of its population living below the poverty line?
   - (A) Victoria
   - (B) Queensland
   - (C) New South Wales
   - (D) Australia

2. The difference between the percentage of people living below the poverty in Tasmania and the average for all of Australia is:
   - (A) 2.6 per cent
   - (B) 2.2 per cent
   - (C) 1.9 per cent
   - (D) 1.5 per cent.

3. Spatial inequality:
   - (A) means we are spaced at unequal distances from each other
   - (B) means we are not all equal
   - (C) describes where different people are located
   - (D) describes where inequalities occur and the reasons for these inequalities.

4. The letters RAP stand for:
   - (A) recycling and pollution
   - (B) research action plan
   - (C) renewable air policy
   - (D) renew Australia's parks.

5. Most air pollution is caused by:
   - (A) the burning of fossil fuels
   - (B) the ozone layer
   - (C) cigarettes
   - (D) bushfires.

6. The greater metropolitan region of Sydney, Newcastle, Wollongong and the Central Coast contains:
   - (A) 50 per cent of the New South Wales population
   - (B) 25 per cent of the New South Wales population
   - (C) 85 per cent of the New South Wales population
   - (D) 75 per cent of the New South Wales population.

7. In 2008, the fastest growing Australian capital cities were:
   - (A) Sydney and Brisbane
   - (B) Darwin and Adelaide
   - (C) Darwin and Perth
   - (D) Sydney and Perth.

8. The human poverty index measures:
   - (A) access to education and health
   - (B) minimum income and education level
   - (C) GDP per capita
   - (D) life expectancy, literacy and standard of living.

9. The services and programs provided by Australian governments and non-government organisations to alleviate poverty are known as:
   - (A) social justice
   - (B) income support
   - (C) social welfare
   - (D) the age pension.

10. A growing component of waste in developed countries is:
    - (A) cigarette butts
    - (B) e-waste from electronic goods
    - (C) plastic bags
    - (D) motor vehicle parts.

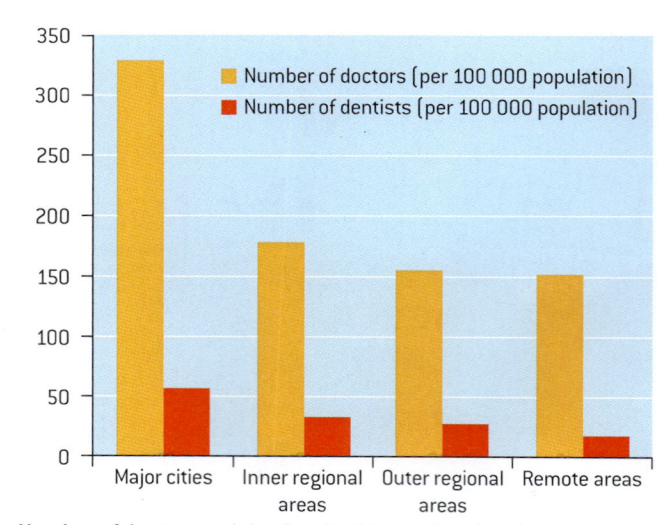

*Number of doctors and dentists in cities and regional areas*

188  Geoactive 2

## SHORT RESPONSE

11. What is the difference between the numbers of doctors and dentists in major cities and remote areas? Suggest how this gap could be reduced.

12. Discuss spatial inequality between rural/remote areas and capital cities in Australia. Include employment, education and health in your answer.

## EXTENDED RESPONSE

13. As the photo below shows, many people in developing countries live in, or make a living from, garbage tips. Discuss the nature of the issue and the impacts of it on society as well as the responses by individuals, groups and governments to the issue. In your answer include: What is waste?, Why has waste increased over the last 100 years?, What are the impacts of waste on people and the environment?, How could garbage be sustainably managed? and What is being done about waste?

14. Refer to the poster and design a RAP about littering. Include the impact of littering on people and the environment, and the actions you recommend for fixing the problem. Use both primary and secondary material; the local council and Clean Up Australia are good resources to start with.

*Part of the statewide campaign in Victoria to reduce cigarette butt litter*

*People scavenging in a landfill site in the Philippines*

CHAPTER 7 | Geographical issues

189

# 8 Land and water management

### INQUIRY QUESTIONS

+ What is the nature of land and water management?
+ What are the impacts of humans on land and water resources?
+ Why is it important to manage both land and water for sustainability?
+ What are the responses of individuals, groups and governments to land and water issues?

The management of Australia's land and water resources is a major geographical issue. Water shortages and increasing salinity in the Murray–Darling Basin, along with the expected impacts of climate change, are urgent issues facing Australia in the twenty-first century. Each Australian uses more land and water per person than in the UK, China and India. Overuse and misuse of water, the clearing of native vegetation and wetlands, and overcropping and overgrazing the land have contributed to a large and unsustainable ecological footprint. The unsustainable exploitation of land and water resources requires immediate action by individuals, groups and governments to bring about the sustainable management that is essential to Australia's future.

### GEOskills TOOLBOX

+ Collecting and using digital images (page 199)

*Aerial view of Tintaldra, on the Murray River, New South Wales*

## KEY TERMS

**billabong:** small wetland associated with a river channel that is isolated during low-flow periods and can be flushed during a flood

**carbon neutral:** describes an outcome in which carbon emissions are balanced by carbon reductions to achieve zero net emissions of carbon dioxide

**catchment:** extent of land where water from rain or snow melt drains downhill into a body of water, such as a river, lake, reservoir, estuary or wetland

**drought:** extended period of months or years when a region experiences a deficiency in its water supply

**drowned river valley:** melting of continental icecaps following the last ice age, which saw sea levels rise and drown coastal river valleys

**ecotourism:** ecologically sustainable tourism, with a primary focus on experiencing natural areas, that fosters environmental and cultural understanding, appreciation and conservation

**flood plain:** part of a river valley covered by water during floods

**geographic information systems (GIS):** set of computer programs designed to deal with databases able to collect, store, retrieve, manipulate, analyse and display mapped data

**global warming:** increase in the average temperature of the Earth's air and oceans since the mid twentieth century and its projected continuation

**ground water:** water under the surface of the ground that has seeped through soil and rock; often used for drinking and irrigation

**intertidal zone:** area between low and high water marks that is exposed at low tide

**Landcare:** group formed to protect the land

**land degradation:** loss in quality of the land and the consequent reduction in its ability to sustain agriculture or support native vegetation

**salinity:** presence of salt on the land's surface, in soil or rocks, or dissolved in water in rivers and ground water

**soil:** naturally occurring, unconsolidated or loose covering of broken rock particles and decaying organic matter on the surface of the Earth that is able to support life

**sustainable management:** management that meets the needs of the present population without endangering the ability of future generations to meet their own needs

**topsoil:** layer of soil that contains most of the nutrients required for the healthy growth of plants

**water footprint:** indicator of water use

**water table:** the upper limit of the ground water

**wetland:** area covered permanently or occasionally by fresh or salt water up to a depth of six metres

# 8.1 Land and water interactions

Humans depend on both land and water to provide basic needs such as food. Land and water are interconnected: a change to the land affects water and vice versa. For example, Australia, the driest inhabited continent, has recently experienced prolonged **droughts**. Reduced precipitation results in less run-off into rivers and the death of vegetation, which in turn leads to increased soil erosion and more dust storms. Sustainable management requires an understanding of land–water interactions, especially the anticipated impacts of **global warming**.

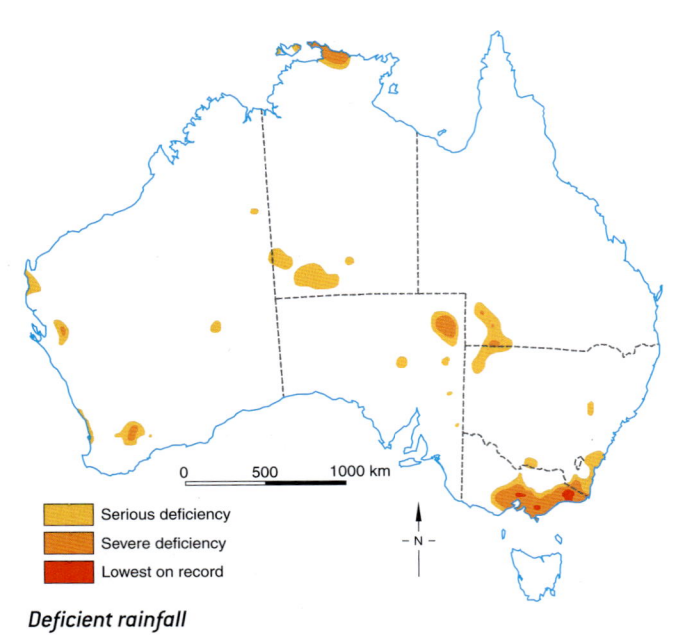

**Deficient rainfall**
- Serious deficiency
- Severe deficiency
- Lowest on record

Source: Australian Bureau of Meteorology.

## Catchment management

Catchment management aims to coordinate land and water resources. A **catchment** is an area of land, bound by higher areas such as mountains from which water flows to the lowest point, such as a lake, river or sea. Catchments are connected from top to bottom, so what happens to the land and water upstream has a large influence on what happens downstream. No matter where a person lives, they live in a catchment and have some responsibility for its **sustainable management**.

The New South Wales Government has 13 Catchment Management Authorities (CMA) to handle land–water issues. CMAs work in partnership with farmers, Aboriginal communities, local governments and industries to develop programs:

- *Land management* focuses on conserving soil and land resources (timber, minerals). Some programs have filled in gully erosion, thus decreasing the amount of sediment in rivers and maintaining marine species.
- *Water management* focuses on improving water quantity and quality. Some programs have built artificial wetlands to reduce nutrients such as nitrates and phosphates entering rivers, resulting in healthier marine ecosystems.

Individuals are part of catchment management. The Sydney catchment has 8800 volunteers involved in Bushcare and Landcare activities every year. Over 21 000 volunteers helped manage beaches, bushlands and parklands in 2008.

### Water linked to land

| Water … | … Land |
|---|---|
| Water cycle flows of precipitation, evaporation, transpiration and condensation … | … allow water to infiltrate into ground water and run-off into rivers, lakes and oceans. On the way, it erodes soil. |
| Acid rain … | … falls onto the ground causing acid soils and acid lakes. This can kill trees and marine species. |
| Heavy precipitation such as floods … | … increases erosion of soil, which is washed into rivers. |
| Little precipitation such as droughts … | … reduces the amount of vegetation so that the soil is subject to increased water and wind erosion. |

### Land linked to water

| Land … | … Water |
|---|---|
| Land cleared of vegetation for urban and rural development … | … increases erosion by water. Sediments are deposited in rivers and lakes. |
| On steep slopes … | … rivers flow faster, increasing the risk of soil erosion. |
| Excess fertiliser and pesticide on crops … | … runs off into rivers and lakes, causing blue-green algae that poisons marine food webs. |
| Overgrazing and compaction of soil by animals and heavy machinery damages soil structure … | … which increases run-off and soil erosion, thus reducing farm productivity. |

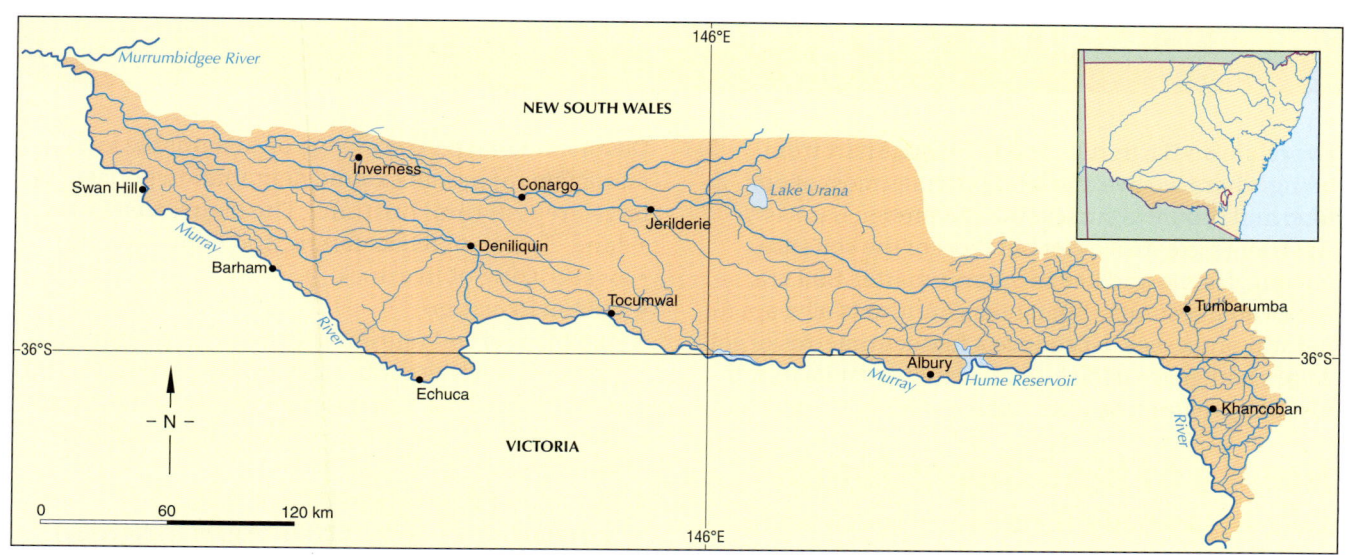

*The Murray River catchment*

## SAMPLE STUDY

### Land–water–air management: Murray catchment

The Murray catchment is bound by the Murray River to the south, the Murrumbidgee River catchment divide to the north and the Australian alps to the east, spanning an area of 35 170 square kilometres. Deniliquin is a settlement of approximately 8000 located in the Murray catchment. Until 2008 it had the largest rice mill in the southern hemisphere, which processed grain grown in the catchment to satisfy the needs of 21 million Australians and export its surplus overseas. Unfortunately six years of drought reduced Australia's rice crop by 98 per cent, leading to closure of the mill. The prolonged drought severely affected Deniliquin, and in 2008 it experienced dust storms over three times the recommended health limit for airborne particles. The dust storms were comprised of **topsoil** from bare paddocks affected by droughts, overgrazing and overcropping. The top few centimetres of soil is made up of nutrients and their loss reduced agricultural productivity.

Today, only 3.3 per cent of the original vegetation in the Murray catchment remains. To reduce the clearing of vegetation, the Murray Catchment Management Authority (MCMA) undertakes ground-cover surveys and enforces the *Native Vegetation Act 2003* (NSW), requiring approval before clearing. The work of the MCMA resulted in more landholders increasing ground-cover on their land to more than 50 per cent. The MCMA also holds drought management workshops and has installed DustTrak instruments to measure airborne dust concentrations.

## ACTIVITIES

### UNDERSTANDING

1. Why is it difficult to study water and land in isolation?
2. Discuss the importance of catchment management for land and water issues.
3. Explain the impacts of drought on land and water resources in the Murray catchment.

### THINKING AND APPLYING

4. What effects might the closure of Deniliquin's rice mill have had on the local community?

### USING YOUR SKILLS

5. Use the table on page 192 to discuss the impacts on the land of too much water and too little water.
6. Refer to the map of deficient rainfall and an atlas. List three locations experiencing severe deficiencies in rainfall over 16 months. Explain why serious rainfall deficiencies occur inland rather than on the coast.

## GEOTERMS

**catchment:** extent of land where water from rain or snow melt drains downhill into a body of water, such as a river, lake, reservoir, estuary or wetland

**drought:** extended period of months or years when a region experiences a deficiency in its water supply

**global warming:** increase in the average temperature of the Earth's air and oceans since the mid-twentieth century and its projected continuation

**sustainable management:** management that meets the needs of the present population without endangering the ability of future generations to meet their own needs

CHAPTER 8 | Land and water management

# 8.2 Land degradation

Everyone on Earth relies on the land. Apart from being where we live, the land provides most of our food and products such as oil and timber. Land is Australia's greatest asset but most of the soils are ancient, fragile and low in organic matter. Soil is a renewable resource, but it takes hundreds of years for natural processes to produce a few centimetres of soil. At present, increasing human activity results in soil loss at a greater rate than nature's ability to replace it.

## Nature of land degradation

**Land degradation** is the decline in quality of the land. It means the land is less able to produce crops, feed animals and renew its natural vegetation. Of the five million square kilometres used for agricultural and pastoral activities, more than half has been affected by, or is in danger of, degradation. Poor management practices have resulted in six tonnes of topsoil lost for every tonne of produce grown.

Despite increased knowledge of sustainable land management practices, land degradation persists in large areas of rural Australia. The main causes are:
- land clearance (clear felling and deforestation)
- overgrazing of livestock
- excess irrigation
- depletion of soil nutrients through poor farming practices such as continually growing a single crop over a large area, a practice known as monoculture
- conversion of farms into urban, industrial and mining uses
- disposal of waste (landfill)
- introduction of exotic plants (e.g. blackberries) and feral animals (e.g. rabbits, sheep)
- tourism.

*Drought* leaves the land vulnerable to wind and water erosion. This results in dust storms and sediment in rivers that kills marine species. **Management:** Revegetate affected areas.

*Clearing vegetation* on steep slopes leads to mass wasting, landslides and rock falls. **Management:** Revegetate steep slopes.

*Tourism* encourages clearing of sand dunes for high-density housing and mountain slopes for ski runs. **Management:** Rehabilitate sand dunes and build avalanche barriers.

*Salinity* occurs naturally in areas where there is low rainfall and high evaporation, and also where the land was below the sea millions of years ago. It is also caused by excess irrigation and clearing natural vegetation. In some cases, the water table rises, bringing salt to the surface. **Management:** Replant with salt-tolerant plants and reduce irrigation.

*Overgrazing* of land leads to nutrient-rich humus being washed or blown away. This decreases the amount of food produced. **Management:** Reduce the number of cattle, especially during droughts.

*Introduced animal species* such as rabbits eat grass and other vegetation, which exposes the soil to erosion. Their burrows increase erosion as they destabilise the soil. **Management:** Eradicate feral animals and revegetate affected areas.

*Hard-hoofed animals* such as sheep and cattle eat and trample the vegetation and compact the soil. This leads to increased run-off after heavy rain. **Management:** Reduce overgrazing and replant native vegetation.

# Impacts of land degradation

Land degradation in Australia has accelerated soil erosion by wind and water, and has increased salinity and desertification. As land productivity decreases and crop yields drop, farmers add more fertiliser to the topsoil. When it rains or the crops receive too much water, nutrients are washed into rivers and out to sea. These nutrients cause blue-green algal blooms that kill marine species. Even a dog that licks itself after swimming in this water can die.

Overlogging, overcropping, overgrazing and over-irrigating the land have resulted in short-term economic returns but long-term ecological damage to the land, which then needs to be managed sustainably by individuals, groups and governments.

*Urban, industrial and mining developments* clear land and remove vegetation. Concrete paths and impervious roads increase run-off, clogging waterways with silt. **Management:** Replant native species, construct pavements that allow water penetration, and restrict development density.

*Climate change* will affect land degradation in the future. Higher sea levels will flood low coastal areas. **Management:** Reduce the use of fossil fuels and build coastal barriers.

*Waste* deposited in landfills seeps into ground water and runs off into rivers and eventually into the sea, killing marine species. **Management:** Rethink, reduce, reuse, repair and recycle.

*Introduced plant species* such as blackberries and Salvation Jane (Paterson's curse) compete with native vegetation. **Management:** Kill exotic species.

*Acid sulfate soils* contain iron sulfides, which produce sulfuric acid and release iron, aluminium and heavy metals when exposed to air after being disturbed. Flood plains and wetlands in low-lying coastal areas are ideal for acid sulfate soil formation. **Management:** Analyse soil in coastal areas before development.

## ACTIVITIES

### UNDERSTANDING

1. Explain why land degradation is a current geographical issue.
2. List five causes of land degradation.
3. How does tourism contribute to land degradation and how can this be managed?
4. Outline the impacts of land degradation on water resources.

### THINKING AND APPLYING

5. *Fieldwork and RAP:* Many school grounds are eroded where students walk and play games. Investigate land degradation in your school or local area. Observe, collect and analyse primary data. Here are some suggestions to help you with your investigation.
    a. Draw a map to show areas of land degradation, such as waste disposal, clearing land for buildings, movement of soil or rocks downhill, erosion of sand dunes, saline or acid soils, introduced species and bare areas caused by overuse.
    b. Take three soil samples in different locations: one exposed to sunlight, one shaded by buildings and one used by many students, such as a pathway. Place samples in plastic bags. Describe the colour (black, red, grey, yellow) and the texture (sandy, clay, moist, dry) of each sample.
    c. Collect a bucket of soil from different places and count the number of earthworms. Compare your results. What is the significance of earthworms?
    d. Describe the strategies used to manage land degradation in the school or local areas such as retaining walls and rubbish bins.
    e. Visit the local council and write a report on how they manage land degradation in the area you studied.
    f. Write an email to your local council about the land degradation problems you observed and your suggested strategies for improvement.
6. Use the illustration on these pages and other research to write an extended response discussing the nature, impacts and sustainable management of land degradation. Include examples, maps, sketches and fieldwork.

### GEOTERMS

**land degradation:** loss in quality of the land and the consequent reduction in its ability to sustain agriculture or support native vegetation

# 8.3 Soil erosion

**Soil** is loose, broken rock particles and decaying organic matter on the surface of the Earth, capable of supporting life. In many parts of Australia, it takes more than 1000 years for natural processes to produce three centimetres of soil.

The most common way the land is degraded is through soil erosion. While soil erosion occurs naturally through the effects of wind and water, the process has been accelerated by human activities such as clearing land for mines, farms and buildings.

There are many types of soil erosion, including sheet, rill, gully, tunnel and wind erosion. Generally, dry inland areas are subject to greater wind erosion, whereas wetter coastal areas are affected by sheet and gully erosion. The amount of soil eroded depends on the gradient of the slope, type of soil, whether the slope is vegetated and how heavy the rainfall is.

Soil erosion is a slow process. One rainstorm can wash away topsoil to a depth of one millimetre. This amounts to 13 tonnes of topsoil from a hectare of land. It would take 20 years of natural processes to replace the loss.

Soil erosion has adverse impacts on the economy, such as less arable land for crops and livestock. Wind-blown soil causes air pollution and increases respiratory problems, and water erosion causes soil and fertiliser to move into rivers, causing silt and nutrient levels to increase.

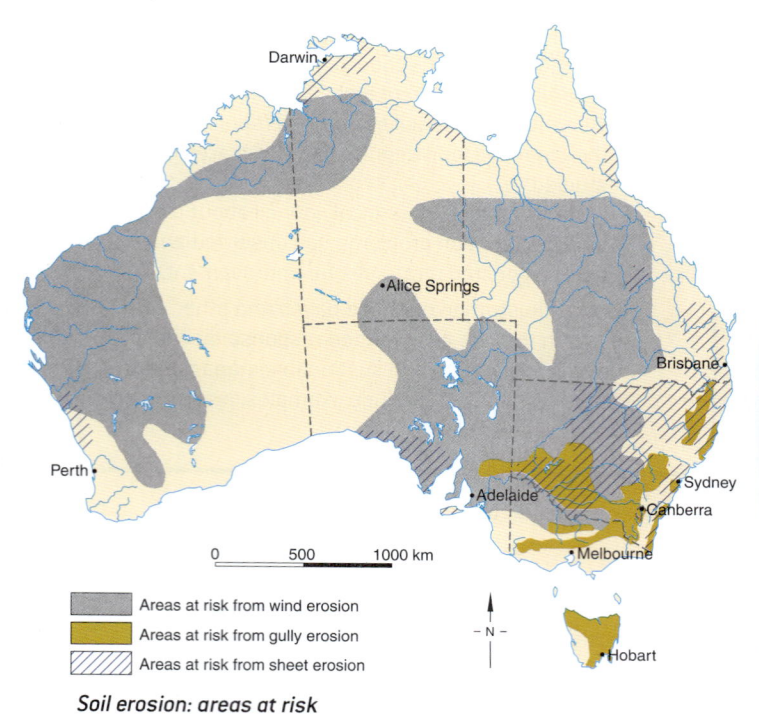

*Rill erosion occurs when channels less than 30 centimetres deep are formed. These deepen over time and become gullies.* **Management:** *Till the soil (turn it over before planting crops) or build contour banks to reduce the speed of water flowing over the surface.*

*Sheet erosion occurs when water flows over the surface, removing a large, thin layer of topsoil.* **Management:** *Plant slopes with vegetation, and add mulch (organic matter such as chopped grass) to exposed soil to absorb water.*

*Gully erosion occurs when rills grow larger and become gullies. Soil is washed into rivers, killing marine species. Large gullies need bridges or ramps to allow vehicles and livestock to cross.* **Management:** *Build dams across gullies; fill in gullies; plant vegetation to soak up excess water before it reaches the gully; or build diversion banks to channel water away from the area.*

*Soil erosion: areas at risk*
- Areas at risk from wind erosion
- Areas at risk from gully erosion
- Areas at risk from sheet erosion

Wind erosion occurs when wind blows away fine soil particles sitting on the ground. This is more common during droughts or when land is overgrazed. **Management:** Plant bare areas with vegetation; build wind breaks; contour plough the land; use strip farming; mulch exposed soil; and avoid overgrazing and overcropping.

## ACTIVITIES

### UNDERSTANDING

1. Describe four types of soil erosion.
2. Explain the long-term processes that occur to the soil when vegetation is cleared.
3. Discuss the importance of sustainably managing soil.
4. Read the sample study and explain the causes of the dust storm in September 2009.

### THINKING AND APPLYING

5. What sort of human-caused activity do you think contributes most to soil erosion? Justify your view.
6. *Fieldwork:*
   a. Draw a map of soil erosion in the school or local area.
   b. Develop a management plan to rehabilitate the area.
   c. Present the plan as a PowerPoint or annotated visual display.

### USING YOUR SKILLS

7. Sketch the photograph of gully erosion. Include labels showing how the site could be rehabilitated.
8. Refer to the map of areas in Australia at risk of soil erosion. Describe the spatial distributions of the areas at risk of wind erosion and water erosion. Explain why they differ.

### GEOTERMS

**soil:** naturally occurring, unconsolidated or loose covering of broken rock particles and decaying organic matter on the surface of the Earth that is able to support life

## SAMPLE STUDY

### Red alert as big dust storm blankets Sydney

BY RICHARD MACEY AND NATASHA WALLACE

Eight years of drought and record temperatures that have baked outback soils bone dry were blamed for yesterday's dust storm that turned Sydney's sky red and the sun blue.

Scientists estimated 75 000 tonnes of dust were being blown across NSW every hour in what may have been the most severe dust storm Sydney has seen since the droughts of the 1940s.

Department of Environment and Climate Change scientist John Leys said NSW was experiencing 'something like 10 times more dust storms than normal'.

'In the last two months we have been getting a major dust storm once a week', he said.

NSW Bureau of Meteorology regional director Barry Hanstrum said rain in the past six months over the border region covering far north-west NSW, north-east South Australia and south-west Queensland was in the lowest 10 per cent on record.

With the soil so dry, whenever strong winds blew 'you would have a dust storm, any time', he said.

Sydney University soil scientist Stephen Cattle estimated yesterday's dust storm stripped several millimetres of topsoil from hundreds of square kilometres of NSW farms. 'This will reduce the productivity of their soil, certainly', he said.

By noon, satellite imagery showed the dust stretching over thousands of kilometres, from the Victorian border, north to Goondiwindi and Bundaberg in Queensland.

Scientists are already studying tell-tale red dust that fell over New Zealand's snowfields last week.

Air quality in Sydney's east yesterday was about 40 times what is regarded as 'poor' and about 20 times the 'hazardous' level — the worst conditions in about 70 years.

The Health Department advised people not to exercise — even indoors — and sent an advisory to preschools and schools to keep children inside.

The director of the Environmental Health branch of NSW Health, Dr Wayne Smith, said the pollution was as bad as a 'heavy bushfire' day.

A NSW Health spokeswoman said there was a 'significant increase' in the number of people going to hospital emergency departments and some hospitals had to set up respiratory clinics.

*Source: The Age, 24 September 2009.*

*A blanket of dust covers Sydney.*

**CHAPTER 8** | Land and water management

# 8.4 Salinity

Every hour, an area equal to one football oval is lost to salinity in Western Australia's wheat belt; by 2100, there could be 5 million hectares of saline soils in the Murray–Darling Basin. While salt is naturally present in soil, excessive salt contributes to land degradation and deteriorating water quality.

## Nature of salinity

**Salinity** is the presence of salt on the land's surface, in soil or rocks, or dissolved in river water or ground water. Salinity is not new in Australia as it dates back 140 million years, when parts of Australia were covered by shallow seas. The seas dried up and salt was left behind in underground water and rocks. Even when Charles Sturt discovered the Darling River, he found the water too salty to drink. However, increasing human activity has contributed to two types of soil salinity:

- *Dryland salinity* occurs when native vegetation is cleared and European farming practices replace deep-rooted native vegetation with shallow-rooted crops and pastures.
- *Irrigation salinity* (wetland salinity) occurs when irrigation is used to grow crops, pastures and trees.

Both shallow-rooted crops and excess irrigation increases the amount of **ground water** and raises the salty **water table** to the soil surface.

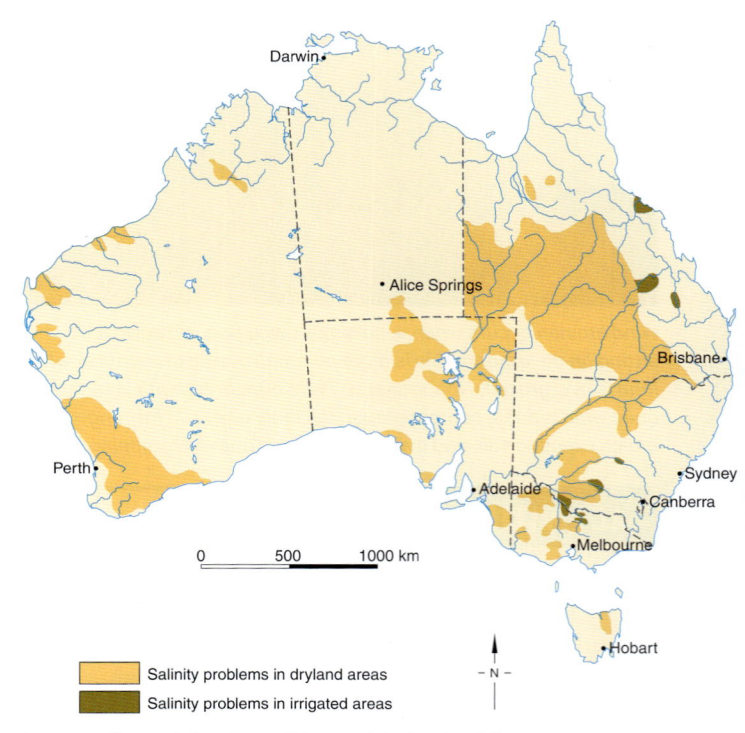

*Areas suffering irrigation salting and dryland salting*

- Salinity problems in dryland areas
- Salinity problems in irrigated areas

*A former freshwater lake affected by dryland salinity. The high salt levels have killed the native eucalypts; the smaller plants are salt tolerant varieties.*

## Impacts and management

About 2.5 million hectares of land in Australia are estimated to be affected by salinity caused by changing land use and poor management. Salinity damages buildings, roads, underground pipes, gardens and domestic appliances. It affects drinking water; if not managed sustainably within 20 years, the salt content in Adelaide's drinking water will exceed the World Health Organization's desirable standard. In Western Australia, 450 plant species are in danger of extinction due to dryland salinity. Salinity has caused agricultural production to decline $190 million annually and is increasing in urban areas (western Sydney, Wagga Wagga and Dubbo). In the Murray–Darling Basin, 68 towns suffer from dryland salinity; by 2050, 200 towns will be affected.

The Australian Government's National Action Plan for Salinity and Water Quality tackles salinity across Australia. State and local governments have placed water restrictions on irrigated crops and planted salt-resistant species such as saltbush. Microwave energy from NASA aircraft monitors salinity, and **geographic information systems (GIS)** are used map areas at risk of salinity, so that action can be taken before further problems develop. This information is available to farmers via satellite images and digital elevation models (DEMs).

## SAMPLE STUDY

### Salinity in the Murray–Darling Basin

The Murray–Darling Basin drains one-seventh of the Australian land. The basin's crop producers use 70 per cent of Australia's irrigation to produce 40 per cent of the nation's food. Parts of the basin are in danger of declining agricultural productivity due to saline soils and saline water. The decline is happening in this area for a combination of reasons: it was once under the sea; it has a low rainfall and high evaporation; it is often irrigated with more water than the crop needs; and native vegetation has been cleared and replaced with salt-intolerant crops.

In nearly half of the water management areas in Australia, including the Murray–Darling Basin, irrigation licences have been capped to stop any increase in water use. The Basin Salinity Management Strategy for 2001–2015 guides communities and governments to use measures that control salinity, such as constructing groundwater schemes to intercept salt flow into rivers. The 2008 Australian government's Water for the Future project aims to invest $3 billion in restoring Murray–Darling Basin rivers by reducing the over-allocation of irrigation water and purchasing water from farmers to be put back into rivers. The impacts of climate change on water availability and salinity will determine how land and water resources are managed in the future.

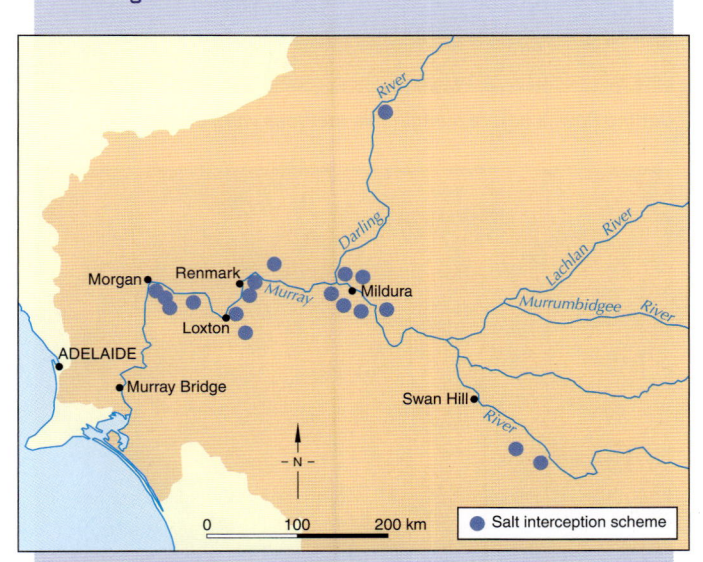

Salt interception schemes remove over 500 000 tonnes of salt annually from ground water and drainage basins. Prior to the Woolpunda and Waikerie schemes, the Murray River carried 250 tonnes of salt per day past Woolpunda and 100 tonnes a day past Waikerie. Recent surveys show that salinity levels have decreased to less than 10 tonnes a day in each area.

## GEOskills TOOLBOX

### COLLECTING AND USING DIGITAL IMAGES

A collection of digital images sourced from reliable websites is an effective way to present information on a geographical issue. Ensure the websites are authoritative; for example, from government departments and non-government organisations. Choose images to suit your audience and purpose. Download the images and keep a record of the source and the date accessed. Categorise the images and write captions to explain them.

## ACTIVITIES

### UNDERSTANDING

1. Describe how the physical and human elements of the environment have contributed to high salinity levels in Australia.
2. Explain the nature and impacts of salinity in the Murray–Darling Basin.
3. Discuss the responses of governments to salinity problems.

### THINKING AND APPLYING

4. Use the photograph on the previous page to explain why salinity is called the 'silent white death'.

### USING YOUR SKILLS

5. Use the map on the previous page to estimate the percentage of Australia affected by salinity. Describe the distribution of dryland salinity. Suggest reasons for salinity in irrigated areas.
6. Conduct an internet image search using the key words *salinity in Australia*, and prepare a PowerPoint presentation of the images with explanatory captions to share with the class.
7. Refer to the map of the Murray–Darling salt interception scheme on the left. What is the aim of such schemes? Explain why they are an effective management strategy. Discuss their impact on river ecosystems.

### GEOTERMS

**ground water:** water under the surface of the ground that has seeped through soil and rock; often used for drinking and irrigation

**salinity:** presence of salt on the land's surface, in soil or rocks, or dissolved in water in rivers and ground water

**water table:** the upper limit of the ground water

# 8.5 Sustainable land management

Australia's Indigenous people evolved with the land, changing it and changing with it. To them, the land is not just soil but the whole environment, so their management was ecologically sustainable. When Europeans arrived in 1788, they regarded the land as a resource to be owned, improved and exploited. Large areas of natural vegetation were cleared for crops and animals. They overgrazed and overcropped the land, especially during droughts. Their practices became unsustainable when land became less productive.

Land management has spatial and ecological dimensions. Spatially, managers of land resources map and locate areas with problems, such as soil erosion, salinity and desertification. From an ecological dimension, managers need to understand how people interact with the land and how it impacts on water, air and plant and animal species.

## Sustainable agriculture

Land and water degradation and the loss of native vegetation are significant problems in Australia. As a result, more farmers use sustainable farming methods. These include minimal use of mechanical cultivation, contour ploughing, mulching and leaving stubble to cover the ground after harvesting crops such as wheat and rice. *Farm planning, farm management, whole farm planning* and *land management planning* are some of the terms used in the practice of sustainable farming. The aim of sustainable farming is to farm and graze in ways that:
- save or improve the soil
- protect or restore the diversity of plants and animals
- protect or increase the supply of clean water.

Local, state and federal governments have established a number of programs, including One Billion Trees, Save the Bush and Landcare. **Landcare** aims to protect and repair the environment. More than 4000 volunteer community landcare groups (bushcare, urban landcare, rivercare, coastcare) and sustainable agriculture groups actively tackle land degradation around Australia. More than 40 per cent of farmers practise landcare farming, which has reduced soil erosion and salinity on farms.

The federal government has set targets for significant changes in the way Australia manages its land, water and vegetation resources. In 2005, there was no net loss of native vegetation and, if this trend continues, a decline in land degradation is anticipated by 2015.

## The Darling Downs

The Darling Downs is a farming region on the western slopes of the Great Dividing Range in southern Queensland. Since the 1850s, European farming methods have contributed to the severe soil erosion of 30–60 tonnes per hectare. Since the 1950s, most farmers have adopted soil conservation measures such as contour banks, which trap 80 per cent of the soil, and grassed waterways, which divert run-off to reduce soil loss.

*Darling Downs before sustainable methods were used*

*Darling Downs after sustainable methods were used*

**Unsustainable land management**

1. Stream and gully erosion.
2. Crop stubble removed by burning or ploughing-in exposes soil to erosion.
3. Cultivation up and down the slope increases run-off and erosion of topsoil.
4. Decline in soil structure from over-cultivation and compaction by heavy machinery, increased soil acidity from overuse of fertilisers, and contamination by pesticides and herbicides.
5. Dust storms remove topsoil.
6. Mass movement caused by land clearing and overgrazing.
7. Development can cause erosion, localised flooding, sedimentation in rivers and a decline in water quality and biodiversity.
8. Habitat loss due to land clearing.
9. Bioaccumulation of pesticides in food webs.
10. Irrigation increases amount of ground water, can lead to waterlogging and rise in watertable.
11. Replacement of trees and deep-rooted native vegetation with shallow-rooted crops and pastures. Allows watertable to rise, salinity to increase, and vegetation to die.
12. Large areas devoted to monoculture (one crop), stubble removed, increased run-off and erosion.
13. Vegetation removed from stream banks causes severe erosion.
14. Run-off of fertilisers can cause eutrophication and algal blooms in waterways.
15. Sedimentation from erosion, silt builds up in river.

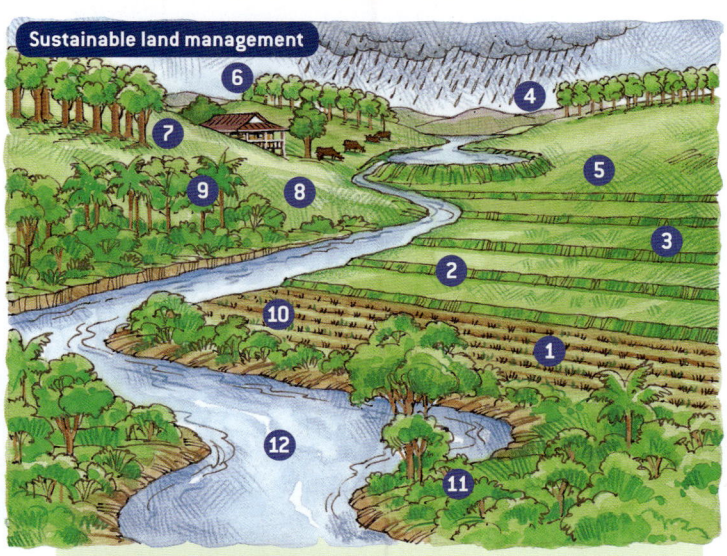

**Sustainable land management**

1. Minimum tillage preserves soil structure and reduces erosion.
2. Contour ploughing and contour banks built across the slope trap soil and run-off.
3. Stubble left on the ground after harvesting to protect soil from erosion.
4. Trees planted.
5. Exposed surfaces stabilised by revegetation or mulching.
6. On steep slopes, tree roots hold soil and protect it from heavy rain, reducing erosion and run-off.
7. Large trees have deep roots that take water from the soil and maintain stable watertable.
8. Land clearing and irrigation kept to a minimum to keep watertable below the surface.
9. Diverse habitats, maintenance of biodiversity.
10. Flat ground planted with strips of different crops to reduce run-off. After harvesting, stubble is left on the ground or the area is mulched.
11. Dense and varied vegetation on banks keeps the soil together and prevents erosion.
12. Clean water in river maintained by controlling erosion, run-off and sedimentation.

### Are dung beetles a solution?

Dung beetles feed on dung and decomposed leaves. The digging activity of tunnelling beetles aerates the soil and transfers the nutrients into the soil. They also reduce nutrient run-off into rivers, increase water infiltration through the soil, increase soil fertility and reduce the need for chemical fertilisers.

*Dung beetles shape dung into balls, which they roll away or pack into burrows tunnelled under the dung pat.*

## ACTIVITIES

### UNDERSTANDING

1. Describe how dung beetles improve land productivity.
2. Explain why land degradation was not a major issue for Australia's Indigenous people before European settlement.
3. Explain why effective land management requires an understanding of the spatial and ecological dimensions of land degradation.

### THINKING AND APPLYING

4. Draw a diagram to show five major causes of land degradation.
5. *Fieldwork and RAP:* Research the nature of land degradation and its impacts on the physical and human elements of the environment in your local area. Describe the responses of individuals, groups and governments to the issue. Propose actions to promote sustainability. For background information, use your library, the internet or the **Land management** weblink in your eBookPLUS.

### USING YOUR SKILLS

6. Compare the aerial photos of the Darling Downs. Describe unsustainable farming practices and their impact on land and water resources.
7. Compare the diagrams of sustainable and unsustainable land management.
    a. What problems occur when trees are removed?
    b. Explain the benefits of contour ploughing.
    c. How can urban and industrial development reduce land degradation?
    d. How is water quality affected by farming practices?
    e. Suggest strategies that could be adopted to ensure sustainable land management.

CHAPTER 8 | Land and water management

# 8.6 Nature and impacts of tourism on land

## Environmental impacts

The impacts of tourism on the environment can range from minimal to extreme. Large numbers of tourists have the potential to create a negative impact, especially on environmentally sensitive areas. Strategies to reduce tourism's impact include educating visitors and using paths and barriers to control people's movement. New technologies, such as geographic information systems (GIS) and satellite imagery are increasingly being used to identify tourism's impacts on natural and built sites.

One positive impact of tourism, which is often overlooked, is that some areas have been protected from other forms of development because people have argued that the area should be managed in a way that allows for conservation and sustainable tourism. In the 1980s, the Franklin River in south-west Tasmania was to be dammed to produce hydro-electric power but this decision was overturned. Many people from all over the world supported the campaign to protect this wilderness area, which is now a popular tourist destination.

## How much is too much?

The term *carrying capacity* describes the level of recreational use an area can support before there is significant damage to the environment. It varies from site to site and over time. For example, in winter the ski resort of Falls Creek in Victoria attracts thousands of visitors. In summer there are fewer visitors but the environmental impact is greater. Bushwalkers and campers spread out over a wider area, and summer tourists can easily damage the environment by lighting camp fires, trampling fragile vegetation and leaving their litter and wastes behind.

*The Gold Coast, 1950*

*The Gold Coast today*

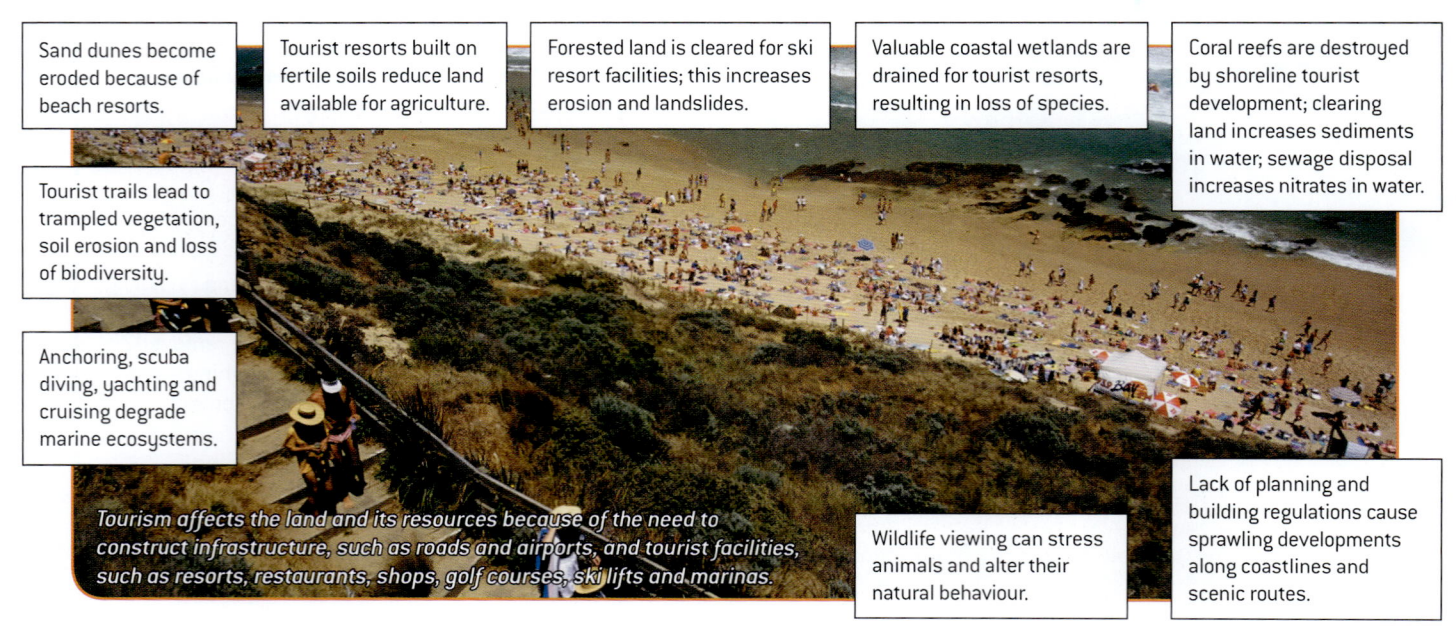

- Sand dunes become eroded because of beach resorts.
- Tourist resorts built on fertile soils reduce land available for agriculture.
- Forested land is cleared for ski resort facilities; this increases erosion and landslides.
- Valuable coastal wetlands are drained for tourist resorts, resulting in loss of species.
- Coral reefs are destroyed by shoreline tourist development; clearing land increases sediments in water; sewage disposal increases nitrates in water.
- Tourist trails lead to trampled vegetation, soil erosion and loss of biodiversity.
- Anchoring, scuba diving, yachting and cruising degrade marine ecosystems.
- Wildlife viewing can stress animals and alter their natural behaviour.
- Lack of planning and building regulations cause sprawling developments along coastlines and scenic routes.

*Tourism affects the land and its resources because of the need to construct infrastructure, such as roads and airports, and tourist facilities, such as resorts, restaurants, shops, golf courses, ski lifts and marinas.*

# Tourism and Aboriginal sites

Non-indigenous Australians have only recently begun to recognise the importance of Aboriginal sites as part of our cultural heritage. To Indigenous people these sites have always been special. The land is the home of their ancestors, and places such as Uluru, Kakadu, the Blue Mountains and Katherine Gorge are linked to the Dreamtime. Often they are also popular tourist sites and this has led to conflict between Indigenous communities and the tourism industry. Commercial interests want to develop areas for tourists but, from the perspective of Indigenous people, this has the potential to affect their relationship with the land and the integrity of sacred sites.

## SAMPLE STUDY

### Uluru–Kata Tjuta National Park

Uluru–Kata Tjuta National Park is located close to the centre of Australia. The area is very arid and consists mostly of red sand plains and rolling sandhills. Out of the vast expanse of the Western Desert rise the giant monoliths of Uluru and Kata Tjuta. Uluru is one of Australia's best recognised icons. Tourists want to see this unique geological landform and to climb it. For the Anangu people of the area, the landscape is integral to their spiritual, cultural and social life. The rock has many sacred sites. The 2009 draft plan for the park included a proposed ban on climbing. Most traditional owners support this proposal.

The Uluru–Kata Tjuta Aboriginal Land Trust owns the park and leases it to the federal government. The park is an example of successful cooperation between Indigenous and non-Indigenous people. Traditional land management practices (including firing of vegetation and care of waterholes) and protection of Aboriginal heritage are part of the cultural values that gained Uluru its place on the World Heritage List. Almost 400 000 people visit the park each year and the number is rising.

*Tourists climbing Uluru*

## ACTIVITIES

### UNDERSTANDING

1. Make a list of ten places you would like to visit. What impact do you think you would have on the land?
2. Describe the link between land and tourism to Aboriginal sites.

### THINKING AND APPLYING

3. In pairs or small groups, develop solutions to the following problem. You are managing a rainforest area and you estimate that the visitor site has a daily carrying capacity of 280 people. You find that up to 500 people arrive on some days. Brainstorm possible strategies to control the number of people visiting. Discuss which solutions are best. Share your results with other groups.
4. Tourists visit outstanding World Heritage land sites such as the Greater Blue Mountains Area, Kakadu National Park, Tasmanian Wilderness, Wet Tropics of Queensland and Fraser Island. Research one of these sites and discuss how managers are sustainably managing the impacts of tourism on the land resources.
5. Read the sample study on Uluru–Kata Tjuta. Why would the Anangu people want people not to climb Uluru? Would you climb Uluru? Give reasons for your answer. Why is Uluru–Kata Tjuta National Park cited as an example of a successful response to a geographical issue?

### USING YOUR SKILLS

6. Refer to the two photographs of the Gold Coast in Queensland. List the changes that have occurred between 1950 and today. Describe the positive and negative impacts of tourism on this site. What might be the impacts of climate change on the land?

# 8.7 Ecotourism: the sustainable alternative

**Ecotourism** promotes natural and cultural conservation and encourages small-scale, low-volume tourism that has minimal impact on the environment. It began when people realised that mass tourism was adversely affecting many physical environments and the culture of local communities. At the same time, experienced tourists and affluent people were becoming dissatisfied with packaged holidays. Ecotourism has become the fastest growing sector in the tourism industry, increasing at around 15 per cent every year. Recent surveys have shown that many international tourists, especially Germans and Americans, visit Australia to experience our natural environment. They are looking for something different from resort-style holidays. They want to go to places where the physical environment is still in its natural state and where cultural experiences are authentic rather than packaged.

## The Australian experience

Australia is popular with ecotourists because it provides ecotourism opportunities. These visitors want to see our national parks and World Heritage sites and experience wilderness or adventure tours. Ecotourism often involves activities such as walking, diving, cycling, animal and bird watching, and photography. More adventurous activities like rock climbing, hang-gliding and whitewater rafting are also popular. Many ecotourists want to know more about traditional Indigenous culture including artworks, ceremonies and bushcraft.

When there are too many tourists, the original appeal of a site can be destroyed. Ecotourism Australia (EA) defines ecotourism as ecologically sustainable tourism that fosters environmental and cultural understanding, appreciation and conservation. There is growing concern that some ecotours are not following the EA's code of practice and that there should be stricter guidelines. Some people argue that ecotourism should exclude activities such as fishing, rock climbing and abseiling because they have the potential to harm the environment.

### Tourism's carbon footprint

The report entitled *The carbon footprint of Australian tourism* informs governments and industry of the impacts of tourism on climate change. Tourism is the seventh highest contributor to Australia's greenhouse gas (GHG) emissions, producing 3.93 per cent of the country's carbon emissions. Transport is the greatest contributor to tourism's carbon footprint accounting for 82.2 per cent of tourism's GHG emissions compared with accommodation (4.5 per cent), other industries (8.6 per cent) and retail (3.4 per cent).

### SAMPLE STUDY

#### The Overland Track

The Parks and Wildlife Service Tasmania is responsible for land and water management of this environmentally sensitive area. Management issues and strategies include:

- **Track erosion.** Boarded tracks, boardwalks across muddy areas and bridges over streams have been constructed to slow down erosion.
- **Fires.** Open fires are banned and this is a 'fuel-stove only' area.
- **Wastes.** Walkers must carry out all of their rubbish. Fact sheets are available on minimising pollution, including what to do where there are no toilets.
- **Education.** Visitor centres and rangers promote concern for wildlife and environmental issues. Brochures and videos are available.
- **Funding.** Park entry fees have increased and are used to fund trainee programs for rangers and to construct and maintain walking tracks, car parks, toilets, and picnic and camping facilities.
- **Quotas.** It may be necessary to limit the number of walkers in the future to ensure sustainability.

To find out more, use the **Minimal impact** weblink in your eBookPLUS.

*The Overland Track in the Tasmanian wilderness runs for 60 kilometres through varied environments including alpine and rainforest vegetation and lakes formed by the action of glaciers. The trip takes about six days for a fit walker.*

### Code of practice for ecotourism operators

- Strengthen the conservation effort for, and enhance the natural integrity of, the places visited.
- Respect the sensitivities of other cultures.
- Be efficient in the use of natural resources.
- Ensure waste disposal has minimal environmental/aesthetic impact.
- Develop a recycling program.
- Support businesses that have a conservation ethic.
- Keep abreast of current political and environmental issues, particularly of the local area.
- Try to use distribution networks and retail outlets to raise environmental awareness by giving guidelines to consumers.
- Support ecotourism education/training for guides and managers.
- Employ ecotour guides well versed in and respectful of local cultures and environments.
- Give clients appropriate educational material and guidance on the natural and cultural history of the areas visited.
- Use locally produced goods that benefit the local community, but do not buy goods made from threatened or endangered species.
- Never intentionally disturb wildlife or wildlife habitats.
- Keep vehicles to designated roads and trails.
- Abide by the rules and regulations applying in natural areas.
- Ensure truth in advertising.
- Maximise the quality of experience for hosts and guests.

*Source:* **Ecotourism Australia.**

### Earthwatch — the ultimate ecotour?

The Earthwatch Institute is an international non-profit scientific research organisation. It aims to involve people 'in scientific field research and education to promote the understanding and action necessary for a sustainable environment'. It does this by providing money for research and inviting volunteers to join expedition teams to take part in scientific fieldwork. Earthwatch has research teams working in more than 50 countries. Volunteers can join a team and be part of a project, usually for a period of about 10 to 14 days. Anyone can apply as long as they are at least 16 years old. Volunteers make their own arrangements to get to a research country and pay a share of other costs such as food and accommodation. Earthwatch provides training so that volunteers can actively contribute to research projects.

Current research projects include:
- surveying the ecological resources of undeveloped Caribbean islands to plan for sustainable tourism
- exploring how Australia's arid lands functioned before the introduction of exotic mammals
- discovering the impact of wilderness roads on desert stream ecology
- mapping water resources and assessing human and wildlife use to avoid potential conflicts.

[To find out more about Earthwatch expeditions, use the **Earthwatch** weblink in your eBookPLUS.]

### GEOTERMS

**ecotourism:** ecologically sustainable tourism, with a primary focus on experiencing natural areas, that fosters environmental and cultural understanding, appreciation and conservation

## ACTIVITIES

### UNDERSTANDING

1. List the reasons why Australia has a lot to offer ecotourists.
2. What are the advantages of an ecotourism code of practice, program and logo?
3. Discuss the positive responses by individuals, groups and government organisations to ecotourism in Australia.
4. Refer to the sample study about the Overland Track.
   a. What activities attract tourists to the Tasmanian wilderness?
   b. How do different activities affect the environment?
   c. What strategies could manage such problems?
   d. Describe different perspectives on this issue that might be held by a national park ranger, a tourist, a tour operator and a person who lives near the park.

### THINKING AND APPLYING

5. Design a poster promoting Australia as an ecotourist destination.
6. Describe how tourism contributes to global warming. Suggest management strategies to reduce its carbon footprint.
7. Read the article about Earthwatch. Create a multimedia presentation or a document with weblinks that describes how Earthwatch expeditions could help to improve land and water management. Select one expedition and explain how the research could contribute to sustainability.
8. Discuss the nature, impacts and responses to sustainable tourism. The following scaffold will help you with your answer.

**NATURE**
- Define sustainable tourism (ecotourism)
- Types of ecotourism

**IMPACTS**
- Natural environment: land for hotels and roads; carbon footprint
- Communities: local, Indigenous people
- Cultures: sensitivity

**RESPONSES**
Tools for management such as:
- EIA (environmental impact assessment)
- carrying capacity (maximum number before damage to environment)
- area protection (World Heritage sites, national parks, boardwalks)
- code of practice for ecotourism operators
- eco certification program and logo (assists tourists to experience authentic tours, attractions, cruises and accommodation that is environmentally, socially and economically sustainable).

CHAPTER 8 | Land and water management

# 8.8 Managing the Australian alps

## Where are the Australian alps?

The Australian alps are located in south-eastern Australia, extending from the Brindabella Range near Canberra to Mount Baw Baw east of Melbourne.

The word *alpine* generally means mountain area. Specifically, it refers to the area above the tree line. In the Australian alps the tree line is at about 1400 metres above sea level. Included in the Australian alps are tableland areas below the alpine zones. Compared with other continents and their mountain ranges, Australia has only a small area of alps and its mountains are not very high. Mount Kosciuszko has an altitude of only 2228 metres, compared with Mount Everest in the Himalayas with an altitude of 8848 metres.

*A view over part of Kosciuszko National Park*

## How were land and water managed in the past?

The first people we know of to use the alps were the Indigenous people. In late spring, groups from the upper Murray River used to travel to the Snowy Mountains and surrounding areas to hunt the Bogong moth, which was considered a food delicacy. They were followed in the 1800s by explorers who mapped parts of the alps. From the 1820s, pastoralists began to spread into the alps, ignoring any occupancy rights of the Indigenous people. This resulted in large areas of the foothills and tablelands being cleared, burned and fenced.

Miners and timber loggers also left their imprint on the land. The result was the widespread destruction of native vegetation, which led to increased water run-off and soil erosion.

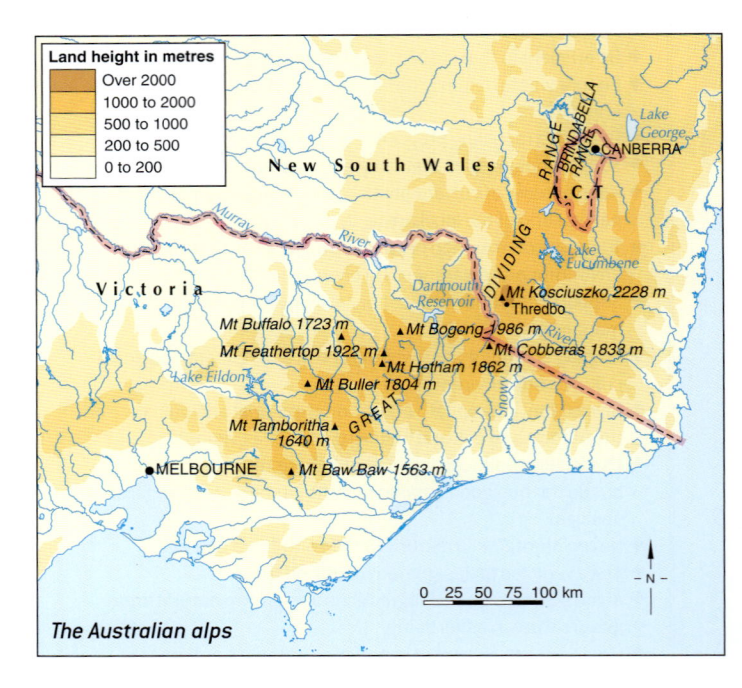

*The Australian alps*

In the 1940s and 1950s, large-scale water conservation projects were undertaken, including the massive Snowy Mountains Scheme, with the aim of storing water then redirecting it for use in inland irrigation schemes. More recently, the improved road systems brought a range of users and community interest groups to the area, including bushwalkers and skiers, and their numbers continue to grow rapidly. This recreational use of the Australian alps, particularly for skiing, became increasingly important from the 1960s and continues to the present. Access roads were developed as more settlements were established, such as at Thredbo.

Among the many groups using the alps, a common concern arose that damage to the physical environment (such as soil erosion and the destruction of native vegetation) would affect their long-term use and interests. The movement for conservation grew and national parks, such as Kosciuszko National Park, were established.

## Responses to the issue

The alpine areas of Australia are easily damaged by humans due to the steep slopes and thin soils. Once soils and vegetation are damaged, they take a long time to recover. Few areas of the alps remain unaffected by the activities of humans.

Management of an area in which there is conflicting use is difficult. For example, on the one hand the ski resort operators might want to expand accommodation; clear more vegetation for ski runs and car parks; and expand the road network. On the other hand, conservationists who believe it should be a wilderness area want it to be allowed to return to its natural state.

At present the alps are managed by separate state governments. However, there are various management objectives that have been agreed on for the national parks in the alps. They include the following:
- conserving and protecting natural ecosystems
- supplying water to catchment areas
- protecting archaeological and historic sites
- promoting low-impact visitor use
- promoting an appreciation and understanding of the alpine environments
- protecting areas from fire and eradicating pest plants and animals
- encouraging scientific research and cooperating with governments and other organisations to coordinate planning and resource management.

## Impact of climate change

Even though Australia's alpine region covers only 0.15 per cent of the continent, its land and water resources are expected to be affected by climate change. The average snowline, which is now at 1412 metres above sea level, is predicted to rise to 1600 metres by 2020. Mount Kosciuszko at 2228 metres will be adversely affected. Already, artificial snow is used in ski resorts, and millions more dollars will be required to supply water and electricity to make snow in the future, further adding to global warming and misuse of water.

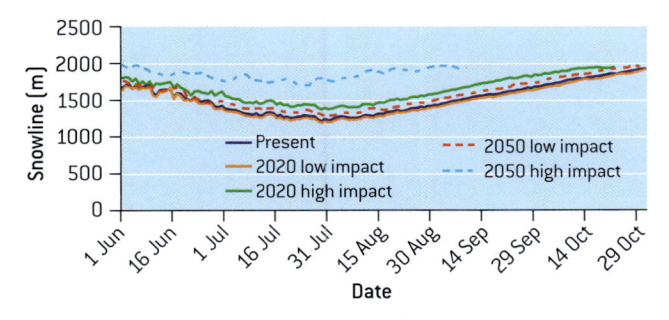

*Predicted changes to snowline, Mt Kosciuszko*

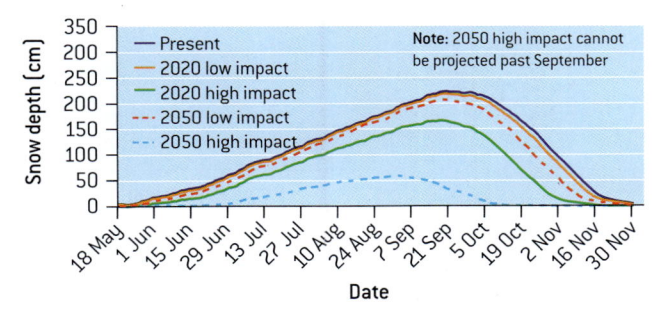

*Predicted changes to snow depth, Mt Kosciuszko*

*Thousands of skiers flock to Thredbo and other alpine villages for the snow season.*

### ACTIVITIES

**UNDERSTANDING**

1. List the ways in which sheep grazing damaged the physical environment.
2. Describe the early forms of land use in the alps. Explain why some forms of land use were in balance with the physical environment.
3. Describe how climate change will affect land and water resources in the alps.

**THINKING AND APPLYING**

4. Explain why parts of the Australian alps are considered suitable for water conservation projects. What damage could these projects cause to both the land and the built environment?
5. Imagine you are the managing director of a company that wants to expand its ski resort in a national park area. In what ways might your plans conflict with national park objectives? How would you solve this conflict?
6. Using the resources in your library and/or on the internet, find a mountain national park in another country. Write a brief report about management of this park. In your answer, cover the following:
   a. physical and human aspects of the environment
   b. impacts of human interactions
   c. different perspectives on its management
   d. actions that promote sustainable management.

**USING YOUR SKILLS**

7. Refer to the map on the previous page to describe the location of Australia's alpine region. Name the three highest peaks and give their heights. Name two large lakes. Do you think these are natural or human-made lakes? Why?
8. Refer to the diagram on the left. Describe the present snowline for Mount Kosciuszko and how it is predicted to change depending on whether climate change has a low or high impact. Discuss the sustainability of the ski industry in the light of this.

**CHAPTER 8** | Land and water management

# Working geographically

## BROADSHEET: LAND MANAGEMENT AND WILDLIFE HABITATS

Poor land management leads to a decline in native vegetation and loss of biodiversity. Native species such as the koala are innocent victims when land is cleared of native vegetation.

Pottsville, a small coastal town located on the north coast of New South Wales, has a stable breeding population of 30–50 koalas. The proposed Koala Beach housing estate could endanger the territory required by the koalas for food and shelter and to breed. Research has found that even a minor habitat disturbance could have disastrous consequences for the koala population.

Topographic map extract of the Pottsville area. The red outline shows the area of the aerial photograph above right.

208  Geoactive 2

*The yellow lines show the range of movement required by koalas for mating, food and shelter. The shaded section shows a possible location of a wildlife corridor in the Pottsville area.*

## KNOWLEDGE AND UNDERSTANDING

1. How might a new housing estate affect the koala population at Pottsville?

## FIELDWORK AND RAP

2. Research the impacts of clearing land on native species in your local area or another area cleared for housing, industrial or tourist development. Propose actions that promote sustainability.

## USING YOUR SKILLS

3. Refer to the topographic map of the Pottsville area.
   a. List five natural features on the map.
   b. What are the landforms in AR5460 and AR5661?
   c. In what direction does Christies Creek flow?
   d. What is the local relief between GR556624 and GR565620?
   e. What is the aspect of the slope at '285' in AR5562?
   f. Calculate the gradient of the slope from GR555621 to the caravan park at Hastings Point.
   g. What is the straight-line distance from Pottsville tennis courts to the garbage depot?
   h. Calculate the distance by road from Pottsville sports ground to Hastings Point caravan park.
   i. What is the density of buildings in AR5662?
   j. Give the grid reference of the highest point.
   k. List the area references of five sites where humans have cleared the land.
   l. Draw and label a cross-section from A to B.
   m. Construct a transect from C to D.
   n. What is the bearing of the caravan park at Hastings Point from Round Mountain dip in AR5362?
   o. Construct a land-use map of the area inside the four red lines.

4. Study the aerial photograph and the topographic map.
   a. What is the town shown in the aerial photograph?
   b. Describe the vegetation in the koala's home-range.
   c. Describe the land over most of the area shown in the aerial photograph.

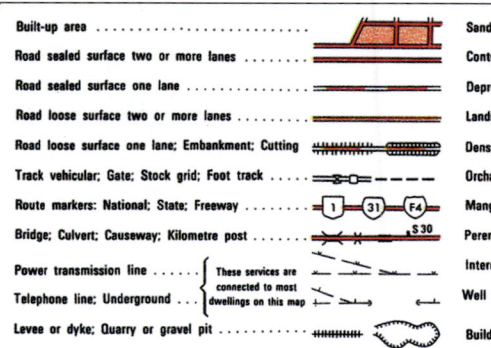

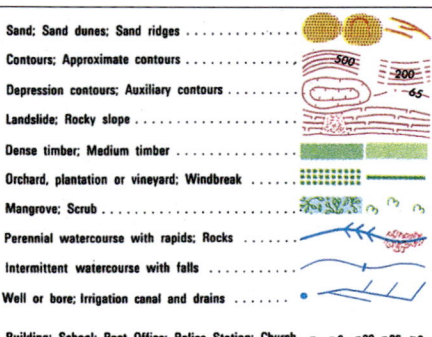

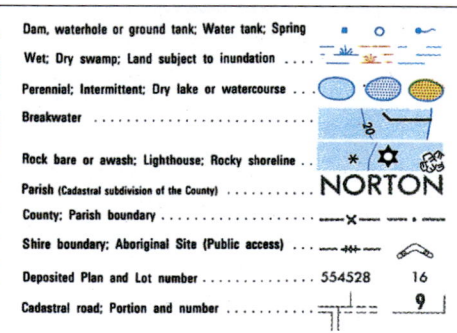

**CHAPTER 8** | Land and water management

# 8.9 Water: nature, impacts and management

## The water cycle

The water cycle is the circulation system that carries water from the oceans, through the atmosphere, to the land and back to the sea. The basic processes in the water cycle are evaporation, condensation, precipitation, infiltration and run-off. When we are studying water in rivers, for example, we are concerned with the run-off stage of the water cycle.

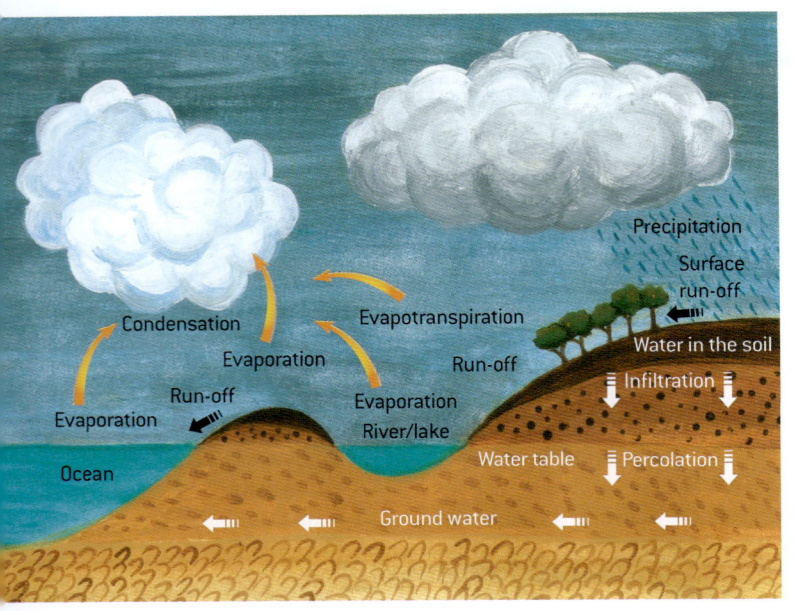

When precipitation occurs on areas higher than sea level, and if the water does not infiltrate the ground, it will move overland towards the sea as surface run-off. Most of this run-off will find its way into streams and rivers, which may be permanent (water in them all year) or intermittent (water in them after rain). Some rivers drain towards the ocean, like the Murray–Darling; while others drain inland and dry up as salt lakes. Run-off is a most important part of the cycle for communities because a lot of fresh water is obtained from rivers. Streams and rivers are also important areas for community activities and recreation.

## Why manage water quantity and quality?

Australia has the lowest and most variable rainfall of the inhabited continents. It has the least river water, the lowest run-off, the most variable streams, the smallest area of permanent wetlands and the smallest area of freshwater lakes. It is clear that water is a resource that requires careful management in contemporary Australia, particularly because of recent long-lasting droughts.

The 'health' of rivers in Australia depends on the amount of water taken from them and the amount and type of waste dumped into them. Problems with water quality and reduced flows, due to irrigation and damming, are affecting many of our rivers.

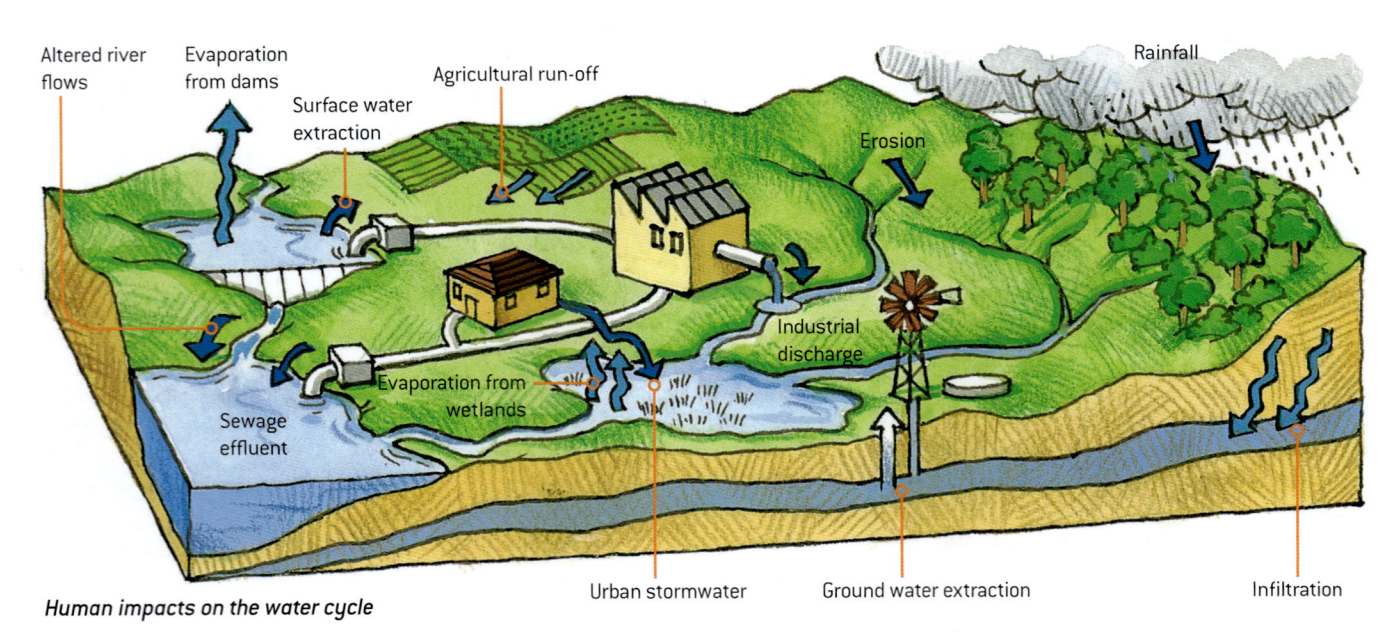

*The water cycle*

*Human impacts on the water cycle*

People who depend on rivers for their livelihood or for enjoyment are becoming increasingly aware of this. They want clean water and healthy rivers for good health, pleasure and prosperity. In modern times, this is virtually impossible without sound, sustainable management.

## Management issues

When Europeans arrived in Australia, they cleared natural vegetation from large areas of land and began European farming methods with European crops and animals. Over the next 200 years or so, in an attempt to overcome the variability of rainfall and river flow, various types of water storages were constructed. These ranged from small on-farm dams to large-scale storages for irrigation, industrial and mining use, and to provide urban supplies. Ground water from sources such as the Great Artesian Basin was tapped as well, mainly as drinking water for stock. These storages have affected the natural flow of rivers, water temperatures and chemistry. In addition, waste disposal into rivers from rural, urban and industrial activities has polluted rivers, lakes and wetlands.

We are now starting to realise the full environmental effects of the rapid development of Australia's water resources and traditional management methods. These effects on the physical environment have included:
- disappearing wetlands
- rivers containing too little water at appropriate times for various fish and bird species to breed
- salinisation of irrigation areas
- the development of blue-green algae in many streams during periods of drought
- ground water being used faster than it is being replenished in many basins.

## Towards sustainability

The effective management of water quantity and quality is an urgent challenge facing Australia, especially given the expected impacts of climate change. In response, state and federal laws have been passed and regulatory bodies established; these include the Australian government's Department of the Environment, Water, Heritage and the Arts; the NSW Department of Water and Energy; Sydney Water; and the Lower Murray Darling Catchment Management Authority. The National Water Commission drives water reform policies such as water trading, water pricing, recycling and provision of water for wetlands. The $12.9 billion national water plan, Water for the Future, provides rebates to households that install rainwater tanks and aims to recycle 30 per cent of waste water by 2015. Other changes include:
- catchment management: managing the catchment area as a whole rather than its individual parts
- water conservation: increasing the price of water, implementing flood control, buying back water entitlements from irrigators in the Murray–Darling Basin to be returned to the river
- biological conservation: creating programs such as Waterwatch and Frogwatch
- water quality control: setting guidelines for drinking water, recreational use of rivers and recycling waste water to reduce infections from faecal contamination (*E. coli*)
- action by individuals: growing native vegetation, mulching gardens and using water-saving devices such as showerheads.

### GEOfacts
Australian scientist Tim Flannery predicts that within 50 years Perth could become a ghost metropolis — an abandoned city with no water to sustain its population. Rainfall loss due to climate change is the main cause.

### ACTIVITIES

**UNDERSTANDING**
1. Describe the links between water and land.
2. Explain why Australia is the driest inhabited continent but has the highest per capita water storage.
3. Describe the impacts of traditional forms of water management on the physical environment.
4. Discuss the actions of individuals, groups and governments to sustainably manage water quantity and quality in Australia.

**THINKING AND APPLYING**
5. Make a list of ways you could reduce the amount of water used around the home and school.

**USING YOUR SKILLS**
6. Refer to the diagram on the previous page of the water cycle.
   a. What are the main processes in the water cycle?
   b. Why is run-off such an important part of the water cycle?
7. Refer to the diagram on the previous page of human impacts on the water cycle. List four ways human activities affect the water cycle. Describe how you interacted with the water cycle over the last week.

# 8.10 Rivers out of balance

Rivers are complex systems that depend on a balance between inputs and outputs. Any changes in river flow and water quality can affect the health of habitats in streams and on riverbanks.

The water in many of Australia's major rivers is nearly all being used. This means that a large amount of water has been diverted away from them.

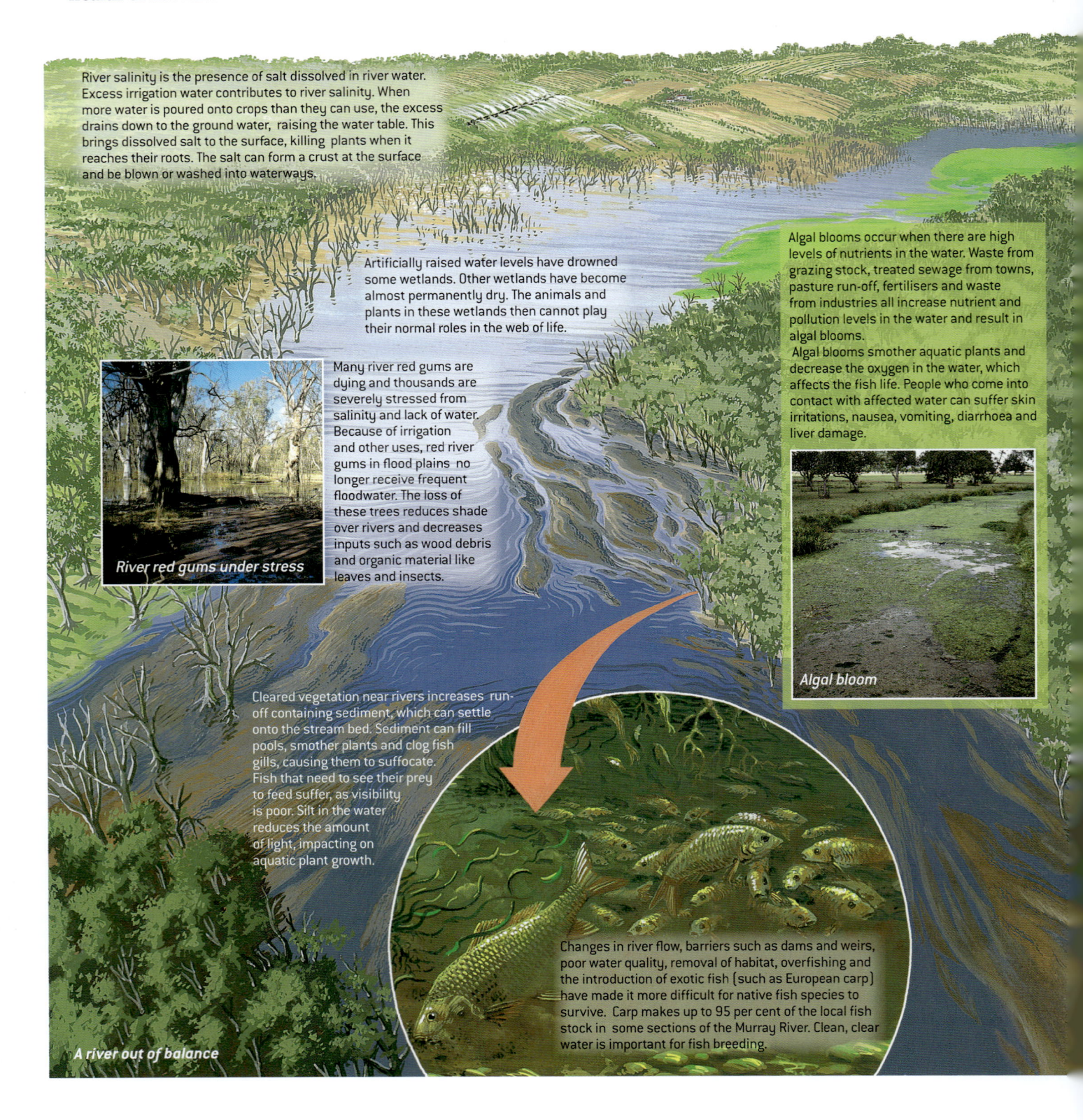

River salinity is the presence of salt dissolved in river water. Excess irrigation water contributes to river salinity. When more water is poured onto crops than they can use, the excess drains down to the ground water, raising the water table. This brings dissolved salt to the surface, killing plants when it reaches their roots. The salt can form a crust at the surface and be blown or washed into waterways.

Artificially raised water levels have drowned some wetlands. Other wetlands have become almost permanently dry. The animals and plants in these wetlands then cannot play their normal roles in the web of life.

Algal blooms occur when there are high levels of nutrients in the water. Waste from grazing stock, treated sewage from towns, pasture run-off, fertilisers and waste from industries all increase nutrient and pollution levels in the water and result in algal blooms.
Algal blooms smother aquatic plants and decrease the oxygen in the water, which affects the fish life. People who come into contact with affected water can suffer skin irritations, nausea, vomiting, diarrhoea and liver damage.

Many river red gums are dying and thousands are severely stressed from salinity and lack of water. Because of irrigation and other uses, red river gums in flood plains no longer receive frequent floodwater. The loss of these trees reduces shade over rivers and decreases inputs such as wood debris and organic material like leaves and insects.

*River red gums under stress*

*Algal bloom*

Cleared vegetation near rivers increases run-off containing sediment, which can settle onto the stream bed. Sediment can fill pools, smother plants and clog fish gills, causing them to suffocate. Fish that need to see their prey to feed suffer, as visibility is poor. Silt in the water reduces the amount of light, impacting on aquatic plant growth.

Changes in river flow, barriers such as dams and weirs, poor water quality, removal of habitat, overfishing and the introduction of exotic fish (such as European carp) have made it more difficult for native fish species to survive. Carp makes up to 95 per cent of the local fish stock in some sections of the Murray River. Clean, clear water is important for fish breeding.

*A river out of balance*

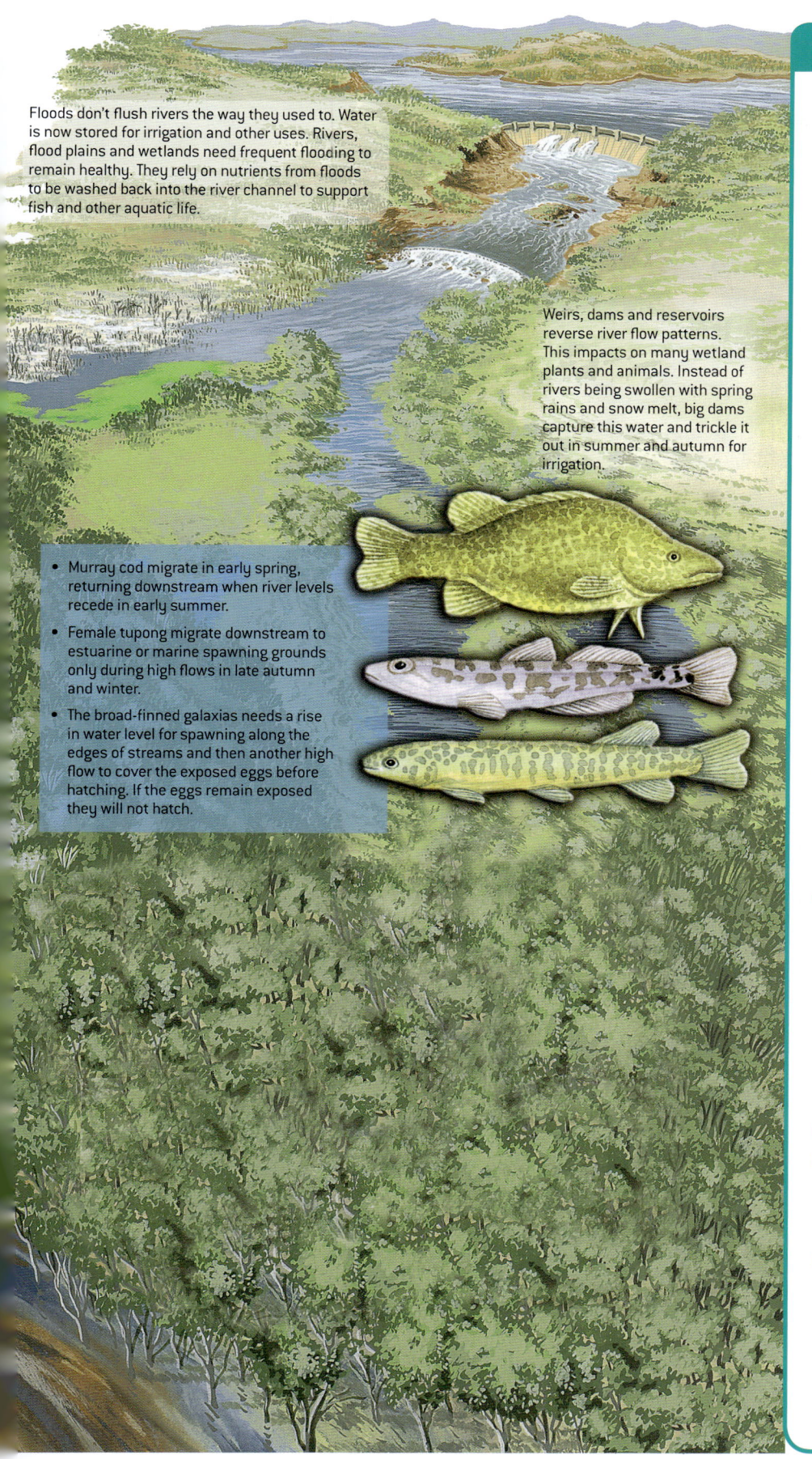

Floods don't flush rivers the way they used to. Water is now stored for irrigation and other uses. Rivers, flood plains and wetlands need frequent flooding to remain healthy. They rely on nutrients from floods to be washed back into the river channel to support fish and other aquatic life.

Weirs, dams and reservoirs reverse river flow patterns. This impacts on many wetland plants and animals. Instead of rivers being swollen with spring rains and snow melt, big dams capture this water and trickle it out in summer and autumn for irrigation.

- Murray cod migrate in early spring, returning downstream when river levels recede in early summer.
- Female tupong migrate downstream to estuarine or marine spawning grounds only during high flows in late autumn and winter.
- The broad-finned galaxias needs a rise in water level for spawning along the edges of streams and then another high flow to cover the exposed eggs before hatching. If the eggs remain exposed they will not hatch.

## ACTIVITIES

### UNDERSTANDING

1. Draw up a table with two columns listing a river's inputs and outputs.
2. What is algal bloom? What are its causes? How does it impact on water quality? What can be done about it?
3. Why are naturally occurring floods important to a river?
4. What are the advantages of river red gums? Why are they dying? Suggest how this trend could be reversed.
5. Describe the impacts of dams on river flow, wetlands and fish. Suggest how these issues could be better managed.
6. Discuss the impacts of human interaction on fish species.

### THINKING AND APPLYING

7. Identify the factors that result in a river and a wetland being out of balance. For each one, describe the changes required to bring it back into balance.
8. As a concerned Adelaide resident, write a letter to a newspaper describing how you feel about the quality of your drinking water and what could be done to improve it.
9. *Fieldwork and RAP*: Research the health of a river or stream in your local area. Describe the impacts of human activities and propose actions to promote sustainability. To find out if the New South Wales Government has plans for your site, use the **Rivers** weblink in your eBookPLUS.

### USING YOUR SKILLS

10. Draw a flow diagram showing how clearing vegetation impacts on run-off, river quality and marine species.
11. Imagine you were employed to improve the health of the river and wetlands illustrated on these pages. Redraw the river, indicating what actions you would take and where you would take them.

CHAPTER 8 | Land and water management    213

# 8.11 The Georges River catchment

The Georges River begins south of Sydney in upland swamps on the Woronora Plateau and meanders across its **flood plain** through the Sydney suburbs, including Liverpool and Bankstown. It completes its 97-kilometre journey by flowing through a broad, **drowned river valley** into Botany Bay.

The catchment has an area of 920 square kilometres and is an incredibly varied place. It has some of Sydney's oldest and newest suburbs, the nation's largest tip and Australia's only nuclear reactor at Lucas Heights. It contains Aboriginal art sites, sandmines and coalmines, endangered plant and animal communities and a military firing range. Fortunately for the Georges River, approximately 40 per cent of its catchment comprises bushland. Water that is filtered through bush and swamp remains clean. The Woronora River, one of the main tributaries, provides many homes in southern Sydney with clean drinking water.

With already more than one million people in the catchment, urban run-off and sewer overflows are a problem. Thousands of new houses will be built. Although there are more than 350 sewer overflow points in the catchment, it is the impact of polluted run-off from streets, roofs and other hard surfaces that is the biggest contributor to poor water quality in the river. The catchment is under pressure and needs to be managed in a sustainable manner. Key issues include urban development, water quality, erosion, loss of biodiversity, floods, mining and the need to conserve special places.

As part of the management of water catchments, it is important to educate residents and the community in general about matters that affect their water supply. The Georges River Environmental Education Centre at Chipping Norton is available for school visits and provides field studies and excursions. The centre is a joint initiative of the NSW Department of Education and Training and Liverpool City Council (the centre can be contacted on 02 9755 3189). It has a fully trained teaching staff and uses sites on the river and in the surrounding wetlands, mangroves, bushland and urban communities.

[The authors are grateful to Sharyn Cullis of the Georges River Environmental Education Centre for assistance in compiling the information on these pages.]

## ACTIVITIES

### UNDERSTANDING
1. What is a catchment? (See page 192.)
2. Explain the importance of catchment management.
3. Describe the location of the Georges River catchment.

### USING YOUR SKILLS
4. Study the map on the next page.
   a. What is the main reservoir in the catchment?
   b. List nine suburbs in the Georges River catchment.
   c. What is the name of the catchment to the north of the Georges River catchment?
   d. Name three tributaries of the Georges River.
   e. Which tributary of the Georges River is most likely to be affected by industrial pollution?
   f. Where does the water of the catchment end up?
   g. Describe the nature of human interaction in the Georges River catchment. What impact does this have on the quality of the water?
5. Refer to the photographs on the next page.
   a. How many waterfalls can you see in the photograph from the upper catchment?
   b. Is the photograph of flood in the mid catchment an oblique or ground view?
      i. Make a sketch of this photograph as it might appear when not in flood. Show the normal course of the river, main transport routes, industrial land and residential land.
      ii. What type of land use do you think takes place on the area covered by floodwaters?
   c. The background of the mid-catchment photograph (far right, top) gives a clue to why the foreground is so important. Explain.
   d. What evidence relating to water quality is provided in the photograph of the stormwater pipe in the mid catchment?
   e. What impact on the water system is shown in the ground level photograph of new housing developments on the riverbank?
   f. Rank the photographs from low impact on the environment to high impact.
   g. Suggest different management strategies for the upper, mid and lower catchments.

### GEOTERMS

**drowned river valley:** melting of continental icecaps following the last ice age, which saw sea levels rise and drown coastal river valleys

**flood plain:** part of a river valley covered by water during floods

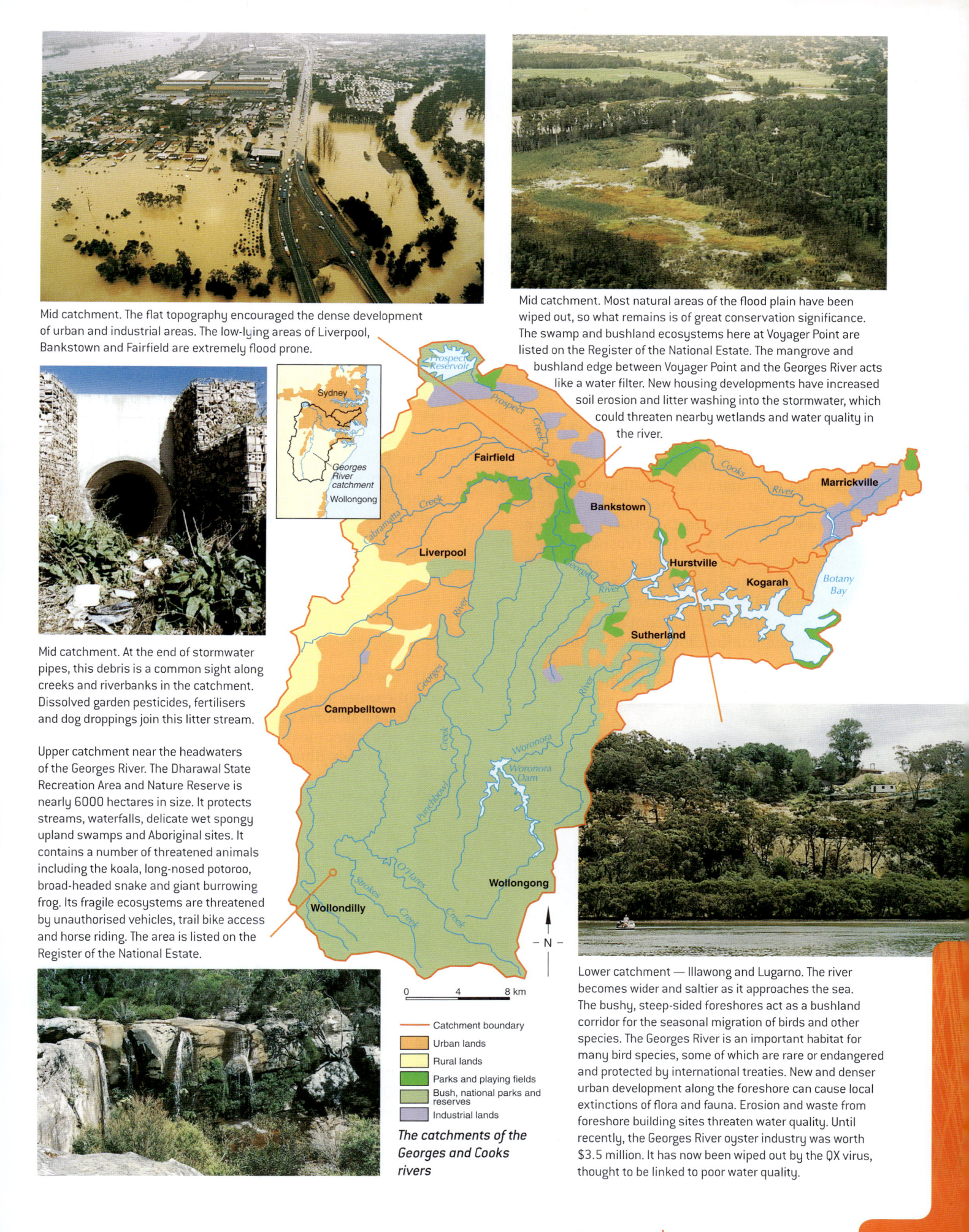

Mid catchment. The flat topography encouraged the dense development of urban and industrial areas. The low-lying areas of Liverpool, Bankstown and Fairfield are extremely flood prone.

Mid catchment. Most natural areas of the flood plain have been wiped out, so what remains is of great conservation significance. The swamp and bushland ecosystems here at Voyager Point are listed on the Register of the National Estate. The mangrove and bushland edge between Voyager Point and the Georges River acts like a water filter. New housing developments have increased soil erosion and litter washing into the stormwater, which could threaten nearby wetlands and water quality in the river.

Mid catchment. At the end of stormwater pipes, this debris is a common sight along creeks and riverbanks in the catchment. Dissolved garden pesticides, fertilisers and dog droppings join this litter stream.

Upper catchment near the headwaters of the Georges River. The Dharawal State Recreation Area and Nature Reserve is nearly 6000 hectares in size. It protects streams, waterfalls, delicate wet spongy upland swamps and Aboriginal sites. It contains a number of threatened animals including the koala, long-nosed potoroo, broad-headed snake and giant burrowing frog. Its fragile ecosystems are threatened by unauthorised vehicles, trail bike access and horse riding. The area is listed on the Register of the National Estate.

**The catchments of the Georges and Cooks rivers**

- Catchment boundary
- Urban lands
- Rural lands
- Parks and playing fields
- Bush, national parks and reserves
- Industrial lands

Lower catchment — Illawong and Lugarno. The river becomes wider and saltier as it approaches the sea. The bushy, steep-sided foreshores act as a bushland corridor for the seasonal migration of birds and other species. The Georges River is an important habitat for many bird species, some of which are rare or endangered and protected by international treaties. New and denser urban development along the foreshore can cause local extinctions of flora and fauna. Erosion and waste from foreshore building sites threaten water quality. Until recently, the Georges River oyster industry was worth $3.5 million. It has now been wiped out by the QX virus, thought to be linked to poor water quality.

# 8.12 Managing Sydney's water

Supplying Sydney with abundant, fresh, high-quality water is an important geographical issue. Although Sydney's average rainfall is above world standards, it is unreliable. For this reason, its dams store eight years of water compared with twelve weeks' storage in London. The 2006 Sydney Water Plan aims to provide high-quality water to meet the needs of a growing city, taking into account the impacts of El Niño, droughts and climate change.

## Managing quantity and quality

The Sydney Catchment Authority includes Sydney, Illawarra and the Blue Mountains. The four main rivers in the catchment are the Upper Nepean, Warragamba, Woronora and Shoalhaven rivers. The largest dam is Warragamba, storing four times the amount of water held in Sydney Harbour, and the main distribution reservoir is at Prospect.

In 1998, micro-organisms called *Cryptosporidium* and *Giardia* were detected in Sydney's drinking water. An inquiry into the incident led to the creation of the Sydney Catchment Authority, which works with communities, local councils, industries, environmental groups, government agencies and landowners to manage and protect the catchment. Sydney Water buys untreated water from the Sydney Catchment Authority and treats the water at filtration plants. Treated water is distributed to 4.3 million customers via 21 000 km of water mains, 261 reservoirs and 155 pumping stations.

Sydney dwellers have a large unsustainable **water footprint**. The average daily water consumption is 1610 megalitres — enough to fill the Olympic Stadium at Homebush Bay to the top of its highest stand 100 times over. Saving water is part of the government's plan for a sustainable water supply. Already, the quantity of water used today is less than in 1970, even with an extra one million people. The reduction in water use per person is due to the responses of individuals, groups and governments with strategies such as:

- the distribution of 90 000 Do-It-Yourself Water Saving Kits
- mandatory water-restrictions, which have reduced water use by 15 per cent
- installation of water-efficient taps and fittings in 500 000 households
- the Every Drop Counts Business Program, which saves 38 million litres of water every day.

## Recycling, desalination and carbon trading

By 2015 the Sydney catchment will recycle 12 per cent of the water supplied. In 2009, 160 000 homes in Sydney's new suburbs received recycled water. The use of waste water meant that Sydney Water's largest customer, BlueScope Steel at Port Kembla, reduced the amount of drinking water drawn from the Avon Dam by 7.3 billion litres a year. Sydney Water's Replacement Flows project saves drinking water and provides 18 billion litres of recycled water each year to the Hawkesbury–Nepean river system.

In 2007, dams were only 34 per cent full. To reduce fears of running out of water, the government is constructing a desalination plant, powered by renewable energy. It aims to produce 15 per cent of Sydney's water supply. Sydney Water uses one per cent of all the energy consumed in New South Wales. By 2020, it aims to be **carbon neutral** by eliminating 400 000 tonnes of carbon dioxide each year — equivalent to taking 100 000 cars off the road. It also aims to use renewable energy from cogeneration and hydro-electricity. Cogeneration harnesses biogas, a waste product of the waste-water treatment process at Malabar.

*Warragamba Dam, looking upstream*

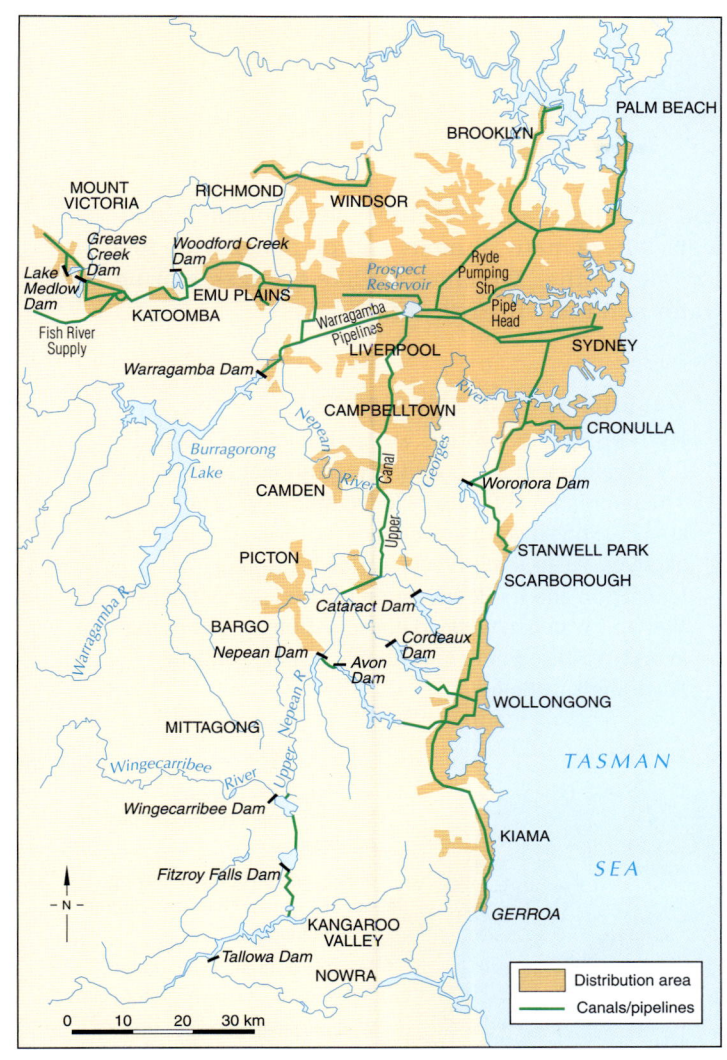

*The Sydney water supply system*

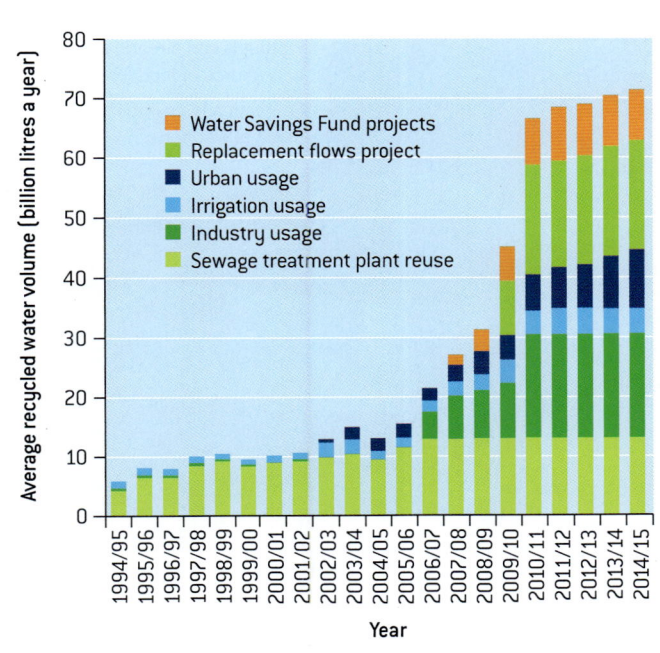

*Recycled water in Sydney: 70 billion litres a year by 2015*

## GEOfacts

**Sydney Water:**
- supplies 1.4 billion litres to 1.7 million homes and businesses a day
- collects and treats 1.3 billion litres of waste water a day
- recycles 58 million litres of waste water a day.

## ACTIVITIES

### UNDERSTANDING

1. Describe the functions of Sydney Water, Sydney Catchment Authority and Sydney Water's Replacement Flows project.
2. Explain why Sydney's water should be managed sustainably.
3. Discuss how recycling, desalination and carbon trading can reduce Sydney's large water and carbon footprints.
4. Discuss the responses of individuals, groups and governments to the sustainable management of Sydney's water quantity and quality.

### THINKING AND APPLYING

5. As groups, design and implement a water audit of your school. Discuss how the school could reduce its water footprint. Present findings as a report to the principal. For more help use the **Sustainable Schools**, **Every Drop Counts in Schools** and **Rainwater Tanks in Schools** weblinks in your eBookPLUS.

### USING YOUR SKILLS

6. Refer to the photograph on the previous page. Sketch the Warragamba Dam. Label the spillway (channel that carries away surplus water from the top of the dam wall), the dam wall, Burragorang Lake (formed by the dam), roadways and natural vegetation. From what direction is the photograph taken?
7. Refer to the map on this page of Sydney's water supply system. Use it to sketch a map of Sydney's water supply system. Label the main streams, dams and pipelines. Shade in the main distribution area. Explain the journey of water from its source to a home in Palm Beach, Kiama and Campbelltown. What is the length of the Upper Canal? What direction does the canal run from Wollongong to Gerroa?
8. Refer to the graph of recycled water. Compare water use and water recycling in 1995 with 2015. How much recycled water is attributed to the Water Savings Fund from 2008 to 2015? How much water did the Replacement Flows project recycle from 2010 to 2015? Describe the impacts of recycled water on the environment.

**CHAPTER 8** | Land and water management

# 8.13 Nature of wetlands and inland rivers

Wetlands and inland rivers are special environments in Australia. They function very differently but both are important aquatic habitats.

## Wetlands

A **wetland** is an area of land covered by water at least some of the time. **Billabongs** and **intertidal zones** are wetlands that are covered by water only some of the time. Wetlands can also be natural or artificial.

Billabongs, swamps, estuaries and flood plains are all examples of different types of wetlands. They have different names depending on their size, the amount of water they contain or whether they contain fresh or salt water. Nutrients in the flowing water mean that wetlands support many plants and animals — and sometimes very complex food webs where many animals and plants provide food for one another. Wetlands act like sponges, storing water and reducing run-off.

### Wasteland to valuable resource

By 1993, half the world's wetlands had been drained for development or flooded as recreational lakes. The international Ramsar Convention (1971) aims to conserve 65 Australian wetlands, covering 7.5 million hectares. Australia protects wetlands through legislation and implementation of management plans. Wetland Watch, a wetland conservation project of the World Wildlife Fund, aims to rehabilitate some of Australia's wetlands.

- Wetlands support many important animals.
- Muddy and dirty water moving out of a wetland has been filtered and cleaned.
- Many birds breed in Australia's wetlands, including migratory birds.
- Wetlands help to reduce the impact of floods.
- Many native animals and plants will breed and feed in wetlands.
- Wetlands can directly and indirectly be a source of food for people.
- Recreation is an important use made of wetlands.

*Wetlands are valuable places that need to be conserved.*

Lake Eyre in flood 2009

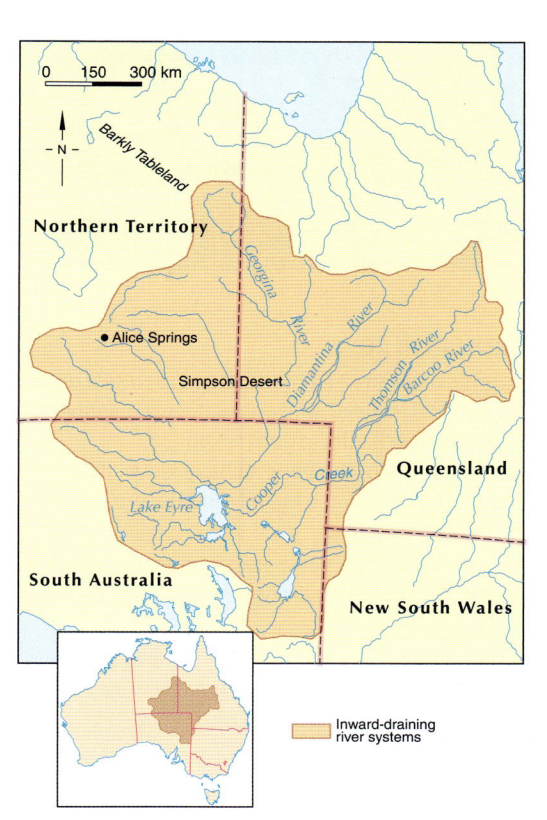

The Lake Eyre Basin and the inward-draining rivers

# Inland rivers

Although many of Australia's rivers flow out to sea, there are also a number that flow inland to the Lake Eyre Basin, one of the world's largest internally draining river systems. The Cooper and the Diamantina rivers are two of the most variable large rivers in the world. These rivers are ephemeral (they last only for a short time, often not flowing for months on end) but can then experience extreme flooding to levels greater than those on the Nile River.

The Lake Eyre Basin covers one-sixth of the continent. It is situated in the most arid part of Australia with an annual rainfall of less than 125 millimetres and a very high evaporation rate. Lake Eyre, 15 metres below sea level, is Australia's lowest point.

The level of water in Lake Eyre was at its highest in 1974. To keep this record level constant, Lake Eyre would need a river with the average flow of the Murray River flowing into it.

When in flood, such as in 2009 after record rainfall in western Queensland, the basin's flood plains extend over tens of thousands of kilometres. During the 'boom' time of floods, the waters support a huge amount of life — algae, plankton, crustaceans, fish, tortoises, water rats and birds. Hundreds of thousands of birds arrive to feed and breed, including waders from Siberia.

When the 'bust' occurs and the rivers and flood plains dry up, some species hide (frogs can burrow); some die, leaving eggs behind for the next 'boom'; and others, such as birds, leave.

## ACTIVITIES

### UNDERSTANDING
1. Explain the importance of wetlands.
2. Discuss the impacts of humans on wetlands.

### THINKING AND APPLYING
3. What does it mean for a wetland to be in a boom or bust cycle? Refer to the photograph above of Lake Eyre in flood and list evidence to support either a boom or a bust time.

### USING YOUR SKILLS
4. Refer to the map above. List the names of five rivers that drain into Lake Eyre. What is the length of the Diamantina River? What is the area of Lake Eyre?

## GEOTERMS

**billabong:** small wetland associated with a river channel that is isolated during low-flow periods and can be flushed during a flood

**intertidal zone:** area between low and high water marks that is exposed at low tide

**wetland:** area covered permanently or occasionally by fresh or salt water up to a depth of six metres

CHAPTER 8 | Land and water management

# Working geographically

## BROADSHEET: CRISIS IN THE MURRAY–DARLING BASIN

### EXTENDED RESPONSE

1. Use the material presented on these pages to write a report on the geographical issue of land and water management in the Murray–Darling Basin. In your response:
   - describe the nature of the geographical issue, its impacts and the responses by individuals, groups and governments to the issue
   - describe how the interaction between the physical and human elements of the environment has contributed to the issue
   - explain how effective various strategies have been in managing the issue. What still needs to be done?

### Murray–Darling Basin

In 2007, the Basin was in a critical condition as a result of a prolonged drought. The federal government proposed a $10 billion take-over of the Murray–Darling Basin (MDB), arguing that effective management could not be undertaken by competing state governments (NSW, ACT, Queensland, Victoria, South Australia). Australia's *Water Act 2007* now enables water resources in the MDB to be managed in the national interest. The Act established an independent Murray–Darling Basin Authority with powers to ensure that water resources are managed in an integrated and sustainable way. However, the first Basin Plan is not expected to start until 2011.

### Solving the crisis in the lower lakes

No water is flowing to the sea at the Murray mouth, and Lakes Alexandrina and Albert are currently below sea level. Barrages prevent sea water from reaching the lakes, but the freshwater lakes are at risk. Possible solutions include:
- releasing some fresh water from places like the Menindee Lakes on the Darling River to try to raise the lakes above sea level
- opening the barrages to sea water, which would affect freshwater habitats and species
- a government buy-back of water licences to reduce water extracted by irrigators
- supplementing the lake water with ground water pumped from nearby aquifers
- cloud seeding to try to boost rainfall over the lake.

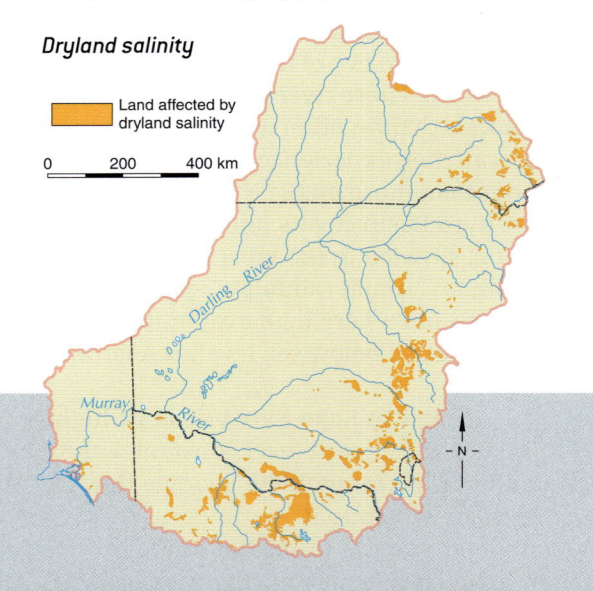

*Dryland salinity*

Land affected by dryland salinity

0  200  400 km

## Big dry to hit Murray system

**BY ASA WAHLQUIST**

Climate change will be one of the greatest challenges for the new Murray–Darling Basin Authority, which begins operations this week.

Wendy Craik, chief executive of the Murray–Darling Basin Commission for the past four years, warned that the potential climate changes could be 'quite significant', particularly in the south of the basin.

The Rudd Government's white paper says average streamflow in the Murray–Darling Basin is projected to drop by 10 to 25 per cent, while the frequency of drought could increase 40 per cent by 2030. Irrigated agriculture in the basin would virtually end, suffering a massive 92 per cent fall.

'You can't rely on the averages', Dr Craik said.

'You have to be cautious even about the extremes. We were caught out in 2006–07 when inflow went below the minimum we used for planning.'

Inflow into the basin rivers fell to an unprecedented low in 2006–07 — less than 60 per cent of the previous minimum . . .

There has been a sharp drop in autumn and late-winter rainfall over the basin. 'This is associated with the intensification of the sub-tropical ridge, which is associated with global warming'. Average rainfall no longer resulted in average inflow, Dr Craik said.

'For every degree centigrade rise in temperature, you get a 15 per cent reduction in inflows. Overall rainfall in this drought in volume is not so different from previous droughts, but the inflows have been a lot different. You would have to say there is something else at play here.'

*Source: Sydney Morning Herald, 20 March 2009.*

## Too much water under the bridge

BY ASA WAHLQUIST

Under natural conditions, before the Murray River was dammed and its waters taken for towns and farms, an average of 12 890 billion litres (gigalitres) flowed through the lower lakes, out the mouth and into the sea south of Adelaide.

The lower lakes were a natural estuary, fed by the fresh waters of the Murray, with some tidal or seawater incursions. But settlement along the river began to change the balance. By the 1890s more and more fresh water was being taken, and the lakes were becoming more saline. Salt water, at times, went up the river as far as Murray Bridge, about 100 km from the mouth, threatening the local water supply.

Between 1932 and 1940, barrages were built, separating the salt water of the Coorong from the fresh water of the lower lakes. This resulted in an ecological change for the lower lakes, from an estuary to fresh water.

It has been more than a decade since 12 890 GL flowed into the Murray itself, let alone through the mouth. Over the past decade inflows into the Murray River have fallen 38 per cent. Drought and over-allocation of water closed the mouth in 2002. It has been kept open since only by constant dredging.

No one saw the long drought coming. But governments have known for 20 years that too much water was being taken from the river. They agreed water had to be returned to the environment, but they argued the details long and hard, and hesitated again and again to act.

Any changes have been, to quote the late Peter Cullen, glacially slow.

Take 'The Living Murray': the $700 million program aims to return 500 GL to six sites on the river. Five years later, it is highly unlikely to reach its target of 500 GL next year. And 500 GL is only a fraction of what is needed; the independent Murray–Darling Basin Commissioner, Ian Kowalick, thinks 2500 GL must be returned to the river.

There is not enough water in storage to save the lower lakes. Meeting human needs this year will be a challenge, and heaven help those who depend on the Murray if next year's rainfall is a repeat of the past two years.

That means there is only one solution to preventing the lower lakes drying out and acidifying, and suffering irreversible damage. That solution is opening the barrages, and letting salt water in.

That will also necessitate building a weir where the river enters the lower lakes, to prevent salt water travelling up the river and affecting the water that supplies almost all of South Australia.

Letting in salt water would be the third huge ecological shock the lower lakes have experienced in 120 years — from estuary to fresh water, to salt water. The damage would be incalculable, but the alternative, acidification, is worse.

That it has come to this is a terrible indictment of how Australians have managed one of our greatest natural assets.

*Source: The Australian, 8 August 2009.*

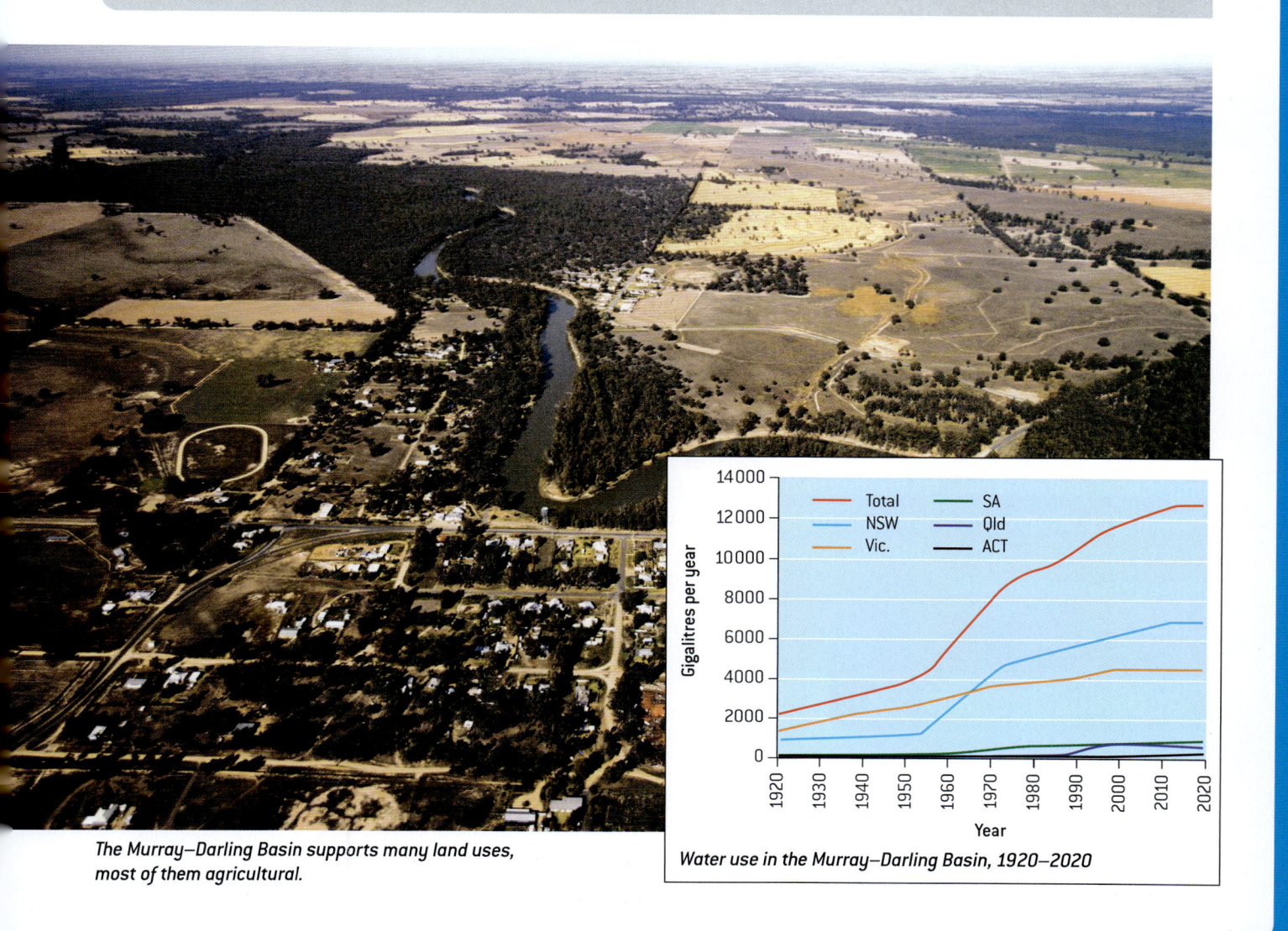

*The Murray–Darling Basin supports many land uses, most of them agricultural.*

*Water use in the Murray–Darling Basin, 1920–2020*

# 9 Coastal management

**INQUIRY QUESTIONS**

+ Which coastal processes erode and build coastlines?
+ What are the impacts of physical and human elements on coastal processes?
+ Why is it important to manage land, water and waste for sustainable coastal ecosystems?
+ How do individuals, groups and governments respond to coastal issues such as climate change and pollution?

Australia has 37 000 kilometres of coastline, 11 000 beaches, and stunning coastal landforms such as the Twelve Apostles, the Nullarbor Coast and Fraser Island. Despite their beauty, coastal environments are under stress from natural processes such as cyclones and storm surges. Wetlands and dunes have been cleared for development as more people settle in coastal areas. Understanding coastal processes and the impacts of polluted coastal waters and global warming on people and environments will lead to informed, sustainable and equitable management strategies.

## GEOskills TOOLBOX

**GEOskillbuilder** Coastal fieldwork and research action plan (pages 248–49)

+ Reading and interpreting a synoptic chart (page 228)
+ Interpreting a vegetation transect (page 235)

*Perhaps Australia's best known beach, Bondi Beach is a one-kilometre-long stretch of sand surrounded by development in Australia's most populous city.*

### KEY TERMS

**back dunes:** dunes that develop behind the fore dunes. They may be stabilised by small shrubs and trees.

**beach nourishment:** artificial placement of sand on a beach

**blowhole:** a hole in the roof of a coastal cave, produced by wave erosion, through which compressed air and water are forced as waves break into the cave

**blowout:** a bare depression in a sand dune caused when loose sand is blown from the dune because vegetation has been removed

**climate change:** a long-term, significant change in the average weather that a region experiences

**deposition:** the laying down of material carried by rivers, wind, ice, ocean currents and waves

**dune (coastal):** a mass that forms along shorelines, usually composed of sand formed from loose particles of rock and other materials such as shells and coral

**ecosystem:** a system formed by the interactions between the living organisms (plants, animals, humans) and the physical elements of an environment (land, water)

**environmental impact statement (EIS):** investigation of the impact of building development on the physical environment, as well as the social and economic impacts

**erosion:** the wearing away of soil and rock by wind and water

**estuary:** tidal mouth of a river where the salt water of the tide meets the fresh water of the river current

**fore dunes:** sand dunes closest to the surf

**global warming:** the increase in average temperature of the Earth's atmosphere and oceans since the mid twentieth century, and its projected continuation

**longshore drift:** the movement of sand and other materials along the shore

**perspective:** a way of viewing the world

**spit:** narrow deposit of sand and other materials that extends out into a body of water

**stack:** a column of rock, isolated from the shore by the corrosive action of waves

**storm surge:** a dome of water, about 60 to 80 kilometres across and two to five metres higher than the normal tide level, resulting from an intense storm system

**sustainable development:** development that meets the needs of the present population without endangering the ability of future generations to meet their own needs

**tide:** the daily rise and fall of the ocean and its inlets, due to the attraction of the moon and sun

**tsunami:** an ocean wave caused by an earthquake or volcanic eruption beneath the sea, travelling at high speed and causing massive destruction along coasts

**wave-cut notch:** a hollow eroded by the impact of waves at the foot of a cliff

# 9.1 Coastal management: a geographical issue

Nine out of ten Australians live within 50 kilometres of the coast. By the year 2030, it is estimated that 21 million people are likely to live near the coast. As well as being the favourite place to live, the coast is the most popular destination for tourists and visitors of all ages. Industry is also drawn to coastal areas because of access to transport. Nearly 50 per cent of Australia's gross domestic product is produced in coastal urban areas. All of the activities impact on coastal environments and **ecosystems** as well as on the quality of life we experience as residents or visitors. It is clear that Australia's coasts need to be managed.

### GEOfacts
- All urban centres in Australia with populations of more than 500 000 are located on the coastal fringe of the continent.
- Between 1974 and 1989, one-third of the coastal vegetation along the south-east coast of Queensland was removed.
- Around Perth, 70 per cent of the original wetlands have been cleared.

## The coastal zone

The coastal zone includes the coastal hinterland and the inner continental shelf as well as everything in between, such as beaches and estuaries. The coast is the interface where the ocean meets the land. Within Australia's coastal zone there are many different environments, including mountain ranges, flood plains, rivers and lakes, rainforests, wetlands, mangrove areas, estuaries, beaches, coral reefs, seagrass beds and the continental shelf.

All these environments must be managed in a sustainable manner to enable future generations to enjoy Australia's natural beauty. **Sustainable development** and management means that our use of coastal resources must meet the needs of the present population without endangering the ability of future generations to meet their own needs.

*The coast is the interface where the ocean meets the land. This aerial photograph shows the coastline between the Nullarbor Plain and the Great Australian Bight.*

The majority of Australia's World Heritage sites are located in the coastal zone. For example, the Great Barrier Reef, Lord Howe Island, Fraser Island and Shark Bay are part of Australia's cultural and natural heritage. Many Aboriginal and Torres Strait Islander heritage sites are found within the coastal zone. The identification and preservation of middens, art sites, fish traps, stone and ochre quarries, burial and religious sites must be considered when developing management plans.

Coastal environments have not always been managed sustainably. In the past, decision makers had limited knowledge about the fragile nature of many coastal ecosystems and they had different **perspectives** about the use of coastal areas. Their aim was to develop coastal areas for short-term economic gains. This was based on the belief that nature's resources were limitless. Building high-rise apartments and tourist resorts on sand dunes seemed a good idea — until they fell into the sea when cyclones eroded the shoreline.

*The Great Barrier Reef was placed on the World Heritage List in 1981.*

## SAMPLE STUDY

### Coastal erosion leads to action

From 1967 to 1974, erosion events along the east coast were so severe that they changed ideas about coastal management. Communities and governments wanted to know more about coastal processes to help them manage the problems. Information was gathered from new systems such as wave-rider buoys (which measure wave height and period), time-lapse photography, storm surge recordings and sediment analysis. This information was used to plan and manage programs such as **beach nourishment**.

There was also a growing awareness that coastal management must consider the perspectives of different communities, interest groups and individuals to ensure social justice and equity. The New South Wales Coast Government Policy stated: 'The government [must] ensure the responsible and productive management of the 1100-kilometre strip of land along the New South Wales coast. The efficient management of this land has been plagued by a history of haphazard development and the absence of a clear conservation strategy. This is not acceptable.'

*Bilgola 1974*

1. Homes rebuilt on fore dune since 1974
2. Coastal development
3. Headlands eroding
4. Increased width of beach — erodes easily after storms.

*Bilgola Beach 2008. Homes worth millions of dollars have been rebuilt on the fore dune. Pittwater Council continually adds sand to the beach after storms.*

Over time, people have realised that coastal management requires an understanding of the processes that affect coastal environments. To manage the coast sustainably we need to understand:
- the coastal environment and the effect of physical processes
- the effect of human activities within the coastal zone
- the different perspectives of coastal users
- how to achieve a balance between conservation and development
- how decisions are made about the ways in which coasts will be used
- how to evaluate the success of individuals, groups and the levels of governments in managing coastal issues.

## ACTIVITIES

### UNDERSTANDING

1. When do you visit the beach, and why?
2. Describe the changes in the attitudes of communities and governments, following erosion along the east coast from 1967 to 1974.
3. Discuss the impacts of erosion on homes built on fore dunes.

### THINKING AND APPLYING

4. Draw a mind map showing the impacts of humans on coastal environments.
5. Collect five articles on coastal development. Select one article and present your information using the geographical issues scaffold (see section 7.1).
6. Explain why an understanding of coastal processes is essential for sustainable management.

### USING YOUR SKILLS

7. Sketch the photographs of Bilgola Beach in 1974 and 2008. What conclusions can you reach about the change over time?

### GEOTERMS

**ecosystem:** system formed by the interactions between the living organisms (plants, animals, humans) and the physical elements of an environment (land, water)

**sustainable development:** development that meets the needs of the present population without endangering the ability of future generations to meet their own needs

CHAPTER 9 | Coastal management — 225

# 9.2 Coastal landforms

About 85 per cent of Australia's population lives in coastal towns and cities (more than 25 per cent within three kilometres of the coast). This means that beaches and other coastal landforms are familiar sights for most people. Most of the coastal features we see today were formed in the last 6000 years, after the sea reached its present level.

Coastal landforms are formed by two main processes — *erosion* and *deposition*. Some of the landforms resulting from erosion are cliffs, rock platforms, headlands, caves, blowholes, stacks and arches. In places sheltered from strong winds and wave attack, sediments are deposited to form features such as beaches, *spits*, *dunes*, *estuaries* and lagoons.

## Builders and destroyers

How is it that waves can both erode and build coastlines? Wind and waves transfer energy to the coast. (If you've ever been dumped by a large wave, you will be aware of how much energy it contains!)

When the weather is very windy and waves are large, energy transferred to the coast can erode rocks and move sediment. Such waves are called destructive waves. Some coastal rocks are harder than others and resist erosion; other rocks are softer and erode more easily.

Constructive waves are smaller and contain less energy — they carry sand or other material up the beach in the swash and deposit it there. (Beaches are formed by constructive waves.) Destructive waves carry more material to deep water in the backwash.

Storm surges are a build-up of water in the coastal zone by strong winds blowing from the sea towards the land. Storm surge waves can cause severe erosion.

Dune **blowouts** occur when loose sand is blown from the dune because vegetation has been removed.

Waves are refracted (bent towards) a headland and release energy either side of it. Caves will be formed where weak rocks are eroded on each side of a headland.

Over time the caves will erode on either side of a headland and join to form an arch.

Erosion between low and high tides undercuts rocks and a rock platform develops. This undercut section eventually becomes weak and collapses, creating a cliff.

Estuaries are the parts of a river that are tidal and occur at the sea. They catch mud, sand and nutrients.

A lagoon is formed when a sandbar begins to develop, eventually closing an estuary.

Beaches are formed when material is brought to the shore by waves. The material can be sand, stones or pebbles.

Further erosion of the rock supporting the arch will cause it to collapse, leaving a stack.

Dunes are formed when sand on a beach is stabilised by vegetation.

*Coastal landforms*

## How are sand dunes formed?

Sand dunes are formed by the wind when dry sand is blown to the back of the beach and trapped. The initial dune is called the fore dune. Back dunes may develop behind the fore dune. Grass such as spinifex usually traps the sand. Over time other vegetation, such as shrubs and trees, will grow helping to stabilise the back dunes.

### GEOTERMS

**deposition:** laying down of material carried by rivers, wind, ice, ocean currents and waves

**dune (coastal):** a mass that forms along shorelines, usually composed of sand formed from loose particles of rock and other materials such as shells and coral

**erosion:** the wearing away of soil and rock by wind and water

**estuary:** tidal mouth of a river where the salt water of the tide meets the fresh water of the river current

**spit:** narrow deposit of sand and other material that extends out into a body of water

Longshore drift moves sand and other material along a beach. If this drift occurs mainly in one direction, sand may extend along the coastline forming a spit.

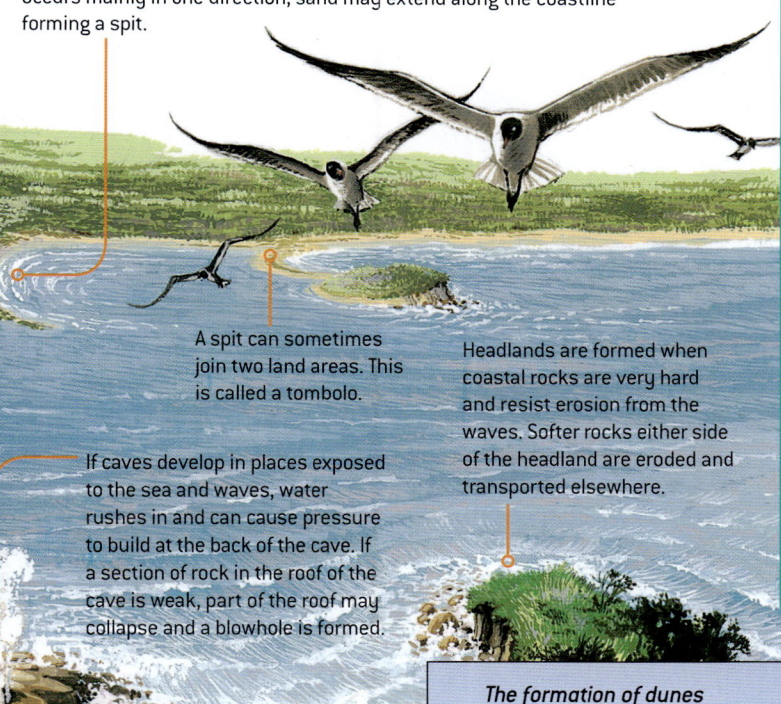

A spit can sometimes join two land areas. This is called a tombolo.

Headlands are formed when coastal rocks are very hard and resist erosion from the waves. Softer rocks either side of the headland are eroded and transported elsewhere.

If caves develop in places exposed to the sea and waves, water rushes in and can cause pressure to build at the back of the cave. If a section of rock in the roof of the cave is weak, part of the roof may collapse and a blowhole is formed.

### GEOfacts

New South Wales has 1100 kilometres of coastline with 721 ocean beaches.

### ACTIVITIES

**UNDERSTANDING**

1. What are the two main coastal processes that form coastal landforms?
2. Describe the type of weather and waves that erode coasts.
3. Explain how waves can both build and destroy coastlines.

**THINKING AND APPLYING**

4. Why might surfers flock to a beach after a storm at sea?
5. Redraw the coastal landforms illustration after the impacts of climate change. In your drawing, indicate the landforms that could be under the sea and those still above the sea.

**USING YOUR SKILLS**

Refer to the coastal landforms illustration and answer the following questions.

6. Select either true or false for the statements below. Rewrite the false statements to make them true.
   a. Headlands are made of softer rock than the surrounding landscape. T/F
   b. Rock platforms are usually submerged during low tide. T/F
   c. Caves form in the weakest part of a headland. T/F
   d. Beaches are an example of a deposition feature. T/F
   e. A spit is formed when a sandbar closes an estuary. T/F
   f. Estuaries trap nutrient-rich sediments. T/F
7. Explain why stacks provide evidence that the coastline was once further out to sea.
8. Discuss what happens over millions of years to eroded material that falls into the sea.
9. Explain how vegetation helps dune formation. What might happen if vegetation is removed?

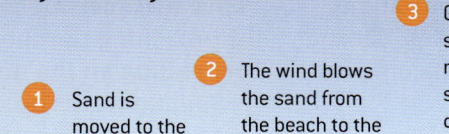

### The formation of dunes

1. Sand is moved to the beach in the swash.
2. The wind blows the sand from the beach to the fore dune.
3. Grasses such as spinifex and marram bind the sand to form a dune.
4. Small plants and shrubs grow to form a back dune.

Sea — Beach — Fore dune — Back dune

**CHAPTER 9** | Coastal management

# 9.3 Transportation processes

To manage the coast in a sustainable manner we need to understand the effect of physical processes on the coastal environment. Coastal landforms are produced by the processes of erosion, transportation and deposition, mainly through the action of waves, **tides** and currents. Landforms produced by erosion make up 27 per cent of Australia's coastlands and include cliffs, arches, caves and blowholes. Landforms produced by deposition make up 73 per cent of the coast and include alluvial plains and swamps (41 per cent), beaches, dunes, tombolos, spits and bars (24 per cent) and estuaries, lakes and lagoons (8 per cent).

## Ocean processes

The oceans occupy 71 per cent of the Earth's surface and therefore have a major influence on what happens on the remaining 29 per cent of the surface. This applies especially along coasts, the intersection point where ocean meets land. The eastern coast of Australia is influenced by processes taking place in the Pacific Ocean, the largest of all the oceans. The Pacific covers nearly one-third of the surface of the planet and includes the Tasman and Coral seas. Ocean processes that can have a major impact on coasts include waves, tides, currents, water temperature, salinity and tectonic forces.

## How are waves formed?

Waves are formed in the ocean and may originate thousands of kilometres away from the beach. Waves are usually formed by the wind blowing over the ocean. The size of a wave depends on the:
- wind velocity. Wave height increases exponentially as velocity increases. This is why waves associated with cyclones are larger than normal waves.
- length of the stretch of ocean over which the wind blows
- duration of time that the wind blows.

The largest waves are produced by strong winds blowing in a constant direction for a long time over a wide expanse of ocean.

Waves vary over time and space. This is called the wave climate and explains seasonal variations in the size, character and direction of waves. There are four main weather systems that produce waves along the New South Wales coast:
- tropical cyclones
- east coast lows
- mid-latitude cyclones
- high pressure systems.

### GEOskills TOOLBOX

**READING AND INTERPRETING A SYNOPTIC CHART**

Synoptic charts feature isobars. These are lines that join places with the same atmospheric pressure. Pressure readings above 1013 millibars are said to be high pressure regions. In the southern hemisphere, winds rotate in an anticlockwise direction. Low pressure regions are those below 1013 millibars. Winds in low pressure systems rotate in a clockwise direction in the southern hemisphere. Cold fronts are another key feature on Australian synoptic charts. These show the 'line' where an approaching mass of cold air meets warm air. The front moves in the direction shown by the arrowheads.

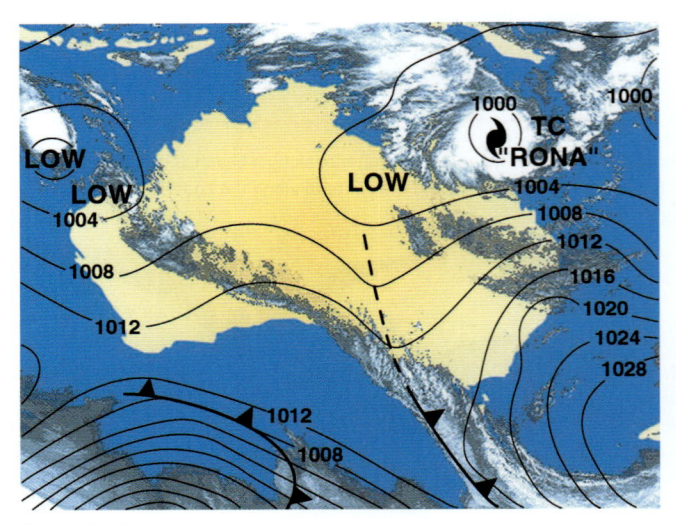

*Synoptic chart*

## What happens when waves reach the coast?

The water particles in a wave actually move in orbits within the wave. This orbital movement is interrupted by the seabed as the wave moves into shallow water. The base of the wave is slowed down by friction against the seabed while the top of the wave keeps going at the original speed. The wave becomes higher and then breaks. Waves approaching the shore break in different ways depending on the underlying topography offshore.
- *Spilling* waves occur where the seabed rises gently and the waves rise and break gently over a distance of several metres.
- *Plunging* waves are what surfers know as tubing waves because the waves curl over at the crest.

228  Geoactive 2

These waves occur where the seabed rises steeply causing waves to rise and break within a few metres.
- *Surging waves* occur where waves run up a very steep slope without appearing to break.

*Spilling wave*

*Plunging wave*

*Surging wave*

## Constructive and destructive waves

Coasts are built and eroded by the energy of waves. The water that rushes up a beach after a wave breaks is called the swash. The swash, which picks up sand and other material, travels up the beach in the same direction as the breaking wave. When this water returns down the beach to the sea it is called the backwash.

When waves are large and steep, the backwash becomes more powerful. These waves remove sand and other material from the beach and are called destructive waves. In contrast, constructive waves are lower and flatter and carry sediment up the beach. Steep destructive waves cause erosion of sand from beaches, whereas flatter, smaller constructive waves build up beaches.

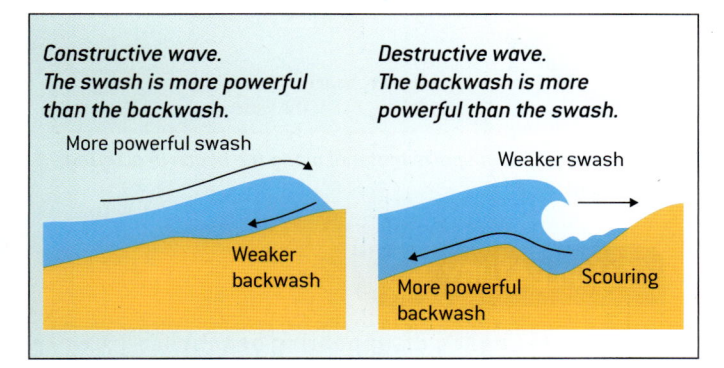

*Constructive wave. The swash is more powerful than the backwash.*

*Destructive wave. The backwash is more powerful than the swash.*

## Longshore drift

In addition to moving material into and out of beaches, waves move material along the shore. Waves rarely approach a beach at right angles. They usually approach at an angle that depends on the direction of the wind. The swash travels up the beach in the same direction as the breaking wave. Due to gravity, the direction of the backwash and any material it is carrying tends to be straight down the beach. The result is that material is transported along the beach in a zigzag movement. (You may have experienced this when you have ended up some distance along the beach from where you left your towel and entered the water.) This movement of material is called **longshore drift** and is usually in one direction only — that of the prevailing wind.

To reduce the loss of sand from longshore drift groynes (rock walls) are built from the land out into the water. The beaches to the south of the

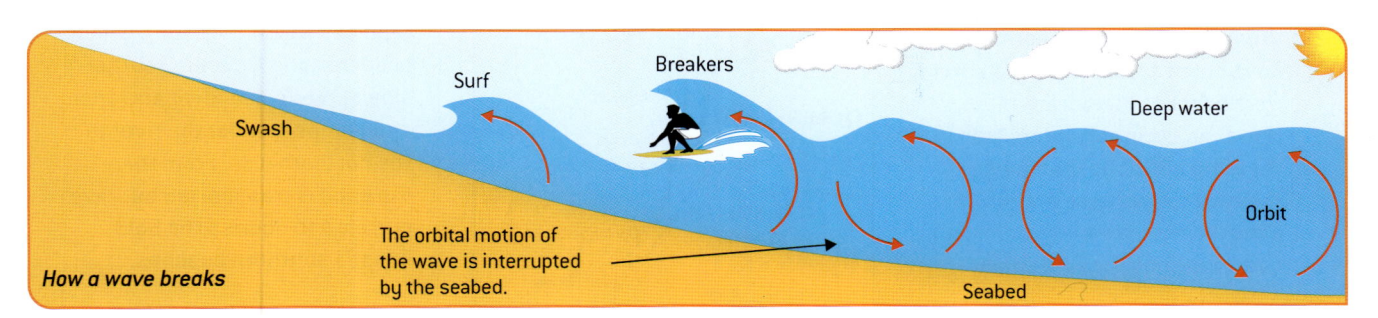

*How a wave breaks*

CHAPTER 9 | Coastal management

Maroochy River at Maroochydore on Queensland's Sunshine Coast experienced substantial erosion. This prompted the construction of four groynes and a seawall, which has successfully retained a wide beach.

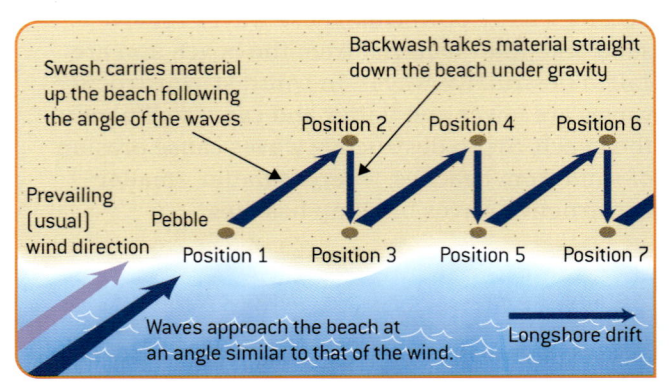

*Longshore drift transports material along the beach in a zigzag movement.*

*Managing longshore drift at Maroochydore*

### SAMPLE STUDY

**The Gold Coast's disappearing beaches: a geographical issue**

Some of the most popular beaches in Australia are located on the Gold Coast, the narrow coastal strip from the New South Wales border to Southport in Queensland. Over nine million visitors each year are attracted to its warm climate, good surfing waves, sandy beaches and theme parks, such as Movie World, Dreamworld, Wet'n'Wild and Sea World.

The Gold Coast is threatened by erosion. In 1967 five cyclones and four intense low pressure systems caused very destructive waves and severe erosion. Storm surges up to 0.9 metres threatened to sweep buildings into the sea. Property owners and businesspeople demanded action to protect their interests. The Gold Coast Council commissioned a report to investigate the problem. The report found two main problems:

1. Long-term erosion due to waves moving sand along the beaches in a northerly direction (longshore drift). This sand would normally have been replaced by sand arriving from beaches further south. However, the breakwaters built in the early 1960s at the mouth of the Tweed River were trapping the sand that would have replenished beaches along the Gold Coast.

2. Short-term erosion due to offshore–onshore movement of material. During calm seas, gentle constructive waves deposited material onto the beach but, during storms, destructive waves eroded the beach. A large amount of sand was eroded during storms and moved offshore where it was deposited as sandbars. Erosion takes only a short time. It takes a much longer time for constructive waves to gradually move this sand back to the beach.

Various management strategies have been tried, including:
- beach nourishment programs, such as revegetation, costing millions of dollars
- groynes built at right angles to the beach to help prevent longshore drift
- a protective boulder wall built along the Surfers Paradise esplanade in 1967. This prevented further damage to buildings and roads behind the beach but unfortunately it also interfered with the ability of the beach to rebuild itself from constructive waves.
- the Tweed River Entrance Sand Bypass Project (TRESBP), which collects sand from the southern side of the Tweed River entrance and pumps it under the river to the northern side. From there the sand is transported by wave currents to nourish the Gold Coast's southern beaches.

## Rips

Rips also move sediment. Rips are localised, fast-flowing currents that run out towards the sea. Rip currents depend on the height and duration of the waves and on the contours and shapes of the seabed. Many Australian beaches have dangerous rips, and too many people have died at our beaches simply because they did not swim in a safe area between the flags. Swimmers who are caught in a rip should not swim directly against the current. Most rips are fairly narrow so if they swim across the main direction of the current they should soon find themselves out of the rip and able to swim back to shore.

## Tides

Tides are due to the gravitational force of the moon and the sun acting on the rotating Earth. New South Wales tides are classified as micro-tidal, as the range (difference between high tides and low tides) is less than 2 metres. The mean average is 1.3 metres. Tides can move a lot of sediment into and out of bays and estuaries. Animals and plant life living in estuaries and tidal wetlands rely on this steady stream of water to help them survive.

## Storm surges

A **storm surge** is a rise in sea level resulting from the effects of intense storm systems. Cyclonic spinning winds whip up the ocean surface, and low pressure systems can exert less pressure, or weight, on the sea allowing the surface of the sea to actually rise. If a storm surge reaches the coast at the same time as an incoming tide, or meets the discharge from a flooded river, then severe damage can occur. The Bureau of Meteorology tries to predict storm surges so that communities know whether it is necessary to evacuate low-lying areas.

### GEO*facts*

- The world's biggest waves occur in the Indian Ocean between Australia and Antarctica. The average height of waves in the Indian Ocean is 6 metres but they can be as high as 30 metres.
- A 50-metre-wide rip can carry swimmers beyond the breakers within 30 seconds.
- Rogue waves are large and occur spontaneously. Sometimes referred to as hundred-year waves, they can be walls of water that kill fishermen on rock platforms and can be a threat to ocean liners.

### ACTIVITIES

#### UNDERSTANDING

1. Define the terms *wave climate*, *swash*, *backwash*, *longshore drift*, *rip*, *tide* and *storm surge*.
2. Explain the ocean processes that affect the east coast of Australia.
3. Explain how sand moves along a beach.
4. Describe how waves are formed and the type of wave most suitable for surfing.
5. Compare the impacts of constructive and destructive waves on coastal landforms.

#### THINKING AND APPLYING

6. Why does a surfer stay almost in the same place while waiting for a good wave? Use a diagram to assist your explanation.
7. Discuss why rips are dangerous for inexperienced swimmers. What would you do if caught in a rip?
8. Explain why there is more sand at the northern end of most beaches on the east coast of Australia.

#### USING YOUR SKILLS

9. Refer to the synoptic chart on page 228.
   a. What is the air pressure in Sydney?
   b. Where is the pressure gradient the steepest? What is its effect on waves?
   c. Which direction is Sydney's wind coming from?
   d. What do you think TC 'Rona' refers to? What impact will it have on waves and coastal processes?
   e. Explain how coasts are affected by different weather conditions.
10. Read the sample study about the Gold Coast's disappearing beaches. What caused the destructive waves in 1967? What was the impact on the coastal environment? Explain how the Tweed River breakwaters reduced the amount of sand deposited on Gold Coast beaches and the management solution.
11. Refer to the aerial photograph of the Maroochydore groynes. Draw and label a line diagram of Maroochydore's coast. Discuss the advantages of building groynes to reduce longshore drift.

### GEOTERMS

**longshore drift:** movement of sand and other materials along the shore

**storm surge:** rise in sea level resulting from the effects of intense storm systems

**tide:** the daily rise and fall of the ocean and its inlets, due to the attraction of the moon and sun

# 9.4 Processes of coastal erosion

The three main ways in which the sea can erode the land are through:
- *hydraulic action* — that is, the sheer force of the waves hitting the shore
- *corrasion* — when waves hurl material such as sand or rocks against the shore or when waves roll particles back and forth across the shore. Sand and rock particles are very effective tools for abrading (or wearing down).
- *corrosion* — when weaker layers of rock dissolve in sea water or disintegrate because of salt crystallisation.

The amount of wave energy determines whether deposition or erosion takes place. In calm conditions, wave energy may be too low to erode or transport material so deposition occurs. When wave energy is high — for example, in storm conditions — it is used to erode and move materials. Corrasion is also more active because the waves pick up more sand and rock particles.

## Headlands and bays

Soft rocks are eroded more quickly by wave erosion than harder rocks. Headlands and bays form along coasts that have alternating resistant (harder) and less resistant (softer) rock. Where there is resistant rock, the coast is worn away more slowly leaving a headland that juts out into the sea. Where there is softer rock, wave erosion is more rapid and a bay will form.

As a headland becomes more exposed to the full force of the waves, it becomes more vulnerable to erosion than the sheltered bay. As waves approach the coast, the wavefront bends to reflect the shape of the coastline. This bending of the waves is called *refraction* (see the diagram bottom left). Wave energy is concentrated around headlands, which are eroded forming landforms such as cliffs, rock platforms, caves, arches, stacks and blowholes.

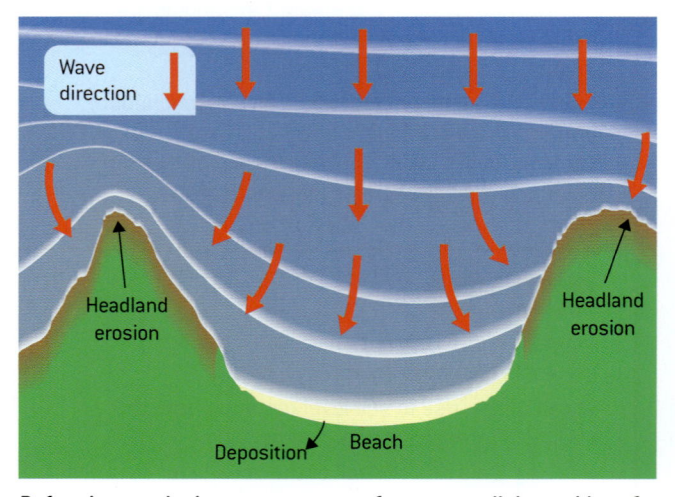

## Cliffs and rock platforms

The impact of waves at the foot of a cliff forms a **wave-cut notch**. Wave erosion enlarges the notch, the cliff is undercut and eventually the cliff collapses. As this process is repeated the cliff slowly retreats inland. The rate of retreat depends on the

*Blowhole at Quobba Point near Carnarvon, Western Australia*

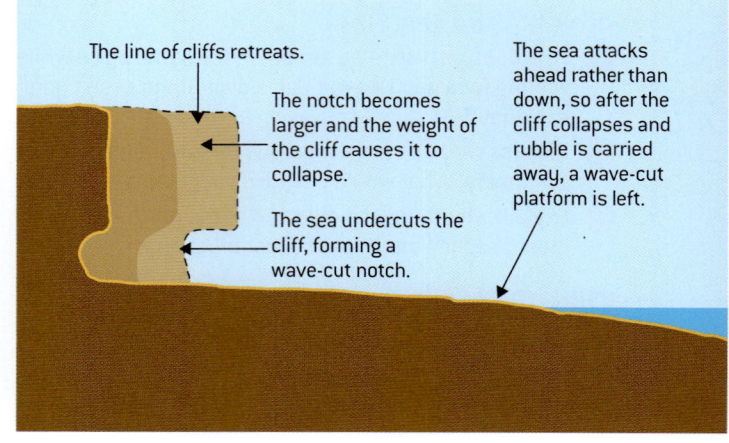

*Refraction results in a convergence of waves on all three sides of a headland.*

*Formation of cliffs and rocky platforms*

Tasman Arch, Tasmania

hardness of the rocks and the power of the waves. The rock platform that remains can be further shaped by the abrasion of rock fragments dragged back and forth by waves.

## Caves, arches, stacks and blowholes

Headlands and cliffs often contain weak areas such as faults or softer rock. Sea caves are formed because weaker areas are the first to be worn away. If sea caves form on both sides of a headland, or if the waves erode through the sea cave to the other side, an arch or bridge is formed. Further erosion of the rock supporting the arch may then cause it to collapse, leaving a **stack**.

When water rushes into a sea cave, it can cause pressure to build at the back of the cave. If a section of rock in the roof of the cave is weak, part of the roof may collapse and a **blowhole** is formed. At Kiama in New South Wales, sea water shoots many metres into the air through the blowhole in the rock.

## ACTIVITIES

### UNDERSTANDING

1. Copy the table below and link each formation with the sentence that best describes how it occurred.

| arch | A notch forms at the base of a cliff face when undercut by waves. |
| --- | --- |
| stack | The entire roof of a cave collapses. |
| headland | Two caves erode enough to join together. |
| rocky platform | A hard, rocky formation remains after the softer rock in adjoining bays has eroded. |

2. Distinguish between hydraulic action and corrosion.
3. Describe the effects of high-energy waves on coasts.
4. Explain how blowholes are formed.

### USING YOUR SKILLS

5. Refer to the photograph of Tasman Arch. Explain what this coastal feature may look like in 1000 years. Give reasons for your answer.
6. Refer to the diagram on wave refraction. Why are headlands more vulnerable to erosion than bays?
7. Refer to the diagram showing the formation of cliffs and rocky platforms. Use the labels to write a brief paragraph explaining the process.

### GEOTERMS

**blowhole:** a hole in the roof of a coastal cave, produced by wave erosion, through which compressed air and water are forced as waves break into the cave

**stack:** a column of rock, isolated from the shore by the corrosive action of waves

**wave-cut notch:** a hollow eroded by the impact of waves at the foot of a cliff

# 9.5 Processes of coastal deposition

Over millions of years, sediments have accumulated along the Australian coast. Sediments were transported to the coast by rivers and were also produced by the erosion of coastal landforms such as cliffs. Some of these sediments were deposited on the shore by waves and currents. The most common depositional features are beaches, dunes, bars, barriers and spits.

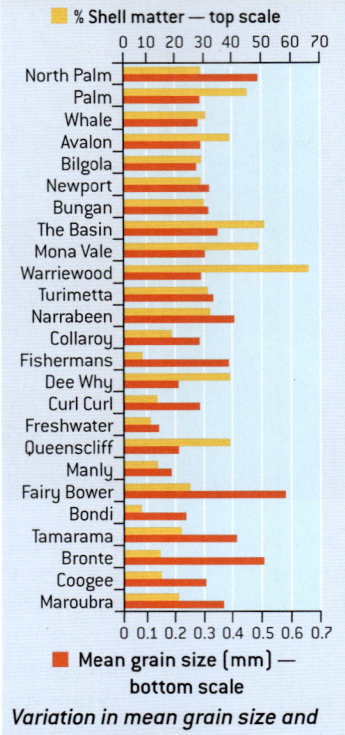

## Beaches are dynamic

A beach is a wave-deposited accumulation of loose sediment (usually sand or rocks). Beaches are constantly changing because of the processes of erosion, transportation and deposition. Under storm conditions, waves remove material from the beach. In contrast, gentle winds produce waves that are low and flat, leading to sand movement onshore.

The New South Wales coast has approximately 720 beaches. We can enjoy sandy beaches and making sandcastles, but in other parts of the world — for example, in England — beaches often consist of hard material such as rocks or pebbles. Our beaches are mainly composed of quartz sand grains. Notice the size of the sand grains next time you visit the beach. Larger grain sizes, for instance, produce steeper slopes. The percentage of shell content also varies and this affects the colour and feel of the sand. This information is important when coastal managers plan to replenish sand on beaches after storms. The wrong choice of sand for a particular beach will simply wash away.

## Sand dunes and coastal management

Accumulated sand is necessary to form dunes. Dunes are formed where dry sand is blown from the shore to the back of the beach. Varieties of dunes include **fore dunes**, parallel dunes and parabolic dunes. Fore dunes are the dunes closest to the surf. Parallel dunes are formed when successive fore dunes develop and are stabilised by vegetation. Dune blowouts occur when the vegetation cover is removed, either naturally or by human interaction. The loose sand is blown from the dune leaving a bare depression.

Stable and well-vegetated dunes are a barrier to erosive waves, stop sand from being blown inland and act as a buffer zone that protects land and property. Vegetation on the fore dune has to grow in sand that is very low in nutrients and dries out quickly. It has to cope with exposure to sun, salt and wind-blown sand. Spinifex and marram grass are often the first species to colonise the fore dune, beginning the process of stabilisation because their roots bind the sand. Spinifex grass has fine hairs that protect the leaves from wind and blowing sand.

In the lee at the back of the fore dune there is more protection from wind and salt, allowing small plants and shrubs to become established. Once the fore dune is stabilised there are opportunities for bigger plants to colonise the **back dunes**. These include small trees that have special adaptations to help them cope

*Variation in mean grain size and composition of sand on Sydney beaches*

*(Above) Barrenjoey Head, north of Sydney, was once an island. It is now joined to the mainland by a spit. This is called a tombolo.*

*(Below) A spit is an extension of the coastline.*

with low nutrients and dry salty conditions. Banksias, tea trees and acacias have tough leathery leaves that slow down transpiration. Acacias can acquire nitrogen from the atmosphere with the help of soil bacteria. Behind these grow larger trees, such as dry sclerophyll forest species. The variety of plant species attracts native fauna and increases biodiversity.

Human access often has to be restricted to allow dune vegetation to regenerate. The fore dune is particularly fragile and cannot withstand activities such as pedestrian traffic or trail bikes. To effectively manage this problem, access tracks with board and chain walkways need to be constructed, as well as fences to exclude people from sensitive areas.

## Other depositional landforms

Other depositional landforms include bars, spits, tombolos and lagoons.

- *Bars* and *barriers* are offshore deposits of sediment, lying roughly parallel to the beach.
- *Spits* are continuations of beaches that diverge from the coast. They are generally formed by longshore currents. For example, Noosa in south-east Queensland is largely built on a spit across the mouth of the Noosa River.
- *Tombolos* are formed when spits link an island to a mainland, such as at Palm Beach in New South Wales.
- *Lagoons* are usually formed behind depositional features such as spits. Lagoons are normally cut off from the sea and therefore contain fresh water. Where a lagoon is open to the sea, its salinity is highest where it is closest to the sea. Human intervention can drastically affect lagoon ecosystems. When an artificial entrance to Gippsland Lakes was constructed at Lakes Entrance in Victoria, the increased water salinity killed the freshwater vegetation.

*Dune stabilisation begins when sand and salt-tolerant grasses, such as spinifex or marram grass, trap and bind the sand.*

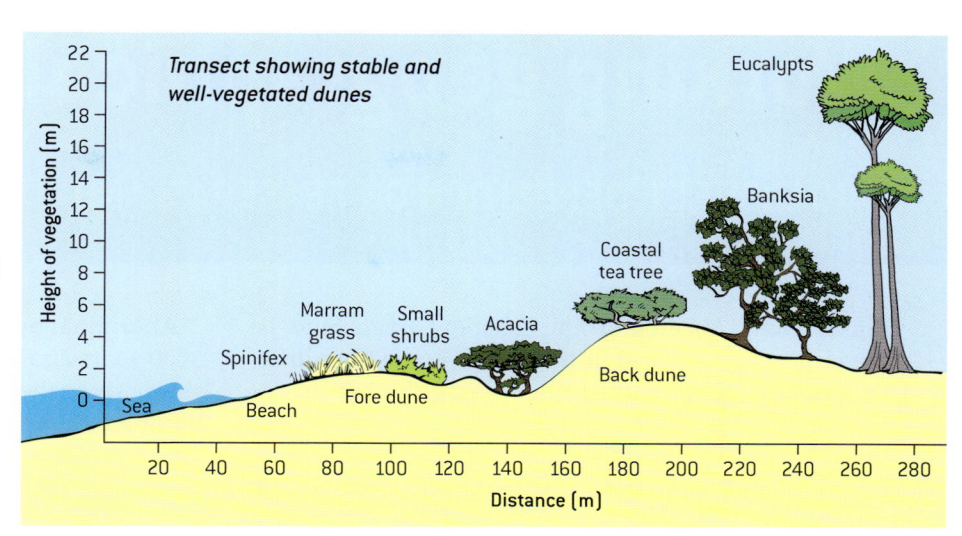

### GEOskills TOOLBOX

**INTERPRETING A VEGETATION TRANSECT**

A transect is a cross-section diagram on which information about the area is written or drawn, such as landforms, vegetation and land use. The transect above shows stable, well-vegetated dunes. (For information on how to draw a transect, see page 28.)

### ACTIVITIES

**UNDERSTANDING**

1. List five depositional landforms.
2. Explain how a lagoon is formed.
3. Discuss how fore dunes could be managed sustainably.

**USING YOUR SKILLS**

4. Refer to the graph opposite. Compare shell matter and grain size between Warriewood, Maroubra, Bondi and Manly. Why do they differ and why is this information necessary to effectively manage the beaches?
5. Draw and label a sketch of the tombolo and spit in the photographs on page 234. What is the difference between a beach and a spit? Discuss how a spit could become a tombolo over time. Label the direction of longshore drift on each sketch. Discuss how longshore drift has formed each feature.
6. Refer to the vegetation transect. Explain why the size and type of vegetation varies from the seaward side of the fore dune to the back dune. How has the dune vegetation adapted to dry, windy coastal environments? What would happen to the vegetation on the back dune if all the vegetation was removed from the fore dune?

# Working geographically

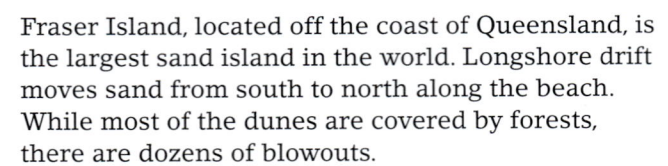

## BROADSHEET: DEPOSITION ON FRASER ISLAND

Fraser Island, located off the coast of Queensland, is the largest sand island in the world. Longshore drift moves sand from south to north along the beach. While most of the dunes are covered by forests, there are dozens of blowouts.

Aboriginal people first inhabited the island over 5000 years ago. Today, it has become an eco-tourism venue since the disbandment of the timber and sand-mining industries. Increasing tourism has resulted in land degradation, increased traffic and disturbance to ecosystems. Lake McKenzie attracts 2000 visitors a day in peak periods, which many people consider unsustainable. The Queensland Government aims to address environmental degradation by sustainably managing development on Fraser Island.

### USING YOUR SKILLS

1. Use the map to answer the following.
   a. What is the latitude and longitude of Fraser Island?
   b. Name one river that runs east and two rivers that run west.
   c. What is the direction of Happy Valley from Kingfisher Bay?
   d. What is the bearing of Moon Point from Dilli Village?
   e. How far is Indian Head from Hook Point?
   f. Write the scale as a representative fraction.
   g. Use your atlas to find out how far the southern tip of Fraser Island is from Brisbane.
   h. Describe the vegetation on the island.

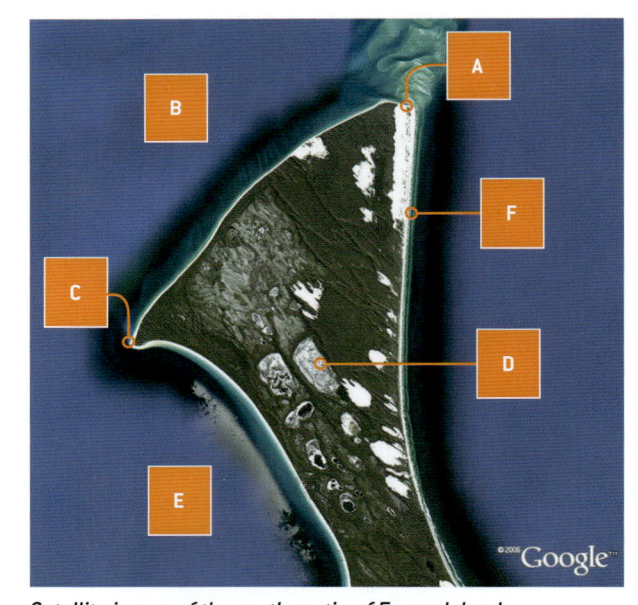

*Satellite image of the northern tip of Fraser Island*

2. Use the satellite image, map and photo above right to answer the following.
   a. What is located at A, B, C, D and E?
   b. Discuss what seems to have happened at F. Suggest two sustainable management strategies.

c What is the name of the beach on the east side of the island and the bay on the west side of the island?

*One of the island's many sand blows (blowouts). The shape of the dunes indicates the direction of the prevailing wind.*

3 Refer to the photograph above. This blowout is on the eastern side of the island.
   a What is the main direction of the wind?
   b How do you think the blowout occurred?
4 Re-draw the table below as a climatic graph. Answer the questions that follow.
   a Which season receives the highest rainfall?
   b What is the average monthly minimum temperature?
   c What is the range of temperature in January and June?
5 Refer to the article above right. What problems does tourism cause for a World Heritage site? Discuss the impacts of urine on water ecosystems and how the problem could be better managed.

## GEOfacts

- Fraser Island was inscribed as a World Heritage site in 1992.
- The island is over 123 kilometres in length, 22 kilometres at its widest point, and covers an area of 184 000 hectares.
- The island's sand dunes rise to as high as 250 metres.
- There is a 75-kilometre-long white beach flanked by coloured-sand cliffs (e.g. Rainbow Gorge) and over 100 freshwater lakes.
- Fraser Island is the only place in the world where rainforests grow on sand dunes up to 200 metres high.

## Please tourists, don't pee in the lake

So, we're sure your momma told you not to pee in the swimming pool — but did she also tell you it's bad to pee in a lake? Down in Australia, the beautiful Basin Lake on Fraser Island off Queensland isn't doing well these days, and one of the causes is high levels of urine in the water. The official word is that too many tourists are using the lake as a toilet and that's led the Queensland Parks and Wildlife Service to consider closing one of the access tracks to reduce visitor numbers. Right now 35 000 people visit the lake every year and since there's no in- or outflow from the lake; whatever goes in, stays in. Our alternative suggestion is to simply stick up a big notice advertising the current urine levels in the lake. We're fairly sure most people would skip the swim.

*Source: Fraser Island Travel Guide, 17 October 2008.*

*Basin Lake on Fraser Island*

### Climate: Sandy Cape Lighthouse

|  | Jan. | Feb. | Mar. | Apr. | May | Jun. | Jul. | Aug. | Sep. | Oct. | Nov. | Dec. | Annual |
|---|---|---|---|---|---|---|---|---|---|---|---|---|---|
| Mean maximum temperature (°C) | 29.4 | 29.3 | 28.5 | 26.8 | 24.1 | 21.7 | 21.1 | 22.3 | 24.3 | 26.1 | 27.6 | 28.9 | 25.8 |
| Mean minimum temperature (°C) | 22.3 | 22.4 | 21.7 | 19.9 | 17.5 | 15.2 | 14.3 | 15.0 | 16.8 | 18.7 | 20.3 | 21.6 | 18.8 |
| Mean rainfall (mm) | 160.3 | 168.4 | 153.8 | 121.5 | 117.9 | 110.6 | 90.4 | 64.0 | 51.7 | 59.5 | 72.4 | 96.9 | 1267.4 |

CHAPTER 9 | Coastal management

# 9.6 Managing the impact of global warming on coasts

In 2008, Australian coastal environments were not only subject to tropical cyclones and three **tsunamis**, but to a rising sea level. Global sea level rose 17 centimetres (from a range of 12–22 centimetres) during the 20th century. As the Earth continues to heat up, sea levels are estimated to rise between 18 centimetres and 59 centimetres by the year 2100 as glaciers melt and oceans expand. While the figure sounds small, a one-centimetre sea-level rise can cause erosion effects of up to one metre.

## Impacts of global warming

**Global warming** is predicted to cause tropical cyclones to move further south towards New South Wales and more extreme coastal weather conditions leading to an increase in storm surges, coastal inundation and endangered marine habitats. Areas affected by global warming will include the World Heritage-listed Sydney Opera House and Great Barrier Reef, and low-gradient beaches such as at the Gold Coast and Narrabeen. As many as 711 000 residences within three kilometres of the coast and below six metres above sea level, will be flooded. It is predicted that by 2050 most of Sydney's 150 major beaches will require thousands of tonnes of extra sand to maintain their current condition.

## Management of impacts

The Council of Australian Governments (COAG), the Natural Resource Management Ministerial Council (NRMMC) and the Department of Climate Change all consider the impacts of **climate change** on the coastline a management priority. Local councils are currently incorporating sea-level rise projections into their planning codes. Obviously, rising sea levels are a global issue. Two small low-lying islands in the South Pacific nation of Kiribati disappeared beneath waves in 1999. As sea levels rise, climate refugees or eco refugees will also increase.

*Life's a beach, and then it disappears. (Left) The Narrabeen coastline today. (Right) Digitally altered image showing what Narrabeen might look like in 2050*

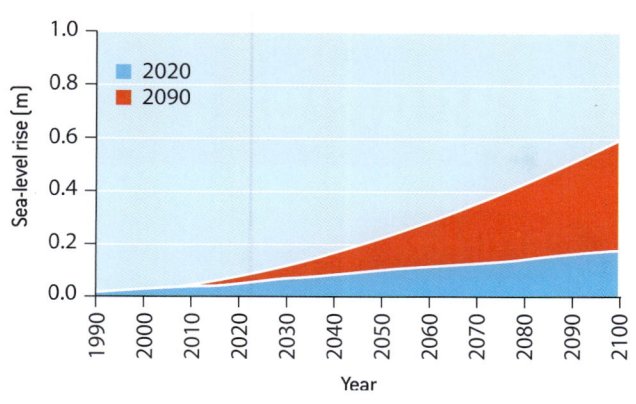

*Future scenarios for sea-level rise*

**Impact of climate change on Australian coasts**

| Nature | Impacts |
|---|---|
| Sea-level rise | Increases in:<br>• coastal erosion<br>• flooding of coastal wetlands and lowlands<br>• salinisation of surface and ground waters<br>• destruction of coastal housing and infrastructure |
| Sea-surface temperature rise (1–2°C, with greatest warming in south-eastern Australia/Tasman Sea) | Increases in:<br>• coral bleaching<br>• migration of marine species<br>• algal blooms |
| Wave–climate alteration | Alterations to erosion and deposition processes |
| Extreme weather events – altered frequency | Southward movement of:<br>• cyclone zones<br>• destructive waves and storm surges<br>• increased coastal erosion (especially in NSW) |

*Artificial rock wall, Wetherill Street, Narrabeen, showing close proximity of the ocean to the houses*

# ACTIVITIES

## UNDERSTANDING
1. Explain the links between global warming and a rise in sea level.
2. Describe the responses of governments to potential coastal flooding.

## THINKING AND APPLYING
3. As a group, develop a policy to reduce the impacts of global warming on Australian coastlines. Present your management strategies as a report to the federal government.
4. Research five low-lying world cities threatened by rising sea levels, such as:
    - London
    - Venice
    - New Orleans
    - Alexandria
    - Shanghai.
   
   Find out what management strategies have been implemented to reduce the impact of potential disaster.
5. Research one organisation involved in sustainably managing the impacts of global warming on coastal environments and one organisation involved in managing coastal pollution.

## USING YOUR SKILLS
6. Refer to the line graph on rising sea levels. What is the range of anticipated sea-level rise in 2020 and 2090? Explain why the range increases over time.
7. Refer to the table on climate change impacts. Discuss the impacts on the New South Wales coast in the next 100 years.
8. Refer to the two photographs of the Narrabeen coastline.
    a. Why is the beach disappearing?
    b. What would be the impact on people and infrastructure?
    c. Suggest both local and global management strategies to avoid such a disaster.
9. Study the photograph showing the Wetherill Street artificial wall in Narrabeen. Discuss whether this is an effective long-term management strategy considering the sea level will continue to rise. Suggest other solutions.

## GEOTERMS

**climate change:** long-term significant change in the average weather that a region experiences

**global warming:** increase in the average temperature of the Earth's air and oceans since the mid twentieth century, and its projected continuation

**tsunami:** an ocean wave caused by an earthquake or volcanic eruption beneath the sea, travelling at high speed and causing massive destruction along coasts

# 9.7 Coastal pollution: nature, impacts and management

Polluted coastal waters are a major potential problem for a nation such as Australia, with its many thousands of kilometres of coastline and a concentration of settlements along the coast. Polluted coastal waters can cause a decline in marine species and diseases like hepatitis can occur. The nature of the pollution varies, from litter and debris such as plastic, household and industrial rubbish, stormwater litter and sediment, to contaminating substances such as oil, raw sewage, pesticides, fertilisers and toxic chemicals.

## Management of coastal pollution

To deal with the issue, a national Coastal Catchments Initiative (CCI) protects water quality by reducing sedimentation, algal blooms, discharges of polluted water into coastal waters, and high-coliform (harmful bacteria) concentrations that require beach closures. Permits are required from the Department of Environment, Water, Heritage and Arts for any activity that may put coastal marine areas at risk, including ocean disposal, dredging operations, artificial reef creation, the dumping of vessels, and sea burials. Australia is party to the Protocol to the Convention on the Prevention of Marine Pollution by Dumping of Wastes and Other Matter, which limits the types of materials disposed in the ocean.

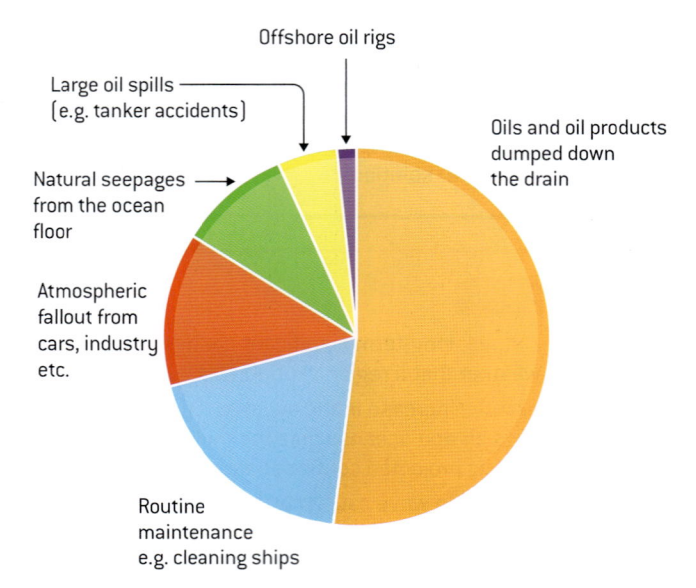

> **GEOfacts** There are about three or four sea burials in Australian waters each year. The burial location chosen must ensure that the body will not be carried in to shore by currents or picked up by fishing vessels. This requires a minimum water depth of 1000 metres. Around Sydney, this would mean a site at least 60 kilometres out from the mainland.

## Integrated coastal zone management (ICZM)

Integrated coastal zone management (ICZM) maintains and restores coastal zone ecosystems. Coastal zone management involves the coordination of individuals, groups and governments in maintaining the quality of coastal environments, in events such as Clean Up Australia Day and coastal land care.

About half of Australia's Aboriginal and Torres Strait Islander population live near the coast. Many depend on the coast for their livelihood and sustainably manage its resources.

*Pie graph on coastal pollution* — segments labelled: Offshore oil rigs; Large oil spills (e.g. tanker accidents); Natural seepages from the ocean floor; Atmospheric fallout from cars, industry etc.; Routine maintenance e.g. cleaning ships; Oils and oil products dumped down the drain.

### ACTIVITIES

**UNDERSTANDING**

1. List the effects of the Queensland oil spill on both the physical and human environments.
2. Why are polluted coastal waters potentially a problem for Australia?
3. Refer to the pie graph on coastal pollution. What factor contributes to marine pollution (a) the most, and (b) the least? Give reasons for your answers.

**THINKING AND APPLYING**

4. Research the ways in which Indigenous Australians traditionally managed the coastal environments where they lived. Compare these with contemporary management policies of Australian governments.

**USING YOUR SKILLS**

5. Refer to the map opposite showing the extent of the oil spill in Queensland. Estimate the total area affected.
6. Make a line drawing of the oblique aerial photograph opposite showing the oil spill on Moreton Island. Label your sketch.

## SAMPLE STUDY

### Oil spill in Queensland

In March 2009, parts of coastal Queensland around Bribie Island, Moreton Island and the southern area of the Sunshine Coast were declared a disaster area. During Cyclone Hamish, more than 270 000 litres of oil were spilled from a cargo ship damaged by rough seas. Thirty-one containers of fertiliser (ammonium nitrate) also went overboard and have not been recovered from the ocean floor. The Queensland Government responded quickly, declaring the area a disaster zone. A large-scale clean-up operation commenced, using hundreds of emergency workers and council personnel. The thick oil slick killed many fish and affected birds, turtles and sea snakes. Formerly pristine beaches, usually busy with tourists, were closed. The Environmental Protection Agency and the RSPCA warned of potential long-term effects to the marine food chain. The annual migration of whales through the area could also be affected by residual oil. The cost of the clean-up was approximately $31 million and the captain of the ship was charged with illegally spilling oil in Queensland waters. Costs to the tourism industry were expected to continue for many months.

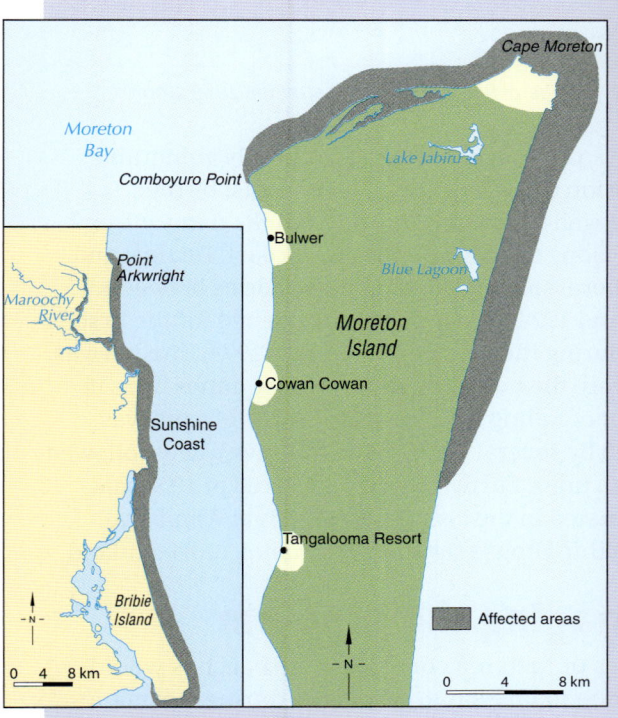

*An oil-stricken pelican rescued by a wildlife ranger*

*Map showing location of oil slick*

*Oil slick on Moreton Island*

**CHAPTER 9** | Coastal management

# 9.8 Coastal management case study: Wamberal and Terrigal

## Who manages the coast?

All levels of government have some responsibility for coastal management. Traditionally, under the Australian Constitution, the states have the greatest power over the use of the coastal zone. However, it is not always easy to work out whether federal, state or local government is responsible for a particular area because responsibilities are fragmented and often overlap. In addition, certain areas are managed according to the traditional decision-making processes of Aboriginal and Torres Strait Islander peoples.

Australia is a member of the global community and there are some international conventions that influence the decisions made by our government. In 1997 the United Nations Convention on the Law of the Sea allowed Australia to declare a 370-kilometre exclusive economic zone (EEZ) around the continent and the territories under its responsibility. At the 1992 Earth Summit, Australia signed the Convention on Biological Diversity. International commitments influence decisions made by our national, state and local governments.

## Different perspectives

People have different and often conflicting perspectives about how the coast should be used and managed. Opinions may be expressed by various stakeholders, such as local residents, shopkeepers, engineers, hotel owners, teenagers, senior citizens and marine scientists. To ensure social justice and equity, all perspectives need to be considered and, before development applications can be approved, an **environmental impact statement (EIS)** must be prepared. An EIS shows the likely impacts on the physical environment as well as social and economic impacts. The study is distributed and responses invited. Interest groups include local, state and federal governments, the community, environmental groups, local businesses, and recreation and sporting associations.

The challenge is to resolve the conflicting perspectives of the stakeholders. The future of our coasts depends on informed and aware citizens making decisions based on the information available from sources such as governments and scientists. Responsible media reports can also play a role in presenting different perspectives and avoiding bias.

## Erosion at Wamberal and Terrigal

Wamberal and Terrigal beaches are located near Gosford, 80 kilometres north of Sydney. In the early 1900s, several guesthouses and some holiday cottages were built on the dunes and along the beach. The fore dunes had been densely vegetated. During the 1960s many more houses were built along the beach. Demand for housing increased until, in 2004, a house on the fore dune at Terrigal sold for four million dollars.

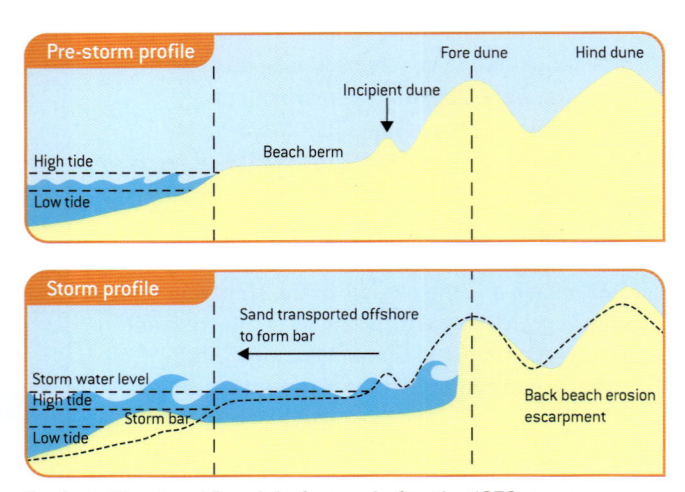

*Terrigal–Wamberal Beach before and after the 1978 storm*

The coastline in this area is naturally vulnerable to erosion but was protected in the past by the stable, well-vegetated fore dunes. Like many other areas along the New South Wales coast, Terrigal and Wamberal suffered erosion from storms between 1967 and 1974. Houses were threatened for the first time during the storm of 25–26 May 1974. Erosion was so severe the homes built on the fore dunes were in danger of falling into the sea. The loss of sand was caused by several weeks of destructive waves followed by high tides. Further storms occurred in 1978 that culminated in the loss of two houses at Wamberal, with a third house saved only by being moved inland.

## Managing the problem

Studies of the area concluded the beaches would continue to lose sand, especially during storms. Coastal managers predicted that over the next 50 years, parts of Wamberal Beach would recede by

*Storm erosion claims a house at Wamberal Beach, 1978. A second house on the left was lost later during high tide. A house on the far left was saved by being relocated.*

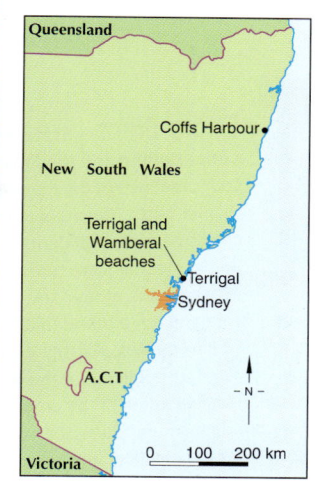

*Location of Terrigal and Wamberal beaches*

20 to 50 metres, resulting in the loss of buildings along the beach. At Terrigal the beach was expected to recede by about three metres.

The community expected that the government would manage the problem and protect their property. However, the responsibility of governments does not usually extend to private property. In 1970, the State Planning Authority prepared a plan to manage the erosion. Suggested measures included beach nourishment, groynes, sea walls, offshore breakwaters and purchasing threatened properties. The costs of managing coasts in this way are enormous. For Wamberal Beach, estimates were $21.4 million dollars for sea wall and sand nourishment; $21 million for sand dune nourishment; $17.7 million for acquisition of land; and $63 million for ongoing management costs.

Advantages and disadvantages of five protection measures are shown in the table on page 245.

# A contemporary geographical issue

Beach erosion along the Central Coast remains a contemporary geographical issue. A storm in 1991 threatened the Wamberal Lake foreshore. In June 1995, king tides contributed to the worst erosion experienced at Terrigal since 1974. In 1996 at Jenny Dixon beach, due to undercutting of the cliffs by wave erosion, a huge boulder almost the size of a house fell 25 metres onto the beach.

The impacts of global warming will continue to threaten coastal homes located on the fore dunes, requiring immediate action.

## ACTIVITIES

### UNDERSTANDING

1. What is an EIS? Explain why an EIS is essential before approval is given for coastal development.

### THINKING AND APPLYING

2. At a local council meeting, a proposal is made to 'take action to control erosion at Wamberal and Terrigal beaches, funded from rates'.
   a Refer to the roles outlined on page 244 and consider other views that might be relevant. As a group, roleplay the views for and against the proposal.
   b At the end of the meeting, everyone votes on whether or not to proceed with the proposal.
   c After the vote, discuss the following issues.
      i What primary and secondary data are required before making an informed decision?
      ii Who else should have been consulted?
      iii What compromise solution could be reached?
      iv In a democracy, are citizens able to express their views on issues that concern them?

### USING YOUR SKILLS

3. Refer to the photograph of Wamberal Beach in 1978.
   a Discuss the events that led to the scene in the photograph.
   b Imagine you own one of the collapsing houses. Who do you think has the responsibility to pay for the damage to your home?
   c Explain the predicted impacts of climate change on this beach.
   d Discuss the steps you would take to prevent the problem from occurring again.

4. Refer to the cross-section (page 242). Discuss the changes to the coastline after the storm in 1978. Where does the sand dune disappear to during a storm?

5. Refer to the series of diagrams showing beach-protection measures on page 245. What alternatives do you think would be:
   a most economical
   b best for the natural environment
   c the most easily achieved?

CHAPTER 9 | Coastal management

### Eddie Elect — State Minister for Conservation and the Environment

Your presence at the meeting is important to your party. You are sympathetic to the concerns of the residents and express this in most sincere terms. You also see the value of tourism to this coastal area and understand that it should be preserved. Also, further loss of beach and homes would produce negative publicity for the government nearing election time. However, most of the proposals will cost a lot of money and your department does not have the funds to help at the moment. After the election, and with a new budget, you may be able to give a more positive response. At present, you must convince the meeting of the need for further study into the most appropriate scheme and that more time can be taken to reach a decision.

### Grant Green — conservationist

You sympathise with residents whose homes are located on the eroding foreshore, but are concerned that most of the schemes proposed will interfere with nature. It is natural for a beach to erode. In doing so, sand and other material is transported to other beaches, which build up over time. Some of the solutions have negative effects on the environment. Beach nourishment will affect other environments that will supply the sand; groynes, an offshore breakwater and sea walls are a visual eyesore and interfere with the natural cycle of material. There is also no guarantee of any scheme succeeding in the long term. You believe properties should be bought by council and the residents compensated. This will leave the beach in a more natural state and coastal processes can continue unimpeded. Buildings in the back dune area can be protected by long-term planting of vegetation.

### Belinda Builder — engineer

You are an expert in the field of engineering, especially relating to marine projects. You have studied this coastal area extensively and believe it is possible to stabilise the dune area with a combination of a sea wall and beach nourishment scheme. This would stabilise the dunes for about 50 years. You work for a firm that has not been too successful in bidding for contracts recently and you are determined to convince the meeting to proceed with your proposal. You intend to play on the negative publicity the council will receive if more houses are threatened or lost. The attraction for tourists is also important to the council.

### Helena Holliday — regular visitor

This is a location you visit for holidays each year. It is attractive to you because of its proximity to Sydney and its size. The area is not as busy as many other more popular resorts. You are concerned about the erosion as it destroys the very beach you come to enjoy. You would like the council to undertake any measure possible to protect the beach. If this is not done, you will stop coming for holidays and think others will do the same.

### Lou Loner — local inland resident

You moved to this area many years ago seeking a quiet, peaceful lifestyle, away from busy Sydney. Your house is three kilometres inland from the coast and not threatened by erosion. You feel that the people who built or bought houses so close to the beach should have considered the likelihood of erosion. You are against any scheme proposed to reduce erosion because it means your rates will need to increase to pay for them. You are also unconcerned about the possible reduction in tourists to the area because this location has become very popular and is overcrowded with visitors. Anything that increases your peace and quiet is agreeable to you.

### Cliff Topper — fore dune resident

You are one of the many residents who have homes along the eroding dune. You are concerned about the safety of the beach, especially as it is popular with holiday makers and tourists. If the erosion is not stopped, many buildings will eventually be destroyed. You believe the council is partly to blame for granting building permits on these sites. You also feel that local governments have responsibility to protect ratepayers from such disasters.

### Des Agree — chairperson

You are a local councillor sympathetic towards the home owners on the dune but also aware that the council does not have sufficient funds to meet the requirements of the schemes outlined. You will listen carefully to the speakers and ask further questions where necessary. After a brief summary at the end of the presentations, you will conduct a vote among the audience for and against the proposal. In the event of a tie, you will cast your vote according to the most convincing arguments presented.

**Possible management solutions to reduce the impacts of erosion**

| Solution | Description | Diagram | Advantages | Disadvantages |
|---|---|---|---|---|
| Beach nourishment | The artificial placement of sand on a beach. This is then spread along the beach by natural processes. | | Sand is used that best matches the natural beach material. Low environmental impact at the beach | The sand must come from another beach and may have an environmental impact in that location. Must be carried out on a continuous basis and therefore requires continuous funds |
| Groyne | An artificial structure designed to trap sand being moved by longshore drift, therefore protecting the beach. Groynes can be built using timber, concrete, steel pilings and rock. | | Traps sand and maintains the beach | Groynes do not stop sand movement that occurs directly offshore. Visual eyesore |
| Sea wall | Structure placed parallel to the shoreline to separate the land area from the water | | Prevents further erosion of the dune area and protects buildings | The base of the sea wall will be undermined over time. Visual eyesore. Will need a sand nourishment program as well. High initial cost. Ongoing maintenance and cost |
| Offshore breakwater | A structure parallel to the shore and placed in a water depth of about 10 metres | | Waves break in the deeper water, reducing their energy at the shore. | Destroys surfing amenity of the coast. Requires large boulders in large quantities. Cost would be extremely high |
| Purchase property | Buy the buildings and remove structures that are threatened by erosion | | Allows easier management of the dune area. Allows natural beach processes to continue. Increases public access to the beach | Loss of revenue to the local council. Possible social problems with residents who must move. Exposes the back dune area, which will need protection. Cost would be extremely high. Does not solve sand loss |

CHAPTER 9 | Coastal management

# 9.9 Managing Sydney Harbour: a geographical issue

## The nature of Sydney Harbour

Sydney Harbour is the largest natural harbour in the world. Over one million people live in the 25 council areas in the Sydney Harbour catchment, which includes the waters and foreshores of Sydney Harbour, Parramatta River and Lane Cove River, their tributaries and catchments.

The harbour has changed environmentally, socially and economically from the impacts of urban growth, industry, commerce, transport, recreation and tourism. The challenge faced by the City of Sydney Council, local governments, state government departments and city dwellers is how to manage the harbour sustainably, so that future generations can enjoy ferry trips across the harbour to Manly, watch whales, sail boats or have access to the foreshore for picnics.

## Managing the Sydney Harbour catchment

The Sydney Harbour catchment covers an area of 600 square kilometres, containing all the rivers and creeks that flow into the harbour stretching from North Head and South Head to Blacktown, Hornsby and Bankstown. This huge area and diversity of human interactions make management difficult. Originally, each government department looked after shipping, or water, or parks; and each local council their own stretch of foreshore. Today, there is a whole-of-government catchment management approach that treats Sydney Harbour as one system in which each decision from the different levels of government affects all decisions. The focus of management is to create collaborative workable solutions, ensuring equity and social justice, so the shared use of the harbour can achieve sustainable environmental standards. In 2000, the 'Our Harbour' Agreement enabled 19 councils in the Sydney Harbour catchment to be directly involved in harbour planning and management.

*Sydney Harbour*

## Sharing the harbour

After consulting with a wide range of harbour users, the New South Wales Government developed the Sharing Sydney Harbour Regional Action Plan, which aimed to ensure that everyone had access to information, decision making and use of harbour resources. This form of governance promoted collaboration by bringing together groups, 19 local governments, 20 state agencies and three Commonwealth agencies that aimed to:
- conserve strategic sites
- improve stormwater quality

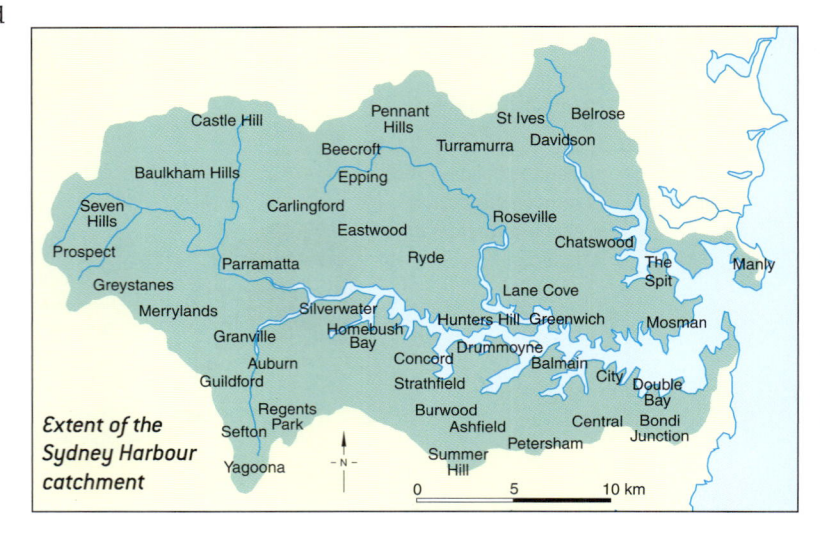

*Extent of the Sydney Harbour catchment*

- regenerate and conserve native bushland
- supply land for a working harbour
- audit over 60 cultural assets and organise programs such as festivals
- redevelop a 'spirit of place' in consultation with the Indigenous community
- improve recreational facilities on the foreshore
- exchange information about the harbour.

## Sydney Water, Harbourwatch and Streamwatch

Sydney Water conducts water quality testing in Sydney Harbour, as pollution threatens coastal ecosystems and our enjoyment of coastal environments. Sydney Water continually measures pH, temperature, dissolved oxygen, sediment content, nutrients and bacteria in the harbour. Over time, water quality measurements have improved but the harbour continues to be polluted from stormwater outflows, sewer overflows, land contamination and ships.

In 2007, Harbourwatch found Darling Harbour to be the most polluted site in Sydney Harbour with elevated faecal coliform levels. In 2008 Streamwatch found copper, lead and zinc in the Blackwattle Bay catchment, which drains into the harbour near the Sydney Fish Market.

Another problem facing Sydney Harbour is that the low-lying waterfront areas such as the Sydney Opera House are expected to be inundated with water as sea levels rise due to global warming, requiring urgent management.

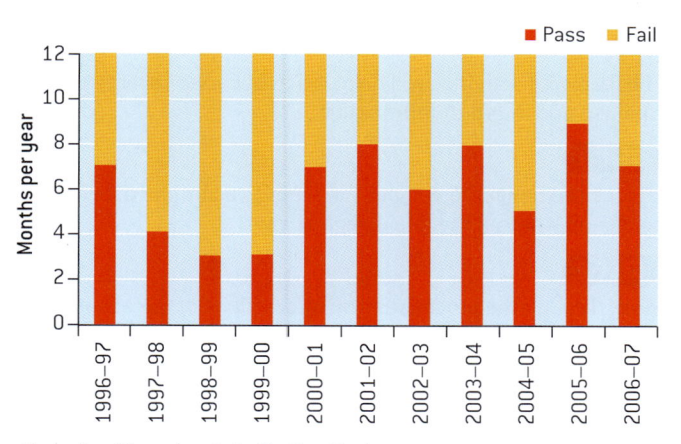

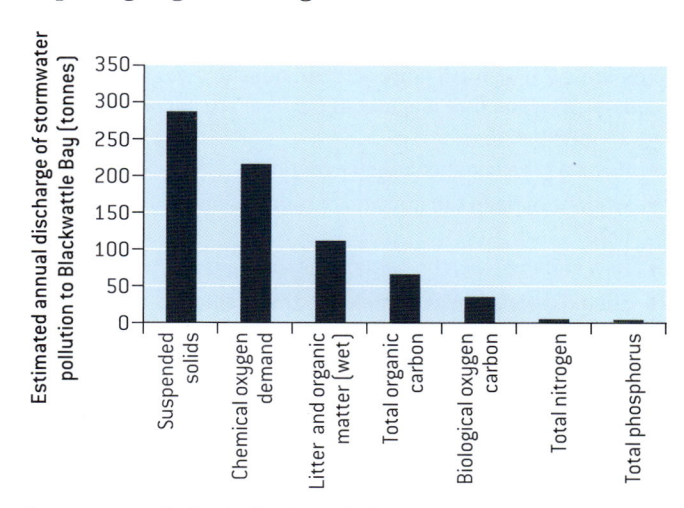

*Faecal coliform levels in Darling Harbour*

*Stormwater pollution in Blackwattle Bay*

### ACTIVITIES

**UNDERSTANDING**

1. List ten human impacts on Sydney Harbour, then create a collage showing these impacts.
2. All stakeholders want Sydney Harbour to be managed sustainably. What does this mean?

**THINKING AND APPLYING**

3. Discuss how individuals, groups and governments work to sustainably manage Sydney Harbour. Prepare your answer as a poster, multimedia presentation or web page.
4. Propose actions to promote equal access to Sydney Harbour.

**USING YOUR SKILLS**

5. Refer to the photograph opposite. Draw a land-use map of Sydney Harbour. Include waterways, famous landmarks, CBD, wharves, parks, harbour suburbs (particularly northern suburbs) and main transport links. Which areas will be subject to climate change? Explain your answer.
6. Study the map opposite. What is the breadth and length of the Sydney Harbour catchment? You may not live beside Sydney Harbour, but live in the catchment — for example, Blacktown, Hornsby, Warringah or Bankstown. How do your actions impact on water quality? What can you do to improve water quality in the harbour?
7. Refer to the graph showing faecal coliform levels. Looking at the years 2000–01 and 2006–07, how many months were faecal levels in Darling Harbour too high to be acceptable? Discuss the causes and impacts of high faecal levels on health. Suggest management strategies.
8. Refer to the graph showing estimated annual discharge of stormwater pollution in Blackwattle Bay. What was the total discharge of stormwater pollution (in tonnes)? What are the impacts on the environment? Suggest management strategies.

# 9.10 GEOskillbuilder

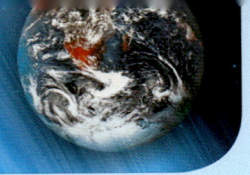

# Coastal fieldwork and research action plan

Geographers are interested in where things are, why they are there and how humans interact with the environment. The development of a research action plan (RAP) allows students to apply fieldwork techniques such as observing, measuring, collecting and analysing primary data. By investigating coastal processes and human impacts in the field, students are able to understand the importance of active, responsible and informed citizenship for a sustainably managed, socially just and equitable coastal zone.

## Pre-fieldwork activities

### STEP 1
Prepare a RAP using fieldwork techniques to investigate a coastal area and how it is managed. Here are some possible focus questions:
- How has the coast changed over time?
- What have been the impacts of humans on the coast over time?
- How can the coast be sustainably managed?
- Should development continue in the coastal area?
- What are the effects on local ecosystems?
- How can the dunes be rehabilitated?
- Has everyone access to the coastal areas?
- What are the roles of individuals, groups and governments for a more sustainable coast?

### STEP 2
Discuss human interactions over time in coastal areas — from Indigenous people to a future scenario.

### STEP 3
Take notes from videos, and research current coastal issues from newspapers, journals, CD-ROMs and websites to obtain perceptions from different groups — for example, sewage outfall and the building of high-rise apartments on fore dunes.

### STEP 4
Complete activities using topographic maps, Google Earth and geographic information systems (GIS). Calculate the density of features, such as homes around coastal areas. Calculate the local relief, identify the aspect of slopes, measure bearings, draw a cross-section, calculate the gradient of slopes, construct a vegetation transect and a land use map. Identify and locate physical features (such as cliffs and beaches) and human features using latitude, longitude, and area and grid references.

### STEP 5
Read and interpret synoptic maps, such as those with a cyclone around a coastal area. Identify the effects on the physical and human elements of environments and how individuals, groups and governments can manage the issue. Compare weather patterns and their effects on the formation of constructive and destructive waves.

### STEP 6
Construct and interpret graphs and statistics, such as population change over time.

### STEP 7
Collect and use digital images showing the impacts of humans on coasts, the changing coastal process (before and after a storm) and how active citizens have improved a coastal area (for example, the Clean Up Australia campaign, revegetation of fore dunes).

## Fieldwork

The following activities will help you to observe, collect, record, analyse and interpret information.

### STEP 1
Before you begin the activities in step 2, record the date and time, and whether the tide is high or low.

### STEP 2
Work through the processes and interactions of the coastal zone you are investigating. Follow the sequence outlined below, answering the questions as you go.

### Beach environment
1. Determine wind direction with a compass or a wind vane.
2. Determine the temperature on the shoreline and on the fore dune. Give reasons for the difference.
3. What fraction of the sky is covered by clouds?
4. Use a camera to record wave and weather conditions and landform and vegetation features.
5. Make line drawings of coastal landforms. Add any relevant details and label all of the features.

### Longshore currents
1. Throw a paddlepop stick raft into the waves to determine the direction the current is flowing.
2. Throw in an orange at three different places along the beach. Follow each orange for one minute. Calculate how far each one travels. Compare their movements and give reasons for any differences.

### Human interaction
1. List examples of human interaction on the beach.
2. List examples of human interaction in the area inland.
3. Form into groups of five students and collect ten items of rubbish on the beach. Sort it into these categories: glass, tin, paper, plastic and other. Graph the results. Which was the most common type of rubbish?

## Waves

1. Are the waves breaking at right angles or obliquely?
2. Use a compass to find the direction the waves are coming from.
3. Use a compass to find the wind direction.
4. Is there a correlation between wind direction and wave direction?
5. Estimate the height of the waves.
6. What is the time between waves?
7. What is the wave shape (for example, smooth, choppy, white caps)?
8. Are the waves spilling, plunging or surging?
9. Do waves break offshore at a sandbar?
10. Can you see a rip? Where is it located?
11. Can you can see a group of surfboard riders? Why are they located in that part of the surf?
12. How and why do the surfboard riders make use of wave refraction?
13. Use a thermometer to determine the water temperature.
14. How good is the water clarity (for example, clean, dirty, polluted, sandy)?
15. What evidence can you see that sand is moved in the surf?
16. Do the waves run up the beach evenly or are there any indentations (cusps) at regular intervals?
17. Estimate how far the water runs up the beach.
18. Is the beach patrolled? Where are the flags located?

## Water table on the beach

Use a small shovel to dig a hole in the sand near the water's edge until you reach water. Measure the distance from the top of the sand to the water table. Do this every two metres from the water level towards the fore dune. Record and explain your results.

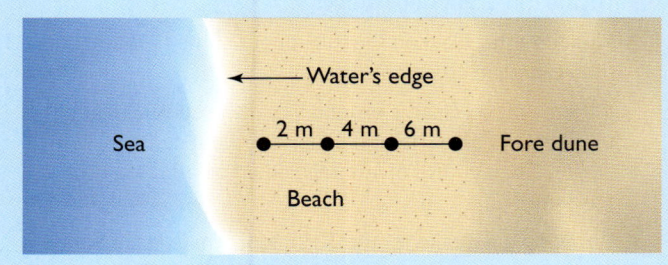

## Sand dunes and vegetation

1. Observe the plants growing on the sand dunes. How many of the following can you identify?

   spinifex      pennywort        banksia
   marram grass  beach daisy      coastal wattle
   pig face      native rosemary  beach bean
   sesuvium      pandanus         casuarina
   snake vine    bitou bush

2. Sketch four of the plants. Explain how they have adapted to this environment.
3. Draw a sketch of the sand dune showing the distribution of vegetation from the front to the back of the dune. Which plant is dominant near the sea? Which plant is dominant near the land?
4. Explain the relationship between the size of the plant and its position on the dune.
5. Which is the best plant to hold the sand together?
6. Does the amount of organic matter change as you go inland?
7. Is there evidence of beach erosion? If so, where?

*Collecting and recording data from a survey on sand dunes*

## Headland

1. Draw a sketch of the headland and label the following: cliff, wave-cut notch, rock platform.
2. What evidence is there that the headland is eroding?

## Sand

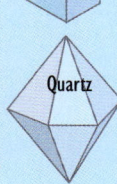

1. Collect a handful of sand close to the shore. Using sieves of various sizes, sieve the sand and separate out the particles. Now look carefully for shells and other minerals. Using a magnifying glass, identify any quartz and felspar (see the sketches). Record what you observe.
2. Repeat the activity above, this time with sand from the fore dune. Record what you observe.
3. What differences are there between the sand from the two locations? Give reasons for the differences.

### STEP 3

Use the information you have gathered to present a report that communicates your findings to other people. Interpret the data and organise the information under headings and subheadings. Describe the weather, waves, landforms, sand dune stability and vegetation, and how people use the beach. Comment on any issues you think could be improved by better management. Include a location map and illustrate your report with sketches, graphs, diagrams and photographs.

## Post-fieldwork activities

Put all your primary and secondary data together in a research action plan. Process and analyse the data to answer your focus question. Present your plan as a report, video, poster, PowerPoint show or multimedia display. Where appropriate, propose individual and group action.

# Working geographically

## BROADSHEET: TSUNAMIS

### AUSTRALIAN TSUNAMI

In the last few thousand years the Australian coast may have experienced large tsunami, as evidenced by shell, coral and boulder deposits found well above sea level and several kilometres inland.

Minor tsunami are recorded about once every two years in Australia, but most are small and present little threat to our coastal communities. The tsunami threat to Australia varies from 'relatively low', for most of our coastline, to 'moderate' on the north-west coast of WA due to its proximity to Indonesia and other countries in that region prone to large earthquakes and volcanic activity.

Several large tsunami have hit Australia's north-west coast—the largest at Cape Leveque, WA, in 1977, with a 6 m wave height. Further south in the Onslow-Exmouth region, in June 1994, tsunami waves with over 4 m 'run-up' (i.e. it travelled inland to a point 4 m above sea level) appeared out of a calm sea and washed 300 m inland. Both of these WA tsunami were generated by earthquakes in Indonesia.

In May 1960, a great earthquake in Chile generated the largest recorded tsunami along the east coast of Australia. The event generated tsunami waves of just under a metre (trough to crest) at the Fort Denison tide gauge in Sydney Harbour. Slight to moderate damage (mainly to boats) resulted in harbours at Lord Howe Island, Evans Head, Newcastle, Sydney and Eden.

*Figure 7:* Australia's region of highest tsunami risk is the north-west coastline.

**Figure 8:** Unusual tidal fluctuations were recorded in Augusta, South Australia, during the December 2004 tsunami. The strong currents caused by the tsunami dragged bathers out to sea, but they were either rescued or made it back to shore on their own. (Images courtesy Dave Piper)

*An extract from the Australian government brochure 'Tsunami Awareness'*

### SHORT RESPONSE

**Use the resources on these pages to answer the following.**

1. What was the cause of the tsunami?
2. Locate three Seaframe stations.
3. What country blocked the full impact of the tsunami on the Australian coast?
4. If there was a volcanic eruption near the south coast of Indonesia or an earthquake near the west coast of New Zealand, what parts of Australia could be affected by a tsunami?
5. How long did it take for the 2007 tsunami to leave South America and arrive along the Australian coast?

### EXTENDED RESPONSE

6. **a** Tsunamis affecting the Australian coast have always occurred. Use the **Australian Government Geoscience** weblink in your eBookPLUS to find out more about the impact of tsunamis on the Australian coast. Discuss the impacts of these tsunamis and their management.
   **b** Use the **Pacific Tsunami Warning Centre** weblink in your eBookPLUS to find out about tsunamis that have occurred in the last 90 days. Describe the source, severity and impacts of the tsunamis that have affected the world during that time.

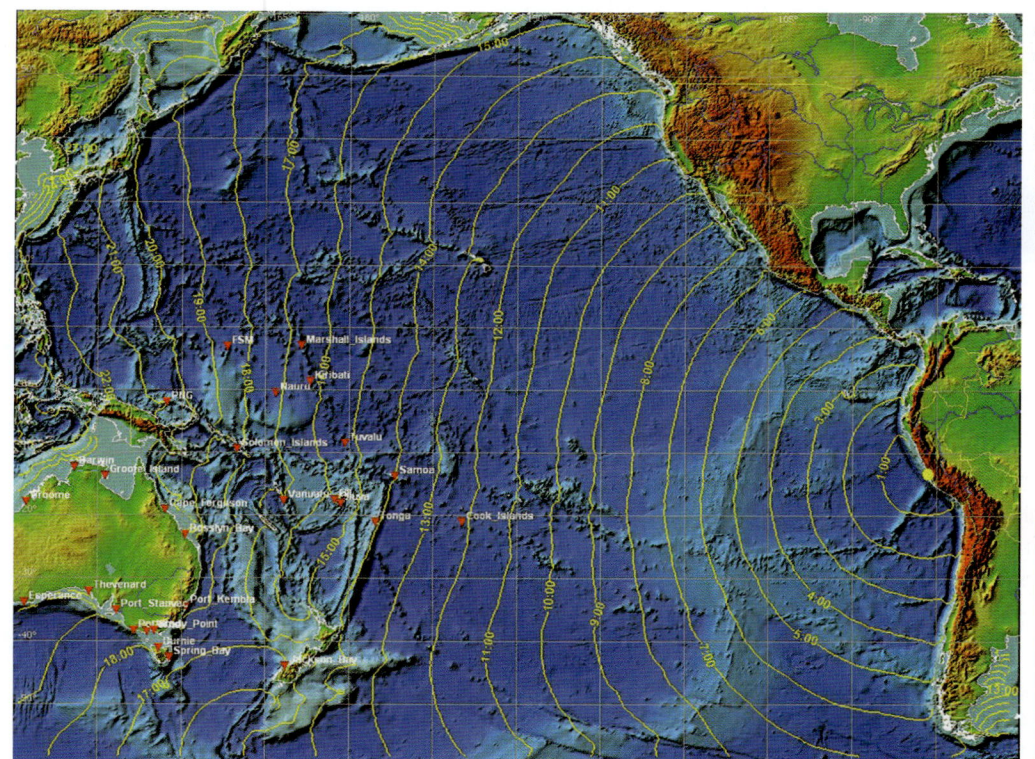

A magnitude 8.0 earthquake occurred on 15 August 2007 near the coast of Peru. A tsunami was detected by Seaframe (sea level fine resolution acoustic measuring equipment) stations located on Pacific islands. A small tsunami was detected at Port Kembla.

**Key**
- Tsunami travel time contours (hours)
- Earthquake near coast of central Peru
- SEAFRAME stations operated by the Bureau of Meteorology

## Tsunami exercise tests Australia's warning system

Attorney-General Robert McClelland today delivered the findings of Exercise Ausnami, a comprehensive test of the Australian Tsunami Warning System (ATWS).

The aim of the national exercise was to allow the government to test the effectiveness of the Australian Tsunami Warning System's communications for delivering and managing tsunami warnings for Australia.

'Exercise Ausnami' was conducted on 15 and 16 June 2009 and simulated a magnitude 9.0 earthquake in the Pacific affecting the east coast of Australia and a magnitude 9.0 earthquake off Indonesia, affecting Western Australia, South Australia and relevant offshore islands.

The test reaffirmed that in the event of a tsunami, the Australian Government is ready to protect the Australian community.

The test confirmed:
- the capability of the system to detect and verify tsunami threats from earthquakes;
- that warnings could be issued within thirty minutes of an undersea earthquake; and
- the timely provision of information to affected jurisdictions and relevant government agencies.

The capability of the states to provide timely warnings to potentially affected coastal communities is also important. That capacity will be significantly enhanced by work being undertaken by the states to develop a national telephone-based emergency warning system.

The Federal Government is contributing $27 million to this project, including $11.3 million to build a secure database of phone numbers for the system to use and conduct research into mobile location-based warnings.

'Exercise Ausnami' involved Geoscience Australia, the Bureau of Meteorology, the Attorney-General's Department and state and territory emergency management agencies from Western Australia, South Australia, Queensland, Victoria and New South Wales.

The ATWS is provided through the Joint Australian Tsunami Warning Centre which operates 24-hours a day, seven days a week to detect and verify tsunami threats to Australia as a result of earthquakes.

The ATWS provides a comprehensive warning system capable of delivering timely and effective tsunami warnings to affected populations. It also supports international efforts to establish an Indian Ocean tsunami warning system, and contributes to the facilitation of tsunami warnings for the South-West Pacific.

Similar tests of the ATWS will continue on a regular basis in the future. In addition, Australia will also take part in Pacific and Indian Ocean tsunami exercises with our international counterparts.

*Source: www.attorneygeneral.gov.au, 19 June 2009.*

# ICT activities

## projects*plus*

## Coastal Management
**SEARCHLIGHT ID: PRO-0032**

### YOUR TASK
Create a website that outlines the views of a specific stakeholder in regards to a high rise resort development. The development will be built on an undeveloped coastal area in the local community of the coastal town of Seaton.

### SCENARIO
You live in a quiet coastal town called Seaton on the east coast of Australia. The local community experiences a small amount of tourism each summer, and is well known for its beautiful bays and local fishing industry. A large-scale coastal resort development company — *Sea Breezes* — has indicated that they plan to build a high rise resort development on pristine coastal land in your local community.

The location of the development will be on the secondary and tertiary dunes and swampy mangrove land right next to the local estuary. The creek that feeds this estuary runs through the national park. The land is also ideal as it is right near the beach, as well as close to major roads and is in walking distance of the town's commercial district. This land is owned by the local council, and has been officially unused since the town was settled although many locals use the area of land to access the beach and they also enjoy walking through the area.

The news of this development caused quite a bit of controversy and conflict at the last town meeting. Members of the Seaton community are divided, as a coastal development of this size could offer both positive and negative impacts on the town and surrounding areas. At the end of the meeting a number of lobby groups (both for and against the development) quickly formed. The local council indicated that all lobby groups would need to forward a submission to the council in the next two weeks if they wanted their views to be considered in the decision-making process.

Your group has decided that the development of a website is the most effective way of promoting the views of your lobby group, as well as gathering the support of others in Seaton and the surrounding local communities. The website should contain your group's perspectives on the development, as well as arguments against the perspectives of other stakeholders in the development.

The website your group creates will need to be very clear and contain evidence to support your argument. It is also important that it stands out from the others, in terms of the accuracy and wide audience appeal. The website should adhere to common conventions of good website design; more information on this can be found in the Additional Resources section.

The choices of lobby groups include:
- Local residents for the development
- Local residents against the development
- Local businesses for the development (shops in the commercial district)
- Local businesses against the development (other tourism accommodation operators and any ecotourism businesses)
- Environmentalists
- the Developer (*Sea Breezes*)

### PROCESS
- Open the ProjectsPLUS application for this chapter located in your eBookPLUS. Watch the introductory video lesson and then click the 'Start Project' button to set up your project. Your group can have any number of members but each student can be a member of only one group. Save your settings and the project will be launched.

- Your teacher will assign your group to create a website for one of the lobby groups listed in the Scenario. Navigate to your Research Forum which has been set up so you can enter your ideas and research in the form of a SWOT analysis of your position.
- Consider your stakeholder's perspective and viewpoints in terms of this coastal development. To help you with this, a SWOT analysis tool is available in your Media Centre. You will also need to research and brainstorm arguments against the other stakeholders of the development. From this analysis, share your ideas with your other group members by entering them in your Research Forum. Look for examples of other coastal developments and consider their arguments. You will need facts and evidence that is accurate to support your arguments. The weblinks in your Media Centre will help you get started. You can view and comment on other group members' articles and rate the information they have entered.
- When your research is complete, navigate to your Media Centre and download the Website Model and Website Planning Template to help you build your website. Your Media Centre also includes images, video and audio files to help bring your site to life. You could also film some of your own videos and create your own audio files.
- Use the Website Planning Template to create a design specification for your site. You should have a home page and at least three other pages. These pages could include a place to vote for or against the proposal, an outline of your group's arguments, links to other developments and a forum to create discussion. Remember the three-click rule in web design — you should be able to get anywhere in a website (including back to the home page) in a maximum of three clicks.
- Use FrontPage, Dreamweaver, iWeb or other website building software to build your website. Remember to consider the layout and design of your website — the main focus should be on the viewpoints of your stakeholder.
- Print out your Research Report from ProjectsPLUS and hand it to your teacher with your website.

**SUGGESTED SOFTWARE**
- ProjectsPLUS
- Word
- FrontPage, Dreamweaver, iWeb or other web-building software

**MEDIA CENTRE**

Your Media Centre contains:
- a topographic map of the proposed development site
- a SWOT analysis template
- a website planning template
- images to add richness to your website
- weblinks to other resort developments
- an assessment rubric.

Your ProjectsPLUS application is available in this chapter's Student Resources tab inside your eBookPLUS. Visit www.jacplus.com.au to locate your digital resources.

## eLesson

### LAND DEGRADATION

Land degradation is the process that reduces the land's capacity to produce crops, support natural vegetation and provide fodder for livestock. In this video lesson we explore some of the factors that contribute to land degradation such as poor agricultural practices and management, the removal of vegetation and urban development.

SEARCHLIGHT ID: ELES-0261

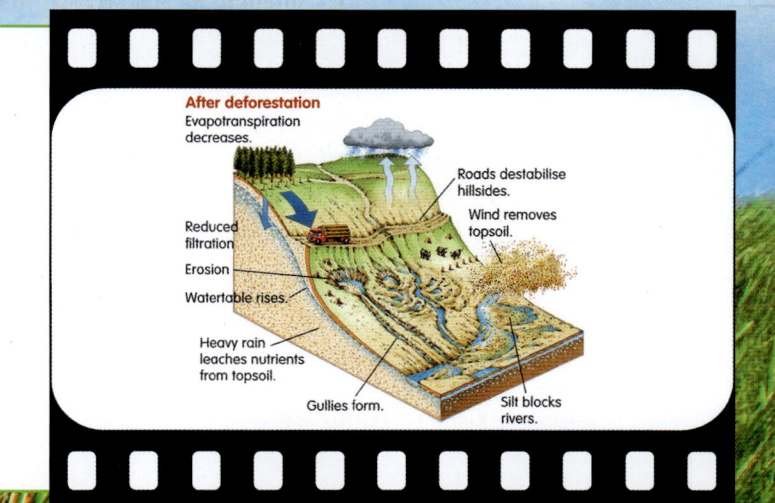

# 10 Australia in its regional and global contexts

**INQUIRY QUESTIONS**

+ What is Australia's place in the world?
+ What are Australia's global and Asia–Pacific regional links?
+ How are these links established and maintained and what are their implications for Australia, the region and the world?

Despite Australia's geographical isolation, it is connected to the rest of the world by trade, defence, diplomacy, tourism, sport, culture, aid, migration and communication.

Since Britain joined the European Economic Community in 1973 (now the European Union), Australia has increased its links with countries in the Asia–Pacific region. Through these cultural, economic and geopolitical links, Australia aims to work for an equitable and socially just world.

*The Australian, US and Russian teams celebrate on the podium after the women's basketball gold medal match of the Beijing Olympic Games, 23 August 2008.*

### KEY TERMS

**Asia–Pacific region:** area covering North-East Asia, South-East Asia, Australasia, Melanesia and Polynesia

**Australasia:** area that includes Australia, New Zealand, Papua New Guinea and neighbouring islands in the Pacific Ocean

**climate refugee:** person displaced by climate-change-induced environmental disasters

**cultural diversity:** cohabitation of people from different ethnic and/or religious–cultural backgrounds within the same geographic location

**culture:** system of shared beliefs, values, customs, behaviours and artefacts used by members of a society to interact with one another and with the outside world

**equity:** the concept of fairness, ensuring an even share

**exclusive economic zone (EEZ):** sea zone over which a country has sovereign rights to explore, exploit and conserve its natural resources

**globalisation:** breakdown of traditional barriers between nation states, allowing the movement of goods, capital, people and information

**intellectual property:** output from creative workers as protected by copyright, patents or trademarks — for example, the concept for a TV show

**migration:** movement of people into a country (immigration) and out of a country (emigration)

**non-government organisation (NGO):** not-for-profit organisation, usually with a charitable, community or environmental focus

**social justice:** the just and fair treatment of individuals and groups within a society

**sovereign rights:** power or authority over a territory

**tourism:** the practice of travelling temporarily to destinations not normally visited in the course of one's work or life

**transnational corporation (TNC):** company or organisation that owns and controls the means of production, such as factories, mines, farms and financial organisations, across more than one country

**treaty:** formal agreement between two or more independent countries, which is binding under international law. Treaties take a variety of forms, including conventions, protocols, agreements, exchanges of notes and exchanges of letters.

# 10.1 Australia's place in the world: territorial boundaries

Australia is an isolated island continent located in the Asia–Pacific region. Its territorial boundaries are located in the surrounding Pacific and Indian Oceans. Within these boundaries Australia has **sovereign rights** to billions of dollars worth of marine, mineral and petroleum resources. Global **treaties** such as the United Nations Convention on the Law of the Sea (UNCLOS) and organisations such the International Maritime Organisation (IMO), the International Seabed Authority (ISA) and the International Whaling Commission (IWC) oversee the management of Australia's marine boundaries and resources. Australia's Oceans Policy (1998) coordinates government bodies such as the Department of Environment, Water, Heritage and Arts, and **non-government organisations (NGOs)** such as the Australian Marine Environment Protection Association, to sustainably manage marine resources.

## Maritime boundaries

Australia's maritime boundaries are defined by their distance from land. This is measured from the territorial sea baseline (TSB), which corresponds roughly with the low-water line, and includes the

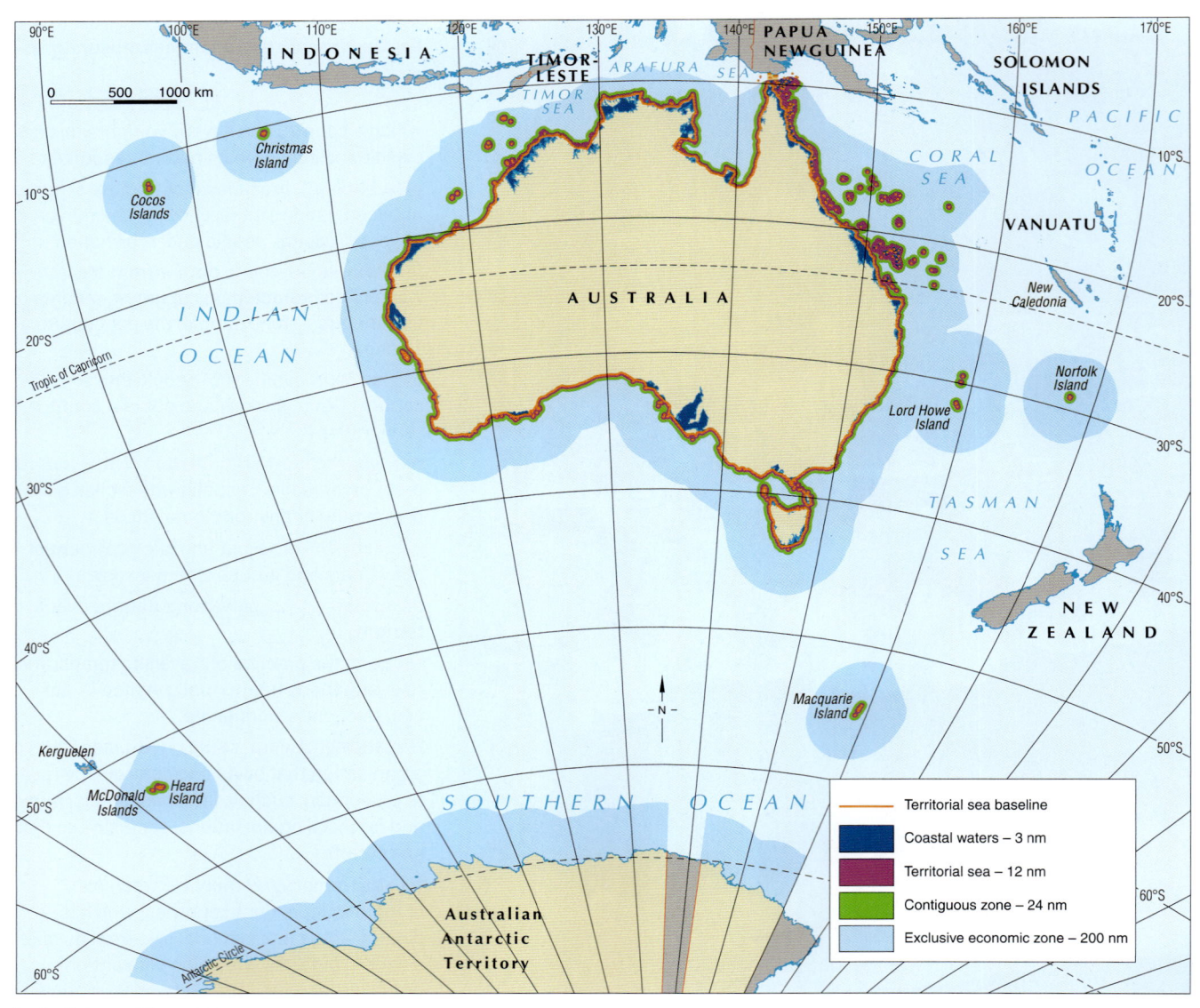

*Australia's maritime zones*

coasts of islands such as Lord Howe Island. The zones are divided into the following:
- *coastal/internal waters* — first three nautical miles (nm) from TSB
- *territorial sea/waters* — 0 to 12 nautical miles from TSB. Australia has rights over this area and allows 'innocent passage' (i.e. with no harmful purpose) for foreign ships.
- *contiguous zone* — 12 to 24 nautical miles from TSB. In this zone, Australia may punish infringements of customs, money or sanitary regulations.
- *exclusive economic zone (EEZ)* — 12 to 200 nautical miles from TSB. Australia has exclusive use of marine life and oil and gas reserves in the EEZ unless it grants access to another country.
- *Australian fishing zone* — 3 to 200 nautical miles from TSB. Generally the outer limit of this zone is the same as the EEZ boundary. In this zone Australia regulates fishing by all countries.
- *continental shelf* — an area of seabed extending outward from Australia and roughly the same as the EEZ. Australia has sovereign rights over the continental shelf for exploiting mineral and marine organisms.

In 2008 the United Nations expanded Australia's rights to oil, mineral and biological resources by an extra 2.5 million square kilometres of continental shelf, in nine marine regions.

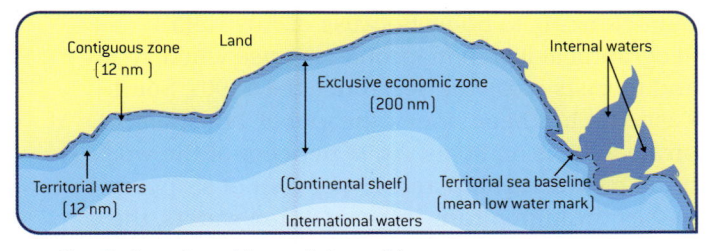

*Detailed section of Australia's maritime zones*

## Treaties and agreements

Australia's exclusive economic zone (EEZ) is a sea zone over which the country has sovereign rights to explore, exploit and conserve its natural resources. Australia has the third largest EEZ in the world (after the United States and France) with an area larger than its land territory. To avoid conflict over the use of resources Australia has maritime boundary agreements with Indonesia, Papua New Guinea, the Solomon Islands, France (New Caledonia) and New Zealand.

The 1978 Torres Strait Treaty (TST) between Australia and Papua New Guinea (PNG) covers the management of the Torres Strait, a 150-kilometre wide shallow passage, between the two countries. The treaty describes two different boundary lines (the seabed line and fishing line) and the Torres Strait Protected Zone (TSPZ), and allows Indigenous people from both countries to move freely for traditional activities such as fishing for food. The boundaries are managed by the Protected Zone Joint Authority (PZJA).

Conflict has occurred over the ownership of oil and gas in the Timor Gap between Australia and Timor-Leste (formerly East Timor). These resources are located in a shared zone known as the Joint Petroleum Development Area (JPDA). Under the Timor Sea Treaty (2002) revenue from the oil and gas is shared between Timor-Leste and Australia. In return Australia provides billions of dollars in development aid to Timor-Leste.

### ACTIVITIES

#### UNDERSTANDING
1. Describe the different types of maritime boundaries.
2. Discuss the importance of border treaties and agreements.

#### THINKING AND APPLYING
3. Indicate whether the following statements are true or false.
   a. A foreign vessel carrying legitimate cargo can be intercepted and searched in the EEZ. **T/F**
   b. A foreign vessel suspected of carrying drugs can be searched and intercepted in the contiguous zone. **T/F**
   c. Australia can permit an oil company to drill for oil in the EEZ. **T/F**
   d. Part of the territorial sea baseline could be observed from a coastal headland on a clear day. **T/F**
   e. A foreign vessel wishing to fish in the Australian fishing zone can do so under international law. **T/F**
4. Australia, like most nations, restricts the right of people from other countries to enter our boundaries. In groups, discuss arguments for and against restricted entry of immigrants. Summarise your findings as an oral report.
5. Read the information about oil in the Timor Sea. Using the internet or library, describe the progress of the project and how the revenue is shared between Timor-Leste and Australia.

#### USING YOUR SKILLS
6. Refer to the map of Australia's maritime zones.
   a. List the islands and countries close to Australia's EEZ.
   b. Describe the area of the EEZ.
   c. Explain why the EEZ is important to Australia.

# 10.2 Protecting territorial boundaries

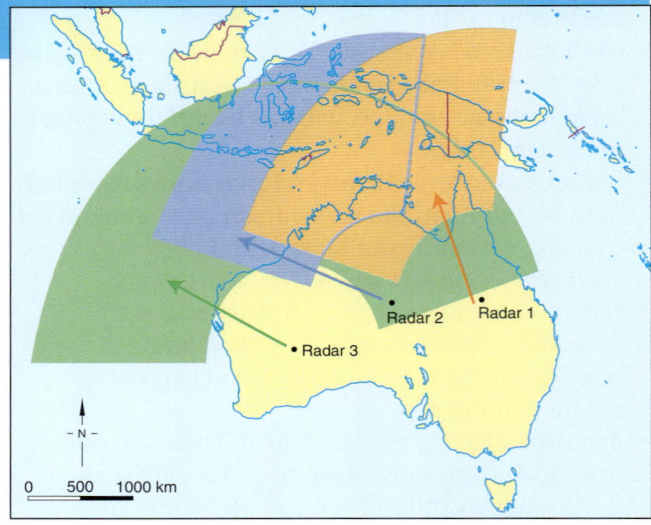

Australia's geographical isolation and vast territorial borders require the coordinated management of Australian government departments such as Customs, Immigration and Citizenship, Foreign Affairs and Trade, Defence, and the Maritime Safety Authority. Customs Coastwatch and navy vessels patrol Australia's maritime boundaries and respond to illegal fishing, drug smuggling, people smuggling, piracy, terrorist threats and the dumping of toxic waste. The United Nations Convention on the Law of the Sea (UNCLOS) bans piracy, the slave trade and trafficking in narcotic drugs, and grants Australia the right to intervene in such activities. Also the Bali Process, involving Australia and 41 other countries, aims to combat people smuggling in the Asia–Pacific region.

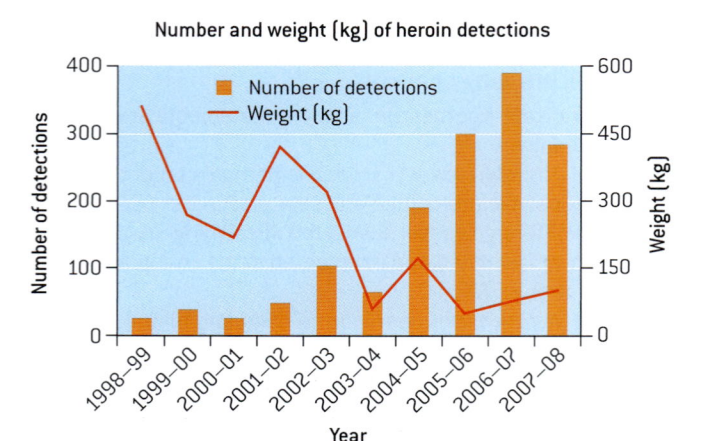

*The Jindalee Operational Radar Network (JORN) uses radar at Longreach in Queensland (1), Laverton in Western Australia (2), and Alice Springs in the Northern Territory (3). This enables the Australian military to observe air and sea activity north of Australia to a distance of at least 3000 kilometres. It takes in all of Java, Irian Jaya, Papua New Guinea and the Solomon Islands, and halfway across the Indian Ocean.*

*In 2008 the total weight of heroin detected at Australia's border was 99.3 kilograms. A sizeable detection of 24.9 kilograms was made by Customs in February 2008.*

The Jindalee Operational Radar Network (JORN) monitors air and sea movements across 37 000 kilometres of unprotected Australian coastline and 9 million square kilometres of ocean. It detects suspicious aircraft activity, curbs people smuggling and spies on neighbouring nations from at least 3000 kilometres away. In 2008 its technology contributed to the interception of unauthorised boatloads of people off the north-west coast of Australia, as well as 156 illegal vessels and 1217 foreign fishers in Australian waters. Targeting such activities within Australia's EEZ led to stronger links with Indonesia's maritime security agency, Bakorkamla.

## Piracy on the open sea

All waters beyond Australia's national boundaries or EEZ are international waters — free to all nations but belonging to none. Because of Australia's geographical isolation, problems arise when goods and tourists cross the sea. Since the 1990s, South-East Asia has been one of the global 'hot spots' of pirate attacks on boats. As 90 per cent of the world's trade moves via ship and 45 per cent of shipping passes through pirate-infested Asian waters, the risk of attack is of global concern. To reduce the threat Australia, as a member of the Five Power Defence Arrangement, participates in anti-piracy and anti-terrorism activities with Malaysia, New Zealand, Singapore and the United Kingdom.

*Twenty-first century pirates*

## Sustainable oceans

State and federal governments aim to sustainably manage the ocean zone that surrounds the Australian continent. In Australian waters, the *Environment Protection and Biodiversity Conservation Act 1999* regulates actions that adversely impact on threatened migratory species. The NSW Marine Parks Authority aims to conserve the diversity of marine life, and Australia, as a member of the International Maritime Organisation (IMO), aims to prevent marine pollution and reduce greenhouse emissions from ships. Of concern is the capacity for oil spills from tankers plying coastal waters and threatening Australian coral reefs and wetlands.

## International Whaling Commission

In 2008 the Japanese whaling fleet moved back into Australia's territorial waters. The anti-whaling protest ship, *Steve Irwin*, requested their removal by the Australian government. Japan hunts about 1000 whales per year, mostly in the Southern Ocean Whale Sanctuary where commercial whaling is banned. They hunt under International Whaling Commission (IWC) rules that allow hunting for scientific purposes. The Border Protection Command and the Enforcement and Investigations Division of Australian Customs monitor Japanese whaling activities in the Southern Ocean. Despite strong protest activity by Greenpeace during whale hunts, Japan has killed 6500 minke whales in the Southern Ocean Whale Sanctuary since 1987. These actions violate the Whale Sanctuary, the Antarctic Treaty, International Maritime Law and the moratorium of the International Whaling Commission. Prime Minister Kevin Rudd argues that although Australia has strong economic, diplomatic and security links with Japan, it is important for Australia to oppose Japan's annual whale hunt.

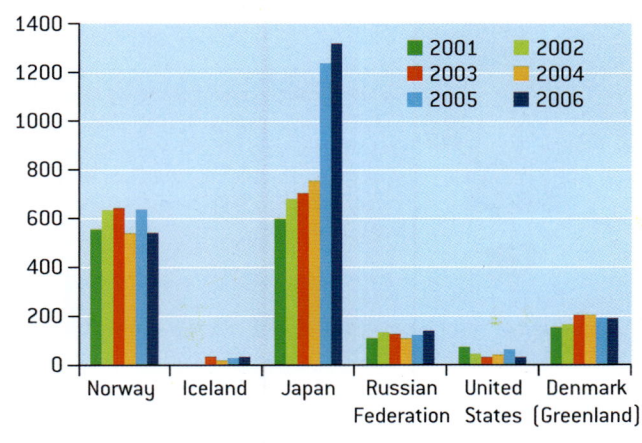

*Annual whale harvest, 2001–06*

*In 2008 Japan resumed whale hunting in the Southern Ocean Whale Sanctuary.*

**GEOfacts** In the open sea, Australia conducts peaceful military activities. Australia assists its neighbour Kiribati in the surveillance of its EEZ and assists Micronesia by patrolling its waters to stop illegal fishing of tuna.

### ACTIVITIES

**UNDERSTANDING**

1. Explain the management of Australia's territorial boundaries.
2. Describe the threats to Australia's boundaries.

**THINKING AND APPLYING**

3. Crimes at sea — including piracy, maritime terrorism, drug trafficking, people smuggling, illegal fishing and illegal dumping — are on the increase. Research two of these crimes and find out how the Australian government contributes to managing the issue nationally and globally.
4. On 16 April 2009, 47 asylum seekers, two crew and Australian navy personnel were on board a vessel when it exploded in flames at Ashmore Reef, north-west of Darwin. Three people were killed and two were believed to have drowned. Many suffered serious burns. Research the incident and decide what approach you would have taken if you were the Australian government.

**USING YOUR SKILLS**

5. Refer to the graph on border heroin detection. Calculate the number of heroin detections in 1998–99 and 2007–08. Describe the change in the number and weight of heroin detections in 1998–99 and 2007–08. Account for the changes.
6. Refer to the graph on whale harvesting.
    a. Calculate the countries with the largest whale harvest in 2001, 2004 and 2006.
    b. Name the country with the largest whale harvest increase between 2001 and 2006.
    c. Explain why whale harvest figures are high for Norway and Denmark (Greenland).

**CHAPTER 10** | Australia in its regional and global contexts

# 10.3 Australia's changing place in a globalised world

After European settlement in 1788, Australia's links with the rest of the world were restricted by its isolation. In recent decades, the situation has changed dramatically. Australia has become increasingly connected with the rest of the world through trade, tourism, sport, migration, culture, defence, aid and communications.

## Links with old friends

Geographically, Australia is part of the Asia–Pacific region. Yet for over 200 years, it had strong links with Europe, especially the United Kingdom. These links weakened when:
- Australia and the United States forged a strong defence link in the Pacific region in World War II.
- The United Kingdom entered into a trading agreement with many western European countries, leading to the creation of the European Economic Community (now called the European Union or EU) in 1973.

Today, links to the United Kingdom are both cultural and economic: English laws, language, religion and literature have shaped our culture; the largest group of overseas-born residents in Australia comes from the United Kingdom; Australia participates in sporting competitions such as the Ashes cricket tests; tourism is still strong between the two countries; and the UK is Australia's seventh-largest trading partner.

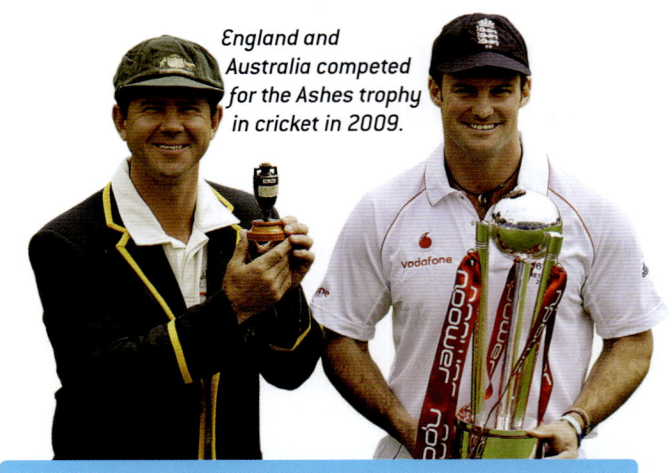

*England and Australia competed for the Ashes trophy in cricket in 2009.*

**Environmental links: the global commons**
Water cycles (river systems); ecosystems (rainforests, soil nourishment); the atmosphere (global warming, pollution, radiation); geological factors (earthquakes, tsunamis); weather patterns (storms, cyclones); marine, bird and animal life (fishing grounds, endangered species); microbes and diseases (SARS, swine flu)

**Economic, trade and tourism links**
Importing and exporting; multilateral and bilateral trade agreements; trade organisations (International Monetary Fund, APEC, ASEAN); the Stock Exchange; transnational corporations (Nike, Rip Curl); travel and hospitality industries; transport (A380 airbus, super tankers); international trafficking

**Global citizenship: government and non-government organisations**
AusAID, Austrade, World Vision, AUSTCARE, UNICEF, Amnesty International, Red Cross, Greenpeace, Civil Society Organisations, overseas volunteer organisations

**Communications: global organisations**
United Nations (UN), World Trade Organization (WTO), World Bank, Organisation for Economic Co-operation and Development (OECD), International Monetary Fund (IMF), Australian Department of Foreign Affairs and Trade (DFAT), diplomatic missions, international agreements

**Cultural and sporting links**
Cinema, TV and music; food and clothing; sport (Olympic Games); education (student exchanges); religion, language and cultural identity (cultural festivals, Indigenous movements/rights); information/ideas (national and international conferences); architecture; growth of global citizenship (internet)

**Defence, aid and migration links**
Wars (Vietnam, Iraq); Australian peacetime alliances (United Nations); government foreign aid (AusAID); migration (Department of Immigration and Citizenship); refugees (Refugee Council of Australia)

**Communications and technology links**
Global media networks; the internet; mobile phones; cable and satellite technology; mapping and location sytems (GIS, GPS); social networking (MySpace, Facebook, blogs, YouTube)

**Treaties and agreements links**
Environmental (Kyoto Treaty and Montreal Protocol); weapons and arms control (Nuclear Non-Proliferation Treaty); war (Geneva Conventions); trafficking and organised crime; human rights and development (Universal Declaration of Human Rights 1948, UN Millennium Development Goals 2000–15)

*Australia's regional and global links*

Many Australians are also descended from Europeans, such as the Germans who settled in the Barossa Valley in the mid 1800s, and this has contributed to our culturally diverse society. The European Union is Australia's largest trade and investment partner, and over 700 000 Australians travel to Europe each year.

## Australia's global links

In a globalised world, Australians are affected by rising oil prices and falling share prices. Our country exports minerals, imports cars, gives aid after disasters, fights in overseas wars, participates in world sporting events, accepts refugees and protects against illegal drugs entering the country. Australians eat McDonald's hamburgers, watch *The Simpsons*, wear Nike shoes and obtain information via mobile phones, the internet and geographic information systems (GIS). Australia is a member of the United Nations and has signed global treaties/agreements such as the Universal Declaration of Human Rights (1948) and the Millennium Development Goals (2000–15). As a member of the Organisation for Economic Co-operation and Development (OECD), Australia maintains communication with development agencies in over 100 countries.

**Globalisation** is a two-way process, as Australian products such as Rip Curl and entertainment groups such as The Wiggles are sold overseas. Australian films, artists and inventions have won global awards. The 2008 Beijing Olympics Swimming Cube was designed by Australians, and Ian Thorpe and Nicole Kidman are global names. Australian wool is used in high-fashion clothing designs in Milan, Australian wines are drunk in Paris restaurants and Aboriginal paintings are displayed in world-famous galleries.

## Advantages and disadvantages of global links

Some aspects of globalisation are disliked, such as the Americanisation of our culture. On the other hand, people employed in the tourist industry favour globalisation, as it provides a livelihood. Australians benefit from globalisation, in terms of exports, skilled immigrants, and the internet as a source of information and communication via social networking sites such as MySpace. Australia's aid helps reduce poverty in developing countries and the defence force participates in the United Nations global peacekeeping force.

From an equity and social justice perspective, Australians dislike the loss of jobs when **transnational corporations (TNCs)** move out of Australia, while others protest over the exploitation of low-paid workers when TNCs move into developing countries.

### GEOfacts

- Japan is Australia's top export market.
- Australia's 2020 summit in 2008 recommended we strengthen links with our Asia–Pacific neighbours. Kevin Rudd also aims to create an Asia–Pacific Community, modelled on the EU, to deal with future economic, political and security challenges in the region.

### ACTIVITIES

**UNDERSTANDING**

1. Describe the changes to Australia's place in the world since 1788.
2. Explain what is meant by the term *globalisation*.
3. Discuss the advantages and disadvantages of globalisation to Australia and its citizens.

**THINKING AND APPLYING**

4. Globally, the United States may be the economic superpower and China the new manufacturing powerhouse. Describe what contribution Australia could make to the world.
5. Research a global company that has strong Australia–global links, for example, Rip Curl or Coca-Cola. On a blank map of the world, mark the countries where this company has manufacturing sites.

**USING YOUR SKILLS**

6. Refer to the diagram that shows examples of global links. Using the diagram, and drawing from your own knowledge, complete the following.
   a List ten Australian global sporting links.
   b Explain how improved communications have increased Australia's global links.
   c Describe how Australia's culture has spread around the world.
   d List Australia's recent defence links.
   e Explain how treaties/agreements can improve equity and social justice around the world.

### GEOTERMS

**globalisation:** breakdown of traditional barriers between nation states, allowing the movement of goods, capital, people and information

**transnational corporation (TNC):** company or organisation that owns and controls the means of production, such as factories, mines, farms and financial organisations, across more than one country

# 10.4 Strengthening links in the Asia–Pacific region

Australia is located in the Southern Hemisphere and is part of the **Asia–Pacific region**, covering North-East Asia, South-East Asia, **Australasia**, Melanesia and Polynesia. During the late twentieth century, links were strengthened between Australia and countries in the Asia–Pacific region.

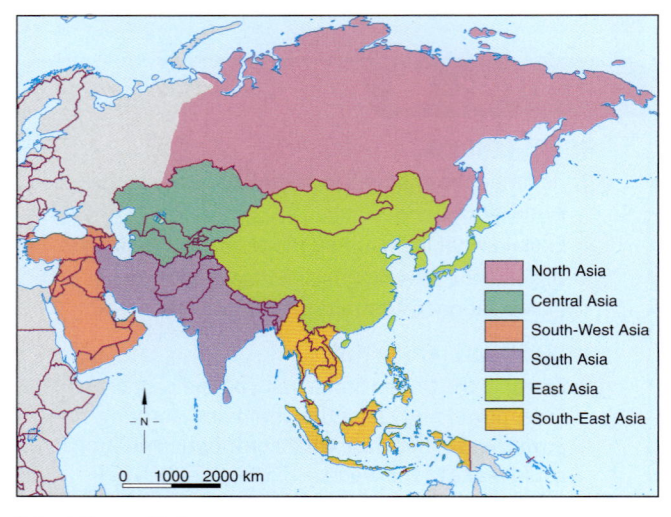

**Sub-regions of Asia**

## North-East and South-East Asian links

Asia is the world's largest and most populous continent, covering 29.4 per cent of the Earth's land area and containing over 60 per cent of the world's population. Australia's economic future is tied to Asia as it buys 60 per cent of Australian exports and provides half of all our imports. The main Asia–Australia links are with:

- *South-East Asia*. The mainland countries of Cambodia, Laos, Myanmar, Thailand and Vietnam, and the maritime countries of Brunei, Timor-Leste, Indonesia, Malaysia, the Philippines and Singapore make up the South-East Asian region. Singapore is the fifth wealthiest country in the world (GDP) and the 2003 Singapore–Australia Free Trade Agreement (SAFTA) strengthened trade and investment links between the two countries.
- *North-East Asia*. China, Japan, North and South Korea and Taiwan make up the North-East Asian region. Japan is Australia's third largest source of tourists and 60 000 Japanese live in Australia. Australia and Japan share the United States as their most important strategic ally and cooperate through Trilateral Strategic Dialogue ministerial meetings. Whaling is one of the few issues about which Australia and Japan disagree.

The cooperative relationship between Australia and its Asian neighbours is important for several economic, cultural and strategic reasons.

- Japan, China and North Korea are Australia's top three export markets.
- Australia's aid to Timor-Leste in 2008–09 was $96.3 million.
- Australia is the second largest provider of defence training to the Philippines.
- 177 000 Vietnamese-born immigrants live in Australia.
- The Thailand–Australia Free Trade Agreement aims to eliminate tariffs on imported goods from Australia by 2010.
- 1.4 million tourists arrive annually from North-East Asia.
- Australia participates in South-East Asian sports (Hong Kong Sevens Rugby).
- Asian culture is evident in Australia, with Buddhist temples, Muslim mosques, Chinatowns and the celebration of cultural events such as Chinese New Year. The Australia–China Council (ACC) encourages cultural exchanges through its Youth Exchange Programs.

## Pacific region links

Australasia includes New Zealand, Australia, Papua New Guinea, and the neighbouring islands in the Pacific Ocean. Papua New Guinea and the Pacific islands, with their range of landforms and resources, are divided into three sub-regions based on ethnic groups:

- *Melanesia* ('black islands'), which includes New Guinea, New Caledonia, Vanuatu, Fiji and the Solomon Islands
- *Polynesia* ('many islands'), which includes New Zealand, Samoa, Tonga and Tuvalu
- *Micronesia* ('small islands'), which includes Guam, Kiribati, Nauru and the Federated States of Micronesia. Most of these islands lie north of the Equator.

Until recently, Australians learned more about countries on the other side of the world than their own regional neighbours, and our understanding of the Pacific is sometimes based on stereotypes from

The regions, nations, territories and dependencies of Oceania. (The flags belong to the countries and territory highlighted in red.)

| Australia | Melanesia | Micronesia | Polynesia |
|---|---|---|---|
| • Australia<br>• Christmas Island (Australia)<br>• Cocos (Keeling) Islands (Australia)<br>• Norfolk Island (Australia) | • Fiji<br>• Indonesia — Oceanian part only*<br>• New Caledonia (France)<br>• Papua New Guinea<br>• Solomon Islands<br>• Vanuatu | • Federated States of Micronesia<br>• Guam (USA)<br>• Kiribati<br>• Marshall Islands<br>• Nauru<br>• Northern Mariana Islands (USA)<br>• Palau | • American Samoa (USA)<br>• Chatham Islands (NZ)<br>• Cook Islands (NZ)<br>• Easter Island (Chile)<br>• French Polynesia (France)<br>• Hawaii (USA)<br>• New Zealand<br>• Niue (NZ)<br>• Pitcairn Island (UK)<br>• Samoa<br>• Tokelau (NZ)<br>• Tonga<br>• Wallis and Futuna (France) |

*Irian Jaya and Maluku Islands, for example

television such as sun, surf, grass huts and exotic fruits. Recently, Australia's knowledge of and relationship with the Pacific islands has increased through:

- *aid* to Pacific islands such as Papua New Guinea
- *defence* personnel deployed to assist in restoring law (e.g. following the Tongan riots in 2006)
- *immigration* (e.g. more than 7000 Tongan-born immigrants live in Australia)
- *foreign investment*, especially in Fiji, where Australia is the largest foreign investor
- *exports* of food and other goods
- *tourism* (e.g. Australians make up 66 per cent of long-stay tourists in Vanuatu)
- *communication* links via the internet
- *sports* such as Rugby with Tonga and Samoa
- *cultural* displays from New Zealand's Maori culture, New Guinea and the Pacific.

## Asia–Pacific Economic Cooperation

Australia is a member of the Asia–Pacific Economic Cooperation (APEC). The 21 Pacific Rim countries account for 41 per cent of the world's population, 55 per cent of the world's GDP and 49 per cent of the world's trade. APEC aims to increase economic growth, cooperation, trade and investment in the Asia–Pacific region. Australians require a better understanding of culturally appropriate behaviour within these nations for improved future links.

### GEOTERMS

**Asia–Pacific region:** area covering North-East Asia, South-East Asia, Australasia, Melanesia and Polynesia

**Australasia:** area that includes New Zealand, Australia, Papua New Guinea, and neighbouring islands in the Pacific Ocean

## ACTIVITIES

### UNDERSTANDING

1. List the countries that are part of the Pacific Rim.
2. Describe the location of the Asia–Pacific region. What links does Australia have with this region?
3. Account for the growing importance of the Asia–Pacific region for Australia.
4. Refer to the table of regions in Oceania. Name two countries in Melanesia and two in Polynesia.

### THINKING AND APPLYING

5. Brainstorm the qualities that make a good neighbour. Describe the qualities that make Australia a good neighbour to countries in the Asia–Pacific region.
6. Discuss the cultural, economic and geopolitical advantages of Asia–Pacific links to Australia.
7. Plan a two-week holiday to five islands located in the Asia–Pacific region. Complete a table that lists the following for each island:
   • name of country • latitude and longitude
   • time difference • distance from Sydney to the capital city • climate • landforms • natural disasters (if relevant) • culture • sights you would visit • activities you would participate in.

### USING YOUR SKILLS

8. Study the map opposite. List three countries in North-East Asia and three countries in South-East Asia.
9. Use an atlas to:
   a. calculate the distance from Sydney to Vanuatu and Tonga
   b. determine the direction of Tuvalu from New Zealand
   c. calculate the bearing of Papua New Guinea from Samoa
   d. name Australia's six closest neighbours.

CHAPTER 10 | Australia in its regional and global contexts

# 10.5 Australia's connection to ASEAN countries: Indonesia

The South-East Asian region is located north of Australia. The region covers an area of 4 523 000 km², has a population of 568 300 000 culturally diverse people, and a mixture of developed countries (such as Singapore) and developing countries (such as Indonesia). A large proportion of Australia's exports and tourists either go to or pass through these countries. Over the last 20 years, Australia has increased its links with South-East Asia via non-government organisations (NGOs) and treaties/agreements for economic and geopolitical advantages.

## Association of South-East Asian Nations

The Association of South-East Asian Nations (ASEAN) promotes economic growth, cultural development and regional peace among its ten members — Brunei, Burma, Cambodia, Indonesia, Laos, Malaysia, the Philippines, Singapore, Thailand and Vietnam. Western countries have criticised ASEAN for being too soft over human rights abuses in Myanmar and refusing to suspend its ASEAN membership. Australia, as one of ASEAN's Dialogue Partners, aims to liberalise trade, expand security, increase environmental protection, and stop illegal immigrants, transnational crime, piracy and terrorism. Australia has strengthened its relationship with ASEAN countries via several different links:

- *Aid.* Australia provides investment and communication technologies through its aid programs to ASEAN countries. In 2009 Australia provided Cambodia with $55 million to reduce rural poverty and infant mortality rates.
- *Trade.* ASEAN receives 12 per cent of Australia's exports and aims to complete free trade agreements with China, Japan, South Korea, India, Australia and New Zealand by 2013. Vietnam's rapid economic growth has increased the demand for Australian metals, wheat, dairy produce, machinery, petroleum-based products and live animals. The Australian–ASEAN–New Zealand Free Trade Agreement (AANZFTA) strengthens Australia's economic and strategic engagement within the region.
- *Education.* Education services are Australia's largest service export to ASEAN. Australia provides on- and off-shore education services to 70 000 students.
- *Tourism.* Increasing travel between Australia and ASEAN countries has improved cultural understanding, especially through tours by performing arts groups.
- *Defence.* Australia participated in the Vietnam War and the ASEAN Regional Forum (ARF) promotes regional security.
- *Migration.* In 2008, 14 per cent of immigrants in Australia came from South-East Asia. Vietnamese Australians constitute the seventh largest ethnic group in Australia and the sixth most widely spoken language in the country.
- *Future.* A plan of action to implement the ASEAN–Australia Comprehensive Partnership (2008–13) aims to achieve the United Nations Millennium Development Goals (2000–15) and to establish an ASEAN Economic Community by 2015.

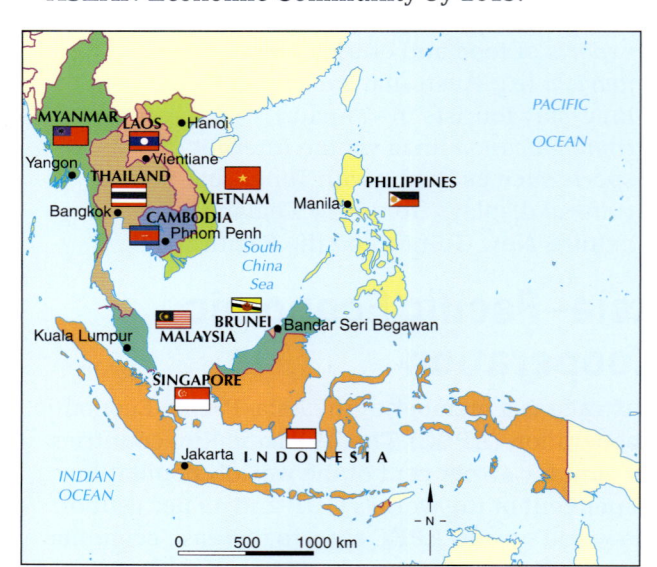

ASEAN's ten member countries

### ASEAN's main trading partners 2007

| ASEAN's principal export destinations, 2007 | | |
|---|---|---|
| 1 | United States | 16.3% |
| 2 | Japan | 13.4% |
| 3 | China | 12.2% |
| 4 | Hong Kong, SAR | 8.8% |
| 5 | Repub. of Korea | 4.8% |
| 6 | Australia | 4.8% |

| ASEAN's principal import sources, 2007 | | |
|---|---|---|
| 1 | Japan | 16.2% |
| 2 | China | 15.8% |
| 3 | United States | 12.7% |
| 4 | Repub. of Korea | 6.5% |
| 5 | Germany | 4.1% |
| (7) | Australia | 2.6% |

# Indonesian links

Indonesia, closely located to the north of Australia, is part of South-East Asia. It is an archipelago of 13 667 islands located along the Equator. It supports a population of 222 million people, with 60 per cent living on the island of Java. Australians who visit Bali for a holiday are made aware that the death penalty applies to the smuggling of drugs into the country. Illegal boat people arrive on our shores via Indonesian islands. AusAID assisted Indonesian people after the 2004 tsunami disaster and after the Bali terrorist bombings of 2002, which killed many Australian tourists and local Balinese. Australia and Indonesia cooperate on counter-terrorism, illegal fishing, people smuggling, avian influenza management, climate change and interfaith dialogue.

In 2009 Indonesia was the largest recipient of Australian aid, as 17 per cent of its population live below the poverty line. Indonesia is Australia's thirteenth largest trading partner and 400 Australian firms operate there. The Australia–Indonesia Institute promotes improved communication links through 'people exchanges'. In 2008 the cultural diplomacy program IN2OZ enabled Australian writers to participate in Indonesia's annual Ubud Writers and Readers Festival. The Australia–Indonesia Partnership Country Strategy 2008–13 tackles poverty and promotes regional peace, stability and prosperity. The Australia–Indonesia Lombok Treaty coordinates defence, including military training and maritime patrols.

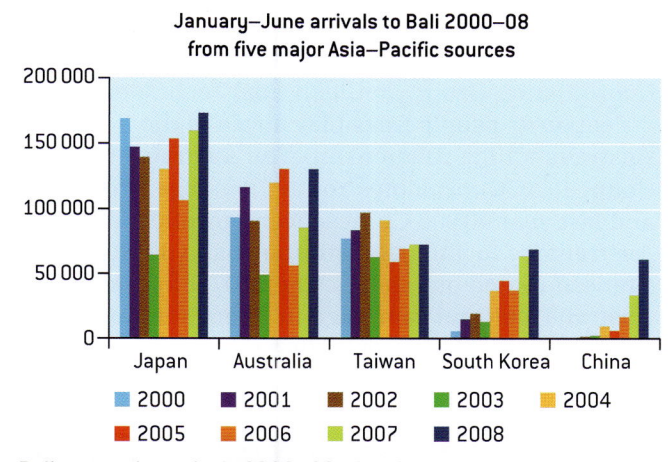

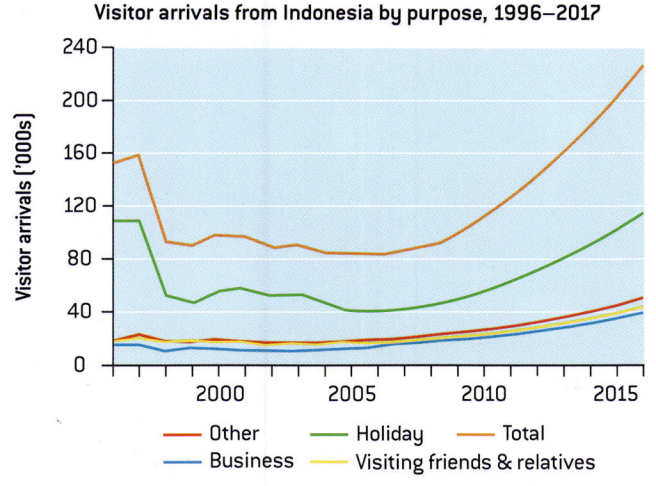

*January–June arrivals to Bali 2000–08 from five major Asia–Pacific sources*

**Bali top tourist arrivals 2000–08, showing an increase since the bombings**

*Visitor arrivals from Indonesia by purpose, 1996–2017*

**Indonesian tourism to Australia**

## ACTIVITIES

### UNDERSTANDING
1. Describe five ASEAN links with Australia.

### THINKING AND APPLYING
2. Analyse the advantages and disadvantages of Indonesia's links with Australia.
3. Select two ASEAN countries and complete the table below, illustrating their links with Australia. The website of the Department of Foreign Affairs (Country Information) is a good starting point.

| Links with Australia | Country A | Country B |
| --- | --- | --- |
| Aid | | |
| Communication | | |
| Culture | | |
| Defence | | |
| Migration | | |
| Tourism | | |
| Trade | | |
| Sport | | |
| Agreements and treaties | | |

### USING YOUR SKILLS
4. Refer to the map of ASEAN nations opposite. List the members of ASEAN. Using an atlas, redraw the map and label the countries, the capital cities, one line of latitude and one line of longitude.
5. Refer to the table showing ASEAN's main trading partners. Describe the importance of Australia to ASEAN trade.
6. Refer to the graph showing tourism arrivals in Bali. Discuss the impacts of the 2002 and 2005 bombings on Australian tourists to Bali. Describe the economic impact on the country.
7. Refer to the graph showing Indonesian tourism to Australia. Calculate the difference between the total number of tourists from Indonesia in 2003 and those projected for 2015. Discuss the advantages of tourism to the Australian economy.

# 10.6 Links with a future superpower: China

Since the 1970s, China's economy has developed so fast that it is now the fourth largest economy in the world after the United States. Of China's 1.4 billion people, 400 million labourers aged between 20 and 39 contributed to its economic growth. As a result, Chinese factories produce 70 per cent of the world's toys and 60 per cent of its bicycles. Some forecast that China is emerging as both a military and an economic rival to the United States — heralding a shift in global power. The Australian government acknowledges the rising importance of the People's Republic of China and aims to strengthen its links to the country. This is because China:

- is a major contributor to global wealth (GDP)
- plays an important role in global trade
- contributes to regional security through its important role in the Six Party Talks aimed at dismantling North Korea's nuclear weapons program
- contributes to global peace initiatives by taking action to support international arms control and non-proliferation of nuclear weapons
- participates in counter-terrorism work.

Australia pursues relations with China on the basis of mutual respect. Both countries recognise shared interests and differences. Australia is aware that any breakdown in stability in North-East Asia would have a devastating effect on Australia.

## Australia–China links

Many Chinese were lured to Australia by the gold rush in the 1850s. The White Australia policy of the early twentieth century curtailed the development of Chinese communities until the advent of multiculturalism, a 1970s Australian government policy. Over time, Chinatowns developed in Australia's capital cities with Chinese restaurants and religious temples forming the main cultural hubs. Today China is the third major source of immigrants to Australia, Chinese is the most widely spoken foreign language in Australian homes, and Australians celebrate Chinese New Year.

In 2008 AusAID provided aid to China after the Chengdu earthquake and Australia participated in the Beijing Olympic Games. Communication via the media enables Australians to be knowledgeable about air pollution in China, human rights abuses by the Chinese in Tibet, and the rural migration of 8.5 million Chinese to cities every year.

Over the last ten years China's importance to Australia has grown economically, politically and socially. Both countries have bilateral agreements on trade, aid, security and human rights. China is Australia's second biggest export market (wool, raw hides and skins, cotton, minerals and fuel) and in 2005, both countries commenced negotiations on a Free Trade Agreement. Environmental concerns over Australia's coal exports to China and its links to global warming led to the 2007 Australia China Joint Coordination Group on Clean Coal Technologies.

People-to-people links play a role in the Australia–China relationship. The Australia–China Council (ACC) promotes Youth Exchange Programs and last year 90 000 Chinese were enrolled at Australian educational institutions and 300 000 Chinese visited our shores. The 2007 'Experience Australia' cultural campaign in Shenzhen raised Australia's profile by promoting tourism and business links between the countries.

*Prime Minister Kevin Rudd meets the Chinese President Hu Jintao in Beijing in 2008.*

### New South Wales' trade with China

**Two-way trade**
- China is New South Wales' largest trading partner, with $16.4 billion two-way merchandise trade in 2007.

**Goods exports**
- China is New South Wales' fourth largest goods export destination.
- New South Wales' goods exports to China were worth $2.3 billion in 2007 (13 per cent average annual growth since 1998).
- New South Wales' top 10 goods exports to China in 2005 were:

| | |
|---|---|
| Copper ores | $504m |
| Wool | $235m |
| Coal | $131m |
| Aluminium | $129m |
| Non-ferrous metal waste | $118m |
| Medicaments (including veterinary) | $88m |
| Cotton | $86m |
| Civil engineering equipment | $54m |
| Integrated circuits | $45m |
| Copper | $45m |

Other fast-growing New South Wales goods exports included leather valued at $20 million (178 per cent average annual growth since 2002) and pulp and waste paper valued at $43 million (69 per cent average annual growth since 2002).

**Services exports**
- New South Wales' top services exports to China were education and tourism.
  - New South Wales hosted 46 per cent of the 107 000-plus Chinese student enrolments in Australian educational institutions in 2007.
  - New South Wales received 269 000 or three-quarters of all Chinese visitors to Australia in 2007 (150 per cent increase since 2003).
- New South Wales has direct air services from Sydney to Beijing, Shanghai and Guangzhou.

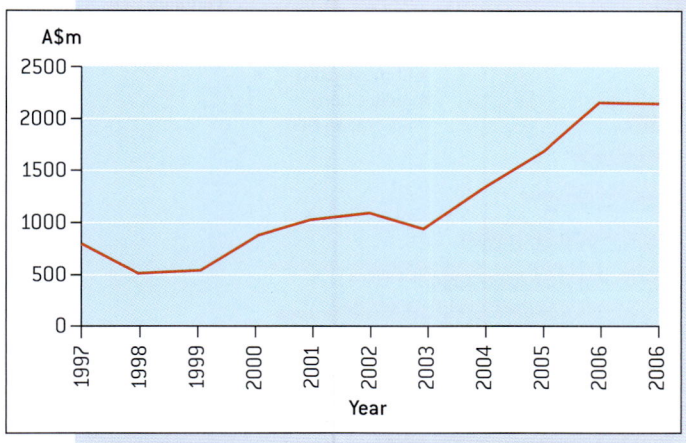

*New South Wales' merchandise exports to China by value*

## Future links

The World Expo to be held in Shanghai in 2010 will promote Australian cities (which are ranked among the most liveable in the world) as great places to study, live and work. Mandarin-fluent Prime Minister Kevin Rudd aims to build a stronger relationship with China, and the 2020 Australia Summit supports Chinese communities, especially their social inclusion in our culturally diverse country.

The Community Engagement Strategy run by the Fairfield Council in Sydney supports social justice and equity by providing language aids and a multilingual website to communicate with the local Chinese community.

### GEOfacts

Chongqing in China is the fastest growing urban centre on Earth. Its population, bigger than Peru and Iraq, has half a million people arriving every year in search of a better life.

### ACTIVITIES

**UNDERSTANDING**
1. List as many Australia–China links as you can.
2. Explain the reasons for supporting stronger Australia–China links.

**THINKING AND APPLYING**
3. Name five famous Chinese-born Australian residents.
4. Make a list of Chinese goods in your home.
5. Discuss the role of the Australia–China Council (ACC), especially its goal to foster cultural, economic and geopolitical advantages to both countries. To find out more, go to the **Australia–China Council** weblink in your eBookPLUS.
6. Research Australia's links with the 2008 Chengdu earthquake, Olympic Games and Tibetan protests.
7. Explain why the links between Australia and China are not always smooth.

**USING YOUR SKILLS**
8. List the trade links between New South Wales and China.
   a. Draw the top ten exports to China as a column graph.
   b. Calculate the change in exports to China from 1997 to 2007.
   c. Explain why coal, cotton and wool are exported to China.

# Working geographically

## BROADSHEET: AUSTRALIA–CHINA LINKS

### USING YOUR SKILLS

1. Use an atlas to find a map of China. Then complete the following.
   a. Draw an outline of the map.
   b. On the map, locate Beijing, Hong Kong, Guangzhou, Shanghai, Yangtze River, Great Wall of China, Three Gorges Dam, Gobi Desert, Plateau of Tibet and Chengdu.
   c. Include the following on the map: scale, two lines of latitude and two lines of longitude.
   d. List the countries that border China.

2. Use the topographic map of the Three Gorges Dam to complete the following.
   a. Calculate the density of towns and villages in AR5040.
   b. Measure the bearing of Zhaotziadian from the Three Gorges Dam.
   c. Calculate the local relief from GR4941 to GR5041.
   d. Identify the aspect of the slope at GR514410.
   e. Construct a cross-section from AR5040 to AR5042.
   f. Calculate the gradient of the slope from spot height 1342 to spot height 563 in AR4940.
   g. Construct a transect from AR5242 to GR535395.
   h. Construct a land-use map of the topographic map extract.

**Refer to the pyramid graph on Chinese-Australian ancestry.**

3. Answer True or False to the following.
   a. There is a larger percentage of Chinese-born women than Australian-born women over 90 years. **T/F**
   b. Australian-born families have more children under the age of 10 years than Chinese- and Indian-born families. **T/F**
   c. The largest percentage of Chinese-born residents is between 20 and 29 years. **T/F**

4. Calculate the percentage of Chinese-born males and females aged between 10 and 19 years. Compare the percentage with the Australian-born population.

5. Determine the percentage of Chinese-born residents within the working age of 20 to 59 years. Describe the advantages of this age group to the Australian economy.

6. Explain the shape of the population pyramid for the Chinese-born population.

7. Refer to the pie graph on Australia–China tourism to answer the following.
   a. Calculate the percentage of Chinese tourists who visit Australia for a holiday.
   b. Explain why a large percentage of Chinese visit Australia to see friends and relatives.

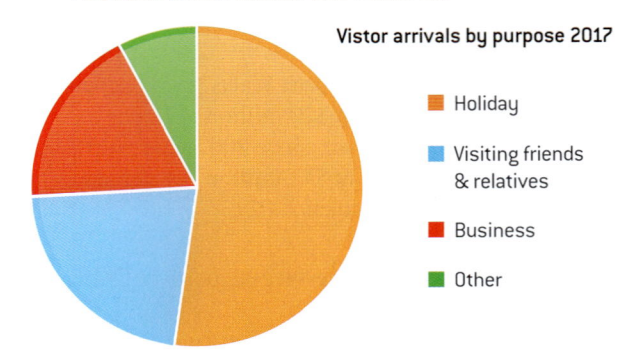

*Visitor arrivals by purpose 2017*
- Holiday
- Visiting friends & relatives
- Business
- Other

*Australia–China tourism forecast, 2017*

8. Use the internet to complete the following. Collect ten digital images of China's cultural and economic links in Australia. Discuss the advantages of the links to both Australia and China. Present your images as a poster, PowerPoint presentation or on an interactive whiteboard.

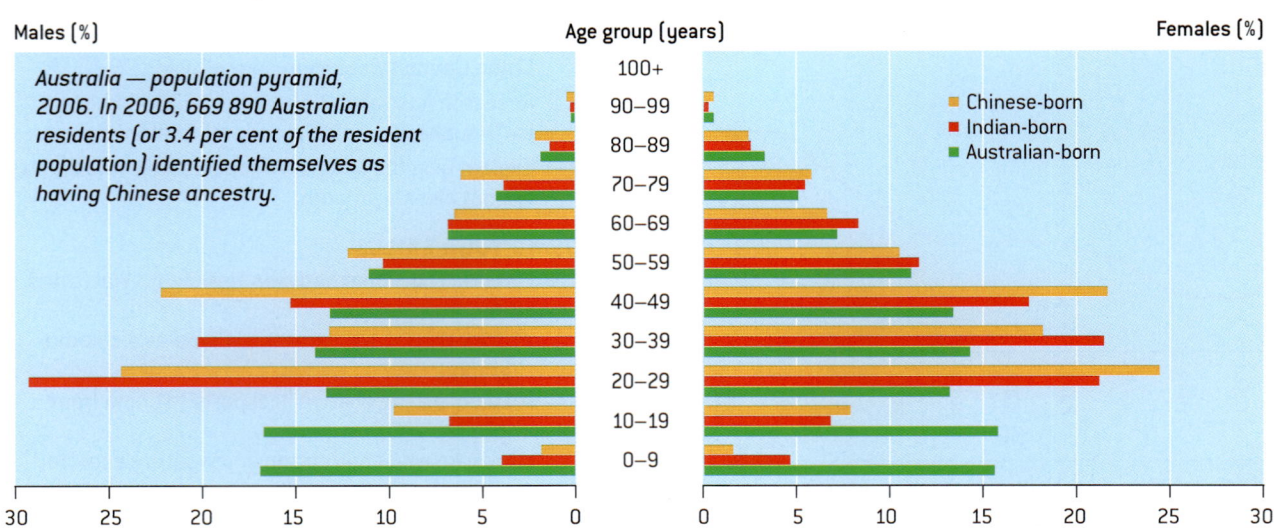

*Australia — population pyramid, 2006. In 2006, 669 890 Australian residents (or 3.4 per cent of the resident population) identified themselves as having Chinese ancestry.*

- Chinese-born
- Indian-born
- Australian-born

Topographic map of the Three Gorges Dam and surrounding region

SCALE 1 : 250 000

**Key**

| sealed | unsealed | |
|---|---|---|
| ▬▬▬ | ━ ━ ━ | Principal road; Built-up area |
| ─── | ─ ─ ─ | Secondary road |
| ┼┼┼┼┼ | | Railway; Station or siding |
| ○ ○ ✴ | | Town; Village; Shrine |
| | | Contour with value (interval 200 metres) |
| •730 | | Spot height (metres) |
| | | Forest, wood or scrubland |
| | | Watercourse (presence of water not implied) |
| | | Perennial lake; Dam |

## Three Gorges Dam

Australians cruise along the Yangtze River and visit the world's largest hydro-electric power project, the Three Gorges Dam in China. The construction of the 663 kilometre-long dam controls flooding and generates hydro-electric power for the growing population. The dam's construction caused 1.2 million Chinese to be relocated and environmental problems have emerged, including endangered species, landslides and water pollution.

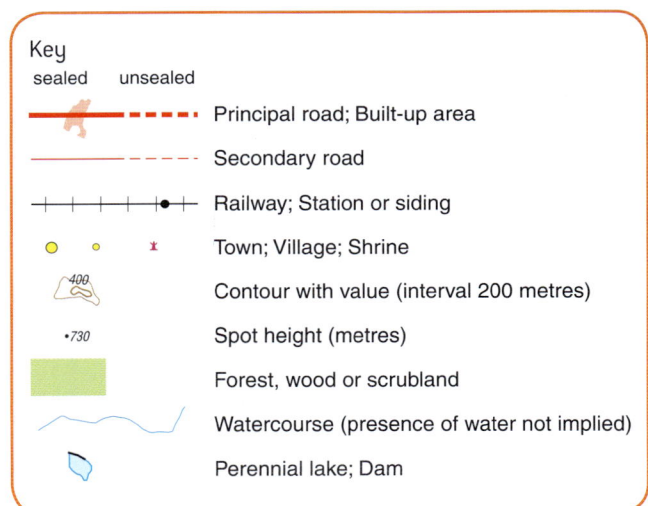

**CHAPTER 10** | Australia in its regional and global contexts

# 10.7 Our Pacific island neighbours: Nauru and Tuvalu

Australia is linked to its Pacific neighbours via aid, culture, defence, migration, sport and trade, and communicates via diplomatic missions and agreements. Australians holiday in Fiji, experience French culture in Vanuatu and play rugby with New Zealand. Australian tourists follow the Kokoda Track in Papua New Guinea, and the Australian Defence Force Operation HELPEM FREN (Helping Friend) assisted the Solomon Islands government to restore law and order after conflict.

Exotic cultures, and sun and surf attract Australians to these Pacific islands. For some islands, tourism generates up to 50 per cent of GDP. However, despite a diversity of resources some of the islands experience negative economic growth and poverty. Unsustainable logging, mining, fishing and agriculture have caused environmental degradation in some areas. By 2050, hundreds of thousands of people living on low-lying Pacific islands are expected to be flooded from rising sea levels. The impacts of global warming place pressure on Australia to help sustain these fragile communities or otherwise accommodate future **climate refugees**.

Pacific countries like the Solomon Islands are classified by the World Bank as a Low Income Country Under Stress (LICUS) because the government is unable to provide security, good governance and economic growth for its citizens. In some Pacific islands water supplies are erratic, sanitation systems are not maintained and power supplies are unreliable. Social and economic problems arise where teachers have few resources, doctors have insufficient medicines and there is no municipal body to repair buildings, sweep streets or manage rubbish. Australian aid, trade and investment aims to reduce inequity by improving the lives of the people of these islands.

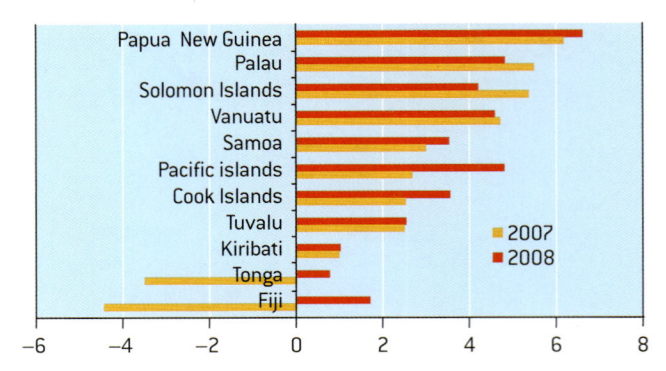

*Economic growth in Pacific island countries, 2007 and 2008*

## Small islands: Nauru and Tuvalu

On the small Pacific islands of Nauru and Tuvalu most of the population lives below the poverty line as the islands possess few natural resources. They have also suffered environmental degradation due to mining and other commercial activity and are particularly vulnerable to the effects of natural disasters (e.g. cyclones).

**Pacific development indicators 2009**

| Country | GDP per capita A$ | Literacy rate (% of adult population) | % safe water access | Life expectancy (years) |
|---|---|---|---|---|
| Australia | 30 500 | 99 | 100 | 80.2 |
| **Melanesia** | | | | |
| PNG | 2 650 | 57 | 39 | 55.1 |
| Solomon Islands | 1 900 | 30 | 70 | 62.2 |
| Vanuatu | 3 150 | 34 | 60 | 68.4 |
| Fiji | 6 150 | 93 | 47 | 67.8 |
| **Polynesia** | | | | |
| Tonga | 7 900 | 99 | 100 | 72.1 |
| Samoa | 5 700 | 99 | 88 | 70 |
| **Micronesia** | | | | |
| Kiribati | 2 900 | 93 | 65 | 65 |

Nauru, a phosphate rock island, is the world's smallest island nation, covering 21 square kilometres. About 80 per cent of the land was degraded after a century of mining. The run-off of silt and phosphate into the surrounding Exclusive Economic Zone killed 40 per cent of marine life. With 70 per cent of the population unemployed it accepted aid from the Australian government and in return Nauru became a detention centre, holding and processing asylum seekers trying to enter Australia from 2001 to 2008.

Tuvalu, comprising nine low-lying coral atolls, is the third-least populated independent country in the world. Most of the population is involved in subsistence fishing and agriculture, and the marketing of its internet domain name '.tv' contributes to government revenue. Tuvalu's low-lying terrain makes it especially vulnerable to the effects of global warming. In 2006 the Australian government established the South Pacific Sea Level and Climate Monitoring Project to enable Tuvalu to make informed decisions about managing its coastal resources.

**Development indicators of Nauru and Tuvalu and links to Australia, 2009**

| Development indicators | Nauru | Tuvalu |
|---|---|---|
| Population | 9000 | 12 000 |
| Literacy | 97% | 95% |
| Life expectancy women | 56 years | 71 years |
| Life expectancy men | 49 years | 66 years |
| Infant mortality rate | 10 per 1000 | 18.9 per 1000 |
| GDP | $27 million | $20 million |
| GDP per capita | $3000 | $1600 |
| Currency | Australian dollar | Australian dollar |
| Diplomatic relations | Diplomatic missions with Australia and Taiwan | Close relations with Fiji, New Zealand and Australia |
| Major aid donor | AusAID provides millions of dollars, with the aim of reducing poverty and improving education and training in skills required to live sustainably. | |

*Tuvalu. Naseli Kaitu, chief and elder of the Funafuti people, goes fishing. In parts of the Pacific, the chief system is still part of community life. With their knowledge of customary law, chiefs and elders are called upon to maintain social order and uphold traditional values.*

**Nauru and Tuvalu trade with Australia**

| Nauru | | | |
|---|---|---|---|
| **Major Australian exports, 2007–08* (A$'000)** | | **Major Australian imports, 2007–08 (A$'000)** | |
| Refined petroleum | 3597 | Crude fertilisers | 4979 |
| Goods vehicles | 2151 | Rotating electric plant and parts | 276 |
| Rotating electric plant and parts | 836 | Telecom equipment and parts | 41 |
| Medicaments (incl. veterinary) | 709 | Wood- and resin-based chemical products | 40 |

*Includes A$7.5m of confidential items and special transactions, 31% of total exports.

| Tuvalu | | | |
|---|---|---|---|
| **Major Australian exports, 2007–08* (A$'000):** | | **Major Australian imports, 2007–08 (A$'000):** | |
| Meat (excl. beef) | 635 | Orthopaedic appliances | 708 |
| Refined petroleum | 277 | Prams, toys, games & sporting goods | 54 |
| Sugar, molasses & honey | 267 | Railway or tramtrack fixtures & fittings | 87 |
| Tobacco, manufactured | 226 | Paper and paperboard | 37 |

*Includes A$1.5m of confidential items and special transactions, 37% of total exports.

*Satellite image of Nauru*

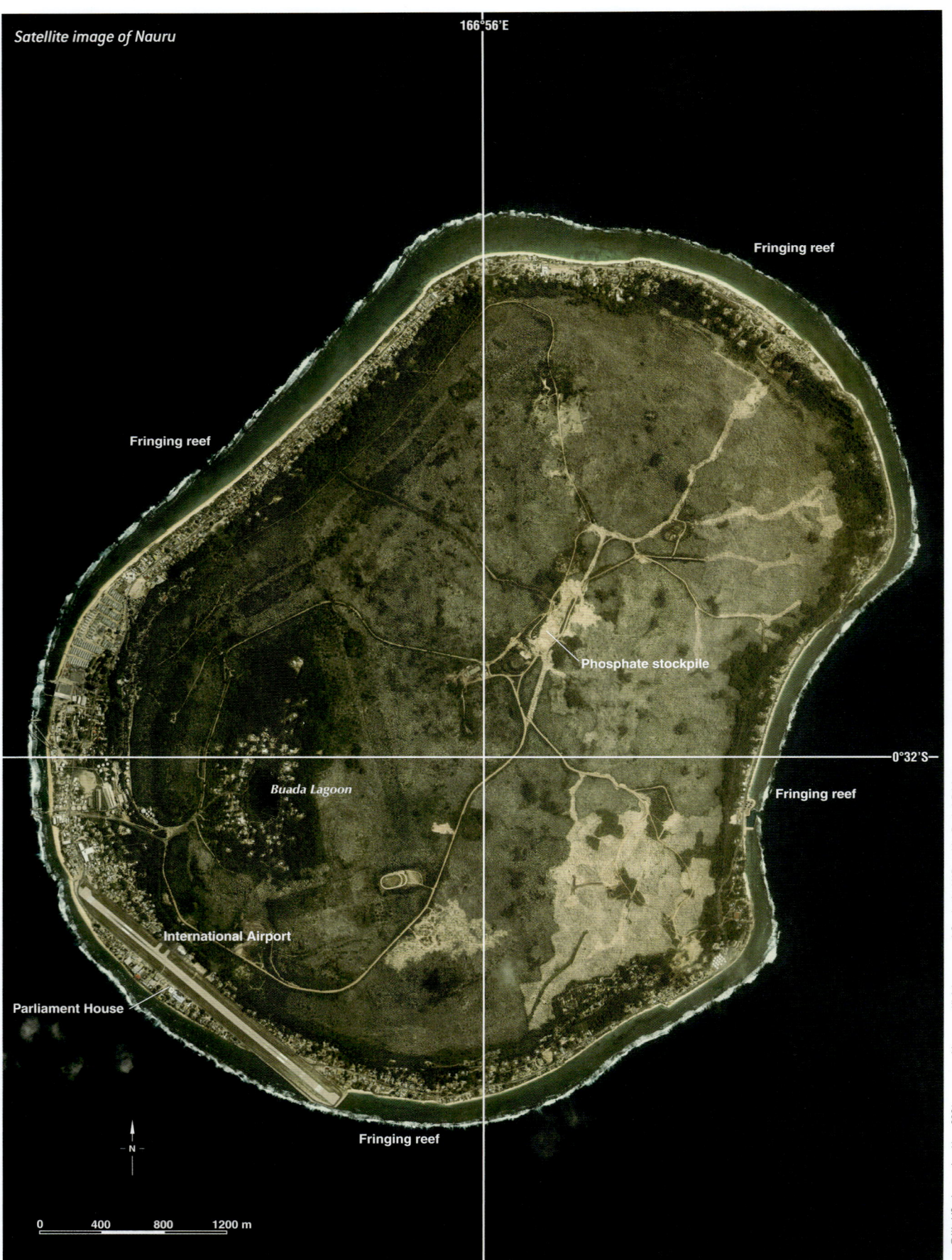

166°56'E

Fringing reef

Fringing reef

Phosphate stockpile

0°32'S

Fringing reef

*Buada Lagoon*

International Airport

Parliament House

Fringing reef

N

0  400  800  1200 m

### Perspectives on the Pacific

*You must walk the Kokoda Trail. It was great fun. It gave me an interest in our past defence links with PNG.* — Australian tourist

*Australia should look after its neighbours who are not as wealthy as us.* — Global citizen

*We are not a government organisation but work hard to reduce poverty and improve health and education in Pacific islands.* — NGO spokespeson

*As a wealthy government we give aid to Pacific countries suffering poverty.* — AusAID

*My child cannot go to school as my husband is unemployed since there are no more phosphate resources to be mined.* — Nauru mother

*I moved to the city to get a job. There are no jobs. I became bored and started to drink. I miss my life on the farm.* — Unemployed teenager, Pacific islander

*We need to poach the adult turtles for meat, shells and leather to sell so I can survive.* — Pacific fisherman

*I am worried that the sea level will rise and cover my island. What will I do?* — Tuvalun inhabitant

## Pacific Islands Forum

Australia is one of sixteen members of the Pacific Islands Forum, which is the region's main political and economic organisation. The Forum's Pacific Plan aims to stimulate growth via the following trade and economic agreements.

- The *Pacific Island Countries Trade Agreement (PICTA)* establishes a free trade area in goods, and in future services, among the forum island countries (FICs).
- The *Pacific Agreement on Closer Economic Relations (PACER)* promotes economic and trade cooperation and agreement between FICs, Australia and New Zealand.

In 2008 the Pacific Islands Forum and the European Union endorsed a joint declaration on climate change.

### GEOTERMS

**climate refugee:** person displaced by climate-change-induced environmental disasters

## ACTIVITIES

### UNDERSTANDING

1. Explain the links between Australia and the Pacific region.
2. Describe the purpose of the Pacific Islands Forum and its advantages to Australia and the other Pacific island countries.
3. Discuss the positive and negative aspects of living on a Pacific island.

### USING YOUR SKILLS

4. Refer to the graph showing economic growth in the Pacific islands.
   a. List the Pacific island countries that experienced negative growth from 2007 to 2008.
   b. Which country had the largest increase in the rate of economic growth?
   c. Discuss the advantages of economic growth to the islands.
   d. Suggest strategies Australia could take to help our poor neighbours.
5. Refer to the table listing Pacific development indicators.
   a. Compare Australia with the Solomon Islands and Kiribati.
   b. Account for the differences.
   c. Draw GDP per person as a line graph and access to safe water as a column graph.
   d. If you were an aid worker for an Australian non-government organisation, what would you do to improve social justice and equity in the poorest Pacific islands?
6. Refer to the table listing development indicators for Nauru and Tuvalu. Imagine you had a choice to live in either Nauru or Tuvalu. Looking at the indicators, make a choice and justify your reason.
7. Refer to the table showing Australia's trade with Nauru and Tuvalu.
   a. Calculate the total exports to Tuvalu and Nauru from Australia.
   b. List the products and services Australia buys from Tuvalu and Nauru.
   c. Discuss the benefits of trade to Australia and these two countries.
   d. Explain how trade could reduce poverty in these countries.
8. Refer to the satellite image of Nauru.
   a. What is the latitude and longitude of Nauru?
   b. Determine the direction of the phosphate stockpile from Parliament House.
   c. Calculate the distance from the dot indicating the international airport to Buada Lagoon.
   d. Calculate the area of the island.

# 10.8 Communication links

Australia is an isolated continent thousands of kilometres from Europe. In 1919 a flight from the United Kingdom to Australia took 30 days, and in the 1940s a boat trip took from four to six weeks. Over time, communications technology, such as telephone, wireless and television, reduced Australia's global isolation. Recent technology, such as satellite communication, the internet and mobile phones, enables almost instantaneous high-speed communication around the world.

## Satellite technology

A communications satellite, or COMSAT, is an orbiting device in space that creates communication links. Information is transmitted from a ground station to a satellite (uplink), followed by a retransmission of the information from the satellite back to the ground (downlink). Today satellite communication has grown into a multi-billion-dollar business. The sky is littered with 550 COMSATS, of which 356 are for commercial use and 80 for military use.

COMSATS provide a variety of communication needs, including communicating with ships and planes, weather forecasting, navigation, locating illegal drugs, protecting vessels from piracy, and observing changes to the land caused by natural disasters and climate change.

Today, the international communications company Inmarsat has a broadband global area network (BGAN), which enables television broadcasters to beam breaking news live via videophone into millions of homes. Satellites communicate information to geographers via geographic information systems (GIS), global positioning systems (GPS) and Google Earth.

## Australia's global communications

New technologies such as cable TV, the internet and mobile phones have made Australia's global communications easier, faster and more effective. The Australian Communications and Media

### SAMPLE STUDY

**Climate change expedition and Inmarsat BGAN**

/// There are not many places in the world more remote than the Greenland ice sheet, which ensures that any communication with the wider world is limited.

In 2006, an international group called the Climate Change College took six young ambassadors to Greenland for a field trip to study the effects of climate change on the island's ice sheet. Climate change is immediately evident in Greenland, so the field trip represented an opportunity to raise awareness of its impact.

The CCC used BGAN, a mobile satellite service created by the Inmarsat company, to provide a mobile broadband link to get the message about climate change in Greenland out to the world. Team members sent emails, made voice calls and updated blogs from a remote area in central Greenland. The technology also made possible a live video transmission from the camp to an early-morning Dutch television program.

Authority (ACMA) is responsible for regulating broadcasting, the internet, radio communications and telecommunications. Whether it is via email, BlackBerry, television, radio, broadband or mobile phone, ACMA represents Australia's communication interests internationally.

## Regional and global links

The Australian Satellite Service provides services to *Safe Caledonia*, a vessel in the Timor Sea, where hundreds of mining staff work on oil and gas platforms. Inmarsat's high-speed data service offers global mobile satellite services on land, at sea and in the air. It also enables instantaneous reporting of military activities at the frontline. The Global Maritime Distress and Safety System (GMDSS) has saved thousands of lives, and Inmarsat mobile satellite phones work in remote areas after disasters. In 2008 a distress call via Inmarsat saved 89 tourists when a boat ran aground in Antarctica.

## Social justice and equity

The right to communicate freely is a basic human right. Australians' rights in this area are partly covered by the *Telecommunications Act 1997*.

In 2007 Australia entered a bilateral agreement with the United States to gain access to the Wideband Global Satellite Communications System. The agreement aims to have six satellites operating by 2013, and these will meet the needs of the Australian Defence Force until 2024. Australia's military commitments rely on satellite communications to control and protect our forces in Afghanistan, Iraq, Timor-Leste, and the Solomon Islands.

The Australian government, through AusAID, supplies modern communications technology to the Asia–Pacific region to reduce the communications gap during critical events (such as the 2004 Indonesian tsunami and 2008 Chinese earthquake) and daily in remote communities in Papua New Guinea. It also provides money to improve transport infrastructure (planes, roads) to ensure greater communications mobility. Inmarsat sponsored the NGO Télécoms Sans Frontières by providing free equipment to restore communications after disasters in Bangladesh, the Solomon Islands and Pakistan.

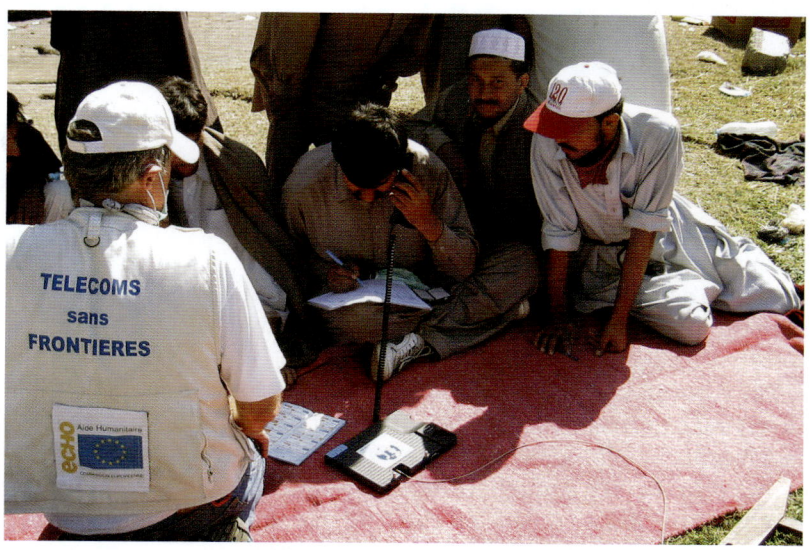

*Télécoms Sans Frontières provided satellite phones to people cut off by a massive earthquake in Pakistan in 2005, allowing them to communicate with family in other areas. (Photo courtesy Télécoms Sans Frontières, www.tsfi.org)*

### GEO*facts*

- In 1861 the cost per word for a telegraph message from London was equivalent to the average weekly wage.
- Australia has 20 broadband subscriptions per 100 people but more mobile phones than the population (105 per 100 people).

### ACTIVITIES

#### UNDERSTANDING

1. Explain how communications technology has reduced Australia's geographical isolation.
2. Describe the responsibilities of the ACMA.
3. Describe how modern technology has improved the work of AusAID, the Australian Defence Force and NGOs that work towards peace, social justice and equality.

#### THINKING AND APPLYING

4. Read the sample study. Imagine you are reporting from an isolated and dangerous place.
   a. Describe your location and the situation.
   b. Prepare a two-minute telecast to the world.
   c. Explain how frontline reporting using satellite broadband increases our understanding of world problems and contributes to active citizenship.
5. Refer to the photograph above and explain how new communications technology improves the lives of vulnerable people.

# 10.9 Australia's cultural links

**Culture** is the system of shared beliefs, values, customs, behaviours and tools used by members of a society to cope with their world and with one another. It is transmitted from generation to generation through learning. **Cultural diversity** is part of Australia's national identity and all governments support an inclusive, tolerant and culturally diverse society through legislation and programs.

The Aboriginal culture is one of the world's longest surviving cultures, with over 500 different nations and hundreds of languages. In the late eighteenth century the British brought Christianity and the English language to Australia. The British culture is reflected in Australia's laws, architecture and recreation. Today, immigrants from over 200 countries have enriched our culture, for example, through Buddhist temples, Japanese gardens, Vietnamese food and Bollywood movies.

## Australia's unique culture

Australia's culture is an evolving blend of global influences from the internet, media, migration and tourism. The young follow overseas trends in dress, and American jeans, baseball caps and Halloween have all made inroads into Australian culture. Despite these influences Australia has developed its own distinctive culture. This is evident in our literature and our distinctive accent, and in sayings such as *She'll be right, mate*, *G'day* and *Fair dinkum*. An essential part of our culture is the belief in a 'fair go' for all citizens, a sense of justice shown by support for the 'underdog', and the value we place on mateship. These principles stress the importance of equality and friendship. Australians, according to overseas opinions, are tolerant, easygoing and make great sportspeople and soldiers.

## Culture: a two-way process

Not only has Australia absorbed aspects of many different cultures, it has also made an impact on cultures in other countries through its global cultural links. *Home and Away*, Wolfmother, Cate Blanchett, Kylie Minogue and The Wiggles all have a high profile internationally. Aboriginal artefacts are displayed in overseas museums and 51 per cent of overseas visitors attended at least one of our cultural attractions in 2008. Australians are also known for their love of sport, and Australian teams compete successfully in many competitions, both at home and abroad. Teams from overseas also visit Australia and experience our way of life.

## Australian cultural exports

Much of what Australia exports culturally takes the form of **intellectual property**, or creative output, an example of which is the concept for a locally created and produced TV program. *Wheel of Fortune* was the first Australian television format to be sold and shown overseas. The children's entertainment program *Hi-5* is another successful Australian concept that has been sold internationally, and the comedy series *Kath and Kim* is licensed in the United States.

### Australia's global cultural 'exports'

| | |
|---|---|
| **Entertainment** | • Dame Edna Everage (Barry Humphries), Kylie Minogue, Nicole Kidman, Cate Blanchett, Hugh Jackman, The Wiggles<br>• *Neighbours*, *Hi-5*, *Home and Away*<br>• *Crocodile Dundee*, *Strictly Ballroom*, *Australia*<br>• Gillian Armstrong, Baz Luhrmann<br>• David Helfgott, Joan Sutherland |
| **Heroes and heroines** | Don Bradman, the Anzacs, Nancy Bird Walton, Charles Kingsford Smith, Steve Irwin |
| **Music** | *Waltzing Matilda*, didgeridoo |
| **Artists** | Sidney Nolan, Brett Whiteley, Indigenous artists |
| **Sport** | • Australian Rules Football, surf lifesaving<br>• Cathy Freeman, Ian Thorpe |
| **Food and food products** | Vegemite, Arnott's biscuits, Uncle Toby's, meat pies |
| **Inventions** | bionic ear, black box flight recorder, TV 'race cam' (for car and motorbike racing) and 'stump cam' (for cricket) |
| **Cultural icons** | Akubra hat, Sydney Opera House, Qantas flying kangaroo, Holden |
| **Natural icons** | Uluru, Great Barrier Reef, koala, kangaroo |

## Globalisation of culture: citizenship

The globalisation of culture has both advantages and disadvantages. In a few generations, 50 per cent of around 7000 global languages will disappear and, with them, a great part of their unique cultures. In response, the 2001 United Nations Universal Declaration on Cultural Diversity was adopted by 185 countries, and the United Nations declared 2008 the International Year of Languages. The non-government organisation Survival International and the UN Educational, Scientific and Cultural Organisation (UNESCO) work towards preserving threatened cultures. The 2005 UNESCO Cultural

**Advantages**

- Greater intercultural understanding reduces global tension.
- Selling Australian culture overseas results in income and employment in the country.

**Disadvantages**

- Globalisation of culture develops a monoculture.
- Americanisation of the global culture and reduction of local culture
- Disappearing cultures

*Advantages and disadvantages of cultural globalisation*

Diversity Treaty helps governments protect their cultures from foreign competition. Australia, with a culturally diverse population and disappearing Indigenous languages, supports these treaties, agreements and organisations.

## Exporting Australian surf culture

Most Australian teenagers have at least one big-brand surf T-shirt or cap. Open up Dad's wardrobe and you may find a Billabong T-shirt and a pair of Rip Curl shorts. Little sister has her eye on a pair of Roxy board shorts. Surfing is part of Australian culture and represents a healthy, easygoing lifestyle. Globalisation has seen Australian-owned surfing brands such as Rip Curl, Mambo, Quiksilver and Billabong become leaders in a multi-billion-dollar global business.

### GEOTERMS

**cultural diversity:** cohabitation of people from different ethnic and/or religious–cultural backgrounds within the same geographic location

**culture:** system of shared beliefs, values, customs, behaviours and artefacts used by members of a society to interact with one another and with the outside world

### ACTIVITIES

#### UNDERSTANDING

1. Outline what is meant by culture and cultural diversity.
2. Explain the values promoted by Australian culture.
3. Discuss how tourism, migration and communication links have contributed to a culturally diverse Australian society.
4. Describe the importance of Australian government treaties/agreements and non-government organisations in relation to the globalisation of Australian culture.

#### THINKING AND APPLYING

5. Culture is a two-way process. Discuss the global impacts on our culture and Australia's cultural impact on overseas countries.
6. Outline the aspects of our culture that are strongly influenced by the United States, Britain and Europe.
7. Research one agreement and one organisation that Australia supports, which aims to preserve Indigenous cultures. Describe the organisation, including its aims and activities and the successes it has achieved.

# 10.10 Australia's migration links

Australia is a nation built on immigration. Indigenous Australians date their ancestry back to the Aboriginal Dreamtime over 50 000 years ago. Other Australians are descended from more recent arrivals. It is believed that as many as 60 nationalities, mainly from the British Isles and Europe, were transported to Australia on the First Fleet in 1788. Later, Chinese mined the gold fields in the 1850s and Afghans were camel drivers in the 1860s. Since World War II, 5.6 million immigrants from up to 200 countries have made Australia their home. Today the largest group of overseas-born Australian immigrants are from the United Kingdom, followed by New Zealand, Italy and China.

Even though the percentage of overseas-born Australians remained almost the same in 1901 (22.8 per cent) and 2008 (22 per cent), the composition of immigrants changed. The White Australia policy (1901–73) and the *Immigration Restriction Act 1901* ensured immigrants were of European origin and predominantly from the United Kingdom. A dictation test further restricted the entry of non-European immigrants. Today an increasing number of Asian immigrants and Middle Eastern refugees have settled in Australia

## Government agreements and social justice

The Department of Immigration and Multicultural and Indigenous Affairs (DIMIA) develops policies under the *Migration Act 1958*. It allows people to live permanently in Australia under the Migration Program (e.g. skilled and family links) and Humanitarian Program (e.g. refugees). Those who enter Australia without authority or overstay their visa are called illegal migrants.

Since the end of World War II, more than 690 000 refugees and people in humanitarian need have settled in Australia. Australia signed the 1951 United Nations Convention relating to the Status of Refugees and the 1976 United Nations Protocol accepting responsibility for resolving refugee problems. Australia protects refugees according to its commitment to the United Nations High Commissioner for Refugees (UNHCR) and allocated 13 000 places in 2008–09 under the Humanitarian Program. Today's refugees were mainly born in the Middle East (38 per cent), Sub-Saharan Africa (33 per cent), South-East Asia (16 per cent) and Central Asia (13 per cent).

## Australia's migration program

Australia's **migration** program balances the government's social, economic, political, humanitarian and environmental objectives. Changes in migration policy as well as national and international events (e.g. racial tensions, terrorism, human rights abuses and wars) influence the number, nationality and types of immigrants.

Australia's current skills crisis is addressed by the Temporary Skilled Migration Program. In 1996 skilled immigration was 23 per cent of total immigration, but by 2008 it grew to 67 per cent (decreasing in 2009 with the financial crisis). Most skilled immigrants come from the United Kingdom

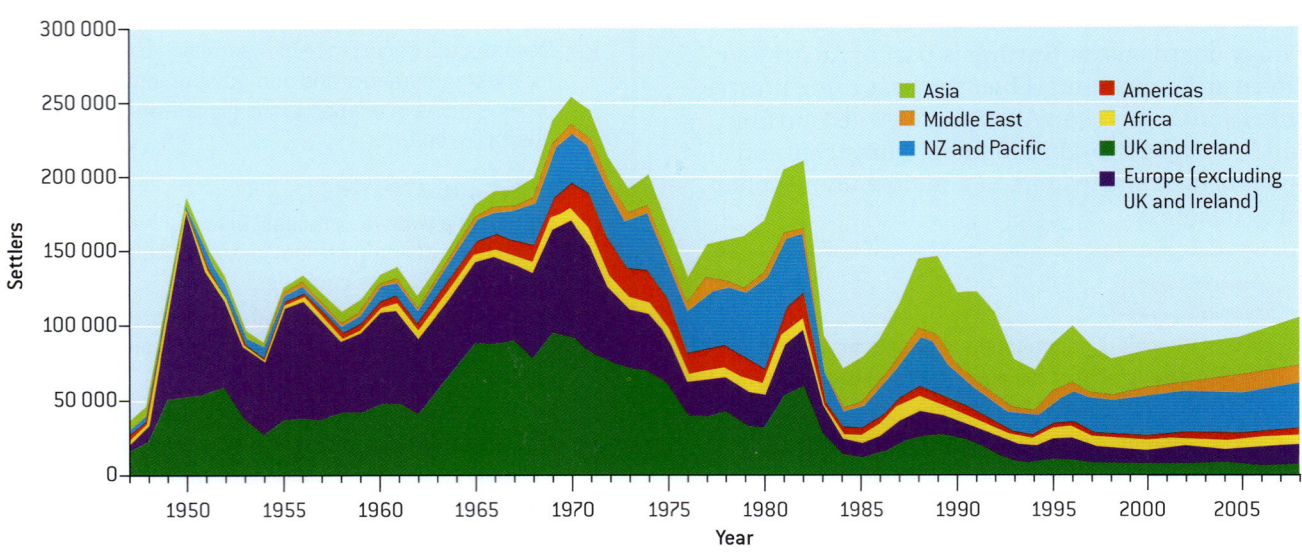

*Settler arrivals by region of last residence, 1947–2008*

(25 per cent), India (16 per cent) and China (15 per cent). The program takes into account business globalisation, which results in people moving in and out of the country. In 2008, of the 77 000 people who emigrated, 49 per cent were born overseas and the largest groups to leave were from New Zealand.

Immigration has been a significant contributor to Australia's population growth. But the rate varied from 23 per cent of population growth in 1993 to 59 per cent in 2009. Immigration brings cultural, economic and geopolitical advantages and disadvantages to Australia but, with an ageing population, immigration's contribution to population growth is expected to increase over the next 30 years.

In a culturally diverse country, **social justice** and **equity** are promoted by a national action plan (NAP) to build on social cohesion, harmony and security. Racist behaviour is against the *Racial Discrimination Act 1975*, and the *Racial Hatred Act 1995* balances the right to communicate freely and the right to live free of harmful language.

### Timeline of changing migration links and government policies

|  |  |
| --- | --- |
| 40 000–60 000 years ago | Aboriginal people first inhabit Australia. |
| 1788 | First Fleet arrives, containing up to 60 nationalities. |
| 1830s | Labourers are brought from Asia and South Pacific Islands. Germans settle in South Australia (Barossa Valley). |
| 1840s | Upheavals in Europe bring migrants from Greece, Italy, Hungary, Germany and China. Some Spanish missionaries settle in Western Australia. |
| 1850s | Australian gold rushes (from 1849) attract Chinese goldfields labourers. Irish Potato Famine (1845–50) brings influx of Irish refugees. |
| 1860s | Afghan cameleers arrive. South Pacific Islanders are kidnapped to work in Australia. |
| 1870s | Peak migrant numbers arrive from Ireland. |
| 1880s | Legislation restricts future immigration, especially Chinese. |
| 1890s | Immigration is reduced due to the Depression. |
| 1900s | White Australia policy is introduced. The *1901 Immigration Restriction Act* is passed. Pacific Islanders are deported. |
| 1910s | Immigration is halted during World War I. Enemy aliens are interned. |
| 1920s | Immigration increases, favouring the British, then Europeans. |
| 1930s | The Depression causes anti-immigration feeling among Australians. Australia accepts Jewish refugees. |
| 1940s | Post–World War II 'populate or perish' immigration program is set up. The Adult Migration Scheme begins. |
| 1950s | International concern over Australia's handling of 'non-white' people. Assisted migration is introduced, allowing immigration from specific countries such as Britain. |
| 1960s | Policy of integration is introduced. South Australia becomes first state to pass anti-racism legislation. |
| 1970s | Increase in migrants from non-European countries. Multiculturalism is introduced and *Racial Discrimination Act* is passed. Indochinese refugees arrive. |
| 1980s | SBS multicultural television station begins. Human Rights and Equal Opportunity Commission (HREOC) is established. |
| 1990s | *Racial Hatred Act 1995* is passed. Temporary protection is granted to refugees from Kosovo and East Timor. |
| 2000s | Boat people are placed on Christmas Island and Pacific islands such as Nauru — the Pacific Solution. Protests against immigration detention centres take place. Skilled migration and family reunions increase. Refugees arrive from Pakistan, India, Africa, Jordan, Lebanon, Syria, Iran, Sudan, Iraq and Afghanistan. |

## ACTIVITIES

### UNDERSTANDING

1. Distinguish between immigration and emigration.
2. Briefly explain the difference between migration and humanitarian programs.

### THINKING AND APPLYING

3. Discuss the reasons why people immigrate to and emigrate from Australia.
4. Explain how Australia is a nation built on immigration.
5. Suggest strategies to promote Australia as the best place in the world to live.

### USING YOUR SKILLS

6. Refer to the graph showing settler arrivals.
   a. Compare the changes in immigration patterns from the United Kingdom and from Asia in the years 1948 and 2008. Give reasons for the changes.
   b. Discuss how Australia's immigration links with countries in the Asia–Pacific region are increasing.
   c. Describe how this might strengthen Australia's cultural links with the Asia–Pacific countries.
7. Refer to the timeline.
   a. List the countries that have had immigration links to Australia since 1788.
   b. Name the Acts or laws concerning migration since 1901.
   c. Explain the reasons for declining immigration numbers to Australia.
   d. Discuss how migration links moved from predominantly European to Asia–Pacific countries over time.

### GEOTERMS

**migration:** movement of people into a country (immigration) and out of a country (emigration)

# 10.11 Australia's tourism links

**Tourism** is the practice of travelling temporarily to destinations not normally visited in the course of one's life or regular work. It includes temporary travel for business, leisure, education, religious gatherings, sporting and cultural events, and visits to family and friends. Tourism is both inbound and outbound and involves domestic travel (within one's own country) and international travel. It also includes the consumption of goods and services, such as transport, accommodation, entertainment, dining and souvenir purchases.

*Some of Australia's tourism campaigns have been less successful than others.*

## Growth of tourist links

Tourism is the world's largest industry and a source of employment and economic growth. In 2008 Australians made a total of 4.7 million trips overseas. New Zealand, followed by the United States, the United Kingdom, Indonesia and Thailand, were the most popular destinations. Tourism's recent high share of Australia's GDP was attributed to the impact of the 2000 Sydney Olympics. Since then, however, the 2002 and 2005 Bali bombings; the 2005 and 2006 London bombings; the SARS (Severe Acute Respiratory Syndrome) and swine flu scares; and the 2009 recession have caused a decline in the number of international visitors. They have also reduced the willingness of many Australians to travel overseas.

Today's traveller is more aware of the world via TV and the internet. An increase in leisure time and incomes, faster air transport such as the A380 airbus, the spread of satellite communication and improved tourist accommodation, infrastructure and services have contributed to stronger Australia–global tourist links. In an unpredictable, globalised world these links are never secure, as tourist numbers are influenced by oil prices, terrorism, recession and exchange rates.

## Australia: tourist destination

A recent survey conducted by Lonely Planet found travellers from 170 countries rated Australia as the number-one place they most wanted to visit. In 2008, 5.9 million international tourists visited Australia, generating employment and economic growth. The Australian summer is the most popular period for visitors (28 per cent) and autumn the least popular (23 per cent). Inbound tourism traditionally came from Europe and North America but the fastest growing source is from Asia–Pacific countries, with the expansion of low-cost carrier routes in Asia and an emerging affluent middle class. While New Zealand has the most visitor arrivals to Australia, Japan is Australia's largest financial tourist market. New South Wales attracts more than half of Australia's overseas visitors, a high percentage of whom visit Sydney for the purpose of a holiday.

Improvements in international understanding occur through conferences, family visits and educational tourism. Backpackers, mostly young people from Western European countries (particularly the United Kingdom), are a major source of tourists who stay longer and explore more of the country. Educational tourism accounts for 6 per cent of all international visitors and 27 per cent of total visitor nights stayed. World Youth Day in 2008, which featured a visit to Sydney by Pope Benedict XVI, attracted 531 600 overseas visitors to Australia, the highest July figure ever recorded.

## Tourism and Aussie culture

Australia is a unique, diverse and sophisticated tourist destination. Visitors are attracted to Australia's beaches, unique fauna, friendly people and relaxed atmosphere. Tourists get into the Aussie spirit by attending events such as the Imparja Camel Cup at Alice Springs, the Melbourne Cup, the Sydney–Hobart Yacht Race and the Dreaming Festival. Australia's cultural diversity and tolerance play a role in making international visitors feel welcome. For example, Tourism Australia launched a guide for Muslim visitors, providing information about *halal* food outlets and the location of mosques.

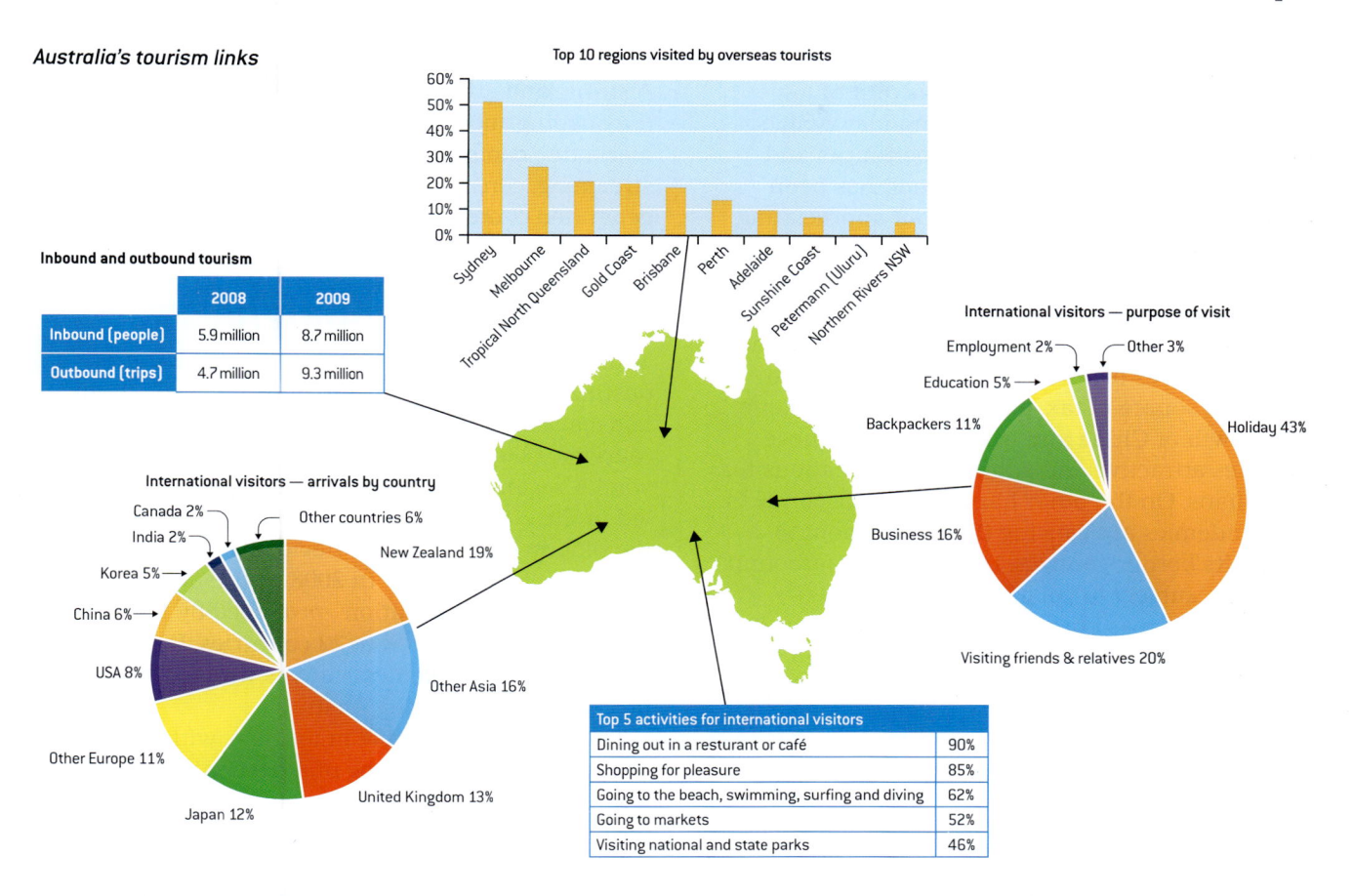

*Australia's tourism links*

**Inbound and outbound tourism**

|  | 2008 | 2009 |
|---|---|---|
| Inbound (people) | 5.9 million | 8.7 million |
| Outbound (trips) | 4.7 million | 9.3 million |

Top 10 regions visited by overseas tourists: Sydney, Melbourne, Tropical North Queensland, Gold Coast, Brisbane, Perth, Adelaide, Sunshine Coast, Petermann (Uluru), Northern Rivers NSW

International visitors — arrivals by country: Canada 2%, India 2%, Korea 5%, China 6%, USA 8%, Other Europe 11%, Japan 12%, United Kingdom 13%, Other Asia 16%, New Zealand 19%, Other countries 6%

International visitors — purpose of visit: Employment 2%, Other 3%, Education 5%, Backpackers 11%, Business 16%, Visiting friends & relatives 20%, Holiday 43%

| Top 5 activities for international visitors | |
|---|---|
| Dining out in a resturant or café | 90% |
| Shopping for pleasure | 85% |
| Going to the beach, swimming, surfing and diving | 62% |
| Going to markets | 52% |
| Visiting national and state parks | 46% |

# ACTIVITIES

**UNDERSTANDING**

1. Define tourism.
2. Outline the reasons for the global growth of tourism.
3. Explain why predicting Australia's future tourism links is a difficult task.

**THINKING AND APPLYING**

4. Research and report on one of the following: an international hotel, the Blue Mountains World Heritage Site, the Sydney Opera House or the Rocks area.

**USING YOUR SKILLS**

5. Refer to the table on inbound and outbound tourism. Compare the difference between inbound and outbound tourists in 2008 and 2009.
6. Refer to the table of top 5 visitor activities.
   a. Draw the table as a column graph.
   b. List the activities that would attract you if you were an overseas visitor to Australia.
7. Refer to the pie graph of visitor arrivals by country.
   a. Rank in order from largest to smallest the top international visitor arrivals by country.
   b. Compare the percentage from Europe and the United Kingdom with Asia–Pacific countries.
8. Refer to the bar graph on top 10 regions visited.
   a. Why do you think Sydney ranks the highest? Name five places in Sydney that would attract tourists.
   b. Explain why cities are popular tourist destinations.
   c. List the tourist attractions along Australia's coast and inland areas.
9. Refer to the pie graph showing purpose of visit.
   a. List the three top reasons to visit Australia.
   b. Explain the advantages of backpackers to the Australian economy.

**GEOTERMS**

**tourism:** the practice of travelling temporarily to destinations not normally visited in the course of one's life or regular work

# 10.12 Future tourism links and trends

Tourism styles have changed over time. Once, the most popular form of tourism was the 'bucket and spade' holiday, which meant setting off for two weeks of sun, sand and surf. The advent of low-cost airlines created the package holiday, which often became a race to tick off experiences and destinations. More recently, the trend has been towards 'deep' travel, which is about appreciating the factors that make a place unique. This form of travel is anticipated to become the most popular form of tourism by 2020.

Australia depends on all these travel experiences as expenditures by foreigners. They provide an important source of tax, employment and income. The growth of China and India is making these countries attractive and accessible destinations for Australians. On the other hand terrorism, conflicts and pandemics are causing the government to tighten its border controls. Inbound and outbound tourism is subject to volatile globalisation processes, such as changing exchange rates and rising oil prices, requiring the government to plan for these changes, as well as future shocks such as recessions.

## Digital future

Evolving media technologies have seen consumers become more discerning about where and how they travel. Travel blogs and video-sharing websites allow tourists to share their experiences of distant places with more and more people. Each week the TripAdvisor website is visited by 11 million travellers in more than 160 countries and the website Photobucket has 43 million members. The numbers of international visitors using the internet for information before coming to Australia has increased from 22 per cent in 2003 to 65 per cent in 2008. A strong and effective digital presence is critical to the ongoing success of Tourism Australia's global marketing campaigns. Innovative sites offer video streaming, consumer chatrooms and consumer-generated content. Web technology transferred to mobile phones ensures 24-hour accessibility.

## Marketing campaigns

Tourism Australia markets Australia as a tourist destination. The 1980s campaigns focused on our laid-back lifestyle, featuring Paul Hogan telling tourists: 'I'll slip an extra shrimp on the barbie for you.' A recent decrease in tourism's share of GDP led to the 2006 controversial campaign 'So where the bloody hell are you?', viewed by 200 million people in 11 countries. In 2008, Tourism Australia launched 'Transformation', produced by Baz Luhrmann and viewed in 22 countries. It presented stories of overworked executives whose lives were transformed by visiting Australia.

The media plays a role in tourism, with consumers gaining an understanding of a destination through television, film or the internet, and then visiting the destination. For example, Tourism Australia entered into a partnership with Twentieth Century Fox's film *Australia*, to promote the country as the 'must visit' destination for travellers around the world. The term *walkabout* in the campaign is a way of describing what an Australian holiday should be — a time of joy, discovery and reconnection with our selves and loved ones.

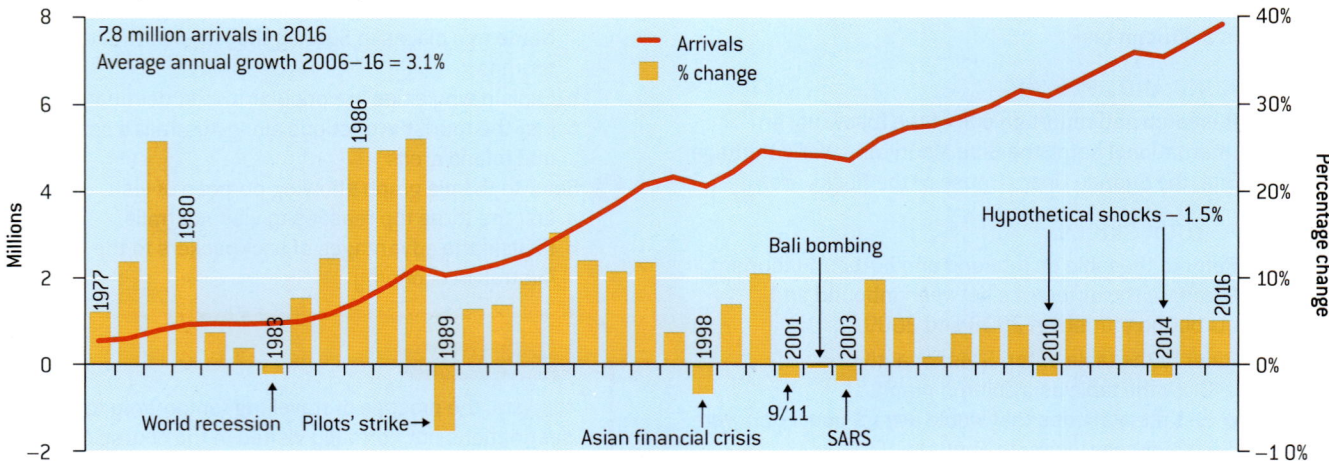

Visitor arrivals (shock in 2010 and 2014)

*Australia's past and future tourism trends. The future scenario shows two hypothetical shocks.*

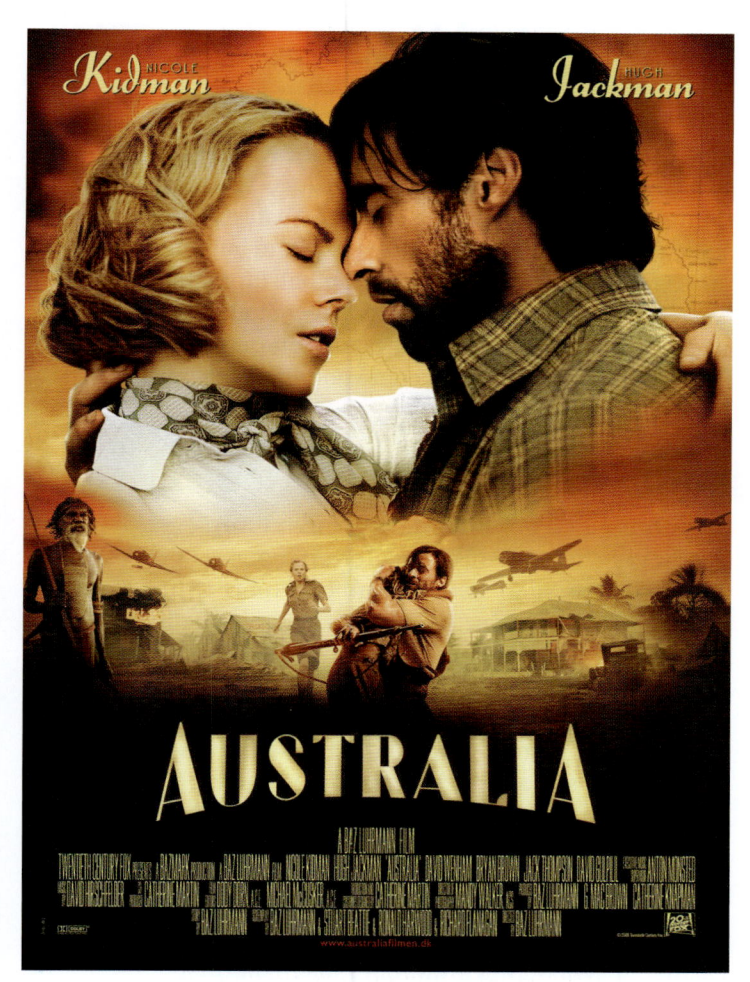

*Tourism Australia secured permission to use promotional artwork for the movie* Australia *in their marketing activities in Australia and overseas.*

## Towards sustainable tourism

Tourism is a double-edged activity. It contributes to socioeconomic progress but uncontrolled tourism growth can cause environmental degradation. The sustainable tourism mantra of 'leave nothing but footprints, take nothing but photographs' holds value in a world experiencing global warming.

Climate change is affecting tourism trends and travel behaviour. Coral bleaching, coastal erosion and a rise in sea levels threaten beach destinations. Australia's geographical isolation and dependence on air travel, contributes to global warming. Virgin Blue, Qantas and Jetstar operate Greenhouse Friendly voluntary carbon offset programs. Each airline prices the carbon footprint of an air journey and passengers have the option when booking their flight to offset the emissions by contributing to government-recognised carbon abatement projects.

Future tourism aims to be both sustainable and responsible, with a focus on preserving cultures and conserving what is distinctive about a place.

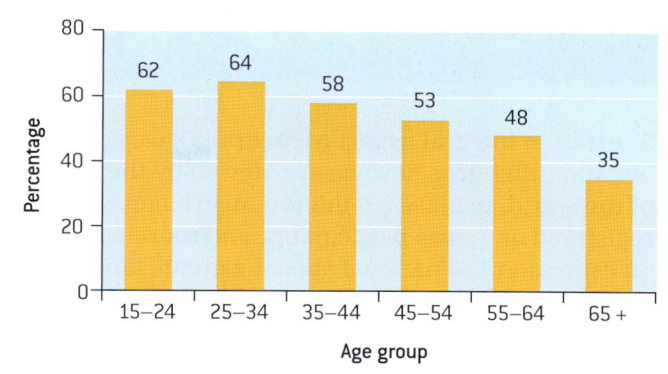

*International tourist internet use by age*

| Age group | 15–24 | 25–34 | 35–44 | 45–54 | 55–64 | 65+ |
|---|---|---|---|---|---|---|
| Percentage | 62 | 64 | 58 | 53 | 48 | 35 |

## ACTIVITIES

### UNDERSTANDING

1. Explain the importance of modern digital technology for Australia's future tourist industry.
2. Discuss how Australia's overseas tourist links are subject to volatile global influences.

### THINKING AND APPLYING

3. Indigenous culture is a unique attraction for the Australian tourism industry. Design a poster promoting Indigenous culture.
4. In groups, discuss the strategies Australian tourism needs to adopt to become more internationally competitive — in terms of experience offered, product and service. Present your findings as a multimedia PowerPoint or interactive whiteboard.

### USING YOUR SKILLS

5. Refer to the graph showing tourism trends.
   a. What is the average annual tourism growth rate predicted between 2006 and 2016? Explain the impact of this growth on the Australian economy.
   b. Which years had the highest and lowest numbers of overseas visitors?
   c. Describe the impact of the 2000 Sydney Olympics.
   d. List the factors that have caused decreases in tourism to Australia since 1977.
   e. Suggest four potential future shocks.
   f. Explain why globalisation has made the forecasting of future tourism trends a difficult task.
6. Refer to the poster of the film *Australia*.
   a. What is the poster's message?
   b. Who is the poster appealing to?
   c. Explain how the film's promotion aims to attract tourists to Australia.
7. Refer to the graph showing international tourist internet use by age. Account for the varied levels of internet use by different age groups.

# 10.13 Australia's sporting links

Sport is an integral aspect of Australia's way of life and influences how we are viewed by the rest of the world. In 2008, 6.5 million Australians were registered as sports participants, and there were an estimated 120 national sporting organisations along with thousands of local sports bodies. The Australian Sports Commission is responsible for distributing government funds, and it guides sporting activities in Australia. It funds the Australian Institute of Sport (AIS) in Canberra, which trains 700 top athletes in 26 different sports.

Whether as spectators or participants, most Australians are affected by sport in their everyday lives. The media shows Australian sportspeople participating at international level in events such as the Tour de France, World Surfing Championships, Paralympics, World Snowboard Championships and Rugby World Cup. These global sporting links not only increase Australia's international status but have:
- assisted in building a strong national identity
- established goodwill and cooperation among nations
- increased tourism and trade in related products (e.g. Rip Curl sportswear).

## Global links

Australia competed in the first modern Olympics in 1896, and hosted the Games in 1956 and 2000, as well as the Commonwealth Games in 1938, 1962, 1982 and 2006. The Australian Tennis Open is the first of the four international grand slam tennis events held each year. Australia stages the Cricket World Cup and Formula 1 Australian Grand Prix, and hosted the Rugby Union World Cup in 2003. Australia's Tour Down Under is the first ProTour cycling race to be held outside Europe. Australia's global sporting links have increased as modern venues such as Sydney Olympic Park have become available to provide a safe, crowd-friendly environment. Our international team names are identified with Australian natural and cultural icons, such as the Wallabies and Opals.

Even before Federation in 1901, Australia competed internationally. Our oldest sporting links are with the United Kingdom, in test cricket, tennis, rugby and the Commonwealth Games. Today, Australia's sporting links have extended to include Asia–Pacific countries, with the Asia Cup, Asia Pacific Games and Pan Pacific (Pan Pacs) swimming. Australia's links with the Asian Football Confederation (AFC) aim to build an Australian–Asian sporting culture and to increase trade and business in the region. This is referred to as 'football diplomacy'. Australia plays Tonga, Samoa and New Zealand in rugby union and rugby league competitions, and some Polynesian players have become popular, high-profile players in Australian teams.

## Equity and social justice

Preventing and eliminating discrimination and harassment ensures greater enjoyment. Organisations such as the Disability Sport Unit of the Australian Sports Commission ensure all Australians have an opportunity to participate in sporting activities at the level of their choice. Recreational Link (Reclink), a non-profit organisation, brings sport to every person who experiences social disadvantage, such as the homeless, unemployed and those who suffer from substance abuse and mental illness. The Homeless Football World Cup was held in Melbourne in 2008.

In 2009 young athletes throughout the world competed in the fifth Australian Youth Olympic Festival. Participants attended *Live Clean Play Clean* drug education presentations, teaching young athletes about the moral, ethical, social and physical implications of performance-enhancing drugs. In 2007 the Australian government announced funding for 6000 tests of illicit drugs.

*Australian Andrew Burton competes in the Halfpipe Snowboard World Cup in 2005.*

| Rating | Competitor | Roxy Pro Gold Coast | Rip Curl Pro Bell's Beach | Billabong Girls Pro Brazil | Rip Curl Pro Mademoiselle Hossegor, France | Beachley Classic Sydney, Nth Beaches | Movistar Classic Mancora, Brazil | Roxy Pro Sunset Beach, Hawaii | Billabong Girls Pro Honolua Bay, Hawaii | Total points | 2008 earnings | Career earnings |
|---|---|---|---|---|---|---|---|---|---|---|---|---|
| 1 | Stephanie Gilmour (AUS) | 9 | 1 | 1 | 3 | 9 | 1 | 1 | — | 6348 | $61 500 | $217 100 |
| 2 | Sofia Mulanovich (BRA) | 1 | 2 | 9 | 2 | 3 | 5 | 13 | — | 5233 | $45 900 | $343 100 |
| 3 | Silvana Lima (BRA) | 9 | 9 | 3 | 5 | 2 | 2 | 2 | — | 5138 | $41 500 | $147 750 |
| 4 | Layne Beachley (AUS) | 5 | 3 | 2 | 3 | 5 | 3 | 5 | — | 5006 | $36 100 | $641 135 |
| 5 | Samantha Cornish (AUS) | 2 | 5 | 5 | 5 | 9 | 5 | 13 | — | 3882 | $31 900 | $245 700 |
| 6 | Amee Donohoe (AUS) | 3 | 3 | 5 | 9 | 3 | 9 | 17 | — | 3871 | $33 000 | $124 250 |
| 7 | Jessi Miley-Dyer (AUS) | 0 | 5 | 5 | 5 | 9 | 9 | 3 | — | 3364 | $29 100 | $146 650 |
| 8 | Rebecca Woods (AUS) | 5 | 9 | 9 | 9 | 5 | 3 | 13 | — | 3320 | $29 900 | $177 450 |

**The Association of Surfing Professionals (ASP) Women's World Tour ratings 2008**

## GEOfacts

- The 2006 FIFA World Cup was one of the most watched events in television history, gathering 26.29 billion viewers over the course of the tournament.
- The number-one team sport for Australian girls is netball. Soccer is the number-one team sport for boys.
- 3.5 billion people either watch or play football.
- Ian Thorpe (Australia) and Michael Phelps (United States) hold the record of four awards each as World Swimmer of the Year. Thorpe won in 1998, 1999, 2001 and 2002.
- The ten most popular physical activities undertaken by Australians are: walking, aerobics/fitness, swimming, cycling, tennis, golf, running, bushwalking, soccer and netball.

## ACTIVITIES

### UNDERSTANDING

1. Describe Australia's changing global and regional sporting links.
2. Explain how equity and social justice can be integrated within sport.
3. Describe the organisations involved in Australia's global sporting links.

### THINKING AND APPLYING

4. Despite its small population, Australia has produced world champion teams in many sports, including cricket, rugby union, women's basketball, rowing, netball, field hockey, swimming and skiing. Research one world champion team and its links with other countries.
5. The chant, 'Ozzie, Ozzie, Ozzie! Oi, Oi, Oi!', is usually performed by Australian sporting crowds to cheer on an athlete or national sporting team. Write a short chant or slogan for a sports team.
6. Your town or city wants to host the Olympic Games in 2016. You are responsible for planning the proposal. Discuss the following questions with your group and then present your ideas to the class as a PowerPoint presentation.
    - What new sports facilities do you need?
    - Where will the facilities be built?
    - Where will the participants sleep?
    - How many volunteers will you require to help during the Games?
    - What will be the impact on your city if you win the bid?
   
   Design a logo for your city to use for your campaign.

### USING YOUR SKILLS

7. Study the table of ASP ratings. Using an atlas, locate the female ASP world tour locations. Find the latitude and longitude of three places. Calculate the percentage of Australians in the top eight ratings in the surfing professional tour. List the global sponsors.
8. Study the photograph of the snowboarder. Draw a form–line diagram of the photograph. List the advantages and disadvantages of the sport to the snowboarder and to Australia.

# 10.14 Strengthening future sporting links

Research has confirmed that young adults spend too much time in front of the TV, PlayStation and computer, and not enough time on the sporting field or at the swimming pool. Increased time spent on sedentary activities has resulted in fewer Australian children developing the essential sporting skills required to compete internationally in the future. In response, the Australian Sports Commission's (ASC) publication, *Building a Healthy, Active Australia*, aims to combat declining physical activity and poor eating habits among children. The ASC received Australian government funding to coordinate the Active After-school Communities (AASC) program aimed to cover 4000 schools and 200 000 children by 2012.

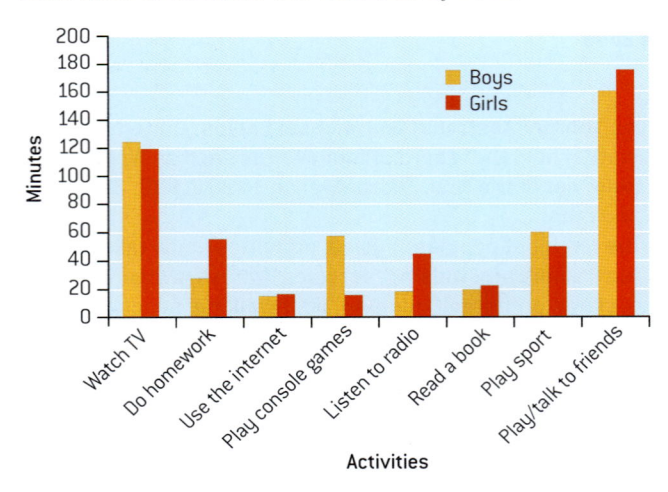

*Minutes per day spent on activities, years 7–10 (2008)*

Equity — participation rate in sport and/or dancing, 5 to 14 years, outside school hours, 2008

|  | Sport | Sport and/or dancing |
|---|---|---|
| Boys | 69.1% | 69.8% |
| Girls | 57.9% | 67.2% |

## Sport linked to economic advantages

Playing sport provides economic benefits to Australia through the production of goods and services, and the generation of tourism and employment. In 2008 over 80 000 Australians were employed in sport and recreation activities, contributing to increased global and regional links such as:
- sports consultancies in Indonesia, the Philippines, South Africa and Thailand
- junior sports programs in Hong Kong, New Zealand, Papua New Guinea and South Africa
- elite athlete training programs in Brunei
- events-management services in the United States.

Both sportspeople and businesses are involved in the Olympic Games. More than 35 Australian companies provided $200 million worth of goods and services for the Athens Olympics in 2004. Australian companies designed stadiums and provided telecommunications for Beijing (2008) and are involved in various projects for the London Olympic Games in 2012.

Globalisation has led to global brands such as Nike, Coca-Cola and Vodafone advertising on Australian sports equipment, clothes and venues. Also, global brands sponsor Australian TV sports shows, sports stars and events. Many sportspeople have become wealthy from sponsorship. The Indian Premier League (IPL) could make Australian cricketers the country's richest sports stars, with top players signing individual IPL contracts of up to $15 million per year.

## Sport linked to aid — equity and social justice

Sport is one of the universal languages that brings people together, helps them overcome ignorance and discrimination and sows the seeds of integration and equality. The United Nations recognises the value of sport as a tool for achieving the Millennium Development Goals (2000–15). The Sport Development Program (2006–11), funded by AusAID and managed by the Australian Sports Commission, builds on existing sport development programs — the Active Community Clubs (Africa), Sport Ability (Africa and Pacific islands) and Pacific Junior Sport. The Australian Sport Outreach Program encourages greater participation in physical activity and addresses HIV/AIDS awareness, youth leadership and personal development. The Pacific Sport Ability Program improves sporting opportunities for people with disabilities, for example, through the paralympic sport of boccia. The government welcomes Pacific athletes to train at the Australian Institute of Sport through the Australia–South Pacific Sports Program.

The United Nations World Food Programme is a humanitarian partner of the International Rugby

Board (IRB). The *Tackle Hunger* campaign fielded an all-star team composed of Rugby World Cup winning captains to educate the world about hunger. High-profile tournaments including the IRB Sevens World Series, the Under 21 and Under 19 World Championships and Women's Rugby World Cup are used as platforms to spread the *Tackle Hunger* message across the world.

In addition the IRB's Total Rugby TV and Total Rugby Radio broadcast in over 120 countries worldwide have showcased the *Tackle Hunger* message.

**Major/jersey:** QBE
**Shorts:** Optus
**Coach:** Ford
**Match ball:** Red Rooster
**Other:** Australia Post, Coca-Cola, Nationwide News, Puma, Star City, Bing Lee, Red Rooster

*Major sponsors of the AFL team the Sydney Swans, 2008*

**Advantages and disadvantages of promoting sporting links**

| Advantages | Disadvantages |
| --- | --- |
| Promotion of sporting links:<ul><li>leads to improved economic, cultural and geopolitical advantages, e.g. football diplomacy</li><li>reduces obesity and improves health, so that less is spent on health services</li><li>encourages mateship and cooperation, especially through team sports</li><li>promotes social equity, e.g. Paralympics, increasing role of women's sports</li><li>promotes social justice by being inclusive of all people</li><li>creates businesses, jobs and economic growth</li><li>improves cultural understanding</li><li>helps improve the lives of individuals, families and communities in developing countries</li><li>provides a means of achieving the UN Millennium Development Goals.</li></ul> | Promotion of sporting links:<ul><li>puts pressure on players to succeed, leading to injuries, violence, corruption and use of performance-enhancing drugs</li><li>increases commercialisation, which attacks sport's central ethos, as well as providing advertising venues for unethical and/or unhealthy products</li><li>creates crowd-control risks such as stampeding and hooliganism</li><li>increasingly links sport to politics, making sporting events a target for political statements</li><li>maintains existing social inequities, e.g. the continued media preference for men's sport over women's sport</li><li>alienates some parents, especially those with sons, due to the machismo associated with elite male commercial sport</li><li>can result in excessive financial outlays on sponsorship, elite salaries and sports funding</li><li>makes it increasingly expensive for poor individuals and countries to participate and succeed.</li></ul> |

## GEO*facts*

- Australian soccer player Craig Johnston invented a soccer boot that was picked up by Adidas. Today it is called Predator™ and worn by David Beckham.
- Seventeen-year-old Sudanese refugee John Athian is the Queensland 3000-metre champion for his age group and won bronze at the Australian All Schools and Youth Athletics Championships in Sydney.

## ACTIVITIES

### UNDERSTANDING

1. Name three disadvantages associated with Australia's sporting links that you think are of most concern. Explain your answer.
2. Explain how sport can promote social justice and equity.
3. Explain the importance of Asia–Pacific regional sporting links to Australia.
4. Discuss how Australia's sporting links are also linked to trade, aid, communication, tourism and migration.

### THINKING AND APPLYING

5. Many people say that sponsorship and money have no place in the Olympics. In small groups, discuss the different perspectives of this issue.
6. Explain why global organisations support sport in Australia. Describe the different views on sport sponsorship by hotels and breweries.
7. Refer to the panel about the Sydney Swans' sponsors.
    a. If you were a sponsor, where would you prefer to advertise: on jerseys, shorts, the coach or at the match?
    b. Give reasons for your answer.
8. The Warlpiri people in the Northern Territory play 'murri murri', in which a disc is rolled between two lines of children who have to spear it quickly. How does this game help them to live in the Australian bush? Find out what other games Australian Indigenous children play.

### USING YOUR SKILLS

9. Refer to the graph.
    a. What is the most time-consuming activity for both boys and girls?
    b. Calculate the proportion of time spent on sport compared to the other activities for boys and girls.
    c. Explain the implications of a sedentary lifestyle on Australia's future sporting links.

# Working geographically

## BROADSHEET: AUSTRALIA'S LINKS

### KNOWLEDGE AND UNDERSTANDING

#### Australia's global soccer links

The British Empire and Spanish Empire helped popularise football, or soccer, around the world via conquests and colonisation. Today 250 million people from more than 200 countries regularly play football. The most prestigious international football competition is the FIFA World Cup, held every four years.

In Australia during the 1950s and 1960s, soccer was mainly popular in British and southern European immigrant communities. Today it is the fastest growing sport among young Australians. The Socceroos secured a place in the 2006 FIFA World Cup and the Matildas regularly qualify for the FIFA Women's World Cup and Olympic Games. Australia is bidding to hold the FIFA World Cup in either 2018 or 2022.

**Refer to the text and select the alternative that best answers the question.**

1. The names of the male and female soccer teams that compete globally for Australia are:
   - (A) Wallabies and Socceroos
   - (B) Matildas and Jillaroos
   - (C) Kookaburras and Hockeyroos
   - (D) Matildas and Socceroos.

2. Australia aims to bid for the World FIFA Cup for:
   - (A) 2012 and 2022
   - (B) 2014 and 2018
   - (C) 2016 and 2022
   - (D) 2018 and 2022.

**Refer to the map and select the alternative that best answers the question.**

3. Countries where football is the most popular sport are:
   - (A) Australia, Brazil, Mexico
   - (B) South America, United Kingdom, India
   - (C) Argentina, Italy, Mexico
   - (D) Canada, Chile, Spain.

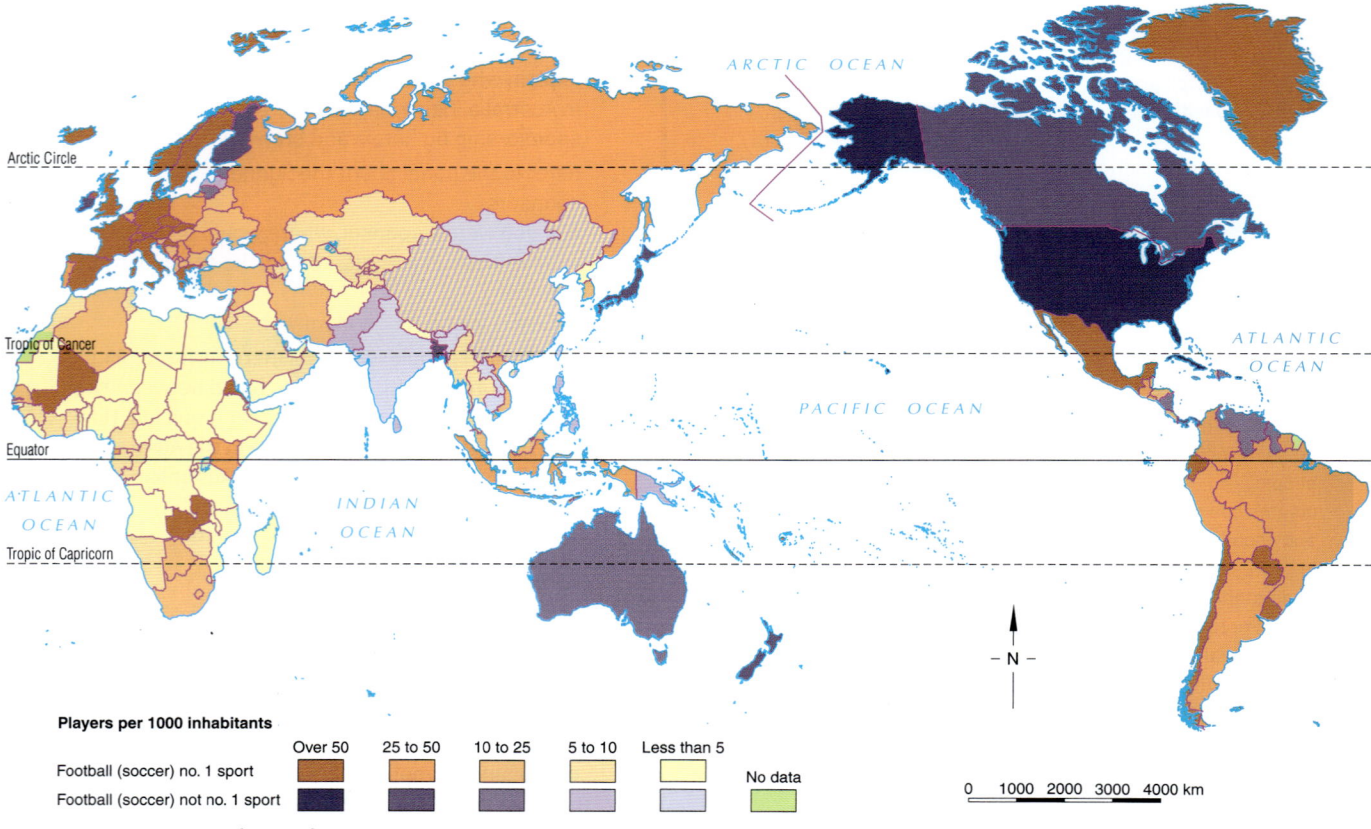

*Popularity of football (soccer) around the world*

4. Players per 1000 inhabitants in Australia are:
   - (A) over 50
   - (B) between 10 and 25
   - (C) over 5
   - (D) over 500.
5. The three countries with the largest number of football players per 1000 population are:
   - (A) USA, Mexico, France
   - (B) India, Tunisia, China
   - (C) Japan, Russia, Australia
   - (D) Argentina, New Zealand, India.

## SHORT RESPONSE

6. Explain why developed countries tend to have more football players than developing countries.

**Use the graphs to answer the following questions.**

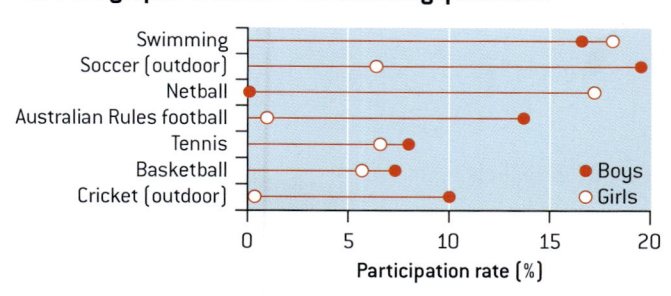

*Australia's sports with most participants among young people.*

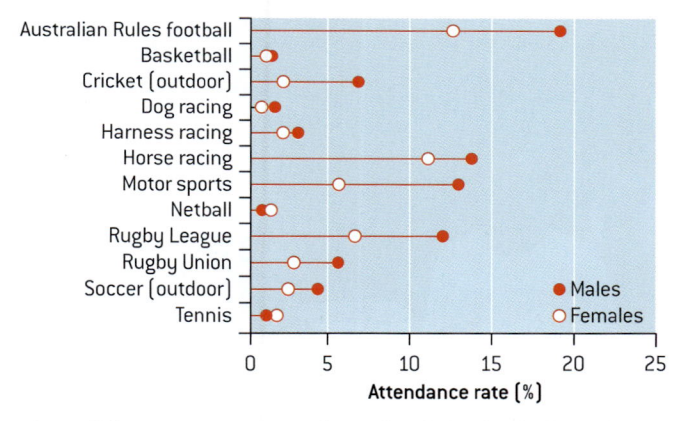

*Australia's sports attendance. Australian Rules football has the highest attendance rate of any sport in Australia. In 2005–06 it was attended at least once by 2.5 million people (16 per cent) aged 15 years and over.*

7. List the three most popular sports for girls and boys.
8. Calculate the gender gap in netball and Australian Rules football.
9. List three sports where the gender gap is small.
10. Explain some possible reasons for the gender gap in sports.
11. What are the three main sports attended by Australians?
12. Determine the percentage rate of men attending Australian Rules football, rugby league and rugby union. Explain why these percentages differ.
13. What is the difference in the rate of men and women attending motor sports? Why do you think there is a large difference?

*Australia not in soccer world* (Cartoon by Nicholson from *The Australian* newspaper: www.nicholsoncartoons.com.au)

**Refer to the cartoon to answer the following.**

14. What is the message of the cartoon?
15. Where is Australia in the cartoon and how is it presented?
16. Where is the rest of the world and how is it presented?
17. Suggest strategies Australia could use to strengthen its soccer links with the rest of the world.
18. Discuss the tourism, communication and cultural advantages and disadvantages of holding a FIFA World Cup in Australia.

## EXTENDED RESPONSE

19. Discuss and report on Australia's changing place in the world and the advantages of increasing its regional and global links. Include details of countries and statistics. Refer to the table provided below to build your response.

| Introduction | Body | Conclusion |
| --- | --- | --- |
| • Location — hemisphere, latitude, longitude, boundaries<br>• Nearest neighbours (Asia–Pacific):<br>– North-East Asia<br>– South-East Asia<br>– Australasia<br>– Melanesia<br>– Polynesia | • Change of focus from Europe to Asia–Pacific region<br>• Australia's global links:<br>– technological (transport, internet, satellite)<br>– economic (trade, tourism)<br>– social/cultural (migration, media, sport, aid)<br>– political (defence, treaties/agreements)<br>– environmental (global commons) | • Reduced isolation<br>• Increased global and regional links:<br>– social advantages/ disadvantages<br>– economic advantages/ disadvantages<br>– political advantages/ disadvantages |

# 11 Trade, aid, defence: global regional links

### INQUIRY QUESTIONS

+ What are Australia's trade, aid and defence links?
+ What are the roles of governments and non-government organisations in relation to these links?
+ What is the importance of treaties and agreements to Australia and the other countries involved in these links?
+ What are the implications of these links for social justice and equity?

Australia has a long history of international trade, aid and defence. Our trade, aid and defence links have been strengthened through agreements focusing on the countries located in the Asia–Pacific region. These links have been beneficial to Australia economically, culturally and politically. Governments and non-government organisations work towards a peaceful, equal and socially just future, regionally and globally.

### GEOskills TOOLBOX

+ Using latitude and longitude (page 319)

*Unloading Australian aid from an RAAF Hercules at Munda, Solomon Islands, after the tsunami in 2007*

### KEY TERMS

**archipelago:** large body of water with many islands

**counter-terrorism:** practices, techniques and strategies that governments, the military, police departments and corporations adopt in response to terrorist threats or acts

**European Union (EU):** political and economic union of 27 member states, located primarily in Europe

**exports:** the goods, services and ideas that Australia sells to other countries

**fair trade:** the organised social movement that advocates payment of a fair price for producers in developing countries. The fair trade movement focuses on exports from developing countries to developed countries, most notably coffee, cocoa, sugar and tea.

**geographic information system (GIS):** set of computer applications designed to integrate, collect, store, retrieve, manipulate, analyse and display mapped data

**governance:** method or system of government, authority or control

**human rights:** concept that all human beings are equal and deserve fair and equal treatment

**imports:** the goods, services and ideas that Australia buys from other countries

**international trade:** movement of goods, services and ideas between countries

**microcredit:** extension of very small loans to those in poverty, enabling them to be self-employed

**Millennium Development Goals (MDGs):** eight humanitarian development goals to be achieved by 2015, as set at the Millennium Summit in 2000 by 189 UN member states and at least 23 international organisations

**quota:** physical limit on the quantity of a goods item that can be imported into a country in a given period of time

**secularism:** the belief that public organisations such as schools and governments should function without religious influence or interference

**subsidy:** financial aid given by a government to an individual producer or group of producers to reduce the price of a good or service

**tariff:** tax imposed on goods when they move across a political boundary, which increases the price for both importer and exporter

**terrorism:** generally defined as the intentional use, or threat, of violence against civilians or civilian targets in order to achieve political ends

**trade deficit:** trade imbalance whereby imports are greater than exports

**United Nations (UN):** intergovernmental organisation (IGO) that promotes equity, human rights, peace and ecologically sustainable environments

# 11.1 Australia's changing trade links

Australia trades with over two hundred countries and contributes one per cent to world trade. It is ranked number 27 as a world exporter and number 20 as a world importer. Australia's diverse export industry incorporates manufacturing products, high-quality food and wine, and services such as education and tourism. Trade is a vital component of Australia's economic prosperity, which is attributed to good infrastructure, stable government, a skilled workforce, and a rich resource and agriculture base. Australia has had a **trade deficit** for the last 50 years, meaning the value of our **imports** is greater than that of our **exports**.

## International trade

Every day Australians benefit from **international trade** when people around the world drink our wine, ride in our fast ferries, use our cochlear implants to improve their hearing, and wear our pink diamonds. In a globalised world, computer access enables Australians to purchase DVDs and PlayStation games via eBay, and have them delivered from anywhere in the world within a few days.

Countries differ in the type of goods and services they produce because natural, human and capital resources are unevenly distributed. Australia, for instance, is rich in coal (a natural resource) that is exported to China and Japan. In return Australia imports cheap toys produced by China's large population (a human resource) and high-value products such as cars made in Japan (a capital resource).

## Changing trade links

One of Australia's earliest exports was wool, from which was born the expression: *Australia rides on the sheep's back*. For many years, Britain was Australia's major trading partner but since it joined the **European Union (EU)** in 1973, we have increased our trading links with countries in the Asia–Pacific region. Agricultural goods and minerals dominate Australia's exports, and service firms such as Qantas are well known overseas. Over the last century, Australia's membership of trading blocs such as Asia–Pacific Economic Cooperation (APEC) and participation in free trade agreements have altered Australia's trading links. These changes include:

- *Trade with other countries*. In 1906 the United Kingdom was Australia's major trading partner accounting for 59 per cent of imports and 49 per cent of exports. By 2009 the United Kingdom accounted for 4 per cent of both imports and exports. China is now Australia's largest two-way trading partner (in imports and exports), followed by Japan, the United States and Korea.
- *Trade in goods*. In 1901 agricultural goods were 54 per cent of Australia's exports, of which wool was 31 per cent. By 2009 agriculture decreased to 4 per cent of exports and wool was 2 per cent. Today coal is the main export and the main exporting sectors are manufacturing (47 per cent) and mining (32 per cent). Australia is an efficient producer of a range of agricultural products. However, many countries such as the United States and Europe subsidise their agriculture, making it difficult for Australia to compete.
- *Trade in services*. In 1901 services were one per cent of total exports but today services are 22 per cent of exports and 19 per cent of imports. Services such as education and tourism are Australia's third and fifth largest export after coal and iron ore. Imported services include overseas business services, computer services and royalties paid to view overseas films.
- *Manufacturing exports*. Originally, Australia made simply transformed manufactures (STMs), which are goods that have undergone minimal changes, such as paper, crude petroleum and minerals. Today, elaborately transformed manufactures (ETMs) account for 65 per cent of Australia's manufactured exports. This includes motor vehicles exported to the Middle East and Papua New Guinea. Australia is also developing a competitive edge in medical and scientific equipment.

The objective of Australian governments in recent decades has been to ensure that all Australians benefit from trade with the rest of the world, especially the expanding Asian market.

### GEOfacts

- Australia imports more goods and services from the United States than from any other country.
- Japan is Australia's largest export market, worth nearly $40 billion in 2007–08.
- China is Australia's fastest growing export market, accounting for over $30 billion in 2007–08.

**Broad composition of exports: 2002–03 and 2007–08**

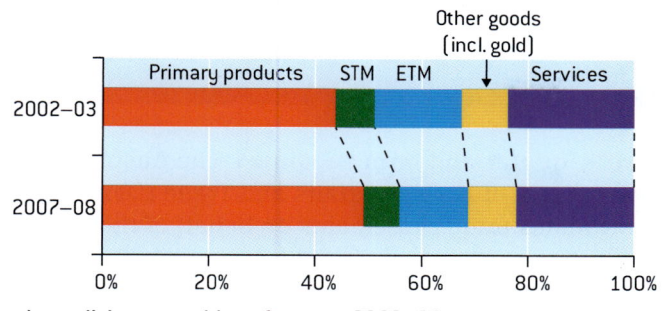

*Australia's composition of exports 2002–08*

Source: www.dfat.gov.au.

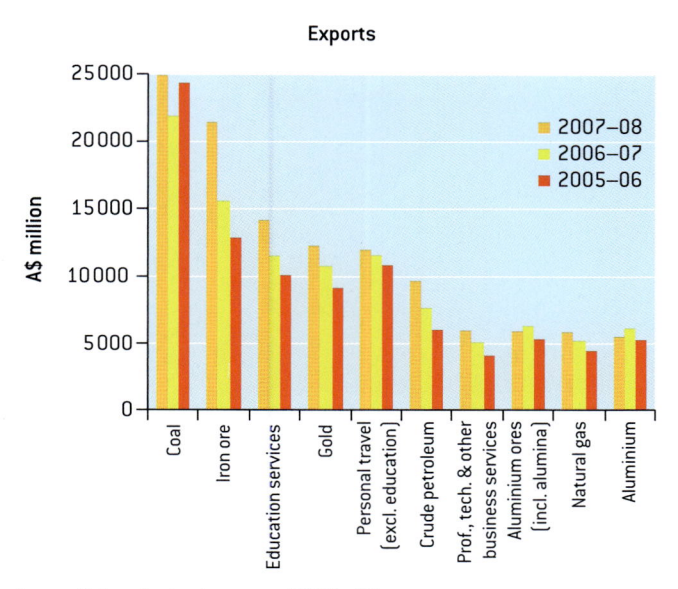

*Australia's principal exports 2005–08*

Source: www.dfat.gov.au.

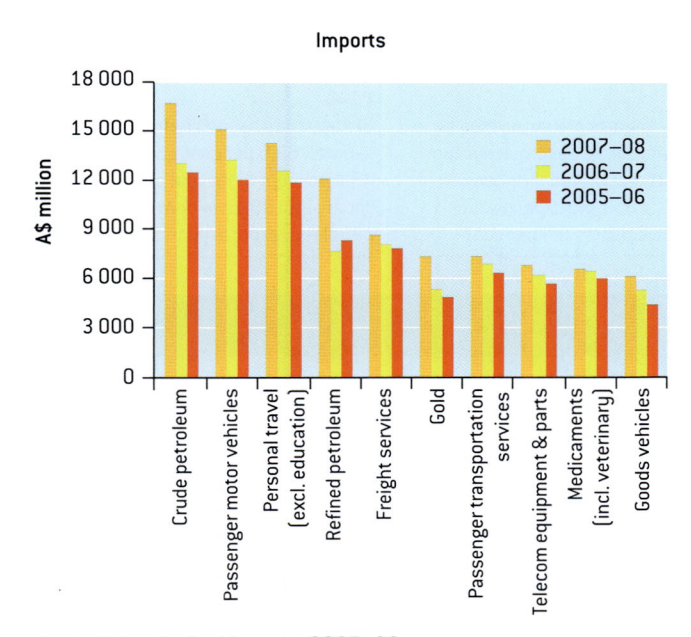

*Australia's principal imports 2005–08*

Source: www.dfat.gov.au.

## GEOfacts

- The United States, Germany and China are the world's top goods-trading countries.
- By 2020, China is anticipated to become the world trade leader and India to generate 10 per cent of world trade.
- International trade increased over the last ten years but decreased during the 2008–09 recession.

## ACTIVITIES

### UNDERSTANDING

1. Explain what is meant by international trade.
2. Discuss Australia's changing trade links over the last century.

### THINKING AND APPLYING

3. Consider Santa Claus as an 'international exporter', who exports goods produced in one country to be delivered to consumers in another country, in a once-a-year night service. List the 'imported goods' you received last Christmas.
4. Discuss the advantages of access to trading with the world, especially the Asian region.

### USING YOUR SKILLS

5. Refer to the graph on Australia's principal exports. List the three largest exports. Calculate the difference between 2005–06 and 2007–08 of iron ore, petroleum, professional business services and travel exports.
6. Refer to the diagram on Australia's principal imports. List the three largest imports in 2005–06 and 2007–08. Calculate the difference between 2005–06 and 2007–08 of medical products, telecom equipment and goods vehicle imports.
7. Refer to the graph of broad composition of exports.
   a Which sector has increased from 2002–03 to 2007–08?
   b Which sector has remained approximately the same over that time?
   c Which sector is the largest in both time periods?

### GEOTERMS

**exports:** the goods, services and ideas that Australia sells to other countries

**imports:** the goods, services and ideas that Australia buys from other countries

**international trade:** movement of goods, services and ideas between countries

CHAPTER 11 | Trade, aid, defence: global regional links

# 11.2 Australia's main trading links: countries, goods and services

Australia is one of the 153 members of the World Trade Organization (WTO), which covers 95 per cent of global trade. The organisation promotes free and fair trade between countries and, since 2001, its Doha Development Agenda has aimed to help the world's poor, by slashing trade barriers such as tariffs, quotas and farm subsidies. The Australian Department of Foreign Affairs and Trade (DFAT) coordinates trade agreements on behalf of the Australian government, and the Australian Trade Commission (Austrade) promotes the export of goods and services.

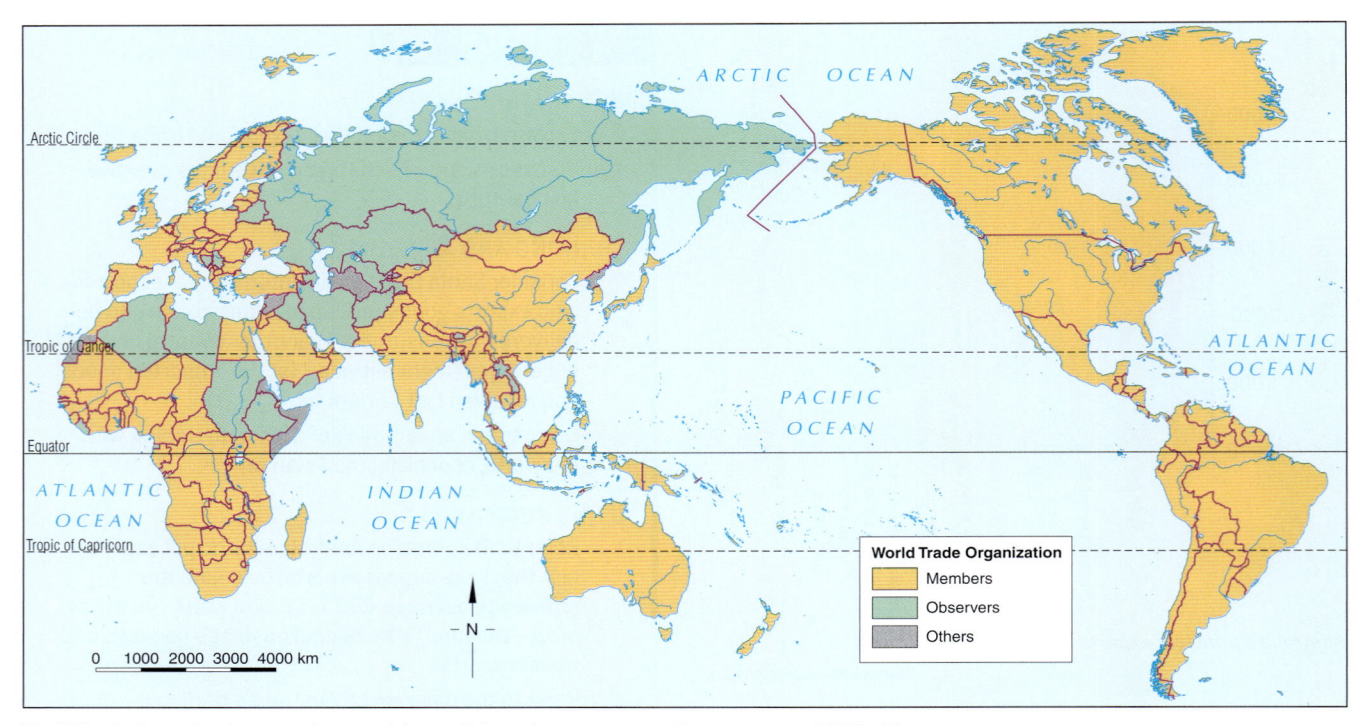

World Trade Organization members and Australia's main two-way trading partners, 2008–09

**1942–43**
World War II leads to high import and export prices, resulting in a 33 per cent trade surplus.

**1943–45**
War affects the safety of shipping, causing a decrease in international trade. Australia's trade surplus falls to 16 per cent.

**1966–67**
When British imports are surpassed by US imports and Japan becomes our top export market, the United Kingdom is no longer Australia's principal trading partner. Trade deficit is 0.4 per cent.

**2008**
Of Australia's refined petroleum exports, 69.9 per cent go to Singapore, 43.4 per cent of its coal exports go to Japan, and 30.1 per cent of its crude petroleum exports go to South Korea.

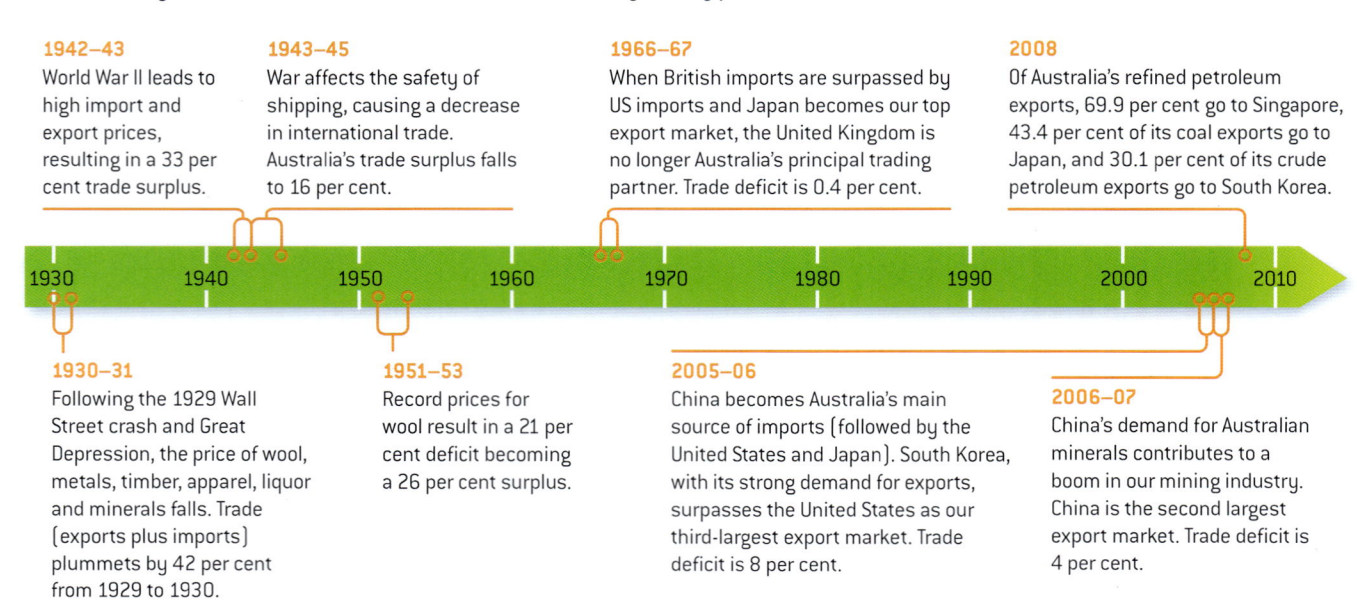

**1930–31**
Following the 1929 Wall Street crash and Great Depression, the price of wool, metals, timber, apparel, liquor and minerals falls. Trade (exports plus imports) plummets by 42 per cent from 1929 to 1930.

**1951–53**
Record prices for wool result in a 21 per cent deficit becoming a 26 per cent surplus.

**2005–06**
China becomes Australia's main source of imports (followed by the United States and Japan). South Korea, with its strong demand for exports, surpasses the United States as our third-largest export market. Trade deficit is 8 per cent.

**2006–07**
China's demand for Australian minerals contributes to a boom in our mining industry. China is the second largest export market. Trade deficit is 4 per cent.

Timeline of key events in Australia's trading history

**Australia's goods and services trade-percentage share, 2008**

| Top 10 two-way trading partners (exports and imports) | Top 10 export markets | Top 10 import markets |
|---|---|---|
| 1. China 12.9% | 1. Japan 16.0% | 1. United States 13.6% |
| 2. Japan 12.1% | 2. China 12.8% | 2. China 12.9% |
| 3. United States 10.6% | 3. United States 7.3% | 3. Japan 8.5% |
| 4. United Kingdom 5.3% | 4. Republic of Korea 7.1% | 4. Singapore 6.5% |
| 5. Singapore 5.0% | 5. New Zealand 6.0% | 5. United Kingdom 5.2% |
| 6. Republic of Korea 4.8% | 6. United Kingdom 5.4% | 6. Germany 4.7% |
| 7. New Zealand 4.8% | 7. India 5.2% | 7. Thailand 4.1% |
| 8. Thailand 3.3% | 8. Singapore 3.3% | 8. New Zealand 3.7% |
| 9. Germany 3.0% | 9. Taiwan 3.0% | 9. Malaysia 3.6% |
| 10. India 2.9% | 10. Thailand 2.4% | 10. Republic of Korea 2.8% |

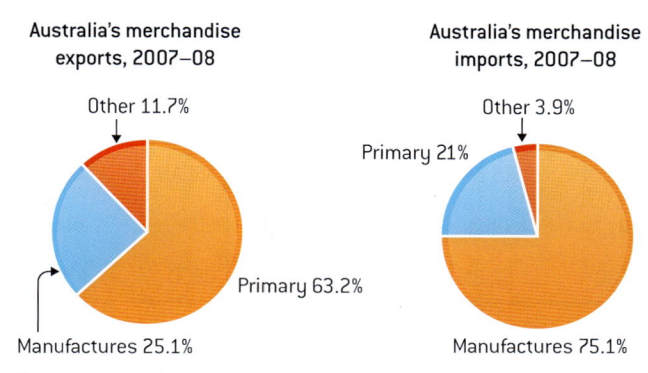

**Australia's merchandise exports, 2007–08**
- Other 11.7%
- Primary 63.2%
- Manufactures 25.1%

**Australia's merchandise imports, 2007–08**
- Other 3.9%
- Primary 21%
- Manufactures 75.1%

*Goods: Australia's exports and imports*

**Australia's exports of services, 2007–08**
- Other 26.3%
- Transportation 18.3%
- Travel 55.4%
  - Business 5.3%
  - Education-related 26.7%
  - Other personal 23.4%

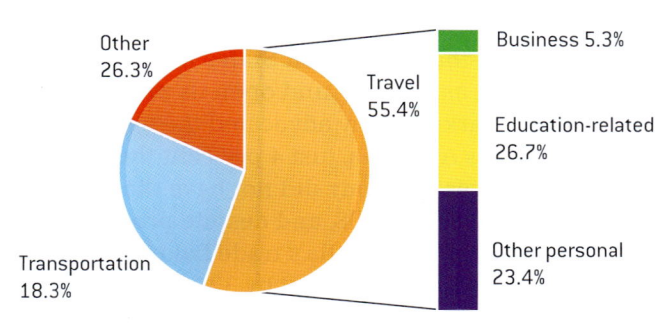

*Services: Australia's exports*

**Australia's imports of services, 2007–08**
- Other 31.1%
- Transportation 32.8%
- Travel 36.1%
  - Business 5.9%
  - Education-related 1.7%
  - Other personal 28.5%

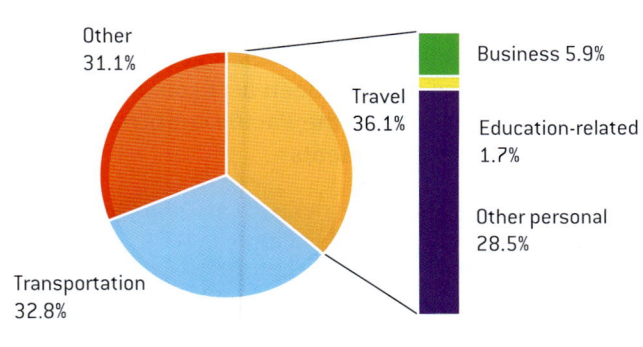

*Services: Australia's imports*

## ACTIVITIES

### UNDERSTANDING
1. Explain the roles of Australian government organisations in relation to trade.

### THINKING AND APPLYING
2. Design a collage of goods imported into Australia.
3. Discuss Australia's main trading links with countries in the Asia–Pacific region.

### USING YOUR SKILLS
4. Refer to the table on Australia's top trading partners.
   a. As Australia's trading partners, list the rankings for China, New Zealand, the United States and the United Kingdom.
   b. What country is our fourth largest export market but our tenth largest import market?
   c. Is Malaysia a larger market for our exports or imports?
   d. What percentage of Australia's trade is with Asian countries?
   e. List the countries where Australia exports more goods than it imports. Explain the economic advantages of this to Australia.
5. Refer to the graphs on Australia's exports and imports of goods.
   a. What is Australia's main exports sector?
   b. What is Australia's main imports sector?
   c. Calculate the difference between Australia's exported and imported manufactured goods and primary goods sector.
6. Refer to the diagrams on Australia's exports and imports of services.
   a. List the components of travel.
   b. Calculate the difference between exported and imported travel services.
7. Refer to the timeline.
   a. Explain the impact of wars and depression on Australian trade.
   b. In which time periods has there been a trade surplus?

# 11.3 Australia's trade agreements

When the United Kingdom's trade with its Commonwealth countries declined, Australia sought closer links with its neighbour, New Zealand. This led to our first trade agreement, the 1965 New Zealand–Australia Free Trade Agreement. This was followed by the 1983 Australia–New Zealand Closer Economic Relations Trade Agreement (ANZCERTA). Since the 1990s free trade in goods and stronger links on migration, tourism and transport have occurred between the two countries.

## Australia's integrated trade policy

Trade agreements are Australia's major international trade link. The Australian government has signed over 580 trade treaties that provide Australians with access to a range of high-quality imported goods and increase the employment prospects for Australians working in export industries. For mainly economic purposes, the government aims to expand Australia's export markets through an integrated trade policy, covering bilateral, multilateral and regional trade agreements. These include:
- *bilateral agreements*, such as the Australia–United States Free Trade Agreement (AUSFTA)
- *multilateral agreements*, such as the Doha Round Trade Agreement between the 153 World Trade Organization members
- *regional agreements*, such as the Asia–Pacific Economic Cooperation (APEC), Association of Southeast Asian Nations (ASEAN) and Organization for Economic Co-operation and Development (OECD).

## Bilateral and regional trade agreements

The Department of Foreign Affairs and Trade (DFAT) coordinated Australia's free trade agreements (FTAs) with New Zealand (ANZCERTA 1983), the United States (AUSFTA 2005), Thailand (TAFTA 2005) and Singapore (SAFTA 2003). These countries agreed to eventually eliminate tariffs and quotas on most (if not all) goods and services between them. At present Australia is negotiating FTAs with China, the Gulf Cooperation Council (GCC) and Japan. Over the last few years, these agreements are claimed to have saved the average Australian family $1000 per year, created employment, improved cultural understanding and contributed to regional security with our Asia–Pacific neighbours.

Today 60 per cent of the world's trade takes place among regional trading blocs, as shown in the table below.

**Australia's goods and services trade with regional organisations, 2008**

| | Two-way trade (imports and exports) | | Imports | | Exports |
|---|---|---|---|---|---|
| APEC | 68.0% | APEC | 67.6% | APEC | 68.7% |
| ASEAN | 15.7% | ASEAN | 19.5% | ASEAN | 11.6% |
| EU | 17.6% | EU | 21.9% | EU | 12.9% |
| OECD | 52.8% | OECD | 53.6% | OECD | 52.0% |

## Equity: lopsided trade agreements

In 2003 Australian entered the Australia–United States Free Trade Agreement (AUSFTA). In addition to a commitment to free trade, there was also an understanding that the United States would look after Australia, as a 'mate', and open its protected agricultural market. Many advocated the agreement was lopsided as Australia, just 4 per cent the size of the United States economy, did not have the same bargaining power. By 2008, and despite promises of economic riches, Australia's trade balance with the United States had declined by 32 per cent. The Australian Manufacturing Workers' Union estimated that over 10 000 jobs were lost as a result of the agreement. Some high-profile Australian actors also spoke out against the agreement, claiming that it would lead to a decrease in Australian film and TV content.

On the other hand, the Australian government is far from innocent and has been accused of similar bullying of Thailand and the Pacific countries, when negotiating trade agreements.

**GEOfacts** In December 2008, Australia signed the Singapore Treaty on the Law of Trademarks and the Patent Law Treaty.

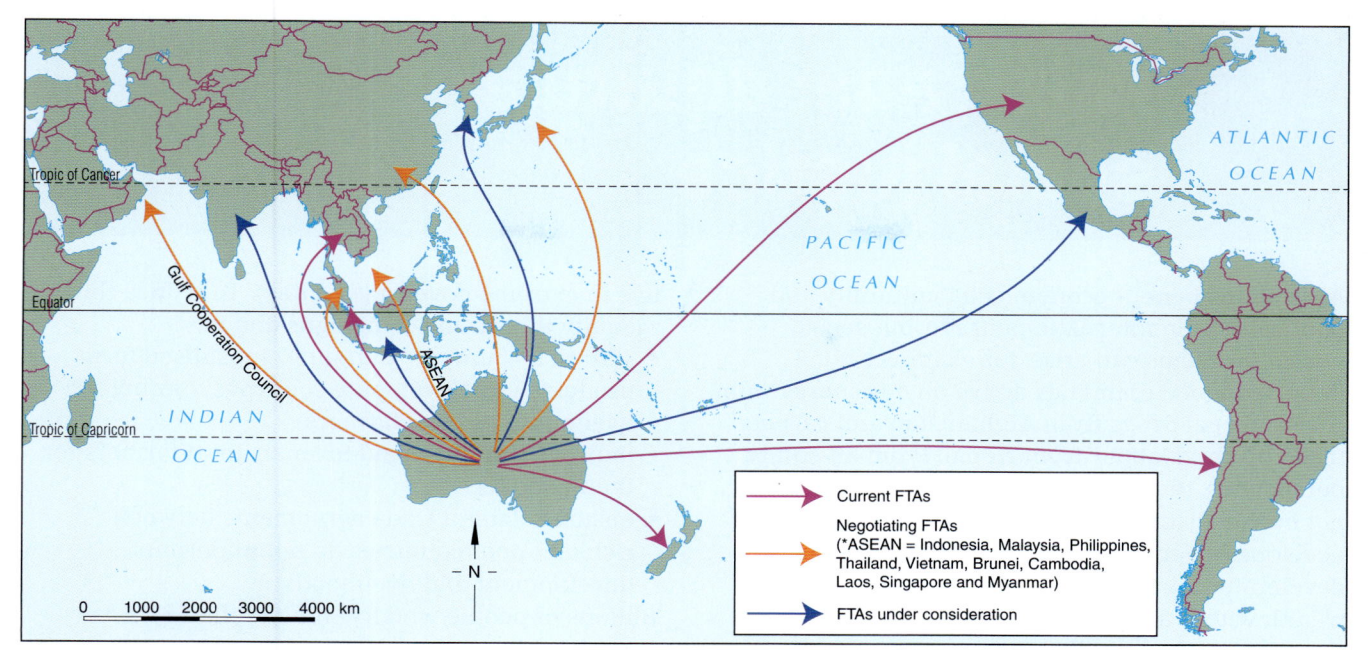

*Australia's Free Trade Agreement agenda*

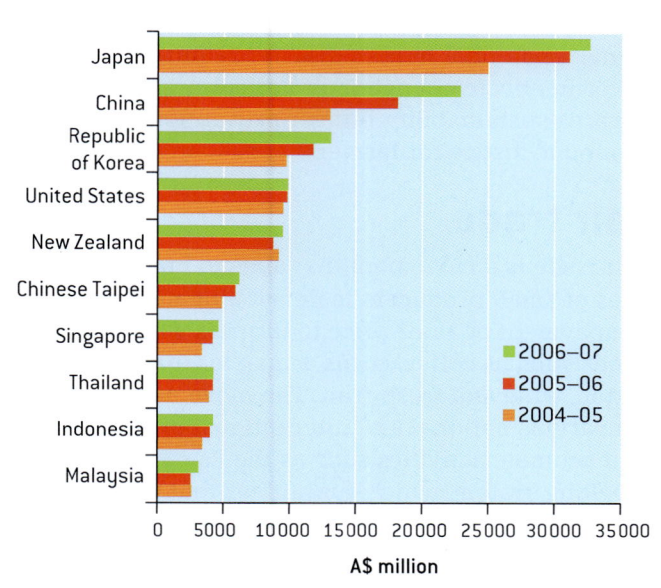

*Australia's top 10 exporting markets in APEC*

*AUSFTA – the trade-off*

## ACTIVITIES

### UNDERSTANDING

1. Describe what is meant by ANZCERTA, APEC, ASEAN, AFTA, OECD, DFAT, TAFTA, SAFTA and WTO.
2. Distinguish between bilateral, multilateral and regional agreements.

### THINKING AND APPLYING

3. Analyse the economic, cultural and geopolitical advantages and disadvantages of trade agreements to Australia.

### USING YOUR SKILLS

4. Refer to the map.
   a. Calculate the number of free trade agreements that are current, under negotiation and under consideration.
   b. List the agreements that involve countries in the Asia–Pacific region.
5. Refer to the table.
   a. Draw Australia's imports and exports with regional organisations as two line graphs.
   b. Discuss the reasons for differences in Australia's trade with the European Union and organisations in the Asia–Pacific Region.
6. Refer to the bar graph.
   a. Between 2004 and 2007, which country had the largest increase in exports from Australia?
   b. Calculate the total Australian exports in goods to the top 10 APEC trading countries in 2006–07.
   c. Explain why trade with APEC countries is important for Australia.
7. Refer to the cartoon.
   a. Explain the message in the cartoon.
   b. Analyse the advantages and the disadvantages of AUSFTA to Australia.
   c. Explain its implications for social justice and equity.

CHAPTER 11 | Trade, aid, defence: global regional links

# 11.4 Fair trade: equity and social justice

Australians benefit economically, culturally and politically from international trade, but social justice problems can arise, for example, when imported blood diamonds arrive on our shores from Africa, illegal drugs from Afghanistan and carpets made by child labour from Nepal. From an equity perspective, the benefits of international trade are not evenly distributed as such trade favours large, developed countries to the detriment of small developing countries. Unfair distribution of trade wealth within a country can lead to conflict, as was the case in Bougainville where most trade money ended up in transnational corporation's bank accounts and little in the workers' hands.

## Non-government organisations

Free trade is the trade of goods and services between countries, unhindered by government restrictions such as tariffs, quotas or government assistance to farmers. Two-thirds of Australia's agricultural products are exported but as Australian farmers do not receive agricultural subsidies they find it difficult to compete with, for example, the $2555 government subsidy per cow in Japan and $1057 in the United States.

Non-government organisations (NGOs) such as Oxfam and World Vision support **fair trade** and oppose socially unjust trade agreements. They oppose attempts by developed countries to block agricultural imports from developing countries and to unfairly subsidise their own farmers while demanding that poor countries keep their agricultural markets open. Even though the World Trade Organization (WTO) promotes a fair trade system, smaller countries often bow to pressure from larger, wealthier countries with more influence.

Oxfam argues that international trade in agricultural products is unjust, forcing millions of farmers to live in extreme poverty ($1 a day). To reduce this inequity their trade campaigns aim to:
- stop rich countries 'dumping' subsidised farm products into developing countries, ruining the livelihoods of local farmers
- improve the price paid to small, local farmers for their products
- ensure bilateral trade agreements between rich and poor countries do not undermine development and livelihoods.

Billions of people who live on less than $2 a day are sliding into hunger as the cost of basic food skyrockets around the world. Population growth, global warming and food crops used for biofuel signal a potential human disaster requiring governments to change their agricultural policies towards sustainability, hunger prevention, and economic justice for farmers.

## Fair trade

Fair trade is a movement that aims to improve the lives of small producers in developing nations by the payment of a fair price to farmers who export goods such as coffee, cocoa, sugar, tea, bananas, cotton, wine and fresh fruit. The movement operates via various national and international organisations that promote activities such as the Fair Trade labelling system, which guarantees that the income generated from these products will go back to the farmers and their communities.

Australia is a member of the International Fair Trade Association (IFAT). By 2009 Australian sales

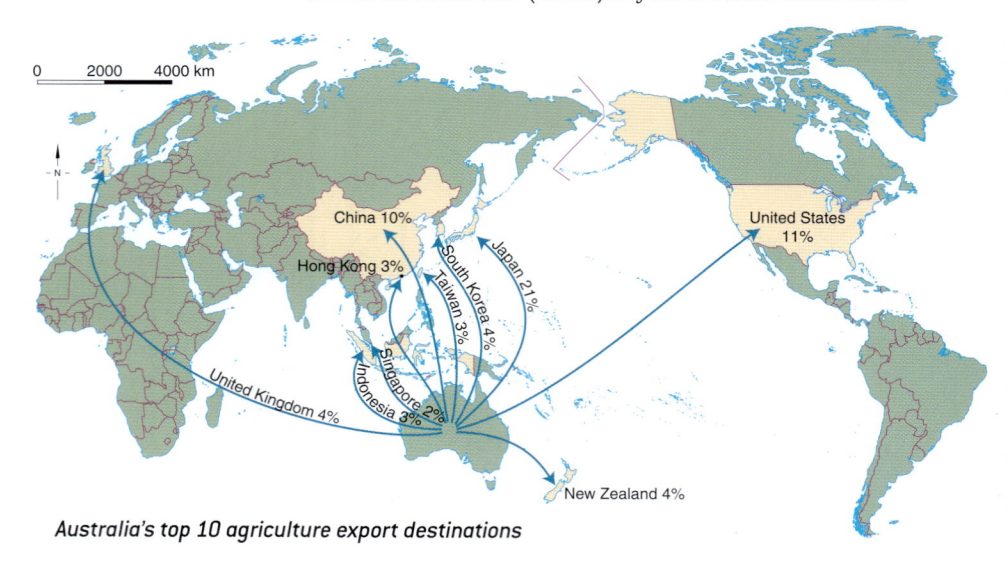

**Australia's top 10 agriculture export destinations**

of products carrying Fair Trade labelling reached $11 million. Coffee accounted for 75 per cent of sales, followed by chocolate, tea and sports balls. On a global scale, eight million producers and their families have benefited from fair-trade-funded infrastructure and community development projects.

The Fair Trade Association of Australia and New Zealand (FTAANZ) reports that 284 000 children in West Africa were working in dangerous conditions on cocoa farms. Many were subjected to forced labour and earned $30 per year. In January 2009, FTAANZ joined the international *Stop the Traffik* campaign to hold Australia's largest chocolate fondue party to raise awareness about child exploitation and trafficking in the West African cocoa trade.

*Active global citizenship: 'Australia's largest fondue party' raises awareness of the need for fair trade.*

At this factory in Ghana, pineapple is cut and packaged and shipped directly to retailers. By shipping a value-added product, the company's workers and partner growers receive a better return for their labour than by simply shipping a commodity.

### Social advantages and disadvantages of international trade to Australia

| Social advantages | Social disadvantages |
| --- | --- |
| • Greater variety of, and access to, goods and services | • Necessity for Australian companies to compete with cheaper imported goods |
| • Greater access to cheaper goods and services from overseas | • Increased balance-of-payment debts when resource prices (e.g. coal) or exchange rates worsen |
| • Continued benefits to the one-in-five Australians, and 80 per cent of small- and medium-sized businesses, engaged in export industries | • Overreliance on essential imports (e.g. oil), which are vulnerable to disasters, wars or price increases |
| • Potential for the limited Australian market to reach up to 7 billion people worldwide | • Difficulty entering some overseas markets due to tariffs, quotas and subsidies |
| • Greater productivity motivation due to overseas competition. | • Increased opportunity for importation of illegal and unethically produced goods. |

## ACTIVITIES

### UNDERSTANDING

1. Explain how tariffs, quotas and subsidies restrict trade.
2. Discuss the principles of fair trade.
3. Explain the role of NGOs such as Oxfam in relation to trade.

### THINKING AND APPLYING

4. Australia has made stronger regional trade links with its neighbours and lowered its tariffs against imported textiles, clothing and footwear (TCF).
   a. Make a list of five items of personal clothing that are imported.
   b. Explain how these imports might present equity and social-justice issues for workers who were previously employed in Australia's TCF industries.
   c. Suggest how some of these local TCF industries have survived in fiercely competitive markets.
5. In theory, every country — rich or poor — should have the opportunity to benefit from international trade. But the reality is very different. Discuss.

### USING YOUR SKILLS

6. Study the map on the previous page.
   a. Rank in order from highest to lowest the percentage of Australia's agricultural exports.
   b. Calculate the total percentage of agricultural goods exported to the top 10 countries.
   c. Draw the percentages as a bar graph.
7. Refer to the poster *Australia's largest chocolate fondue party*.
   a. What is the message about our trade in chocolate?
   b. List the sponsors of the chocolate fondue party.
   c. How does the poster appeal to us as responsible, active citizens?

### GEOTERMS

**fair trade:** the organised social movement that advocates payment of a fair price for producers in developing countries

# 11.5 Helping hand: Australia's foreign aid links

Campaigns such as Make Poverty History, the Live 8 Concerts and World Vision's annual 40 Hour Famine have brought poverty and aid into the international spotlight. The Australian Agency for International Development (AusAID) manages the Australian government's official overseas aid program, which is aimed at reducing poverty and promoting sustainable development in poorer countries. It aims to achieve these goals by working with Australian businesses, non-government organisations such as CARE Australia and international agencies such as the United Nations (UN) and World Bank.

## AusAID links: official development assistance

Overseas aid is the transfer of money, food and services from developed countries like Australia to developing countries such as Papua New Guinea. The Australian government's overseas aid or official development assistance (ODA) is distributed in a number of forms. These include:
- *Bilateral aid agreements*. This is aid given by one government to another government. For example, the Australian government has given aid to the Afghanistan and Iraq governments for war and post-war reconstruction.
- *Multilateral aid agreements*. This is aid given by governments of many countries to be distributed through international organisations. For example, AusAID distributes food through the United Nations World Food Programme. Multilateral aid programs enable Australia to contribute to projects that would otherwise be too large (e.g. the UN High Commissioner for Refugees) and to target problems requiring international efforts (such as the UN Environment Program to combat climate change).
- *Emergency humanitarian relief agreements*. This form of aid helps communities recover from disasters and conflict. Food, medicine and shelter were supplied by AusAID to affected populations after the 2004 Indian Ocean tsunami, the Indonesian earthquake and the Samoan tsunami in 2009.
- *NGO partnership agreements*. These take the form of grants to NGOs to deliver AusAID programs. For example, AusAID works with World Vision to reduce child labour in developing countries.
- *Community involvement agreements*. These involve funding education programs and support the many thousands of Australian volunteers who have worked overseas since the 1960s.

## Millennium development goals: global citizenship

In 2000, all world leaders adopted the United Nations Millennium Declaration, committing their nations to reduce extreme poverty by 2015. The declaration consists of eight Millennium Development Goals (MDGs) that aim to reduce poverty, hunger and disease (HIV/AIDS) while promoting gender equality, health, education and environmental sustainability. The MDGs embody basic human rights such as the right of each person to health, education, shelter and security. The achievement of the eight MDGs by 2015 requires the combined efforts of governments, NGOs and the private sector.

Millennium Development Goals (MDGs):
1. Eradicate extreme hunger and poverty
2. Achieve universal primary education
3. Promote gender equality and empower women
4. Reduce child mortality
5. Improve maternal health
6. Combat HIV/AIDS, malaria and other diseases
7. Ensure environmental sustainability
8. Develop a global partnership for development

*UN Millennium Development Goals (2000–15)*

The Australian aid program supports the MDGs and in 2008–09 Australia's official development assistance (ODA) was 0.32 per cent of gross domestic product (GDP) or $2.40 per person per week. The amount is anticipated to reach 0.5 per cent by 2015. The AusAID budget focuses on ensuring that money for hospitals, schools and refugees reaches the poorest people and does not find its way into the bank accounts of corrupt officials. The largest proportion of the AusAID budget is allocated to countries in the Asia–Pacific region.

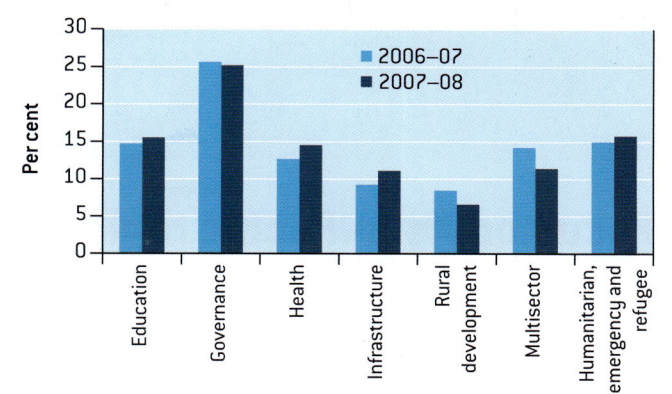

*Breakdown of Australian ODA by sector 2006–08*

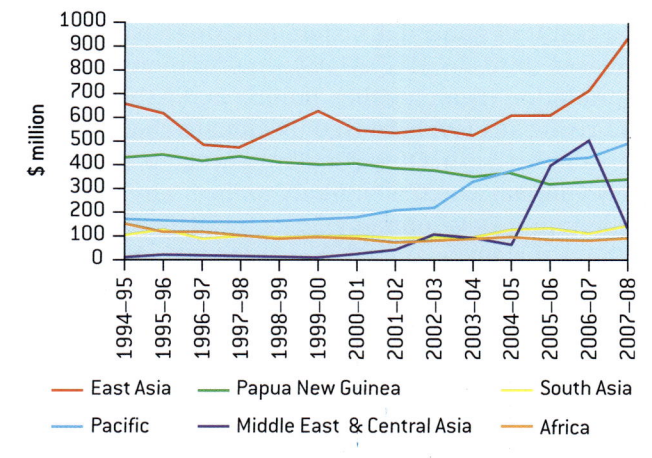

*Trends in Australian ODA by region 1994–2008*

*Australian assistance to UNICEF helps to fund food-distribution projects such as this refugee therapeutic feeding centre at Iriba Hospital, Sudan.*

## ACTIVITIES

### UNDERSTANDING

1. What organisation manages Australia's official overseas aid program?
2. List two international agreements relating to equity and social justice.
3. Discuss how the Australian government distributes aid.

### THINKING AND APPLYING

4. Collect five articles written in the last year where reference is made to the provision of aid by AusAID in the Asia–Pacific region. After reading each article, answer these key questions: What is the issue? Where is it located? What was done? What were the advantages to the country and to Australia?
5. Design an advertisement encouraging people to donate money to help developing countries achieve their Millennium Development Goals by 2015.

### USING YOUR SKILLS

6. Refer to the diagram of UN Millennium Development Goals. List the eight goals and outline the purpose of the Millennium Development Declaration.
7. Refer to the photograph.
    a. What is the location?
    b. What has happened to create this situation? How did it affect people?
    c. What should be done by global organisations to improve the life of these people?
    d. Imagine you are one of the people in the photograph. Describe your life.
8. Refer to the column graph.
    a. Calculate the percentage of the AusAID budget allocated to education and health in 2006–07 and 2007–08.
    b. Explain why the **governance** sector receives the largest percentage.
    c. What was the percentage given to humanitarian relief in 2007–08?
    d. List three countries that you think received humanitarian aid.
    e. Explain why rural development is important to reduce poverty and hunger.
9. Refer to the line graph.
    a. Calculate the changes in aid to Papua New Guinea, East Asia and the Pacific from 1996–97 to 2007–08.
    b. Explain why aid to the Middle East and Central Asia increased sharply during 2005–07.
    c. Discuss how AusAID focuses on the Asia–Pacific region.

# 11.6 Australian government aid links at work

## Focus on Asia–Pacific region

For geopolitical, economic and cultural reasons over 80 per cent of Australia's official development assistance (ODA) is distributed between 45 countries in the Asia–Pacific region. The geographic focus makes sense as 640 million people living in the region survive on $1 a day. Many suffer as a result of natural disasters (cyclones, tsunamis), diseases (bird flu, HIV/AIDS), environmental degradation (from logging, mining and fishing) and rising sea levels caused by climate change (Tuvalu, Kiribati). Of particular concern is Papua New Guinea, which is unlikely to meet any of the Millennium Development Goals by 2015.

Since the 1980s AusAID has lifted 500 million people in the Asia–Pacific region out of extreme poverty, by providing **microcredit**, education, shelter, health services, clean water, sanitation, food and modern technology. AusAID's efforts wiped out polio from the Pacific region and reopened 980 schools in Timor-Leste. These humanitarian links have also improved cultural understanding and regional security.

### 1 INDONESIA

After the 2004 tsunami, Australia gave $1 billion under the Australia Indonesia Partnership for Reconstruction and Development (AIPRD) agreement. AusAID worked alongside communities to rebuild hospitals, schools and infrastructure.

The bombing of the Sari nightclub in Bali in 2002 killed 88 Australians, 75 other nationalities and 39 Indonesians. AusAID provided $10.5 million to improve Bali's health system. An Australian Memorial Centre (2004) was built on the site of the old burns unit in Denpasar and staff were trained by Australian nurses. The centre provides a mobile eye clinic.

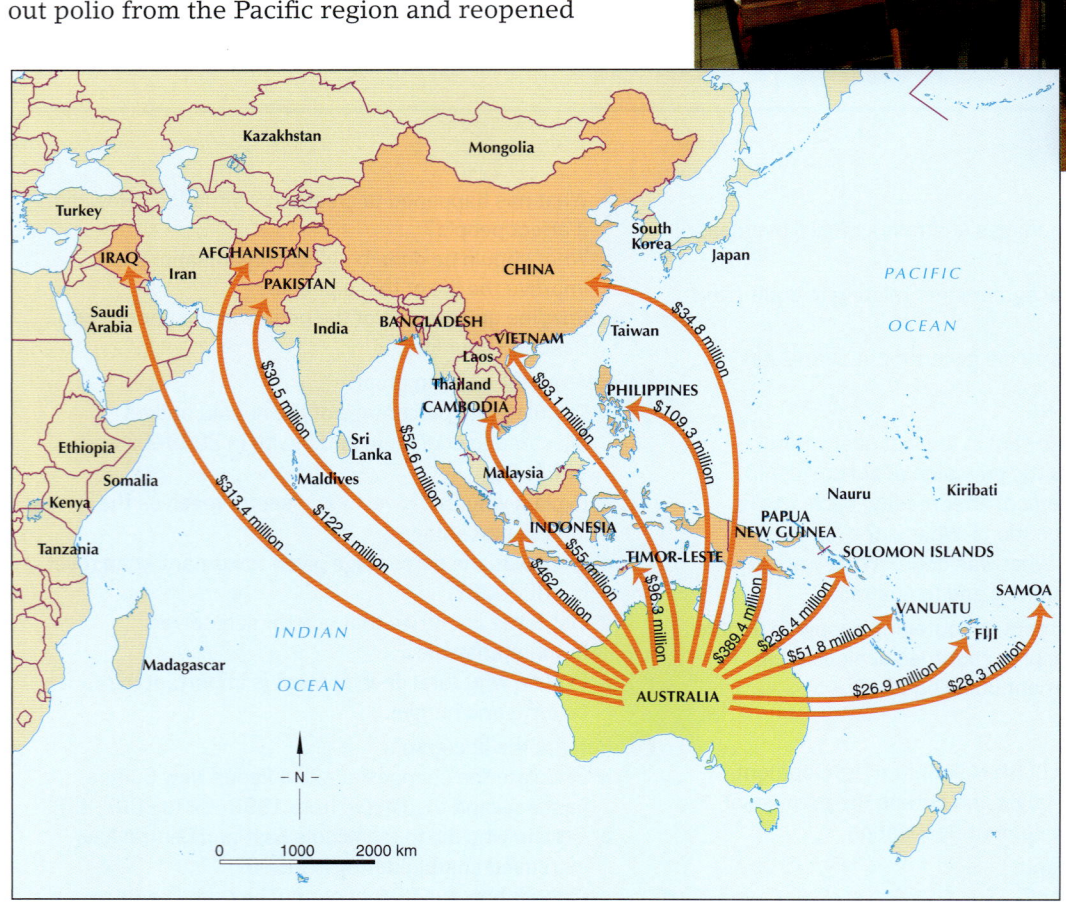

*Top 15 recipient countries for Australian government aid, 2008–09*

### 2 PAPUA NEW GUINEA

AusAID supports Anglicare's StopAIDS program which includes prevention education, blood tests, support and counselling.

The Bougainville Peace Agreement (2001) between Bougainville, Papua New Guinea and regional partners including Australia, included the provision of aid to restore basic services and stimulate economic growth.

### 3 IRAQ

The 2007–10 goal of the program is to support the reconstruction of Iraq, strengthen its governance and security and improve the quality of life for Iraqi people. Australia supports a joint Iraq–United Nations project aimed at reducing violence against women.

### 4 SOLOMON ISLANDS

The Kastom Gaden Association is a community development charity supported by AusAID to preserve traditional sustainable farming methods through education.

The RAMSI program in the Solomon Islands aims to restore stability by improving health services, tackling health issues such as HIV/AIDS and providing disaster management assistance. AusAID also gave assistance and support after the 2007 tsunami.

### 5 AFGHANISTAN

Australian aid to Afghanistan aims to improve security, governance, human rights and economic and social development. AusAID, through the Red Cross, provides emergency medical care in remote and conflict-affected areas. The most vulnerable, including women and children, are a priority for AusAID's health services.

### 6 PHILIPPINES

Masabud in Mindanao is an isolated island surrounded by rivers. The Philippines–Australia Local Sustainability Program constructed eight hanging bridges allowing 900 residents better access to markets and schools.

### 7 TIMOR-LESTE

AusAID and the UN Development Program (UNDP) has funded the development of a democratic parliament, as well as schools, hospitals and infrastructure.

### 8 VIETNAM

Disadvantaged street children learn skills at the Know One, Teach One (KOTO) restaurant vocational training program. To date 100 per cent of KOTO graduates have found employment in hotels and restaurants. It is funded by AusAID and an Australian charity, Street Voices.

### 9 CAMBODIA

Cambodia has one of the heaviest concentrations of landmines in the world. Each year these explosive devices kill or injure hundreds of people. Since 1996 AusAID has been the main supporter of the Cambodian National Volleyball League (Disabled). One of the teams reached number one in the Asia–Pacific Region in 2007.

AusAID's Agriculture Quality Improvement Project (AQIP) has helped develop seed-producing businesses and sells high-quality rice seeds to help farmers make a better livelihood from the land.

### 10 BANGLADESH

AusAID assisted people affected by Cyclone Sid, which devastated the southern coast of Bangladesh in 2007. It delivered training to 16 500 members of School Management Committees and over 120 000 primary school teachers, as well as giving 40 000 women access to microcredit.

### 11 VANUATU

AusAID and the Vanuatu Women's Centre aim to change community attitudes about violence against women and children.

### 12 CHINA

AusAID-funded Xinjiang HIV/AIDS Prevention and Care Project involves 35 Imams educating their followers in HIV prevention.

### 13 PAKISTAN

AusAID focuses on basic health care and education, through programs such as Australia Pakistan Scholarships, and supporting reconstruction following the 2005 earthquake. Australia provides support to reduce poverty in Pakistan's border areas with Afghanistan, where its poorest and most marginalised populations live.

An AusAID-funded field hospital in Battagram also acted as short-term housing for the families of those injured by the earthquake in 2005.

### 14 SAMOA

Australia contributed A$7 million to Samoa to support recovery and reconstruction after a tsunami in 2009. The aid was intended to rebuild houses and restore utilities such as water and power. AusAID was also active immediately after the disaster, providing 108 emergency and medical personnel and 29 tonnes of supplies to treat the injured. Search and rescue personnel were sent to help locate and treat people in the affected areas.

### 15 FIJI

Working with Fiji's justice and local communities, an Australian government program is building a better future for youths grappling with unemployment. The Nepani Youth Club gives the unemployed an opportunity to develop new skills. Many have gone on to find jobs in construction and other industries and improved community safety in a former high-crime suburb.

## ACTIVITIES

### UNDERSTANDING

1. List the different types of AusAID links.
2. Explain why AusAID focuses on the Asia–Pacific region.
3. Explain the role and actions of the Australian government when providing aid to developing countries.
4. Discuss the advantages to Australia of maintaining these aid links.

### USING YOUR SKILLS

5. What are the advantages of Australia's aid links to the people living in Indonesia, Samoa, Fiji and Vietnam?
6. What are the gender issues addressed by AusAID?
7. Describe how aid contributes to peace, reconstruction and stability after war and conflict.
8. Calculate the total AusAID money given to the top 15 countries. Draw the aid amounts as a column graph. Explain why more money is given to the top three countries.

# 11.7 Indonesia–Australia aid links

Australia's close neighbour Indonesia declared its independence from Dutch colonial rule in 1945. In 1949 the Republic of Indonesia was officially recognised. Since then, Australia has maintained firm diplomatic relations with Indonesia and has been a major aid donor, especially during times of humanitarian crisis such as the 2004 Indian Ocean tsunami and the 2009 Sumatran earthquake. Today, Indonesia is headed by a president, Susilo Bambang Yudhoyono, who was directly elected for a five-year term. As our regional neighbour, it is in Australia's interests that Indonesia has good governance, economic stability, and an effective ability to respond to emergencies. As well as securing strong relationships through trade and membership of international treaties and agreements, Australia and Indonesia work together to address issues such as counter-terrorism, people smuggling, illegal fishing and climate change. Australia is a popular host country for Indonesian students continuing their studies abroad.

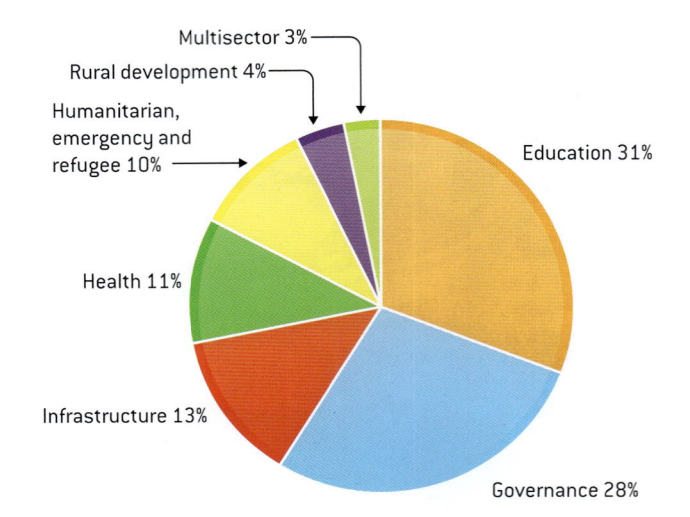

Estimated AusAID programs in Indonesia by sector, 2006–07

- Multisector 3%
- Rural development 4%
- Humanitarian, emergency and refugee 10%
- Health 11%
- Infrastructure 13%
- Governance 28%
- Education 31%

However, Australia's involvement with Indonesia is not universally welcomed within that country. Australia's support for the independence in 1999 of Timor-Leste (or East Timor as it was then) and the recent granting of refugee status to West Papuan asylum seekers has caused diplomatic tensions with the Indonesian government. Australia promotes democracy, **secularism** and other Western ideals, and this stance is believed to have motivated Islamic extremists to carry out terrorist attacks upon Australian targets and tourists.

## GEOfacts

Indonesia is:
- the world's largest **archipelago** nation, comprising 17 508 islands, of which 6000 are inhabited
- the fourth most populous country in the world, with a population of almost 240 million people
- a secular republic, with 300 distinct ethnic groups, 742 linguistic groups and an 86 per cent Muslim majority
- vulnerable to natural disasters such as earthquakes and tsunamis.

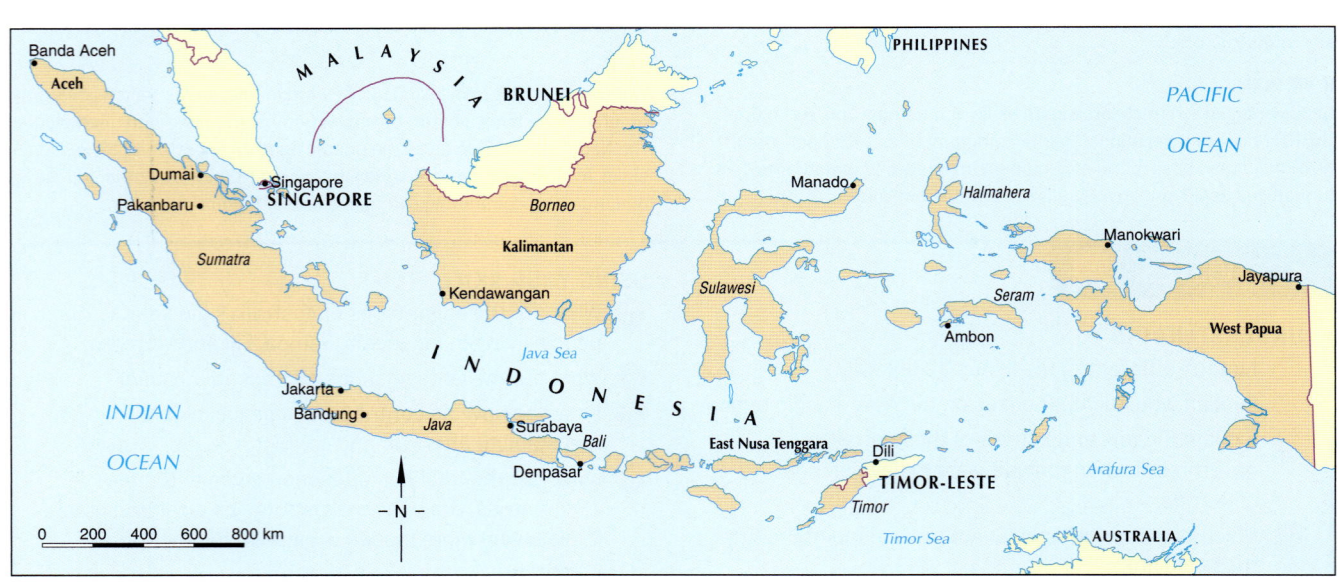

Indonesia: Australia's near neighbour

## Australia Indonesia Partnership Country Strategy

In 2008 Australia and Indonesia announced a bilateral five-year plan (2008–13) for the distribution of Australian aid valued at $2.5 billion to specific programs within Indonesia. These programs promote health, education, political stability and disaster preparedness. Australia has selected two moderate local Islamic organisations to assist in the programs, which hope to make practical improvements to the lives of the 100 million Indonesians who live in extreme poverty. The strategy has three main goals:

- to create a prosperous Indonesia
- to establish justice and democracy for all Indonesian citizens
- to ensure a safe and peaceful Indonesia.

Education is seen as a key pillar in achieving these goals. Australia is helping Indonesia achieve at least nine years of basic education for its children. This involves the building or expansion of 2000 junior secondary schools over 21 Indonesian provinces.

In 1998 the World Bank ranked Indonesia within the worst corruption category. This means that the effective distribution of aid has required significant changes within Indonesian governance. Another challenge is that some of Indonesia's most economically poor regions experience civil unrest. Papua and Aceh have ongoing movements for independence, and Ambon suffers from religious-based violence.

*Australian Prime Minister Kevin Rudd at the opening of an Indonesian primary school rebuilt with Australian aid money after it was destroyed in 2004 by a tsunami*

### GEOTERMS

**archipelago:** a large body of water with many islands

## ACTIVITIES

### UNDERSTANDING

1. List the reasons why it is strategic for Australia to support Indonesia.
2. Describe some of the challenges Australia faces in providing support to Indonesia.

### THINKING AND APPLYING

3. Explain why education is an important pillar of the Australia Indonesia Partnership Country Strategy.
4. Considering Indonesia's physical geography, and its political and economic situation, why might it be difficult to distribute effective health, education and aid programs?

### USING YOUR SKILLS

5. Refer to the graph showing AusAID programs in Indonesia.
   a. List the five main sectors benefiting from Australia's aid.
   b. Describe the types of programs that could be included in each sector.
6. Refer to the map of Indonesia.
   a. Estimate the distance from the northern tip of Australia to **i** Banda Aceh **ii** Java **iii** Manado.
   b. Which geographic description best fits Indonesia?
   **i** A group of islands **ii** An archipelago **iii** A continent
   c. Name two other nations that share a border with Indonesia.

# 11.8 Australian government links with Papua New Guinea

The mainland of Papua New Guinea (PNG) and its 600 islands has a population of 6.1 million people. Papua New Guinea's society ranges from traditional subsistence and small cash-crop agriculture, to modern urban life in the capital, Port Moresby. About 85 per cent of the population derive their livelihood from farming.

## Traditional links

Geographic proximity and historical links give PNG a special place in Australia's foreign relations. In 1906 Australia assumed responsibility for the administration of Papua (formerly British New Guinea) and in 1920 the League of Nations made the former German New Guinea an Australian territory.

Australians also fought in PNG during World War II. The Kokoda Track, the scene of major confrontations between Australian and Japanese forces, has become a focus for Australian patriotism and walking the track has become a popular tourist activity. Since independence in 1975, Australia's links have continued in trade, defence and aid. Australia is PNG's largest source of imports and largest export market, and Australia assists in its military training under the bilateral Defence Cooperation Program. PNG is Australia's second largest receiver of aid, with the largest proportion allocated to governance.

AusAID assisted Bougainville's recovery from armed conflict (1989–98) by rebuilding roads and wharves and helping to restore the production and export of cocoa to pre-crisis levels. AusAID coordinated these programs with the United Nations Development Program (UNDP) and the European Union (EU).

Today, 80 per cent of Bougainville's population has access to a road within seven kilometres of their home.

## Papua New Guinea–Australia Development Cooperation Strategy

Under the terms of the Treaty on Development Cooperation (2000) Australia agreed to maintain a bilateral program of aid to PNG. The treaty, supported by the Papua New Guinea–Australia Development Cooperation Strategy 2006–10, is driven by PNG ownership and leadership.

The 'strategy' focuses on effective aid that reduces poverty and promotes sustainable development. It does this by improving democratic governance, human rights, equity, education, health, infrastructure, rural development and an effective coordinated response to the HIV/AIDS epidemic. During 2008–09, AusAID assisted in the building of clinics to treat sexually transmittable diseases, in partnership with the Clinton Foundation and the Asian Development Bank.

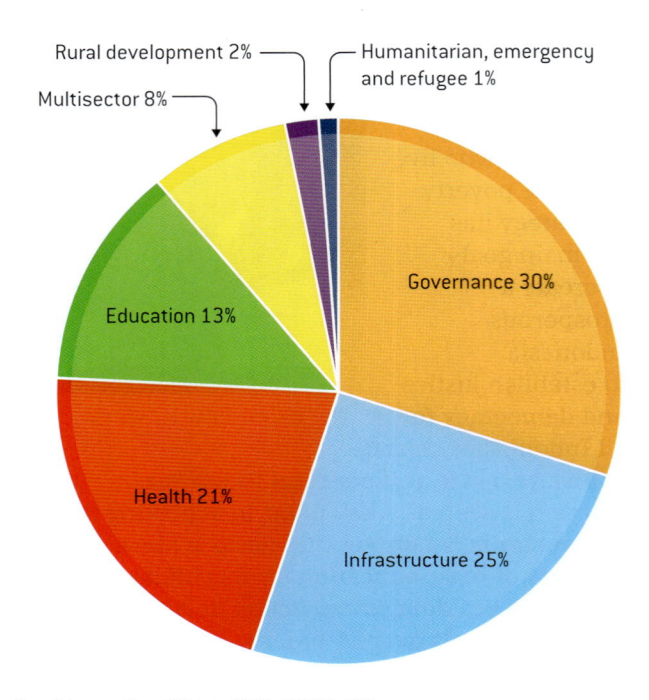

*Total Australian ODA to PNG, 2007–08*

- Governance 30%
- Infrastructure 25%
- Health 21%
- Education 13%
- Multisector 8%
- Rural development 2%
- Humanitarian, emergency and refugee 1%

## Millennium Development Goals

About 40 per cent of the PNG population lives on less than US$1 a day. Women remain the most disadvantaged — in education, access to employment and political representation. AusAID programs address gender inequality, especially sexual and domestic violence. Delivering effective aid in PNG is a problem, with 700 cultural groups living in remote, rugged areas. Service delivery is expensive and most communities have difficulty accessing health care, education and transport.

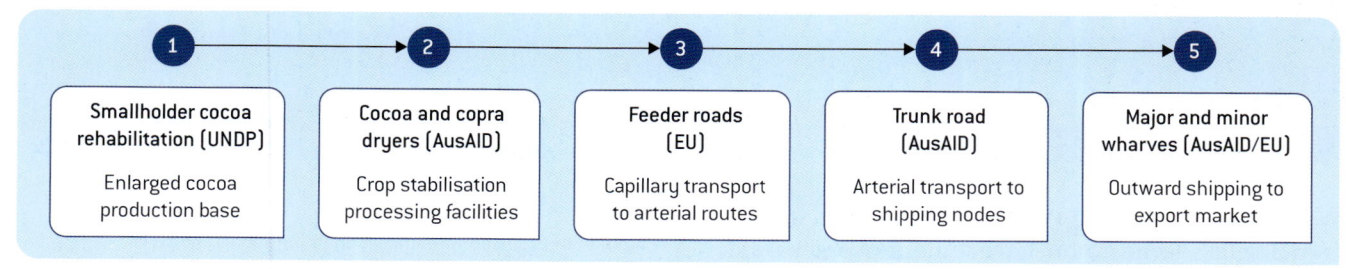

| 1 → | 2 → | 3 → | 4 → | 5 |
|---|---|---|---|---|
| Smallholder cocoa rehabilitation (UNDP) | Cocoa and copra dryers (AusAID) | Feeder roads (EU) | Trunk road (AusAID) | Major and minor wharves (AusAID/EU) |
| Enlarged cocoa production base | Crop stabilisation processing facilities | Capillary transport to arterial routes | Arterial transport to shipping nodes | Outward shipping to export market |

*Post-conflict agriculture market chain rehabilitation links. Australia's roads, wharves and agriculture projects complemented the work of other donors, notably that undertaken by the UN Development Program (UNDP) to restore Bougainville's cocoa tree stock.*

Since PNG gained independence, AusAID and various NGOs have contributed to improved life expectancy, literacy levels, infant mortality rates and school participation rates. Even though the economy is growing by 2.6 per cent per year, the country is unlikely to meet any of the Millennium Development Goals by 2015. The 2008 Port Moresby Declaration commits the Australian government to improved cooperation with the Pacific island nations – including PNG – to reduce inequality and social injustice.

**Towards the Millennium Development Goals**

| Indicators | 1990 | 2009 |
|---|---|---|
| Proportion of population below $1 per day | 24% | 39% |
| Prevalence of child malnutrition (under 5 years) | 36% | 24% |
| Enrolment in primary education | 66% | 73% |
| Girls enrolled in primary school | 61% | 69% |
| Births attended by skilled staff | 20% | 39% |
| Infant mortality rate (per '000 live births) | 82% | 69% |
| Access to improved sanitation | 82% | 45% |
| Access to an improved water source | 42% | 39% |

*Papua New Guinea woman in the Simbu province of Papua New Guinea*

## ACTIVITIES

### UNDERSTANDING
1. Describe Australia's links with Papua New Guinea.
2. Discuss the advantages of Australian aid to PNG.

### THINKING AND APPLYING
3. Suggest strategies to improve the lives of Papua New Guineans so that their development goals could be reached by 2015.
4. Explain how the Australian government contributes to social justice and equity in PNG.
5. Research how AusAID projects in PNG are addressing **a** HIV/AIDS and **b** gender inequality.
6. Describe the life of the woman in the photograph. Compare her life with yours.

### USING YOUR SKILLS
7. Refer to the pie graph. Rank the aid by sector from largest to smallest. Explain why governance is a large component of the budget.
8. Refer to the diagram on market chain rehabilitation links in Bougainville. Explain how the coordination of aid contributed to the export of cocoa and improvements to the lives of farmers.
9. Refer to the table on Millennium Development Goals. What targets have not improved since 1990? Explain why some targets have improved while others have deteriorated.

# 11.9 A non-government organisation: World Vision Australia

World Vision Australia (WVA), which began in 1965, is Australia's largest non-government overseas-aid organisation. It addresses the causes of poverty in overseas communities in three main ways — providing short-term emergency relief, creating long-term community development projects and conducting advocacy and education activities within Australia. WVA is part of World Vision International. It is a member of the Australian Council for International Development (ACFID) and works with AusAID and United Nations agencies such as the World Health Organization.

World Vision Australia works with people of all cultures and faiths to achieve social justice and equity. In 2008 WVA assisted 20.4 million people around the world through 735 projects in over 90 countries. Approximately 2.8 million people received emergency relief, 400 000 children were sponsored, 270 000 participated in the 40 Hour Famine and 3808 people worked as volunteers. In 2007 WVA's total income was $356.5 million, with 53 per cent received from child sponsorship. The WVA sponsorship network contributes to assistance programs that benefit the child, the child's family and the community. The sponsorship link also helps Australians understand what life is like for families living in extreme poverty.

## Global citizenship: equity and social justice

World Vision Australia supported the Make Poverty History movement and concert, which reached 1.5 million Australians, and supports Stand Up Against Poverty, an annual event calling on individuals to take the challenge to put an end to poverty. World Vision encourages supporters to lobby the Australian government on issues that affect the poor, and is involved in campaigns against landmines, child labour, child soldiers and debt.

The work of World Vision Australia focuses on social justice and equity issues — children who are exploited, orphaned, homeless or disabled; education, to enable people to participate more fully in society and in decision making; gender, where the poorest are usually females and the main carers of children and families; HIV/AIDS awareness and prevention; and food, water and sanitation problems, to assist people in achieving food security and better health.

**India**
Community-based performance monitoring (CPBM) projects

**Uganda**
Rural water and sanitation education programs

**Cambodia**
Working with people in rural communities to clear landmines from schools, villages and communal areas

**Afghanistan**
AusAID-funded improved-livelihoods project

**Vietnam**
Innovative teacher training using creative methods such as puppetry and roleplay

**Timor-Leste**
Vocational training, helping troubled teenagers to turn their lives around

**Solomon Islands**
Earthquake relief and reconstruction training to families

**Australia**
Health and social support programs for adult members of the Stolen Generations

**Lesotho**
Nutrition education for mothers in drought- and HIV-affected communities

**Brazil**
Community centres and sponsorship programs in Brazilian slums

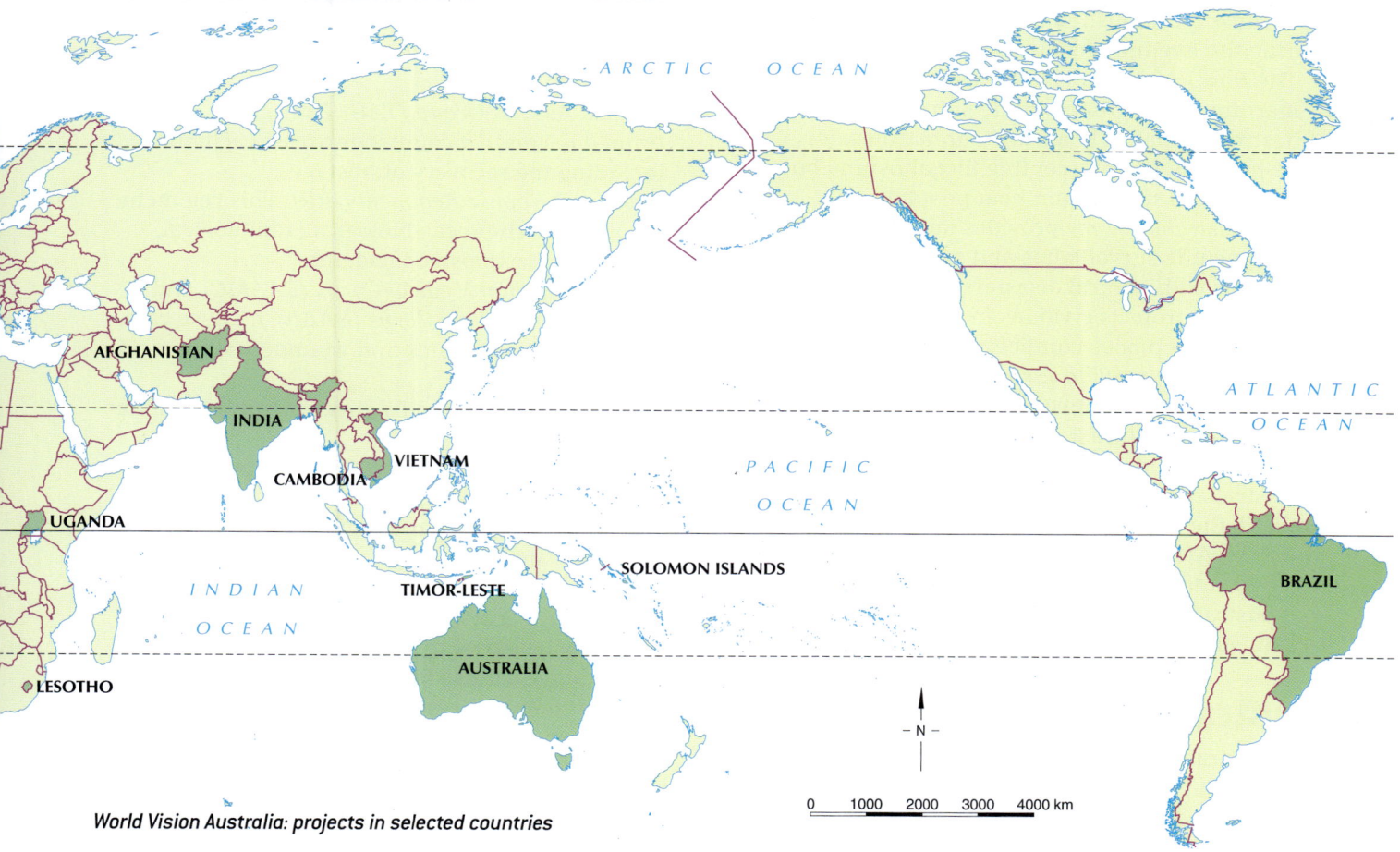

*World Vision Australia: projects in selected countries*

## ACTIVITIES

### UNDERSTANDING
1. What is the role of World Vision Australia (WVA)?
2. Describe WVA's aid links with the rest of the world.

### THINKING AND APPLYING
3. Explain how WVA contributes to social justice and equity.
4. Using the internet, research another Australian NGO and how it contributes to a better life for poor people living in developing countries (e.g. CARE Australia).

### USING YOUR SKILLS
5. Refer to the map.
    a. List the countries that receive aid from WVA.
    b. What do these countries have in common?
    c. Describe how WVA contributes to improved health, food, education, water and sanitation in developing countries.
    d. Explain WVA's aid projects in Cambodia, the Solomon Islands and Timor-Leste.

CHAPTER 11 | Trade, aid, defence: global regional links

# 11.10 Australia's defence links

The Australian Defence Force (ADF) is the military organisation responsible for defending Australian territory and contributes to maintaining peace and resolving conflicts around the world, especially in the Asia–Pacific region.

## Tri-service defence

To enable Australians to live in one of the most secure countries in the world the Australian government established the following three services during the twentieth century.

- The *Royal Australian Navy (RAN)* provides maritime forces that operate ships, guided-missile destroyers, patrol boats and submarines. It is responsible for intercepting illegal fishing boats and asylum seekers (or 'boat people').
- The *Australian Army* provides land operations that include surveillance and special recovery. It helps with natural disasters in Australia and overseas, protects civilians in conflict zones and helps to keep post-conflict zones safe.
- The *Royal Australian Air Force (RAAF)* plays a role in air surveillance and intelligence gathering. It responds to disasters by transporting aid, personnel and medical supplies and evacuating Australian citizens in emergencies.

By 1976 the importance of joint warfare led to the Navy, Army and Air Force services combining under a single headquarters, or tri-service, called the Australian Department of Defence which administers the Australian Defence Force (ADF).

## Australian Defence Force

The Australian Department of Defence and the Department of Foreign Affairs and Trade are responsible for the protection of Australia and our national interests. In 2009 the ADF employed 51 500 full-time active personnel and 19 500 reservists. This includes 10 000 women currently serving in the Navy (18 per cent), Army (12 per cent) and Air Force (17 per cent). Australia has a small defence force compared to the global figure of 17 442 000 active troops. The amount and percentage of military expenditure per GDP is also smaller than most countries. The government aims to increase defence expenditure by 3 per cent each year until 2016 to fund resistance to potential terrorist attacks; to purchase new destroyers and fighter planes; and to provide assistance after natural disasters.

Throughout its history, the ADF has established special military forces to help protect Australia's interests. These include:

- *Australian Reserve Forces*. These served in China during the Boxer Rebellion, in South Africa during the Boer War and in both World Wars. They assist after disasters and provide security at major events.
- *Special Operations Command (SOCOMD)*. This force is trained for unconventional warfare and counter-terrorism. It is involved in Timor-Leste, Afghanistan and Iraq and provided security for the Commonwealth Games (2006) and Rugby World Cup (2003).
- *Tactical Assault Group (TAG)*. This group is trained to conduct counter-terrorism activities including the recovery of hostages.
- *Incident Response Regiment (IRR)*. This regiment responds to chemical, biological, radiological, nuclear and explosive incidents.
- *Royal Australian Medical Corps (RAAMC)* and *Royal Army Nursing Corps (RAANC)*. These care, treat and evacuate sick and wounded soldiers and civilians.

The ADF is supported by government bodies that include:

- Australian Federal Police (AFP), for people-smuggling and terrorism
- Australian Defence Force Academy (ADFA), for military training
- Australian Security Intelligence Organisation (ASIO), for gathering information about criminal activity or security threats
- Australian Customs Service, Australian Quarantine and Inspection Service and Department of Immigration and Multicultural Affairs, for border security
- Australian Government Aid Agency (AusAID), for humanitarian relief to people affected by conflict.

## Non-government organisations

Non-government organisations (NGOs) play an important role in Australia's defence. For example, the Returned Services League (RSL) provides welfare to war veterans; Legacy provides financial assistance to war widows and children; the Australian Defence Association (ADA) presents information to parliament on defence and security issues; Amnesty International monitors and raises awareness about human rights abuses in connection with military activity and conflict zones; and the Red Cross and Salvation Army assist people affected by conflict.

**Defence world overview 2009**

| Active troops* ('000s) | Reserve troops ('000s) | Defence budget ($ billion) | Tanks | Aircraft carriers | Cruisers | Destroyers | Frigates | Corvettes | Nuclear submarines | Submarines | Fighter aircraft | Nuclear weapons |
|---|---|---|---|---|---|---|---|---|---|---|---|---|
| 17 442 | 44 925 | 1200 | 86 681 | 24 | 28 | 204 | 319 | 335 | 134 | 259 | 17 489 | 26 291 |

*China has the largest number of active troops and South Korea the largest number of reserve troops.

Infrastructure, transport and energy $10.3 billion
Industry and workforce $11.6 billion
Defence $17.8 billion
Education $18.7 billion
Health $46.0 billion
Community services and culture $6.1 billion
Social security and welfare $102.4 billion
General government services $79.2 billion

Australian budget 2008–09

### GEOfacts
North Korea devotes 22.9 per cent of GDP on military expenditure, compared to 1.9 per cent by Australia.

*An Australian Army tank performing on its first exercise*

## ACTIVITIES

### UNDERSTANDING
1. Describe Australia's main defence forces.
2. Explain the roles of government and non-government organisations in relation to defence links.

### THINKING AND APPLYING
3. Discuss the problems faced by the Australian government in trying to protect a vast coastline of 36 735 kilometres.
4. Discuss the impact on a population when its government spends more on the military as a percentage of GDP than on infrastructure, education and health.
5. Choose two of the following defence non-government organisations: Australian Peacekeeper and Peacemaker Veteran's Association, Australian Red Cross, Legacy, Australian Defence Association, Amnesty International, Returned Services League, Peace Organisation Australia.
   a Explain the aims of the organisation.
   b Discuss the importance of the organisation in relation to Australia's defence links.
   c Explain how the organisation addresses social justice and equity.
6. Debate the topic *Women in Australia's defence forces should not be allowed to serve in combat roles*.

### USING YOUR SKILLS
7. Refer to the pie graph.
   a Calculate the proportion of money spent on defence compared to health, education and social services.
   b Imagine you were in charge of the defence budget. Explain how you would allocate the money to ensure a secure Australia.

# 11.11 Australia's defence agreements

Australia's major defence agreements show a process of change — from our commitment to the United Kingdom in the nineteenth and early twentieth centuries, to the United States during the Cold War (1945–91), then towards countries in the Asia–Pacific region in the late twentieth century.

## Australia's diverse defence policy

Even though defeating terrorism and countering the proliferation of weapons of mass destruction remains high on Australia's defence policy agenda, its main objectives are to:
- protect and defend Australia's land and marine territories
- keep Australia and the Australian people safe from attack or the threat of attack, and from economic and political coercion
- support and maintain strategic stability and peace in the Asia–Pacific region
- support the international community to uphold global security organisations such as the United Nations.

These objectives form the basis of Australia's defence agreements — bilateral (joint military activities with the United States, Canada, Singapore, New Zealand, Britain and PNG), multilateral (United Nations) and regional (ANZUS) defence agreements.

## Defence agreements with Asia–Pacific countries

Australia has an obligation to its Asia–Pacific neighbours to assist in maintaining peace under the following agreements:
- *ANZUS (Australia, New Zealand, United States)*. Beginning in 1952, the ANZUS treaty promotes regional security through peaceful means.
- *Closer Defence Relations (CDR)*. This is an informal agreement entered into with New Zealand during the 1990s and emphasises intelligence sharing and joint exercises between the two countries.
- *Five Power Defence Arrangements (FPDA)*. This arrangement between the United Kingdom, Australia, New Zealand, Malaysia and Singapore was adopted in 1971. It involves consulting each other if there is a threat to attack Malaysia or Singapore.
- *ASEAN Regional Forum (ARF)*. The principal security forum in the Asia–Pacific region, the ARF fosters dialogue on political and security issues of common concern.

Under the 1989 Joint Declaration of Principles (JDP), Australia agreed to commit forces to resist external aggression against Papua New Guinea. The Australia–Indonesia Security Agreement (2007) focuses on reducing international terrorism and transnational crime and the JANZUS Agreement between Japan, Australia, New Zealand and the United States (2007) aims to develop closer security ties with Japan. Australia participates in joint exercises with South-East Asian countries, deploys warships and aircraft to patrol Pacific waters and is responsible for the defence of Nauru.

## Nuclear and landmine agreements

The atomic bombs that were dropped on Hiroshima and Nagasaki in Japan in 1945 bring fear to people's minds that this type of military action could occur again. Over 2000 nuclear tests have been conducted since 1945. North Korea tested a nuclear weapon in 2009 and the International Atomic Energy Agency was unable to verify in 2008 whether Iran's nuclear activities were exclusively peaceful. Australia participates in the UN Disarmament Commission and signed the United Nations Treaty on the Non-Proliferation of Nuclear Weapons (NPT) which provides global nuclear safeguards and is part of the South Pacific Nuclear Weapons Free Zone.

*The front page of the* Herald Sun *shows Darwin within range of North Korea's missiles. North Korea tested a nuclear bomb in October 2006, and again in May 2009.*

## SAMPLE STUDY

### Landmines in Cambodia

Approximately 15 000 to 20 000 people die or receive injuries from landmines or unexploded ordnances each year. Those who survive often require amputations. Australia signed the 1997 Ottawa Convention to prohibit the use, stockpiling and production of mines, and is involved in landmine clearance programs in Cambodia. The treaty is supported by NGOs (Human Rights Watch and Save the Children) and AusAID assists the Cambodian National Volleyball League for the Disabled. **Geographic information systems (GIS)** assisted the Cambodian government to clear landmines, contributing to reduced deaths and accidents.

In Cambodia 6422 villages are contaminated with landmines and 5.1 million people are considered at risk.

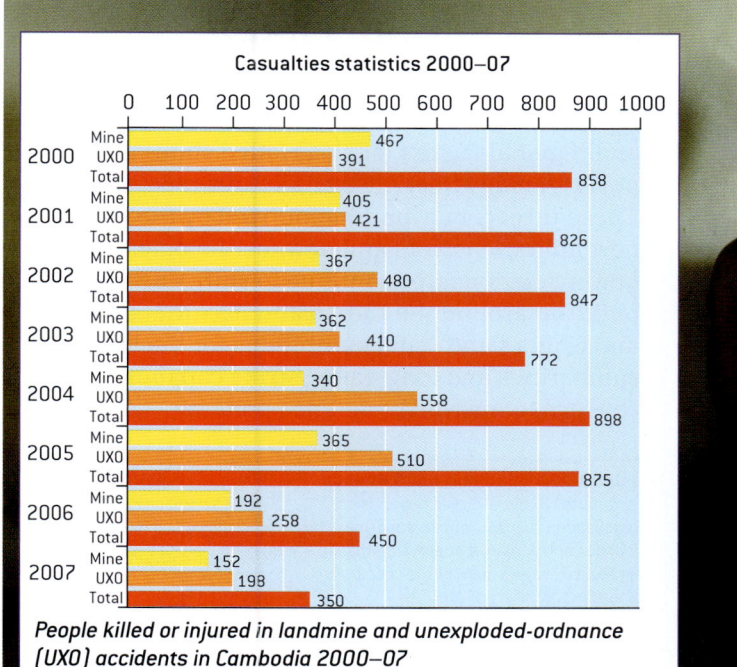

**Casualties statistics 2000–07**

| Year | Mine | UXO | Total |
|------|------|-----|-------|
| 2000 | 467 | 391 | 858 |
| 2001 | 405 | 421 | 826 |
| 2002 | 367 | 480 | 847 |
| 2003 | 362 | 410 | 772 |
| 2004 | 340 | 558 | 898 |
| 2005 | 365 | 510 | 875 |
| 2006 | 192 | 258 | 450 |
| 2007 | 152 | 198 | 350 |

*People killed or injured in landmine and unexploded-ordnance (UXO) accidents in Cambodia 2000–07*

*Impact of landmines on children. This fifteen-year-old lost a foot and is permanently blinded.*

## ACTIVITIES

### UNDERSTANDING

1. What are Australia's three main types of defence agreements?
2. Explain the main focus of Australia's defence policy.
3. Discuss the importance of Australia's defence agreements with countries in the Asia–Pacific region.

### THINKING AND APPLYING

4. Discuss how the impact of war continues after conflicts cease.
5. Discuss the advantages of defence agreements to countries like Australia, being an isolated island nation with a small population.
6. Should the world community try to prevent any new nuclear nations? How could this be achieved?
7. Celebrities such as Princess Diana and Paul McCartney have campaigned against landmines. Do you think that celebrity involvement such as this is a good way of increasing awareness of the issue?

### USING YOUR SKILLS

8. On a blank map of the world draw Australia's defence links as outlined on these pages.
9. Refer to the bar graph in the sample study.
   a. Calculate the total mine/UXO casualties in Cambodia from 2000 to 2007.
   b. Explain the reasons for the decline of deaths and injuries from mine and UXO accidents from 2005 to 2007. Discuss how international agreements contributed to this decline.

CHAPTER 11 | Trade, aid, defence: global regional links

# 11.12 From frontline to peace building

In 2009 the Australian Defence Force (ADF) had 3800 members deployed to eleven overseas operations and 500 personnel involved in domestic operations ranging from protecting Australia's borders and patrolling Australian waters to providing assistance to Indigenous communities in the Northern Territory.

## Peace-building links

Despite the strengths of our defence links, it is always less costly, both in human and financial terms, to prevent and resolve conflicts before they lead to violence. Australia recently supported the Aceh, Bougainville and Solomon Islands Peace Agreements. Australia is part of the 63 UN peacekeeping operations around the world. Peacekeepers' tasks vary depending on different conflicts but generally include policing buffer zones, demobilisation and disarmament of military forces, establishing communication between parties, and protecting the delivery of humanitarian assistance.

Peace building is a lengthy process requiring the reintegration of soldiers and refugees, demining and removal of war debris, emergency relief, the repair of roads and infrastructure, and economic and social rehabilitation. The Australian government's peace-building initiative aims to avert conflict where possible and addresses the causes of conflict such as social injustice and inequity.

## Future defence links

Global factors (such as terrorism, pandemic diseases, resource depletion and impacts of climate change) and regional factors (such as failed states and poverty) may affect Australia's future security links. These threats may be compounded by the rise of new military powers and new technologies as global power relationships continue to shift. The military build-up around the Indian and Pacific oceans, and China's and India's ambitions for nuclear submarines and long-range strike capabilities, are of concern to Australia's defence policy.

**1 Operation Resolute: border protection**
Responsible for activities within Australia's Exclusive Economic Zone (EEZ). It deals with unauthorised arrivals, illegal fishing and smuggling, and protects Australia's gas and oil infrastructure.

**2 Operation Catalyst: Iraq**
Contributes to the rehabilitation and reconstruction of Iraq.

**3 Operation Astute: Timor-Leste**
Assists in restoring of peace and stability in Timor-Leste.

**4 Operation Slipper: Afghanistan**
Prevents acts of terrorism around the world.

**5 Operation Anode: Solomon Islands**
Aims to restore law and order and improve economic governance through the Australian-led Regional Assistance Mission to Solomon Islands (RAMSI).

**6 Operation Outreach: Indigenous Affairs**
Supports the Northern Territory Emergency Response Task Force. It assists police and civilian health teams. The unit has a high proportion of Aboriginal soldiers as it relies on local knowledge.

**7 Operation Mazurka: the Sinai**
Assists the peace process by monitoring the border and preparing daily operational briefings.

**8 Operation Paladin: Israel/Lebanon**
Contributes to the UN Truce Supervision Organisation (UNTSO) with Israel, Syria, Lebanon and Jordan. It supervised the agreed truce agreement at the conclusion of the first Arab/Israeli War.

**9 Operation Azure: Sudan**
Deploys personnel to the peacekeeping United Nations Mission in Sudan (UNMIS).

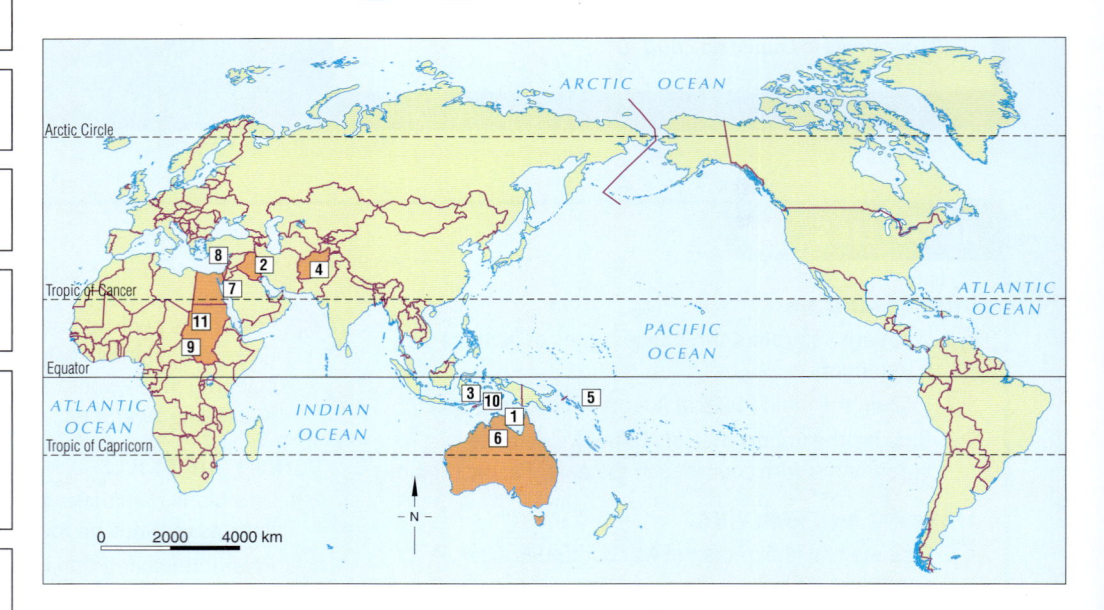

**10 Operation Tower: Timor-Leste**
Supports the on-going UN mission to Timor-Leste and supports the Timorese Defence Force under the regional Defence Cooperation Program.

**11 Operation Hedgerow: Darfur**
Deters the resurgence of violence in Darfur by stabilising the region and providing support for an effective peace process.

*New Years Day on the frontline, 2009*

**Some arguments for and against Australia's defence links**

| | In favour | Against |
|---|---|---|
| Economic | The ADF develops important trade and professional skills and provides employment to many thousands of Australians. | Maintaining the ADF is very costly and diverts government funding away from education, health, transport and other infrastructure. |
| Cultural | The ADF protects the democratic way of life around the world and has played an important role in forging Australia's national identity.<br><br>The ADF defends vulnerable Indigenous and poor communities within Australia and defends social justice and equity around the world through participation in UN peacekeeping activities.<br><br>The ADF accompanies and protects overseas aid projects and post-conflict reconstruction. | The presence of heavily armed soldiers in countries where the ADF is deployed can have an intimidating effect on local populations, creating tensions and poor cultural interaction.<br><br>The dangers of military activity can cause fatalities in local populations, creating resentment and anger towards Australian troops. Fatalities among Australian troops create severe emotional distress for family and friends.<br><br>Controversy surrounding some unpopular overseas military engagements creates divisions within Australian society. |
| Political | The ADF maintains stability in the Asia–Pacific region and protects Australia from transnational crime and terrorist attacks.<br><br>The ADF has a commitment to support peaceful resolution to conflict rather than military involvement.<br><br>The ADF helps to maintain agreements aimed at reducing nuclear, chemical, biological and landmine warfare. | Some Australians believe the ADF is involved in too many overseas conflicts, making it less available to respond to emergencies and threats within Australia.<br><br>Australia's military role in the US-led 'war on terror' has created resentment in some countries, negatively affecting Australia's standing in the world. It is also believed to have attracted hostility from extremist groups, thus increasing the likelihood of terrorist attacks on Australians. |

## SAMPLE STUDY

### Timor-Leste: crises and peace

Timor, one of our closest neighbours to the north, was colonised by the Dutch and Portuguese over three centuries ago. The country was divided into the Dutch-controlled west and Portuguese east. In 1949 West Timor became part of the Republic of Indonesia. The Portuguese neglected East Timor, resulting in poverty, lack of infrastructure and poor governance. In 1975, only days after declaring itself independent, East Timor was invaded by Indonesia, resulting in the deaths of 60 000 people. Under Indonesian occupation, the people suffered human rights abuses, and non-Timorese were given preferential treatment.

Pressure from the global community in 1999 led to the Indonesian government allowing the people of East Timor to vote. People chose independence, but celebrations were brief as violence broke out. Thousands became refugees in desperate need of food, shelter and protection. Global pressure led the Indonesian government to allow a UN peacekeeping force to restore law and order. Australia's defence forces assisted the UN Mission in Support of East Timor (UNMISET) by providing 5000 Australian troops. AusAID and NGOs such as CARE Australia and World Vision assisted in its restoration. In 2002 the people changed the name of their country to Timor-Leste.

## ACTIVITIES

### UNDERSTANDING
1. List Australia's peacekeeping links.
2. Explain the role of the Australian Defence Force in supporting peacekeeping agreements.

### THINKING AND APPLYING
3. Use the internet to write a short report on the current situation in Timor-Leste. Include a map, the Australian government department links, Australian NGO links, progress made, and problems that still remain.
4. Analyse the table, outlining advantages and disadvantages of defence links to Australia. Which side do you think is stronger? Explain your decision.

### USING YOUR SKILLS
5. Refer to the map.
   a. List Australia's frontline links.
   b. Where are Australian troops based in the Asia–Pacific region?
   c. Write a short description of a country where Australian troops are at the frontline. List reasons for the conflict or tensions and who is involved.
   d. Discuss whether the response might lead to peace and other methods which could be used to stop the conflict.

# 11.13 Global links: the war on terrorism

**Terrorism** is the intentional use, or threat of the use, of violence against civilians or civilian targets in order to achieve political ends. Terrorism is not new but extensive media coverage in recent years has helped create a climate of fear about terrorism in the population. In the fight against terrorism, Australia strives to bring international terrorists to justice, works to undermine the political credibility of terrorist networks and encourages responsible citizens to notify the government of suspected activities.

## Australia's response to 9/11

On 11 September 2001 (9/11), al-Qaeda terrorists hijacked four passenger planes. Two were then flown into New York's World Trade Center. Another hijacked plane flew into the Pentagon building in Washington DC and the fourth crashed into a field in Pennsylvania, possibly due to an onboard struggle. The attack sparked a 'war on terrorism', beginning with the US-led attack on Afghanistan in 2002, where the Saudi Arabian leader of al-Qaeda, Osama bin Laden, was based. This resulted in the overthrow of Afghanistan's Taliban government. The Australian Defence Force (ADF) responded with Operation Slipper and Operation Palate, and supported the UN Assistance Mission in Afghanistan.

Following 9/11, the United States saw Iraq as a potential terrorist threat, as it feared the regime possessed weapons of mass destruction and posed a serious threat to the security of the United States and its allies. As a result, the United States led an invasion of Iraq by the Coalition of the Willing (the United Kingdom, Australia, Poland and Denmark) in 2003. The invasion overthrew the government of Iraq and eventually led to the capture and execution of its president, Saddam Hussein.

The ADF's Operation Catalyst has contributed to the reconstruction of Iraq. AusAID and NGOs (UNICEF, CARE Australia) committed millions of dollars towards humanitarian assistance and rehabilitation. Australia provided $150 million to Afghanistan under a bilateral aid agreement, to set up surgical, obstetric and paediatric services in 50 health clinics and to shelter refugees made homeless by or fleeing the conflict.

*The terrorist attack on New York's World Trade Center on 11 September 2001 is regarded as one of the worst terrorist attacks in history. Almost 3000 lives were lost.*

*Aerial view of Ground Zero, site of the 9/11 attacks*

## Australia's response to terrorism in Indonesia

Terrorist attacks in Indonesia, at the Australian Embassy in Jakarta (2004) and in Bali (2002, 2005), were attributed to the al-Qaeda-affiliated Jemaah Islamiyah terrorist group. In response, the Australian government provided $100 million to Indonesia for counter-terrorism actions to strengthen airports, immigration and customs services.

Australia also signed counter-terrorism agreements and participated in forums. These included:
- *bilateral agreements* with Indonesia, the Philippines, Malaysia, Cambodia, Thailand, Brunei, Fiji, Papua New Guinea, Timor-Leste, India, Pakistan, Afghanistan and Turkey
- *multilateral forums* with the United Nations, ASEAN and APEC
- *regional forums* such as the Bali Regional Ministerial Meeting on Counter-Terrorism (2004) and the Sub-Regional Ministerial Conference on Counter-Terrorism (2007).

In 2008 Australia hosted the Trilateral Counter-Terrorism Consultations (Australia, Japan and the United States) to promote security, especially in the Asia–Pacific region.

**Worst terrorist attacks**

| Incident | Date | Deaths |
| --- | --- | --- |
| World Trade Center in New York destroyed | 2001 | 2749 |
| Truck bombings in Al-Qataniyah and Al-Adnaniyah, Iraq | 2007 | 520 |
| Hostage siege in Beslan, Russia | 2004 | 350 |
| Car bombs destroy US embassies in Kenya and Tanzania | 1998 | 224 |
| Car bombs destroy two Bali nightclubs | 2002 | 202 |
| Bombings on commuter trains in Mumbai, India | 2006 | 200 |
| Train bombs explode during rush hour in Madrid | 2004 | 191 |
| Gun/grenade attacks and hostage takings in Mumbai, India | 2008 | 174 |

*One of Mumbai's luxury hotels, the Taj Mahal Palace, under terrorist attack in November 2008. Of the 174 people killed in the attack, two were Australian.*

## Counter-terrorism agreements

**Counter-terrorism** refers to the strategies that governments, the military, police departments and corporations adopt in response to terrorist threats and/or acts. Australian anti-terrorist organisations include the Australian Federal Police and the Australian Protective Service. Australia's *Anti-Terrorism Act (2005)* allows police to detain suspects for up to two weeks without charge, and to electronically track suspects for a year. The ADF is called upon to resolve a domestic terrorist incident only when police and emergency services are unable to cope. The Australian Department of Foreign Affairs and Trade supports international counter-terrorism initiatives; supports the fight against chemical, biological, radiological and nuclear terrorism; monitors and responds to threats from suspected terrorist groups; administers laws to freeze terrorists' assets; advises Australian residents about terrorist threats when travelling overseas; and secures Australia's passport system and embassies.

### ACTIVITIES

**UNDERSTANDING**

1. Define terrorism and counter-terrorism.
2. List groups involved in terrorist activities.
3. Explain the role of Australian government organisations (e.g. AusAID, DFAT, ADF, customs, Australian Federal Police) in response to terrorism.
4. Explain why terrorism is a global defence link.
5. Describe the events that led to the US-led coalition invasion of Iraq in 2003.
6. Discuss the treaties and agreements relevant to terrorism.

**THINKING AND APPLYING**

7. Terrorism generally involves violence, often by individuals or groups using a disguise, and the effect of the attacks impart fear to the affected country and its people. Explain this, using examples of recent terrorist attacks.
8. Explain the counter-terrorism advice *Be alert but not alarmed*.

**USING YOUR SKILLS**

9. Refer to the aerial photograph of Ground Zero.
   a. Work out the area destroyed in the terrorist attack.
   b. Imagine you were the city planner. Draw what you think should be placed at this site. Justify your decision.

# 11.14 Regional defence links: helping a friend

The Solomon Islands is a sprawling archipelago of nearly a thousand islands to the north-east of Australia. The capital is Honiara, located on the island of Guadalcanal. The country is classified by the World Bank as a low-income country under stress (LICUS). It is one of the 49 least developed countries in the world with income per capita of $2031 per year. With weak security, poverty and a corrupt government, the Australian Defence Force acknowledges that neglecting the Solomon Islands could endanger regional stability.

## Solomon Island 'tensions'

Violent conflict in the Solomon Islands, referred to as 'the tensions', began in Honiara in 1998 when militant Guadalcanal youths attacked Malaita islanders who had migrated from a neighbouring island. Their actions were prompted by the failure of successive governments to address issues such as poverty, the killing of indigenous residents, and migrants from other provinces owning land on Guadalcanal. The tensions resulted in 25 000 Malaitans fleeing the island and another 11 000 fleeing Honiara for the safer Guadalcanal interior.

In 2000 violence escalated when the Malaita Eagle Force (MEF) took control of Honiara. The Australian and New Zealand governments failed to negotiate a ceasefire between Guadalcanal and Malaitan militant groups. Further negotiations resulted in the signing of the Townsville Peace Agreement (TPA) and the establishment of the International Peace Monitoring Team (IPMT), comprising 50 police and civilians from Australia, New Zealand and Pacific Island countries. Weapons were collected and reconciliation ceremonies facilitated. However, as militant leaders had hidden their guns, rampart lawlessness, extortion, theft and beatings, soon became commonplace.

## RAMSI: Helpem Fren

In 2003 a multinational force consisting of 15 Pacific nations, called the Regional Assistance Mission to the Solomon Islands (RAMSI), arrived in the country to assist the government in restoring order. The contingent was led by 2200 Australian police and troops. Their contribution was named Operation Helpem Fren, and its aim was to:
- strengthen law and justice
- improve economic management
- maintain access to basic services (especially health)
- support peace building and civil-society development.

## RAMSI: the Australian government and NGOs

Australia's contribution to RAMSI is a whole-of-government approach involving the Australian Federal Police, the Customs Service, AusAID and the Departments of Treasury and Finance and Administration. The Australian government's Cooperation Agreement with the Solomon Islands supports 20 Australian NGOs that promote peace, reduce poverty and involve the community in the peace-decision process, especially women. These NGOs undertake activities such as agriculture, disaster management, education, governance, health, water and sanitation. They work in partnership with the Solomon Islands government and local communities and support AusAID's Solomon Islands Community Sector Strategy (2007–11).

By 2009 RAMSI had restored law and order, economic growth was 6.1 per cent, the government's revenue had tripled, 332 new police officers had graduated, over two thousand public servants received training, and tourist boats had started visiting the islands.

## Preventing future tensions

Poverty, crime and government corruption continue to undermine stability in the Solomon Islands. In 2006 Prime Minister Snyder Rini used bribes from Chinese businessmen to buy the votes of parliament members. This led to mass rioting in Honiara and most of Chinatown was destroyed. Australian, New Zealand and Fijian troops were dispatched to quell the unrest and Rini eventually resigned. The future of the Solomon Islands is unpredictable, as unsustainable logging and fishing practices are anticipated to increase poverty, resulting in further tensions.

### GEOfacts
- Life expectancy in the Solomon Islands is 63.2 years.
- The population of the Solomon Islands is 584 000 (2008 estimate).

Map of the Solomon Islands

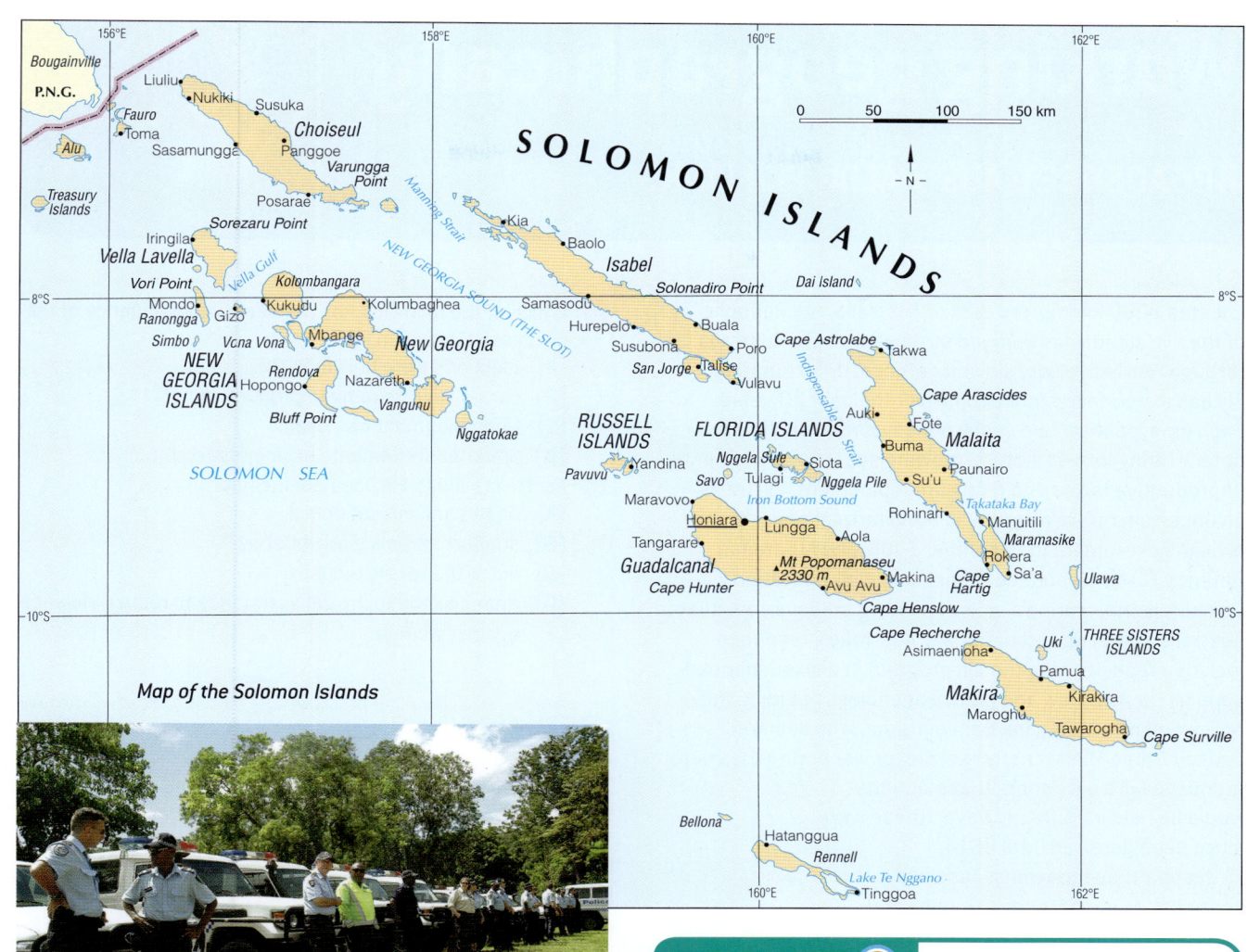

RAMSI Participating Police Force

## GEOskills TOOLBOX

### USING LATITUDE AND LONGITUDE

Latitude and longitude help you to pinpoint places with accuracy.

Lines running east–west across the map are called parallels of latitude. They are measured in degrees north and south of the Equator (0° latitude). Lines running north–south down the map are called meridians of longitude. They are measured in degrees east and west of Greenwich (0° longitude). Latitude is always given before longitude.

To help pinpoint particular locations, each degree of latitude can be further divided into 60 small sections, which are known as minutes. For example, the settlement of Honiara is located at 9.28°S 159.52°E.

## ACTIVITIES

### UNDERSTANDING

1. List the tensions that led to numerous conflicts in the Solomon Islands.
2. Explain the benefits of the defence and aid links between Australia and the Solomon Islands, to both countries.

### THINKING AND APPLYING

3. Discuss the roles played by AusAID and NGOs in assisting the peace process by improving social justice and equity.

### USING YOUR SKILLS

4. Refer to the map of the Solomon Islands.
    a. Name the six largest islands.
    b. What is the latitude and longitude of Malaita?
    c. What is the direction of the Three Sisters Islands from Isabel?
    d. Determine the bearing of Uki from Honiara.
    e. Calculate the distance from Liuliu to Cape Surville.
    f. Why could the country be difficult to govern?
    g. Explain why the security and stability of the islands is important to Australia.

**CHAPTER 11** | Trade, aid, defence: global regional links

# Working geographically

## BROADSHEET: AUSTRALIA–FIJI LINKS

Located 2000 kilometres east of Australia, the Republic of the Fiji Islands has enjoyed strong links with Australia through tourism, trade, aid and defence. Unfortunately, Fiji has experienced four coups over the past 20 years. Each time, political and social upheaval has resulted in deteriorating infrastructure, growing squatter settlements, unproductive farms and rising unemployment. Fiji faces an uncertain future after the last military takeover of the civilian government in December 2006. The Australian Defence Force responded to the coup with Operation Quickstep and, fearing a violent military takeover, evacuated Australian citizens and nationals. Australia's response included repositioning the aid program. It also suspended support for most law and justice agencies, including the police and prisons. Frank Bainimarama, who declared himself Prime Minister after seizing power during the coup, promised Fiji's aid donors that elections would be held in 2009. However, these have since been deferred until 2014.

Despite these tensions, Australia continues to support social justice and equity in Fiji by providing aid for health, education, community development, the textile industry, HIV/AIDS prevention and the scholarships program. AusAID supports gender equality and provides financial and technical assistance to the Fiji Women's Crisis Centre to reduce the incidence of violence against women.

### KNOWLEDGE AND UNDERSTANDING

**Read the text above and select the alternative that best answers the question.**

1. How many political coups has Fiji experienced over the last 20 years?
   - (A) Three
   - (B) None
   - (C) Four
   - (D) Twenty
2. Operation Quickstep was:
   - (A) an Australian aid program to Fiji
   - (B) a peacekeeping operation
   - (C) a trade agreement with Fiji
   - (D) an evacuation of Australian citizens after the 2006 coup.
3. Which of the following has not been a consequence of the successive coups in Fiji?
   - (A) Elections were held in 2009.
   - (B) Farms have become unproductive.
   - (C) Unemployment has risen.
   - (D) Squatter settlements have increased.
4. Australia's aid to Fiji does not include:
   - (A) health and education aid
   - (B) support for police and prisons
   - (C) aid to the textile industry
   - (D) financial and technical assistance to reduce violence against women.

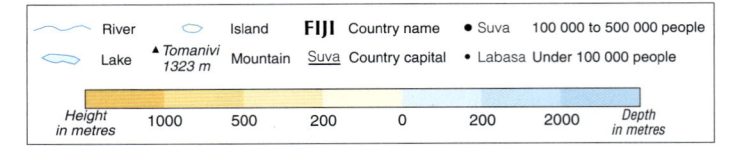

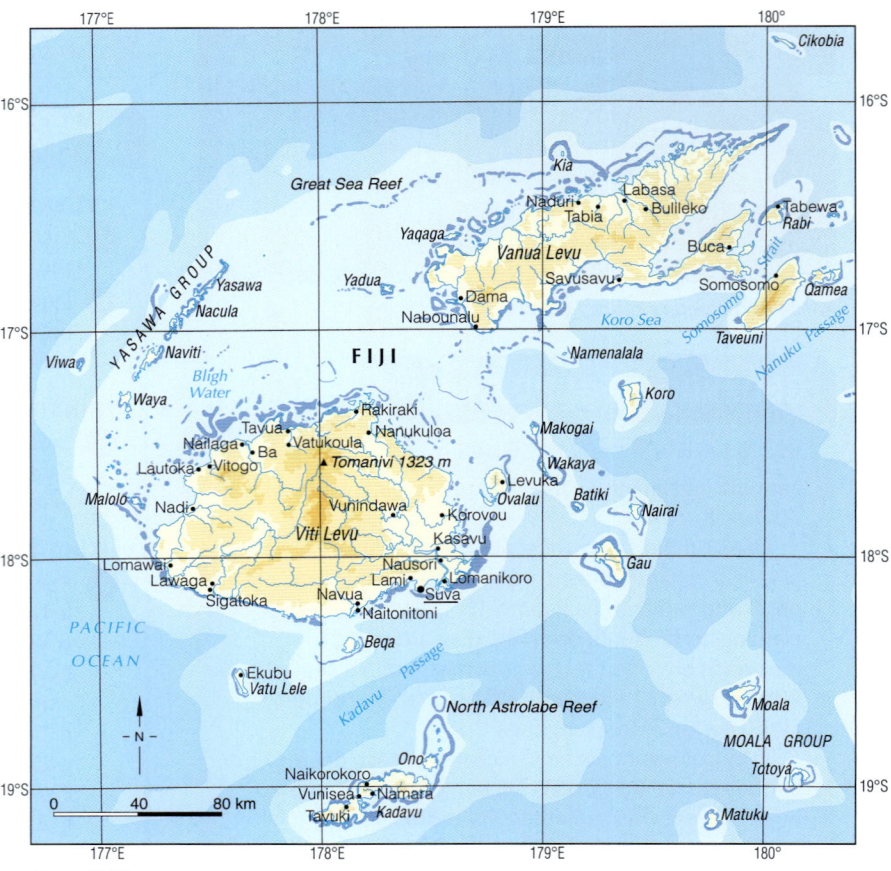

Map of Fiji

## USING YOUR SKILLS

5. Refer to the map on the previous page.
   a. Name the settlements located at:
      i. 18.08°S 178.25°E
      ii. 19.04°S 178.21°E
      iii. 17.46°S 177.27°E.
   b. Name the landforms located at:
      i. 17.48°S 179.22°E
      ii. 17.48°S 178.05°E
      iii. 18.43°S 178.44°E.
   c. What is the latitude and longitude of Makogai Island?
6. What is the direction of Suva from Lautoka?

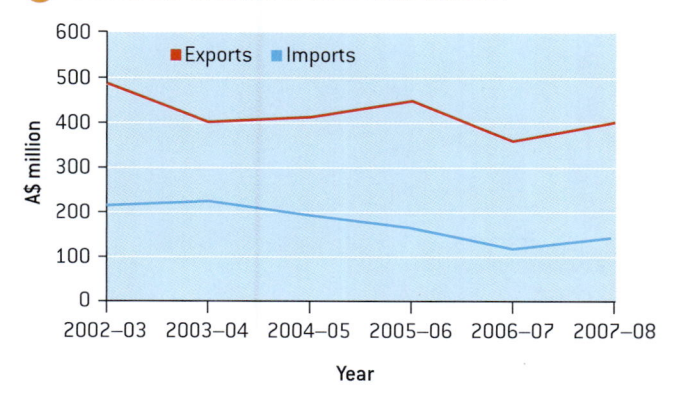

| Major Australian imports, 2007–08 (A$m) | |
|---|---|
| Clothing | 73 |
| Cereal preparations | 15 |
| Vegetables | 5 |
| Made-up textile articles | 4 |
| **Major Australian exports, 2007–08\* (A$m)** | |
| Liquefied propane and butane | 13 |
| Wheat | 12 |
| Cotton fabrics, woven | 10 |
| Man-made fabrics, woven | 10 |

*Includes A$72m of confidential items and special transactions, 20% of total exports.

*Australia's trade with Fiji. Australia is Fiji's fourth largest export market and second largest source of imports. The countries share the bilateral Australia–Fiji Trade and Economic Relations Agreement (AFTERA) of 1999.*

### Use the line graph and table above on Fiji–Australia trade to answer the following questions.

7. Calculate the difference between imports and exports in:
   a. 2007–08
   b. 2005–06.
8. Account for the trade links between Australia's exported cotton fabrics and imported clothes and articles.
9. Why do you think Australia's imports from Fiji have not exceeded exports to Fiji over the time period shown on the graph?
10. Explain why AusAID supports the Fijian textile industry.
11. What correlation can you see between Australia's import of 'cereal preparations' and one of Australia's exports?

*Satellite image from NASA satellite of Cyclone Ami over Fiji, showing the position of the main Fiji islands. The cyclone, which hit Fiji in 2003, killed several people, flattened homes and schools, and destroyed crops, plantations, infrastructure and fresh water supplies. The eastern islands were also hit by massive waves.*

### Use the satellite image of Cyclone Ami to answer the following questions.

12. Name the two Fijian islands superimposed on the satellite imagery.
13. In what direction were the winds moving around the cyclone?
14. Explain the impact of a cyclone on low-lying coral islands.
15. The Fiji and Australian Red Cross provided effective emergency relief and AusAID provided finance and funded a helicopter. Imagine you were in charge of the emergency. Explain how you would allocate funds a immediately and b over the long term.

### EXTENDED RESPONSE

16. Discuss the impacts of conflicts on tourism, trade, aid, defence and migration links.
17. Use the internet to find out more about Operation Quickstep. Describe the operation and evaluate its impact on Australia's relations with Fiji. Use the **Operation Quickstep** weblink in your eBookPLUS to find out more.

CHAPTER 11 | Trade, aid, defence: global regional links

# 12 Future challenges: population

### INQUIRY QUESTIONS

+ What are Australia's current and future population growth rates and trends?
+ What are the government's population policies on refugees and immigrants?
+ Where do Australians live and where are they moving to?
+ What are the implications of population trends for ecological sustainability?

The inaugural Australia 2020 Summit in 2008 aimed to prepare Australia for future challenges. These include the management of population growth, urbanisation and coastal development, while ensuring ecological sustainability. The key goal of the summit was to adopt a national sustainability, population and climate change agenda and to develop a national system to reduce water and energy consumption and minimise waste.

### GEOskills TOOLBOX

+ Statistical data and combined graphs (page 325)
+ Constructing a population pyramid (page 329)

*Australia's population is increasing at a rate faster than that of China.*

### KEY TERMS

**assimilation:** absorption into, and adoption of, the host country's culture

**asylum seeker:** refugee who seeks official shelter or protection in a foreign country under international law

**carbon footprint:** greenhouse gas emissions caused by an individual, organisation, event or product

**census:** a population count conducted every five years that captures details of age, sex, employment and other social indicators

**diaspora:** the spreading of people from their original location

**ecocity:** a city dedicated to minimising inputs (energy, water and food) and waste outputs (heat, air pollution and water pollution)

**ecological footprint:** a measure of human demand on the Earth's ecosystems

**ecological sustainability:** the needs of the present population being met without endangering the ability of future generations to meet their needs

**emigration:** movement of people out of a country

**fertility rate:** average number of children born to a woman over her lifetime

**immigration:** movement of people into a country

**integration:** respect for source country's and host country's cultures and their dynamic blending; aimed at greater inclusiveness

**life expectancy:** average number of years a person can be expected to live

**liveability:** comfort and convenience of an area, assessed on living conditions such as safety, education, hygiene, recreation, politico–economic stability and public transport

**Local Agenda 21 (LA21):** a program, run by the United Nations, for implementing sustainable development at the local level

**migration:** the permanent and semipermanent movement of people from one location to another

**multiculturalism:** respect and maintenance of source countries' cultures and the official Australian government policy since the 1970s. It means that communities keep their native language, rituals, religion and cultural ways while remaining loyal to Australia and its values.

**natural increase:** excess of births over deaths, usually expressed as a percentage

**net overseas migration:** immigration minus emigration

**people smugglers:** individuals or groups paid by those who wish to enter another country, but who do so without permission

**population:** total number of people inhabiting an area

**spatial distribution:** distribution of a population across a country

**water footprint:** volume of fresh water used to produce the goods and services consumed by an individual or community or produced by a business

# 12.1 Australia's population is growing

Before 1788, Australia's **population**, which consisted entirely of Indigenous Australians, is estimated at between 300 000 and 750 000. By the end of 2009, the population had grown to 22 million, and it is expected to reach 24 million by 2020. Australia's population is increasing at a rate of 1.8 per cent per year — faster than China (0.6 per cent) but slower than Papua New Guinea (2.7 per cent).

In 2008, Australia's population grew at its fastest rate in nearly 20 years, with immigration being the main driver. In that year, Western Australia recorded the fastest population growth at 2.7 per cent, followed by Queensland (2.3 per cent).

Today, Australia is the fifty-third most populous country in the world: 2.5 per cent of Australia's population are Indigenous, 40 per cent have at least one parent born overseas and 91 per cent live in urban areas.

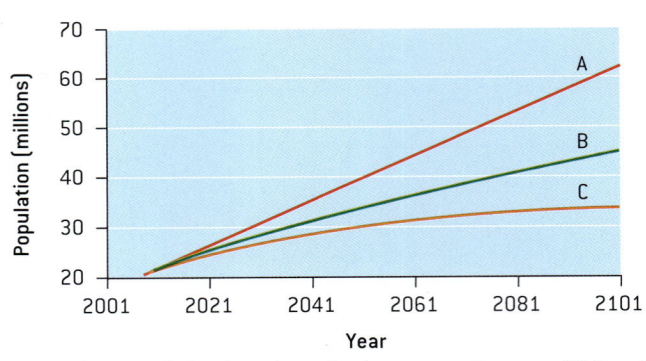

## Current and future population trends

Population growth or decline is the product of four factors: births, deaths, **immigration** (arrivals from other countries) and **emigration** (Australian residents moving overseas). The rate of **natural increase** is births minus deaths, and **net overseas migration** is immigration minus emigration.

Australia's population clock indicates that one more person is added to the Australian population every 1 minute and 31 seconds as there is:
- one birth every 1 minute and 51 seconds
- one death every 3 minutes and 48 seconds
- a net gain of one international migrant every 2 minutes and 38 seconds.

In 2008, net overseas migration contributed to 59 per cent of population growth, with the remainder (41 per cent) coming from natural increase.

*Australia's population is projected to increase to between 33.7 and 62.2 million people by 2101. Line A shows the highest growth estimates, line C shows the lowest estimates, and line B is based on current population growth patterns.*

Australia's current population trend indicates an ageing population with declining fertility rates. If this trend continues without an increase in immigration, deaths will exceed births by 2041 and Australia's population will decline.

Every five years, the Australian Bureau of Statistics (ABS) conducts a **census** to collect information about Australia's population, such as size, rate of change, spatial distribution, age structure and **migration**. This information enables governments to predict

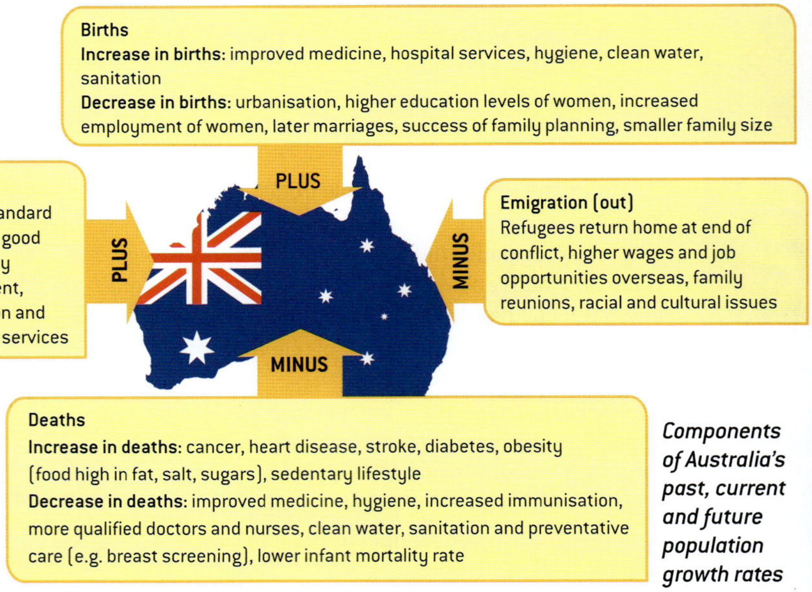

**Births**
Increase in births: improved medicine, hospital services, hygiene, clean water, sanitation
Decrease in births: urbanisation, higher education levels of women, increased employment of women, later marriages, success of family planning, smaller family size

**Immigration (in)**
Employment/jobs, high standard of living, political stability, good human rights record, family reunions, clean environment, democracy, good education and health facilities and social services

**Emigration (out)**
Refugees return home at end of conflict, higher wages and job opportunities overseas, family reunions, racial and cultural issues

**Deaths**
Increase in deaths: cancer, heart disease, stroke, diabetes, obesity (food high in fat, salt, sugars), sedentary lifestyle
Decrease in deaths: improved medicine, hygiene, increased immunisation, more qualified doctors and nurses, clean water, sanitation and preventative care (e.g. breast screening), lower infant mortality rate

*Components of Australia's past, current and future population growth rates*

*Million milestones: Australian population trends*

| Million | 1 | 2 | 3 | 4 | 5 | 6 | 7 | 8 | 9 | 10 | 11 | 12 | 13 | 14 | 15 | 16 | 17 | 18 | 19 | 20 | 21 | 24 (estimated) |
|---|---|---|---|---|---|---|---|---|---|---|---|---|---|---|---|---|---|---|---|---|---|---|
| Year | 1858 | 1877 | 1889 | 1905 | 1918 | 1925 | 1939 | 1949 | 1954 | 1959 | 1963 | 1968 | 1972 | 1976 | 1981 | 1986 | 1990 | 1995 | 1999 | 2003 | 2007 | 2020 |

## Population — Australia's 'big threat'

BY PETER KER

Prominent Australians have thrown their support behind a controversial new book which argues that population growth is the biggest threat to environmental sustainability in this country.

The book *Overloading Australia* by Mark O'Connor and William Lines argues that pro-immigration and 'baby bonus' policies are at odds with plans to reduce carbon emissions and secure water supplies.

'The task of simultaneously increasing population and achieving sustainability is impossible', the book argues.

Predicting Australian cities will suffer more congestion, pollution, loss of biodiversity and diminished services, the authors argue there is no point conserving water 'until we get restraint in population'.

The Australian Conservation Foundation has also called for a reduction in the nation's skilled migration program, stating that 'population increase makes it harder for Australia to reduce carbon pollution levels and is placing stress on state and regional planning, infrastructure and ecological systems'.

Adapted from *The Age*, 24 January 2009.

---

future population trends, determine where to build new schools and hospitals, and assess where there will be increased need for housing and transport. Generation Z (those born after 2000) will live longer and will most likely pay higher taxes to cover the costs of an ageing population.

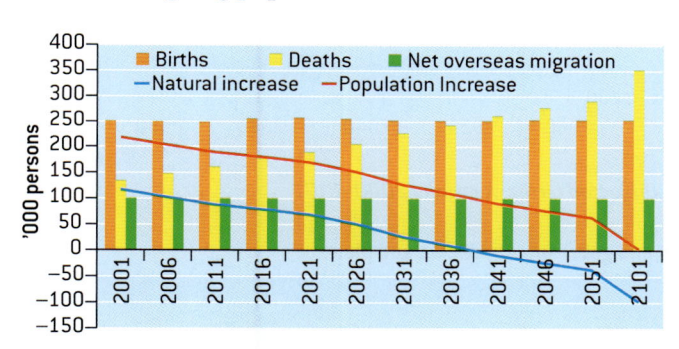

*Future trends: deaths may exceed births in 30 to 40 years.*

### GEOskills TOOLBOX

**STATISTICAL DATA AND COMBINED GRAPHS**

Statistical data are very useful for showing change over time. When comparing sets of data from different years, check that each data set is measuring the same things — otherwise it will not be a valid comparison.

Statistical data is often presented in a visual format, such as a line, bar or column graph. The combined line and column graph above shows projected changes over time in Australia's population, and makes it possible to show a lot of statistical information in one graph.

## Future challenges

The federal government has identified three population challenges: to support the elderly; sustain a demographically diverse population; and protect the environment. A key question is the number of people that Australia can sustain ecologically.

### ACTIVITIES

**UNDERSTANDING**

1. List the main factors that determine population.
2. List Australia's future population challenges.
3. Describe the current trends in the Australian population.
4. Explain the importance of census information for governments.

**THINKING AND APPLYING**

5. Debate the statement: 'Australia's current and future population is unsustainable'.

**USING YOUR SKILLS**

6. Refer to the graph of future trends.
   a. Calculate the expected population growth from 2021 to 2101.
   b. What population component is anticipated to make up the largest percentage of future population growth? Give reasons for your answer.
   c. How do you account for the downward trend in natural increase from 2001?

### GEOTERMS

**census:** a population count conducted every five years that captures details of age, sex, employment and other social indicators

**emigration:** movement of people out of a country

**immigration:** movement of people into a country

**migration:** the permanent and semipermanent movement of people from one location to another

**natural increase:** excess of births over deaths, usually expressed as a percentage

**net overseas migration:** immigration minus emigration

**population:** total number of people inhabiting an area

## 12.2 Age structure trend: fewer babies

As with most of the developed world, Australia's major population trends include a declining **fertility rate** and increasing life expectancy. These changing age structure trends are partly due to governments' policies of increased investment in health (immunisation, medicines), education (especially women) and infrastructure (hospitals, water).

*Trends in Australia's age structure: young children and older people as a percentage of the Australian population*

### Marrying later — having fewer babies

In 2008, 3.2 million Australian families had children under the age of 15. Most children lived in New South Wales (1.3 million), Victoria (950 400) and

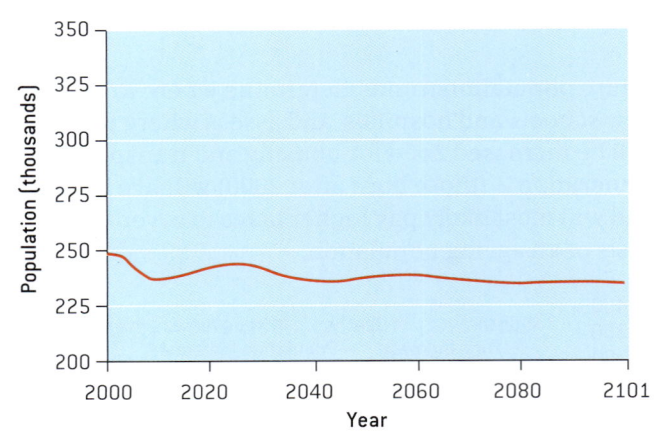

*Projected births: Australia 2000–2101*

**Declining fertility rates — current and future trends, spatial distribution and government policies and plans**

| Current and future trends | Reasons for current and future trends | Spatial distribution | Government policies and plans |
|---|---|---|---|
| • If current trend continues 31 per cent of men and 26 per cent of women will never marry.<br>• Employment of women of child-bearing age (15–44 years) rose from 59 per cent to 72 per cent between 1980 and 2009.<br>• 34 per cent of families with children are now one-child families — 20 years ago it was 21 per cent.<br>• The average age of women at the birth of their first child is 30 years.<br>• 27 per cent of men and 21 per cent of women aged 18–24 expect not to have children. | • Equal pay for men and women<br>• Greater choice in lifestyle — travel, entertainment<br>• High cost of homes and mortgage repayments<br>• Family planning gives people a choice over their fertility<br>• Increased cost of child rearing — childcare, education<br>• Increased education of women and employment<br>• Later marriages<br>• Juggling work and family is difficult<br>• Risk of unemployment in a recession — unable to support child<br>• Women often jeopardise career prospects and their lifetime earnings when they leave the workforce to have children. | Young families with children live in the outer western suburbs of Sydney, where houses are cheaper and governments provide more schools and baby health services.<br><br>Remote areas of Western Australia such as the Pilbara and Kimberley areas have the youngest populations in Australia. | • Maternity allowance<br>• Family tax benefits<br>• Childcare and parenting payments<br>• Baby bonus tax<br>• Paid parental leave (from 2011)<br><br>Other suggestions:<br>• Paternity leave<br>• Work and family packages<br><br>Australia 2020 proposal is to create high-quality parent and child centres for all 0–5-year-old children. |

Queensland (806 500). Since the early 1900s, Australia's fertility rate has declined. In 1961, there were 3.6 children per woman; this figure fell to 1.73 in 2001 but increased to 1.93 in 2008. This increase caught governments by surprise, placing a strain on maternity and early childhood services and infrastructure. The rate of 1.93 children per woman is still below the population replacement rate of 2.1 children per woman required to offset the natural population reduction; if the trend continues, Australia will have a declining population.

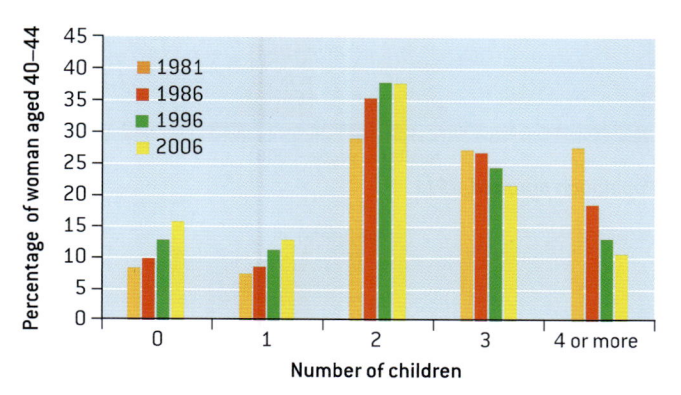

*Trend to smaller families*

The declining fertility rate is caused by a combination of economic, biological and social changes; it is predicted to continue in the future, resulting in smaller families. To reverse this long-term population trend, one politician suggested that Australian families have three children: 'one for your husband, one for your wife and one for your country'.

*In its 2009 Budget, the federal government announced that a paid parental scheme would be introduced nationally from 2011. The government sees this as essential in helping Australia prepare for the challenges of an ageing population. The Baby Bonus will continue for mothers not in paid employment. Whether the scheme will affect Australia's declining fertility rate remains to be seen.*

*The family in this photograph exceeds the national average of 1.93 children.*

## ACTIVITIES

### UNDERSTANDING

1. List the two main population trends globally and in Australia.
2. Explain why knowing the spatial distribution of young families is essential for effective government planning.
3. Explain the current and future child-bearing trends in Australia.
4. Discuss the reasons for declining fertility rates.
5. Discuss Australia's current and future population trends and government population policies to support young families.

### THINKING AND APPLYING

6. Imagine you are a shop owner in the year 2100. Suggest five profitable retail businesses you would invest your money in.

### USING YOUR SKILLS

7. Refer to the graph on the left on the opposite page. In which year will the number of children 0–14 years be the same as the number 65 years and over?
8. Discuss the changes to family sizes from 1981 to 2006. Which group had the largest increase since 1981? Suggest reasons for people planning to have no children.

### GEOTERMS

**fertility rate:** average number of children born to a woman over her lifetime

CHAPTER 12 | Future challenges: population

# 12.3 Implications of an ageing population

Australians have the fifth highest average **life expectancy** in the world. By 2051, the average life expectancy is anticipated to be 83 years for men and 86 years for women.

**Australia: life expectancy at birth — past, current and future**

| Year | Males | Females |
|---|---|---|
| 1901 | 55.2 | 58.8 |
| 1960 | 67.9 | 74.2 |
| 1995 | 75.7 | 81.4 |
| 2051 | 83.3 | 86.6 |

*Source:* Australian Bureau of Statistics.

The increase in life expectancy and fall in the fertility rate have resulted in an ageing population. Centenarians (people who are 100 years old or over) are the fastest growing age group and are expected to number 38 000 by 2051.

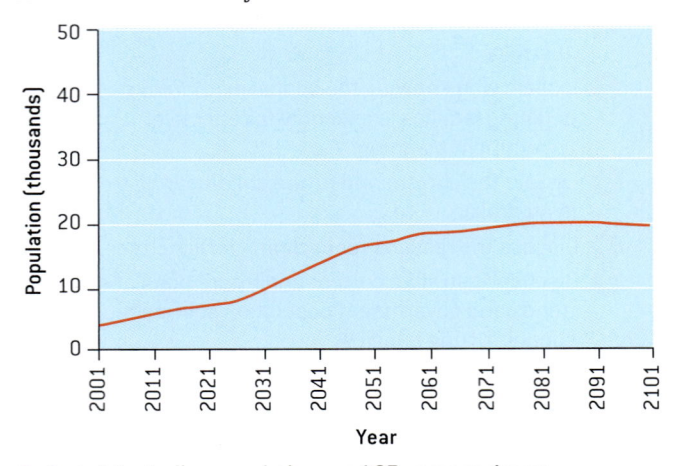

*Projected Australian population aged 85 years and over*
*Source:* Australian Bureau of Statistics.

## Age structure trends: population pyramids

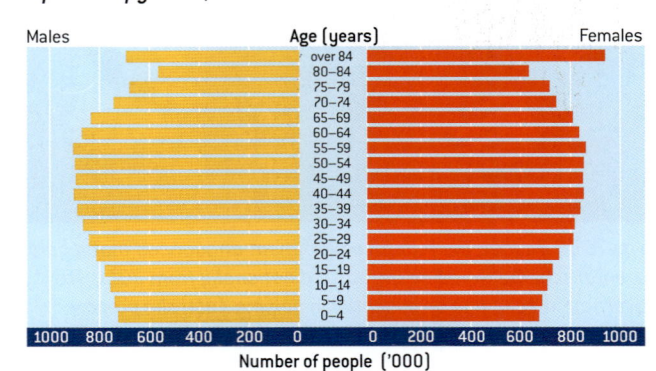

Past and current population trends are used to estimate Australia's future population and age distribution; these are shown graphically as population pyramids.

Australian governments analyse the trends in population age structure to guide future policies including spending on aged care and childcare. The spatial distribution of the population's age structure helps governments determine where to spend the money, including the locations of planned childcare facilities and retirement villages.

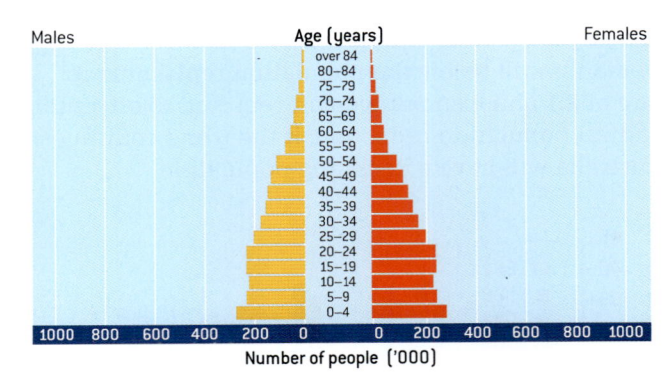

*Population pyramid, 1911*

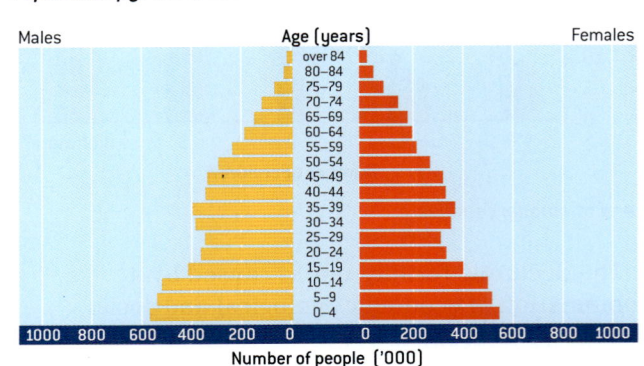

*Population pyramid, 1961*

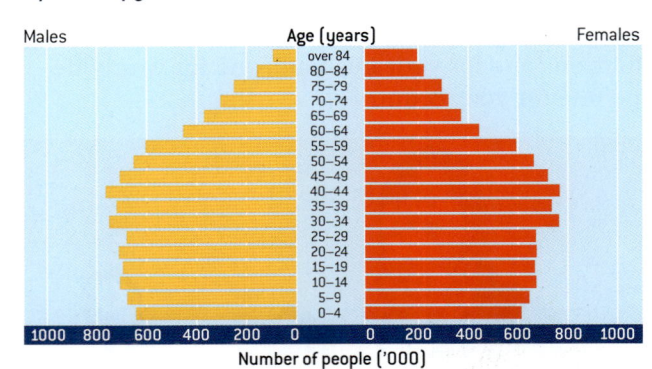

*Population pyramid, 2004*

*Population pyramid, 2051*

**Ageing Australia: current and future trends, spatial distribution and government policies and plans**

| Reasons for current and future trends | Implications of the ageing population | Governments' policies and plans | Spatial distribution |
|---|---|---|---|
| • Improved living conditions — clean water, sanitation<br>• Improved nutrition<br>• Exercise — gyms, walking clubs<br>• Decreased smoking — linked to lung cancer<br>• Improved medicines — reduce strokes, heart attacks and diabetes<br>• Improved food — heart-approved food<br>• Increased social activities — improved mental health | • Disposable incomes are higher than for older people than in previous generations. This generates demand for services such as leisure and tourism.<br>• Drift to coastal areas — demand on services<br>• Greater awareness of age-related health problems<br>• Some people on pension experiencing poverty<br>• Rise of grey power<br>• Increased learning, such as University of the Third Age<br>• Increased travel including the 'grey nomads' | • Department of Health and Ageing and Aged Care Australia<br>• Compulsory superannuation<br>• Aged pensions<br>• Aged care program — residential, long and short term<br>• Medicare<br>• Public hospitals<br>• Community support — senior concessions<br>• Encouraging older people back to work — retraining and employment<br>• Provide support so older people can stay at home<br>• Retirement villages | • Many older people have retired to the coast (sea change)<br>• Queenscliff (Victoria), Victor Harbor (South Australia) and Bribie Island (Queensland) have the oldest populations with one-third aged 65 years and over.<br>• Mornington Peninsula in Victoria and the Great Lakes area in New South Wales have a higher than average proportion of their population aged 65 years and over. |

## GEOskills TOOLBOX

### CONSTRUCTING A POPULATION PYRAMID

Population pyramids are simply two bar graphs that are drawn on a vertical axis. They show the age and sex distribution of the population and the size of the dependent population as a proportion of the total population. Young populations are indicated by a wide base. Old populations are indicated by a vase shape, with a small base, larger middle and small top.

For the steps in constructing a population pyramid, see page 101.

## ACTIVITIES

### UNDERSTANDING

1. What is a centenarian?
2. How many countries have citizens with a higher life expectancy than Australia?

### THINKING AND APPLYING

3. Explain the implications of an ageing population on government policies.

### USING YOUR SKILLS

4. Refer to the table on the previous page. Calculate the difference in life expectancy between males and females in 1901 and 2051. Explain the reasons for an increasing life expectancy. Draw the table on the previous page as a column graph.

Refer to the population pyramids on the previous page to answer questions 5 to 10.

5. Describe the long-term trend in the population aged 85 years and over. Discuss the economic and social implications for governments.
6. Where did this information come from? How many age groups are shown? Explain why the 2051 population pyramid is only one possible scenario.
7. Calculate the difference between the number of children under 4 years and the number of people over 80 years in 1911. Explain the reasons for the triangle-shaped graph.
8. Calculate the number of children under 14 years in 1961. If you were born in 1961, how old would you be in 2004 and 2051?
9. Explain the large bulge in the middle of the graph in 2004. What are the advantages of a larger number of people in the working age group? Explain the changes to the number of children under 4 years and people over 80 years between 1911 and 2004.
10. Why do you think the 2051 graph is referred to as 'coffin shaped'? How many children are under 4 years and how many people are over 80 years? Draw a sketch of a hypothetical population pyramid for the year 3000 (assuming no immigration).

### GEOTERMS

**life expectancy:** average number of years a person can be expected to live; affected by nutrition, occupation, heredity and other factors

# 12.4 Government migration policies

Overseas migration has been a significant component of Australia's population growth. Over 6.6 million people have migrated to Australia since 1945, including 675 000 humanitarian arrivals. Migration accounted for 56 per cent of Australia's population increase in 2009; it is expected to provide over 90 per cent by 2050. Net overseas migration (NOM) describes the permanent or semipermanent movement of people into and out of a country.

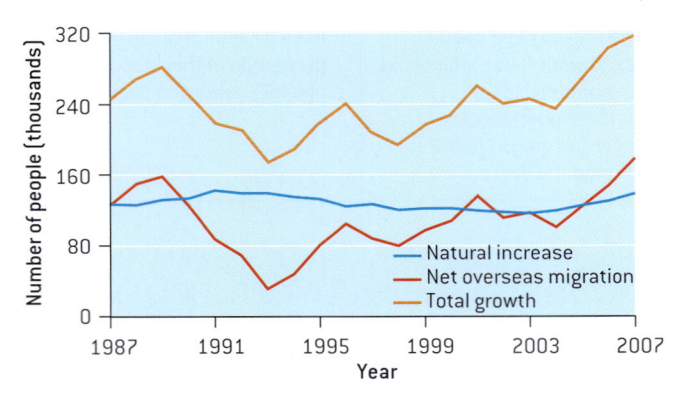

*A 2009 Border Protection Command photo of an asylum seekers' boat, with Australian Defence Force personnel on board, minutes before it caught fire and sank*

*Growth and components of Australia's population change — net overseas migration and natural increase*

The majority of migrants enter Australia through the skilled migrant program. Most are in the working age group, which supports the government's objective to increase this segment of Australia's population.

Population trends such as decreasing fertility rates and an ageing population point to a future reduction of people in the working age group. While some argue that future high levels of migration are ecologically unsustainable and will contribute to Australia's already large **ecological footprint** (EF), the immigration policies of successive governments have reflected the view that migration is vital to sustain our current economic standards.

## Government policies

The Department of Immigration and Citizenship (DIAC) develops policies that help support the government's overall social, economic, humanitarian and environmental objectives. Under the *Migration Act 1958*, DIAC oversees a range of programs that allow certain people to live permanently in Australia. The Migration Program (for skilled workers and their families) currently provides 158 800 places a year, and the Humanitarian Program (for refugees forced to flee their homeland) provides a further 13 000 places. **Asylum seekers** in Australia are provided with temporary residence in detention centres until their application to stay is processed. The Australian *Criminal Code Act 1995* prohibits **people smuggling**.

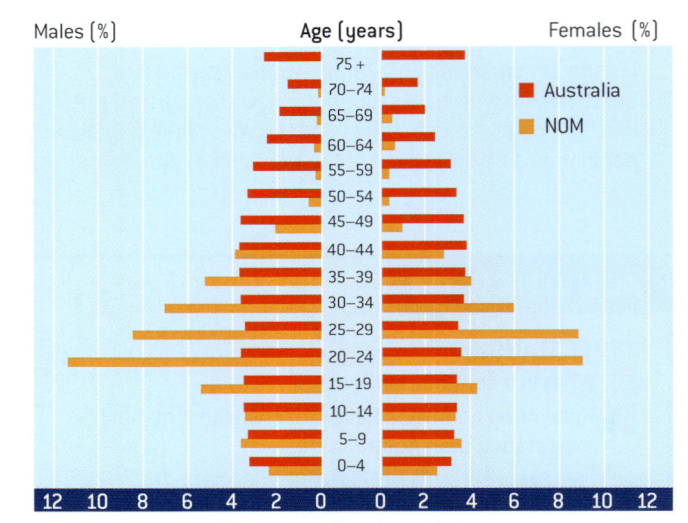

*Population pyramid — Australian and net overseas migration age structures, 2005–06*

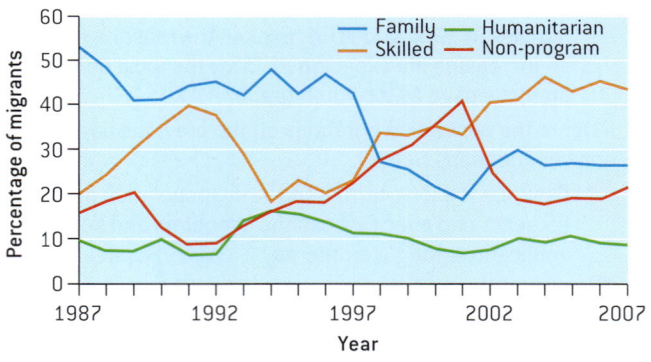

*Government policy — eligibility categories of settler arrivals*

## Spatial distribution

Along with internal population movements, the **spatial distribution** of Australia's population is shaped by where migrants decide to live. Job location, migrant networks and settlement areas of people from their former country all influence where migrants settle. Western Australia has the highest proportion of people born overseas (26 per cent), and Sydney's Fairfield–Liverpool area has a high concentration of overseas migrants (49 per cent).

Over three-quarters of Australia's migrants in 2008 settled in New South Wales, Victoria and Queensland. Around 81 per cent settled in urban areas such as Sydney (31 per cent) and Melbourne (24 per cent). Government policies support a more even distribution of migrants across Australia. Under the Regional Sponsored Migration Scheme (RSMS), employers nominate skill vacancies in regional and remote areas that can be filled by migrants. In 2009, migrants with skills in construction were in demand as part of the government's stimulus package to overcome the threat of recession.

## Becoming a citizen

The Department of Immigration and Citizenship (DIAC) encourages migrants to become Australian citizens. Since the enactment of the *Australian Citizenship Act 1948*, 3.5 million people have become Australian citizens — over 75 per cent of those eligible to do so. These new citizens pledge to uphold values such as loyalty to Australia and its people, a belief in the democratic process, respect for the rights and liberties of others and a commitment to obey Australia's laws.

**GEOfacts** The lowest immigration intake was 52 752 in 1975–76. The highest since World War II was in 1969–70 (185 099).

### ACTIVITIES

**UNDERSTANDING**

1. Define net overseas migration.
2. Discuss the contribution of migration to Australia's population growth rate.
3. How do the majority of migrants enter Australia?

**THINKING AND APPLYING**

4. Imagine you were an agricultural scientist from the Ivory Coast who is in a refugee camp in Sudan. After researching on the internet:
   a. describe the life you left behind
   b. describe the journey you made to a refugee camp in Sudan
   c. describe the conditions in the refugee camp
   d. explain why you decided to come to Australia
   e. explain the difficulties you might face in obtaining humanitarian migration to Australia.

   Present your research as a PowerPoint presentation.

**USING YOUR SKILLS**

5. Refer to the graph of net overseas migration (NOM) and natural increase. During which years did NOM make a greater contribution to population growth than natural increase? Explain the trends in NOM.
6. Refer to the population pyramid. List the five main age groups that had more migrants (NOM) than Australians.
7. Refer to the graph of eligibility categories of settler arrivals. Discuss the changing humanitarian migration trends, and suggest reasons for the changes. Explain the increase in skills migration and its economic importance to Australia.
8. Refer to the table below. Describe the spatial distribution of migrants.

**GEOTERMS**

**spatial distribution:** distribution of a population across a country

**Spatial distribution of migrants, top five countries by birth by state/territory, 2008**

| ACT | NSW | NT | Qld | SA | Tas. | Vic. | WA | Other territories |
|---|---|---|---|---|---|---|---|---|
| United Kingdom | United Kingdom | United Kingdom | United Kingdom | United Kingdom | United Kingdom | United Kingdom | United Kingdom | Malaysia |
| New Zealand | China | New Zealand | New Zealand | Italy | New Zealand | Italy | New Zealand | United Kingdom |
| China | New Zealand | Philippines | South Africa | Germany | Netherlands | New Zealand | South Africa | Singapore |
| India | Vietnam | United States | Germany | New Zealand | Germany | Vietnam | Italy | New Zealand |
| Vietnam | Philippines | East Timor | Philippines | Greece | United States | China | Malaysia | Indonesia |

*Source:* Australian Bureau of Statistics.

## 12.5 Humanitarian migration

### Australia's humanitarian program

As a signatory to the United Nations Convention Relating to the Status of Refugees (1951), Australia is obliged to provide asylum to refugees who seek protection due to a well-founded fear of being persecuted for reasons of race, religion, nationality, membership of a particular social group, or political opinion. Australia's current humanitarian program assists up to 13 000 refugees and asylum seekers each year in two ways:
- The *Refugee Program* provides resettlement for people who are subjected to persecution in their home country.
- The *Special Humanitarian Program* assists people who have suffered discrimination that presents a gross violation of human rights in their home country. Applicants must be sponsored by an Australian resident, citizen or organisation operating in Australia.

### Iraqis in Australia

The people who have fled from the Republic of Iraq to countries such as Australia are referred to as the Iraqi **diaspora**. They began leaving during the reign of Saddam Hussein (1979–2003), whose regime supported arbitrary killings, torture, abuse of women and the persecution of the Kurds and Shia. The outflow spiked during the Iraq war of 2003, and continues due to the aftermath of the war, such as ongoing terrorist attacks. In all, 2.2 million Iraqis have been forced to flee their country, most to neighbouring Jordan and Syria. Another two million are displaced within the country. Thousands of Iraqis migrated to Australia under the humanitarian program, with 85.3 per cent becoming Australian citizens.

About 97 per cent of Iraqis seeking asylum in Australia are unable to obtain a passport from the Iraqi government to allow them authorised entry into Australia. Their desperate need to escape causes many Iraqis to turn to people smugglers. In 2008, 40 Iraqis were stranded on a remote Indonesian island on their way to Australia, and an Iraqi citizen was charged with smuggling 900 people from Iraq and Afghanistan into Australia.

Asylum seekers are transferred to a detention centre while their applications are processed. Although the government has softened mandatory detention laws for those caught entering Australia without a visa, people smugglers face up to 25 years in prison.

*Iraqi refugees Adnan and Ikhlas Algahazar with their children Lubna and Ahmed at their home in Shepparton, Victoria*

The Iraqi population living in Australia jumped from 2273 in 1976 to 39 000 in 2008. The majority of Iraqis migrated here after 1991. Most (63 per cent) have settled in New South Wales, are Catholic (36.7 per cent), male (52 per cent) and in the working age group of 15 to 65 years (85 per cent).

**Iraqi-born Australians**

| Year | Population |
| --- | --- |
| 1976 | 2273 |
| 1986 | 4516 |
| 1991 (End of first Gulf War) | 5186 |
| 2001 | 24 760 (0.6% of the overseas-born population) |
| 2006 | 32 520 (increase of 31.3%) |
| 2008 | 39 000 |

*Source:* Australian Bureau of Statistics.

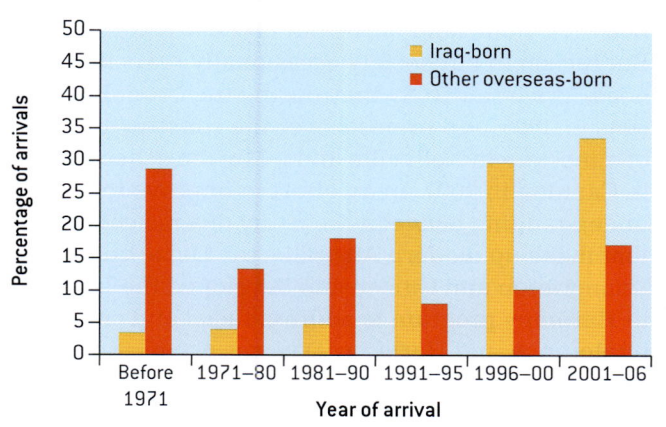

*Immigration of Iraqis to Australia*

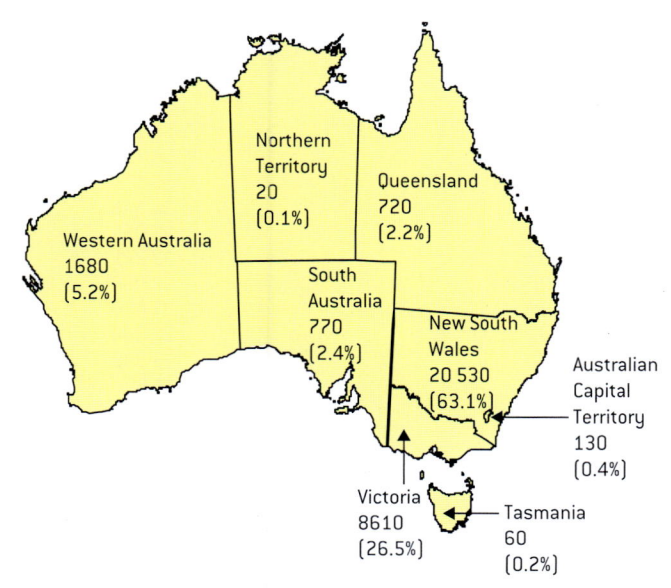

*Spatial distribution of Iraqis living in Australia, 2006*

- Northern Territory 20 (0.1%)
- Queensland 720 (2.2%)
- Western Australia 1680 (5.2%)
- South Australia 770 (2.4%)
- New South Wales 20 530 (63.1%)
- Australian Capital Territory 130 (0.4%)
- Victoria 8610 (26.5%)
- Tasmania 60 (0.2%)

The median age of Iraqi-born Australians is 35.7 years, compared with 46.8 years for all overseas-born Australians and 37.1 years for the total Australian population.

Iraqi immigrants also arrive under the family and skilled migration programs. Iraqi employees and their families, who supported Australian troops in Iraq, can apply for resettlement in Australia. The community is supported by organisations such as the Australian Iraqi Forum, and other cultural and religious associations.

### GEOfacts

Australia hosts one refugee for every 1583 Australian people (1 : 1583) compared with Iran (1 : 36), Sudan (1 : 76) and the United States (1 : 572).

### ACTIVITIES

**UNDERSTANDING**

1. Under which convention is Australia obliged to admit Iraqi asylum seekers?
2. Outline the Australian government's humanitarian program.
3. Why have Iraqis sought refuge in Australia?
4. What is a detention centre?

**THINKING AND APPLYING**

5. Discuss the economic, cultural and political advantages of Iraqi immigration for Australia.
6. Captain Cook in 1770, the Vietnamese in 1970s and Iraqis in 2000 can be seen as 'boat people'. Research the problems of entering Australia without a visa by boat or air.
7. Australia has received international criticism for detaining the children of asylum seekers in detention centres. Research the issue and how it is being resolved.
8. Most Iraqis in Australia are in their thirties and forties. What advantages are there for the Australian economy in this statistic?

**USING YOUR SKILLS**

9. Refer to the graph above left. List the years when the percentage of Iraqi-born migrants was higher than for other overseas-born migrants. Explain why more Iraqis came to Australia after 1990. Describe how Iraqis have contributed to Australia's population growth rate.
10. Refer to the map on the left. Discuss the spatial distribution of Iraqis in Australia. If you were employed as a social worker, how would you describe the types of support required by these migrants, especially children without parents?

# 12.6 Culturally diverse Australia

The Australian government's migration policies over the last hundred years have been central to the evolution of a culturally diverse Australian population. In partnership with state and local governments and community organisations, the federal government's programs seek to promote unity for all Australians. Today, Western Australia is home to people born in more than 200 different countries; 60 per cent of Sydney residents are first- or second-generation descendants of migrants; Chinese is the most common foreign language spoken in the home; and Islam is the fastest growing religion.

## Migration trends

Although the percentage of the Australian population who have immigrated from the United Kingdom (UK) has declined from 73 per cent in 1947 to 17 per cent in 2009, the UK is still the country that supplies the most immigrants. Today, most immigrants arrive from Asia–Pacific countries such as New Zealand and China. The newest and fastest growing groups are from Sudan, Afghanistan, Somalia and Iraq. Future eco-refugees are anticipated from Pacific Islands, such as Tuvalu, where sea level rises are expected to make their islands uninhabitable.

Since the late 1800s, the Australian government has adopted a range of policies to manage cultural differences; these include the White Australia policy (see page 136), assimilation, multiculturalism and integration. Today's multicultural policy promotes a culturally integrated and inclusive society, with freedom to express and share cultural values, respect for parliamentary democracy and the rule of law, freedom of speech and religion, and acceptance and equality.

Racial discrimination complaints are taken to the Human Rights and Equal Opportunity Commission (HREOC). The National Action Plan to Build on Social Cohesion, Harmony and Security addresses religious and political extremism, and the Australian government's Access and Equity strategy promotes equality in the delivery of government services. There are numerous local government efforts to improve cultural diversity, such as the Canterbury Inter-Faith Harmony project.

## Citizenship: Harmony Day

Rarely are the conflicts that cause immigrants to flee their homeland borne out on Australian streets. But racism in our society occasionally rears its ugly head, as we saw in Sydney during the Cronulla riots in 2005, and protests over the construction of a mosque in Kellyville and a Muslim school in Camden in 2007. In an effort to improve the understanding between the many diverse cultures that make up modern Australia, the Department of Immigration and Citizenship developed the Living in Harmony program to address racial and cultural intolerance, and Harmony Day was established to celebrate our cultural diversity.

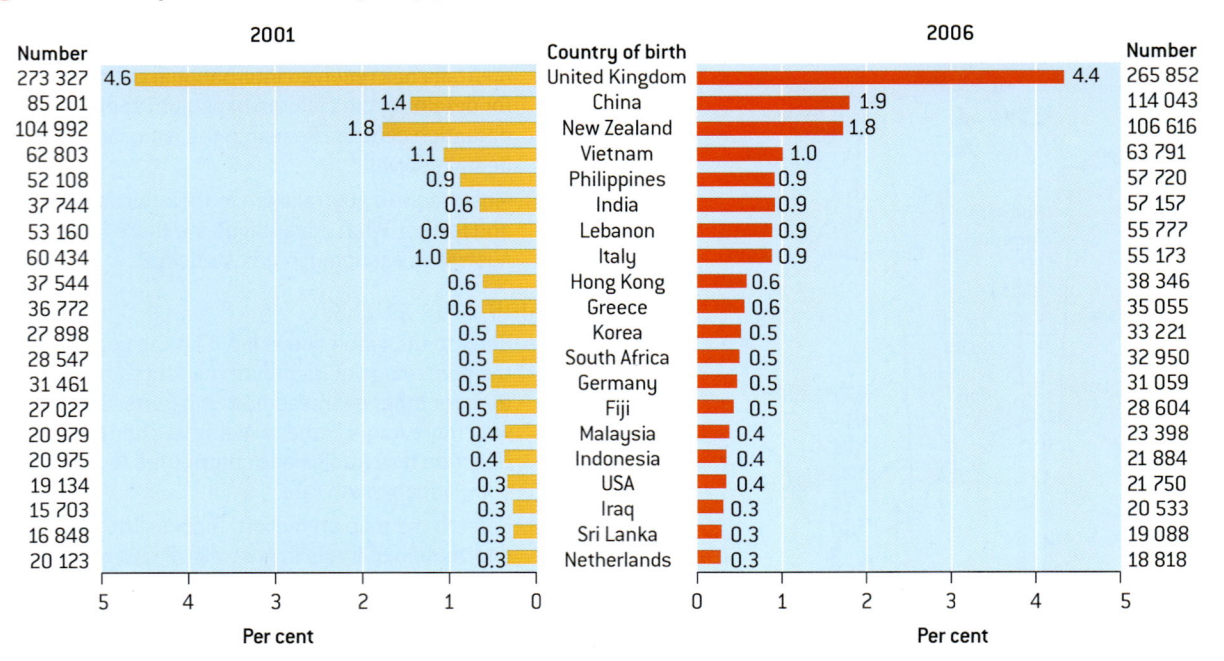

| Country of birth | 2001 Number | 2001 Per cent | 2006 Per cent | 2006 Number |
|---|---|---|---|---|
| United Kingdom | 273 327 | 4.6 | 4.4 | 265 852 |
| China | 85 201 | 1.4 | 1.9 | 114 043 |
| New Zealand | 104 992 | 1.8 | 1.8 | 106 616 |
| Vietnam | 62 803 | 1.1 | 1.0 | 63 791 |
| Philippines | 52 108 | 0.9 | 0.9 | 57 720 |
| India | 37 744 | 0.6 | 0.9 | 57 157 |
| Lebanon | 53 160 | 0.9 | 0.9 | 55 777 |
| Italy | 60 434 | 1.0 | 0.9 | 55 173 |
| Hong Kong | 37 544 | 0.6 | 0.6 | 38 346 |
| Greece | 36 772 | 0.6 | 0.6 | 35 055 |
| Korea | 27 898 | 0.5 | 0.5 | 33 221 |
| South Africa | 28 547 | 0.5 | 0.5 | 32 950 |
| Germany | 31 461 | 0.5 | 0.5 | 31 059 |
| Fiji | 27 027 | 0.5 | 0.5 | 28 604 |
| Malaysia | 20 979 | 0.4 | 0.4 | 23 398 |
| Indonesia | 20 975 | 0.4 | 0.4 | 21 884 |
| USA | 19 134 | 0.3 | 0.4 | 21 750 |
| Iraq | 15 703 | 0.3 | 0.3 | 20 533 |
| Sri Lanka | 16 848 | 0.3 | 0.3 | 19 088 |
| Netherlands | 20 123 | 0.3 | 0.3 | 18 818 |

Top 20 populations by country of birth, living in New South Wales, 2001 and 2006

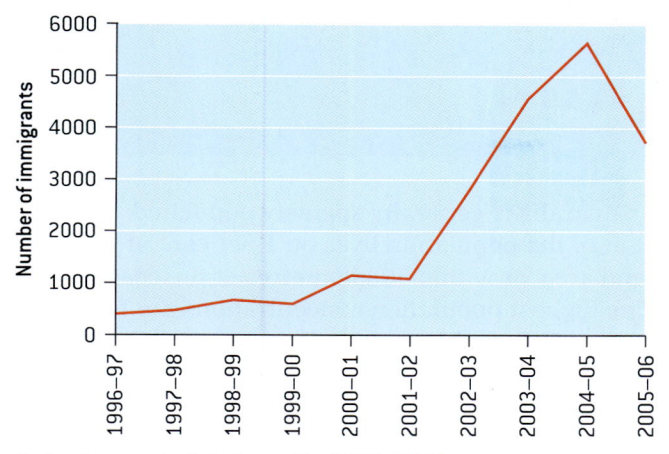

*Sudan-born arrivals in Australia, 1996–2006*

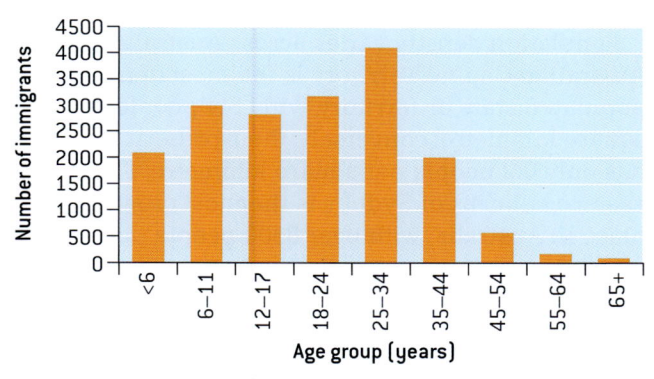

*Age of Sudan-born entrants on arrival in Australia, 2001–2006*

## SAMPLE STUDY

### New and emerging Sudanese immigrants

From 1983 to 2005, two million people were killed in conflicts between Sudan's Muslim government and non-Muslim rebels. A further 4.4 million fled their homes, and 15 000 people were abducted by militiamen and used as slaves.

Many Sudanese sought to escape the violence, with more than 20 000 being accepted by the Australian government under the Humanitarian Program since 1996–97. During the past 10 years, the number of immigrants from Sudan has increased 34 per cent each year. Today, Sudanese immigrants are our fastest growing ethnic group.

Most Sudanese immigrants are Christians, are in the working age group and live predominantly in Victoria (36 per cent) and New South Wales (24 per cent), mostly in cities such as Melbourne (33 per cent). Their community is supported by the Sudanese Australian Integrated Learning Program and the Sudanese Lost Boys Association of Australia, which provides programs for young people separated from their family by war.

## ACTIVITIES

### UNDERSTANDING

1. Distinguish between the following government policies: White Australia, assimilation, multiculturalism and integration.
2. Explain how Australia is a culturally diverse country.
3. Describe the focus of Australia's multicultural policy.
4. Discuss the Australian government's policies and programs to improve social harmony and equity.

### THINKING AND APPLYING

5. Design a survey to give to your family, a relative, a neighbour and a friend. Include questions such as: Where were you, your parents and grandparents born? Discuss whether your sample is a good representative of a culturally diverse Australia.
6. Compile a collage using digital images of a culturally diverse Australia.
7. *Citizenship*. Design a poster or present a video or play promoting Harmony Day. Use the **Harmony Day** weblink in your eBookPLUS to help you.
8. Go to the **Cultural Diversity** weblinks in your eBookPLUS. Analyse three of the websites. Discuss the ethics of each organisation. Include the reliability of the information (bias, exaggeration, up to date), its relevance (whether you can use it in your geography assignments) and inclusion of geographical tools (maps, graphs, statistics).

### USING YOUR SKILLS

9. Refer to the bar graph on the previous page. Calculate the percentage changes to the numbers of people who have migrated from the United Kingdom, China, Italy, India and Iraq between 2001 and 2006. Calculate the total number of immigrants from Asia–Pacific countries.
10. Refer to the graphs on this page.
    a. What is the range in the number of Sudanese immigrants between 1996 and 2006? Explain the push and pull forces of Sudanese immigrants living in Australia.
    b. Calculate the total number of Sudanese immigrants aged between 18 and 54 years. Discuss how they might contribute to the Australian economy.

### GEOTERMS

**multiculturalism:** respect and maintenance of source countries' cultures and the official Australian government policy since the 1970s. It means that diverse communities keep their native language, rituals, religion and cultural ways as long as the loyalty (commitment) to Australia and its values (civic responsibilities) are clear.

# 12.7 Where we live: spatial distribution

Australia is a large and sparsely populated country; our population density of 2.84 people per square kilometre is much lower than the world average of 45.2 people per square kilometre. Population density varies across Australia because of biophysical, socioeconomic, historical, political and environmental factors.

**Biophysical** — moderate/hot temperature; sufficient/insufficient precipitation; undulating/steep landforms; fertile/saline soils; frequent natural hazards (floods, droughts); lack/plenty energy resources (electricity); raw materials (employment in coal, iron ore)

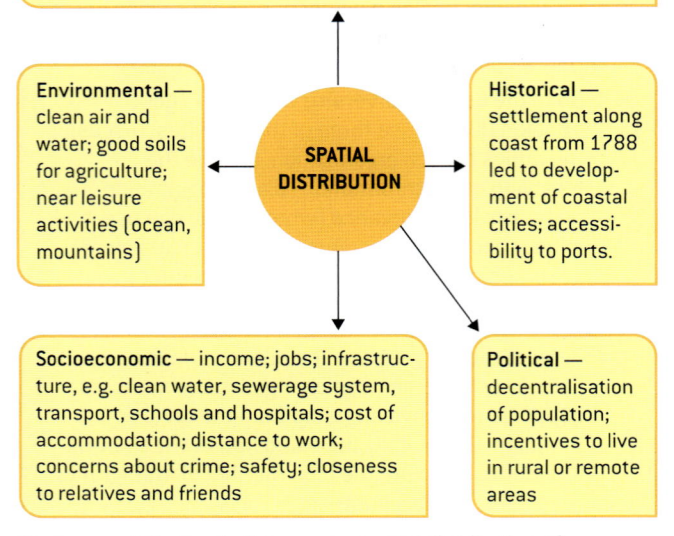

**Environmental** — clean air and water; good soils for agriculture; near leisure activities (ocean, mountains)

**SPATIAL DISTRIBUTION**

**Historical** — settlement along coast from 1788 led to development of coastal cities; accessibility to ports.

**Socioeconomic** — income; jobs; infrastructure, e.g. clean water, sewerage system, transport, schools and hospitals; cost of accommodation; distance to work; concerns about crime; safety; closeness to relatives and friends

**Political** — decentralisation of population; incentives to live in rural or remote areas

*Factors contributing to the uneven spatial distribution of Australia's population*

Australia is generally sparsely populated; 85 per cent of the population lives on 1 per cent of the land area, or within 50 kilometres of the coast. The highest population concentrations are found around Sydney, Melbourne, Brisbane and Perth. Just 0.3 per cent of the population lives in half the area of Australia because of factors such as arid and semi-arid climate, infertile soils for agriculture, poor infrastructure (such as transport) and lack of services (such as hospitals).

Population density varies across Australia. The Australian Capital Territory is the most densely populated state or territory, with 144 people per square kilometre; conversely, the Northern Territory has only 0.2 people per square kilometre. The inner eastern suburbs of Sydney is the most crowded place in Australia, with over 8300 people per square kilometre.

## Spatial distribution

The centre of population describes the spatial distribution of the Australian population. This centre marks the average latitude and longitude around which the population is distributed. In 2008, the centre was located 53 kilometres east of Ivanhoe in western New South Wales. This centre reflects the concentration of the population in south-east Australia, particularly in Sydney and Melbourne. Between 2002 and 2008, the centre moved 12 kilometres north as a result of population growth in northern Australia.

*Spatial distribution of Australia's population, 2008*

| State/territory | Population | % total population | Density (persons per km$^2$) | Capital city | Population 2008 | % of state population |
|---|---|---|---|---|---|---|
| New South Wales | 6 967 200 | 32.6 | 8.6 | Sydney | 4 336 374 | 62.8 |
| Victoria | 5 297 600 | 24.8 | 22.9 | Melbourne | 3 806 092 | 73.1 |
| Queensland | 4 279 400 | 20.0 | 2.4 | Brisbane | 1 857 594 | 44.4 |
| Western Australia | 2 163 200 | 10.1 | 0.8 | Perth | 1 554 769 | 73.8 |
| South Australia | 1 601 800 | 7.5 | 1.6 | Adelaide | 1 158 259 | 73.1 |
| Tasmania | 498 200 | 2.3 | 7.2 | Hobart | 207 484 | 42.1 |
| Australian Capital Territory | 344 200 | 1.6 | 144.1 | Canberra | 339 573 | 99.9 |
| Northern Territory | 219 900 | 1.0 | 0.2 | Darwin | 117 395 | 54.6 |
| Australia[a] | 21 374 000 | 100.0 | 2.84 | | | |

(a) Including other territories

*Source:* Australian Bureau of Statistics.

New South Wales is Australia's most populous state or territory, with Sydney being the largest capital city in Australia. The largest regional cities in New South Wales are Newcastle (524 000 people) and Wollongong (280 000 people). Together with greater Sydney, they account for three-quarters of the New South Wales population.

## Distribution of Indigenous people

According to the 2006 census, there were 517 200 Indigenous Australians, equating to 2.5 per cent of the total population. Most lived in New South Wales (148 200), followed by Queensland. About 74 per cent lived in major cities or regional areas, while the remaining 26 per cent lived in remote and very remote areas.

**Population distribution by remoteness category, 2001**

| Location | Indigenous population | Non-Indigenous population |
|---|---|---|
| Major cities | 30.2% | 67.2% |
| Inner regional | 20.3% | 20.7% |
| Outer regional | 23.1% | 10.1% |
| Remote | 8.8% | 1.5% |
| Very remote | 17.7% | 0.5% |

*Source:* Australian Bureau of Statistics 2003.

Almost one-fifth (93 000) of Australia's Aborigines and Torres Strait Islanders live in separate Indigenous communities. About 85 per cent of these communities are located in remote or very remote locations, with 15 per cent in major cities or inner/outer regional areas, such as Redfern in Sydney.

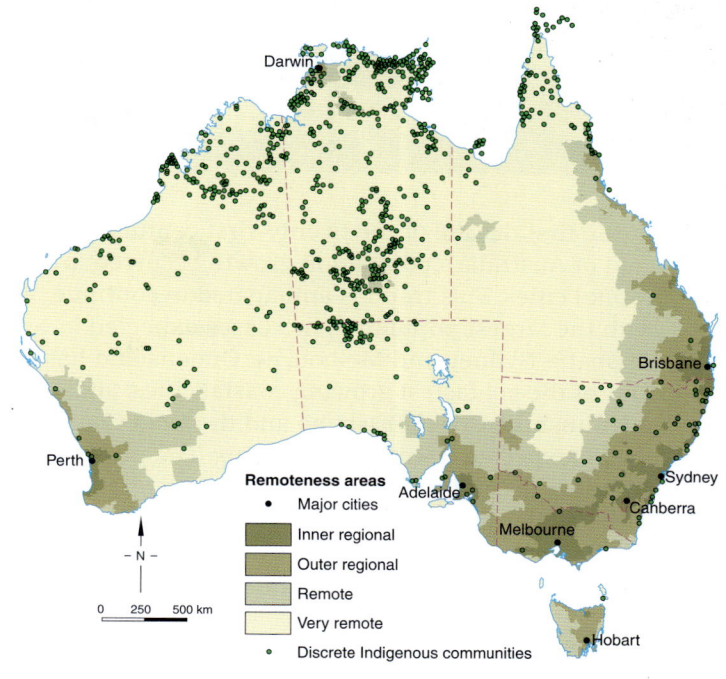

*Spatial distribution of discrete Indigenous communities, 2001*

The Northern Territory has the highest proportion of Indigenous communities, with 81 per cent located in remote or very remote areas. See pages 108–9 for more about the Indigenous population.

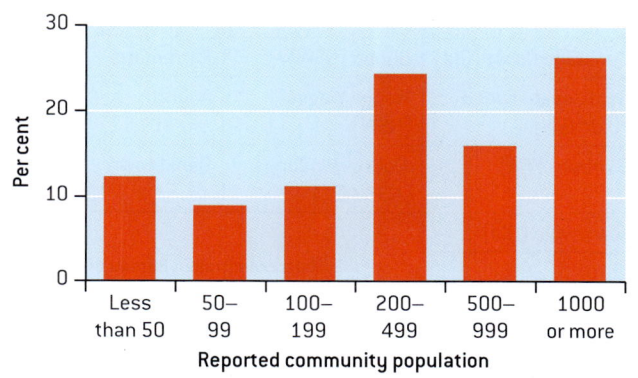

*Population distribution of remote Indigenous communities, 2006*

### ACTIVITIES

**UNDERSTANDING**

1. Describe the factors that explain why most Australians live along the coast.
2. Explain why Australia is a sparsely populated country.
3. Compare the population density of Australia against the world average.

**THINKING AND APPLYING**

4. Imagine you have been asked to give a short talk to a group of tourists from Japan on the current distribution of the Australian population. In preparation, write a short paragraph on each of the following:
   - distribution of population
   - factors contributing to uneven distribution
   - reasons for the unequal distribution of infrastructure and services.

**USING YOUR SKILLS**

5. Refer to the table on the previous page. Discuss Australia's current spatial population distribution. Include statistics in your answer. Draw the state/territory population as a bar graph and the population percentage of capital cities as a line graph.
6. Refer to the table on this page. For both Indigenous and non-Indigenous people, calculate the population in very remote areas as a percentage of the population in major cities. Suggest reasons for the difference.
7. Refer to the graph above. What is the size of the Indigenous communities with the most people? What percentage of people lives in communities with fewer than 50 people?

CHAPTER 12 | Future challenges: population

# 12.8 Population movements

In the first decade of the twenty-first century, 66 per cent of Australia's population growth occurred in capital cities. This trend is anticipated to continue, with the largest population increases expected in Brisbane, Sydney and Melbourne. Queensland has four of the six fastest growing coastal cities, and the Sunshine Coast, Brisbane and the Gold Coast are all expected to continue growing. The projected growth will comprise mainly interstate migration, with smaller growth expected from natural increase (births minus deaths) and net overseas migration (immigration minus emigration).

**Australia's fastest and largest growth areas, 2008**

| Fastest growing areas | Fastest growing regional areas in NSW | Largest local council growth in NSW (all in Sydney) |
|---|---|---|
| Mandurah (WA) | Nowra–Bomaderry (NSW) | Blacktown |
| Hervey Bay (Qld) | Port Macquarie (NSW) | Sydney |
| Sunshine Coast (Qld) | Dubbo (NSW) | Parramatta |
| Gold Coast–Tweed (Qld/NSW) | Wagga Wagga (NSW) | Auburn |
| Bunbury (WA) | Albury–Wodonga (NSW/Vic.) | Bankstown |
| Townsville (Qld) | | |

*Source: Australian Bureau of Statistics.*

## Future: moving north and urban consolidation

Internal migration occurs when people change their place of residence. Australia has one of the highest rates of internal migration in the world; nearly 50 per cent of Australians changed their address between 2001 and 2006, with the trend expected to continue. Internal migration takes three broad forms:

- *Interstate migration* is the movement of people to another state. Queensland is the most popular destination, contributing to the growth of Brisbane and nearby coastal cities. In 2007–08, Western Australia attracted an influx of people lured by high-paying jobs during the resources boom. (See page 110 for more on interstate migration.)
- *Rural–urban migration* is the movement of people from rural to urban areas because of jobs, specialist services or lifestyle. This contrasts to *urban–rural migration*, which is the movement of people out of cities (counter-urbanisation) for reasons including the high cost of housing, traffic congestion and poor air quality. Today, there is a small drift from declining rural areas to coastal urban areas.
- *Intra-city migration* is the movement of people within a city. Significant movement to new suburbs (suburbanisation), such as Camden in Sydney, usually leads to an increase in government expenditure on roads, schools, water and hospitals in that area. Others move to inner suburbs that have been transformed from urban decay to urban renewal, such as Balmain, and renovate old terrace homes and factories (gentrification). Today, urban planners support urban consolidation, which increases population density in existing areas.

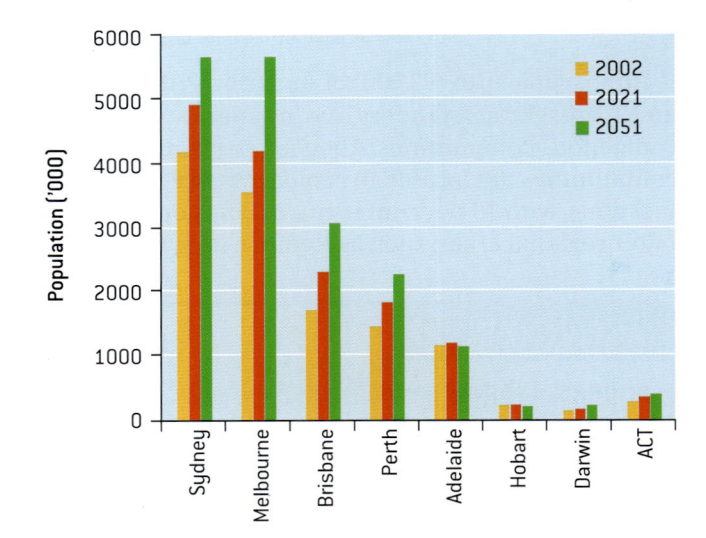

*Capital cities: future growth and distribution of population, 2002–2051*

**Components of current population growth rates, 2005–06**

|  | NSW % | Vic. % | Qld % | SA % | WA % | Tas. % | NT % | ACT % | Australia % |
|---|---|---|---|---|---|---|---|---|---|
| Natural increase | 0.60 | 0.63 | 0.73 | 0.38 | 0.76 | 0.52 | 1.37 | 0.87 | 0.64 |
| Net overseas migration | 0.63 | 0.76 | 0.53 | 0.61 | 1.07 | 0.14 | 0.41 | −0.03 | 0.66 |
| Net interstate migration | −0.35 | −0.04 | 0.64 | −0.18 | 0.15 | 0.01 | −0.19 | 0.08 | |
| Total population growth | 0.91 | 1.52 | 2.14 | 0.99 | 2.07 | 0.70 | 1.98 | 1.24 | 1.43 |

# Crowded coast

The number of people who moved to the coast increased by 2 per cent in 2008, compared with a national growth rate of 1.2 per cent. This sea-change trend is anticipated to continue, attracting free migrants (those whose lifestyle does not bind them to big cities, such as retirees and internet commuters) and forced migrants (those pushed out of big cities due to the high cost of housing). Sea changers are motivated by *pull factors* (improved environment and lifestyle, cheaper housing, employment, family reasons) and *push factors* (including high housing costs, traffic congestion and crime). The influx of people is transforming sleepy coastal towns into areas of high-density development.

The National Sea Change Taskforce (NSCT) aims to sustainably manage population growth in coastal Australia. Local councils such as Noosa in Queensland are attempting to limit future population growth because the water supply cannot meet the demand. The New South Wales Inquiry into Infrastructure Provision in Coastal Growth Areas aims to manage the impacts of climate change on the increasing coastal population.

*Residents of Byron Bay protest over a proposed resort development.*

**Types of coastal population growth and government policies and plans**

| Coastal community | Description | Examples in NSW | Government focus | Government and businesses |
|---|---|---|---|---|
| Coastal commuters | Urban communities within daily commuting distance of a capital city | Woollongong and Central Coast (Wyong, Gosford) | Efficient, cheap public transport and motorways/freeways to link community to city. Parking facilities at railway stations, e.g. Gosford | Infrastructure (transport, water, sewerage, electricity), community services and social services, shopping centres, post offices, banks |
| Coastal getaway | Within three hours drive of a capital city and easy weekend access to a holiday home | Port Stephens | Good transport links, entertainment activities, parks, cycling and walking paths | |
| Coastal cities | Greater than 10 000 people (regional urgan centres) | Newcastle | Hospitals, schools, higher education, central business district | |
| Coastal lifestyle | Tourism-dominated communities | Byron Bay, NSW | Hotels, restaurants, entertainment | |

## ACTIVITIES

### UNDERSTANDING
1. Describe where most Australians live.
2. Describe where population growth rates are highest in Australia.
3. Discuss the different population movements within a city.

### THINKING AND APPLYING
4. Design a poster to attract sea changers to a coastal area of New South Wales.
5. Refer to the table on this page. Create a graphic organiser to display the information.

### USING YOUR SKILLS
6. Refer to the table at the bottom of the previous page. Which state or territory is growing the fastest by:
   a natural increase
   b net overseas migration
   c net interstate migration
   d total population growth?
7. Refer to the table at the top of the previous page. Locate the fastest growing places on a blank map of Australia. Research one location in Queensland and one in New South Wales and give reasons for their growth.

# 12.9 Population movement and urban planning

The population in Australia's urban areas is expected to grow by 4 million in the next 25 years, putting pressure on transport, energy, and air and water systems, as well as threatening the **liveability** of Australia's urban spaces. The high urban growth rate has made it difficult for governments to supply adequate infrastructure and services, resulting in:
- a large ecological urban footprint — soil erosion, water and air pollution, and accumulation of waste
- socioeconomic exclusion — lack of infrastructure and the development of enclaves of poverty
- unsustainable development — unaffordable housing, inadequate access to education and welfare services, danger due to proximity of housing to industrial- and hazardous-waste disposal sites.

Australian cities are increasingly characterised by spatial inequality, with higher income groups moving into the better serviced inner suburbs, and lower income groups forced to occupy lower cost housing in the more poorly resourced outer suburbs.

## Planning for urban movement

Planning for the long term is difficult due to constantly changing population size, family structure, housing types and locations. Town planners, engineers, architects and local communities work with urban ecologists to design and develop urban projects. Developers influence the way the city changes and where people live by purchasing land and constructing houses and some infrastructure; governments affect the city by providing transport routes, schools and hospitals. Urban planners promote urban consolidation by redeveloping inner and middle suburbs, and aim to improve public transport in outer suburbs.

## Planned development of an urban village

Urban planners face the difficult task of designing new urban areas with a high degree of liveability. The development of an urban village aims to improve liveability through:
- a mixture of land uses (residential, commercial and recreational)
- reducing carbon and water footprints
- people of different age groups
- emphasis on public transport
- pedestrian-friendly traffic systems and bike paths
- attractive places for people to meet.

## Backyard bliss

The development of low-density suburbia and the so-called 'quarter-acre block' is part of the traditional Australian landscape. Despite the prevailing views that it is ecologically unsustainable, a large percentage of urban dwellers are expected to live in the outer suburbs by 2050.

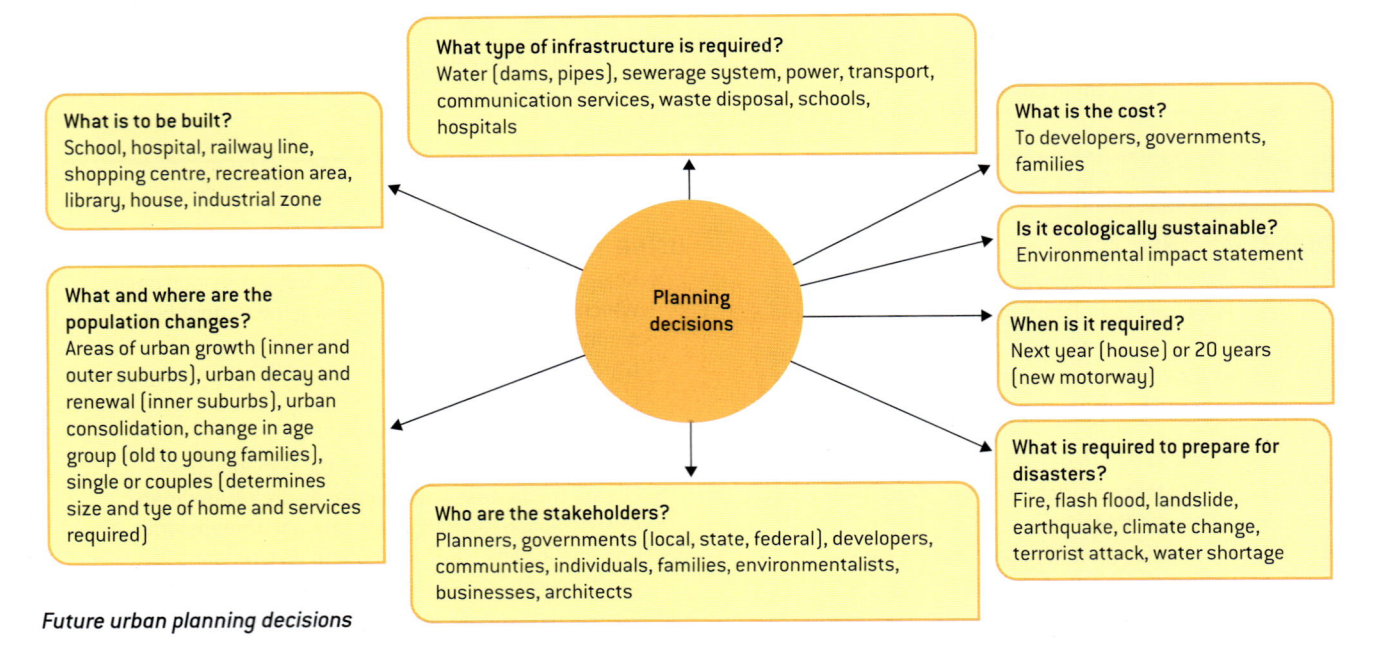

**Planning decisions**

**What is to be built?**
School, hospital, railway line, shopping centre, recreation area, library, house, industrial zone

**What and where are the population changes?**
Areas of urban growth (inner and outer suburbs), urban decay and renewal (inner suburbs), urban consolidation, change in age group (old to young families), single or couples (determines size and tye of home and services required)

**What type of infrastructure is required?**
Water (dams, pipes), sewerage system, power, transport, communication services, waste disposal, schools, hospitals

**Who are the stakeholders?**
Planners, governments (local, state, federal), developers, communities, individuals, families, environmentalists, businesses, architects

**What is the cost?**
To developers, governments, families

**Is it ecologically sustainable?**
Environmental impact statement

**When is it required?**
Next year (house) or 20 years (new motorway)

**What is required to prepare for disasters?**
Fire, flash flood, landslide, earthquake, climate change, terrorist attack, water shortage

*Future urban planning decisions*

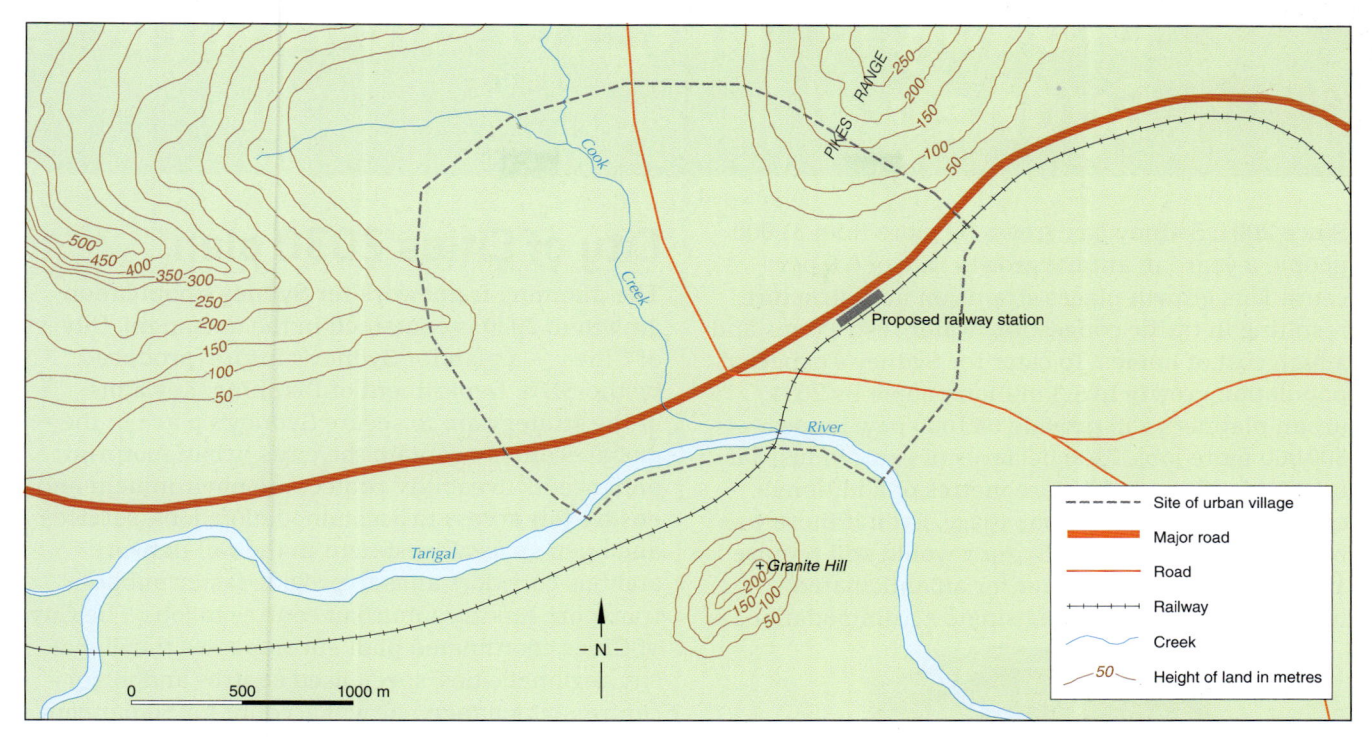

*Base map of the proposed urban village in Blissville*

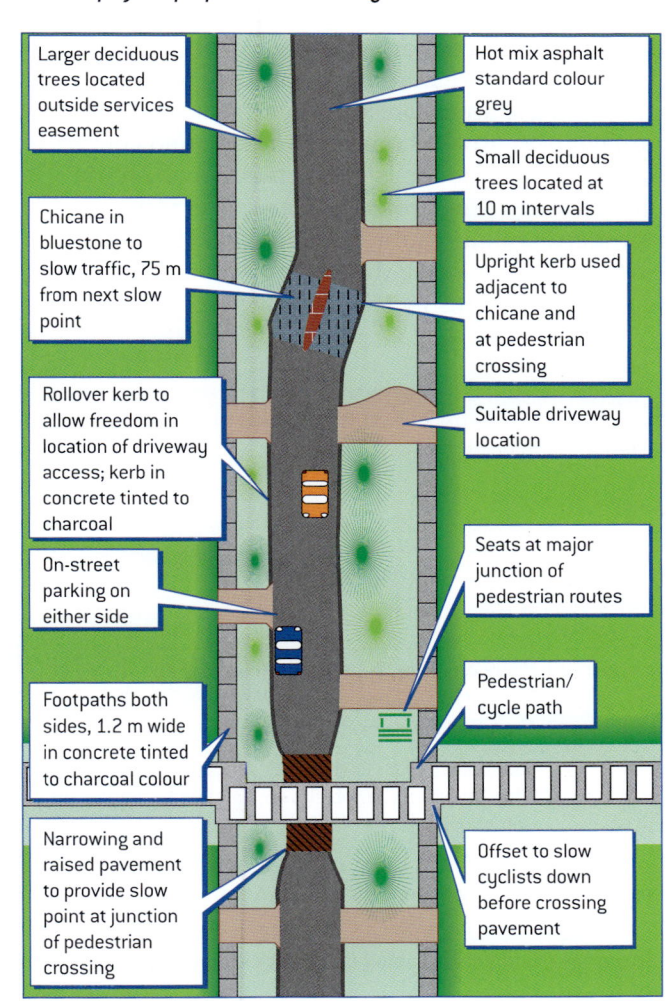

*Streetscape sketch for an urban village*

Labels on streetscape:
- Larger deciduous trees located outside services easement
- Chicane in bluestone to slow traffic, 75 m from next slow point
- Rollover kerb to allow freedom in location of driveway access; kerb in concrete tinted to charcoal
- On-street parking on either side
- Footpaths both sides, 1.2 m wide in concrete tinted to charcoal colour
- Narrowing and raised pavement to provide slow point at junction of pedestrian crossing
- Hot mix asphalt standard colour grey
- Small deciduous trees located at 10 m intervals
- Upright kerb used adjacent to chicane and at pedestrian crossing
- Suitable driveway location
- Seats at major junction of pedestrian routes
- Pedestrian/cycle path
- Offset to slow cyclists down before crossing pavement

## ACTIVITIES

### UNDERSTANDING

1. List some of the problems of past urban planning.
2. Discuss how urban plans led to different patterns of population growth within cities.

### USING YOUR SKILLS

3. Working in teams, read the following scenario; then plan an urban village using the instructions below.

   *Scenario.* Blissville is an imaginary city on the east coast of Australia. It has a population of 2 million and is becoming a centre of information and high-tech industries. The government wants new suburbs to be ecologically sustainable and planned around the idea of an urban village. The area for the urban village is 30 kilometres from Blissville's central business district alongside a new railway line that provides fast access to the city. Incentives will be offered for industries to move near the new urban village.

   *Planning stages.* Examine the map showing the area in which the urban village is to be located. Brainstorm ideas for the plan. Assess the range of ideas, and then agree on a plan.

   *Presentation.* Allocate the following tasks to group members: an introduction to the plan, setting out the village's aims; a copy of the base map with a plan of the village, including key, scale, north point and drainage features; a labelled streetscape for a small part of the map; models and sketches to supplement the map and streetscape; an oral report to the class with an invitation for questions and comments.

CHAPTER 12 | Future challenges: population

# 12.10 Urban planning for the future: Sydney

Since 2001, Sydney has grown by more than 31 000 people a year (an annual growth rate of 0.8 per cent). This growth places strains on infrastructure, resulting in traffic congestion, water restrictions and a high cost of homes. To cater for Sydney's expected population growth to 5.3 million people by 2031, urban planners will provide 640 000 new homes, 500 000 more jobs, 7500 hectares of extra industrial land and millions of square metres of additional commercial and retail floor space. Even if there was zero population growth, Sydney would still require 190 000 new homes to cater for an anticipated increase in people seeking single accommodation.

*These heritage buildings in Glebe, Sydney, have been preserved.*

## City of Cities 2030 plan

The planning framework for Sydney's population growth to 2030 is contained in the document 'City of Cities — a plan for Sydney's future' produced by the NSW Department of Planning. Key aims of the strategy are to secure Sydney's place in the global economy, contain the city's urban footprint, enhance its liveability, protect the environment and ensure fair access to accommodation, jobs, services and open space. Investment in the rail network and bus corridors aims to provide faster public transport, linking suburban centres to jobs. The City of Cities coordinated plan encompasses the global city, regional cities, specialised centres and major centres, which together will account for 50 per cent of new homes and 50 per cent of new jobs by 2030.

The Metropolitan Strategy aims to accommodate around 70 per cent of Sydney's growth in existing areas, with the remaining 30 per cent located in new-release areas. The new-release areas cover an area of over 10 000 square kilometres and comprise 43 local government areas, including two on the central coast. The area is too large and complex for metropolitan planners to manage effectively; instead, they oversee the implementation of subregional plans by local governments.

**Sydney's City of Cities coordinated plan 2030 for strategic centres**

| Strategic centre | Functions | Examples |
| --- | --- | --- |
| Global Sydney | Increase Sydney's role as a global city by providing professional services, specialised health care, education, shops, and cultural and entertainment facilities and attracting tourists. | Sydney city, North Sydney |
| Regional cities | Provide a range of business, government, retail, cultural, entertainment and recreational activities and provide jobs linked by transport. | Parramatta, Liverpool, Penrith |
| Specialised centres | Provide global links through airports and ports and provide hospitals, universities and research and business activities. | Macquarie Park, St Leonards, Olympic Park–Rhodes, Port Botany, Sydney Airport, Westmead, Bankstown Airport–Milperra, Norwest |
| Major centres | Provide major shopping and business centres for the surrounding area (shopping malls, office and residential buildings), community facilities and a minimum of 8000 jobs. | Bankstown, Blacktown, Bondi Junction, Brookvale–Dee Why, Burwood, Campbelltown, Castle Hill, Chatswood, Hornsby, Hurstville |
| Planned major centres | Provide future locations for shopping and services in residential growth areas. | Rouse Hill, Leppington, Green Square |
| Potential major centres | Provide transport or open space for potential shopping and service hubs to cater for increased residential development. | Sutherland, Cabramatta, Mt Druitt, Fairfield |

**Subregional planning — employment capacity targets, 2031**

| Subregion | Local government area | Employment targets |
|---|---|---|
| Sydey City | Sydney City | 58 000 new jobs |
| Inner North | Lane Cove, North Sydney, Ryde, Willoughby, Hunters Hill, Mosman | 54 000 new jobs |
| Inner West | Ashfield, Burwood, Canada Bay, Leichhardt, Strathfield | 10 000 new jobs |
| South | Kogarah, Hurstville, Canterbury, Rockdale, Sutherland, Marrickville | 21 000 new jobs |
| East | Botany Bay, Randwick, Waverley, Woollahra | 17 500 new jobs |
| North East | Pittwater, Warringah, Manly | 16 000 new jobs |
| North | Hornsby, Ku-ring-gai | 8000 new jobs |
| North West | Baulkham Hills, Blacktown, Blue Mountains, Hawkesbury, Penrith | 99 000 new jobs |
| West Central | Auburn, Bankstown, Fairfield, Holroyd, Parramatta | 35 000 new jobs |
| South West | Wollondilly, Camden, Campbelltown, Liverpool | 80 000 new jobs |
| Central Coast | Gosford, Wyong | 55 000 new jobs |

## The rise of high-rise

About 36 per cent of owners of owner-occupied homes in Sydney intend to move during the next ten years, with a quarter of them seeking medium- or high-density accommodation. Under a 2009 transport plan developed by state and federal governments, Sydney will be 'reinvented' as a high-density metropolis serviced by mass-transit subways. The new push is to model Australian cities on London, Tokyo and Singapore, which have twice as many people and jobs per hectare as Sydney. Heritage inner-west suburbs such as Glebe, Leichhardt, Rozelle and Camperdown would face radical changes as part of the proposed $4.8 billion CBD Metro project, including the development of 15-storey apartment towers. The proposed $8.1 billion West Metro will transport up to 30 000 people an hour from Parramatta to the CBD in less than 27 minutes, stopping at nine underground stations.

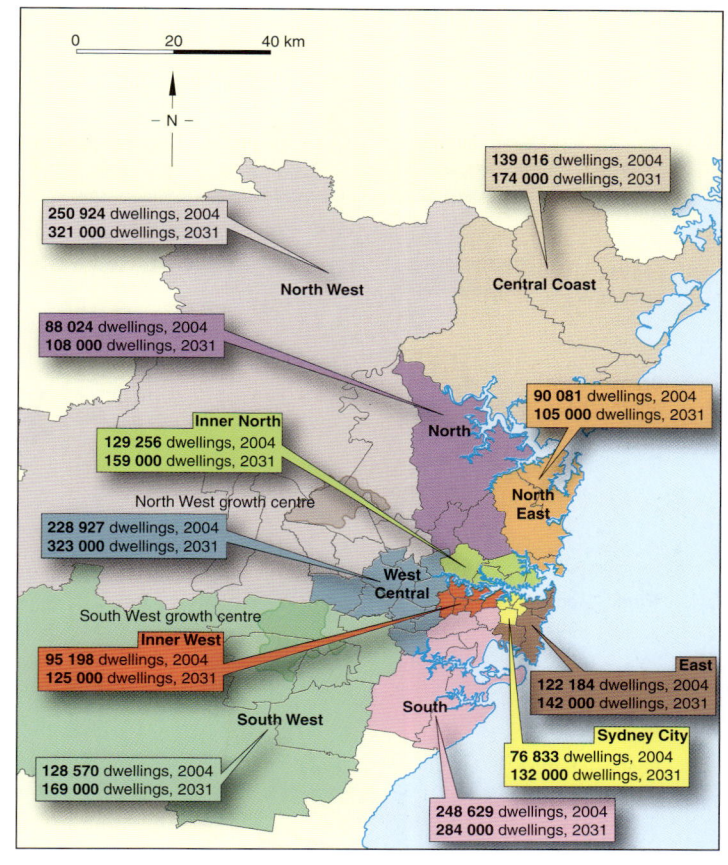

*Subregional planning — housing capacity targets, 2031*

Dwellings data by subregion:
- North West: 250 924 dwellings, 2004 / 321 000 dwellings, 2031
- Central Coast: 139 016 dwellings, 2004 / 174 000 dwellings, 2031
- Inner North: 129 256 dwellings, 2004 / 159 000 dwellings, 2031
- North: 90 081 dwellings, 2004 / 105 000 dwellings, 2031
- West Central: 88 024 dwellings, 2004 / 108 000 dwellings, 2031
- South West: 228 927 dwellings, 2004 / 323 000 dwellings, 2031
- Inner West: 95 198 dwellings, 2004 / 125 000 dwellings, 2031
- East: 122 184 dwellings, 2004 / 142 000 dwellings, 2031
- Sydney City: 76 833 dwellings, 2004 / 132 000 dwellings, 2031
- South: 128 570 dwellings, 2004 / 169 000 dwellings, 2031
- North East: 248 629 dwellings, 2004 / 284 000 dwellings, 2031

## ACTIVITIES

**UNDERSTANDING**

1. Explain the City of Cities 2030 Plan.
2. Discuss the coordination of urban consolidation and the 2009 future transport plan.

**THINKING AND APPLYING**

3. Analyse Sydney's future population trends and their implications for urban planning.

**USING YOUR SKILLS**

4. Refer to the table on the previous page. Find the example locations on a map of Sydney. Explain the advantages of regional cities for people who live in the outer suburbs. Discuss the advantages of specialised centres and how they can help Sydney keep pace with other major global cities. Research one of the example locations and the implications of the City of Cities 2030 Plan.
5. Refer to the table above. Calculate the total number of new jobs that will be created in Sydney by 2031. List the three regions that will supply most of the jobs. Discuss the advantages of jobs close to residential areas.
6. Refer to the map above. Rank the subregions from highest to lowest number of dwellings in 2031. List two regions experiencing suburbanisation. Explain the urban process occurring in the Inner North and Inner West.

# 12.11 Ecological sustainability

**Ecological sustainability** ensures that the needs of the present population can be met without adversely affecting the needs of future generations. One of the challenges facing Australia is how to manage population growth, especially in urban areas, while ensuring ecological, social and economic sustainability (referred to as the triple bottom line).

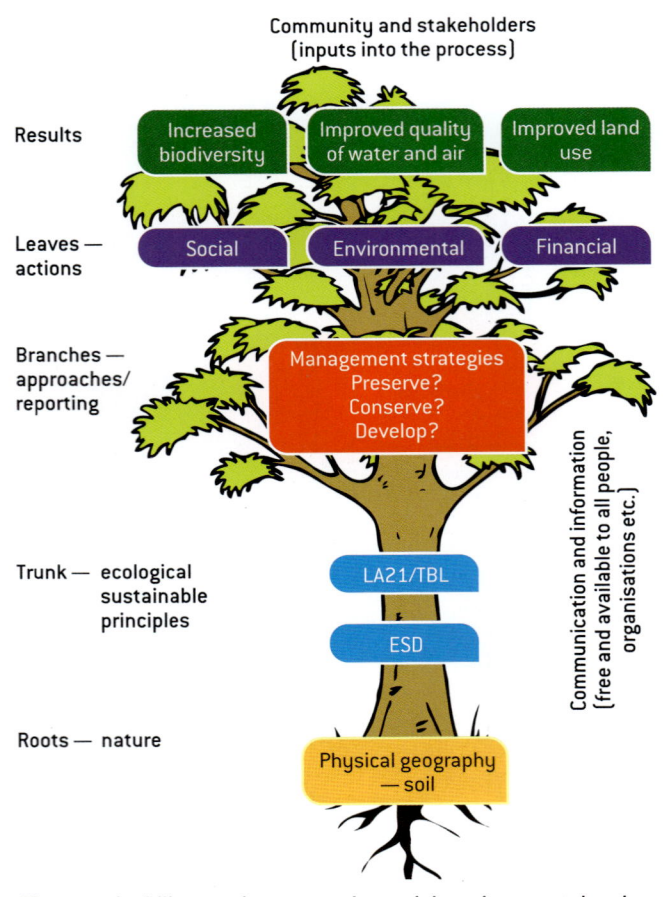

*The sustainability tree integrates the social, environmental and economic dimensions — the triple bottom line (TBL). It is based on the principles of ecologically sustainable development (ESD) incorporating Local Agenda 21 (LA21), ecological footprinting and the natural step model (which determines the minimum conditions for a sustainable society).*

**Local Agenda 21 (LA21)** spells out three broad conditions for an ecologically sustainable population:
- *renewable resources* such as timber should not be used faster than they are renewed
- *non-renewable resources* such as coal should be used only within the rate of substitution by alternatives
- *wastes* such as garbage should be produced only within society's ability to process or assimilate them.

## Ecological footprint

One way of determining whether the Australian population is ecologically sustainable is to use each person's ecological footprint. The ecological footprint (EF) measures the quantity of resources each person or household uses to produce the energy (oil, gas, uranium, timber), food (crops, livestock, fish) and infrastructure (schools, roads, houses) they consume as part of their daily activities. It also calculates the amount of waste people produce, including those found in the air (greenhouse gases, pollutants), water (blue-green algae, toxic chemicals, acid) and soil (garbage, pesticides, fertilisers). The 6.6 billion people on Earth are notionally entitled to an EF of 1.7 hectares of productive land. Australians, with an EF of 7.81 hectares per person, have the fifth largest EF in the world.

**Ecological footprint, 2009**

| Country | Ecological footprint (hectares per person) |
|---|---|
| **Developed countries** | |
| Australia | 7.8 |
| United States of America | 9.4 |
| **Developing countries** | |
| Iraq | 1.3 |
| Afghanistan | 0.5 |
| China | 2.1 |
| Indonesia | 0.9 |
| Papua New Guinea | 1.7 |
| Rwanda | 0.8 |
| Vietnam | 1.3 |
| **World** | **2.7** |

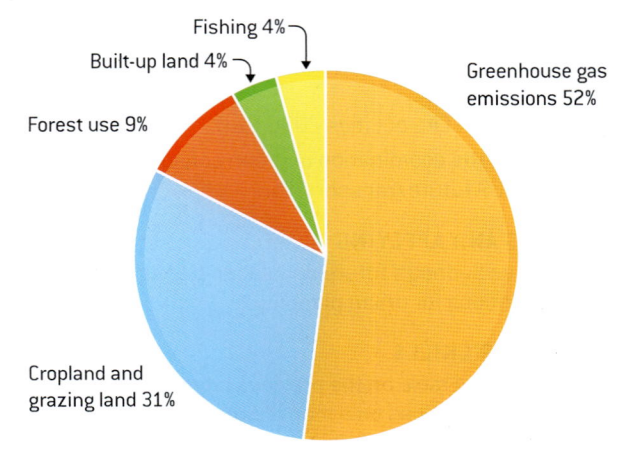

*Composition of Australia's ecological footprint*
- Greenhouse gas emissions 52%
- Cropland and grazing land 31%
- Forest use 9%
- Built-up land 4%
- Fishing 4%

## Carbon and water footprints

Carbon and water footprints are components of an ecological footprint. A **carbon footprint** measures the amount of greenhouse gases produced by humans. In 2008, Australian households produced on average 32 tonnes of carbon per year, one of the largest footprints in the world. Wealthier households generated 58 tonnes of greenhouse gases a year in contrast to 22 tonnes for poorer families. The population's large carbon footprint motivated the Australian government to sign the Kyoto Protocol to reduce greenhouse gas emissions, to establish a carbon pollution reduction scheme and to develop alternative energy sources.

The **water footprint** measures the total volume of fresh water used to produce the goods and services consumed by the community. The world average water footprint is 1.24 million litres per person per year, which is equivalent to half the volume of an Olympic swimming pool. Australia's large water footprint of 1.39 million litres of water per person per year led the New South Wales Government to enforce water restrictions on households and water quotas on agriculture during droughts.

## Implications for future population trends

One of the challenges facing the Australian government is the development of a future population resource plan. The Australian population is predicted to grow to between 25 and 34 million by 2050, and between 44 and 50 million by 2101. If the demand for resources continues to increase at the present rate, coupled with the expected population increase, experts predict an environmental disaster. If Australians want to maintain their large footprint and still have an ecologically sustainable future, a decrease in population is essential. To reduce your ecological footprint, are you, for example, prepared to walk to school instead of taking the bus, or put on more clothes rather than turn on the heater when you're cold?

### GEOTERMS

**carbon footprint:** greenhouse gas emissions caused directly and indirectly by an individual, organisation, event or product

**ecological sustainability:** the needs of the present population being met without endangering the ability of future generations to meet their needs

### GEOfacts

- Water footprint — It takes 120 litres of water to produce one glass of wine, 40 litres to produce one slice of bread and 4100 litres to produce one cotton T-shirt.
- Carbon footprint — Producing a traditional Christmas dinner results in the emission of 26 kilograms of carbon dioxide.

### ACTIVITIES

**UNDERSTANDING**

1. What is ecological sustainability?
2. Explain the broad conditions of ecological sustainability.
3. Distinguish between Australia's water and carbon footprints.
4. Discuss government plans to reduce Australia's ecological footprint.
5. What three broad conditions are required for an ecologically sustainable population, according to Local Agenda 21?

**THINKING AND APPLYING**

6. Explain Australia's large ecological footprint and its spatial distribution across Australia.
7. Imagine you were employed to administer a future ecologically sustainable population plan. What would you change: population, ecological footprint, or both? Explain the reasons for your decision.
8. Write a letter to a politician promoting a water footprint on food labels similar to the energy labels on whitegoods. Use the **Food Labelling** weblink in your eBookPLUS to help you.

**USING YOUR SKILLS**

9. Refer to the sustainability tree on the previous page. What are the principles behind sustainable development? Explain why sustainable development is more than an ecological concept. Suggest government plans to promote a sustainable population. Describe actions you could take to reduce your ecological footprint. Discuss the use of the tree to describe the complex concept of sustainable development.
10. Refer to the table on the previous page. What is an ecological footprint? Draw the ecological footprints of the countries as a column graph; draw the world footprint as a line across the middle of the graph. Provide reasons for the larger footprint in developed countries.
11. Refer to the graph opposite. Rank the main components of Australia's ecological footprint from largest to smallest. Explain how active citizens could reduce their footprint.

CHAPTER 12 | Future challenges: population

# 12.12 Towards the ecocity: sustainable Sydney

A region's ecological footprint (EF) changes with population size, average consumption per person and resource efficiency. Sydney's population of 4.4 million people have an EF of 7.5 hectares per person, and they depend on food, energy and timber resources from other parts of New South Wales, Australia and overseas. The footprint varies spatially across Sydney with the largest EF of 14.7 hectares occurring in wealthy Mosman. Population-resource planners are concerned that Sydney's large EF is already unsustainable, but it is expected to worsen with the population predicted to reach six million by 2036, and 6.9 million by 2049.

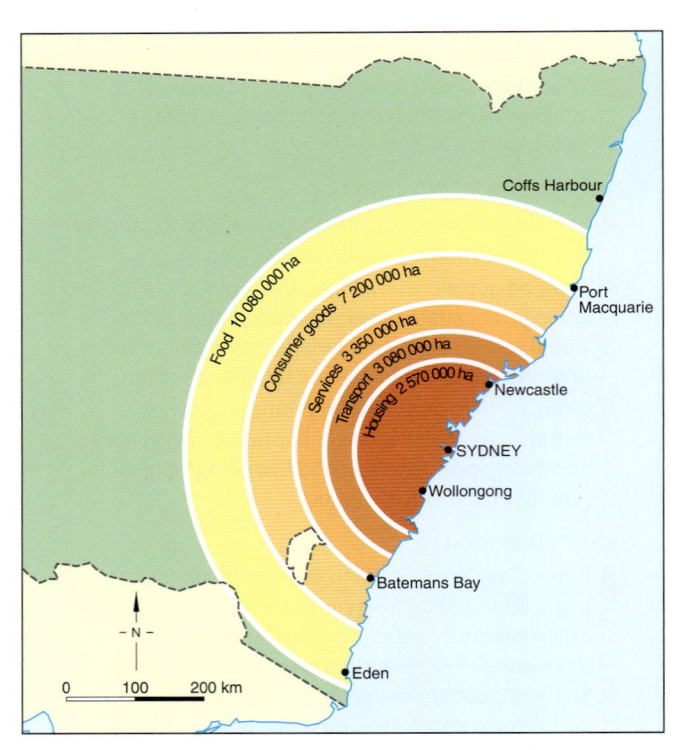

*The amount of land and water required to sustain Sydney's population*

## Eco-city: Sustainable Sydney 2030

A sustainable city, called an **ecocity**, minimises energy, water and wastes. These cities create smaller EFs for their residents by feeding the population from within and generating their own power. To reduce its ecological footprint, the city of Sydney aims to redesign Sydney's central business district (CBD) into an environmentally sustainable city.

By 2030, the 'grand makeover' will see tree-lined streets connecting parks for pedestrians and cyclists, and Sydney's White Bay transformed into the state's first ecologically sustainable city. The 80-hectare White Bay ecocity, located in Sydney Harbour, will accommodate up to 22 000 people in mid- to high-density solar districts, with rooftop gardens and recycled water. It envisages a light tram grid and special roads for public GPS-guided stackable mini-cars.

*Stackable cars could be used in White Bay's ecocity and in Sydney to manage traffic congestion. (Image © Franco Vairani, MIT)*

## Reshaping cities: civics and citizenship

Active Australian citizens have lobbied governments for ecologically sustainable urban plans that focus on reducing, reusing and recycling resources, investing in public transport, developing homes and offices with zero carbon dioxide emission, and helping people become responsible for the environment by changing their consumption behaviour.

## Sydney: long-term liveability

With a focus on reducing Australia's carbon footprint, the federal government introduced the Solar Cities program. By becoming a solar city, Blacktown Council in Sydney has reduced emissions equivalent to taking 6000 cars off

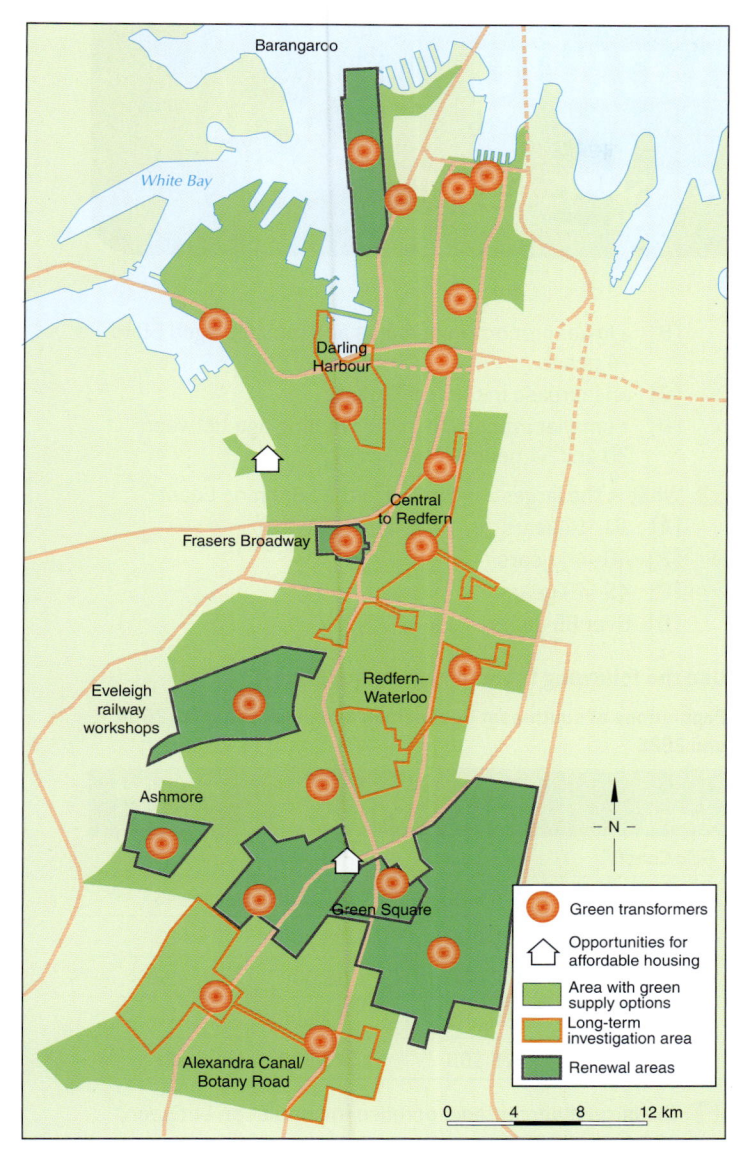

*Sustainable renewal of the city of Sydney. Areas such as Green Square and Barangaroo will provide innovative approaches to energy generation waste and affordable housing.*

Sydney's roads. The New South Wales Government's GoGet project encourages employees to share cars, and Parklea Public School's Walking School Bus promotes a parent–child walking program. The planned community at Ropes Crossing near St Marys focuses on a 'walkable neighbourhood'. Governments encourage industries to minimise their building footprints through a star-rating such as the Nationwide House Energy Rating System (NatHERS).

Efforts to reduce Sydney's waste footprint include the provision of recycling facilities by local councils, reduced packaging use by businesses, and governments charging people and organisations for dumping waste. Today, 30 per cent of municipal waste, 44 per cent of commercial and industrial waste and 57 per cent of construction and demolition waste is recycled.

To reduce the state's water footprint, Sydney Water and the New South Wales Departments of Water and Energy (DWE) and Environment and Climate Change have implemented a variety of measures such as mandatory water restrictions, pay-for-use water pricing, rainwater tank rebates and the Every Drop Counts business program. By 2015, the Western Sydney Recycled Water Initiative will provide 27 billion litres of recycled water a year to new homes, and Sydney Water aims to complete the construction of a desalination plant to secure Sydney's future water supply by 2010.

## ACTIVITIES

### UNDERSTANDING

1. Which suburb of Sydney has the largest ecological footprint?
2. Explain what is meant by an ecocity.
3. Suggest strategies to support urban ecological sustainability.
4. Describe the grand makeover of Sydney's CBD by 2030.

### THINKING AND APPLYING

5. Explain how the ecological footprint of a city no longer coincides with its geographic footprint.
6. Explain the statement 'Bigfoot alive and thriving in Mosman'. Suggest strategies to live sustainably in your suburb. Use the **Ecological Footprint** weblink in your eBookPLUS to help you.
7. Explain the advantages of using stackable cars in cities.

### USING YOUR SKILLS

8. Use Google Earth to help you sketch White Bay and surrounding suburbs and islands.
9. Refer to the map on the previous page. Explain why Sydney's ecological footprint extends beyond its geographic boundary.
10. Refer to the map on this page. List the areas that are being renewed. Suggest how development plans could reduce the ecological footprint.

### GEOTERMS

**ecocity:** an entire city dedicated to minimising inputs (energy, water and food) and waste outputs (heat, air pollution as carbon dioxide and methane, and water pollution)

# Working geographically

## BROADSHEET: POPULATION CHANGE — SUNSHINE COAST

### KNOWLEDGE AND UNDERSTANDING

**Read the statement below and answer question 1.**

The Sunshine Coast is located in south-east Queensland. It covers an area of 3130 square kilometres, stretching from Caloundra in the south to Noosa in the north. The Sunshine Coast's population is more than 295 000, or 7 per cent of Queensland's population and is forecast to increase to 483 000 by 2026. The population growth rate is 3.3 per cent each year (Queensland's overall growth rate is 1.9 per cent), with most of the population being under 50 years old. In 2008, the mayor of the Sunshine Coast Regional Council requested a population cap as the rate of population increase was outstripping the capacity to provide the infrastructure.

1. Which statement is the most correct?
   (A) Most people moving to the Sunshine Coast are over 50 years old.
   (B) The population will increase by 188 000 new residents by 2026.
   (C) Caloundra is the most northerly town on the Sunshine Coast.
   (D) The percentage population growth rate of 3.3 per cent is low.

**Use the following graph to answer questions 2 and 3.**

2. Compared with the 2005 population, the 2020 Sunshine Coast population is expected to have:
   (A) a lower proportion of males and females aged 0 to 24 years
   (B) a lower proportion of males and females aged 60 to 74 years
   (C) an increase in the fertility rate
   (D) a smaller proportion in the working age between 30 and 54 years.

3. What is the largest age group in the Sunshine Coast?
   (A) 10–14 years
   (B) 40–44 years
   (C) 45–49 years
   (D) Over 85 years

**Use the following table to answer question 4.**

Populations of south-east Queensland's regional councils, 2004 and 2026

| Council | 2004 | 2026 (predicted) | Percentage change (%) |
|---|---|---|---|
| Gold Coast | 475 500 | 719 000 | +51 |
| Caboolture | 124 500 | 180 500 | +45 |
| Caloundra | 85 000 | 155 500 | +83 |
| Maroochy | 142 000 | 216 000 | +52 |
| Noosa | 48 500 | 52 500 | +8 |
| Total | 875 500 | 1 323 500 | +51 |

4. The largest percentage increase in population between 2004 and 2026 occurred in:
   (A) the Gold Coast
   (B) Caloundra
   (C) Maroochy
   (D) Noosa.

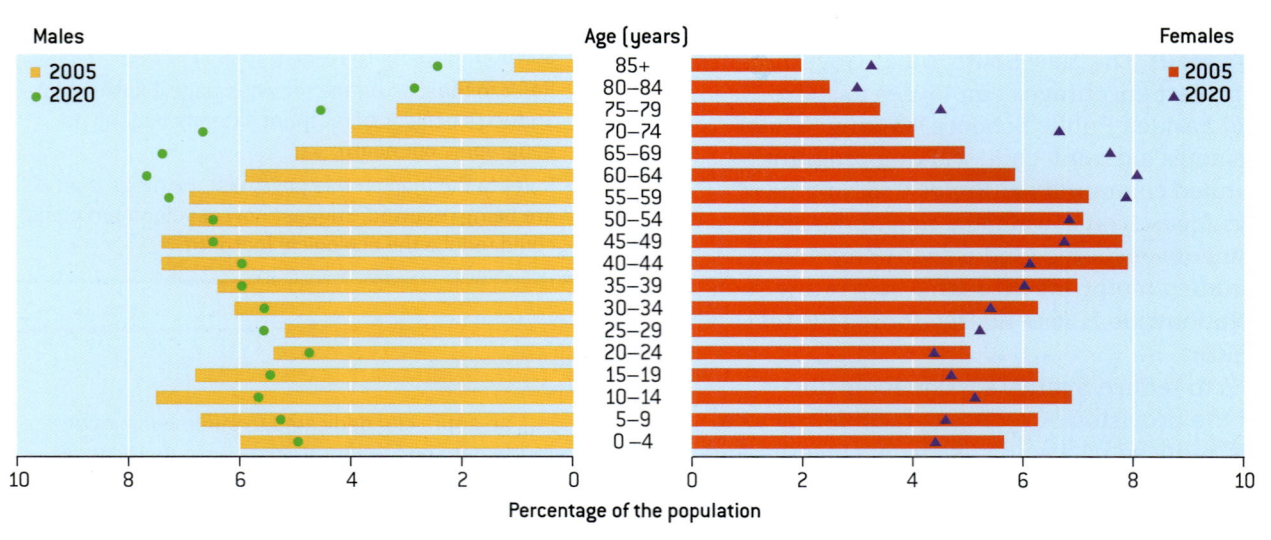

*Population pyramid for the Sunshine Coast, 2005 and 2020*

**Use the map below to answer question 5.**

**5**
a What is the AR of Noosa Heads?
b What is the density of buildings in AR0273?
c What is the area of Lake Weyba?
d What is the direction of Noosa National Park from Tewantin?
e What is the bearing of Noosa Hill to the quarry in AR0076?
f In which direction does Eenie Creek flow?
g What is the land use in AR1079?
h What is the AR of the breakwater?
i Construct a vegetation transect along easting 05 (north to south).

*Topographic map of Noosa*

# 13 Challenges: human rights and reconciliation

## INQUIRY QUESTIONS

+ What are human rights?
+ How do individuals, groups and governments respond to human rights abuses?
+ What are the responses of Australia and other nations to human rights and reconciliation?
+ What strategies can Australia adopt to address human rights and reconciliation in the future?

Everyone in Australia is born free and equal, and is entitled to basic human rights. However, the life expectancy of Indigenous people is 17 years less than non-Indigenous people. It is even less than the life expectancy of 'boat people' and their children who have been detained for long periods in immigration detention centres. The future challenge is for individuals, groups and governments to respond to Indigenous human rights abuses by implementing strategies to ensure that all Australians are treated equally — so that we can move towards creating a reconciled country, which holds a better future for all Australians.

*Reg Edwards, along with several brothers and sisters, was forcibly removed from his parents. He raises his fists in triumph after Prime Minister Kevin Rudd's apology to the Stolen Generations on 13 February 2008.*

### KEY TERMS

**customary law:** law based on tradition and the customary practices of traditional societies, usually passed on orally between generations

**gender equality:** equal valuing of women and men so both sexes are able to equally contribute to and benefit from economic, social, cultural and political developments within society

**genocide:** planned killing of a whole national or racial group

**global gender gap:** World Economic Forum measurement examining inequality between men and women in economic participation, educational attainment, political empowerment, health and survival

**human development index (HDI):** measures human development in three broad dimensions: life expectancy, education and wealth; published by the United Nations Development Programme each year

**human rights:** basic rights and freedoms to which all humans are entitled

**indigenous people:** the descendants of the original inhabitants of the area

**land claims:** claims of Indigenous peoples about their right of ownership of the land they or their ancestors inhabited before the arrival of settlers, primarily Europeans

**life expectancy:** the average number of years a person can be expected to live; affected by nutrition, occupation, heredity and other factors

**reconciliation:** a process that strives to improve relations between Indigenous and non-Indigenous people

**refugee:** a person who is forced to flee their homeland because of a well-founded fear of being persecuted due to race, religion, nationality, membership of a particular social group, or political belief

**self-determination:** the right of a nation or group of people to form their own government

**Stolen Generations:** refers to Aboriginal children who were removed from their families and communities by government or non-government agencies in order to enforce integration into society; this practice continued in some areas until the 1970s

**visa:** a permit that allows the holder to enter a country for a specified period of time

# 13.1 Everyone, everywhere has human rights: agreements

All humans are born equal and entitled to humane, fair treatment and basic freedoms known as **human rights**. These rights are inherent to everyone, everywhere, regardless of nationality, sex, race, colour or religion.

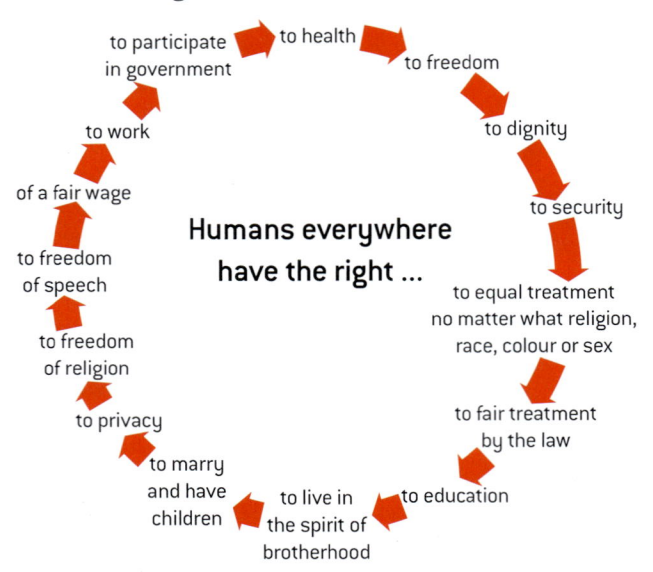

Humans everywhere have the right ...
- to participate in government
- to health
- to freedom
- to dignity
- to security
- to equal treatment no matter what religion, race, colour or sex
- to fair treatment by the law
- to education
- to live in the spirit of brotherhood
- to marry and have children
- to privacy
- to freedom of religion
- to freedom of speech
- of a fair wage
- to work

*Everyone, everywhere has these rights.*

## United Nations Universal Declaration of Human Rights

In 1948, the United Nations adopted the Universal Declaration of Human Rights and urged all 192 member nations to protect 30 basic human rights.

For example:
- *Civil and Political Rights* (Articles 2–21), including the right to:
  – choose how a country is run
  – be protected from wrongful arrest
  – have a fair trial
  – own property
  – work
  – have freedom of thought, religion and expression
  – hold meetings
  – join groups
  – have freedom from slavery and torture.
- *Economic, Social and Cultural Rights* (Articles 22–28), including the right to achieve a minimum standard of living by having food, clothing, medical care, welfare, education and housing, and to enjoy the culture of one's people.

Even though everyone deserves these rights, they are not applied in every country — one billion people live on a US$1 a day, many work as slaves, and some are killed because of their religious beliefs.

## Human rights agreements

To clarify the complex Universal Declaration of Human Rights agreement, a number of conventions were developed. These conventions include the Status of Refugees (1954); Civil and Political Rights (1966); Economic, Social and Cultural Rights (1966); Elimination of All Forms of Racial Discrimination (1969); Elimination of All Forms of Discrimination against Women (1981); Against Torture and Other

---

- Gay student bullied
- War on terror eroded human rights in the name of national security.
- Middle Eastern women's rights ignored
- Five HIV-positive children barred from school in Pampady, India.
- 300 000 CHILDREN ARE CHILD SOLDIERS.
- 74 countries have HIV-related travel restrictions.
- Killing of Buddhist priests in Tibet
- 93 million children of primary-school age are out of school
- 211 million children aged 5 to 14 yrs forced to work
- Girls forced to marry at 6 years
- 2.5 million children die from diarrhoea linked to unclean water each year.
- 17-year life expectancy gap between Indigenous and non-Indigenous Australians
- 27 MILLION SLAVES AROUND THE WORLD
- 777 million hungry people live in developing countries

*Human rights are not universally accepted.*

Cruel, Inhuman or Degrading Treatment or Punishment (1984); Rights of the Child (1990); and Protection of the Rights of all Migrant Workers and Members of their Families (2003).

Countries can either sign and/or ratify agreements. A country signs an agreement to declare it will abide by it, and ratifies an agreement by making it law. The Australian government has signed all international human rights agreements/conventions; it has ratified all except the Rights of all Migrant Workers and Members of their Families (2003). Australia signed and ratified the 1988 treaty creating the world's first independent International Criminal Court (ICC) to try crimes such as **genocide**. Australia also signed the United Nations Millennium Development Goals (2000–2015), which aims to improve social and economic equality.

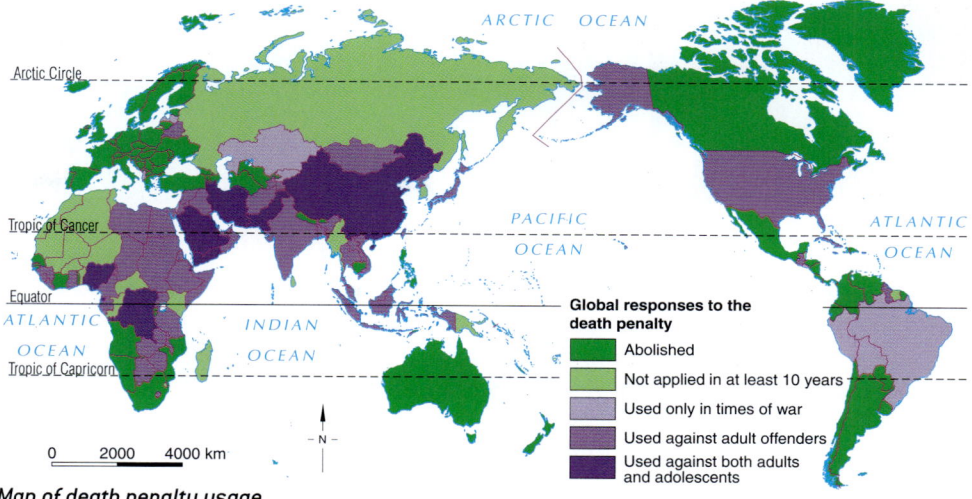

*Map of death penalty usage*

Global responses to the death penalty
- Abolished
- Not applied in at least 10 years
- Used only in times of war
- Used against adult offenders
- Used against both adults and adolescents

## Implementation and monitoring

The United Nations established bodies such as the Human Rights Council (HRC) and the Office of the High Commissioner for Human Rights (OHCHR) to support the implementation of the Universal Declaration of Human Rights. Established in 2006, the Universal Periodic Review (UPR) assesses human rights in all member states once every four years. In Australia, the Human Rights Commission promotes and protects human rights by reviewing legislation, conducting inquiries and investigating complaints.

## The right to life

The most fundamental right is the 'right to life'; yet, in 2007, there were 1252 people officially executed in 24 countries and 3347 people sentenced to death in 51 countries. Saudi Arabia has the highest number of executions per capita. Many countries execute people for crimes not commonly considered criminal in Australia — Ja'Far Kiani was stoned to death for adultery in Iran and Mustafa Ibrahim was beheaded for sorcery in Saudi Arabia. When the Universal Declaration of Human Rights was adopted in 1948, eight countries had abolished the death penalty in law or practice. Sixty years later, as of December 2008, the number stands at 137. The death penalty was abolished in Australia in 1973.

### GEOTERMS

**genocide:** planned killing of a whole national or racial group

**human rights:** basic rights and freedoms to which all humans are entitled

### ACTIVITIES

#### UNDERSTANDING

1. Explain the Universal Declaration of Human Rights.
2. Identify human rights agreements that Australia has ratified.
3. Describe the importance of the right to life.
4. Discuss how human rights are implemented and monitored.

#### THINKING AND APPLYING

5. Collect a media file of ten recent human rights abuses. Include date and source. Determine whether each article is factual or biased.

#### USING YOUR SKILLS

6. Refer to the diagram opposite showing human rights. Describe what is meant by human rights. Discuss whether you do or do not have these rights.
7. Refer to the collage of newspaper headlines. In pairs, choose two headlines and answer the following key geographical questions: What is the issue? Where is it happening? How does it affect people? How should their rights be protected? What are the responsibilities of governments? What responsibilities do you have to yourself and others? Present your thoughts as a poster, PowerPoint or on an interactive whiteboard.
8. Refer to the map and list two countries that do not have the death penalty. Which countries allow the execution of minors? Compare the responses of the following countries to the death penalty: Australia, the United States, China, Papua New Guinea, Indonesia, Saudi Arabia and Argentina.

CHAPTER 13 | Challenges: human rights and reconciliation

# 13.2 Abuse of human rights: global community

Amnesty International, a worldwide movement of 2.2 million people in 151 countries, publishes a report each year on human rights abuses around the world. The 2008 report noted torture occurred in 81 countries and unfair trials were held in 54 countries. These abuses occurred despite the Declaration of Human Rights Article 5, stating *'torture is forbidden at all times'*, and Article 10 stating *'everyone has the right to a fair trial'*. Instead of being tortured or killed, people are taken hostage or simply 'disappear'. About 30 years ago, 30 000 people disappeared in Argentina. In 2008, hundreds of Tamils disappeared in Sri Lanka as did thousands of Falun Gong followers in China.

Human rights organisations focus on countries like Myanmar and Zimbabwe, but less well known abuses occur in El Salvador and Saudi Arabia.

Amnesty International works to reduce human rights abuses by placing pressure on governments, political groups and companies via demonstrations, letter-writing campaigns, awareness-raising concerts and email petitions. It supports human rights groups such as the Buddhist monks in Myanmar, lawyers in Pakistan and women activists in Iran. Amnesty International challenges China to allow free speech and Australia to close immigration detention centres and reduce the gap between Indigenous and non-Indigenous people.

Another Amnesty International campaign demanded the closure of the US detention centre at Guantanamo Bay, where people were illegally detained, tortured and denied the right to a fair trial.

### 1. Iran
*Challenge:* Amnesty International says Iran is second only to China in the number of executions recorded annually, including those of children. After elections in June 2009, the right of free expression by dissenters was brutally squashed. Demonstrators were arrested and killed. The regime attempted to shut down communications but many examples of abuse were transmitted via the internet all around the world.
*Strategy:* The Iran Human Rights Documentation Center, based in the US, is documenting the abuses. Its goal is to encourage informed dialogue among scholars and the general public both in Iran and abroad.

### 2. Zimbabwe
*Challenge:* Human rights defenders and political dissidents were attacked, tortured and thrown into prison without a fair trial. ZANU-PF members set up torture camps for people suspected of voting against President Mugabe in the 2008 election.
*Strategy:* Amnesty International calls on governments to use their influence to bring an end to the violations. The UN imposed sanctions on anti-human rights activists by freezing their assets.

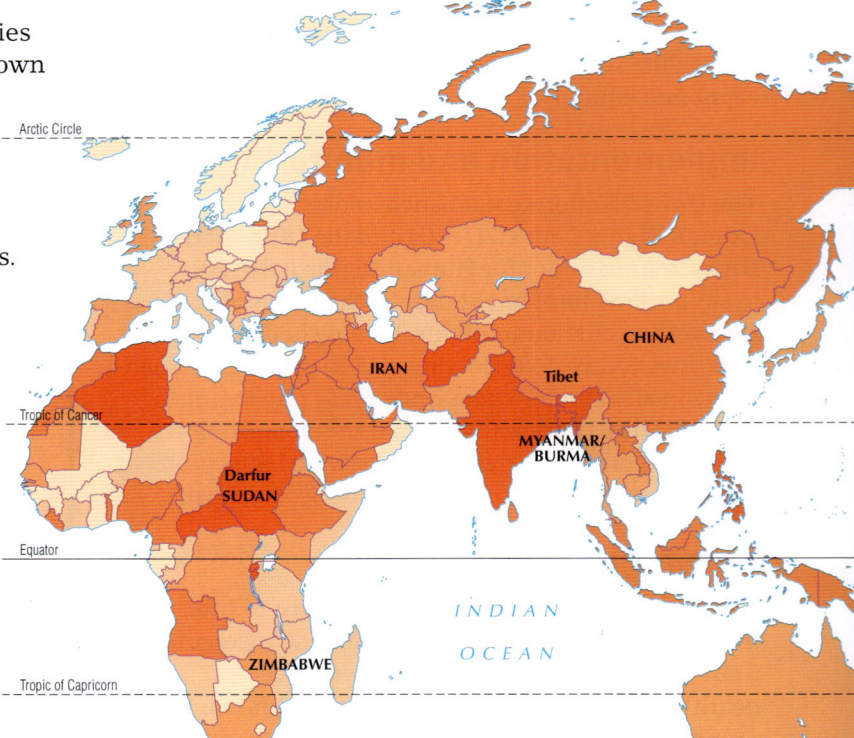

*Global overview of human rights abuses: challenges and strategies*

### 3. Tibet
*Challenge:* In 1951, the Chinese government occupied Tibet. In 1959 after a failed uprising, the Dalai Lama fled to India. In 1991 he alleged that Chinese settlers in Tibet were creating Chinese apartheid, which the Chinese call segregation and assimilation. He believes the Chinese government denies Tibetans equal social and economic status and their human rights are violated by discrimination.
*Strategy:* Pressure on China from individuals, groups and governments. For example global protests during the 2008 Beijing Olympic Games.

### 4. El Salvador
*Challenge:* Sixteen years after the end of El Salvador's civil war, the fate of hundreds of children who disappeared during the conflict remains unknown.
*Strategy:* The government established a national commission on disappearing children, a DNA database and a web database. Three years after the ruling, very few of these obligations have been fulfilled.

### 5. Darfur, Sudan
*Challenge:* Of the four million people affected by conflict in Darfur, 1.8 million are children.
*Strategy:* The United Nations African Union deployed a peacekeeping force to Darfur. Unfortunately, little has changed for the children. The Sudanese government, instead of disarming the militias, continues to arm them.

### 7. China
*Challenge:* Human rights issues include the Tiananmen Square protests of 1989, capital punishment, one-child policy, policies in Tibet and Sudan, and restrictions on Chinese journalists and internet users.
*Strategy:* As the 2008 Olympic flame travelled around the world, strategy included global protests (sometimes violent) and media coverage over China's human rights abuses.

**Forms of human rights abuse:**
* torture or ill-treatment by security forces, police and other authorities
* detention without charge or trial
* people sentenced to death
* human rights violations such as killing of civilians, torture and hostage-taking by armed opposition groups.

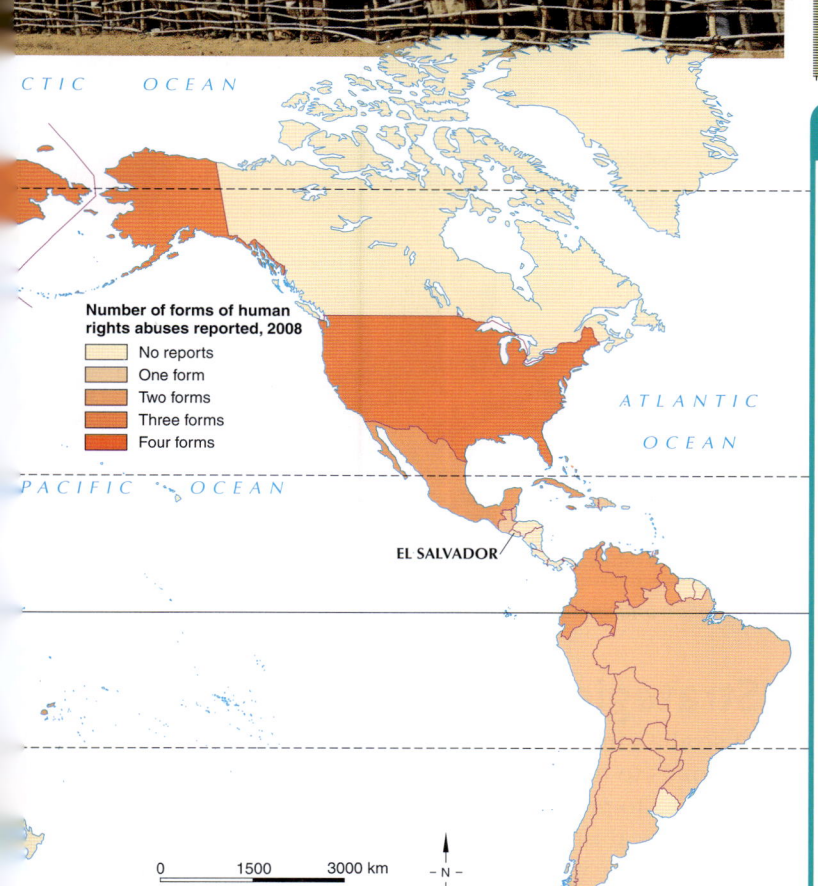

**Number of forms of human rights abuses reported, 2008**
- No reports
- One form
- Two forms
- Three forms
- Four forms

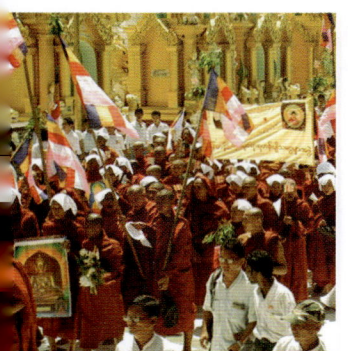

### 6. Myanmar/Burma
*Challenge:* Monks protested over the repression and impoverishment of their people and in return were brutally attacked by the military junta.
*Strategy:* International protests to release Aung San Suu Kyi and other prisoners of conscience and bring about change.

## ACTIVITIES

### UNDERSTANDING
1. List ten human rights you enjoy in Australia.
2. Discuss, as a class, why human rights organisations such as Amnesty International and Human Rights Watch play an important role in today's world.

### THINKING AND APPLYING
3. In groups, brainstorm what is meant by the abuse of human rights. Place your definitions on a large poster and display in the classroom. Summarise into a class definition.
4. In pairs, debate whether peaceful demonstrations and symbolic acts (such as not buying goods from a country that practices human rights abuses) are significant ways of highlighting the violation of human rights. Present your thoughts as an oral report.
5. Draft a letter to the United Nations Office of High Commissioner for Human Rights (OHCHR) expressing your feelings on a human rights abuse issue and your ideas for future action.

### USING YOUR SKILLS
6. Refer to the world map and information in the text and list examples of human rights abuses.
7. Refer to the map and an atlas.
   a. Identify the four forms of human rights abuses on the world map.
   b. Name five countries that received the 'worst report card' for these human rights offences.
   c. What score did Australia receive? Explain the human rights abuses you think occurred in Australia.

**CHAPTER 13** | Challenges: human rights and reconciliation

# 13.3 Human rights for Australians

Human rights are an important part of our lives; yet in Australia, we often take them for granted. Consider how often you eat good food, drink clean water, and speak or write what you think. All these everyday activities depend on the protection of our human rights. The rights of individuals in Australia are promoted and protected by instruments including the Australian Constitution, an independent judiciary, democratically elected governments, a free and questioning media, a strong civil society, non-government organisations such as Amnesty International, and common and statute laws. The laws protecting our rights include the *Racial Discrimination Act 1975*, the *Human Rights and Equal Opportunity Act 1986*, the *Workplace Relations Act 1996*, the *Public Service Act 1999* and the *Equal Employment Opportunity Act 1987*.

## Responses

Individuals, groups and governments respond to human rights abuses in Australia. The non-government organisation Human Rights Council of Australia (HRC) protects human rights in Australia and the Asia–Pacific region and monitors governments' compliance with international human rights agreements. The Australian Human Rights and Equal Opportunity Commission (HREOC) investigates infringements such as discrimination on the grounds of race, colour, ethnic origin, sex, marital status, pregnancy or disability; racial vilification; and sexual harassment. The government recently suggested the addition of 'sexuality' and/or 'gender identity' to anti-discrimination legislation.

## Future challenges and strategies: charter of rights

Australia has a good — but not perfect — human rights record; the mandatory detention of asylum seekers and their children, and the 17-year life expectancy gap between Indigenous and non-Indigenous Australians are two examples of areas we can improve. An outcome of Australia's 2020 Summit was a push to improve the rights of Indigenous and disabled people, and to establish a federal charter of rights to incorporate international agreements into Australian law. The case for a charter has accelerated with the creation of charters of rights in the Australian Capital Territory and Victoria. Some argue that a charter of rights does not guarantee against human rights abuses. For example, the USSR's 1977 Bill of Rights guaranteed freedom of expression and worship and the preservation of the cultures of ethnic minorities. All these rights were later abused.

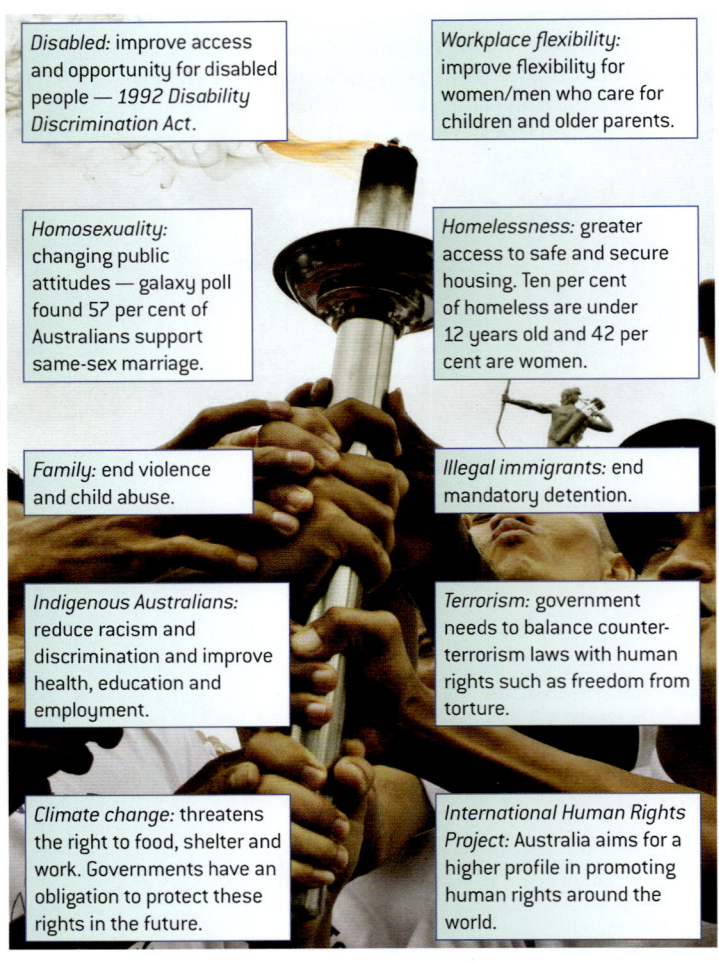

*Disabled:* improve access and opportunity for disabled people — 1992 Disability Discrimination Act.

*Workplace flexibility:* improve flexibility for women/men who care for children and older parents.

*Homosexuality:* changing public attitudes — galaxy poll found 57 per cent of Australians support same-sex marriage.

*Homelessness:* greater access to safe and secure housing. Ten per cent of homeless are under 12 years old and 42 per cent are women.

*Family:* end violence and child abuse.

*Illegal immigrants:* end mandatory detention.

*Indigenous Australians:* reduce racism and discrimination and improve health, education and employment.

*Terrorism:* government needs to balance counter-terrorism laws with human rights such as freedom from torture.

*Climate change:* threatens the right to food, shelter and work. Governments have an obligation to protect these rights in the future.

*International Human Rights Project:* Australia aims for a higher profile in promoting human rights around the world.

Australia's anticipated future human rights strategies
Source: The Epoch Times.

## Strategies for the region

Australia's international aid program, AusAID, responds to human rights abuses by undertaking activities to protect economic, social, cultural, civil and political rights, especially in the Asia–Pacific region. These include:

- *Asia Pacific Forum of National Human Rights Institution:* AusAID helped establish human rights institutions in Korea, Malaysia and Thailand.
- *Human Rights Small Grants Scheme (HRSG):* AusAID provided training in Indonesia on human rights abuses and supported victims of child trafficking in Thailand.
- *Australia–China Human Rights Technical Cooperation Program:* AusAID promoted women's, children's and minority rights.

## Australia's response to torture and the war on terror

The so-called 'war on terror' led to the torture of terrorists and other human rights abuses, as depicted by the 'ladder of torture' diagram below. Australia's humanitarian program contributed to improved human rights for people escaping death and torture in their country of origin. Australia ratified the Convention against Torture and Other Cruel, Inhuman or Degrading Treatment or Punishment (CAT) in 1989; torture is now a criminal offence under Australian law. To support human rights, Australia introduced safeguards to govern how the Australian Security Intelligence Organisation (ASIO) questioned people suspected of terrorism.

**Step 6:** Person plants bomb and admits it. *Response:* Torture them to find out details and save lives.
**Step 5:** Person suspected of planting a bomb. *Response:* Torture to find if it is true.
**Step 4:** Person is friendly with someone suspected of planting a bomb. *Response:* Torture them to discover where the suspect is.
**Step 3:** Person may be thinking of planting a bomb. *Response:* Torture them to discover if it is true.
**Step 2:** Person goes to meeting attended by people who criticise government. *Response:* Torture person to find out whether acts of terrorism were planned.
**Step 1:** Person refuses to tell police whether they attended certain meetings: *Response:* Torture person just in case they are hiding something dangerous.

*The torture steps (adapted from Amnesty International)*

### A better life for Aluong

Aluong loves living in Australia. She now has a life which is very different to the war and persecution which killed her parents and forced her to flee to a refugee camp.

After starting a new life in Australia, she's found that a relaxing walk in the park is her favourite thing about Australia, simply because she can do it without fear . . .

'Following the death of my parents, I left Sudan and went to the Kakuma refugee camp in Kenya where I lived for two years before coming to Australia.

'I knew about Australia, I'd heard it was a wonderful country and I wanted to come and start a new life here,' she said.

That new life began when she arrived in Australia in November 2003 . . .

Since her arrival in 2003, Aluong has started going to school, something she didn't get to do in Sudan.

'I'm a student and I'm learning maths, science and English,' Aluong said.

'I want to learn English so I can speak it perfectly, and then when I'm finished at school I can get a job. I don't really mind what I do because I'll be happy just to be working and living in Australia.

'In the meantime, I'm happy to be able to just walk through a park without having to fear for my life,' she said.

*Like Aluong, these three young Sudanese refugees are happy to have the chance to go to school.*

## ACTIVITIES

### UNDERSTANDING

1. Explain how rights are protected in Australia.
2. Describe the purpose of the Human Rights and Equal Opportunity Commission (HREOC).
3. Discuss how Australia's aid program (AusAID) responds to human rights in developing countries.

### THINKING AND APPLYING

4. Australia is the only Western democracy without a Human Rights Act or similar legislation. Argue *for* and *against* a bill or charter of rights for Australia.
5. Mandatory detention of refugees around the world tends to be acceptable for a short period in order to conduct security, identity and health checks. What type of security checks should be made? If a refugee is a suspected terrorist, suggest strategies that should be used.
6. Discuss Australia's future human rights challenges. Imagine you were the Prime Minister of Australia. Suggest strategies you would adopt to address these challenges.
7. In groups, discuss your views on each step on the ladder of torture. At each step, discuss whether you agree or disagree if torture should be used. Give reasons for your decision. Present your thoughts to the class as an oral report.
8. Refer to Aluong's story. Compare the responses of Sudan and Australia to human rights.

# 13.4 Human rights and refugees: Australia responds

Australia has a strong tradition of resettling **refugees** who have fled their homeland to escape torture and conflict. Since the end of World War II, over 675 000 refugees and people in humanitarian need have resettled in Australia. In 2008, Australia accepted 13 000 of the world's 11.4 million refugees.

## Refugees' right to asylum

Article 1 of the Convention Relating to the Status of Refugees (1951) defines a refugee as a person who is forced to flee their homeland because of a well-founded fear of being persecuted due to race, religion, nationality, membership of a social group, or political belief. Article 14 of the UN Declaration of Human Rights states that anyone who flees their home because of human rights abuses has the right to seek safety, or asylum, in another country.

## Responding to the challenge

The Department of Immigration and Citizenship's Humanitarian Program responds to refugees seeking asylum in Australia via two programs:
- *Offshore resettlement:* allows legal arrivals with a permanent protection **visa** to stay in Australia
- *Onshore protection:* allows people already in Australia to seek protection under the Convention Relating to the Status of Refugees. These people may have overstayed their visa or entered Australia without authorisation.

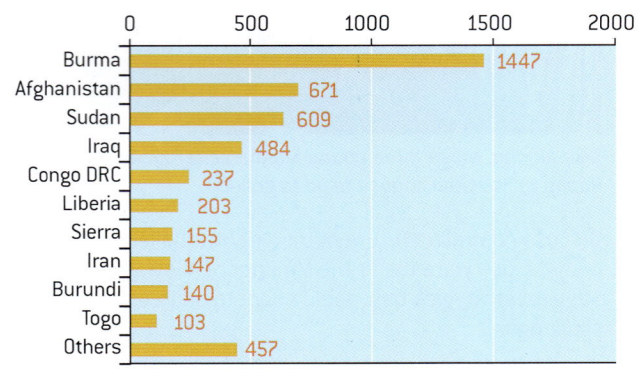

| Country | Visa grants |
|---|---|
| Burma | 1447 |
| Afghanistan | 671 |
| Sudan | 609 |
| Iraq | 484 |
| Congo DRC | 237 |
| Liberia | 203 |
| Sierra | 155 |
| Iran | 147 |
| Burundi | 140 |
| Togo | 103 |
| Others | 457 |

*Australia's offshore visa grants by top ten countries of birth, 2007–08 Humanitarian Program*

In Australia, asylum seekers are placed in detention centres where they undergo security, identity and health checks, and their claims for asylum or refugee status are checked. In 2001, the *Tampa*, a Norwegian vessel, rescued 433 refugees in a sinking boat near Christmas Island. New Zealand and Nauru offered to take them in. After the *Tampa* incident, Australian laws excised certain Australian territories such as the Christmas and Cocos Islands. An unauthorised person who arrived in an excised territory would be unable to acquire an Australian visa. This was referred to as the 'Pacific Solution' and led to global criticism. The Pacific Solution was disbanded in 2008.

## Global comparisons

Though nations accept refugees on a temporary basis during the early phase of a crisis, fewer than 20 nations take part in UNHCR resettlement programs by accepting quotas of refugees on an annual basis, such as Australia's quota of 13 000 and New Zealand's 750. Canada has no mandatory detention system and asylum seekers have the right to work and access health and education services while their applications are processed. In Sweden, refugees live freely in the wider community. During the application process for permanent residence, about 70 per cent of asylum seekers in Sweden stay with family and friends, and the remainder stay in government-funded housing. Government allowances are made to those who have no other support.

**Responses — individuals, groups and governments**

| Individuals and groups | Australian government |
|---|---|
| • Amnesty International Australia<br>• Australian Council for International Development<br>• AUSTCARE<br>• Children out of Detention<br>• Rural Australians for Refugees<br>• We are All Boat People — aims to create a change in government policies and legislation | • Signed and ratified international agreements<br>• Human Rights and Equal Opportunity Commission<br>• Department of Immigration and Citizenship — Humanitarian Program<br>• AusAID human rights programs<br>• *Migration Act 1958* and amendments<br>• Border control, Customs and Australian Defence Force<br>• Detention centres<br>• Australian Cultural Orientation Program<br>• Local councils — resettlement programs |

In 2001, Australia established the Woomera Housing Trial based on the Swedish Group Home

System. Women and children were transferred to an alternative detention arrangement. At present, there is growing pressure for the Australian government to allow asylum seekers to live in community accommodation or to be issued with a bridging visa.

### A story of strength, courage and spirit

When she was just seven years old, Acee and her family fled their native war-torn country of Liberia in search of a safer place to live.

Her new life in Ivory Coast was disrupted in 2002 when soldiers came into 19-year-old Acee's school and began shooting. Fearing for her life, she ran from the school and fled to Guinea, carrying her six-month-old daughter Deybeh with her and leaving behind her parents and five sisters.

'It was very hard to separate from each other but I just had to run for my life,' Acee said. 'I was very afraid. They killed many people.'

She hasn't seen her family since …

It wasn't until she arrived in Australia that Acee was able to sleep soundly with four walls around her. She was resettled here in October 2005 as a refugee under the Humanitarian Program …

Acee is still adjusting to life in Australia and finds the Australian way of speaking particularly difficult to understand. She is learning English though, and wants to study beauty care and eventually become a beautician.

She is happy to be in Australia and grateful for the opportunities that she and her daughter will have in the future.

## Active citizenship

Individuals, groups and governments support refugees seeking asylum in Australia. A number of strategies have been suggested and implemented to enable refugees to maintain their culture, integrate with Australian society and receive just and compassionate treatment consistent with human rights laws.

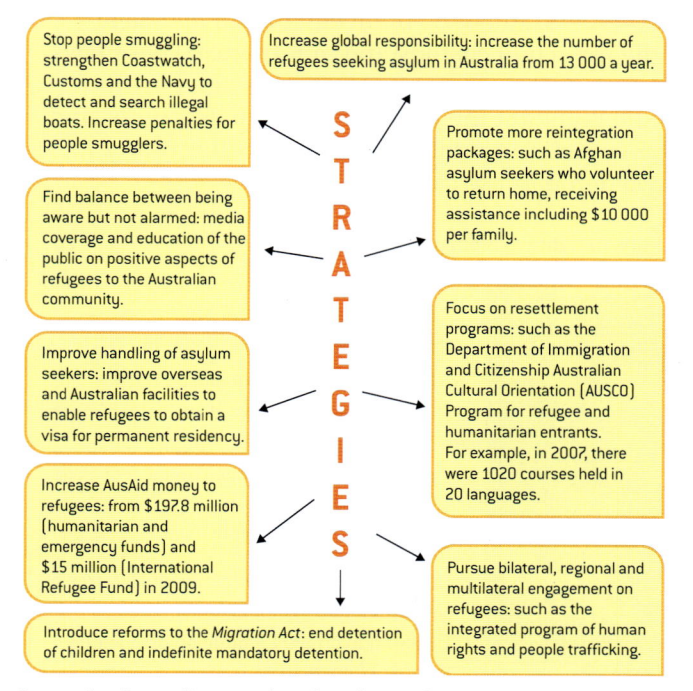

**Strategies:**

- Stop people smuggling: strengthen Coastwatch, Customs and the Navy to detect and search illegal boats. Increase penalties for people smugglers.
- Find balance between being aware but not alarmed: media coverage and education of the public on positive aspects of refugees to the Australian community.
- Improve handling of asylum seekers: improve overseas and Australian facilities to enable refugees to obtain a visa for permanent residency.
- Increase AusAid money to refugees: from $197.8 million (humanitarian and emergency funds) and $15 million (International Refugee Fund) in 2009.
- Introduce reforms to the *Migration Act*: end detention of children and indefinite mandatory detention.
- Increase global responsibility: increase the number of refugees seeking asylum in Australia from 13 000 a year.
- Promote more reintegration packages: such as Afghan asylum seekers who volunteer to return home, receiving assistance including $10 000 per family.
- Focus on resettlement programs: such as the Department of Immigration and Citizenship Australian Cultural Orientation (AUSCO) Program for refugee and humanitarian entrants. For example, in 2007, there were 1020 courses held in 20 languages.
- Pursue bilateral, regional and multilateral engagement on refugees: such as the integrated program of human rights and people trafficking.

*Strategies Australia can adopt for a better future*

## ACTIVITIES

### UNDERSTANDING

1. Define the term *refugee*. How does a refugee differ from a migrant?
2. List two components of Australia's Humanitarian Program.
3. Explain why the *Tampa* incident and the Pacific Solution was criticised by the global community.
4. Compare treatment of asylum seekers in Sweden and Australia.

### THINKING AND APPLYING

5. Many children have been detained for three years in immigration detention centres in Australia. Describe how their lives differ from yours. Develop a way of providing more humane treatment for children, which protects their human rights.
6. *Citizenship*: In groups develop a plan to promote Refugee Week in your school (speaker, cultural event, raise money for a refugee organisation). Present your plan to the class.

### USING YOUR SKILLS

7. Refer to the graph showing offshore visa grants. Which four countries had the largest number of grants? Explain why these people were leaving their country.
8. Refer to the table of responses. Describe how individuals, groups and governments in Australia have responded to refugees.
9. Examine the strategies for a better future. If you were Prime Minister of Australia, suggest strategies you would adopt for a better future for refugees living in Australia. Present your findings as an oral report.

### GEOTERMS

**refugee:** person who is forced to flee their homeland because of a well-founded fear of being persecuted due to race, religion, nationality, membership of a particular social group, or political beliefs

# 13.5 Gender: women's rights

**Gender equality** means women and men have equal opportunities to realise their potential, to contribute to their country's development and to benefit from their participation in society. Laws in Iran and Saudi Arabia treat women as legal minors under the guardianship of male family members, and deny them equality in marriage, divorce, child custody and inheritance. These laws ignore international human rights agreements, and highlight the need for individuals, groups and governments to take action for a better future for women in these countries.

**Human rights agreements**

| Articles from the Universal Declaration of Human Rights, 1948 | 2: Rights and freedoms to all people — cannot be taken away because of your sex |
| --- | --- |
| | 3: Right to life, liberty and security |
| | 7: Right to be treated equally by the law |
| | 17: Right to own goods, land and other property |
| | 21: Right to take part in the government of your country and to have equal access to services in your country |
| | 26: Right to an education |
| United Nations agreements | • Convention on the Elimination of All forms of Discrimination against Women 1979 |
| | • Declaration on the Elimination of Violence against Women 1993 |
| | • Millennium Development Goals (2000) |

## Violence against women: responses

A life free from violence is a basic human right, yet women were raped during armed conflict in Rwanda in 2004, are still burned for their dowry in India, and six year olds are still forced to marry in Ethiopia.

In 2008, the UN Secretary-General, Ban Ki-moon, launched a campaign to end violence against women by 2015. He said, 'At least one out of every three women is likely to be beaten, coerced into sex or otherwise abused in her lifetime'. Violence against women exists in all countries and across all levels of education, income, race and culture. The crimes go unpunished, the perpetrators are freed and few women seek justice, either because of fear or lack of money.

In 2008, 39.9 per cent of Australian women experienced at least one incident of physical or sexual violence. The non-government organisation Amnesty International responded with its 'Stop Violence against Women' campaign and its National Plan of Action which works with 100 organisations to end violence against indigenous, disabled and lesbian women. The White Ribbon Foundation of Australia aims to eliminate violence against women by promoting changes in culture.

## Equal rights: responses

A global poll found that most people thought women should have equal rights, and that governments and the United Nations should be the main organisations responsible for preventing discrimination. The 1979 United Nations Convention on the Elimination of All Forms of Discrimination against Women (CEDAW) established national action programs to end discrimination. The Australian government's 1984 Sex Discrimination Act promotes gender equality and eliminates discrimination on the basis of sex. The Act is supported by Australia's Human Rights and Equal Opportunities Commission (HREOC). At the international level, the United Nations Development Fund for Women (UNIFEM) and International Women's Day foster women's empowerment and gender equality.

A 2008 poll across all countries found 84 per cent of men and 88 per cent of women said equality is important.

*United Nations Development Fund for Women (UNIFEM) Goodwill Ambassador, Nicole Kidman*

# Future strategies

Despite improvements in the status of women, seventy per cent of the world's poorest people are female. The 2015 United Nations Millennium Development Goals aim to reduce female poverty (Goal 1), provide universal primary education (Goal 2), promote gender equality and empower women (Goal 3) and improve maternal health (Goal 5). AusAID and Women in Development (WID) responded to the challenge by integrating gender equality into development programs.

Despite advancements in women's rights in Australia, such as the right to vote (1902), women still experience inequality in employment, leadership and political representation. The 2008 Australian Plan of Action Towards Gender Equality aims to:
- increase the number of women in leadership positions
- balance work and family
- reduce the incidence of sexual harassment and the gender gap in retirement savings
- strengthen the 1984 Sex Discrimination Act
- promote progress in health and education.

In 2008, after a reduction of the gender gap in health and education, the **global gender gap** ranked Australia 21 out of 130 countries. Australia aims to improve political empowerment and economic participation of women, as 25 per cent of women and 21 per cent of men stated that women are not treated equally in the Australian workplace.

**Global gender gap 2008 — some international comparisons**

| Country | Rank (130 countries) |
| --- | --- |
| Norway | 1 |
| Finland | 2 |
| Sweden | 3 |
| New Zealand | 5 |
| Philippines | 6 |
| Sri Lanka | 12 |
| Lesotho | 16 |
| Australia | 21 |
| United States | 27 |
| Iran | 116 |
| Saudi Arabia | 128 |

Note: Australia ranked 15 (2006), 17 (2007) and 21 in 2008.
Global Gender Gap 2008 Rating — the lower the number (1) the greater the equality between men and women

### GEOfacts

A survey conducted in various countries asked 'How important is equality between men and women?' The following percentages of people in these countries agreed it was either very or somewhat important:

| | | | |
| --- | --- | --- | --- |
| Iran | 78% | Nigeria | 76% |
| Mexico | 98% | South Korea | 86% |

Zonta is an international non-government organisation of women who work to improve the legal, political, economic and professional status of women, locally and globally. Members of Zonta Northern Beaches, in Sydney, made 8000 birthing kits that were shipped to Vietnam, Madagascar and Papua New Guinea in 2007. Each year members hold an International Women's Day breakfast, participate in the UNIFEM walk and provide funds for the Hamlin Fistula Hospital in Ethiopia. They also support the community by providing student support grants and resources to a women's refuge centre. They distribute white ribbons (promoting the elimination of violence against women) and pink ribbons (promoting breast cancer research).

## ACTIVITIES

### UNDERSTANDING

1. Explain why violence against women is an abuse of their human rights.
2. Describe how individuals, groups and governments have responded to the abuse of women's rights.
3. Compare the response of Australia and other nations to women's human rights.
4. Suggest strategies Australia can adopt to improve the rights of women.

### THINKING AND APPLYING

5. Create a series of questions and answers about the need for, and ways of, overcoming gender inequality.
6. Use the **MDG** weblink in your eBookPLUS to research how countries are progressing or not progressing toward gender equity by 2015. Describe the strategies used to address gender inequality in Australia and other nations.
7. Imagine you are replacing Nicole Kidman as the goodwill ambassador for UNIFEM. Suggest strategies you would adopt to promote gender equality and to empower women.

### USING YOUR SKILLS

8. Refer to the global gender gap table. What region in the world had the highest gender equality ranking? What was the rank of developing countries such as the Philippines and Lesotho? Suggest strategies to improve Australia's global ranking.

# 13.6 Freedom of expression

Freedom of speech is a right in the Universal Declaration of Human Rights and the International Covenant on Civil and Political Rights. It allows everyone, everywhere, to speak freely without censorship or limitation. Freedom of expression includes freedom of speech and freedom of information, meaning people are free to receive and send information. In practice, freedom of expression is limited, as what you say or write may offend or harm a person ('hate' messages) and could lead to social disapproval or even legal action. People are still tortured and killed for their opinions, despite the existence of human rights agreements, as occurred during the leadership of Saddam Hussein in Iraq and Robert Mugabe in Zimbabwe.

*Iraqi families in Canberra, protesting over the conditions of their temporary protection visas*

**Facts and figures — Amnesty International Report 2008**

Prisoner of conscience refers to those who have been imprisoned and/or persecuted for non-violent expression of their beliefs (e.g. political, religious, environment)

| Promise — Universal Declaration of Human Rights | Reality 2008 |
|---|---|
| Article 18. Everyone has the right to freedom of thought, conscience and religion (Falun Gong practitioners were tortured and killed for their belief in China) | **45** countries with prisoners of conscience |
| Article 19. Everyone has the right to freedom of opinion and expression, and to seek, receive and impart information and ideas through any media and regardless of frontiers. | **77** countries restricted freedom of expression |

*Source:* Adapted from Amnesty International.

## Freedom of information: the internet

The internet has opened new possibilities for exercising freedom of information, especially via blogs and social network sites. According to Reporters without Borders, freedom of information is restricted by government censorship of the internet in countries such as Cuba, Myanmar and Vietnam. Barring total control of internet-connected computers, as occurs in North Korea, total censorship of the internet is near impossible. Saudi Arabia blocks pornographic sites; China blocks content relating to Tibetan independence; Iran blocks women's rights sites; and Uzbekistan prevents access to material critical of the government's human rights violations.

The black holes in the map opposite represent 15 countries that limit or prohibit their citizens' access to the internet as a way of censoring the free flow of information. Internet censorship is a strong indicator of press censorship.

Journalists have been thrown in prison for years for a single offending word or photograph. During the Russian and Chechnyan war, 20 journalists were killed. Reporters without Borders and UNESCO fight for freedom of expression and freedom of the press. People who defend human rights injustices such as journalists are protected by the 1998 United Nations Declaration on Human Rights Defenders.

## Strategy: active citizenship

Every person has rights — but with them come responsibilities.

- Governments have a responsibility to ratify the signed human rights agreements and implement basic rights within the country, such as access to clean water.
- Non-government organisations have a responsibility to ensure governments abide by their agreements, and to conduct public awareness campaigns to inform citizens of human rights abuses.

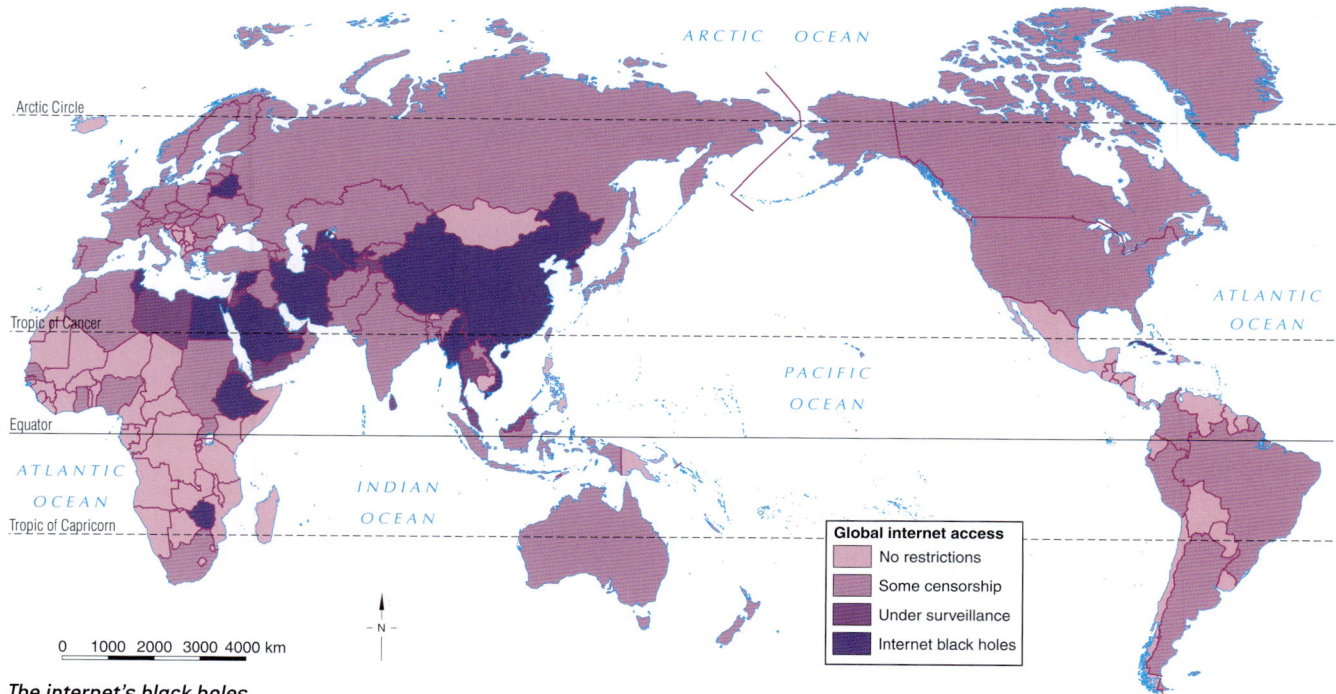

*The internet's black holes*

Legend — Global internet access:
- No restrictions
- Some censorship
- Under surveillance
- Internet black holes

- Individuals have a responsibility to express factual, current and unbiased opinions. Informed, responsible active citizens can express their views in the media or by contacting politicians by phone, email or letter.

Children's physical and intellectual immaturity makes them particularly vulnerable to human rights violations. It is the responsibility of adults, groups and governments to implement strategies for a better future for children.

## ACTIVITIES

### UNDERSTANDING

1. Explain the importance of freedom of expression.
2. Explain why legal systems and societies limit freedom of speech.
3. 'With rights come responsibilities.' What does this statement mean?
4. Discuss how Australia and other nations respond to the right to freedom of expression.

### THINKING AND APPLYING

5. Imagine you are a journalist in a country that suffers human rights abuses.
    a. Write a newspaper report on a country by referring to interviews, photographs, videos, blogs and the internet.
    b. Publishing this information may endanger the people who are suffering human rights abuses. Not publishing means the abuses will continue. Use the chart below to explore the issue of publishing from the perspective of the journalist.

| For publishing | Against publishing |
|---|---|
|  |  |

6. Investigate the Australian government's plan for mandatory internet censorship. The plan is to filter content in all homes, schools and public internet access points, so that no illegal content, such as child pornography, can be accessed. Do you consider censorship of the internet a limitation on freedom of expression?

### USING YOUR SKILLS

7. Refer to the Amnesty International Report 2008.
    a. How would you determine whether the statistics are factual and current?
    b. Distinguish between the promise and reality.
    c. Suggest strategies you would adopt to address these human rights abuses.
8. Refer to the photograph showing a protest over temporary protection visas. What are your opinions on the treatment of refugees in Australia? Explain the advantages of being able to express your opinions on controversial issues in Australia.
9. Refer to the map showing internet black holes. Name ten countries with internet black holes. List three countries with no internet censorship. Explain the reasons for censorship in Australia and three other countries.

**CHAPTER 13** | Challenges: human rights and reconciliation

# 13.7 Indigenous Australians: many nations, one people

Australia is sometimes called the 'lucky country', and perhaps with good reason — we have the third highest **human development index (HDI)** out of 177 countries. However, Aboriginal and Torres Strait Islander peoples, who comprise 2.5 per cent of the population, are not so lucky. If the HDI of **Indigenous people** was calculated separately from the non-Indigenous population, these original inhabitants would rank 104 out of 177 countries. This demonstrates that their basic rights have been ignored — rights such as a standard of living adequate for health and wellbeing, including food and medical care, as listed in Article 25 of the Universal Declaration of Human Rights.

## Not so lucky

Since Europeans arrived in Australia in 1788, many Indigenous people have lost their land and their traditional way of life. Some suffered human rights abuses and loss of culture, and children were taken from families and placed in institutions. For over 150 years, Indigenous people were not recognised as Australian citizens; they were finally given the right to vote in 1962 and included in the national census in 1967. Even today, some Australians treat Indigenous people as inferior citizens — perhaps worthy of sympathy, but not human rights.

As a result of discrimination in basic necessities over many years, Indigenous people have a life expectancy 17 years lower than non-Indigenous people. Many factors have been responsible for racial inequality in **life expectancy**:
- poverty — lack of suitable jobs and high unemployment
- poor education
- substance abuse (smoking, alcohol, illicit drugs)
- poor access to health services (doctors, hospitals) and clean water, and a lack of adequate housing in remote areas
- poor diets (processed food high in sugar, salts and fats).

### Life expectancy inequality, 2009

|  | Indigenous people | Non-Indigenous people |
|---|---|---|
| Life expectancy men | 59.4 years | 76.6 years |
| Life expectancy women | 64.8 years | 82.0 years |

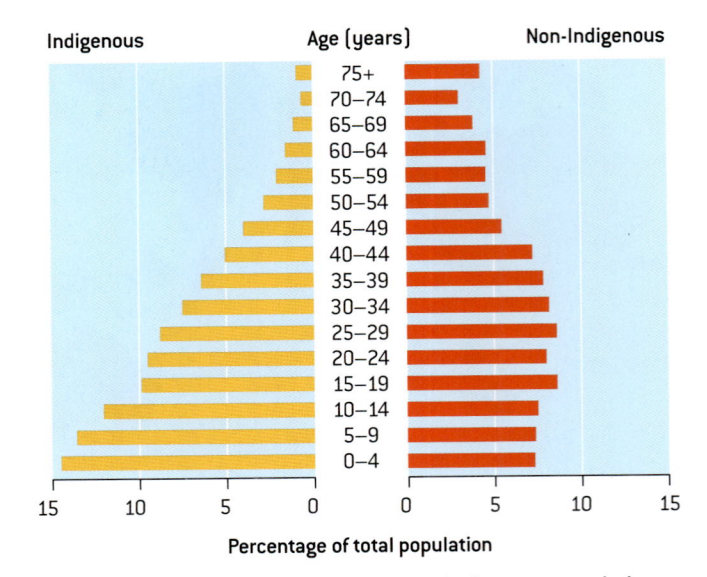

Population pyramid of Indigenous and non-Indigenous populations, 2006 — poor health linked to lower life expectancy
Source: www.healthinfonet.ecu.edu.au

Individuals, groups and governments have developed strategies aimed at creating equality for Aboriginal and Torres Strait Islander peoples.

### Education inequality in Australia, 2009

|  | Non-Indigenous (%) | Indigenous (%) |
|---|---|---|
| Achieved Year 3 benchmarks:<br>• reading<br>• writing<br>• numeracy | 90<br>93<br>93 | 75<br>77 (67% in 1999)<br>78 |
| Achieved Year 5 benchmarks:<br>• reading<br>• writing<br>• numeracy | 89<br>94<br>90 | 68 (59% in 1999)<br>76<br>66 |
| Achieved Year 7 benchmarks:<br>• reading<br>• writing<br>• numeracy | 89<br>91<br>84 | 65<br>72<br>52 |
| Completed Year 12 | 43 | 18 (9% in 1994) |
| Attended university | 23 | 5 |
| Bachelor degree | 16.9 | 3.7 |
| Non-school qualification (e.g. diploma, certificate, bachelor degree) | 40 | 18 |

## Human rights agreements

Every Indigenous person is entitled to human rights on equal terms with other Australians. The human rights of Indigenous people are set out in the Universal Declaration of Human Rights (1948), the International Labour Organisation Indigenous and Tribal Peoples Convention (No. 169, 1991), the Convention on the Elimination of All Forms of Racial Discrimination and numerous international agreements.

Indigenous people also are entitled to specific human rights linked to their identity. These are called indigenous people's human rights, and include:
- the right to a distinct status and culture (Dreamtime)
- the right to self-determination (right to administer their own communities)
- the right to land.

## Responses: citizenship

Since 1975, Australia has submitted reports to the United Nations Committee of Racial Discrimination on the implementation of Aboriginal rights. A recent report recommended that the Australian government:
- reopen discussions on the Native Title Act and find solutions acceptable to all
- ensure sufficient numbers of health professionals provide services to Indigenous peoples
- address harm inflicted by the forced removal of Indigenous children.

In 2008, the Australian government signed the Indigenous Health Equality Summit's Statement of Intent, demonstrating the government's commitment to working in partnership with the Indigenous community and in particular the Indigenous health sector to close the gap in Indigenous life expectancy within a generation.

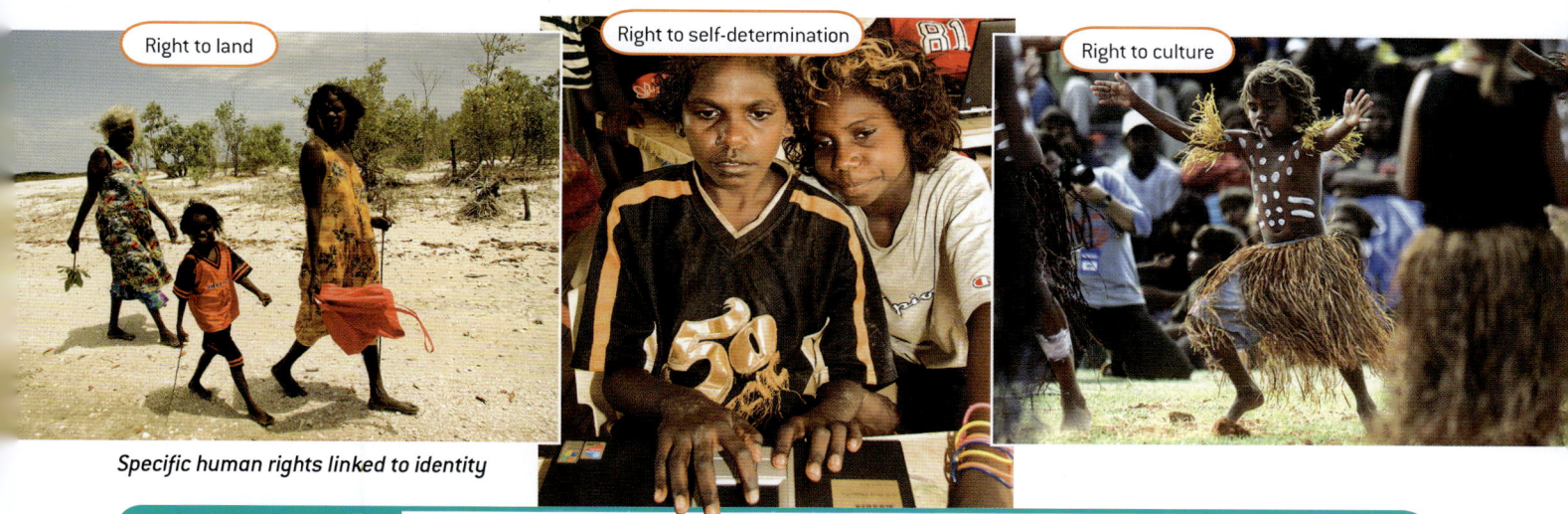

*Specific human rights linked to identity*

### ACTIVITIES

#### UNDERSTANDING
1. Identify the main agreements to protect 'all' Australians' human rights.
2. Describe specific human rights linked to Indigenous identity.
3. Discuss the government response to Indigenous inequality in Australia.

#### THINKING AND APPLYING
4. Write a report on Australia's poor human rights record concerning the Indigenous population. Suggest strategies for a better future. Include statistics and examples. Present the report on PowerPoint or interactive white board.

#### USING YOUR SKILLS
5. Refer to the table on life expectancy. Calculate the average life expectancy for Indigenous and non-Indigenous people. Determine the life expectancy gap. Explain the reasons for the gap.
6. Refer to the population pyramid. Calculate the difference in the percentage of Indigenous and non-Indigenous Australians 0–4 years and 75+ years. Account for the different pyramid shapes. Discuss strategies to improve the life expectancy of Indigenous people.
7. Refer to the table on Indigenous education inequality. Discuss how education is not accessible to all Australians. Explain how education is linked to improved health and employment.

### GEOTERMS

**life expectancy:** the average number of years a person can be expected to live; affected by nutrition, occupation, heredity and other factors

# 13.8 Strategies to 'close the gap'

It's hard to understand how Australia, one of the wealthiest nations in the world, has failed to close the health gap between Indigenous and non-Indigenous Australians, which has led to a 17-year life expectancy gap. These original inhabitants, who constitute 2.5 per cent of the Australian population, have the right to a healthy life — but in reality, they don't have access to equal, fair, acceptable and quality primary health care.

**Equality:** available to all indigenous people — rich and poor

**Fairness:** accessibility to all Indigenous people across Australia — urban to remote areas

**Acceptability:** respect medical ethics as well as the culture of the Indigenous person

**Quality:** qualified doctors/nurses and use of latest medication and technology

*Human right to health*

**Health problems with the highest disparity compared with the non-Indigenous population**

| Health problem | Indigenous compared with non-Indigenous people — times greater |
|---|---|
| Dementia | 26 |
| Circulatory system diseases | 2 to 10 |
| Tuberculosis | 14 |
| Diabetes | 3 to 4 |
| Chronic kidney disease | 2 to 3 |
| Respiratory disease | 5 |
| Communicable diseases | 70 |
| Vision problems | 2 |
| Oral health | 2 |
| Mental health | 2 |
| Infant mortality | 2 to 3 |
| Obesity | 1.2 |

## Strategy: close the gap

Australian governments are obliged to respect, protect and fulfil each citizen's right to health. Strategies for a longer, healthier life for the Indigenous population require individuals, groups and governments to implement strategies that focus on improved access to medicine, doctors and hospitals; housing with access to clean water; sewerage systems in remote communities; and education about the adverse effects of smoking, alcohol consumption, and food high in fat, sugar and salt.

The Close the Gap campaign aims to end health inequality. The campaign is supported by 40 Indigenous and non-Indigenous organisations including the National Aboriginal Community Controlled Health Organisation. It encourages individuals to become active citizens by urging politicians to tackle Indigenous health.

*Aboriginal singer/songwriter Kev Carmody signs on for the Close the Gap campaign.*

## Government's response

In 2008, the Australian government pledged to close the 17-year life expectancy gap between Indigenous and non-Indigenous Australians by 2030. Each year a report is presented to parliament on progress towards 'closing the gap', covering infant and child mortality, literacy and numeracy. At the Council of Australian Governments' (COAG) meeting in 2008, the federal government committed an additional $806 million over four years, with the states and territories also contributing $1.6 billion. Governments have agreed to improve the delivery of services to Indigenous people and fund health-care professionals to treat diabetes, renal failure and substance abuse in inaccessible indigenous areas. It also aims to reduce drug and alcohol use and encourage Indigenous people to become self-sufficient.

### SAMPLE STUDY

**Towards a healthier future for Indigenous people across Australia**

**Northern Territory: Utopia**

Utopia is a former cattle station located 200 kilometres north-east of Alice Springs. It has been an Aboriginal freehold since 1979 and is now home to 1000 people who live at 16 outstations spread across 3000 km². A doctor runs the primary health service with three nursing staff.

Poor education, poor health and petrol sniffing are absent in these outstations. The mortality rate is 40 per cent lower than the rate for Indigenous people in the Northern Territory and there are 40 per cent fewer hospital admissions. The health program has prevented obesity, diabetes and smoking, particularly in women.

If good housing is a precondition for good health, then the picture at Utopia is confusing. The standard of housing is no better at Utopia than in many other Aboriginal communities. However, at Utopia people have access to land for hunting, bush tucker and traditional medicine. This and the successful partnership between Indigenous people and their health service have improved the health in this community.

*Children play at an outstation in Utopia.*

## Strategy: understand culture

The Aboriginal Community Controlled Health Service (ACCHS) and the Aboriginal Medical Service (AMS) provide culturally appropriate primary health-care services operated by local Aboriginal communities. Many Indigenous patients do not seek medical assistance for fear they will never return home. The 2006 death of an elderly Indigenous man left at the Kalkaringi airstrip, 750 kilometres south-west of Darwin, reinforced this fear. The National Strategic Framework commits governments to invest in training Aboriginal health workers and establishing health-care facilities that are locally owned, culturally appropriate and adequately resourced. Strategies focus on working towards a healthier future for Indigenous people.

### ACTIVITIES

**UNDERSTANDING**

1. Explain why many Indigenous people have poor health.
2. Describe the aim of the Close the Gap campaign.
3. Explain why cultural understanding is essential for implementation of Indigenous health and education projects.

**THINKING AND APPLYING**

4. Refer to the campaign poster.
   a Describe its message.
   b Design your own poster to encourage active citizens to work towards a better future for Indigenous people.

**USING YOUR SKILLS**

5. Refer to the table showing health problems.
   a Outline the health problems of Indigenous people.
   b If you were in charge of Indigenous health, suggest strategies you would adopt to reduce health inequality.
6. Referring to the diagram and photo (page 366, top right), explain the human right to good health.

# 13.9 Comparisons: international indigenous communities

There are 370 million indigenous people living in more than 72 countries. They occupy 22 per cent of the Earth's land surface and their traditional lifestyles support the sustainable consumption of natural resources. Despite different geographical and cultural environments, they have one thing in common — the denial of many basic human rights has over time created a gap between indigenous and non-indigenous populations in health, education and income.

## Australia, Canada, the United States and New Zealand

Interactions between indigenous and non-indigenous peoples have often resulted in violence, discrimination and loss of culture. Even though the Australian Aboriginal and Torres Strait Islander peoples, the Canadian Inuits, the Native Americans in the United States and the New Zealand Maoris live in countries with a high human development index, they are likely to be more illiterate, unemployed and live in poverty compared to the non-indigenous population. They also experience higher rates of diabetes, infectious diseases, alcoholism, substance abuse and deaths due to violence.

*New Zealand Maori*

The largest gap between indigenous and non-indigenous peoples in Australia occurs in the areas of:
- *life expectancy* — the difference in life expectancy is 17 years in Australia, compared to 7.5 years in New Zealand and seven years in the United States and Canada
- *birth weight* — indigenous babies in Australia are more than 50 per cent lighter than indigenous babies in the United States
- *infant mortality* — the indigenous infant death rate in Australia is more than 60 per cent higher than for indigenous children in Canada.

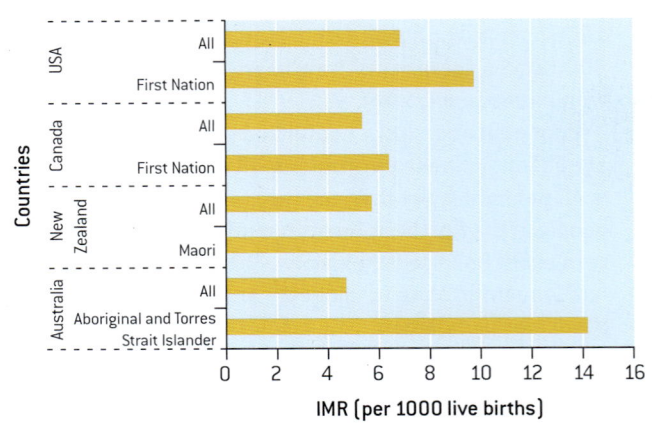

*International infant mortality rate comparisons*

The challenge for governments is to implement strategies to improve access to quality health services for indigenous peoples, while also incorporating traditional community resources such as indigenous healers. A 2005 trilateral agreement between Australia, Canada and New Zealand created a research project to improve indigenous health.

## Response: governments, groups and United Nations

The United Nations 2007 Declaration on the Rights of Indigenous Peoples, signed by 143 countries, outlines the rights of indigenous peoples to identity, culture, language, employment, health and education. Groups and governments respond to human rights agreements by implementing strategies to improve relations between indigenous and non-indigenous people. Two examples include:
- *Canada* — indigenous rights were included in the 1982 *Constitution Act*, the 1999 Marshall decision

## The path towards a more equal, socially just world

**Belize:** Since 2007, the government recognises the indigenous Mayans' tenure to land and is forced to refrain from any act that might prejudice their use or enjoyment of this land.

**Chile:** The 1993 *Indigenous Act* provides protection of indigenous groups in Chile such as the Mapuche people — people cannot be forced to move from their land.

**Pacific:** UNESCO World Heritage Pacific 2009 Program emphasises the role of indigenous communities in the preservation of World Heritage sites such as Tongariro National Park New Zealand.

**New South Wales:** In 2007, the largest native title claim in NSW has given the Githabul people 112 000 hectares of national parks and state forests.

**Botswana:** In 2002, the Kalahari Bushmen were forced off their land. In 2006, the Botswana Court rules that the Bushmen had a right to return to their land in the Central Kalahari Game Reserve.

*Towards a better future for indigenous people: strategies*

regarding fishing rights, and the 2006 Gray decision regarding the right to harvest wood on Crown lands for domestic uses.
- *New Zealand* — the 1840 Treaty of Waitangi signed by Maori chiefs and the Crown provides for Maori seats in parliament and their rights to land, mining, education, health and broadcasting. The Treaty, incorporated into New Zealand law in 1975, established the Waitangi Tribunal with powers to investigate Maori claims against the New Zealand government dating back to 1840. In 1993, the *Maori Land Law Act* strengthened Maori land claims.

## Future challenge: climate change

The close relationship indigenous peoples have with their environment will be affected by the impact of climate change. Today, sea level rises have claimed the land of indigenous Pacific Islanders, melting glaciers have seen the alpine medicinal plants of Tibetan nomadic herders disappear, and breaking ice means the Inuit can no longer hunt safely. It is predicted that climate-related disasters will lead to an increase in indigenous poverty unless immediate, sustainable strategies are implemented to address this challenge.

## ACTIVITIES

### UNDERSTANDING
1. Explain the aim of the Declaration on the Rights of Indigenous Peoples.
2. Outline the history of Maori rights in New Zealand.
3. Explain how climate change might affect indigenous peoples.

### THINKING AND APPLYING
4. Imagine you were responsible for organising activities in your school for the International Day of the World's Indigenous People. Write a report on the strategies you would adopt. Present the strategies as an oral report.
5. As a group, research an indigenous group in the Asia–Pacific region. Draw a map locating where the group lives. List abuses to their human rights. Explain how individuals, groups and governments have responded to these human rights abuses. Discuss reconciliation strategies for a better future.

### USING YOUR SKILLS
6. Refer to the graph of infant mortality rate comparisons. Rank infant mortality rates from lowest to highest. Suggest strategies you would implement if you were responsible for reducing the indigenous infant mortality rate.

# 13.10 Challenge: walking together for reconciliation

**Reconciliation** refers to a process whereby Aboriginal and Torres Strait Islander peoples, non-Indigenous Australians and Australian governments forge a new relationship based on mutual understanding, recognition and respect.

## Council for Aboriginal reconciliation

A formal structure was given to the reconciliation movement in 1991 when the federal government established the Council for Aboriginal Reconciliation. The aim was to increase understanding of Indigenous history, cultures, past dispossession and present disadvantages in the lead-up to the 2001 Centenary of Federation. The preamble to the Act establishing the Council stated:

- to date there has been no formal process of reconciliation between Aborigines and Torres Strait Islanders and other Australians
- by the year 2001, the Centenary of Federation, it is most desirable that there be such a reconciliation.

The Council consulted with thousands of Australians and presented its final report, entitled 'Reconciliation: Australia's Challenge', to the federal government in December 2000. The report included 'Australian Declaration Towards Reconciliation' and the 'Roadmap for Reconciliation'. Key elements were unacceptable to the federal government, in particular an apology to Aboriginal people for past practices such as violence and the Stolen Generations, the concept of **self-determination**, and acceptance of **customary law**.

Many individuals and groups have embraced the concept of reconciliation. In 2000, hundreds of thousands of people across Australia participated in a People's Walk for Reconciliation. In many communities, these walks have become an annual event. Groups such as Amnesty International and the Business Council of Australia have also shown their support for reconciliation.

*The People's Walk for Reconciliation, 2000*

**1911** Federal government assumes legal guardianship of Aboriginal people in parts of Australia.

**1962** Aboriginal people are granted voting rights.

**1967** Referendum amends Constitution to allow Indigenous people to be included in the census.

**1972** Aboriginal tent embassy is established outside Parliament House, Canberra.

**1975** First legally recognised Aboriginal lease is granted to the Gurindji people in the Northern Territory.

**1988** Representatives of Indigenous groups present the Barunga Statement to Prime Minister Hawke, expressing expectations for the future.

**1991** Federal government creates the Council for Aboriginal Reconciliation.

**1992** Mabo judgement overturns concept of *terra nullius* (land belonging to no-one), acknowledging that Australia was occupied by Indigenous people before 1788.

**1993** The federal government passes the *Native Title Act* as a result of the Mabo case. Under the Act, traditional Indigenous owners can make a claim on certain lands.

*Timeline of relationship between Indigenous people and Australian governments*

**Australian Declaration Towards Reconciliation**

We, the peoples of Australia, of many origins as we are, make a commitment to go on together in a spirit of reconciliation.

We value the unique status of Aboriginal and Torres Strait Islander peoples as the original owners and custodians of lands and waters.

We recognise this land and its waters were settled as colonies without treaty or consent.

Reaffirming the human rights of all Australians, we respect and recognise continuing customary laws, beliefs and traditions.

Through understanding the spiritual relationship between the land and its first peoples, we share our future and live in harmony.

Our nation must have the courage to own the truth, to heal the wounds of its past so that we can move on together at peace with ourselves.

Reconciliation must live in the hearts and minds of all Australians. Many steps have been taken, many steps remain as we learn our shared histories.

As we walk the journey of healing, one part of the nation apologises and expresses its sorrow and sincere regret for the injustices of the past, so the other part accepts the apologies and forgives.

We desire a future where all Australians enjoy their rights, accept their responsibilities, and have the opportunity to achieve their full potential.

And so, we pledge ourselves to stop injustice, overcome disadvantage, and respect that Aboriginal and Torres Strait Islander peoples have the right to self-determination within the life of the nation.

Our hope is for a united Australia that respects this land of ours; values the Aboriginal and Torres Strait Islander heritage; and provides justice and equity for all.

# The Roadmap for Reconciliation

The 2000 'Roadmap for Reconciliation' aims to heal past wounds and work towards a future without discrimination, racism, social injustice or the abuse of Indigenous peoples' human rights. It aims to address Indigenous disadvantage in relation to land, housing, law and justice, cultural heritage, education, employment, health, infrastructure and economic development. The Roadmap contains four national strategies:

- sustain the reconciliation process
- promote recognition of Aboriginal and Torres Strait Islander rights
- overcome disadvantage
- promote economic independence.

*Cultural heritage*

**1996**
The High Court finds, in the Wik case, native title can co-exist with the interests of pastoral leaseholders.

**1997**
Release of 'Bringing Them Home' report of the Stolen Generations inquiry. Since early 1900s some Indigenous Australian children were taken away from parents and placed in institutions.

**1998**
Federal government passes legislation that strengthens the rights of pastoral leaseholders. These changes are criticised by the UN.

**2000**
Thousands of people across Australia participate in the People's Walk for Reconciliation.

**2001**
Council for Aboriginal Reconciliation is replaced with a new body: Reconciliation Australia.

**2008**
Prime Minister Kevin Rudd gives a formal apology to the Stolen Generations. Aboriginal Mick Dodson is hired to devise a new organisation to replace Aboriginal and Torres Strait Islander Commission (ATSIC).

**2009**
Mick Dodson is named Australian of the Year.

**Strategies towards reconciliation**

| National strategies | 1. Sustain the reconciliation process | 2. Promote recognition of Aboriginal and Torres Strait Islander rights | 3. Overcome disadvantage | 4. Economic independence |
|---|---|---|---|---|
| Aims | Education and media supports the culturally appropriate teaching of the truth of Australia's history that includes Indigenous perspectives. | Improve community awareness and appreciation of Indigenous people as the first peoples with distinct cultures and rights. | Work towards Indigenous people enjoying a similar standard of living to other Australians, without losing their cultural identity. This strategy focuses on education, employment, health, housing, law and justice. | Ensure Indigenous peoples and communities share the same levels of economic independence. |
| Actions | Leadership (all governments and organisations), education (all levels) and communities support reconciliation. | Legislation to: protect Indigenous intellectual property; observe international Indigenous and human rights obligations; make it unlawful to adversely discriminate against people on the grounds of race | Performance measurement reporting every five years. Human Rights and Equal Opportunity Commission reports on the nation's progress in addressing disadvantage. Businesses and community groups formulate plans to overcome disadvantage. All Australians accept the responsibility to learn more about the causes and extent of disadvantage and reject racism and related behaviour. | Access to jobs and resources; effective business practices; skills development (TAFE, university); joint ventures with Indigenous businesses; development of skills for local markets |

## Meeting the challenges

There are three main strategies Australia can adopt for the future reconciliation journey with Indigenous peoples:
- make a commitment to the Australian Declaration Towards Reconciliation
- follow the Roadmap for Reconciliation. The Roadmap recognises that every Australian has a role to play in making reconciliation a reality.
- make a treaty between the government and Indigenous peoples that recognises the prior occupation and ownership of Australian land by Indigenous peoples, their dispossession of this land, and the rights of Indigenous peoples. This treaty should be part of the Constitution and would not create a separate Aboriginal nation.

## Making a difference

Today, individuals, groups and governments are responding to the challenge of reconciliation by implementing diverse programs and activities. The Across the Great Divide Tour, organised by Australian rock band Powderfinger and featuring silverchair, saw 34 concerts played in 26 towns across Australia in 2007. The tour promoted Reconciliation Australia, which works to reduce the 17-year difference in life expectancy between Indigenous and non-Indigenous Australians.

*The Sea of Hands is a public education initiative that allows individuals to show their commitment to indigenous rights.*

*Groups make a difference.*

*The Aboriginal embassy on the lawn of old Parliament House in Canberra has served for a long time as a symbol for a people who had yet to win full recognition and reconciliation.*

### Individuals make a difference

- Find out the Indigenous traditional owners in your school area.
- Invite traditional owners/elders to perform Welcome to Country at school events.
- Hang Aboriginal and Torres Strait Islander flags beside the Australian flag.
- Celebrate National Reconciliation Week.
- Communicate by email with Indigenous students. Engage in virtual contact and online chatting.
- Invite the local Indigenous traditional owners to speak at assemblies about local history, geography and culture of the area.
- Publish in school newsletter and school website Indigenous events.
- Display Indigenous art in the school and play music at assemblies.
- Name buildings after significant Indigenous community members.
- Establish an Indigenous resources section in the library — Indigenous authors and DVDs on Indigenous issues.
- Participate in fieldwork — visit local Indigenous sites (e.g. National Parks and Wildlife).
- Attend Indigenous cultural events — exhibitions and festivals.
- Visit museums: Australian Museum Aboriginal Heritage.
- Integrate an Indigenous perspective throughout your study of geography.

## ACTIVITIES

### UNDERSTANDING

1. Explain reconciliation.
2. What is the Roadmap for Reconciliation?
3. Discuss future actions proposed for reconciliation.

### THINKING AND APPLYING

4. 'Until we settle on an alternative date for Australia Day, Aboriginal people will always feel excluded ... January 26 was invasion day, the beginning of the philosophy of terra nullius — an unoccupied Australia', *Bev Manton, Chairwoman of the NSW Aboriginal Land Council*. Discuss for and against a changed date for Australia Day. Suggest a date you think would be suitable if it was to be changed. Explain your answer.
5. Collect ten digital images which illustrate important events in Australia's reconciliation process. Label and place these images around the school.
6. You are required to report on the reconciliation process in Australia to your local council. Present your report to the class. Present a proposal to your local council on future strategies it could adopt for a better future.

### USING YOUR SKILLS

7. Refer to the timeline of the relationship between Indigenous people and Australian governments on pages 370–71. When did the formal reconciliation movement begin? Explain how Mabo, Wik and the Native Title Act contributed to the reconciliation process. Discuss the significant movement towards reconciliation in 2008.
8. Refer to the Australian Declaration Towards Reconciliation on page 371. What is meant by 'steps have been taken towards reconciliation'? What does it mean by 'apologises' and 'expresses sorrow'? What is the hope for the future? In groups, discuss how this declaration could be used to assist reconciliation.
9. Refer to the strategies towards reconciliation table on page 372. List four main reconciliation strategies. Suggest strategies to overcome disadvantage.

### GEOTERMS

**customary law:** law based on tradition and the customary practices of traditional societies; usually passed on orally between generations

**reconciliation:** a process that strives to improve relations between Indigenous and non-Indigenous Australians

**self-determination:** the right of a nation or group of people to form their own government

# 13.11 Challenges and strategies for a better future

The UN Permanent Forum on Indigenous Issues (UNPFII) found indigenous peoples are lagging behind the Millennium Development Goal (MDG) targets in the areas of poverty, education and health services in most countries, and also that most indigenous women face gender-based disadvantages and discrimination. The UNFPII states that human rights-based and culturally sensitive strategies are essential if the Millennium Development Goals are to be reached by 2015. These strategies involve the participation of indigenous people in designing, implementing and monitoring MDG-related programs.

The 2007 Overcoming Indigenous Disadvantage Report identified 12 inequality challenges contributing to social and economic disadvantage for indigenous Australians, and developed seven action strategies for overcoming them. The report focuses on providing quality, culturally sensitive social services to indigenous people by involving them in the decision-making and policy implementation processes.

The Australian government recognises that a new attitude to Indigenous affairs is essential. Previous policies and processes have produced poor outcomes for Indigenous Australians, and much can be done to improve this situation.

## Heal the past, embrace the future

The 1997 Human Rights and Equal Opportunities Commission (HREOC) 'Bringing Them Home' report found between 10 and 30 per cent of Aboriginal and Torres Strait Islander children were forcibly removed from families and communities between 1910 and 1970. Many were sexually, physically and

### TWELVE CHALLENGES

Indigenous indicators compared to non-Indigenous indicators:
- Lower life expectancy at birth
- Higher disability and chronic disease
- Lower Years 10 and 12 retention and attainment
- Lower post secondary education — participation and attainment
- Lower labour force participation and unemployment
- Lower householdd and individual income
- Lower home ownership
- Higher suicide and self-harm
- Higher child abuse and neglect
- Higher deaths from homicide and hospitalisation for assault
- Higher family and community violence
- Higher imprisonment and juvenile detention rates

### SEVEN STRATEGY AREAS FOR ACTION

| Early child development and growth (prenatal to age 3) | Early school engagement and performance (preschool to Year 3) | Positive childhood and transition to adulthood | Substance use and misuse | Functional and resilient families and communities | Effective environmental health systems | Economic participation and development |
|---|---|---|---|---|---|---|
| • Injury and preventable diseases<br>• Infant mortality<br>• Birth weight<br>• Hearing impediments<br>• Children with tooth decay | • Preschool and early learning<br>• School attendance<br>• Year 3 literacy and numeracy | • Years 5 and 7 literacy and numeracy<br>• Retention at Year 9<br>• Indigenous cultural studies in school curriculum | • Alcohol consumption and harm<br>• Tobacco consumption and harm<br>• Drug and other substance use and harm | • Children on care and protection orders<br>• Proportion of Indigenous people with access to their traditional lands | • Rates of disease associated with poor environmental health<br>• Access to clean water and functional sewerage<br>• Overcrowded housing | • Employment (full-time/part-time)<br>• Indigenous owned or controlled land<br>• Governance capacity and skills |

### OUTCOMES: TOWARDS A BETTER FUTURE FOR ALL AUSTRALIANS

- Safe, healthy and supportive family environments with strong community and cultural identity
- Improved wealth creation and economic stability for individuals, families and communities
- Positive child development and prevention of violence, crime and self-harm

*Strategies Address Challenges Framework: adapted from Overcoming Indigenous Disadvantage Report 2007*

mentally abused. They and their families have suffered greatly as a result of this policy.

On 13 February 2008, Prime Minister Kevin Rudd made a formal apology to the **Stolen Generations** and said 'SORRY'. By acknowledging past mistakes and paying respect, the government laid the foundations for healing to take place and for a reconciled Australia in which everyone belongs.

*A member of the Stolen Generations accepts the apology on Sorry Day*

The injustices to Aborigines and Rudd's apology reverberated around the globe.

## Reconciliation Barometer

The Reconciliation Barometer is a national research study repeated every two years. It explores the relationship between Indigenous and non-Indigenous Australians and how perceptions affect progress towards reconciliation and the closing of inequality gaps. The Barometer is important for the development and implementation of strategies aimed at producing a fairer, more equal Australian society.

### Indigenous perspectives on the stolen children

**Quote 1**

We may go home, but we cannot relive our childhoods. We may reunite with our mothers, fathers, sisters, brothers, aunties, uncles, communities, but we cannot relive the 20, 30, 40 years that we spent without their love and care, and they cannot undo the grief and mourning they felt when we were separated from them. We can go home to ourselves as Aboriginals, but this does not erase the attacks inflicted on our hearts, minds, bodies and souls, by caretakers who thought their mission was to eliminate us as Aboriginals.

*Link-UP (NSW)*

**Quote 2**

*The Inquiry found that many children were told they were unwanted, rejected or their parents were dead, when this was not true.*

I remember this woman saying to me, 'Your mother's dead, you've got no mother now. That's why you're here with us'. Then about two years after that my mother and my mother's sister came to The Bungalow but they weren't allowed to visit us because they were black.

We were transferred to the State Children's Orphanage in 1958. Olive [aged 6 weeks] was taken elsewhere — Mr L telling me several days later that she was admitted to hospital where she died from meningitis. In 1984, assisted by Link Up (Qld), my sister Judy discovered that Olive had not died but, rather, had been fostered. Her name was changed.

*Source: www.humanrights.gov.au.*

### ACTIVITIES

**UNDERSTANDING**

1. Explain the strategies required for Indigenous people to reach the Millennium Development Goals by 2015.
2. Discuss how Australians can overcome inequality or disadvantage for a reconciled future society.

**THINKING AND APPLYING**

3. Discuss this phrase 'Heal the past and embrace the future'. How do you think this can be applied in reality?
4. Use the **MDG** weblinks in your eBookPLUS to select a country and discuss how its Indigenous population is progressing towards the Millennium Development Goals.
5. Use the **Reconciliation** weblink in your eBookPLUS to develop a Reconciliation Action Plan in your school.

**USING YOUR SKILLS**

6. Refer to the framework developed from the Overcoming Indigenous Disadvantage report. Describe the 12 inequality challenges to be addressed by individuals, groups and governments. In groups, draw a plan to ensure all children grow up physically and mentally healthy, with the necessary skills for future employment.
7. Refer to the quotes in the textbox on the left. What did the inquiry find? What is the significance of 'going home'? Express how you would feel if you were forcibly taken from your family.

### GEOTERMS

**Stolen Generations:** refers to Aboriginal children who were removed from their families and communities by government or non-government agencies in order to enforce integration into society; the practice continued in some areas until the 1970s

# Working geographically

## BROADSHEET: HUMAN RIGHTS AND RECONCILIATION

### KNOWLEDGE AND UNDERSTANDING

**Select the alternative that best answers the question.**

1. Refer to the graph below. The three largest gaps in health between indigenous people and total population are in:
   - (A) Canada, New Zealand and Australia
   - (B) Brazil, Peru and India
   - (C) Uganda, Peru and Brazil
   - (D) India, Uganda and Peru.

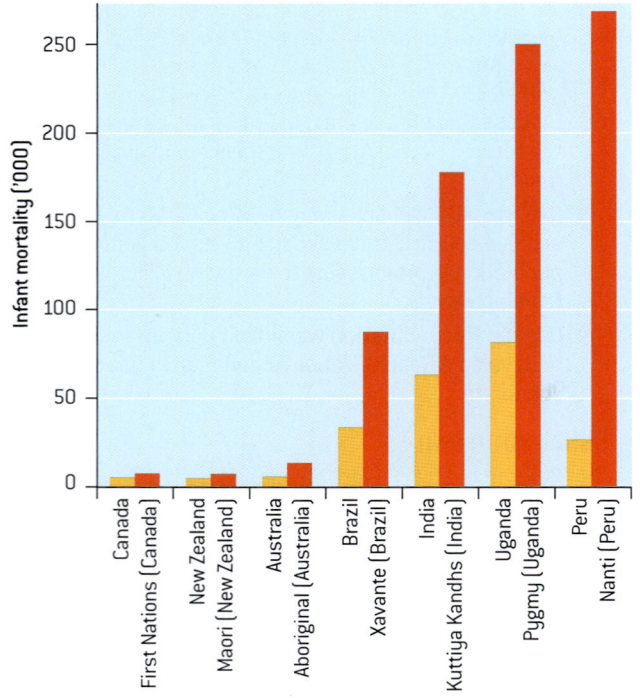

*Source: WHO, Lancet Series on Indigenous Health, vol. 367, June 2006, p. 2022.*

*Infant mortality in indigenous communities and the total population*

2. Refer to the graph at the top of the next column. The percentage of population expected to live to 65 years is:
   - (A) highest for Indigenous Australian males
   - (B) larger for Australia's total population than for the population in India and Vietnam
   - (C) higher for Australia's Indigenous females than for the population in Thailand
   - (D) under 40 per cent in Nigeria.

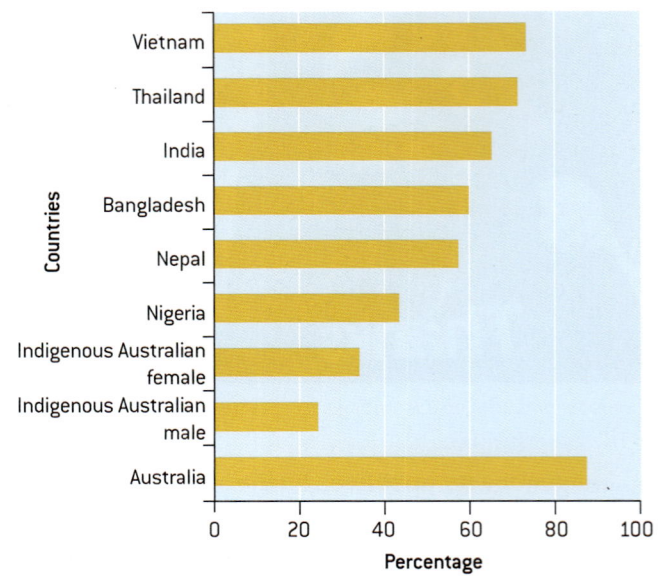

*Percentage of population expected to live to 65 years*

3. Refer to the graph below. Which statement is the most incorrect?
   - (A) Housing is 35 per cent of the budget.
   - (B) Health is 18 per cent of the budget.
   - (C) Education and early childhood is 34 per cent of the budget.
   - (D) Employment is 20 per cent of the budget.

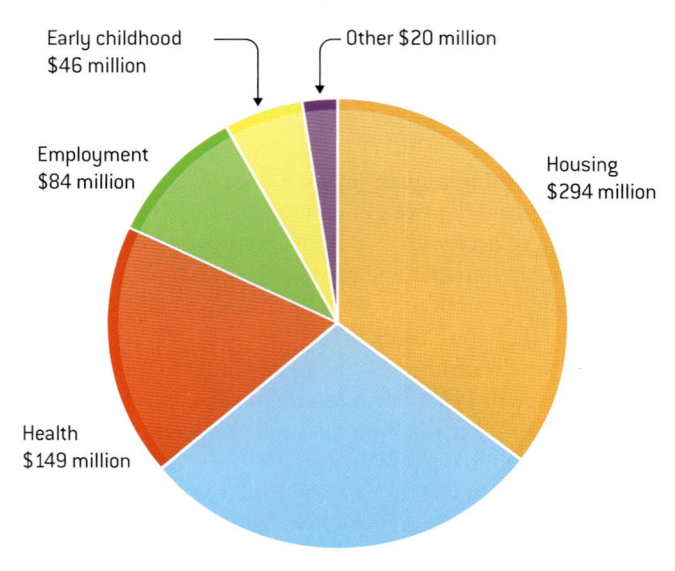

*Government funding for Indigenous Australians, 2008*

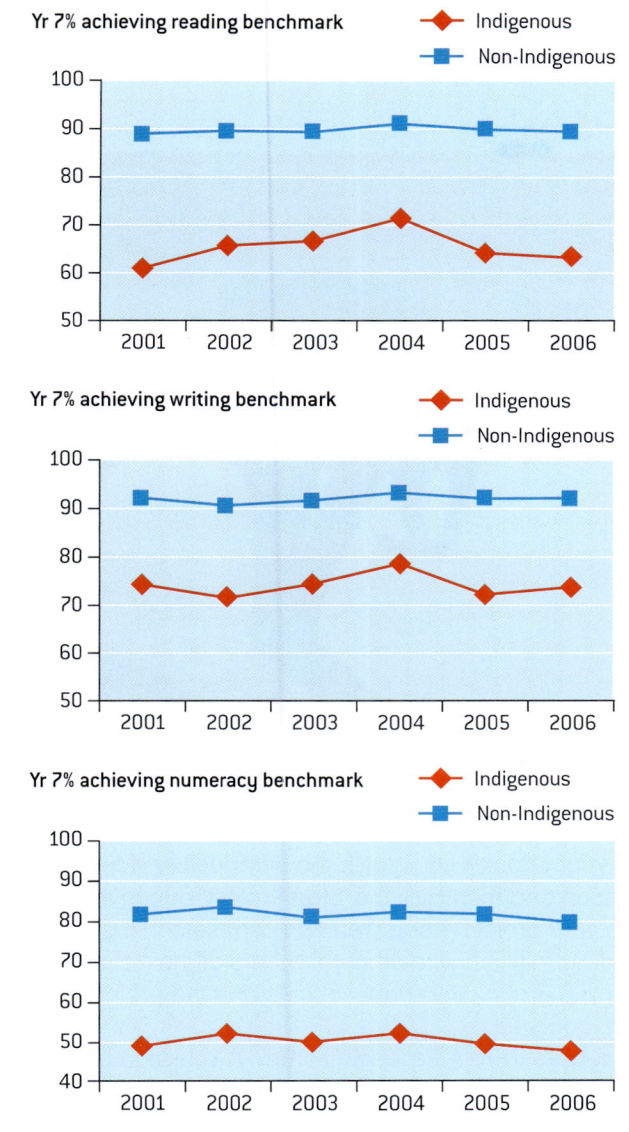

**Yr 7% achieving reading benchmark**
◆ Indigenous
■ Non-Indigenous

**Yr 7% achieving writing benchmark**
◆ Indigenous
■ Non-Indigenous

**Yr 7% achieving numeracy benchmark**
◆ Indigenous
■ Non-Indigenous

*Closing the gap in literacy and numeracy*

**4** Refer to the graphs above. Which statement is the most incorrect?
(A) Non-Indigenous children scored higher than Indigenous children in reading, writing and numeracy.
(B) The gap between Indigenous children and non-Indigenous children is generally largest in numeracy.
(C) Reading and writing in Indigenous children improved in 2004, but numeracy remained stable.
(D) Indigenous children read better than they write.

## SHORT RESPONSE

**5** Access to basic health services is a human right and a Millennium Development Goal. Suggest strategies to reduce the health gap between indigenous and non-indigenous people in Australia and other nations.

**6** Explain why Indigenous Australians do not live as long as other Australians. Discuss how strategies implemented by individuals, groups and governments could improve the life expectancy of Indigenous Australians.

**7** Outline the actions Indigenous people have taken in their struggle for land rights in the post-war period.

**8** Outline some of the changes in government policy affecting Indigenous people since the 1900s.

**9** Suggest strategies for a more equal and socially just future for all Australians.

## EXTENDED RESPONSE

**10** Examine the challenges and responses to reconciliation for Australia.
In your answer provide:
- a definition for 'reconciliation'
- the challenges for Australia
- responses to these challenges by individuals, groups and governments.

**11** Australian Indigenous societies possess a unique body of cultural and environmental knowledge that should be conserved and/or preserved. Discuss using examples.
- Introduction
  – Define: Indigenous Australians.
  – Provide examples of Indigenous communities in Australia.
- Middle section
  – Give examples of unique culture (e.g. art, song, dance, food, shelter, language, Dreamtime, rock carvings).
  – Give examples of environmental knowledge (e.g. water, plants, animals, medicine).
- Conclusion:
  – Give reasons why this knowledge should be conserved and/or preserved (define these terms) for a sustainable future.

**12** In 2008, Australia's Prime Minister, Kevin Rudd, said Indigenous health was a priority, and promised to set benchmarks on Indigenous progress. Write a letter to Mr Rudd, explaining the health problems of Indigenous Australians and emphasise the importance of keeping his promise.

**13** Present a report on inequality between Indigenous and non-Indigenous people and what should be done to create a better future for Indigenous Australians. Use the guidelines below to help you.

| Before | During | After |
|---|---|---|
| Before you start your research, list important things you know about inequality between non-Indigenous Australians and Aborigines and Torres Strait Islanders. | Obtain current information from a variety of sources: online, newspapers, interviews, narratives, journals. Find maps, graphs, statistics, photos, artwork, music, DVDs and poetry to supplement the report. Decide on the format you will use to present it. | Write a story for publication in your school newsletter or local newspaper. What actions will you take to make a difference? |

# ICT activities

**projectsplus**

## Brand Australia
SEARCHLIGHT ID: PRO-0044

### SCENARIO
Your agency, CYBERINKERS, has won a government tender for a new advertising campaign that will rethink and rebrand Australia's international image. The campaign aims to broaden Australia's appeal not just as a tourism destination but also as a centre for business and investment. The government wants the world to recognise that Australia boasts a sophisticated and innovative economy: one that produces top-quality goods and delivers first-rate services in industries such as education, health and engineering. In short, the government wants the campaign to target an audience wider than the holiday-maker.

### YOUR TASK
You are a member of an advertising team that will create a commercial that will rebrand the 'new Australia' as an economic centre. The commercial should run for between 60 and 90 seconds and will screen on television, at the cinema and/or on the internet. Your rebranding must include a catchy slogan or motif in a fashion similar to previous advertising campaigns; for example, Paul Hogan 'slipped an extra shrimp on the barbie for you' or, more recently, we were invited to come 'walkabout' Australia.

### PROCESS
- Open the ProjectsPLUS application for this chapter in your eBookPLUS. Watch the introductory video lesson and then click the 'Start Project' button to set up your project group. You can complete this project individually or invite other members of the class to form a group. Save your settings and the project will be launched.
- Navigate to your Research Forum. A selection of research topics have been loaded to provide you with a framework for your research on rebranding Australia. You should research presentations of the Australian identity that already exist. The following are worth investigating:
    - Pre-existing advertisements for Australia such as the campaign that featured Paul Hogan and the recent Baz Luhrmann productions
    - Statistics sites for Australia, such as those of the ABS (Australian Bureau of Statistics)
    - Images and news stories about Australian industry, technology, Indigenous culture, multiculturalism and creative arts
        - *The Gruen Transfer* television series (ABC television production), particularly season 1, episode 10, featuring two agencies pitching to divert tourism from Australia to New Zealand.

The weblinks in your Media Centre will help you get started. Enter your findings as articles in the Research Forum. You can also rate and comment on the articles posted by other members of your group.

Your ProjectsPLUS application is available in this chapter's Student Resources tab inside your eBookPLUS. Visit www.jacplus.com.au to locate your digital resources.

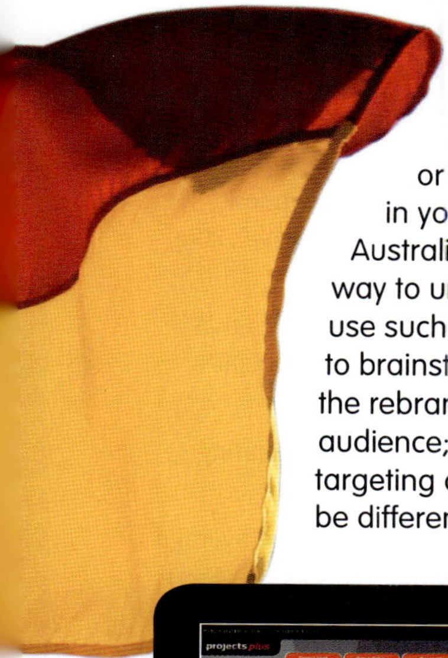

- When your research is complete, download the storyboard template available in your Media Centre and use it to plan your commercial. Remember, the key purpose of your presentation is to persuade your audience about the attractiveness of the 'new' Australia. The target audience is not specifically the tourist market; the ad may be selling Australia as a place to 'work, rest and play' or perhaps to 'invest, live and stay'. It is important to brainstorm slogans or thematic motifs that will feature in your commercial — studying other Australian ID advertisements is a good way to understand how and when to use such techniques. It is also possible to brainstorm different ad formats for the rebranding based on your intended audience; for example, a commercial targeting overseas students would probably be different in form and content from a commercial targeting business interests in Asia.
- Create your commercial. A selection of media has been supplied for you in your Media Centre to download and use along with any media that you create or source for yourself. Allocate roles if working in teams — who is responsible for what job? One way of organising your group is to first 'sign off' on the creative style and slogan for your commercial together and then allocate tasks to each team member. If you need to record a voiceover, you should use Audacity, Garage Band or other voice-recording software but you might prefer to use text on screen and some quintessentially Australian music. Remember, you must acknowledge any music or images you use that you have not created yourself.
- Finally, print your research report from ProjectsPLUS and hand it in to your teacher with your storyboard and completed commercial.

**SUGGESTED SOFTWARE**
- ProjectsPLUS
- Microsoft Word
- Windows Movie Maker, iMovie or other editing software

**MEDIA CENTRE**

**Your Media Centre contains:**
- a bank of media to use in your video
- a storyboard template
- weblinks to research sites on Australian identity
- an assessment rubric.

## Interactivity

### REVELATION: 'IMPORTS AND EXPORTS'

Australia is a major trading nation, importing and exporting goods in order to meet the needs and wants of Australian and overseas consumers. This interactive Revelation game will test your knowledge of Australia's trade system and key trading partners.

SEARCHLIGHT ID: INT-1208

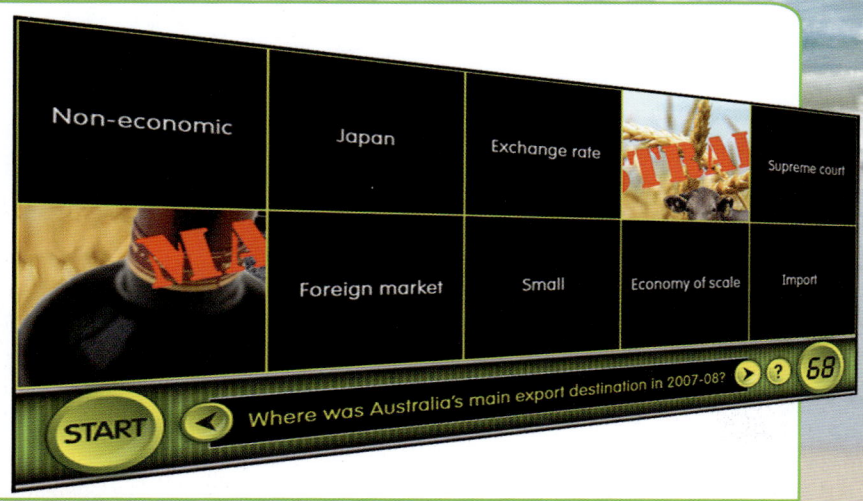

# Glossary

**absolute poverty:** the condition of having so little food, money or resources that the people, no matter where they live in the world, can barely survive (p. 174)

**active citizenship:** involves individuals and groups influencing decision making at local, state, federal and global scales, and actively and responsibly participating in community activities and public affairs (p. 154)

**air pollution:** the build-up of impurities in the air that are likely to be harmful to plants and animals, including humans, once they reach certain concentrations (p. 156)

**alluvium:** the loose material brought down by a river and deposited on its bed, flood plain or delta (p. 79)

**Anglo-Celtic:** describes a person whose origin is the British Isles (pp. 108, 132)

**archipelago:** large body of water with many islands (p. 304)

**Asia–Pacific region:** area covering North-East Asia, South-East Asia, Australasia, Melanesia and Polynesia (p. 262)

**assimilation:** absorption into, and adoption of, the host country's culture (p. 334)

**asylum seeker:** refugee who seeks official shelter or protection in a foreign country under international law (p. 330)

**Australasia:** area that includes Australia, New Zealand, Papua New Guinea and neighbouring islands in the Pacific Ocean (p. 262)

**back dunes:** dunes that develop behind the fore dunes. They may be stabilised by small shrubs and trees. (p. 234)

**beach nourishment:** artificial placement of sand on a beach (p. 225)

**bearing:** an angle, given in degrees and minutes, measured clockwise from north on a compass (p. 171)

**billabong:** small wetland associated with a river channel that is isolated during low-flow periods and can be flushed during a flood (p. 218)

**blocking high pressure system:** a persistent high pressure system that occurs on a large scale, remaining stationary for a period of time, compressing and warming the air below (p. 66)

**blowhole:** a hole in the roof of a coastal cave, produced by wave erosion, through which compressed air and water are forced as waves break into the cave (p. 233)

**blowout:** a bare depression in a sand dune caused when loose sand is blown from the dune because vegetation has been removed (p. 226)

**boom town:** a community that experiences sudden and rapid population and economic growth (p. 165)

**bushfire:** a fire burning out of control in the open; also called a wildfire (p. 62)

**carbon footprint:** greenhouse gas emissions caused by an individual, organisation, event or product (p. 345)

**carbon neutral:** describes an outcome in which carbon emissions are balanced by carbon reductions to achieve zero net emissions of carbon dioxide (p. 216)

**catchment:** extent of land where water from rain or snow melt drains downhill into a body of water, such as a river, lake, reservoir, estuary or wetland (p. 192)

**census:** a population count conducted every five years that captures details of age, sex, employment and other social indicators (pp. 98, 324)

**climate:** the long-term variation in the atmosphere, relating mainly to temperature and precipitation (p. 34)

**climate change:** a long-term, significant change in the average weather that a region experiences (p. 238)

**climate refugee:** person displaced by climate-change-induced environmental disasters (p. 270)

**cold front:** a surface where a cool air mass meets a warmer mass, into which it is advancing (p. 80)

**commodity:** an article such as a raw foodstuff (for example, wheat), or material (such as wool, coal or gold) which is traded internationally (p. 118)

**community:** a group formed by people with something in common and based on shared space and social organisation (p. 114)

**continent:** one of the seven great main landmasses on the Earth (p. 4)

**continental drift:** the theory that describes how continents broke away and drifted from an original landmass (p. 10)

**continental shelf:** the part of a continent found under a shallow sea (p. 5)

**counter-terrorism:** practices, techniques and strategies that governments, the military, police departments and corporations adopt in response to terrorist threats or acts (p. 317)

**crude birth rate:** the number of live births per 1000 population (p. 98)

**crude death rate:** the number of deaths per 1000 population (p. 98)

**cultural diversity:** cohabitation of people from different ethnic and/or religious–cultural backgrounds within the same geographic location (p. 276)

**cultural integration:** communities and governments working together to celebrate diversity, improve community services, meet diverse community needs and address community problems (p. 128)

**culturally diverse:** describes a society that includes many different cultural groups (p. 122)

**culture:** system of shared beliefs, values, customs, behaviours and artefacts used by members of a society to interact with one another and with the outside world (p. 276)

**customary law:** law based on tradition and the customary practices of traditional societies, usually passed on orally between generations (p. 370)

**demographic change:** a change in the characteristics of a population, such as rates of growth, birth, death and migration (p. 128)

**demographic characteristics:** characteristics of a population described by statistics such as births, deaths, marriages and so on (p. 114)

**demography:** the study of populations, including patterns and trends in population data (p. 109)

**deposition:** the laying down of material carried by rivers, wind, ice, ocean currents and waves (p. 226)

**diaspora:** the spreading of people from their original location (p. 332)

**dormitory town:** a place from which many people travel in order to work in a bigger town or city (p. 166)

**drainage basin:** the area of land that feeds a river with water, or the whole area of land drained by a river and its tributaries (p. 20)

**Dreaming:** stories that describe the Dreamtime, a time in which the Aboriginal peoples believe the Earth came to have its present form and in which life and nature began (p. 8)

**drought:** a prolonged period of below-average precipitation (pp. 34, 56, 192)

**drowned river valley:** melting of continental icecaps following the last ice age, which saw sea levels rise and drown coastal river valleys (p. 214)

**dune (coastal):** a mass that forms along shorelines, usually composed of sand formed from loose particles of rock and other materials such as shells and coral (p. 226)

**earthquake:** shaking of the ground that is generated by disturbances in the Earth's crust (p. 84)

**ecocity:** a city dedicated to minimising inputs (energy, water and food) and waste outputs (heat, air pollution and water pollution) (p. 346)

**ecological footprint:** a measure of human demand on the Earth's ecosystems (p. 330)

**ecological sustainability:** the needs of the present population being met without endangering the ability of future generations to meet their needs (p. 344)

**ecosystem:** a system formed by the interactions between the living organisms (plants, animals, humans) and the physical elements of an environment (land, water) (pp. 48, 224)

**ecotourism:** ecologically sustainable tourism, with a primary focus on experiencing natural areas, that fosters environmental and cultural understanding, appreciation and conservation (p. 204)

**El Niño event:** the reversal (every few years) of the more usual direction of winds and surface currents across the Pacific Ocean. This change causes drought in eastern Australia and heavy rain in South America. (p. 58)

**emigration:** the movement of people out of a country (pp. 102, 324)

**endemic:** native to a particular area and found nowhere else (p. 46)

**environmental impact statement (EIS):** investigation of the impact of building development on the physical environment, as well as the social and economic impacts (p. 242)

**epicentre:** the point on the Earth's surface directly above the focus of an earthquake (p. 84)

**equity:** the concept of fairness, ensuring an even share (p. 279)

**erosion:** the wearing away of soil and rock by natural elements such as wind and water (pp. 12, 226)

**estuary:** tidal mouth of a river where the salt water of the tide meets the fresh water of the river current (p. 226)

**ethnically diverse:** describes a population composed of people from different ethnic backgrounds or origins (p. 94)

**European Union (EU):** political and economic union of 27 member states, located primarily in Europe (p. 292)

**exclusive economic zone (EEZ):** sea zone over which a country has sovereign rights to explore, exploit and conserve its natural resources (p. 257)

**exports:** the goods, services and ideas that Australia sells to other countries (p. 292)

**fair trade:** the organised social movement that advocates payment of a fair price for producers in developing countries. The fair trade movement focuses on exports from developing countries to developed countries, most notably coffee, cocoa, sugar and tea. (p. 298)

**fertility rate:** average number of children born to a woman over her lifetime; the average number of babies born to women during their reproductive years (pp. 101, 326)

**fire front:** the edge of a fire that spreads fastest (p. 62)

**firebrand:** aerially burning fuel that blows ahead of a fire front (p. 62)

**firestorm:** an intense fire that may generate strong convection currents and violent winds causing long-range spotting and flame spirals (p. 68)

**flood:** an unusual accumulation of water that overflows from rivers, lakes and the ocean onto land that is not normally covered by water (p. 78)

**flood mitigation:** measures aimed at preparing for floods and trying to reduce their effects, such as constructing artificial levees, strengthening bridges, raising road levels and enlarging drains (p. 80)

**flood plain:** part of a river valley covered by water during floods (pp. 79, 214)

**fore dunes:** sand dunes closest to the surf (p. 234)

**gender equality:** equal valuing of women and men so both sexes are able to equally contribute to and benefit from economic, social, cultural and political developments within society (p. 360)

**genocide:** planned killing of a whole national or racial group (p. 353)

**geographic information system (GIS):** set of computer applications designed to integrate, collect, store, retrieve, manipulate, analyse and display mapped data (pp. 198, 313)

**global gender gap:** World Economic Forum measurement examining inequality between men and women in economic participation, educational attainment, political empowerment, health and survival (p. 361)

**global warming:** the increase in average temperature of the Earth's atmosphere and oceans since the mid twentieth century, and its projected continuation (pp. 192, 238)

**globalisation:** breakdown of traditional barriers between nation states, allowing the movement of goods, capital, people and information; greater movement of people, goods, money and ideas around the world. (pp. 129, 261)

**governance:** method or system of government, authority or control (p. 301)

**gross national income (GNI) per capita:** total value of goods and services produced in a country in one year per person plus net income from abroad (p. 6)

**ground water:** water under the surface of the ground that has seeped through soil and rock; often used for drinking and irrigation (p. 198)

**heatwave:** a prolonged period of very hot weather (p. 63)

**heritage:** assets, traditions or culture that belong to a person, community or nation (p. 114)

**human development index (HDI):** measures human development in three broad dimensions: life expectancy, education and wealth; published by the United Nations Development Programme each year (p. 364)

**human rights:** basic rights and freedoms to which all humans are entitled; concept that all human beings are equal and deserve fair and equal treatment (pp. 300, 352)

**ice age:** a time in which the Earth was colder, resulting in the expansion of glaciers and ice sheets and a fall in sea level (p. 14)

**immigrant:** person who has come to live in a new country (p. 114)

**immigration:** the movement of people into a country (pp. 94, 324)

**imports:** the goods, services and ideas that Australia buys from other countries (p. 292)

**Indigenous people:** the descendants of the original inhabitants of an area (pp. 8, 104, 364)

**infant mortality rate:** the number of deaths per 1000 babies under one year of age (p. 105)

**integration:** respect for source country's and host country's cultures and their dynamic blending; aimed at greater inclusiveness (p. 334)

**intellectual property:** output from creative workers as protected by copyright, patents or trademarks — for example, the concept for a TV show (p. 276)

**international trade:** movement of goods, services and ideas between countries (p. 292)

**internet café:** a place where a person can buy time on a computer with internet access. Often it serves as a regular café serving food and drinks. (p. 130)

**interstate migration:** the movement of people from one state of Australia to another (p. 106)

**intertidal zone:** area between low and high water marks that is exposed at low tide (p. 218)

**intrastate migration:** the movement of people from one location to another within a state of Australia (p. 106)

**isobar:** line drawn on a map joining places of equal barometric pressure (p. 40)

**kinship:** being in a family relationship. A kinship system is the system of relationships traditionally accepted by a particular culture, and the rights and obligations that they involve. (p. 120)

**La Niña event:** a period of well above average rainfall in eastern Australia that often brings floods (p. 58)

**land claims:** claims of Indigenous peoples about their right of ownership of the land they or their ancestors inhabited before the arrival of settlers, primarily Europeans (p. 369)

**land degradation:** loss in quality of the land and the consequent reduction in its ability to sustain agriculture or support native vegetation (p. 194)

**Landcare:** group formed to protect the land (p. 200)

**latitude:** location represented by imaginary lines drawn around the Earth from east to west, which show the distance north or south of the Equator, measured in degrees, minutes and seconds (p. 7)

**life expectancy:** the average number of years a person can be expected to live; affected by nutrition, occupation, hereditary and other factors (pp. 120, 328)

**liveability:** comfort and convenience of an area, assessed on living conditions such as safety, education, hygiene, recreation, politico–economic stability and public transport (p. 340)

**Local Agenda 21 (LA21):** a program, run by the United Nations, for implementing sustainable development at the local level (p. 344)

**longitude:** location represented by imaginary lines drawn around the Earth from north to south, which show the distance east or west of the Prime Meridian, measured in degrees, minutes and seconds (p. 7)

**longshore drift:** the movement of sand and other materials along the shore (p. 229)

**Mabo:** a court case in 1992 in which the High Court of Australia ruled that *terra nullius* (the concept that the land was owned by no-one before European settlement) did not apply (p. 143)

**mantle:** the layer of rock between the Earth's crust and the core (p. 13)

**marsupial:** mammal that keeps and feeds its young in a pouch for a few months after birth (p. 46)

**microcredit:** extension of very small loans to those in poverty, enabling them to be self-employed (p. 302)

**migration:** the permanent and semipermanent movement of people from one location to another (pp. 98, 128, 278)

**Millennium Development Goals (MDGs):** eight humanitarian development goals to be achieved by 2015, as set at the Millennium Summit in 2000 by 189 UN member states and at least 23 international organisations (pp. 300, 374)

**monotreme:** mammal that lays eggs; the only species are the platypus and echidna (p. 46)

**monsoon:** the seasonal change in wind direction that is experienced in much of the tropics (p. 35)

**multiculturalism:** a policy of including many different cultural groups in a society; respect and maintenance of source countries' cultures and the official Australian government policy since the 1970s. It means that communities keep their native language, rituals, religion and cultural ways while remaining loyal to Australia and its values. (pp. 138, 334)

**native title:** the name given by Australian law to Indigenous peoples' traditional rights to their lands and waters (p. 130)

**natural disaster:** an extreme event that is the result of natural processes and causes serious material damage or loss of life (p. 54)

**natural hazard:** an extreme event that is the result of natural processes and has the potential to cause serious material damage and loss of life (p. 54)

**natural increase:** the excess of births over deaths, usually expressed as a percentage (pp. 98, 324)

**net overseas migration:** the number of people migrating to a country minus the number of people emigrating to live in other countries; it is expressed as a percentage of the total population (p. 324)

**non-government organisation (NGO):** not-for-profit organisation, usually with a charitable, community or environmental focus (p. 256)

**nuclear reactor:** a device where a chain reaction is maintained and controlled for the production of nuclear energy or radioactive isotopes (p. 186)

**outstation:** area where a small community of Aboriginal people lives away from larger settlements (p. 121)

**people smugglers:** individuals or groups paid by those who wish to enter another country, but who do so without permission (p. 330)

**perspective:** a way of viewing the world (p. 224)

**population:** total number of people inhabiting an area (p. 324)

**population density:** the number of people living in a given area, usually a square kilometre (p. 94)

**population pyramid:** set of bar graphs that show the age and sex distribution of a population (p. 100)

**quota:** physical limit on the quantity of a goods item that can be imported into a country in a given period of time (p. 294)

**reconciliation:** a process that strives to improve relations between Indigenous and non-Indigenous people (p. 370)

**referendum:** a process through which change can be made to the Constitution, in which electors vote on a particular change (p. 104)

**refugee:** a person who is forced to flee their homeland because of a well-founded fear of being persecuted due to race, religion, nationality, membership of a particular social group, or political belief (pp. 102, 358)

**regolith:** the layer of broken rock and soil on top of the solid rock of the Earth's crust; also known as mantle rock (p. 20)

**relative poverty:** where there is not lack of sufficient resources to meet basic needs, but a lack of resources required to be able to participate in the lifestyle enjoyed by other people in the country (p. 174)

**replacement rate:** a total fertility rate of 2.1. When a population reaches this level, it will remain stable (assuming no immigration or emigration takes place). (p. 101)

**Richter scale:** used to measure the energy of earthquakes (p. 84)

**rural:** describes areas where people live in population clusters of fewer than 1000 people and where primary industry is the main activity (p. 114)

**rural settlement:** site where most of the people are engaged in primary industry, such as farming, fishing or mining (p. 96)

**rural–urban fringe:** an area where growing suburbs meet farmland (p. 162)

**sacred sites:** places where important events in the Dreaming took place (p. 8)

**salinity:** presence of salt on the land's surface, in soil or rocks, or dissolved in water in rivers and ground water (p. 198)

**sclerophyll:** plants found in low rainfall areas; their leathery leaves help reduce water loss (p. 63)

**secularism:** the belief that public organisations such as schools and governments should function without religious influence or interference (p. 304)

**sediment:** material deposited by a stream or other body of water (p. 14)

**self-determination:** the right of a nation or group of people to form their own government (p. 370)

**settlement:** a group of people living in one place or location (p. 96)

**social justice:** the just and fair treatment of individuals and groups within a society (p. 279)

**soil:** naturally occurring, unconsolidated or loose covering of broken rock particles and decaying organic matter on the surface of the Earth that is able to support life (p. 196)

**southern oscillation:** a major air pressure shift between the Asian and east Pacific regions. Its most common extremes are El Niño events. (p. 58)

**sovereign rights:** power or authority over a territory (p. 256)

**spatial distribution:** distribution of a population across a country (p. 331)

**spatial inequality:** the unequal distribution of income, wealth or resources in a geographic area (p. 150)

**species:** a group of plants or animals of the same kind that are able to breed with each other (p. 46)

**spit:** narrow deposit of sand and other materials that extends out into a body of water (p. 226)

**stack:** a column of rock, isolated from the shore by the corrosive action of waves (p. 233)

**standard of living:** the amount of goods and services, mainly food, clothing, housing, education and health, that is available for use in the community per head of population (pp. 94, 118)

**Stolen Generations:** refers to Aboriginal children who were removed from their families and communities by government or non-government agencies in order to enforce integration into society; this practice continued in some areas until the 1970s (p. 375)

**storm surge:** a rise in sea level above the normal tide caused by very low atmospheric pressure and the stress of strong winds on the sea surface when a tropical cyclone approaches or crosses a coastline (pp. 74, 231)

**subsidy:** financial aid given by a government to an individual producer or group of producers to reduce the price of a good or service (p. 294)

**surf lifesaving club:** a club dedicated to the prevention of aquatic injury and drowning through lifesaving and education practices (p. 116)

**sustainable development:** development that meets the needs of the present population without endangering the ability of future generations to meet their own needs (pp. 102, 224)

**sustainable management:** management that meets the needs of the present population without endangering the ability of future generations to meet their own needs (p. 192)

**synoptic chart:** weather map that uses isobars and other symbols to show the movement of weather systems and patterns of temperature and rainfall (p. 40)

**tariff:** tax imposed on goods when they move across a political boundary, which increases the price for both importer and exporter (p. 294)

**tectonic plates:** the various slow-moving plates that make up the Earth's crust. Volcanoes and earthquakes often occur at the edge of plates. (p. 10)

**terrorism:** generally defined as the intentional use, or threat, of violence against civilians or civilian targets in order to achieve political ends (p. 316)

**thunderstorm:** a storm associated with lightning and thunder, occurring with cumulonimbus clouds (p. 70)

**tide:** the daily rise and fall of the ocean and its inlets, due to the attraction of the moon and sun (p. 228)

**topographic map:** a map that shows the relief of an area by use of contour lines (p. 24)

**topography:** physical features (height and shape) of an area of land (p. 14)

**topsoil:** layer of soil that contains most of the nutrients required for the healthy growth of plants (p. 193)

**tourism:** the practice of travelling temporarily to destinations not normally visited in the course of one's work or life (p. 280)

**trade deficit:** trade imbalance whereby imports are greater than exports (p. 292)

**transnational corporation (TNC):** a company or organisation that possesses and controls the means of production, such as factories, mines, farms and financial organisations, in more than one country (pp. 114, 261)

**treaty:** formal agreement between two or more independent countries, which is binding under international law. Treaties take a variety of forms, including conventions, protocols, agreements, exchanges of notes and exchanges of letters. (p. 256)

**tropical cyclone:** a severe weather event that occurs where warm, moist, rising air begins to spiral upwards. Tropical cyclones are often accompanied by very strong winds, heavy rain and rough seas. (p. 74)

**tsunami:** an ocean wave caused by an earthquake or volcanic eruption beneath the sea, travelling at high speed and causing massive destruction along coasts (p. 238)

**United Nations (UN):** intergovernmental organisation (IGO) that promotes equity, human rights, peace and ecologically sustainable environments (p. 300)

**urban:** describes areas where people live in population clusters of more than 1000 people and where either secondary or tertiary industry is the main activity (p. 114)

**urban decay:** occurs when a land use in a part of the city declines where it had previously flourished, leaving behind derelict buildings and vacant sites (p. 164)

**urban settlement:** site where most of the population is engaged in tertiary industries, such as commerce, administration and transport (p. 96)

**urbanisation:** the process by which the proportion of a country's population in urban areas increases (p. 162)

**visa:** a permit that allows the holder to enter a country for a specified period of time (p. 358)

**water footprint:** volume of fresh water used to produce the goods and services consumed by an individual or community or produced by a business (pp. 216, 345)

**water table:** the upper limit of the ground water (p. 198)

**wave-cut notch:** a hollow eroded by the impact of waves at the foot of a cliff (p. 232)

**weathering:** the breakdown of bare rock by water and temperature changes (p. 14)

**wetland:** area covered permanently or occasionally by fresh or salt water up to a depth of six metres (pp. 133, 218)

**White Australia policy:** a law that existed from 1901 to 1973 that restricted the entry of non-white migrants (p. 136)

**World Heritage site:** a place recognised as being of such great value that it should be preserved for all people for all time (p. 140)

# Index

AAQFS (Australian Air Quality Forecasting System)  159, 161
   measurement and prediction of photochemical smog  161
Aboriginal and Torres Strait Islander people
   see Indigenous people
*Aboriginal Land Rights Act 1976*  121
absolute poverty  149, 174, 175
ACOSS (Australian Council of Social Services)  172, 176
active citizenship  149, 154, 155, 299
   fair trade campaigns  299
   freedom of expression and information  362–3
   political involvement  154
   refugees  359
active civil society  154
agricultural practices
   land degradation  200–1
aid
   see foreign aid
air pollution  149, 156–9
   see also air quality
   global city comparisons  157
   health effects  156
   photochemical smog  156, 159, 161
   pollutant concentrations in major cities  157
   pollutants controlled by NEPM (National Environment Protection Measure)  158
   'polluter pays' principle  158, 180
   sources  156–7
air pressure  40
air quality  150, 152, 156, 158–61
   see also air pollution
   AAQFS (Australian Air Quality Forecasting System)  159, 161
   Action for Air program  160
   Cities for Climate Protection  160
   Cool Communities program  161
   greenhouse gas and pollutants in clean and urban air  158
   improvement strategies  158, 159–61
   indoor  157
   measurement  158, 159
   National Environment Protection Measure (NEPM)  158, 161
   National Greenhouse Strategy  161
   'sick building syndrome'  157
   spatial dimension of  156
Air Quality Index (AQI)  159

alluvial fan  16
alluvium  53, 79
Amnesty International  354, 362, 370
Anglo-Celtic community  93, 108, 127, 132, 133
Angourie  165
animals
   see also flora and fauna
   hard-hoofed, effect of  194
   introduced species  194, 212
   overgrazing, effect of  194
ANSTO (Australian Nuclear Science and Technology Organisation)  186
anticyclones  40
*Anti-Terrorism Act 2005*  317
ANZUS Treaty (1952)  312
APEC (Asia–Pacific Economic Cooperation)  263, 292, 296
archipelago  291, 304
ARPANSA (Australian Radiation Protection and Nuclear Safety Agency)  186
ASEAN (Association of South–East Asian Nations)  264–5, 296, 312
   Indonesia, relations with  265
   links with Australia  264–65
Asia–Pacific region  255, 262
   see also APEC; ASEAN; People's Republic of China; Indonesia; Pacific Islands
   defence agreements  312
   North–East and South–East links with Australia  262
   Pacific region links with Australia  262–3
   sporting events  284
aspect of a slope  28
assimilation  323, 334
asylum seeker  323, 330
   see also immigration; refugee
atmospheric hazards  54
AusAID (Australian Agency for International Development)  300–1, 310, 316
   see also foreign aid
   Fiji  320
   human rights protection strategies  356
   Papua New Guinea  306–7
   People's Republic of China  266
   Sport Development Program (2006–11)  286
   telecommunications support  275

   women's rights  361
   World Vision Australia partnership  308
Australasia  255, 262
Australia–China Council (ACC) Youth Exchange Programs  266
Australia–China Joint Coordination Group on Clean Coal Technologies (2007)  266
Australia–Indonesia Institute  265
Australia–Indonesia Lombok Treaty  265
Australia–Indonesia Partnership Country Strategy (2008)  265, 305
Australia–Indonesia Security Agreement (2007)  312
Australia–New Zealand Closer Economic Relations Trade Agreement (ANZCERTA) (1983)  296
Australia–United States Free Trade Agreement (AUSFTA)  296
Australian alps
   climate change, effect of  207
   conservation  206
   land and water management  206–7
   ski tourism  206
   Snowy Mountains Scheme  206
*Australian Citizenship Act 1948*  331
Australian Communications and Media Authority (ACMA)  274–5
Australian Defence Force (ADF)  310
   see also defence; territorial protection
   government agency support  310
   peace-keeping  314–15
   role  310
   services  310
   units  310
Australian Institute of Sport (AIS)  284
Australian Marine Environment Protection Association  256
Australian Satellite Service  275
Australian Security Intelligence Organisation (ASIO)  310, 357
Australian Sport Outreach Program  286
Australian Sports Commission (ASC)  284, 286
   Active After–school Communities (AASC) program  286

Australian Trade Commission (ATC)  294
Australian Tsunami Warning System (ATWS)  251

back dunes  223, 234
bars and barriers  235
beach  234
beach nourishment  223, 225, 230
bearing  26, 149, 171
billabong  191, 218, 219
biological conservation  211, 259
biological hazards  54
Black Saturday  39, 66–8
  see also bushfire
blowout  223, 226
blowhole  223, 233
boom town  149, 165
Budget 2008–09 expenditure  311
Bureau of Meteorology  63, 75, 161
bushfire  53, 54, 62–9
  causes  62, 66–7
  drought  57
  hazard reduction  65
  impact of  64–5
  location  63
  responses  63
  risk areas  62
  types  62
  Victoria 2009, in see Black Saturday

carbon footprint  323, 345
carbon neutral  191, 216
carbon trading see carbon neutral
catchment  191, 192, 193
  Georges River study  214–15
  management programs  192
  Murray River study  193, 220–1
  Sydney Water study  216–17
Catchment Management Authorities (CMA)  192
caves and arches  233
census  93, 98, 99, 323, 324, 325
China
  see People's Republic of China
choropleth maps  72, 122
Cities for Climate Protection  160
citizenship  331
  global  260, 276–7, 300–1, 308
  Harmony Day  334
City of Cities 2030 plan  342–3
Clean Up Australia Day  240
cliffs and rock platforms  232–3
climate  19, 34, 37
  drought  34, 37, 53, 56–61, 191, 192, 193, 194
  heatwave  53, 66
  temperature  36
climate change  14, 38–9, 207, 223, 238, 239
  see also global warming
  Department of Climate Change  238

El Niño event  53, 58, 59
  infrastructure and insurance  38
  La Niña event  53, 58, 59, 79
  land degradation  195
  Pacific Islands Forum and European Union declaration  273
  tourism, effect on  38
  water and primary industries  38
climate refugee  255, 270, 273
climatic graphs  37
'Close the Gap' campaign  366–7
  see also Indigenous people
Closer Defence Relations (CDR) agreement  312
coastal dune  223, 226–7
  formation  227, 234–5
coastal erosion  226, 232–3
  Gold Coast beaches study  230
  sea level rise  238, 239
  solutions  245
  South Pacific Sea Level and Climate Monitoring Project  271
  Wamberal and Terrigal case study  242–3
  wave refraction, by  232
coastal landforms  226–7, 232–3
  beach  234
  dunes  226, 234–5
  sand grain composition and size  234
coastal management  152, 222–53
  beach nourishment program  223, 225, 230
  erosion see coastal erosion
  Fraser Island study  236–7
  global warming, impact of  238–9
  Integrated coastal zone management (ICZM)  240
  oil spill study  241
  parties involved  242
  pollution  240–1
  sediment deposition  234–5, 236–7
  South Pacific Sea Level and Climate Monitoring Project  271
  Sydney Harbour study  246–7
  vegetation  234–5
coastal monitoring  258
coastal urban growth  162, 224–5, 339
  government policy response  339
  National Sea Change Taskforce (NSCT)  339
  sea change  107, 339
  types  339
coastal zone  224–5
cold fronts  35, 53, 80, 81
column graph  120
commodity  113
  prices  118
Commonwealth Games  284
Commonwealth states and territories  5

community  113, 112–25
  changing  114, 128–30
  cultural diversity and integration  122–3, 127, 128, 136–9, 334–5
  demographic change  127, 128, 131
  employment  128
  global  129, 130
  identity and  114
  Indigenous see Indigenous people
  lifestyle expectations  130, 132–5
  occupation as basis  114
  online  130
  rural  114, 115, 118–19
  sporting  116
Comprehensive Nuclear Test Ban Treaty (CTBT) (1996)  185
constructive waves  226, 229
continent  3, 4, 5
continental drift  3, 10–11, 13
continental shelf  3, 5, 257
contour  26
  interval  24
  lines  24, 27
Convention against Torture and Other Cruel, Inhuman or Degrading Treatment or Punishment (UN, 1984)  353, 357
Convention on Biological Diversity  242
Convention on Civil and Political Rights (UN, 1966)  352
Convention on Economic, Social and Cultural Rights (UN, 1966)  352
Convention on Elimination of All Forms of Discrimination against Women (UN, 1981)  352, 360
Convention on Elimination of All Forms of Racial Discrimination (UN, 1969)  352, 365
Convention on Protection of the Rights of All Migrant Workers and Members of their Families (UN, 2003)  353
Convention on the Law of the Sea (UNCLOS)  242, 256, 258
Convention on the Rights of the Child (UN, 1990)  353
Convention on the Status of Refugees (UN, 1954)  278, 352
Cool Communities program  161
Council of Australian Governments (COAG)  238, 367
counter-terrorism  291, 317
  agreements  317
cross-section construction  30–1
crown bushfire  62, 64
crude birth rate  93, 98
crude death rate  93, 98
Cullen Bullen  165

cultural diversity   113, 122–3, 255, 276, 277, 334–5
   see also immigration; population
   Cabramatta study   136–9
   Harmony Day   334
   United Nations Universal Diversity Treaty   277
cultural integration   127, 128
cultural links   122
culture   255, 276–7
   Aussie   280–1
   communities   136–9
   global exports   276
   globalisation   277
   religion   130
   surf   277
customary law   351, 370, 373

Daintree National Park   48
defence
   see also Australian Defence Force (ADF); territorial protection
   Asia–Pacific region agreements   312
   Budget 2008–09 expenditure   311
   future global links   314–15
   non-government organisations (NGOs) role   310
   nuclear agreements   312
   peace-keeping missions   314–15
   policy   312
   RAMSI (Regional Assistance Mission to the Solomon Islands)   318–19
   Timor-Leste study   257, 315
demographic change   109, 127, 128, 131
demographic characteristics   113, 114
demography   93, 109
Department of Climate Change   238
Department of Foreign Affairs and Trade (DFAT)   294, 317
Department of Immigration and Citizenship (DIAC)   330
Department of the Environment, Water, Heritage and the Arts   211, 240, 256
Department of Water and Energy (NSW)   211
deposition   19, 20, 21, 223, 226, 227
desalination plant   216
destructive waves   226, 229
development
   sustainable   93, 103, 166, 171, 224, 225
dormitory town   149, 166, 169
drainage basin   19, 20, 21, 22–3
Dreaming   3, 8–9
   see also Indigenous people
   cultural sites and tourism   203
   map dreaming   8
drought   19, 34, 37, 53, 56–61, 191, 192, 193

bushfire risk   57
   causes   56, 58–9
   dust storm   60
   economic impact   56
   El Niño event   53, 58–9, 60
   environmental impact   57
   Indian Ocean dipole (IOD)   59
   La Niña event   58
   land degradation caused by   194
   National Drought Policy   61
   1991–95, during   60–1
   responses   54, 61
   social impact   57
   southern oscillation   58, 59, 60
drowned river valley   191, 214
dunes   226, 234–5
   back   223, 234
   coastal   223, 226, 227
   fore   223, 234

e-waste   179
earth
   structure of   84
Earth Summit (1992)   242
earthquake   53, 84–6
   causes   84
   epicentre   53, 84, 86
   impact of   84
   measuring   84
   Modified Mercalli scale   84, 85
   Newcastle 1989   54, 85, 86
   Richter scale   84
   risk areas   85
Earthwatch Institute   205
East Timor see Timor-Leste
ecocity   323, 346–7
ecological footprint
   carbon   323, 345
   migration   330
   urban growth   162, 344, 346–7
   water   191, 323, 345, 347
ecological sustainability   323, 344–7
   Sustainable Sydney 2030   346–7
economic activity
   globalisation   127, 129, 260, 261
ecosystem   19, 48, 49, 223, 224, 225
ecotourism   191
   see also tourism
   Earthwatch Institute   205
   Ecotourism Australia (EA)   204–5
   sustainable tourism   283
   The Overland Track study   204
EEZ (Exclusive Economic Zone)   5, 242, 255, 257, 258, 271
EIS (environmental impact statement)   223, 242
El Niño event   53, 58–9, 60
emigration   93, 102, 103, 323, 324, 325
   see also immigration; migration
endemic   19, 46
energy
   renewable   42–3

Environment Protection and Biodiversity Conservation Act 1999   259
EPA (Environment Protection Authority)   152, 183, 241
epicentre   53, 84, 86
EPR (extended producer responsibility)   179
Equal Employment Opportunity Act 1987   356
Equator   7, 95
erosion   3, 12, 13, 223
   see also land degradation; salinity
   coastal   225, 226–7, 230, 232–3
   soil   196–7
estuary   223, 226, 227
ethnic diversity   93, 94, 95, 102, 108
   see also cultural diversity; immigration; population
exports   291, 292, 293
exurbanisation   162, 166

fair trade   291, 298–300
   see also trade
   non-government organisations (NGOs)   298
   Oxfam campaign   298
Fair Trade Association of Australia and New Zealand (FTAANZ)   299
fauna
   see also animals
   birds   48, 49
   Daintree National Park   48
   desert   47
   marsupials   46
   monotremes   47
   reptiles   46, 47, 48
feature area   32
fertility rate   93, 101, 323, 326, 327
fieldwork data collection   139
Fiji   320
fire front   53, 62, 63, 64
   Black Saturday, on   68
firebrand   53, 62, 63, 65
firestorm   53, 68, 69
Five Power Defence Arrangements (FPDA)   312
flood   53, 78–81
   causes   80
   flash   71, 78
   Great Floods of 1990   78
   impact of   80
   La Niña   79
   mitigation   53, 80
   Queensland 2009, in   81
   types   78
flood plain   20, 53, 78, 79, 191, 214
flora   46–9
   introduced species, effect of   195
flow maps   107
fore dunes   223, 234

foreign aid 300–9
   Asia–Pacific region 302–3
   AusAID (Australian Agency for International Development) 266, 275, 286, 300–1, 356
   Papua New Guinea 306–7
   World Vision Australia (WVA) 308–9
Fraser Island 236–7
free trade agreements 296–7
freedom of expression 362–3
   human rights 362
   International Covenant on Civil and Political Rights 362
   prisoners of conscience 362
   UNESCO, role of 362

gender equality 351, 360
   *see also* women's rights
   Australian Plan of Action Towards Gender Equality (2008) 361
   gap 361
genocide 351, 353
gentrification 167
geographical dimensions
   Australia, of 4–5
geographical issues of concern 150–5
   active citizenship, role of 154, 155, 299, 359
   active groups in society, role of 154
   individuals, role of 154
   types 150
geographical issues scaffold 150
geographical location
   Australia, of 6–7, 256
   maritime zones 256–7
geological hazards 54
Georges River 214–15
geothermal energy 42
GIS (geographic information system) 191, 198, 202, 261, 274, 291
global links
   *see also* globalisation
   advantages and disadvantages 261
Global Maritime Distress and Safety System (GMDSS) 275
global positioning systems (GPS) 274
global warming 42, 184, 191, 192, 193, 223, 238–9
   *see also* climate change
globalisation 127, 129, 131, 255, 260–2
   ASEAN country links 264–65
   Asia–Pacific region links 262–3
   communications and technology 260, 274–5
   communities, impact on 129, 130
   culture and citizenship 260, 276–7, 300–1, 308
   defence 260

environmental links 260
Indonesia, links with 258, 265, 304–5
migration *see* migration
organisations 260
Pacific Islands, links with 270–3
People's Republic of China, links with 266–7
sport 260, 284–9
tourism 260
trade 260, 292, 294, 295, 296, 297
treaties and agreements 260
good governance 154
governance 291, 301
government
   powers of 154
gradient 24, 27
Great Artesian Basin 14
Great Barrier Reef 224, 238
Great Dividing Range 20
Green power
   *see* renewable energy
grid north 26
gross national income (GNI) per capita 3, 6
ground water 191, 198, 199

hailstones 71
hailstorm
   causes 72
   Sydney 1999 54, 72–3
HDI (human development index) 351, 361
headlands and bays 232
heatwave 53, 63, 66
heritage 113, 114
   *see also* World Heritage sites
high pressure system 34
   blocking 53, 66, 69
hot spot volcanoes 13
HPI (human poverty index) 172
human rights 291, 300, 351–79, 352, 353
   *see also* freedom of expression; Indigenous people; refugee; women's rights
   Amnesty International 354
   Australia, in 356
   capital punishment 353
   charter 356
   conventions and agreements 352–3
   forms of abuse 355
   global incidents of abuse 354–5
   landmine clearing 313
   monitoring agencies 353, 356
   right to life 353
   United Nations Universal Declaration of Human Rights (1948) 261, 352, 358, 360, 362, 365
   United Nations Universal Declaration of Human Rights Defenders (1998) 362

*Human Rights and Equal Opportunity Act 1986* 356
Human Rights and Equal Opportunity Commission (HREOC) 356, 360, 374
Human Rights Council (HRC) 353, 356
Humanitarian Program 278, 330
hydro-electric power 43
   Snowy Mountains Scheme 206
   Three Gorges Dam 269
hydrological hazards 54

IAEA (International Atomic Energy Agency) 185, 312
ice age 3, 14
Immarsat 274, 275
immigrant 102, 113, 114, 122–3
   *see also* cultural diversity
   population by birth 103, 278, 334
immigration 93, 94, 95, 279, 323, 324–5
   *see also* cultural diversity; migration
   Australian citizenship 331
   humanitarian program 332
   Iraqis 332–3
   pattern 102
imports 291, 292, 293
   Indigenous people 368
Indian Ocean 256
Indian Ocean dipole (IOD) 59
Indigenous Health Equality Summit Statement of Intent 365
Indigenous people 3, 5, 8, 53, 104–5, 108, 120–1, 140–3, 351, 364–76
   Aboriginal Community Controlled Health Service (ACCHS) 367
   *Aboriginal Land Rights Act 1976* 121
   Aboriginal Medical Service (AMS) 367
   age–sex population structure 104–5
   art 9
   'Close the Gap' campaign 366–7
   communities 120–1
   Council of Australian Governments (COAG) funding 238, 367, 376
   cultural and heritage sites 203, 224
   culturally appropriate assistance 367
   customary law 351, 373
   demography 120–1, 240
   Dreaming 3, 8–9, 365
   education inequality 364
   global comparisons on status of 368–9
   health inequality 364, 365, 366
   human development index (HDI) 364
   human rights agreements 365
   ice age migration of 15

Indigenous people (*continued*)
  Indigenous Small Business Fund (ISBF)   176
  infant mortality rate (IMR)   368
  kinship   113
  land claims   351, 365
  life expectancy   120, 172, 364, 367, 368
  *Mabo*   127, 143
  'Making Indigenous Poverty History'   172
  Mirarr community and Jabiluka mine   140–3
  native title   127, 130
  1967 referendum   104
  population   94, 104–5, 108, 337
  poverty   172–5, 364
  reconciliation *see* reconciliation
  self-determination   352, 365, 373
  Stolen Generation *see* Stolen Generation
  strategies to overcome disadvantages   374–5
  Torres Strait Treaty (TST) (1978)   257
  United Nations Declaration on the Rights of Indigenous People (2007)   368
  United Nations Permanent Forum on Indigenous Issues (UNPFII)   374
Indonesia   257, 258, 304–5
  *see also* Australia–Indonesia
  aid   265, 302, 304–5
  tourism   265
  trade   265
  Utopia community   367
infant mortality rate (IMF)   93, 105
inland rivers *see* rivers
Integrated coastal zone management (ICZM)   240
integration   323, 334
  cultural   127, 128
intellectual property   255, 276
International Convention on the Prevention of Marine Pollution by Dumping Wastes (1975)   178
  Protocol   240
International Covenant on Civil and Political Rights   362
International Criminal Court (ICC)   353
International Fair Trade Association (IFTA)   298–9
International Labour Organisation Indigenous and Tribes Peoples Convention (No. 169, 1991)   365
International Maritime Organisation (IMO)   256, 259
International Seabed Authority (ISA)   256

international trade   291, 292–9
  *see also* fair trade; trade
  bilateral trade agreements   296
  exports   295
  fair trade *see* fair trade
  free trade   296–7
  history   294
  imports   295
  partners   294
  regional trade agreements   296
International Whaling Commission (IWC)   256, 259
International Women's Day   360
internet
  broadband   274, 275
  café   127, 130
  censorship   362–3
  freedom of information   362
interstate migration   93, 106, 107, 338
intertidal zone   191, 218, 219
intra-city migration   338
intrastate migration   93, 106, 107
isobar   19, 40, 41

Jabiluka mine proposal
  environmental impact   141
  Jabiluka Long-Term Care and Maintenance Agreement   142
  Mirarr community   140–2
  responses   142–3
  UNESCO World Heritage Committee   141
JANZUS Agreement   312
Jindalee Operational Radar Network (JORN)   258
Joint Petroleum Development Area (JPDA)   257

Kata Tjuta   2, 16
Kimberley   20
kinship   113, 120

La Niña event   53, 58, 59
  floods   79
lagoons   235
Lake Eyre   14
  basin   20, 219
lakes   22, 219, 220
Landcare   191, 200
land–water interactions   192–3
land bridges   15
land claims   351, 369
land degradation   191, 194–5
  *see also* erosion; land management; soil erosion
  carrying capacity   202
  causes   194
  impact of   195
land management   152, 192, 194–209
  Australian alps study   206–7
  Darling Downs study   200
  dung beetles, use of   201
  programs   200

  sustainable agriculture   200, 201
  unsustainable agriculture   201
land maps   119
landmines
  Cambodia, in   313
landforms   20–2
  *see also* coastal landforms; mountain
  calculating area   32–3
latitude   3, 7, 95, 319
life expectancy   108, 113, 120, 323, 328, 329, 351, 367
  low income, effect on   172
lifestyle expectations   130, 132–5
  *see also* standard of living
  factors affecting   130
  Gold Coast study   132–5
liveability   323, 340
Local Agenda 21 (LA21)   323, 344
local relief   28
longitude   3, 7, 95, 319
longshore drift   223, 227, 229, 231
Lower Murray Darling Catchment Management Authority   211

*Mabo*   127, 143
Macdonnell Ranges   12, 20
magnetic north   26
Make Poverty History   300, 308
mantle   3, 13, 84
maps
  choropleth maps   72, 122
  cross-section on   30–1
  flow   107
  land   119
  large scale   96
  physical   22–3
  satellite image   129
  small scale   96
  synoptic chart   19, 41, 228
  topographic   24–9
  weather   40–1
maritime zones   256–7
marsupial   19, 46
migration   93, 98–9, 127, 128, 131, 255, 260, 278–279, 323, 325
  *see also* cultural diversity; immigration; interstate migration; intrastate migration; refugee
  coastal   107
  humanitarian   332–3
  net overseas migration (NOM)   323, 325, 330
  policies   330–1
  spatial distribution   323, 331
  Temporary Skilled Migration Program   278–9, 330
  trends   334
*Migration Act 1958*   278, 330
Millennium Development Goals (UN, MDG) *see* United Nations Millennium Development Goals (MDG)

minerals 44
　global uranium reserves 186
　Jabiluka mine study 140–3
　processing and air pollution 157
Modified Mercalli scale 84, 85
monotreme 19, 46
monsoon 19, 35, 37
Mount Kosciuszko 14
Mount Olga 16
mountain
　see also Australian alps
　formation of 12
　volcanic 13
multicultural 127, 139
　see also cultural diversity; immigration
multiculturalism 138, 139, 323, 334, 335
Murray–Darling Basin 20, 21, 211, 220–1
　Lower Murray Darling Catchment Management Authority 211
　salinity management 199
　water use 221
Murray River 21, 193, 211, 219, 220–1
　see also Murray–Darling Basin; rivers; salinity; water management

National Action Plan for Salinity and Water Quality 198
National Climate Centre in Australia 59
National Drought Policy 61
National Greenhouse Strategy 161
National Water Commission 211
native title 127, 130, 131
　see also Indigenous people
　Jabiluka mine 140–3
　*Mabo* 127, 143
　nature of rights 130
natural disasters 53, 54
　see also natural hazards
natural hazards 52–87
　bushfire 53, 54, 62–9
　cyclone 74–7
　drought 34, 53, 56–61, 191, 192, 193, 194
　earthquake 53, 84–6
　flood 78–81
　risk assessment 54
　storms 70–3, 80
　types 54
natural increase 323, 324, 325
　population, in 98
Natural Resource Management Ministerial Council (NRMMC) 238
natural resources 42–5
　depletion 130
　expansion of usage rights 257
　forests 45
　minerals 44, 94

natural scenery 45
renewable energy 42–3
soils 44
wool 94
Nauru
　links with Australia 270–2
NCAP (National Coalition Against Poverty) 176
NCOSS (Council of Social Service of New South Wales) 176
NEPM (National Environment Protection Measure)
　outdoor air quality 158, 161
net overseas migration (NOM) 98–9, 323, 324, 325, 330
New Zealand
　agreements with Australia 296, 312
　human rights agreements for indigenous people 369
New Zealand–Australia Free Trade Agreement (1965) 296
non-government organisations (NGOs) 105, 153, 154, 176, 255, 256, 316
　defence role 310
　fair trade support 298
　foreign aid agreements 300
　World Vision Australia (WVA) 308–9
north
　grid 26
　magnetic 26
　true 26
nuclear power 149
　agreements 312
　global reactor locations 184
　incidents involving 184, 185
　international responses to use 185
　Lucas Heights reactor 186
　opposition to 185
　uses 186
　weapons 185
nuclear waste 184–5
　disposal methods 184–5, 186
　responses 186–7
　sources 186
　types 184

ocean preservation 259
　International Whaling Commission (IWC) 256, 259
ocean processes 228–31
　longshore drift 229–31
　rips 231
　storm surges 231
　tides 231
　waves 226, 228–9, 232–3
Oceans Policy (1998) 256
Office of the High Commissioner for Human Rights (OHCHR) 353
Official Development Assistance (ODA) 300, 302

　see also AusAID (Australian Agency for International Development); foreign aid
oil spill 241
Olympic Games 284, 286, 288
　Athens 286
　Beijing 266, 268
　revenue 286
　Sydney 280
Operation Helpem Fren
　Solomon Islands, assistance to 217, 270, 318
Organisation for Economic Co-operation and Development (OECD) 261, 296
Ottawa Convention on landmines 313
outstation 113, 121

Pacific Agreement on Closer Economic Relations (PACER) 273
Pacific Island Countries Trade Agreement (PICTA) 273
Pacific Islands 270–3
　development indicators 270
　economic growth 270
　trade 271
Pacific Islands Forum 273
　trade and economic agreements 273
Pacific Ocean 256
Papua New Guinea (PNG)
　AusAID 306–7
　treaties and agreements with 257, 270
Papua New Guinea–Australia Development Cooperation Strategy 306
peace-keeping missions 314–15
　see also defence
people smuggling 310, 323, 330
　Bali Process 258
People's Republic of China 266–7
　see also Australia–China
　aid 266, 300, 303
　ancestry 268
　Free Trade Agreement 266
　future links with 267
　superpower, as 267
　Three Gorges Dam 269
　trade 267
physical maps 22–3
piracy at sea 258
pollution
　see also waste
　air 147, 156–9
　coastal 240–1
population 92–111, 162, 323, 324–5
　see also immigration; migration
　aging 100, 108, 326–9
　change 98–101, 108–9, 325
　crude birth rate 93, 98

Index　**391**

population (*continued*)
  crude death rate   93, 98
  density   93, 94
  ecological sustainability   344–5, 346–7
  ethnicity   102, 108
  fertility rate changes   101, 326–7
  gender distribution   100
  geographic location   130
  growth   98–9, 108, 278–9, 324, 338–9
  Indigenous *see* Indigenous people
  mobile   106
  movement   338–41
  replacement rate   93, 101
  spatial distribution   323, 331, 336–7
  structure   108
  trends   324–5, 334
  urban planning   340–3, 344–7
population pyramid   93, 100, 101, 328, 330, 364
poverty   172–3, 174–5
  *see also* foreign aid; social welfare; social justice; spatial inequality
  absolute   149, 174, 175
  associated social problems   174
  children and youth, impact on   174–5
  indicators   172
  Make Poverty History   300, 308
  relative   149, 174, 175
  social effect   174
  women   361
poverty line   172
pressure systems   34, 40
Prime Meridian   6
prisoners of conscience   362
Protected Zone Joint Authority (PZJA)   257
*Public Service Act 1999*   356

quota   291, 294

*Racial Discrimination Act 1975*   279, 356, 365
*Racial Hatred Act 1995*   279
radioactive waste
  disposal *see* nuclear waste
rainfall   34–5
  low   210
Ramsar Convention (1971)   218
RAMSI (Regional Assistance Mission to the Solomon Islands)   318–19
  Operation Helpem Fren   217, 318
rate
  birth and death trends   99
  crude birth and death   93, 98
  population   338
reconciliation   351, 370–3
  *see also* Indigenous people; Stolen Generation
  Australian Declaration Towards Reconciliation   372

  Council for Aboriginal Reconciliation   370
  People's Walk for Reconciliation   370
  Reconciliation Barometer   375
  Roadmap for Reconciliation (2008)   371, 372
  strategies   371–2
referendum   93
  Indigenous people   104
refugee   93, 102, 103, 278, 351, 358–9
  active citizenship support initiatives   359
  asylum, right to   358
  climate   255, 273
  global responses   358–9
  Humanitarian Program   278, 332, 358
  Iraqi   332–3
  offshore visas   358
  'Pacific Solution'   358
  processing   358
  Sudanese   335
  Swedish Group Home System   358–9
  *Tampa* incident   358
  United Nations Convention on the Status of Refugees (1954)   278
  United Nations High Commissioner for Refugees (UNHCR)   278, 358
  United Nations Universal Declaration of Human Rights   358
  White Australia policy   136
regolith   19, 20, 21
relative poverty   149, 174, 175
renewable energy   42–3
  geothermal energy   42
  solar power   43, 157
  tidal power   42
  wind power   42, 157
replacement rate   93, 101
research action plan   155
Richter scale   53, 84
rips   231
rivers   22
  *see also* lakes; salinity; water management; wetlands
  creation   78
  dams and weirs, effect of   213
  disruption and diversion of flow   212–13
  Georges River   214–15
  inland   219
  monitoring quality   210–11
Royal Australian Air Force (RAAF)   310
Royal Australian Navy (RAN)   310
rural   113, 114, 115
  communities   118–19
  population changes   107
  settlement   53, 93, 96

rural–urban fringe   149, 162, 165
rural–urban migration   166, 338

salinity   191, 198–9, 212
  *see also* water management
  affected areas   198
  annual cost   198
  Basin Salinity Management Strategy for 2001–2015   199
  desalination plant   216
  management   194, 199
  Murray–Darling Basin   199
  National Action Plan for Salinity and Water Quality   198
  types   198
  Water for the Future project (2008)   199, 211
satellite image   129
sclerophyll   53, 63
sea change   107, 339
  National Sea Change Taskforce (NSCT)   339
sea level
  changes   14, 238, 239
  South Pacific Sea Level and Climate Monitoring Project   271
secularism   291, 304
sediment   3, 14
SEIFA (socioeconomic indexes for area)   172
self-determination   351, 365, 370, 373
settlement   93, 96, 97
  nucleated (cluster)   97
  patterns   96–7
  rural   93, 96
  urban   53, 93, 96
sewage
  diseases from by exposure to   182, 183, 216
  recycling waste water   183, 211, 216, 347
  Sydney Water study   183, 216–17
  treatment processes   182–3
Snowy Mountains Scheme   206
social justice   176, 255, 279
  *see also* foreign aid; social welfare
  fair trade   298–9
  international campaigns   308
  refugees *see* refugee
  sport programs   284, 286–7
  technology, role of   275
social welfare   176
  *see also* poverty; spatial inequality
  Budget 2008–09 expenditure   176, 311
  federal government projected payments   177
  government policy advisor groups   176
  volunteers   177
socioeconomic status   130
soil   44, 191, 196, 197
  acid sulfate content   195

soil erosion 196–7
   see also coastal erosion; erosion; land degradation; salinity
solar power 43, 157
Solomon Islands 257
   AusAID Solomon Islands Community Sector Strategy (2007–11) 318
   Operation Helpem Fren 217, 270, 318
   'the tensions' 318
South Pacific Nuclear Weapons Free Zone 312
South Pacific Sea Level and Climate Monitoring Project 271
Southern Hemisphere 6
southern oscillation 53, 58, 59
   El Niño 58, 59, 60
   La Niña 58, 59, 79
Southern Oscillation Index (SOI) 58, 60, 79
sovereign rights 255, 256
spatial distribution 323, 331
spatial inequality 149, 150, 151, 153, 172–3, 175
   government and private strategies to reduce 177
   Indigenous and non-Indigenous people, between 172, 174
   poverty 172
   statistics 173, 174, 175
species 19, 46, 47
spit 223, 226, 227, 234, 235
sport
   advantages and disadvantages of global promotion 287
   advertising 286
   Commonwealth Games 284
   economic advantages 286
   equity and social justice programs 284, 286–7
   global partnerships 284, 286–7
   Olympic Games 280, 284, 286, 288
   soccer study 288–9
   Sport Development Program (2006–11) 286
spot heights 26
stack 223, 233
standard of living 93, 94, 113, 118, 130
   see also lifestyle expectations
Stolen Generations 351, 371, 374–5
   see also Indigenous people; reconciliation
   apology 375
   'Bringing Them Home' report 374
storm surges 53, 74, 223, 231
storms 70–3
   dust 60
   flood, cause of 80
   hail 54, 72–3
   thunderstorm 70–1
   wind 60

subsidy 291, 294
suburbanisation 162, 166, 168
   advantages and disadvantages 168
surf lifesaving club community 113, 116–17
surface bushfire 62
sustainable development 93, 102, 103, 166, 223, 224, 225
   Sydney study 170–1
sustainable energy see renewable energy
sustainable management
   land–water–air interactions 191, 192–3
Sydney Catchment Authority 216
Sydney Water 183, 211, 216–17, 347
synoptic chart 19, 40, 41, 228
   see also weather map

tariff 291, 294
technology
   broadband global area network (BGAN) 274
   effect on communities 130
   geographic information systems (GIS) 274
   global communications 274–5
   global positioning systems (GPS) 274
   satellite 274, 275
tectonic forces 20
tectonic plates 3, 10, 84
Telecommunications Act 1997 275
Temporary Skilled Migration Program 278–9, 330
terra nullius 127, 143
territorial boundaries 256–7
   maritime zones 256–7
   treaties and agreements 257
territorial protection 258–9
   see also Australian Defence Force (ADF); defence
   coastal monitoring 258
   government departments' role 258
   illegal activities 258
   piracy 258
territorial sea baseline (TSB) 256
terrorism 291, 258, 310, 316
   attacks, list of 317
   counter–terrorism agreements 317
   Indonesia 317
   9/11 316
   response 357
   'war on terror' 316–17, 357
thunderstorm 53, 70–1
tidal power 42
tides 223, 228, 231
Timor Gap
   oil and gas revenue management 257
Timor-Leste 257, 315
Timor Sea Treaty (2002) 257

TNC (transnational corporation) 113, 114, 255, 261
tombolo 234, 235
topographic maps 24–5
   area reference 25
   aspect of a slope 28
   contour interval 24, 30
   contour lines 24, 27
   eastings 24
   gradient 27
   grid reference 25
   local relief 28
   northings 24
   transect 28
   using 26–9
   vertical interval 26
topography 3, 14, 15, 19, 20, 21
topsoil 191, 193
tornadoes 71
Torres Strait Islanders see Indigenous people
Torres Strait Protected Zone (TSPZ) 257
Torres Strait Treaty (TST) (1978) 257
tourism 255, 280–1
   Aussie culture 280–1
   carbon footprint 204
   climate change, effect of 38
   ecotourism see ecotourism
   environmental impact 194, 202
   globalisation 260, 280–3
   Gold Coast 134
   greenhouse gas (GHG) emissions 204
   marketing 282
   sustainable 283
   technology, effect of 282
   trends 282–3
   Uluru–Kata Tjuta National Park study 203
towns
   boom town 149, 165
   dormitory 149, 166, 169
trade
   deficit 291, 292
   fair see fair trade
   imports and exports 292–3
   international see international trade
transect 28
treaty 255, 256, 260
   United Nations
   territorial treaties 257
Treaty on the Non-Proliferation of Nuclear Weapons (UN, 1970) 185, 312
triple bottom line 323
tropical cyclone 35, 53, 74–7
   Cyclone Larry 76
   Cyclone Tracy 54, 74, 75–6
   impact 76
   occurrence 74
   paths 74
   responses 76

true north  26
tsunami  223, 238, 239, 250–1
  Australian Tsunami Warning System (ATWS)  251
Tuvalu
  links with Australia  270–1
2020 Summit  322

Uluru  16
UNESCO
  freedom of expression  362
  World Heritage Committee  141
United Kingdom (UK)  260
United Nations (UN)  291, 257, 300
  Conventions *see* entries for Convention
  Local Agenda 21 (LA21)  323, 344
  membership of  261
United Nations Declaration on the Elimination of Violence against Women (1979)  360
United Nations Declaration on the Rights of Indigenous People (2007)  368
United Nations Development Fund for Women (UNIFEM)  360
United Nations Development Program (UNDP)  306
United Nations High Commissioner for Refugees (UNHCR)  278, 358
United Nations Millennium Development Goals (MDG)  261, 286, 291, 300, 306–7, 353, 361, 374
United Nations Permanent Forum on Indigenous Issues (UNPFII)  374
United Nations Treaty on the Non-Proliferation of Nuclear Weapons (1970)  185, 312
United Nations Universal Declaration of Human Rights (1948)  261, 352, 358, 360, 362, 365
United Nations Universal Declaration of Human Rights Defenders (1998)  362
  conventions and agreements  352–3
United Nations Universal Diversity Treaty  277
United Nations World Food Programme  286, 300
urban  113, 114, 115
  settlement  93, 96
urban consolidation  162, 166, 338
urban decay  149, 164, 165, 166
urban decline  164–9
urban growth  153, 162, 163, 166–9, 338–9
urban growth and decline Sydney  166–9
urban planning  340–1
  City of Cities 2030 plan  342–3
  ecocity  346–7

urban renewal  162
  gentrification  167
  redevelopment  167
  Sydney study  170–1
urbanisation  149, 162, 165

vegetation  36
  clearing, effect of  194, 212
  flood reduction method  80
Victorian bushfires 2009, in *see* Black Saturday
visa  351
  offshore grants  358
volcanic mountains  13
volcanoes  13, 14

Walls of Jerusalem  29, 32–3
waste  178
  *see also* air pollution; air quality; pollution
  e-waste  179
  incineration of  178
  landfill, in  178, 195
  nuclear *see* nuclear waste
  sewage *see* sewage
  waterways, disposal in  178, 211, 214
waste management  153, 180–1
  cigarette butts reduction campaign  180
  groups  180
  individual action  181
  plastic bag reduction campaign  180–1
  sewage *see* sewage
  strategies  180
*Water Act 2007*  220
water cycle  210
water footprint  191, 216, 323, 345
water management  152, 192, 210–21
  *see also* rivers and lakes; salinity; sewage
  desalination plant  216
  issues  211
  oil spill  241
  pollution  240–1
  recycling  216, 347
  sustainability initiatives  211, 216
  Sydney Harbour study  246–7
  Water for the Future project (2008)  199, 211
water storage  210, 211
water table  191, 198, 199
wave-cut notch  223, 232, 233
waves  226
  *see also* coastal erosion; coastal landforms; ocean processes; tsunami
  erosion by refraction  232–3
  formation  228
  types  229

weather
  *see also* climate
  anticyclones  40
  cold front  35, 53, 80, 81
  drought  34, 53, 56–61, 191, 192, 193, 194
  maps  40–1
  pressure systems  34, 40, 80
  southern oscillation  53
  storm surge  53, 74, 223, 231
  storms  53, 70–3
  tropical cyclone  35, 53, 74–7
weathering  3, 14, 15
wetlands  127, 133, 135, 191, 218–19
  *see also* lakes; rivers; water management
  Murray Darling  21
  Ramsar Convention (1971)  218
  role  218
  Wetland Watch  218
whale conservation  259
White Australia policy  127, 136, 139, 266, 278
WHO (World Health Organization)  157
Wideband Global Satellite Communications System  275
winds  40
women's rights
  *see also* gender equality
  Australian Plan of Action Towards Gender Equality (2008)  361
  female poverty  361
  global gender gap  361
  International Women's Day  360
  United Nations agreements  360
  United Nations Millennium Development Goals (MDG)  361
  violence against women campaigns  360
Women in Development (WID)  361
*Workplace Relations Act 1996*  356
World Heritage Committee *see* UNESCO World Heritage Committee
World Heritage List sites  127, 140, 143, 152, 224, 238
  coastal zone, on  224, 238
  Lamington National Park  45
  Wet Tropics World Heritage Site  48
World Trade Organization (WTO)  298
  Doha Round Table Agreement  296
  members  294
World Vision Australia (WVA)  308–9
World Wildlife Fund  218

INDONESIA
Sumba
TIMOR-LESTE
Timor
Roti
ARAFURA SEA
Melville Island
Cape Van Diemen
Bathurst Island
Van Diemen Gulf
Wessel Islands
Galiwinku
Darwin
Palmerston
Jabiru
Arnhem Land
TIMOR SEA
Cape Ford
Nauiyu Nambiyu
Wadeye
Daly River
Katherine
Ngukurr
Numbulwar
Alyangula
Cape Londonderry
Cape Voltaire
Kalumburu
Bonaparte Archipelago
Oombulgurri
Wyndham
Kununurra
Victoria River
Larrimah
Timber Creek
Daly Waters
Borroloola
Lake Argyle
INDIAN OCEAN
Cape Leveque
King Sound
Sturt Plain
Newcastle Waters
Kalkaringi
Derby
Halls Creek
Broome
Roebuck Bay
Northern Territory
Tanami Desert
Tennant Creek
Tanami
Lake Gregory
Wauchope
Port Hedland
Shay Gap
Great Sandy Desert
Barrow Creek
Dampier
Karratha
Marble Bar
Percival Lakes
Lake Mackay
Yuendumu
Barrow Island
Nullagine
AUSTRALIA
Pannawonica
Fortescue River
Papunya
Alice Springs
Exmouth
Tom Price
Hermannsburg
Areyonga
Newman
Lake Disappointment
Paraburdoo
Lake Amadeus
Western Australia
Kaltukatjara
Tropic of Capricorn
Gibson Desert
Finke
Gascoyne River
Ernabella
Shark Bay
Carnarvon
Lake Carnegie
Oodnadatta
Wiluna
Steep Point
Meekatharra
Murchison River
Great Victoria Desert
South Australia
Cue
Lake Austin
Manguari
Coober Pedy
Mount Magnet
Laverton
Kalbarri
Yalgoo
Lake Carey
Leonora
Lake Barlee
Maralinga
Andamooka
Geraldton
Menzies
Wynbring
Houtman Abrolhos Islands
Morawa
Cook
Kingoonya
Kalgoorlie-Boulder
Loongana
Koolyanobbing
Coolgardie
Rawlinna
Kambalda
Eucla
Penong
Moora
Widgiemooltha
Coorabie
Ceduna
Lake Gairdner
Lancelin
Merredin
Wanneroo
PERTH
Northam
Norseman
Point Culver
Streaky Bay
Fremantle
Kwinana
Kondinin
Rockingham
Mandurah
Great Australian Bight
Lock
Ravensthorpe
Collie
Wagin
Esperance
Cummins
Bunbury
Katanning
Hopetoun
Port Lincoln
Cape Naturaliste
Busselton
Archipelago of the Recherche
Kangaroo Island
Manjimup
Augusta
Mount Barker
Northcliffe
Albany
INDIAN OCEAN
0
200
400
600
800 km
1 : 16 000 000 — 1 centimetre on the map represents 160 kilometres on the ground.
Equidistant Conic Projection
N
A
B
C
D
1
2
3
4
5
110°E
120°E
130°E
10°S
20°S
30°S
40°S